Lecture Notes in Computer Science 2425

Edited by G. Goos, J. Hartmanis, and J. van Leeuwen

Springer
Berlin
Heidelberg
New York
Barcelona
Hong Kong
London
Milan
Paris
Tokyo

Zohra Bellahsène Dilip Patel
Colette Rolland (Eds.)

Object-Oriented Information Systems

8th International Conference, OOIS 2002
Montpellier, France, September 2-5, 2002
Proceedings

Volume Editors

Zohra Bellahsène
Université Montpellier II, UMR 5506 CNRS
LIRMM - Laboratoire d'Informatique, de Robotique
et de Microélectronique de Montpellier
161, Rue Ada, 34392 Montpellier, France
E-mail: bella@lirmm.fr

Dilip Patel
South Bank University
School of Computing, Information Systems and Mathematics
Centre for Information and Organisation Studies
103 Borough Road, London SE1 0AA, United Kingdom
E-mail: dilip@sbu.ac.uk

Colette Rolland
Université Paris 1, Panthéon Sorbonne
Centre de Recherche en Informatique
90 Rue de Tolbiac, 75634 Paris cedex 13, France
E-mail: rolland@univ-paris1.fr

Cataloging-in-Publication Data applied for

Die Deutsche Bibliothek - CIP-Einheitsaufnahme

Object oriented information systems : 8th international conference ; proceedings / OOIS 2002, Montpellier, France, September 2 - 5, 2002 / Zohra Bellahsène ... (ed.). - Berlin ; Heidelberg ; New York ; Barcelona ; Hong Kong ; London ; Milan ; Paris ; Tokyo : Springer, 2002
(Lecture notes in computer science ; Vol. 2425)
ISBN 3-540-44087-9

CR Subject Classification (1998): H.2, H.3, H.4, H.5, I.2, D.2, D.4, K.4.4, J.1

ISSN 0302-9743
ISBN 3-540-44087-9 Springer-Verlag Berlin Heidelberg New York

Springer-Verlag Berlin Heidelberg New York
a member of BertelsmannSpringer Science+Business Media GmbH

http://www.springer.de

Printed in Germany

Typesetting: Camera-ready by author, data conversion by DA-TeX Gerd Blumenstein
Printed on acid-free paper SPIN: 10873853 06/3142 5 4 3 2 1 0

Preface

The OOIS series of conferences has provided a forum for the presentation and exchange of academic research and industrial experiences within the field of information systems, based on object-oriented technology.

The 8th International Conference on OOIS was held in the University of Montpellier from 2nd to 5th September 2002. The conference focused on the design, maintenance and implementation of web-based information systems. The first day consisted of preconference workshops. The workshop themes included the specialization/generalization hierarchy, reuse, optimization in web-based information systems, and model-driven software development.

The main conference program also included four invited papers, namely "Corporate Semantic Webs" by Dr. Rose Dieng, INRIA, France, "A Framework for Defining E-business Models" by Prof. Yves Pigneur, University of Lausanne, Switzerland, "GRID in E-business" by Pierre Sablonière, IBM, France, and "The Latest Development on Cognitive Informatics" by Dr. Yingxu Wang, University of Calgary, Canada.

The conference attracted 116 papers from more than 20 countries and the program committee accepted 34 regular papers and 17 short papers. The selected papers included the following themes:

- advanced object-information systems,
- web-based information systems,
- knowledge management in object information systems,
- CORBA,
- e-business,
- software metrics,
- object databases.

We would like to thank the members of the program committee and all the other referees who gave up their valuable time to review the papers and helped in putting together an exciting program. We would also like to thank the invited speakers, authors and other individuals who helped, without whom this conference would not have been possible. Finally, our thanks go out to the local organizing committee and all the institutions and organizations that provided financial support.

June 2002

Colette Rolland
Zohra Bellahsène
Dilip Patel

Organization

General Chair

Colette Rolland (Université Paris-Sorbonne, France)

Program Co-chairs

Zohra Bellahsène (LIRMM, France)
Dilip Patel (South Bank University, UK)

Program Committee

Sihem Amer-Yahia (ATT Reaseach, USA)
Motoei Azuma (Waseda University, Japan)
Franck Barbier (University of Pau, France)
Zohra Bellahsène (LIRMM, France)
Elisa Bertino (University of Milano, Italy)
Jean-Louis Cavarero (University of Nice, France)
Sergio de Cesare (Brunel University, UK)
Christine W. Chan (University of Regina, Canada)
Islam Choudhury (London Guildhall University, UK)
Claude Chrisment (IRIT, France)
Christine Collet (LSR-IMAG, France)
Robert B. France (Colorado State University, USA)
Brian Henderson-Sellers (University of Technology of Sydney, Australia)
Danièle H'erin (LIRMM, France)
Keith Jeffrey (CLRC Rutherford Appleton Laboratory, UK)
Donald Kossmann (Technical University of Munich, Germany)
Zoe Lacroix (Arizona State University, USA)
Pece Mitrevski (St. Kliment Ohridski University, Macedonia)
Noureddine Mouaddib (IRIN, France)
Moira Norrie (ETH, Switzerland)
Maria Orlowska (University of Queensland, Australia)
Dilip Patel (South Bank University, UK)
Shushma Patel (South Bank University, UK)
D. Janaki Ram (Indian Institute of Technology, India)
Mike Papazoglou (Tilburg University, The Netherlands)
Colette Rolland (Universit'e Paris-Sorbonne, France)
Michael Rys (Microsoft Research, USA)
José Samos (University of Granada, Spain)

Jeff Sutherland (CTO PatientKeeper Inc., UK)
Zahir Tari (RMIT University, Australia)
Yingxu Wang (University of Calgary, Canada)
Anne-Marie Vercoustre (CSIRO, Australia)
Roberto Zicari (Johann Wolfgang Goethe-University of Frankfurt, Germany)

External Referees

Xavier Baril
Jean Bézivin
Jean-Michel Bruel
Gennaro Bruno
Stefano Cerri
Max Chevalier
Costas Calcanis
Luciano Garcia-Banuelos
Olivier Guyotot
Mountaz Hascoet
Gilles Hubert
Marianne Huchard
Michelle Joab
Daniele Maraschi
Hervé Martin
José Martinez
Olivier Massiot
Ralf Muhlberger
Tanguy Nedelec
Makoto Nonaka
Pierre Pompidor
Richard Raban
Shazia Sadiq
Chantal Soulé-Dupuy
Dalila Tamzalit
Olivier Teste
Genoveva Vargas-Solar
Tuyet-Trinh Vu

Table of Contents

Invited Talks

Developping Web Services

Object Databases

XML and Web

Component and Ontology

UML Modelling

Object Modeling and Information Systems Adaptation

E-business Models and Workflow

Performance and Method Evaluation

Programming and Tests

Software Engineering Metrics

Web-Based Information Systems

Architecture and Corba

Roles and Evolvable Objects

Corporate Semantic Webs

Rose Dieng

INRIA, France

The next generation of the Web will be the semantic Web where semantic contents of the Web resources will be interpretable not only by human but also by machine. One popular approach for Semantic Web consists of describing this semantic contents through metadata. Knowledge Management is one of the key progress factors inorganizations. It can rely on explicit and persistent materialization of knowledge of dispersed groups of people in the organization, so as to improve the activities of the organization. When the organization knowledge is distributed among several experts and documents, an Intranet inside the organization and Web technologies can be a privileged means for acquisition, modelling, management of this distributed knowledge. One promising approach relies on the analogy between the resources constituting a corporate memory and the resources accessible through the Web. A corporate memory can thus be materialised in a "corporate semantic Web" made up of resources (e.g. documents or experts), ontologies and semantic annotations on these resources by using the conceptualvocabulary of the ontologies. I shall present a survey of present research useful for building suchcorporate semantic webs.

Z. Bellahsène, D. Patel, and C. Rolland (Eds.): OOIS 2002, LNCS 2425, p. 1, 2002.

A Framework for Defining E-business Models

Yves Pigneur

HEC Lausanne
yves.pigneur@unil.ch

Nowadays new business models are constantly emerging in electronic commerce and can become a major stake in the e-business game. It is even possible to patent them in some countries. Understanding them and helping to design them are important issues.

We propose a framework or ontology for defining business models. Our e-business model ontology outlines what value a company offers to which customer segments. It describes the architecture of the firm and its network of partners for creating, marketing and delivering value and relationship capital, in order to generate profitable and sustainable revenue streams.

We design this ontology based on an extensive literature review on business model and on enterprise ontology. By merging the conceptually rich business model approach with the more rigorous ontological approach and by applying it to e-business, we achieve an appropriate foundation for tools that would allow the understanding, sharing and communication, change, measuring and simulation of e-business models.

Our e-Business Model Ontology is the conceptualization and formalization into elements, relationships, vocabulary and semantics of the essential objects in the e-business model domain. The ontology is structured into several levels of decomposition with increasing depth and complexity. The first level of decomposition of our ontology contains the four main pillars of a business model, which are the products and services a firm offers, the relationship it maintains with its customers, the infrastructure necessary in order to provide this and finally, the financials, which are the expression of business success or failure (see figure 1).

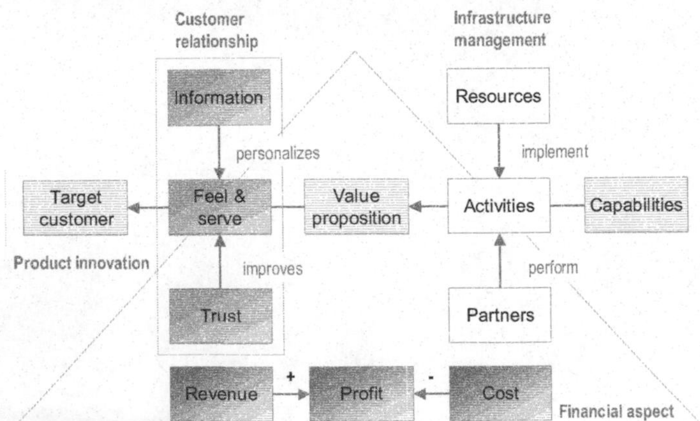

Fig. 1. The main components of the Business Model Ontology

Z. Bellahsène, D. Patel, and C. Rolland (Eds.): OOIS 2002, LNCS 2425, pp. 2-3, 2002.

The **product** component of the e-business model framework describes the *value proposition* a firm wants to offer to a specific *target customer segment*. To deliver this value, the firm has to possess a certain set of in-house and/or outsourced *capabilities*.

ICT offer a range of opportunities to create new and exploit existing **customer** relationships to *feel and serve for* customers and develop an enduring relationship with them. In order to improve the customers experience in doing business, the firm has to gather and exploit *customer information*. More then ever before, the focus has to be on a positive customer relationship which will result in customer *trust* and *loyalty*.

In the product component of the e-business model framework we have described the capabilities which are needed in order to create and deliver the value proposition. The **infrastructure** component describes the value system configuration that is necessary to deliver the value proposition; in other words, the relationship between in-house *resources and assets*, the *activity and process configuration* of the business the firm is operating in and the firms *partner network*.

Of course, the **financial** perspective also belongs to our e-business model framework. Financial aspects can be understood as *costs* required to get the infrastructure to create value and as *revenues* of sold value. The difference between revenues and costs determines the *profitability* of a company.

References

1. Afuah, A., C. Tucci (2001) *Internet Business Models and Strategies*, Boston: McGraw Hill.
2. Osterwalder, A., Pigneur, Y. (2002) An e-Business Model Ontology for Modeling e-Business, *Proc. 15th Bled Electronic Commerce Conference*, June.
3. Gordijn, J., Akkermans, J., van Vliet, J. (2000). What's in an Electronic Business Model?, *Knowledge Engineering and Knowledge Management - Methods, Models, and Tools, LNAI* 1937: 257-273.
4. Hamel, G., (2000) *Leading the revolution*, Boston: Harvard Business School Press.
5. Linder, J.C., Cantrell, S. (2001) *Changing Business Models: Surveying the Landscape*, Working Paper, Institute for Strategic Change, Accenture.
6. Peterovic, O., Kittl, C., Teksten, R.D. (2001) Developing Business Models for eBusiness, *Proc. International Conference on Electronic Commerce 2001*, Vienna, October.
7. Timmers, P. (1998) Business Models for Electronic Markets, *Journal on Electronic Markets*, 8 (2): 3-8.
8. Ushold, M., King, M. (1995) Towards a Methodology for Building Ontologies, *Proc. Workshop on Basic Ontological Issues in Knowledge Sharing*, Montreal, August.
9. Weill, P., Vitale, M.R. (2001) *Place to space: Migrating to eBusiness Models*, Harvard Business School Press.

GRID in E-business

Pierre Sablonière

IBM, France

Ian Foster and Carl Kesselman outlined Grid concepts in 1999 in their book "The Grid Blueprint for a new Computing infrastructure". In a subsequent paper, "the Anatomy of the Grid", the following definition was proposed for Grid as "a Technology that provides coordinated resource sharing and problem solving in dynamic, multi-institutional virtual organizations". Looking further down in actual Grid flavours we have the following functional taxonomy: Compute Grid, Data Grid, Scavenging Grid, Aggregating Grid and Hybrid Grids.

Examples of Compute Grids exist today such as the US TeraGrid, regrouping various Centers for Supercomputing Applications. A data grid example is the US National Digital Mammography Archive system, which provides access to huge and increasing data The recent example of the Dcrypton in France is an example of a virtual dynamic multi organization Grid with tens of thousands PCs federated to build the Proteone database.

In reality these examples are not trivial, as there are many issues to be considered when designing and setting a Grid. A Grid infrastructure has to address: Heterogeneity, integration (OS, protocols) - WANness (bandwidth, latency and disconnects) - Management (autonomy, policy-based) - Dynamic nature (unpredictability, transient) - Large data movement (flat files, RDBMS) - Security (privacy, credentials, authentication) - Large scale serial, batch, parallel processing - Implementing resilience (industrial strength) - Accounting and billing - Guaranteed Quality of Service (QoS).

Today, the existing momentum set by the Internet success and I/T standard adoption thru Open sources and Linux operating system makes possible to envisage standardization of the Grid. This is being addressed by the Grid Global Forum (www.gridforum.org) with a paper "The physiology of the Grid" detailing an "Open Grid Services Architecture". The OGSA is based on a layered architecture and proposes the usage of Web Services standards, UDDI as directory and SOAP for service delivery. The open source Globus package (www.globus.org) is the privileged implementation.

The Grid concepts are hot today. Grid is seen by CIOs as a game changer. For users, Grid provides access to a vast amount of resources. For business people, Grid will tap I/T power on demand like electricity is distributed today. Grid will not eliminate traditional I/T infrastructures it will gradually change the way we see an I/T solution just like the Web changed forever the relationship we have with the Information Technology. More selfishly, for humankind, Grid delivers today with the Dcrypton and the NMDA solution to very serious problems that could not have been solved by other means.

Z. Bellahsène, D. Patel, and C. Rolland (Eds.): OOIS 2002, LNCS 2425, p. 4, 2002.

The Latest Development on Cognitive Informatics

Yingxu Wang
University of Calgary, Canada

Cognitive informatics (CI) is a cutting-edge and profound interdisciplinary research area that tackles the common root problems and foundations of modern informatics, computation, software engineering, AI, and life sciences. CI is a new frontier that studies internal information processing mechanisms and processes of the brain, and their applications in computing, software, and ICT industries. Conventional information theory (Shannon, 1948) treated information as a measure of the probability of messages received from a channel. It was focused on information transmission rather than information itself. Modern information theory perceives information as any aspect of the natural world that can be abstracted and digitally represented. With this orientation, information is regarded as entities of messages, rather than a probabilistic measurement of them as in the classical information theory. However, it is recognized that current information theories are still in a category of external informatics. Complementing to these, there is a whole range of extremely interesting new research areas known as CI, a term which was coined by the author in 2001. 'I think, therefore I am (Rene Descartes, 1596-1650).' CI draws the attention of research on the internal information processing mechanisms of the brain, which are perceived as the foundation of next generation IT and software technologies, such as neural computers, bio-computers, novel methodologies of software engineering, quantum information processing, and powerful ICT systems. This talk focuses on the natural information processing mechanisms and cognitive processes. The latest development on CI at the First IEEE International Conference on Cognitive Informatics (ICCI'02) will be reported. A theoretical framework of CI as an emerging and interdisciplinary research area will be presented. The objectives of this talk are to draw attention of researchers, practitioners and graduate students on the investigation of cognitive mechanisms and processes of human information processing, and to stimulate the collaborative international effort on CI research and engineering applications.

Z. Bellahsène, D. Patel, and C. Rolland (Eds.): OOIS 2002, LNCS 2425, p. 5, 2002.

Pluggable Services for Tailorable E-content Delivery

Christos K.K. Loverdos, Kostas Saidis, Anya Sotiropoulou, and Dimitrios Theotokis

Department of Informatics and Telecommunications
University of Athens
Panepistimiopolis, 157 84 Ilissia, Athens Greece
{loverdos,saiko,anya,dtheo}@mm.di.uoa.gr

Abstract. Delivering e-content as a service to end users involves addressing various cross-cutting aspects, including the heterogeneity of source and data, user needs, business rules as well as the evolution of the content itself. Catering for these aspects when modeling information systems calls for an architecture that accommodates evolution through separation of concerns and tailorability, and provides uniform access to the underlying content. Based on the notions of services and servicing rules, modules, providers, and module composition we show that effective modelling of service-based e-content delivery system is accomplished.

1 Introduction

This work deals with the design and the development of a framework for the delivery of multi-source heterogeneous e-content. From a business perspective, it is necessary to facilitate the incorporation, modification and incremental addition of business logic in a transparent, consistent, and flexible manner. In other words, the system's tailorability is of upmost importance, as it enables its evolution according to emerging business needs. Consequently, the framework must be free of rigid design decisions, and as such abites to the principles of Deffered Design Decisions (DDD) [4].

From the end-user's perspective, as well as that of developers, uniform access to the system's data, whether internal or external, irrespective of their formats, structure and source, is also of great importance. Following this the infrastructure that generates the publishable form of the content from its raw data representation should be as transparent as possible and should not require any special programming skills. That is, an average knowledge of HTML should suffice for this purpose.

To achieve all of the above, it is necessary to separate all such concerns and provide the appropriate infrastructure for their composition into something robust, meaningfull, and well-defined. The system's adaptation is achieved along the following levels: (a) At the programmer level in order to ease the programming cost and minimize editive changes. In effect, the maximization of code

Z. Bellahsène, D. Patel, and C. Rolland (Eds.): OOIS 2002, LNCS 2425, pp. 6–18, 2002.

reusability (modules) and resource transparency (provision) is sought. (b) At the business-logic level to cope with ever changing business requirements (services).

The remainder of this paper is organized as follows. Section 2 focuses on the key concepts of the architecture. In Section 3 the elements of the application framework are presented. Section 4 presents related work. Section 5 concludes the paper and presents future work directions.

2 Key Concepts

A *Service* is a process invoked by a user request, consisting of a set of actions that need to be taken in order to fulfill the request. Services implement business logic and are constructed by the composition of modules.

A *Module* implements an action needed as part of a service. A Module is the fundamental building stone of the architecture and the framework. It describes first level atomic operations, thus wrapping programming logic into reusable, independent units. A module exhibits a well-defined behavior as specified by its input and respective output. Examples of modules include user authorization, user profiling, dynamic HTML creation, database querying etc.

The *Provision* of any resources needed by modules and, consequently, services must be done in an as dynamic and uniform way as possible. Resource handling is, in our opinion, of fundamental value and as a result is treated as a key element in the work presented herein. What follows is a detailed description of the above.

Modules, enable the separation of the servicing process into its operational components. This provides the flexibility to set up new services by composing modules and/or other services. Module composition reflects the adaptability of the approach with respect to the business requirements and usage patterns.

Consider a web application where registered users access a specific service, namely `dbSearch`, and where session management is needed, so that the semantics of "controlled access" business rule are realised. Given the above requirements, we identify the actions, authentication, session management, and reply construction, represented by the modules `Authenticator`, `SessionManager`, and `PageGenerator`, respectively.

Now, assume that the business policy regarding the `dbSearch` service changes to "free access". Consequently, the use of the `Authenticator` and `SessionManager` becomes redundant. Later in this paper we describe a module composition mechanism based on a boolean expressions to model business logic.

To support a unified way of acquiring and manipulating resources, we have based our work on the concept of provision. This is the heart of the proposed architecture, a general concept that can be specialized in more concrete cases, according to the needs of an application. For example, one may refer to the provision of: a set of tuples stored in an RDBMS, text stored in files, XML entities, in-memory objects, the result of a computation, etc.

For identification purposes, resources within the system are supplied with unique identifiers. Grouping of conceptual related resources is achieved in terms of realms. For example, all the modules in the system could belong to the same realm, called `ModuleRealm`. Realms may contain sub-realms, producing in this way a hierarchical model for resource naming. In other words, we define a scheme for supporting *hierarchical namespaces*. Each realm, is administered by an entity called *Provider* which "knows" how to handle and provide objects belonging to that realm. Thus, we can decouple "how to get" data from "where to use" them, allowing for their independent evolution. As long as we keep the same qualified name for a resource, it can be uniformely referenced throughout the system and the editive changes needed in source code are minimized.

3 Key Elements of the Application Framework

Assuming that: (a) modules are composed according to an execution rule – the servicing or business rule – to form a service that fulfills user requests, and (b) provision enables the manipulation of resources as entities grouped into hierarchies we set up an application framework using Java, that can be used to build effective, tailorable, service-based web applications. What follows outlines the framework's key elements: (a) The Provision Mechanism and its core components. (b) The Module Composition Mechanism – how modules are defined and composed, how they communicate and, finally, how they correspond to the execution of a service. (c) The protocol for the Instantiation and Initialization of entities in the framework. (d) The manner through which the Provision Mechanism provides uniform access to data, independently of their source and nature. (e) The Dynamic Content Generation Mechanism.

3.1 Providers and Provider Manager – The Provision Mechanism

A provider is realized as an implementation of the Provider interface (Fig. 1.(a)). This interface defines the most general case of provision, leaving the real "meaningful" specifications to be set by the implementor. We shall see several implementations and specializations of this interface later, as we discuss the functionality of different entities of the framework.

The usage pattern defined by this interface is rather simple: For a client to gain access to a resource it must query the resources's Provider. In doing so it must provide information about the resource it requires, along with a search guideline, namely a *hint*, in order to specialise the provider's response. Thus, it becomes evident that a Provider, although similar to the Factory [1] design pattern it extends it in terms of semantics incorporated in the notion of provision.

Providers register their associated realm in an administration authority called `ProviderManager` (manager). A provider can also act as a manager for specific sub-realms, resulting in a flexible, recursive resource management schema. Any access to resources is done via the `ProviderManager`, using their qualified

```
public interface Provider {
/* Given a description (what) and additional searching hints (hint), provides an object/resource.
 * If for a reason this provision fails, a ProvisionException should be raised, indicating the error. */
 Object provide(Object what, Object hint) throws ProvisionException;
}
```

(a)

```
public interface Module {
/**
 * This method should return true iff the execution succeeds. The SRI object passed as argument
 * provides access to the attributes of the current running state. */
 public boolean execute(SRI runInfo);
}
```

(b)

```
/* A class that implements this interface provides only one instance of itself.
 * If Java supported interfaces with static methods, we could have declared a method:
 *     public static Object getSingleton()
 * Since that is not possible we imply the existence of a static method:
 *     public static Foo getInstance()
 * in every Foo class that implements it. */
public interface Singleton {
 //Empty, just a markup interface
}
```

(c)

```
public interface Initialize {
/**
 * Initialization information is provided through the Map parameter,
 * containing name of attribute/value pairs.   */
 public void init(Map initInfo);
}
```

(d)

```
/**
 * The Provider interface defines the method
 *         public Object provide(Object what, Object hint)
 * Implementations of the DataProvider interface should expect the 'what' object to be an Integer (indexing a
 * specific row of the underlying tabular data) and the 'hint' object either to be of type java.util.Locale
 * for internationalization or null. Also, implementations are advised to return a java.util.Map instance,
 * containing name/value pairs representing the data contained in the requested row. */
public interface DataProvider extends Provider {
  /**
   * This method returns an Enumeration through the names of the resources this provider can handle.
   * For example, the names of the columns occurring in the underlying query that "generates" the data. */
  public Enumeration resourcesProvided();
  /** Returns true if the provider can provide a row with index i. The indexes start from zero. */
  public boolean providesDataWithIndex(int i);
}
```

(e)

Fig. 1. Interface definitions of the framework

names. The `ProviderManager` delegates the provision request to the corresponding provider.

For clarity, examples of resource qualifiers are given below:

db.users.query.userInfo This describes an SQL query which retrieves user information from a database. The manner this specification is parsed and interpreted lies with the specification of the provider associated with the `db` realm. Once the `db` provider is registered with the top-level manager, any `db` prefixed request to the manager is delegated to the `db` provider. This resource is further explained in Section 3.4.

service.request.parameters This identifier represents the parameters provided as part of the user's HTTP request. A more detailed description is provided in Section 3.4.

3.2 The Module Composition Mechanism

The Module Composition Mechanism (MCM) is based on the the following assumptions: (a) Modules should be coded as separate entities that perform a single, well-defined task, in an atomic way, and (b) every module may succeed or fail under certain circumstances, so its execution should be treated as a boolean operation that returns TRUE in case of success and FALSE, otherwise. Furthermore, the MCM should meet the following requirements: (a) Services or modules may change due to business rule modification, and the composition mechanism must be able to easily adapt such changes, and (b) modules that co-operate in a service should be able to exchange information.

In this section we cover in detail the MCM in terms of: how the module composition is specified and executed,how modules communicate, and how all these result in the execution of a service.

MCSL - The Module Composition Specification Language: For the proposed framework we employ a language of boolean expressions, namely MCSL. A module that appears in such an expression corresponds to a boolean variable, as mentioned before. Each service invocation results to the evaluation of such an expression. The boolean expressions supported are build in terms of the following operators, while the MCSL grammar is shown below.

1. Boolean NOT, denoted as '!'.
2. Boolean OR, denoted as '|' and implemented with sequential semantics. This means that an OR expression should succeed as soon as possible — if it succeeds at all.
3. Boolean AND, denoted as '&' and implemented with sequential semantics. This means that an AND expression should fail as soon as possible — if it fails at all.
4. Parentheses '(' and ')', to realise priorities.

```
or_expr  ::= and_expr '|' or_expr | and_expr
and_expr ::= not_expr '&' and_expr | not_expr
not_expr ::= '!' e | e
e        ::= '(' or_expr ')' | IDENTIFIER
```

Communicating Modules - The Service Runtime Information: Module communication is necessary in the context of the execution of a service. For this purpose, we have drawn on the notions behind workflow technology. A workflow, in the higher level of abstraction, consists of rules that govern its execution along with the specification of the data flow between its components. In a similar way, we use the MCSL to define the execution rules of a service and introduce the notion of the Service Runtime Information (SRI) to cover the needs of data communication between each execution step. The similarities between a service process and a workflow process are illustrated in Fig. 2 [3].

We refer to workflow from a rather abstract point of view and use its core semantics. We ommit semantics that are either inapplicable in our context or are unrelated to it such as worklists and BPR and Automation notions.

The SRI Object encapsulates the data associated with a given instance of a service process, acting as the data communication channel between its modules. Every instance of a service is associated with its own SRI object, which is accessible by every module participating in the service execution. A module stores the data it generates in the SRI object. A subsequent module in the execution

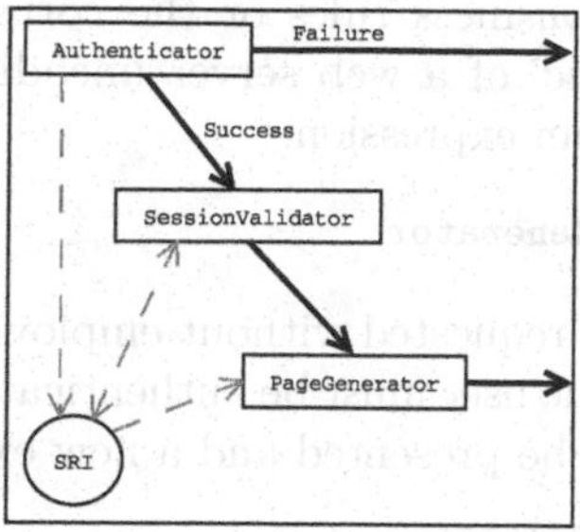

Fig. 2. A Service process presented as a workflow. The black arrows define the execution order – the control flow – while the gray, dashed ones represent the data flow and highlight the data communication channel supplied by the SRI

order requiring the data in question, simply posts a provision request to the SRI object to obtain a reference to them. The framework supports the aforementioned module's interaction is a part of every service execution, but it does not supply a specification scheme for it. It is the implementor of the service and its modules that has the responsibility of the data flow specification.

Module Composition Engine: A module is realized as an implementation of the Module interface presented in Fig. 1.(b). This interface defines the basic operation performed by every module, and ignores issues concerning the instantiation and/or initialization, which are discussed later.

The Module Composition Engine (MCE) is the runtime environment for the execution of modules and services. Its purpose is to evaluate boolean expressions consisting of Modules that represent a service. The evaluation is accomplished as follows:

1. Parse the expression that corresponds to the requested service.
2. Build an equivalent internal representation of the expression which specifies the modules' execution order.
3. Create a new (empty) SRI object.
4. Call the `execute(SRI)` method of the first module in the execution order and store its result (either true for success or false for failure).
5. Remove the module from the execution order.
6. If the expression can not be evaluated because there are modules remaining in the execution order, go to step 4. If its evaluation is possible, perform it by applying to the expression the results available so far and return its value.

Boolean expressions, implementing business logic, define the execution order of the modules that participate in a service. The aim is the evaluation of such expressions to TRUE, indicating an overall successful execution.

A Module Composition Example: Consider the `dbSearch` service example in Section 2. There exist a number of possible implementations of this service, depending either on the business rules or the corresponding modules specifications. The 'business logic' of a web server uncoditionally serving content is implemented by the boolean expression:

```
* = PageGenerator
```

where * refers to any page requested without employing authentication and session management. When the user must be authenticated prior to using the search page, a `LoginPage` should be presented and a new expression is constructed:

```
LoginPage  = PageGenerator
SearchPage = Authenticator & PageGenerator
```

The user reaches the `SearchPage` only if correct username and password values are given in the `LoginPage`. This is reflected in the `Authenticator` module which returns true iff the user's login and password are valid. If session management is needed, this is accommodated by the following definition:

```
LoginPage  = PageGenerator
SearchPage = Authenticator & SessionCreator & PageGenerator
         * = SessionValidator & PageGenerator
```

All visitors should be able to access the `LoginPage`. If they login successfully they are provided with the `SearchPage`. The `SessionCreator` module, creates a new user session, storing in it information provided by the `Authenticator`. This information is available through the SRI object. Finally, all pages appearing after the `SearchPage` should be available only to already authenticated users. That is accomplished by the use of the `SessionValidator`, which succeeds iff a user session is present in the request.

3.3 Instantiation & Initialization Mechanism

The notion of the `InstanceManager` is introduced as a core component of the application framework. It operates on its lowest-level, and in fact is part of the framework's kernel. In accordance with the terminology used so far, it stands for a Provider of instances. The `InstanceManager` provides the functionality of instance creation hiding the underlying details from its clients. It handles the `instance` realm and expects the names of the requested recourses to be the fully qualified Java class names of the associated objects. For example, a provision request `instance.Authenticator` refers to the the class name of the authentication module.

Depending on their usage patterns objects may be multiply or singly instantiated. The latter are named Singletons and comply with the Singleton design pattern [1]. Such Singletons are realized in the framework as implementations of the Singleton interface shown in Fig. 1.(c).

Under our approach initialisation and instantiation are treated as different tasks. For that purpose we introduce the Initialize interface shown in Fig. 1.(d). Using Java's reflection capabilities, the `InstanceManager` can satisfy both instantiation and initialisation needs, by following the steps below:

1. It loads the class that corresponds to the name given,
2. If the class implements the Singleton interface:
   - Obtains a reference to the instance of that class by calling its `getInstance()` method.
   - If the class also implements the Initialize interface it checks if the object needs to be initialized. If so, by means of reflection it calls the instance's `init(Map)` method which it supplies with a Map object that contains initialisation data.

   If not:
   - Assuming that the hint object in the provision request is an object array (`Object[]`), the constructor of the class whose arguments' types match those of the elements of the `Object[]` is reflectively located.
   - Once found, the constructor is called and a reference to the newly created instance is obtained.
3. Returns the instance to the client.

Providers handling external to the system resources are implemented in the framework as Singletons, such as the database data provider. On the other hand, Providers for resources specific to a service execution, such as request parameters, are created upon each service invocation and destroyed after its termination. This makes efficient use of memory.

3.4 Details of the Provision Mechanism – Uniform Access to Data

Data sources are objects that contain or/and generate data. Such data sources could be databases –XML objects, text or binary files, servers residing on the network etc. All these entities are 'external' to the application itself and it is a good practice to decouple the code that accesses them from the code that operates on the data they provide. The same should hold for information that exists "within" the application, such as request parameters session information. However, programmers hard code such accesses to internal resources, causing tight coupling of rather irrelevant to each other tasks and operations.

Instead we use the provision mechanism, to uniformly access both "internal" and "external" data. We introduce an extension to the Provider interface, namely `DataProvider`, illustrated in Fig. 1.(e) that allows one to cycle through the underlying data in a simple and efficient way. Classes implementing this interface act as wrappers of the underlying data, hiding the implementation details of how these are accessed.

Let an SQL query that retrieves user information depending on the username given be:

```
SELECT USERID, UNAME, PASSD FROM USERS WHERE UNAME = '{UNAME}'
```

The results of this query represent a resource, namely `db.users.query.userInfo`. The corresponding Provider of this resource "knows" how to utilise it, hiding from the developer its underlying implemention. The developer treats

```
ProviderManager manager =
        ProviderManager.getInstance();
String username = (String)
        manager.provide(
                "service.request.parameters.username",
                null);
HashMap map = new HashMap();
map.put("USERNAME", username);
DataProvider userInfo = (DataProvider)
        manager.provide(
                "db.users.query.userInfo",
                map);
if (userInfo.providesDataWithIndex(0)) {
        Map userMap = (Map)
                userInfo.provide(new Integer(0), null);
        String password =
                (String)userMap.get("PASSWORD");
        ...
}
else {
        //User's login attempt failed
}
```

(a)

```
<DEFINE>
<TEMPLATE NAME="MENU" WHAT="common/main-menu"/>
<DATASET NAME="BOOK" WHAT="db.books.query.bookInfo"
     HINT="AUTHOR = service.request.parameters.author"/>
<DATASET NAME="REQUEST" WHAT="service.request.parameters"/>
</DEFINE>

<html>
<head><title>Book Search Results</title></head>
<table>
  <tr colspan="2"><td><MENU/></td></tr>
  <tr colspan="2">
    <REQUEST>
      <td>Books written by the author <REQUEST.author/>:</td>
    </REQUEST>
  </tr>
  <tr>
    <BOOK>
      <td><BOOK.TITLE/></td>
      <td><a
href="bookDetails?isbn=<BOOK.ISBN/>">Details</a></td>
    </BOOK>
  </tr>
  <tr colspan="2"><td><MENU/></td></tr>
</table>
</html>
```

(b)

Fig. 3. (a) Code snippet of the authentication module, highlighting the details of data provision, (b)A simple example of an extented HTML template

it as a resource that requires a `UNAME` as an argument, denoted in the SQL code by `{UNAME}`, and returns `(USERID, UNAME, PASSWD)` tuples, wrapped by a `DataProvider` object.

Assume that the Authenticator module in the `dbSearch` example, uses the `db.users.query.userInfo` resource in order to authenticate the user as shown in Fig. 3.(a). The Authenticator module simply requests the provision of named entities from the `ProviderManager`. The latter is accessed when client code requires to a resource and for that reason is implemented as a Singleton object globally available in the system. It delegates each request to the registered provider for the top-level realm specified in its subject. Other implementations could follow different delegation policies according to a more complex lookup.

The role of the hint object in the Provider interface specification (Fig. 1.(a)) is to enable the parameterisation of the provision process. These parameters are represented in the framework as containers of name/value pairs.

The other provision example of Fig. 3.(a) refers to a resource named `service.request.parameters.username`. It corresponds to a parameter provided by the user, encapsulating the `username` input element of the HTML form. We use a Provider to handle the `service` realm and thus represent a service as seen from an HTTP server's viewpoint, consisting of a request, a response and perhaps an associated session. Such providers are automatically created and assigned to every service process by the framework. The flexibility provided by this hierarchical naming scheme is highlighted by the following table, which outlines the results of provision depending on the resource wanted:

Name of resource:	`service.request`
Object returned:	The `javax.servlet.http.HttpServletRequest` object itself
Name of resource:	`service.request.parameters`
Object returned:	A `DataProvider` wrapping all request parameters
Name of resource:	`service.request.parameters.a-param`
Object returned:	The value of the `a-param` request parameter

Simple implementations of the Provider interface are used to wrap various types of data, even components of the system itself, thus, extending and specializing the notion of provision according to a system's needs.

3.5 Dynamic Content Generation

Another goal in the design of the framework was to utilize a powerful yet easy to use mechanism for dynamic content generation. Familiar approaches to ours already exist and some of them are widely used, such as JSP [6], ASP [5] and PHP [7] just to mention a few. Although they provide great functionality and ease of of use, their main characteristic is that they are full fleged programming languages, requiring programming skills. On the contrary, we provide a simple extension to HTML, easily adopted by anyone with its basic knowledge.

The idea is simple and is based on document templates that contain named placeholders of data to be generated on the fly – upon the document's request. Our aim is to separate the details of 'how to get' the content and 'how to render' it, according to the specification of the Model-View-Controller [2] model. The template author, using a language he knows and understands well, is called only to name the data its document needs and specify the places they should appear, *not to program the way they will be accessed.*

The provision mechanism enables us to treat the templates as simple provision specifications. The framework supplies a `PageGenerator` module responsible for the dynamic generation of content according to the following rules: (a) each URL a user requests should correspond to a template stored in the local filesystem, (b) such templates may contain sub-templates, ad infinitum, and (c) the creation of such templates involves specific XML tags.

For that purpose, three XML elements are introduced which define the dynamic content generation process illustrated in Fugure 3.(b). These elements form the aforementioned extension to HTML, but, obviously, are not limited to it. The mechanism can also be used to generate XML, RTF, RDF and any other text-oriented content. In detail these elements are:

DEFINE: This element appears at the top of the template and acts as a container of the other two elements (see Fig. 3.(b)), specifically, it declares the entities that will act as the placeholders in the template. All these entities are supplied with unique identifiers in the scope of the template declared. An occurrence of an element named as any of these identifiers elsewhere in the template, represents a placeholder for the corresponding entity.

TEMPLATE: This element defines a sub-template in a document template. Its syntax is:

```
<TEMPLATE NAME="name-of-template" WHAT="path-to-template-file"/>
```

For example, in Fig. 3.(b), we declare a template named MENU in the body of the DEFINE element, which refers to the contents of the file common/main-menu. In the main body of the template, all occurences of the <MENU/> element will be replaced by the contents of the file it refers to.

DATASET: This element specifies a resource to be used by the template in which it is declared and follows the syntax:

```
<DATASET NAME="entityName" WHAT="resourceName" HINT="f1=val1, f2=val2"/>
```

The DATASET element is also supplied with a unique identifier (the NAME attribute) and specifies a provision request, which will be executed dynamically by the PageGenerator module. Its WHAT and HINT attributes map directly to the parameters of the provide(what, hint) method defined in the Provider interface (see Fig. 1.(a)). The Map object used to encapsulate provision parameters is represented here as name = value pairs separated by commas.

The code shown in Fig. 3.(b) creates a page that displays the results of a book search based on its author. This page supplies the user with a list of the book titles, that matched the given criteria along with a hyperlink to the 'details page' of each book. We declare a dataset named BOOK that refers to an SQL query which returns the title and ISBN of the books written by a given author. The template author needs not to be aware of the details of the query, he is not even expected to know SQL, Java or anything else but HTML, and the fact that the BOOK dataset accepts a parameter named AUTHOR. The content generation mechanism will locate the code enclosed in the <BOOK>, <BOOK/> elements and perform the appropriate substitutions of the placeholders <BOOK.TITLE> and <BOOK.ISBN/> with their corresponding values from the query's results. That task will be repeated as many times as are the rows returned.

The template author is responsible for the implementation of the template generation logic – the templates turn to web pages without the interference of the programmer. Note the use of the hint in the BOOK dataset. It defines a parameter named AUTHOR and dynamically sets it to the value of the author request parameter, reflecting the logic required for the generation of the page.

The use of the PageGenerator module and the content generation mechanism it introduces results in self-contained templates, encapsulating both the rendering information and the content generation logic. The whole process is sped up by the support of sub-templates, which enable code reuse.

4 Related Work

The Turbine servlet-based framework [8] resembles in some aspects our approach for the development of service-based e-content delivery systems. It is of our belief that Turbine addresses the same problems in a far more application-oriented approach. For instance, although the Action, Page, and Layout elements of the Turbine framework are in many ways similar to Modules, Services, and Templates the underlying rationale is different. In Turbine there is no uniformity in accessing the underlying data and there is no provision for a formal approach to module composition. Moreover, and in contrast to our simple yet powerfull content generation mechanism, Turbine utilises yet another custom scripting language for that purpose.

The major difference between the two frameworks however is the lack of a service execution engine in Turbine. This implies that our approach due to the MCSL and the underlying MCE formally defines the notion of a service as a composition of modules and its overall execution.

5 Conclusions and Future Work

We have shown that the underlying notions of services, modules and providers presented here ensure that the framework is flexible enough to accommodate for the evolving requirements of e-content publishing systems.

Finally, our architecture is not limited to e-content delivery, but can be used wherever service-based application are required, because of its modular nature. There is concrete evidence that the framework can be used for any type of service-based applications since only one of the framework's modules is associated with the generation and delivery of content. Substituting it with an appropriate module the framework could act as an FTP, HTTP or LDAP server.

Enhancements of both the architecture and the framework may be carried out, in order to further expand its functionality and application domains. For instance, services may not be resident on the same host as the system. Work is currently undertaken to support distributed services. In order to provide a richer language for expressing business rules and the collaboration of distributed services and modules, extensions to the MCSL are required. Such enhancements will focus on complex module composition as well as the specification of remote modules.

Another area that needs thorough investigation is that of transactional services, so that e-commerce and e-government applications may be realized under the proposed architecture. To formalise module communication it is necessary to provide a data-flow specification scheme, so that module interaction is expressed in a similar way to that of module composition.

References

1. E.Gamma, R.Helm, R.Johnson, J.Vlissides. *Design Patterns Elements of Reusable Object-Oriented Software*. Addison-Wesley, 1997. 8, 12
2. A.Goldberg and D.Robson. *Smalltalk-80. The Language and its Implementation.* Addison-Wesley. 1983. 15
3. D. Hollingsworth, *The Workflow Reference Model*, Workflow Management Coalition, Document Number: TC00-1003, 1995. Available from www.wfmc.org 10

4. D. Stamoulis, D. Theotokis, D. Martakos, and G. Gyftodimos. "Ateleological Development of Design Decisions Independent Information Systems". in Nandish Patel, editor, *Evolutionary and Adaptive Information Systems*, IDEA Publishing Group, 2002. 6
5. http://www.asp.net/ 15
6. http://java.sun.com/products/jsp/ 15
7. http://www.php.net/ 15
8. http://jakarta.apache.org/projects/turbine 16

An Object-Oriented Approach for Designing Administrative E-forms and Transactional E-services

Dimitris Gouscos, Stathis Rouvas, Costas Vassilakis, and Panagiotis Georgiadis

e-Government Laboratory –Dept. of Informatics and Telecommunications
University of Athens, 15771, Ilissia, Athens, Greece
{d.gouscos,rouvas,costas,p.georgiadis}@e-gov.gr
http://www.e-gov.gr/uoalab

Abstract. E-forms are central to the development of e-government, being a basic means for implementing most of the public services considered as required for local and central public administration authorities. In this paper, we present an object-oriented model for e-form-based administrative services, which spans the e-service lifecycle, including development, deployment and use by enterprises and citizens, data collection and communication with legacy information systems. The proposed approach encompasses semantic, structural and active aspects of e-forms, providing thus an inclusive framework for modelling electronic services.

1 Introduction

With administrative services being the most visible and contradictory aspect of Government for the majority of citizens and businesses, e-Government action plans on the national as well as EU level ([9], [3]) recognize the importance of bringing administrative services on-line as a cornerstone of e-Government projects. Administrative forms, on the other hand, are an indispensable part of public administrative services, since delivery of a public administrative service entails, at some point, an application or declaration form that has to be filled, submitted and processed. This situation is well acknowledged by the fact that eEurope benchmarking indicators, as well as the eEurope 4-stage framework for monitoring maturity of on-line public services, both make explicit reference to levels of on-line availability and submission of forms as e-Government indicators ([6], [4], [5]).

Therefore, an important part of public administrative services and information are delivered and represented, respectively, through forms, which means that an approach to better design administrative forms and exploit their informational content can provide substantial benefits. An essential part of designing an administrative form has to do with (i) its structure, i.e. which its component, sections and fields are and how they are nested, and (ii) its semantics, i.e. the intended meaning of each individual field. Field semantics, in particular, determine (a) how input data should be validated when the form is filled and submitted and (b) how input data can be processed and related in back-office operations.

Z. Bellahsène, D. Patel, and C. Rolland (Eds.): OOIS 2002, LNCS 2425, pp. 19-30, 2002.

Controlling the structure of an administrative form allows to have new forms resembling existing ones; in this way forms can have a standardised appearance, which lowers design costs and allows to capitalize on a sharp learning curve due to user familiarization. Most importantly, controlling the structure of a form facilitates the effort to keep the semantics of all forms consistent. Having consistent semantics for corresponding fields in different forms provides two very important capabilities:

1. Common fields of different forms can be identified and eliminated, so that many forms can be re-engineered into a single one; this may the case of an individual public agency reducing its different forms or of different public agencies trying to establish a single shared form in the context of one-stop e-Government services.
2. Fields of different forms can be related; this may be the case of seeking a common field to be used as correlation key, or of trying to make two fields comparable for cross-checking or statistical processing purposes. Both of these functions may be needed either in a back-office setting within a single public agency or in the context of G2G information flows between different agencies.

It is worth noting that the last point about consistent semantics essentially treats administrative forms as generic information sources (e.g. databases). This is due to the fact that, on a conceptual level, an administrative form is nothing more than the schema of an information collection. Therefore, the same issues about semantics consistency arise in both cases. Exploring the implications of this analogy, identification and elimination of common fields during the merging of administrative forms corresponds to schema integration of two information collections; relating fields of different forms for correlation or comparability corresponds to the same operations on, e.g., database tables; validation rules for the data input in administrative forms correspond to constraints and triggers in databases; administrative forms themselves correspond to data entry screens for DB applications.

Therefore, the above discussion about administrative form semantics holds for the semantics of arbitrary information sources as well. Still, our approach focuses on administrative forms because of the additional issues that are raised in this area. Controlling the structure of an administrative form is as important as controlling its semantics, since it allows to re-use components and standardize on user navigation and user support issues.

2 Basic Terms

In this section we present the basic concepts of the electronic service model, regarding the desired functionality, as well as the processes and items involved in the lifecycle of electronic services.

2.1 E-forms

We are concerned with the problem of applying some methodology for designing administrative forms in a systematic way, that allows to control (a) the structure, (b) the appearance and (c) the semantics of a form. In all these aspects, it should be possible to re-use previous designs for standardisation and productivity reasons. Moreover, we address electronically represented administrative forms (e-forms), i.e. forms implemented as web pages in the context of e-Government service offerings.

E-forms are developed and placed on the web site by the service provider. To this end, some experts on the service provider side are assumed who are able to create new e-forms and publish them on the web. In creating a new form, an expert should be able to re-use components of existing forms, whether these have to do with the form's structure, appearance, semantics, user assistance information, validation logic or process logic. What is more, since the creation of e-forms is assumed to be an iterative and collaborative process, there is a need to treat e-forms as artefacts which also have some "life-cycle" information: version, history, author, approver, etc.

The basic user interaction scenario that we assume is that some administrative e-forms are available on the web; an end-user chooses the form of interest, navigates around its structure (sections, sub-sections etc), enters data as appropriate and submits it; a submitted form is processed by the service provider (the corresponding public agency) and some results are returned to the end-user. Input data validation occurs in two phases: some validation checks are applied on individual fields upon data entry whereas some others are performed after submission, since they apply to combinations of fields or may cross-check values with content from other sources (e.g. an administrative registry). It should be noted here that, in order to support these tasks, an e-form must accommodate, apart from its structure, appearance and semantics, also (d) user assistance information as well as (e) the appropriate validation logic. Apart from that, the form should indicate (f) the associated process logic, i.e. it should determine (e.g. by pointing to it) the procedure with which the form should be processed after it is submitted and validated. Finally, processing of submitted forms may produce results or errors, which should be communicated to the users that filled the forms. The overall e-form lifecycle is illustrated in Fig. 1.

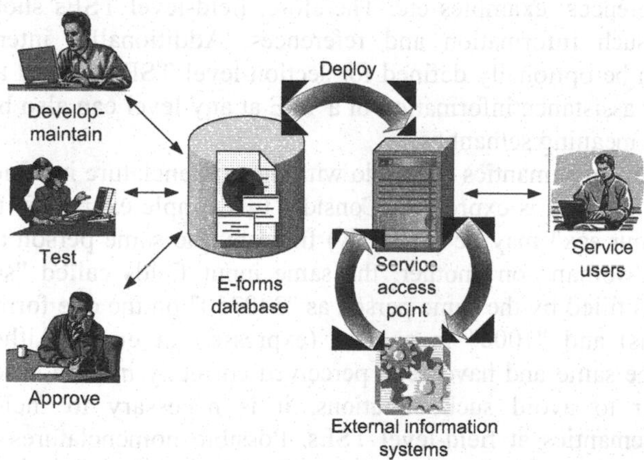

Fig.1. E-form lifecycle

2.2 Transaction Service Elements

A completed e-form, together with its structure, appearance, semantics, user assistance information, validation logic and process logic may be handled as a single entity that can be stored and re-used for generating new e-forms; and of course, this e-form can be published on the web as part of an e-Government service offering for transactional e-services.

As already mentioned, an e-form has some structure, i.e. it consists of sections, subsections, and individual fields just like paper-based administrative forms. Since most of the features of the e-form (appearance, semantics, user assistance info, validation logic) are best defined at the level of the e-form's components, these components (sections, fields) of an e-form are themselves considered as design artefacts which are autonomously created, stored and re-used; this policy evidently increases re-usability potential. Therefore, the term Transaction Service Element (TSE) refers to individual e-form sections and fields, while e-forms are referred to as Transaction Services.

2.3 Semantics

Semantic information as referred to above, has to do with the intended meaning of some values that are expected in the fields of an e-form at data entry time. Only if these semantics are correctly perceived and respected by end users, this a priori intended meaning will also be the actual meaning of the data a posteriori, i.e. when the e-form is inspected or processed after submission and validation. What is more, only if such a condition is met for the corresponding data of all administrative forms that are to be correlated, can such a correlation be successful. In order to facilitate the correct perception by end users of the intended meaning of a data value, this intended meaning can best be associated with the corresponding input field as a description; this description may be complemented by additional aids to the users, including online help references, examples etc. Therefore, field-level TSEs should be able to accommodate such information and references. Additionally, intended meaning descriptions can be optionally defined for section-level TSEs as well as for entire e-forms. The user assistance information of a TSE at any level can also be employed to clarify intended meaning semantics.

A different sort of semantics has to do with the nomenclature in which a value of a given intended meaning is expressed. Consider two simple examples: the same input fields called "your sex" may be (correctly) filled by the same person as "female" on one form and "woman" on another; the same input fields called "salary" may be (correctly again) filled by the same person as "340750" on the one form (expressed in Greek drachmas) and "1000" in another (expressed in euro). Although intended meanings are the same and have been perceived correctly in both cases, data values differ. In order to avoid such situations, it is necessary to included intended nomenclature semantics at field-level TSEs. Possible nomenclatures in which data values are expressed include (a) closed sets of acceptable values, (b) statistical classifications, (c) sets of values from third registries as well as (d) measurement units. Drawing from statistics, it should be noted that the intended nomenclatures of two fields whose values must be compared do not necessarily have to be identical; as long as they are known and at least an one-way mapping exists between them, the field values are comparable.

3 Modelling Transaction Service Elements: An Object-Oriented Approach

According to the above analysis, TSEs at any level, i.e. form-, section- and field-level TSEs must be stored in a way that they can be re-used for designing new e-forms. We adopt an object-oriented approach towards modelling Transaction Service Elements and their attributes. This approach allows, on the one hand, to exploit a significant amount of inheritance and, on the other hand, it facilitates TSE re-use. The resulting object-oriented model, called Transaction Service Object Model (TSOM) incorporates all TSE attributes mentioned above, i.e. structure, appearance, semantics, user assistance, validation logic, process logic as well as life-cycle attributes.

3.1 Modelling of Submitted Forms

Submitted forms, i.e. e-forms that have been filled-in with values by users and submitted, are hosted in TSOM in a special class, which is a specialisation of the respective e-forms class. The additional attributes of a submitted form include, of course, its values, as well submission data and a post-submission trace which is intended as an administrative log for post-submission validation and processing operations (such a trace is necessary in order to produce, e.g., application status reports in an e-Government service context). Providing a special subclass for submitted forms permits for redefinition or cancellation of certain methods defined for the generic class modelling forms. For example, the method catering for the form presentation should now consider the data already typed in by the user; moreover, while a *submit* method is required for e-forms, a submitted form should not have such a method (since it is already submitted!). Through the inheritance mechanism, the specialised class overrides the inherited method to produce an appropriate error.

3.2 Modelling of Agents

As has been discussed, e-forms and TSEs in general are designed by some domain experts on the service provider side. Therefore, the life-cycle information of each TSE also includes some pointers to authors of this TSE and other roles, such as contributors and approvers. On the other hand, form instances are filled and submitted by end-users. For reasons of completeness and uniformity, TSOM includes a sub-hierarchy for modelling all of these roles (TSE authors, etc. as well as end users that fill and submit forms) under the general category of Transaction Service Agents. It is worth noting that this uniform modelling of both e-form authors and users connotes to the possibility of providing, in a real-world setting, a uniform web-based environment both for the authoring of e-forms by experts (possibly external to the public agency) and for the filling and submission of stable and released e-forms by end users in the context of operational e-Government services.

3.3 Modelling of Active Behaviour

Although e-forms may be considered as passive objects being filled-in and submitted by users, they in fact encompass substantial active behaviour in all stages of their usage:

1. When users select an e-form to fill in, the values of various fields may need to be pre-computed before data entry is allowed e.g. for instance, where registry information about the end user is pre-loaded in certain fields of the form.
2. Upon field value modification, certain validations may need to be performed, such as type checks (e.g. only digits are entered in numeric fields), value range assertion, etc. Additionally, some fields may be *read-only* (e.g. fields containing registry data), and consequently appropriate behavioural rules should be defined to prohibit the alteration of their pre-loaded values. Although such checks may be performed when the form is submitted, they are usually performed upon field modification so as to detect errors early and assist thus the user throughout the procedure of form filling.
3. Field value modification may also trigger the updating of the value of other fields. Inter-field dependencies may be necessitated for user convenience, e.g. within a complex multi-page form with many sections that appear through navigation links, it may be arranged that some values are automatically carried on between sections, in order to be readily available for users to look up, without any need for navigating between web pages. Moreover, some fields are automatically calculated via formulas, such as table column sums, VAT amounts corresponding to sales or purchases etc. In these cases, changing the value of any field appearing in the right hand side of the formula should trigger the updating of the field appearing at the left hand side of the formula.
4. Form submission initiates the execution of additional actions, such as field-value correlations, cross-checking of user input with other submitted forms or registries, or even repetition of checks conducted earlier at the organisation's back end environment, since in a web environment front-ends (browsers) are not considered trustworthy and validation checks depending on them may be circumvented.
5. Each step within the processing cycle of a submitted form may trigger a number of actions, such as appending entries to administrative logs for tracing purposes or sending electronic notification to the submitter regarding possible errors.

From the above analysis regarding active features within e-forms, we may derive the following requirements for the TSOM:

1. Since an active feature may involve a single field, a number of fields within the section or the whole e-form, the TSOM should allow the definition of active features in field-, section- and form-level TSEs.
2. TSOM should make provisions for specifying *when* each active feature should be fired. This is a two-fold issue, including the *event* that triggers the active feature (value change, form submission, back-end processing), and a *condition* which must hold (field is not empty, back-end processing resulted to an error etc.)

3. The functions that must be performed as appropriate, may range from simple data type or value-range checks to much more complex validation checks that involve multiple fields or even correlation to information from external sources.

These requirements fit directly to the Event-Condition-Action (ECA) rules paradigm, which is encompassed in the Transaction Service Object Model through a dedicated class sub-hierarchy rooted at the Transaction Service Rules node. This generic category is further specialised to validation, pre-computation, protection, update and processing rules.

At the current state of work, a number of *primitive expressions, functions and constructs* are available for coding conditions and actions; these primitive elements may be combined using *operators*, to form arbitrarily complex constructs. In order to keep the scheme manageable, the number of primitive elements is kept small, sufficing however to model more than 90% of the checks usually encountered in electronic forms. For cases where the supplied expressive power is insufficient, the invocation of external methods is supported, which may be coded in any general-purpose language with unconstrained expressive power. ECA rule execution clearly requires an appropriate engine; the choice of this engine depends on the environment within which the ECA rules will be executed. If the environment is a user's web browser, the Javascript language is a suitable option. Within an organisation's back-end, workflow engines, database triggers or general-purpose languages could be used. In all cases, the ECA rules should be mapped to the target environment.

3.4 Modelling Information Repository Access

While a transaction service is operational, it needs to access information repositories either to retrieve or to store and modify data. For instance, when a user selects to fill in an income tax declaration form, registry data must be retrieved from an information repository and filled in the corresponding form fields before the form is displayed. Subsequently, when the user submits the form, data filled in the various fields should be stored into an information repository, for future processing and/or reference. Data access in the proposed environment is encapsulated in the *Information Repository* object class, which supports methods for invoking *predefined services*. Each such predefined service may accept input parameters and return, besides the execution status, appropriate information. For example, a taxation repository may offer a predefined service that accepts a citizen's tax registration number as an input parameter and returns a structure containing the citizen's data contained in the registry, or a failure indication. An environment offering transaction services may involve multiple instances of *Information Repository* objects, one for each actual information repository that needs to be accessed.

3.5 The Transaction Service Object Model

The class hierarchy of the Transaction Service Object Model is depicted in Fig. 2. The property protocol of TSOM classes is listed in Appendix A.

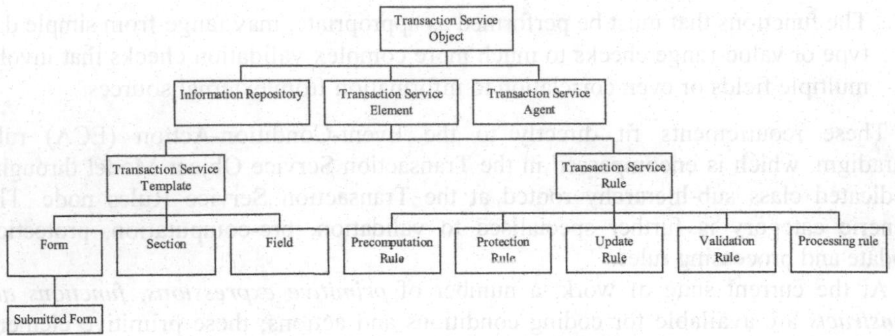

Fig.2. Transaction Service Object Model class hierarchy

4 Sharing and Deployment of TSOM Objects and Services

Form-level TSEs, together with their section- and field-level components, must be publishable on the web as forms that can be filled and submitted. What is more, TSEs at any level may need to be passed on to third parties that exploit a similar, but not necessarily identical approach towards designing administrative e-forms or e-services and could benefit from TSE understanding and re-use. Finally, e-forms may need to be exchanged with third parties in order to investigate capabilities for correlation, and submitted forms may also need to be exchanged in order to actually correlate field values. In the two latter cases, TSEs need to be exchanged together with their associated logic for validation and control, as well as their associated semantics for intended meanings and nomenclatures.

Most importantly, however, the need to exchange e-forms and submitted forms together with their associated logic and semantics calls for representing them by means of a semantics-neutral, syntax-level formalism where TSE attributes can be defined in a straightforward way. In this respect, XML is a natural fit, and has been generally accepted for communication between agencies [10].

The mapping of TSOM instances into XML documents can be approached quite simplistically. An instance o with values v_1, v_2 of an object class C with properties p_1, p_2 can be mapped to some XML code like

```
<instance>
        <of _class> C </of _class>
        <id> o </id>
        <p₁> v₁ </p₁> <p₂> v₂ </p₂>
</instance>
```

Fig.3. XML representation of an instance

While this code excerpt arranges for the transfer of the actual values, communicating entities might also need to exchange schemas of the data transmitted. To this end, XML schemas [13] or XML DTDs [11] may be employed, facilitating the exchange of the data schema descriptions. XML schemas, in particular, may incorporate within data type definitions value constraints that apply to instances.

```
<xs:group name=" TransactionServiceRule">
    <xs:sequence>
        <xs:group ref="TransactionServiceObject"/>
        <xs:element name="trigger" type="Event">
        <xs:element name="condition" type="Expression">
        <xs:element name="procedure" type="ScriptAction">
    </xs:sequence>
</xs:group>
```

Fig.4. Exchanging data schemas through XML

One interesting parameter of TSOM object sharing is that in some cases, certain aspects of the objects need not (or must not) be exchanged for the sake of simplicity, security or information volume reduction purposes. For example, when a tax declaration is forwarded for processing, the presentation details or active features contained within the involved TSOM instances are irrelevant, and may therefore be omitted, without any loss of functionality. Similarly, if the Ministry of Finance has included in its TSEs validation tests to control tax evasion, disclosing of these checks to cooperating taxation agencies (e.g. accountant offices) would void their efficiency. Therefore, the framework should provide the mechanisms for controlling which portions of the Transaction Service Object Model class hierarchy should be exchanged. To this end, a *content negotiation mechanism* is provided, through which the server (i.e. the offering machine) *advertises* the content that is available from it; subsequently, the client requests this data, or a subset of it, possibly providing some authentication credentials. Finally the server, after checking the presented credentials and the access constraints, sends the data or returns an appropriate error either forbidding access or instructing the client to modify its request and ask for a smaller subset. The requesting client may optionally return a reply, either to simply indicate transfer status (success/failure) or to provide any relevant information. Replies, if provided, should be also coded in XML.

The content negotiation mechanism may additionally be used for avoiding to exchange redundant TSOM objects. This applies, for instance, to the case where a new e-form is sent which makes use of section- and field-level TSEs already exchanged. More importantly, this applies to exchanging multiple submitted forms without sending more than once the same e-form. Within the content negotiation phase, the requesting party provides the server with an identification of the objects it already has, so as to enable the server to limit its reply to the objects that will be actually new for the client. In all cases, the main issue is to provide full functionality, with optimisation issues being a highly desirable, but not absolutely necessary feature.

The communication mechanism described above is generic enough to accommodate all circumstances in which electronically submitted forms and/or their data schema need to be exchanged with other information systems. These information systems may be either external to the organisation deploying the electronic service (e.g. governmental agencies, business partners etc.), or internal, such as batch jobs that will process the data (e.g. tax computation procedures).

Service deployment, exploiting the Web as a primary channel, calls for mapping of the object-oriented constructs (i.e. instances of the Transaction Service Object Model) into some mark-up language that can be handled by browsers. The prime candidate for such a mapping is currently HTML since XML and other XML-oriented developments (such as X-Forms [12]) are not fully handled by the majority of browsers. Mapping of TSE information to the appropriate HTML code can be quite straightforward, by employing HTML forms and form elements to facilitate user input, hyperlinks to support navigation between form parts and using visual elements, such as format designators (*<b>*, *<i>*, etc.) or layout specifiers (e.g. *<table>*) to produce the effects designated by the related TSE attributes. A number of active features may also be supported on browser level by means of the Javascript language, which provides modelling constructs for *(event, action)* pairs. Additional active features, such as validation checks or information repository accesses, can be automatically generated for the organisation's back-end, based on the information contained in the TSEs. These features are actually realised through server-side scripting techniques, such as PHP and JSP. These mappings, however, decompose a semantically rich model (the object-oriented one) to low-level formatting and coding constructs, which makes controlling harder and minimises the capabilities for reverse engineering. It is expected that with the advent of the XML and X-Forms standards and their incorporation into browsers, a more straightforward and "non-lossy" mapping may be employed for deploying the electronic services through the Web.

5 Conclusions – Future Work

Work reported in this paper approaches the critical problem of automating the creation, management and processing of electronic administrative forms, in a way that supports the handling of rich form structures together with their associated front- and back-end logic. Object-oriented modelling of e-forms and their active behaviour allows for (a) semantic richness, (b) modelling extensibility, (c) high-level encapsulation of e-forms' data, metadata and associated logic as well as (d) uniform modelling of both submitted e-forms and e-form templates. Mapping of e-forms to XML messages allows forwarding of submitted e-forms to remote sites for processing, which means that front-end submission and back-end processing of an e-form may well be distributed over the web. What is more, XML mapping of e-form templates facilitates the exchange of e-form artefacts for collaborative e-forms design as well as for re-usability purposes.

An important direction of work to carry on, is to elaborate the modelling of e-forms' active behaviour by means of ECA rules and consider additional formalisms of equivalent expressive power (e.g. Horn clauses [8]). Any such representation shall have to be mapped to appropriate XML structures. This mapping may use techniques from existing work (e.g. [1], [2], [7]).

Still another direction of research is that of studying the middleware mechanisms necessary to accept or send e-forms, taking care of issues mentioned in this paper such as management of process traces and content negotiation. The integration of such middleware mechanisms with back-end processing infrastructures is also a subject of investigation.

References

1. J. Bailey, A. Poulovassilis, P.T. Wood "An Event-Condition-Action Language for XML", to appear in the *Proceedings of the WWW2002 Conference*
2. A. Bonifati, S. Ceri, S. Paraboschi, "Active rules for XML: a new paradigm for e-services", VLDB Journal 10(1), pp. 39-47, 2001
3. Commission of the European Communities, "eEurope Action Plan 2002: An Information Society For All", June 2000
4. Commission of the European Communities, "eEurope 2002 Impacts and Priorities", 2001
5. European Commission, DG Information Society, "Web-Based Survey on Electronic Public Services", November 2001
6. European Union Council, "List of eEurope Benchmarking Indicators", November 2000
7. H. Ishikawa, M. Ohta, "An active Web-based Distributed Database System for e-Commerce", Proceedings of the Web Dynamics Workshop, London, 2001
8. J. W. Lloyd, "Foundations of Logic Programming", Springer Series in Symbolic Computation, Springer-Verlag, New York, 1984
9. UK Cabinet Office, "E-Government: A Strategic Framework for Public Services in the Information Age", April 2000
10. UK Cabinet Office, E-Government Interoperability Framework, September 2000.
11. W3 Consortium, "XML 1.0 (Second Edition)", available at http://www.w3.org/
12. W3 Consortium, "XForms-The Next Generation of Web Forms", available at http://www.w3c.org/MarkUp/Forms
13. W3 Consortium, "XML Schema", available at http://www.w3.org/XML/Schema

Appendix A – TSOM Property Protocol

Object class	Properties
object class TransactionServiceObject	• Id
object class TransactionServiceElement	• Name
	• Description
	• Version
	• History
	• Authors
	• Contributors
	• Approvers
object class TransactionServiceTemplate	• AdminName
	• AdminCode
	• AdminDescription
	• Instructions
	• Examples
	• FAQs
	• ApplicableRegulations
	• MoreInfoPointer
	• VisualEffects
	• TransactionServiceRules
object class Form	• SectionSequence
	• Language
	• Provider
	• RelatedForms
	• AdminInfo
	• ProcessingPointer
object class Section	• SubsectionSequence
	• FieldSequence
object class Field	• Nomenclature
	• DefaultValue
	• FormatMask
object class SubmittedForm	• Values
	• SubmittedBy
	• SubmissionTime
	• PostSubmissionTrace
object class TransactionServiceRule	• Trigger
	• Condition
	• Procedure
object class TransactionServiceAgent	• Name
	• ContactCoordinates
	• Credentials
	• Privileges
object class InformationRepository	• Name
	• Services
	• ConnectionDetails

Trust Objects in Electronic Commerce Transactions

Costas Calcanis, Dilip Patel, and Shushma Patel

School of Computing, Information Systems and Mathematics
South Bank University, London, England
{costas,dilip,shushma}@sbu.ac.uk

Abstract. People see trust as an important key issue in embracing electronic commerce. In this paper we review trust within the context of electronic commerce and we propose a trust model, which is based on object-oriented concepts.

Keywords: Electronic commerce, trust, trust objects, object-oriented system, TREN model.

1 Introduction

It is a well known fact that during the past decade people have started to rely totally, plan and depend their lives in using computers. The internet epoch has placed human productivity to its highest level ever. Nowadays, electronic commerce (EC) expands its domain and introduces a new, faster and more practical way to conduct business. With EC people and businesses can engage into commercial exchange of buying and selling products or services using the electronic medium (Ferraro 1998). Every commercial transaction uses the electronic path as a means of communication between the seller and buyer.

However, this new way is still not yet as reliable as the old-fashioned traditional commerce because of a main issue; internet users and particularly EC users are highly concerned with how they should be able to perform online communication, exchanging sensitive information and be assured their communication will be safe and would not be made available to any third parties (Novak *et al* 1998, Ratnasingham 1998). The internet and especially EC lacks of fully securing the electronic medium resulting in raising vulnerability issues (Keen *et al* 2000). An individual or a business organisation using that medium, such as an intended EC consumer or vendor, needs to have a level or certainty for the security that is provided for that medium. Since EC involves the mutual participation between two parties, each party needs to have a level of certainty that the other participating party can be trust to deliver the requested commercial transaction.

Trust is a major requirement in EC. This paper examines trust as an object component, part of an EC system. The need for trust is investigated under the EC plane and the trust objects, required for measuring the level of trust, are identified. Finally, based on these objects, a trust model is presented.

Z. Bellahsène, D. Patel, and C. Rolland (Eds.): OOIS 2002, LNCS 2425, pp. 31-39, 2002.

2 Trust and Electronic Commerce

The notion of trust has been studied and examined under many different disciplines in social sciences (Misztal 1996, Slovic *et al* 2000, Govier 1997). One of the main issues raised in trust is the rational perspective to willingly accept a situation without the need to take risks by accepting that perspective. In other words, trust provides a level of assurance for the achievement of a given situation. On any human conduct it is essential a level of trust to exist. The higher the level of trust the greater the confidence and probability of success for that conduct is achieved. It is proven that there is a direct relationship between trust and risk; the higher the risk, the higher the need for trust (Slovic *et al* 2000, McKnight & Chervany 2000). We can summarise the requirements for trust in a system to the following: *faith, dependability, predictability, competence, persistence, responsibility, privacy* and of course *risk* (Ahuja 2000, Papadopoulou *et al* 2001, Keen *et al* 2000, Slovic 2000, Ackerman *et al* 1999).

Table 1. The trust requirements

Issues	Concern
Faith	Undoubting belief
Dependability	Willingness to rely, importance and uniqueness
Predictability	Certainty for the future
Competence	Expectation of performance, trustworthiness and integrity
Persistence	Attitude in determination and resolution
Responsibility	Who to blame
Privacy	Assurance for safeguarding personal information
Risk	Consequences and losses

Trust issues raised for any commercial information system transaction need to be answered to ensure success for that transaction. The computer world follows the same approach with the real world. Trust is still an important factor that computer users and especially internet users must have when using its medium for their communication. With the introduction of the commercial internet, the "Virtual World" became a new domain in which businesses and individuals emerged into online EC transactions for performing daily tasks, such as exchanging important and sensitive information, buying products or services, and even arranging their finances. Trust in this domain is essential, probably more essential than in the real world, as most of the information exchange takes place using an electronic, lifeless medium.

The EC process between two parties is the result of a successful online transaction. Typically, the transaction process (Ferraro 1998, Calcanis 2000) is based on the following stages: *determination of required service or product, information exchange between interested parties, service or product procurement, financial transaction,* and finally *delivery of requested service or product*. EC organisations and businesses willing to sell their products or services online have to take risks in order to be able to rely on the correctness and trustworthiness of their customers. On the other hand, any potential customers must accept and depend on the proposed and promised services and products offered by the EC businesses or organisations. The risk factor is an essential trust object for any EC transaction (Jones 2000). When performing online transactions in an EC system both participating parties, i.e. the seller and the buyer, must have established some level of trust between each other. Only then the transaction can take place.

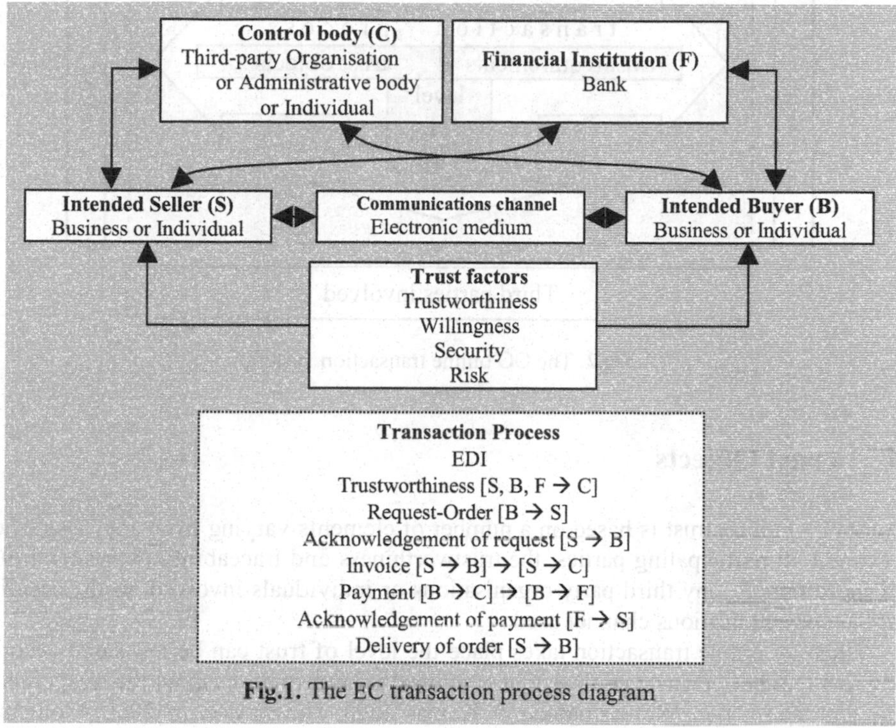

Fig.1. The EC transaction process diagram

3 Object-Oriented Methodology

Trust can be examined using an OO approach. When a transaction process takes place in an EC system, its trust factors can be identified as objects. Every trust object is presented with a set of variables defining its characteristics. For example, the perceived trustworthiness of the transaction is identified by the relationships between the parties involved in the EC system. Each relationship is expressed as an OO process. The OO process model will attempt to describe the trust relationships between the participating parties.

Having identified the key trust objects required for each trust issue, the OO approach is using relationships between the trust objects and issues to valuate the level of trust. The present OO system (as described in section 5 below) attempts to measure the level of trust using the OO approach based on the trust requirements for an online transaction. Figure 2 illustrates the intended approach using a Soft Systems Methodology (Checkland 1999) approach.

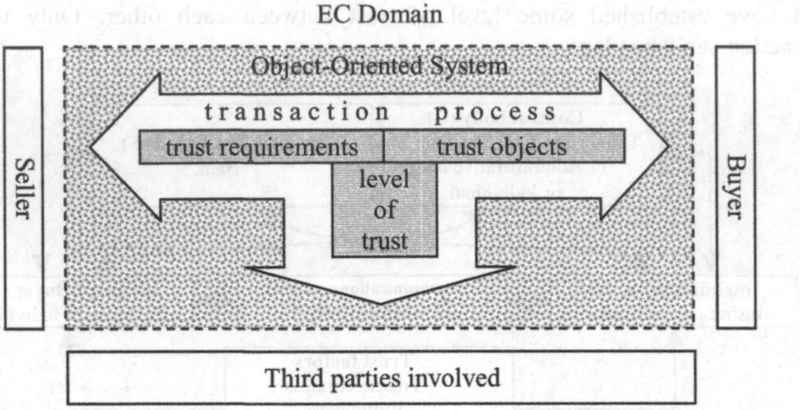

Fig.2. The OO online transaction system

4 Trust Objects

As stated before, trust is based on a number of elements varying from any risks taken between all participating parties, the trustworthiness and traceability (Seinauer 1997) of these parties, any third party organisations or individuals involved, to the security of the communications channel used.

When an online transaction takes place the level of trust can be measured according to a number of trust variables that aim to gather information about the trust objects for that transaction (Ratnasingham & Kumar 2000, Hawkins *et al* 2000, Gollmann 1999). Some of the key trust objects for are *confidentiality, integrity, availability and traceability of sensitive personal information, identification of transaction process and prevention of any possible unauthorised interception,* and finally *delivery of the intended service or products*. Trust objects are considered all elements that their gnosis can be used in establishing a level of trust for a given online transaction.

Table 2. The trust objects

Object	Operation
Confidentiality	How safe and secure is the communications channel used?
Integrity	How safe and secure are the data used?
Availability	Will all the required material be available for the transaction?
Traceability	How trust is enhanced to verify online transactions?
Identification	How well all participating parties involved can be identified?
Prevention	What necessary steps have been taken in order to prevent any implications raised from faults in the transaction process?
Delivery	How the transaction communication, information and product exchange is delivered?

5 TREN Model

To be able promptly and accurately identify and classify trust objects required for performing online transactions in EC the use of the TRust ENvironment model (TREN) is proposed. The presented model is based on an OO framework built between the different trust requirements for a given online transaction process. When an online transaction is requested a TREN environment is formed. This environment is unique for that transaction only. The objective of the TREN model is to satisfy the required trust issues raised for that transaction. The implementation of the proposed model will follow a UML methodology (Eriksson & Penker 1998, Booch *et al* 1999) and modelling process.

When an online transaction between two parties (e.g. a seller and a buyer) takes place there is concern about the finalisation of the transaction process. Based on the trust level between both participating parties the completion and success of the process is depended on. The TREN model aims to provide both parties with a rate of likelihood of success in proceeding with the transaction process. Using an object-oriented approach, trust is expressed using a group of relationships between trust objects (Schoder 2000, Egger 2001, Kim *et al* 2000). The main stages of the TREN model are: *a) to produce a customised trust layout for the particular transaction, b) identify the required key trust objects by which trust can be formed, c) collect the trust elements forming the relationships between the trust objects,* and finally *d) measure the level of trust for the transaction.*

Figure 4 illustrates an outline of the TREN framework. The framework presents an approach to categorise trust requirements (McKnight & Chervany 2000, Slovic 2000, Ratnasingham & Kumar 2000) essential for measuring the level of trust for a given online transaction. These trust requirements are grouped into five main areas; *trust issues; trust considerable, trust elements, trust objects and trust attitudes.*

In the presented OO system, the identified trust considerable are presented as actors and the required trust objects as classes. Each set of the required classes belongs to a given actor. The relationships between the actors and classes depend on the specific requirements for the given online transaction.

The trust objects vary from very generic trust variables (e.g. type of transaction), to very specific for that transaction (e.g. parties personal relationship). Each trust object is directly related with the overall trust state of the transaction. Identifying and collecting the required trust objects the level of trust can be determined.

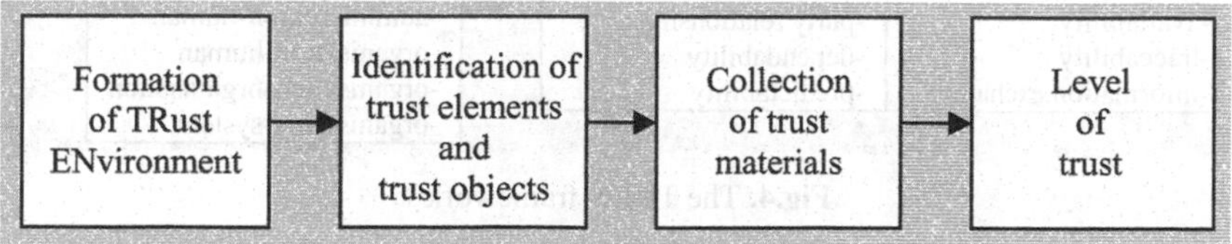

Fig.3. The TREN model

Based on the TREN framework, trust objects are grouped into six main categories. These are called "Trust Considerable". Trust considerable are responsible for identifying the areas, by which trust concerns are raised. Such areas are any factors attached to the transaction, policies that might be enforced, issues involved in the communications channel used, concerns around the transaction process and parties involved, and finally questions raised in relationship levels built for the transaction.

Each trust considerable is identified by a number of trust elements. These elements are responsible for producing a list of specific trust requirements breaking down the trust issues according to the considerable. For example, the Factors considerable is split into trust factor elements, trust human elements, trust medium elements and external trust elements. In the same way, the Policies considerable is broken down to location and legislation trust elements.

Finally, every trust element is acknowledged by its trust objects. The trust objects, as mentioned previously, are responsible in collecting information for every required element that the level of trust can be affected. In table 3, a categorisation approach for the most common trust objects that are considered for the identification of the level of trust within an EC transaction is illustrated.

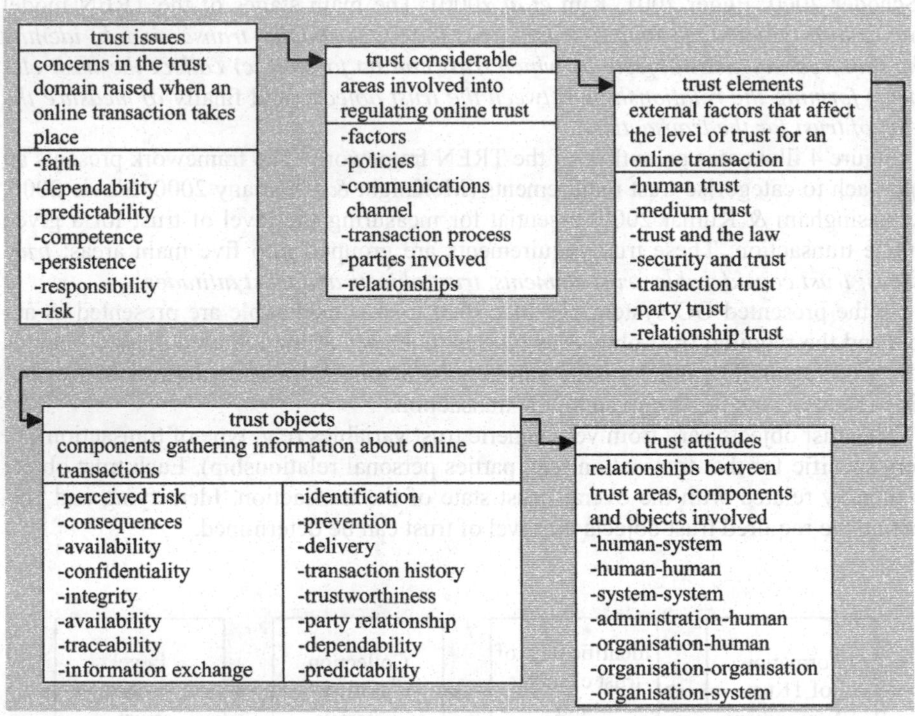

Fig.4. The TREN framework

Table 3. The TREN categorisation

Considerable	Trust Elements	Trust Objects	Attitudes
Factors	• Trust • Human • Medium • External	• Perceived risk • Parties involved • Communication channel	• Human-System • System-System • System-Third party ➢ Trust in system
Policies	• Location • Legal • Available legislation	• Site location • Consequences • Cost • Indemnity • Privacy	• Law-Human • Law-System • Location-Location • Law-Law ➢ Trust in environment
Communication Channel	• Security • Technology used	• Availability • Integrity • Repudiation • Confidentiality • Authentication • Access control	• System-System • Human-System • System-Human ➢ Trust in electronic channel
Transaction Process	• Type • Levels/Stages • Complexity • Repetition	• Transaction history • Type of information exchange • Environment	• EC-System • User-System ➢ Trust in EC process
Parties Involved	• Individuality • Reputation • Achievements & Values • Experience	• Trustworthiness • Business, consumer • Administrative body • Personal and cultural • Ethics and moral	• User-User • User-Third party ➢ Trust in parties
Relationships	• Relationship management • History	• Party relationship • Dependability • Loyalty • Possible implications • Predictability	• Human-Human • User-User • System-System ➢ Trust in relationships

The TREN model table presents an analysis into identifying the possible trust issues and objects required for measuring the level of trust of an online transaction. Having identified these objects, the level of trust can be predicted. Each trust considerable evaluates the attitude of a trust condition. For example, by identifying and collecting all the required trust coefficients for the parties involved we can evaluate the attitude towards trusting the participating parties. When all the trust attitudes have been evaluated the transaction's level of trust can be forecasted.

6 Conclusion

In this paper the notion of trust has been explored particularly focused under the EC domain. Trust is examined as an OO process emphasising the necessity for measuring the likelihood of success for an online electronic transaction. The presentation of TREN, a dynamic net built around an online transaction to measure its level of trust aims to offer a way in securing EC confidence. Businesses and/or individuals wishing to perform EC can assess the likelihood for the success of the intended transaction before the transaction takes place.

References

1. Ackerman, M. Cranor, L. & Reagle, J. (1999) Privacy in E-Commerce: Examining User Scenarios and Privacy Preferences, Proceeding of the ACM Conference on Electronic Commerce, pp. 1-8, ACM Press.
2. Ahuja, V. (2000) Building Trust in Electronic Commerce, IT Pro.
3. Booch, G. Rumbaugh, J. & Jacobson, I. (1999) The Unified Modelling Language: User Guide, Addison-Wesley.
4. Calcanis, C. (2000) Lecture notes in Website Management & Security, South Bank University.
5. Checkland, P. (1999) Systems Thinking, Systems Practice, John Wiley & Sons.
6. Egger, F. N. (2001) Affective Design of E-Commerce User Interfaces: How to Maximise Perceived Trustworthiness, Proceedings of the International Conference on Affective Human Factors Design, Asean Academic Press.
7. Eriksson, H. & Penker, M. (1998) UML Toolkit, John Wiley & Sons.
8. Ferraro, A. (1998) Electronic Commerce: The Issues and Challenges to Creating Trust and a Positive Image in Consumer Sales on the World Wide Web, [Online], Available: http://www.firstmonday.dk/issues/issue3_6/ferraro/index.html [2002, March 27].
9. Gollmann, D. (1999) Computer Security, John Wiley & Sons.
10. Govier, T. (1997) Social Trust and Human Communities, McGill-Queen's University Press.
11. Hawkins, S. Yen, D. C. & Chou, D. C. (2000) Awareness and Challenges of Internet Security, Information Management & Computer Security, Vol. 8, No. 3, MCB University Press.
12. Jones, S. Wilikens, M. Morris, P. & Masera M. (2000) Trust Requirements in E-Business: A Conceptual Framework for Understanding the Needs and Concepts of Different Stakeholders, Communications of the ACM, Vol. 43, No. 12, ACM Press.
13. Keen, P. Balance, C. Chan, S. & Schrump, S. (2000), Electronic Commerce Relationships: Trust by Design, Prentice Hall.
14. Kim, K. & Prabhakar, B. (2000) Initial Trust, Perceived Risk, and the Adoption of Internet Banking, [Online], Available: http://research.is.uc.edu/bipin/Research/TrustIB.htm [2002,March 27].

15. McNight, D. H. & Chervany, N. L. (2000) What is Trust? A Conceptual Analysis and an Interdisciplinary Model, Proceedings of the 6th Americas Conference on Information Systems.
16. Misztal, B. A. (1996) Trust in Modern Societies, Polity Press.
17. Novak, T.P. Hoffman, D.L. & Peralta, M. (1998) Building Consumer Trust in Online Environments: The Case for Information Privacy, [Online], Available: http://elab.vanderbilt.edu/research/papers/html/manuscripts/cacm.privacy98/cacm.privacy98.htm [2002, March 27].
18. Papadopoulou, P. Kanellis, P. & Martakos, D. (2001) Investigating Trust in E-Commerce: A Literature Review and a Model for its Formation in Customer Relationships, Proceedings of the 7th Americas Conference on Information Systems.
19. Ratnasingham, P. & Kumar, K. (2000) Trading Partner Trust in Electronic Commerce Participation, Proceedings of the 21st International Conference in Information Systems.
20. Ratnasingham, P. (1998) The Importance of Trust in Electronic Commerce, Internet Research: Electronic Networking Applications and Policy, Vol. 8, No. 4, MCB University Press.
21. Schoder D. & Yin, P. L. (2000) Building Firm Trust Online, Communications of the ACM, Vol. 43, No. 12, ACM Press.
22. Seinauer, D. D. Wakid, S. A. & Rasberry, S. (1997) Trust and Traceability in Electronic Commerce, Standard View, Vol. 5, No. 3.
23. Slovic, P. *et al* (2000) The Perception of Risk, Earthscan Publications.

OODBMS Metamodel Supporting Configuration Management of Large Applications*

Piotr Habela[1] and Kazimierz Subieta[2]

[1,2] Polish-Japanese Institute of Information Technology, Warsaw, Poland
[2] Institute of Computer Science PAS, Warsaw, Poland

Abstract. Many practical cases of database schema evolution require an effective support from configuration management. Although DBMS construction and software configuration management (SCM) constitute the well established areas of research, they are usually considered in separation from each other. In this paper different issues of SCM are summarized and their relevance to DBMS is investigated. We suggest to extend the OODBMS metamodel to allow recording certain aspects of application-database dependencies in a database schema repository. The extended metamodel contains both typical database metamodel information as well as software configuration information. Such a solution we consider necessary for solving some of schema evolution problems.

1 Introduction

The problem addressed in this paper emerges as an important aspect the definition of a metamodel for object-oriented databases. While the metamodel can be understood as just the description of the data model, in the context of a DBMS it is convenient to understand the term "database metamodel" as the description of all database properties that are independent on a particular database state. Using this view, we can identify the following roles the metamodel for a database system must fulfill:

- **Data Model Description.** The metamodel needs to specify the interdependencies among concepts used to build the model, some constraints, and abstract syntax of data description statements; thus it suggests the intended usage of the model.
- **Implementation of DBMS**. A metamodel determines the organization of a metabase. It is internally implemented in DBMS as a basis for database operations, including database administration, internal optimization, data access and security.
- **Generic Programming**. The metamodel together with appropriate access functions become a part of the programmer's interface for programming through reflection, similarly to Dynamic SQL or CORBA Dynamic Invocation Interface.

* This work is partly supported by the EU 5th Framework project ICONS, IST-2001-32429.

Z. Bellahsène, D. Patel, and C. Rolland (Eds.): OOIS 2002, LNCS 2425, pp. 40-52, 2002.

- **Schema Evolution**. A metamodel equipped with data manipulation facilities on metadata supports schema evolution. Although it is relatively easy to provide the schema modification mechanism itself, the impact of such modifications presents a significant challenge to the configuration management solutions.

As can be seen from the above outline, the database metamodel definition has to address many different and to some extent contradictory requirements. The well known proposals in this area, especially the ODMG [2] standard whose metamodel definition we refer to, are rather far from fulfilling the mentioned roles. Since the mature and well known definition of an OO database metamodel is still not available, we will introduce and briefly describe our own sketch of such metamodel.

In this paper we discuss the consequences of addressing the last of mentioned roles by a database metamodel. This feature is considered to be of great importance for modern DBMS and is supported in a number of commercial products. Unfortunately, the ODMG standard touches this issue only implicitly and, a will be shown, for different reasons inadequately.

The problem of schema evolution remains an active area of research and resulted in many papers (e.g. [3,5,6,13,15,16,17]). The majority of these proposals, although inspiring, can be perceived as too idealistic for today's software development practice. Taking a more pragmatic approach, we would not deal with attempts to automatize the schema evolution process, but instead – propose features of database schema, intended to support Software Configuration Management (SCM). Assuming that in most cases there is only one valid schema version used by a system, our aim is to provide means to easily and reliably extract the information needed to adjust the database applications according to intended schema change.

The paper is organized as follows. Section 2 summarizes the issues of schema evolution, explains why it is inseparable from the SCM area, and presents the requirements of configuration management, identifying the different kinds of configuration information and their relations to the DBMS schema. Section 3 outlines the core elements of proposed object-oriented database metamodel, and identifies possibilities to store configuration information within it. Section 4 concludes and outlines the key issues that need to be considered in the future research.

2 Schema Evolution and SCM

Schema evolution has been recognized as an inevitable aspect of long lived information systems maintenance. The DBMS mechanisms intended to support it are considered mainly in the context of object-oriented databases and became one of the most prominent features to be introduced [1].

Although the research on this subject resulted in more than hundred papers, the problem is far from being solved. Naive approaches reduce the problem to operations on the metadata repository. This is a minor problem, which can be simply solved (with no research) by removing an old schema and inserting a new schema from scratch. If database application software is designed according to SCM principles, then the documentation concerning an old and a new schema must be stored in the

SCM repository. Hence, storing historical information on previous database schemata in a metadata repository (as postulated by some papers) in majority of cases is useless.

The features supporting schema evolution of OO databases has not been effectively standardized so far. The ODMG standard only implicitly assumes such functionality. The interfaces used to define its metamodel provide the modification operations, and their presence is adequate only in the context of schema evolution. However, as already stated, the schema evolution problem cannot be reduced to more or less sophisticated operations on the schema alone. After changes in a database schema the corresponding database objects must be reorganized to satisfy the typing constraints induced by the new schema. Moreover, application programs acting on the database must be altered. For this reasons, serious treatment of SCM excludes ad hoc, undocumented changes in the database schema.

To highlight the real schema evolution problem we present the following real-life example from one of our database applications:

- Altering the schema (in SQL): **10 minutes**
- Preparation and performing of database conversion: ca. **2 days**
- Examination of some 400 potentially affected user screens, altering some of them, updating documentation and system testing: **several person-months**.

This example makes it possible to realize that the schema evolution capabilities in the ODMG standard address only the initial hours of many months of work.

2.1 Views, Wrappers and Mediators

Some papers devoted to schema evolution assume that the problem can be solved by database views. After changing a schema one can define views, which provide virtual mappings from the existing objects to the new schema; hence no changes occur in database object and no changes in existing applications is required. Alternatively, one can convert objects according to the new schema and define views, which preserve the old schema for already defined applications. In both cases, old applications need not be altered, hence the major problem of schema evolution is solved.

In the majority of cases such an approach is idealistic for the following reasons:

- Some changes in a schema stem from unsatisfactory properties of applications, hence changes of applications are inevitable.
- Some changes in a schema stem from changes in business data ontology (e.g. implied by new law regulations). Any automatic mapping of existing data is unable to fulfill new business requirements.
- View definition languages are not sufficiently powerful to cover all possible mappings. There are many mappings not covered by SQL views.
- The view updating problem is solved only in specific cases and (probably) will never be solved in the general case. Hence many applications that require advanced view updating cannot rely on this approach.
- Access to data through views may result in unacceptable degradation in performance. Although materialized views partly solve the problem, this approach implies disadvantages: an additional storage and updating overhead.

- Applications written in languages such as C++ and Java are tightly coupled to physical properties of database objects. Such dependencies (sometimes undocumented and low-level) limit the use of database views.

Another approach to schema evolution can be based on concepts such as wrappers and mediators. The approach is similar to the approach employing database views, but in contrast to database views, which are defined in high-level query languages (SQL), wrappers and mediators are proprietary solutions, tightly coupled to a category of applications and written in lower-level languages (C/C++, Java, etc.). The approach is more realistic than the approach based on database views, but it requires low-level programming. Some of the above mentioned disadvantages of using views are also true for the approach based on wrappers and mediators. In particular, if a change concerns data representation or business data ontology then any kind of wrapper or mediator may be unable to isolate the problem: the change would affect applications.

In summary, although database views provide some hope for schema evolution, according to our experience, this approach is non-applicable in majority of cases. More detailed discussion on this topic can be found in [19].

2.2 Schema Evolution and Software Change Management

Looking at the problem from the software engineering perspective, schema evolution forms a part of a more general topic, which is referred to as *software change management*. It concerns the maintenance phase in the software life cycle. The cost of maintenance is very high and in total can several times exceed the cost of initial software development. Thus some discipline is necessary to reduce the cost. Software change management provides activities during the software development, operation and maintenance to support software changes. It also determines disciplined processes for altering software after changes. Both of these aspects are important. If software developers and clients neglect certain activities addressing future software changes, then the cost of changes can be extremely high. Changes to the software should follow some life cycle to reduce cost and time, and to achieve proper software quality.

Considering schema evolution as a part of the entire change management process we see many change management activities that must be carried out in order to ensure proper conditions for schema evolution. The software change management must also define activities to establish an organized change process, in particular, the following:

- The procedures of reporting software problems or requesting functionality changes.
- Collecting and storing software problem reports; organizing their assessment and qualification according to importance, urgency, cost and the impact of the change.
- The diagnosis of software problems and cost estimations of software changes.
- Decision processes concerning the scope of software changes and/or making new versions of the software.
- Planning, organizing and scheduling concerning the software changes implementation, testing and documentation.

- Testing changed software according to software testing plan including regression testing (testing unchanged modules that can be influenced by the change).
- Documenting of changes, including requirements and other documentation.
- Installation of changed software, training of users and acceptance tests.
- Learning from change, to improve the change processes in the future.

A proposal concerning schema evolution should refer to the activities presented above in software development, to determine a clear goal for the research. It can be formulated in terms of cost, time or quality of particular activities, and/or in terms of software quality. The schema evolution capabilities like that defined in the ODMG standard, have no relationship to activities of the change management processes.

2.3 SCM Repository and a Metabase Repository

SCM is a discipline for establishing and maintaining the integrity of the products of a software project throughout the project's lifecycle [8,9,10,11]. SCM is especially important if a project lasts several years and/or has many versions due to changing user requirements or system requirements. Schema evolution means a new version of a schema and, in consequence, a new version of the database, and a new version of applications. Thus, it must be disciplined by SCM.

A basic entity that SCM deals with is a software configuration item (SCI). An SCI can be atomic or complex. Complex SCIs include all software artifacts that present intermediate or final software products, including source code, documentation, tools, tests, etc. The SCM has to guarantee consistency among SCIs. SCI frozen for changes are called baselines. Some SCIs are called versions, revisions and releases.

All entities that are used or produced within a particular software version must be collected together as SCIs and stored within an SCM repository. This helps to avoid situations where new code is associated with old documentation; old code cannot be re-compiled because a relevant older compiler version is no longer available, etc.

As follows from the above, all versions of a schema must be the subject of SCM. The new schema must be stored within a consistent configuration which includes new requirements, diagnosis and analytical documentation, data conversion code, code of new application modules, new design and implementation documentation, testing code, data and results, software transfer documentation, user documentation, etc. Schema evolution cannot be separated from other SCM aspects and activities.

It is implicitly assumed in the research devoted to schema evolution (in particular, in the ODMG standard) that actions on the database schema repository will immediately change a repository state. Sometimes, it is assumed that the repository will also be prepared to keep historical information on previous schemata. Taking into account software change management and SCM, such an approach is inadequate. A change to a database schema must be carried out on the SCM repository, which should be prepared to keep both old and new schemata. Many other documents are related to this change, including software problem reports, new requirements, managerial decisions, software code, its documentation etc. All of this information must be kept within an SCM repository rather than within a metabase repository.

2.4 Dependencies between Software Units

Some tasks in software change management (like problem diagnosis, change planning and scheduling, implementation, testing, documentation updating etc). are more efficient (in terms of cost, time and quality) if the information on dependencies between software units could be properly organized.

Some dependencies between software units are or can be stored within a metabase repository. Other dependencies can be stored within an SCM repository, in particular, as SCIs. Below we list more important dependencies.

Configuration Dependency: some software and documentation units are dependent because they create a consistent SCI. This dependency is usually stored within a configuration management repository. It is more relevant to SCM.

Forward Dependency between procedural units of the software. The dependency shows which procedural units are called from a given procedural unit. This dependency is easy to discover by analysis of the code.

Backward Dependency is exactly reverse to the forward dependency. It is more valuable than the previous one because it shows which software units calls a given unit. Both forward and backward dependencies are relevant to a metabase.

Event Dependency holds between a unit raising an event and a unit catching it and triggering some action. The case is similar to forward and backward dependency. This information is usually present in the specification of interfaces (CORBA IDL, ODMG ODL), thus it can be stored within a metabase repository.

Parametric Dependency between a given unit and a unit that can be a parameter to that unit. This concerns e.g. *call-by-reference* parameters of methods or parameters of some (generic) software templates. Parametric dependency is relevant to a metabase.

Side Effects Dependency describes all aspects of the data/computer environment that can be affected by a given procedural software unit. Side effects concern operations on a database, global data (shared among applications), hardware devices, catalogs, files, external communication etc. In languages such as Modula-2 and DBPL some side effects are explicitly determined by special programming facilities called import lists. Current object-oriented languages do not determine side effects within class interfaces, hence the programmer and the system is unable to recognize them directly. This can be the source of serious bugs, cf. the Ariane-5 rocket disaster caused by an unspecified side effect. Side effects can be passive (a read-only access), or active (affecting the state of some external resources). Providing the information on those dependencies is an obligatory part of a software unit specification. A metabase repository can store information on those side effects that concern a database. For instance, a part of database can be read and updated by a given method.

Definitional Dependency holds between two data units, where one is a definition and another one is an instance of this definition. The dependency concerns interfaces, classes, types, patterns, skeletons, templates, schemas, specifications, etc. and their instances. Definitional dependency is relevant to a metabase and SCM.

Redundancy Dependency holds between units that contain redundant information; e.g. copies of some data that are introduced to improve performance or to increase safety. Redundancy dependency is relevant to a metabase and SCM.

Taking into account the entire population of software and documentation units we can imagine their structure as a (partly directed) colored graph, where each edge represents some dependency between units and the color of an edge represents a dependency kind. Some dependencies in this graph form subsets of software/documentation units, in particular, configuration and definitional dependency. Some dependencies can be stored within a metabase repository. Other dependencies are more relevant to a software configuration repository.

In summary, the properly defined schema evolution problem should establish dependencies among software and documentation units. It should clearly subdivide the dependencies between a metabase repository and a configuration repository, and should clearly determine benefits of storing the information on dependencies for particular phases and aspects of the software life cycle, including the software change management. None of the above mentioned aspects of schema evolution are taken into account in the metamodel defined by the ODMG standard.

Concluding, the schema evolution problem far exceeds the pure problem of metadata management and should be considered as a part of software change and SCM. While some repository updating operations would indeed be useful, e.g. adding a new attribute or adding a new class, the operations do not solve the essential problem. The major problem of schema evolution concerns altering a database and – most of all – altering applications that operate on the database. This problem is related to software engineering rather than to the pure database domain.

3 Database Metamodel Support for Configuration Management

The main challenge of today's software development is dealing with complexity. In case of SCM this concerns especially the complexity of interdependencies among configuration items. Therefore, in order to better support the SCM aspect, the database metamodel definition should provide means to simplify the management of dependency information. There seem to be two general ways towards this objective:

- **Encapsulation/Layered Architecture**. Applying the encapsulation, both to narrow the interface of particular classes, as well as to isolate the whole layers, allows to shorten the dependency paths.
- **Dependency Tracking**. Even if the dependencies don't span across many configuration items, they still need to be recorded in a way that would guarantee completeness of such information and ability to easily extract it.

Both of these postulates are rather intuitive and are presently treated as a *sine qua non* in the development of large information systems. However, the dependencies between applications and database schema constitute a special kind of dependency that would be much more effectively handled when supported by the core DBMS mechanisms. As certain kinds of dependency information concern directly the database schema elements, storing them within the schema would not significantly complicate the metadata structure.[1] It would be especially advantageous in presence of a DBMS mechanism that would enforce the dependency recording.

3.1 Dependency Kinds Relevant to the Metabase

In the subsections we revisit those of earlier enumerated dependency kinds, we considered relevant to the metabase, looking for optimum way of storing such information within a DBMS schema.

Forward, Backward and Event Dependency

Since these kinds of dependency are mutually symmetrical, they could be registered using single construct, e.g. bi-directional association. Assuming traditional architecture, we would be interested in dependencies between external applications and the database, as well as dependencies within the DBMS (the DBMS dependencies of other system elements, as the least critical, would not be tracked).

The target of the dependency association would be any (that is, behavioral or static) property of the database. The role of a dependent element would be played by either DBMS native procedure / method, or by an external application's procedure or module. Therefore, in addition to the regular database schema elements and dependency association, we need to introduce construct, identifying an external procedure that the schema would be otherwise not aware of.

The optimum level of granularity of such information should be determined. The dependent element would be always a procedure / method. However, in case of external applications' dependencies, it could be practical to use a higher level, e.g. a whole application module. The target of a dependency can be either an interface or – assuming more detailed tracking those of its properties that a given routine accesses.

Concerning the event dependency, it is also desirable to store information on both directions of that dependency that is on both the event producer and event consumer.

Side Effect Dependency

All requests to properties that are non-local for a given procedural unit or interface, can be qualified as side effect dependency. It is desirable to distinguish between passive and active side effects and to include this information in the metabase.

However, it is necessary to note that when we separate interface definition from the structure storing its instances, both the whole metamodel as well as the dependency tracking features, get more complex. The assumption, that the entity definition is inseparable from the set of its instances, is characteristic for the traditional relational model and contributes to its simplicity. We are not going to follow this approach though. The concept of *extent*, being a single structure containing all instances of a given class or interface, becomes problematic in case of distributed environment or (especially) when arbitrarily complex composite objects are supported.

Thus, it is not enough to connect the side effect dependency information with particular interfaces. The side effect dependency record should identify the global property the manipulated properties are accessed through. For example we would like

[1] Making the database aware of its dependent applications has previously been suggested e.g. in [4] through the concept of "application table". Intention of introducing that construct was slightly different though.

to know not only that a given procedure refers to objects of type *Product*, but also that it operates e.g. only on objects stored within the global variable *avaliableProductsCatalog*. Therefore, in order to describe the side effect dependency it is necessary to identify the global variable a given procedure uses to begin its navigation, as well as all properties it then uses to retrieve the target reference. In case of static properties, each such dependency would be marked as read-only or updating.

Parametric Dependency
This kind of dependency seems to be easier to handle than the side effect dependency, because here the dependent procedure does not have to be aware of the origin of provided parameter. No matter what kind of parameter it is: either the procedure reads, updates or returns newly created instance, it is only necessary to guarantee, that the definition of a given type stored in database metamodel has not been changed in a way that affect that procedure. In this case the target of dependency link would be simply a type definition the parameter refers to.

3.2 Proposed Metamodel Extensions

Before illustrating suggested features for dependency tracking, we will briefly describe suggested improvements to the conceptual view of the ODMG's metamodel. For a detailed discussion of the database metamodel roles and the requirements they entail, see [7].

Core Elements of the Suggested Metamodel
The interrelations among the introduced concepts (Fig. 1) are presented in a form similar to the UML standard definition [14]; also, the graphical notation of that language is used. Below outline suggested properties of the improved metamodel.

Clear Separation between Meta-levels. Metamodel does not deal with concepts from other meta-levels, like e.g. *Object*. However, since the database schema has to be aware of the location of user objects and because we are not going to solve this through the *extent* concept, we need to store the declarations of database global variables. If a *StructuralProperty* is connected with a *GlobalDeclaration* metaobject, it means that the former is not a part of Interface definition,[2] but instead it constitutes a global variable declaration (e.g. an entry points for further navigation through the database). Nevertheless, despite the separation of meta-levels, we still assume that both user objects and metaobjects would be accessed in a uniform way.[3]

Lack of the Explicit Collection Concept. It is often necessary to store multiple instances of some type, without necessarily wrapping them into another object. Thus, instead of introducing the concept of collection, the *multiplicity* meta-attribute of a structural property allows to declare it as multivalued (and/or optional).

Object Relativism and Composite Objects. It is desirable to reduce as far as possible the difference in handling of composite and primitive objects. As an important change in comparison to traditional OO programming languages we

[2] Similarly, a *Procedure* can be declared global instead of being a method of a given Interface.

[3] As far as possible we tend to rely on generic query language mechanisms when manipulating the metadata. Note the lack of metadata operations in the presented diagram (Fig. 1).

suggest to allow for arbitrary (perhaps multilevel) nesting of composite objects. Such composition can be declared using the *SubobjectLink* metaobjects.

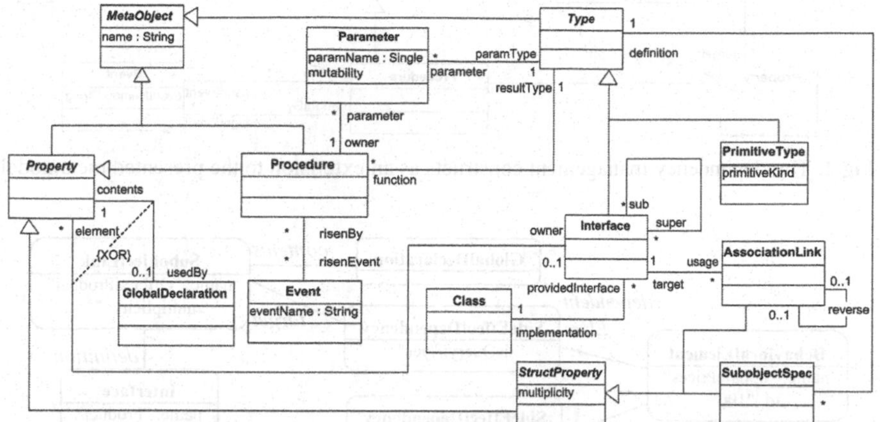

Fig.1. Core elements of proposed metamodel without features specific to SCM support

Metamodel Extensions for Dependency Information Management

Since all constructs needed to describe the targets of different dependencies are already part of the metamodel, adapting it to store the dependency information requires only few additions (see Fig. 2).

Because we are also interested in dependencies of elements located outside the DBMS responsibility (external applications using the database), a *BehavioralElement* concept has been added as a generalization of the *Procedure*. Both elements can be the source of dependency relationship: the former can the external application's elements, while the latter denotes the native procedures stored within the DBMS.

The side effect dependencies are recorded for all elements that are used in navigation or manipulated. For each such dependency a *SideEffectDependency* metaobject connects the dependent element description with dependency target. The *isQuery* meta-attribute determines the character of dependency: either pure read / navigational (value *yes*) or allowing to modify a given element (value *no*). Note that it is not necessary to record the exact path of navigation. It is enough to indicate, whether any part of a given procedure refers to a given property or not. The *isQuery* value is applicable only when the dependency target is a structural property. Parametric dependencies descriptions refer to type definitions (that is, to primitive types or interfaces). Other relevant dependencies (e.g. event dependency and definitional dependency) also can be derived from the outlined metamodel structure.

In Fig. 3 we present exemplary fragment of schema, showing the side-effect dependency of an external procedure *updatePrices*. That method refers to a global variable *OfferedProducts* that is capable of storing arbitrary number of objects described by the interface *Product*. Through this interface, it can modify the subobject (attribute) *Price* of type *Currency*. In contrast, the global variable *OfferedProducts* is never modified by this procedure (it is used only for navigation).

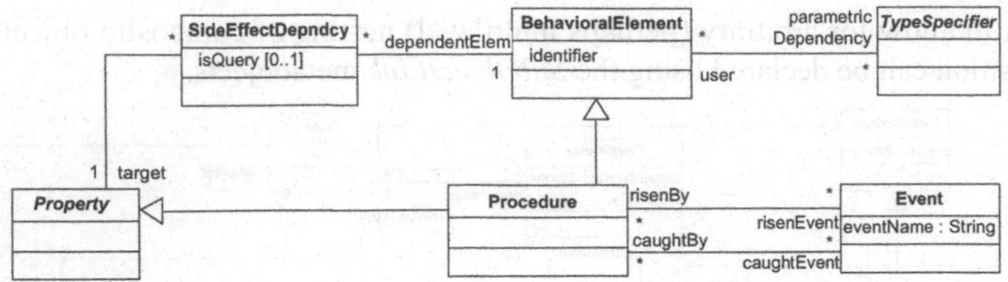

Fig.2. The dependency management constructs as an extension to the presented metamodel

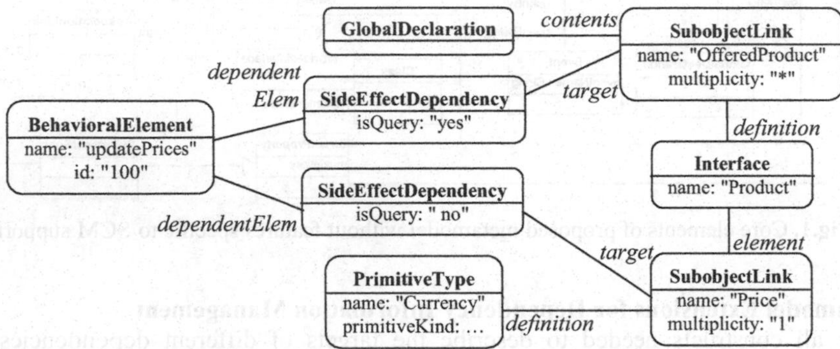

Fig.3. An exemplary fragment of the DBMS schema, containing the side effect dependency information for an external procedure *updatePrices*

Collecting the Dependency Information

In recording the dependency information we have to face the problem similar to the one encountered between SCM system and other tools used in the software development: the development tools are not prepared for providing the information needed for documenting the software configuration. Inability to automatically extract all the dependency information makes it necessary to manually document it, which can be considered as much less efficient and reliable.

Therefore, to make the described feature practically useful, the ability to automatically collect the dependency information seems to be indispensable. In our case, the DBMS could record the dependencies during one phase of the system testing and verify the completeness of collected information during further tests. For each recorded dependency it would need to receive some id of the procedure or unit that performs the database call (e.g. in the form of additional parameter in the statement beginning the given interaction with the database).

Such identification process should be separated from regular database security mechanism in order to not to deteriorate the performance during regular operation.

4 Conclusions

The database schema definition constitutes the critical element of the configuration information that needs to be maintained during the system's lifecycle. Although it is usually relatively stable, it can be also a subject of change. The most significant potential impact of such change concerns the integrity of applications dependent on the schema. This aspect of the schema evolution issue, partly belonging to the SCM area, seems to receive a relatively little attention.

We argue that the database schema would be an appropriate place to store that kind of the dependency information. Therefore the metamodel for ODBMS should provide the necessary constructs. The key advantage in comparison to storing that information in a SCM repository, would be the ability to record it automatically. This would require special mode of work of the DBMS, as well as the means to identify the external programs dependent on to particular properties of the database schema.

The discussion presented in this paper concern core DBMS mechanisms rather then a kind of external extension of existing systems. For this reason we discuss the necessary constructs in the context of new proposals in the object-oriented database area. Other important new features that such DBMS would benefit from include dynamic object roles [12], more powerful view mechanism [19] and the query language seamlessly integrated with the regular programming language constructs [18]. We are currently working on the database metamodel proposal, consistently incorporating the mentioned elements.

References

1. J. Banerjee, H. Chou, J. Garza, W. Kim, D. Woelk, N. Ballou. Data Model Issues for Object-Oriented Applications. ACM TOIS, April 1987.
2. R. Cattel, D. Barry. (eds.) The Object Data Standard: ODMG 3.0. Morgan Kaufmann, 2000
3. K. T. Claypool, J. Jin, E. A. Rundensteiner. OQL SERF: An ODMG Implementation of the Template-Based Schema Evolution Framework. In Centre for Advanced Studies Conference, 1998, 108-122
4. F. Ferrandina, S.-E. Lautemann. An Integrated Approach to Schema Evolution for Object Databases. OOIS 1996, 280-294
5. E. Franconi, F. Grandi, F. Mandreoli. A Semantic Approach for Schema Evolution and Versioning in Object-Oriented Databases. Computational Logic 2000, 1048-1062
6. I. A. Goralwalla, D. Szafron, M. T. Özsu, R. J. Peters. A Temporal Approach to Managing Schema Evolution in Object Database Systems. DKE 28(1), 1998, 73-105
7. P. Habela, M. Roantree, K. Subieta. Flattening the Metamodel for Object Databases. (*To appear in*) ADBIS 2002
8. IEEE Guide to Software Configuration Management, ANSI/IEEE Std 1042-1987
9. IEEE Standard Glossary of Software Engineering Technology, ANSI/IEEE Std 610.12-1990
10. IEEE Standard for Software Configuration Management Plans. ANSI/IEEE Std 828-1990
11. ISO/IEC 12207. Information Technology - Software Life Cycle Processes. ISO/IEC Copyright Office, Geneva, Switzerland, 1995

12. A. Jodłowski, P. Habela, J. Płodzień, K. Subieta. Dynamic Object Roles in Conceptual Modeling and Databases. Institute of Computer Science PAS Report 932, Warsaw, Dec. 2001 (submitted for publication)
13. S.-E.Lautemann. Change Management with Roles. DASFAA, 1999, 291-300
14. Object Management Group: Unified Modeling Language (UML) Specification. Version 1.4, September 2001 [http://www.omg.org/]
15. R. J. Peters, M. T. Özsu. An Axiomatic Model of Dynamic Schema Evolution in Objectbase Systems. TODS 22(1), 1997 75-114
16. Y.-G. Ra, E. A. Rundensteiner. A Transparent Object-Oriented Schema Change Approach Using View Evolution. ICDE, 1995, 165-172
17. B. Staudt Lerner. A model for compound type changes encountered in schema evolution. ACM TODS 25(1), 2000, 83-127
18. K. Subieta. Object-Oriented Standards. Can ODMG OQL Be Extended to a Programming Language? (In) Cooperative Databases and Applications. World Scientific, 1997, 459-468
19. K. Subieta. Mapping Heterogenous Ontologies through Object Views. Proc. of 3-rd Workshop Engineering Federated Information Systems (EFIS 2000), 2000, 1-10

Generic Applications for Object-Oriented Databases*

Mark Roantree[1] and Kazimierz Subieta[2,3]

[1] School of Computer Applications, Dublin City University
Dublin, Ireland
mark.roantree@compapp.dcu.ie

[2] Institute of Computer Science PAS
Warsaw, Poland
subieta@ipipan.pl

[3] Polish-Japanese Institute of Information Technology
Warsaw, Poland

Abstract. It is often necessary to develop database applications with no prior knowledge of the structure of the database. Such applications may be referred to as generic applications, and often they can be required to manipulate multiple (possibly heterogenous) databases across a network. We explore the problems of developing generic applications for the current standard of object-oriented databases, and describe the properties that are needed to build a truly generic application.

1 Introduction

There are many situations in which researchers and companies have a requirement to develop generic applications to run across multiple hardware and software platforms. Generic database applications should be capable of connecting to more than one database during program execution, determining the database's structure, constructing a dynamic query suitable for that particular database, and subsequently utilizing results of the queries within the program. A sample application may be a simple web-based browser that connects to newly discovered relational databases across a network, and dynamically construct queries which may be executed against the database. With conventional relational database technology, such generic applications can be built using dynamic SQL. However the programming is rather difficult as different vendors produced different 'flavors' of relational database products, and quite often, the data dictionaries of some databases contain subtle differences which may make the development of a generic application, as described above, impossible.

This type of genericity is commonly referred to as *reflection*. This term has originated in the programming language community e.g. [6] and denotes the possibility of a dynamic modification of a program being currently executed. More

* (1) supported by Irish Strategic Research Grant ST/2000/091 and (2) partially supported by European 5th Framework project IST-2001-32429.

Z. Bellahsène, D. Patel, and C. Rolland (Eds.): OOIS 2002, LNCS 2425, pp. 53–59, 2002.

recently, the term has found a new use in CORBA [7] and database communities as a means for dynamic construction and invocation of requests. In this paper we investigate the reflection mechanism for ODMG databases and propose a concrete solution which has been implemented in a prototype based on the Versant ODMG database.

In this short paper we provide details of one possible solution for creating generic ODMG applications [3,4,5]. A more complete version of this paper which includes our motiviation, the problems with current ODMG applications, and additional requirements for OODB standards can be found in [8].

2 A Methodology for Making Generic Applications

There are four basic operation types that database systems must support: create, retrieve, update and delete operations. The methodology for making generic applications should support all four types.[1] The difficulty with creating this type of application is that an object's structure and other information can only be determined during run-time. Thus a programmer's thinking can be described as 'second-order': the programmer reasons about a program to generate a subsequent program, which can then be executed. Our experience has shown that such 'second-order' programming is rather difficult and error-prone, and thus may require special methodological support and special utilities within the programming interface.

2.1 Common Operations

All four operation types will require two common steps.

1. Connect to database.
2. Execute metadata queries. These queries will be expressed in OQL and may seek answers to the following: How many classes exist in the schema? What are the names of classes in the schema? For a named class, what are the attributes contained in that class? What are names of superclasses for a named class?

Once this basic information has been extracted, it is then possible to perform those database operations described above. We will demonstrate the methods used for all four, starting with the simplest operation types.

[1] In the following discussion we avoid dynamic updating of relationships, which presents a separate important problem. Although this can be handled similarly to deleting, updating and inserting values, there are peculiarities requiring a longer discussion, which we have considered beyond the scope of this paper.

2.2 Retrieval

The most common possibilities for query results are: the result data may be a set of object references; it may be a set of values (possibly structural values); it may be a single reference; or it may be a single value (possibly an integer which is the sum of all objects). With the first two cases, the application must be able to extract and display actual values from the result set. So the next steps are the following:

3. Construct and execute an OQL query. After step 2, it should be possible to build a query string (or a special structure for queries with parameters) which can be passed to the database.
4. Utilize the result (e.g. display it). If we assume that the result is a collection of object references, it is then a matter of constructing a generic utility to select attribute values (and possibly to convert all types to strings). In this case the information needed for these operations is provided in step 2 above.

The other cases mentioned can be handled in a similar way. In general, when the type of the value returned by the query is a complex structure, it will greatly complicate the programmer's interface, and should possibly be avoided.

2.3 Deleting

In order to delete an object, it is necessary to retrieve that object's reference (i.e. OID), and use it to remove the object from the database.[2] ODMG has complicated this matter with respect to the deletion of elements from collection-valued attributes because they are literals, hence they have no identifiers. Consequently, OQL queries return values of attributes rather than references to these values. This makes it impossible to use OQL queries as the basis for deleting values from collection-based attributes. This may be corrected in future versions (and implementations) of the standard: thus, deletion of objects and deletion of elements of collection-based attributes would be handled in the same way. As SQL makes it possible to delete many tuples in one statement, we assume that the generic utility should enable the programmer to delete many objects (or values) in one run. Further steps are thus as follows:

3. Construct and execute the OQL query. After step 2, it should be possible to build a query string (or a structure for queries with parameters) which can be passed to the database. The query should return references to objects (or values) to be deleted.
4. Delete objects (or values) whose references are returned by the query.

For this method to function correctly, it is necessary to be able to uniquely reference not only objects, but also their individual properties (attributes and

[2] There is the additional problem of deleting links (implied by relationships) leading to the object, as was mentioned earlier.

links (relationships)). A reference to an attribute value can be constructed in many ways. In programming languages a reference is usually a main memory address. This solution is unacceptable for databases, because we would like to build references to values stored on a disk. Another idea is to use the combination of an OID and an attribute name as a reference. Unlike the relational model, this will not work where the attribute is a collection of values. Another solution is to use the OID together with a value offset, but this is tightly bound to physical representations of objects, and may not work in some cases. Hence, references to values should be built on the basis of some higher-level and uniform principle, which should possibly be determined by the ODMG standard. In Loqis [9], a prototype OODBMS implemented by the second author, it has been assumed that each atomic or complex unit can be separately created, retrieved, updated, deleted, locked, indexed, protected, etc. Thus, each of these units must possess a unique internal identifier. Specifically, this identifier exists for an attribute value, the value of a collection-based attribute, a link to another object, a method, or a view. In our opinion, such an improvement of the ODMG object model could much clarify the semantics of future SQL-like imperative statements (creating, inserting, updating and deleting) built on top of OQL.

2.4 Updating

Updating (i.e. assignment) requires an *l-value* (i.e. a reference on the left side of the assignment) and an *r-value* (i.e. a value on the right side of the assignment). In SQL this is wrapped in a special syntax which allows the programmer to express many assignments in one update statement. As previously, the problem made by ODMG concerns lack of identifiers for attribute values; hence there is no way to construct the *l-values* necessary for updating. Once again, it is assumed in the following that this will be corrected in future versions of the standard. Note that during the design of an updating methodology for generic software we should not neglect the updating of values of collection-based attributes.

An initial solution is for the programmer to construct and execute two OQL queries: one for *l-values* and another for r-values. The first disadvantage of this solution is that an *l-value* and *r-value* are frequently dependent, as in the statement SALARY = SALARY + 500. The second disadvantage concerns the case of many assignments in one statement. Here, the first query must return a list of *l-values*, and the second query must return a list of *r-values*, where *l-value*i is assigned to the value of *r-value*i. The size of the lists must be the same and the order of *l-values* and *r-values* must be identical: this is the responsibility of the programmer. Obviously, this solution will be error-prone as for various reasons (e.g. for null values) the size of lists could be different and proper matching of *l-values* and *r-values* could be violated.

Hence we propose a second solution: the programmer will construct one OQL query returning both *l-values* and *r-values*. For example, such a query (increase salaries of all programmers by 500) can look as follows:

```
select x.SALARY, x.SALARY+500
```

```
from EMP as x
where x.Job = 'programmer'
```

Such a query will return a collection of pairs, where in each pair the first element represents an *l-value* and the second element represents an *r-value*. Unlike the previous case, the order of pairs is non-essential, and there is no risk of improper matching of *l-values* and *r-values*.

Further steps are thus as follows:

3. Construct and execute an OQL query. The query must be constructed in such a way that it will return a collection of pairs of *l-values* and *r-values* necessary for updating. As previously, after step 2 it should be possible to build a query string (or a structure for queries with parameters) which can be passed to the database.
4. Iterate over the collection returned by the query and in each iteration step make the assignment of an *r-value* to the value referenced by the corresponding *l-value*.

2.5 Inserting

The process for inserting a new object involves the construction of a new (empty) object, where this operation returns the object reference. At this point the process is similar to updating an existing object.

3. Dynamically construct the ODMG statement for creating a new object of the given type/class.
4. Execute this statement using a special utility for inserting new objects into the proper collection in the database.
5. Where necessary, use updating operations (previously described) to update each attribute's value.
6. Connect the object to other objects through the correct relationships. This requires an additional utility to identify those objects to be connected.

Another insertion case concerns insertion of new values into collection-based attributes. This case can be handled in a similar way to that proposed for assignment. The programmer must construct and execute an OQL query returning a collection of pairs, where the first element of a pair is a reference to a collection-based attribute, and the second element is a new value to be inserted into the collection. The ODMG standard should provide a special utility which will make it possible to iterate over the result returned by the OQL query and in each iteration loop, insert a value into the corresponding collection.

3 Conclusions

With the emergence of distributed technologies such as CORBA, and Web technologies such as XML, it is clear that we are more frequently dealing with data that is not flat in structure (relational-style data) but where linked hierarchical objects are the conceptual units for designers and programmers. In this respect, the ODMG standard presents a homogenous and universal solution, but (in contrast to SQL and CORBA) one that may lead to problems with implementing generic applications requiring strong reflective capabilities. The alternative to 'pure' object storage systems is object-relational systems [10] which are relational databases with added object-oriented functionality. While they are currently preferred by industrial database users (due to the close association with their relational counterparts), they lack many features required by object-oriented software engineers. For example, they contain no support for classification and thus, encapsulation of behavior cannot exist. The data definition language deals with tables rather than classes. There is support for object identifiers and relationships, and in products such as Informix there is support for inheritance [1]. However, as this technology is still in the early phase of development, there is a considerable difference between products, both in terms of how they interpret the object-relational model and those features they support [2]. Consequently, a similar argument could be made for developing a generic interface to object-relational databases also.

In this short paper we have described the issues involved in building such applications and have discussed several improvements that are required to facilitate them. We argue that regardless of a data storage paradigm (object-relational databases, persistent Java solutions, pure o-o databases, XML, etc.), the presence of complex objects implies similar problems and the requirements that are listed in this paper. The need for a simple standard interface to schema repositories is one requirement both for reflective capabilities in software applications and in providing interoperability between heterogeneous data sources. Other requirements focus on standard utilities for the dynamic construction of requests (queries, in particular), converting them to a proper run-time format, executing them, and utilizing their results.

References

1. Brown P. *Object-Relational Database Development.* Informix Press, 2001. 58
2. Cattel R. *Object Data Management.* Addison-Wesley, 1994. 58
3. Cattel R. et. al. (eds.) (2000). *The Object Data Standard: ODMG 3.0*, Morgan Kaufmann. 54
4. Cattell R. and Barry D. (eds) (1987), *The Object Database Standard: ODMG 2.0.* Morgan Kaufmann. 54
5. Jordan D. (1998) *C++ Object Databases: Programming with the ODMG Standard*, Addison Wesley. 54
6. Kirby G. N. C. and Morrison R. Variadic Genericity Through Linguistic Reflection: A Performance Evaluation. *Proceedings of the 8th International Workshop on Persistent Object Systems (POS8) and Proceedings of the 3rd International Workshop on Persistence and Java (PJW3)*, Tiburon, California, 1998, pp.136-148 Morgan-Kaufmann 1999. 53
7. Orfali R. and Harkey D. (1998) *Client/Server Programming with Java and CORBA*, Wiley. 54

8. Roantree M. and Subieta K. Generic Applications for Object-Oriented Databases. *Technical Report No. ISG-02-06*, Dublin City University, June 2002. 54
9. Subieta K., Kambayashi Y., and Leszczylowski J. (1995) Procedures in Object-Oriented Query Languages. *Proceedings of the 21st International Conference on Very Large Databases*, Morgan Kaufmann. 56
10. Stonebraker M. *Object-Relational DBMSs: The Next Great Wave.* Morgan Kaufmann, 1995. 58

Validated Cost Models for Parallel OQL Query Processing

Sandra de F. Mendes Sampaio[1], Norman W. Paton[1], Jim Smith[2], and Paul Watson[2]

[1] Department of Computer Science, University of Manchester
Manchester, M13 9PL, UK
{sampaios,norm}@cs.man.ac.uk
[2] Department of Computing Science, University of Newcastle upon Tyne
Newcastle, NE1 7RU, UK
{Paul.Watson,Jim.Smith}@newcastle.ac.uk

Abstract. Query cost models are widely used, both for performance analysis and for comparing execution plans during query optimisation. In essence, a cost model predicts where time is being spent during query evaluation. Although many cost models have been proposed, for serial, parallel and distributed database systems, surprisingly few of these have been validated against real systems. This paper presents cost models for the parallel evaluation of ODMG OQL queries, which have been compared with experimental results obtained using the Polar object database system. The paper describes the validation of the cost model for a collection of queries, using three join algorithms over the OO7 benchmark database. The results show that the cost model generally both ranks alternative plans appropriately, and gives a useful indication of the response times that can be expected from a plan. The paper also illustrates the application of the cost model by highlighting the contributions of different features and operations to query response times.

1 Introduction

The development of cost models for query performance is a well established activity. Cost models are an essential component of optimisers, whereby physical plans can be compared, and they have been widely used for studying the performance of database algorithms (e.g. [5]) and architectures (e.g. [2]). However, cost models are only as reliable as the assumptions made by their developers, and it is straightforward to identify situations in which researchers make seemingly contradictory assumptions. For example, in parallel join processing, some researchers use models that discount the contribution of the network [7], while others pay considerable attention to it [11]. It is possible that in these examples the assumptions made by the authors were appropriate in their specific contexts, but it is easy to see how misleading conclusions could be drawn on the basis of inappropriate assumptions. It therefore seems surprising that validated cost models for database systems are relatively few in number. This paper

Z. Bellahsène, D. Patel, and C. Rolland (Eds.): OOIS 2002, LNCS 2425, pp. 60–76, 2002.

presents a cost model that characterises the evaluation of ODMG OQL queries in a parallel environment, and illustrates the validation of the model against empirical results.

The setting for the experimental work is the Polar parallel object database system [10]. Polar has a shared-nothing architecture, and has been implemented on a PC cluster. As Polar uses mainstream algebraic query processing techniques, the cost model presented here should be straightforward to adapt for use with other object algebras, for example, in a distributed setting (e.g. [4]).

An early result on cost models for database algebras compared six navigational joins, three sequential pointer-based joins and their value-based counterparts [9]. The model takes account of both CPU and IO costs, but has not been validated against system results. More recent work on navigational joins is reported in [1], in which new and existing pointer-based joins are compared using a comprehensive cost model that considers both IO and CPU. A portion of the results were validated against an implementation, with errors in the predicted performance reported in the range 2% to 23%. The work most related to ours is probably [5]. In [5], several parallel join algorithms, including the hash-loops join used in this paper, are compared through an analytical model. The model in [5] considers only IO, and its formulae have been adapted for use in this paper. As we use only single-pass algorithms, our IO formulae are simpler than those in [5]. The model, however, has not been validated against system results, and a shared-everything environment is assumed. In our work, a shared-nothing environment is used.

The remainder of the paper is structured as follows: Section 2 describes the Polar system and its platform. Section 3 describes the cost model. The experiments used in the validation of the cost model are described in Section 4. Finally, Section 5 presents some conclusions.

2 Technical Context

Polar is a shared-nothing ODMG compliant object database server. For the experiments reported in this paper, it was running on a cluster of 7 PCs. One of these processors serves as a coordinator, running the compiler/optimiser, while the remaining six serve as object stores, running an object manager and query execution engine. The compiler/optimiser compiles ODMG OQL queries into parallel query execution plans (PQEPs) expressed in an object algebra [8]. The join operators supported include parallel versions of hash-join, which is a value-based join, and of hash-loops and tuple-cache hash-loops, which are pointer-based. The implementation of the operators is essentially sequential, and most of the functionality that relates to parallelism, such as flow control, inter-process communication and data distribution, is encapsulated in a single operator, the exchange operator, following the operator model of parallelisation [6]. Object identifiers in Polar contain a volume identifier, and a logical identifier within the volume. Tables are maintained that allow the node of a volume to be identified from the volume id, and that allow the page of an object to be identified from its logical identifier.

The environment used in the experiments is a cluster of 233MHz Pentium II PCs running RedHat Linux version 6.2, each with 64MB main memory and a local disk, connected via a 100Mbps Fast ethernet hub. For each experiment, data is partitioned in "round robin" style over all the disks, of which there is one at each node, each being a MAXTOR MXT-540SL. All timings are based on cold runs of the queries, with the server shut down and the operating system cache flushed between runs. In each case, the experiments were run three times, and the average time obtained is reported.

3 Cost Model

The cost model covers the complete parallel object algebra defined in [8], and estimates query response times on an unloaded server. The cost of executing each operator depends on several system parameters and variables, which are described in Tables 1 and 2. The values for the system parameters have been obtained through experiments and are presented in seconds, unless otherwise stated.

In the model, *partitioned parallelism* is captured by estimating separately the costs of the instances of a query subplan running on different nodes of the parallel machine, and taking the cost of the most costly instance as the cost of the particular subplan, i.e., $C_{subplan} = \max_{1 \leq i \leq N}(C_{subplan_i})$, where N is the number of nodes running the same subplan. *Intra-node pipelined parallelism* is supported by a multi-threaded implementation of the iterator model. Currently, multi-threading is limited as it only happens between operators running in distinct subplans linked by an exchange. *Inter-node pipelined parallelism* is implemented within the exchange operator (described in Section 3.7). Due to the limitations of multi-threaded execution in Polar, it is assumed that the costs of the operators of a subplan running on a particular node represent the cost of the subplan, i.e., $C_{subplan_i} = \sum_{1 \leq j \leq K}(C_{operator_j})$, where K is the number of operators of the subplan. IO, CPU and communication costs are all taken into account in the estimation of the cost of an operator, i.e., $C_{operator_j} = C_{io} + C_{cpu} + C_{comm}$. *Independent parallelism* is captured by enabling subplans neither of which uses data produced by the other may run simultaneously on distinct processors, or on the same processor using different threads. The cost formulae for each operator are described in the rest of this section.

3.1 Sequential-Scan

The seq-scan operator retrieves all the objects of an extent, by accessing local disk pages sequentially. For each page read into memory, it maps each of the objects in the page into tuple format, and evaluates a predicate over the tuple. Seq-scan does not perform communication operations and, therefore, does not incur any communication costs.

Table 1. System parameters

Name	Description	Default value (in seconds)
C_{seek}	average read seek time of disks	0.0085
$C_{latency}$	average latency time of disks	0.0048
$C_{rotation}$	average rotation time of disks	0.0024
C_{eval}	average time to evaluate a one-condition predicate	7.0000e-06
C_{copy}	average time to copy one tuple into another	3.2850e-06
C_{conv}	average time to convert an OID into a page number	3.8000e-06
C_{look}	average time to look up a tuple in a table of tuples and retrieve it from the table	3.6000e-07
C_{pack}	average time to pack an object of type t into a buffer	(depends on t)
C_{unpack}	average time to unpack an object of type t from a buffer	(depends on t)
C_{map}	average time to map an attribute of type t from store format into tuple format	(depends on t)
$C_{hashOnNumber}$	average time to apply a hash function on the page number or OID number of an object and obtain the result	2.7000e-07
$C_{newTuple}$	average time to allocate memory space for an empty tuple	1.5390e-06
$C_{projAttr}$	average time to project one attribute from a tuple	2.9350e-06
$Net_{overhead}$	space overhead in bytes imposed by Ethernet related to protocol trailer and header, per packet transmitted	18
Net_{band}	network bandwidth in Mbps	100

Table 2. System variables

Name	Description
$Inum_{left}, Inum_{right}$	cardinality of the left and right inputs.
P_{len}, R_{card}	length of the predicate, and cardinality of a relationship .
$O_{type}, O_{num}, O_{refnum}$	type of an object, number of objects and number of referenced objects, respectively.
$extent, Page_{num}$	extent of the database and number of pages, respectively
$H_{size}, Bucket_{size}$	number of buckets in a hash table and number of elements in a bucket, respectively.
W_{num}, W_{size}	number of windows of input and number of elements in a window, respectively.
$Col_{card}, Proj_{num}$	cardinality of a collection and number of attributes to be projected, respectively.
T_{size}, T_{num}	size of a tuple (in bytes), and number of tuples, respectively.
$Pack_{num}$	number of packets to be transmitted through the network.

CPU cost: The main CPU operations performed by seq-scan are: mapping of objects from store format into tuple format and predicate evaluation over tuples. Hence:

$$C_{cpu} \quad = \quad mapObjectTuple(O_{type}, O_{num}) \quad + \quad evalPred(P_{len}, O_{num}) \quad (1)$$

Map object into tuple format: The cost of mapping objects from store into tuple format depends on the type and the number of objects to be mapped. Large objects with multiple valued attributes, relationships and large strings are more costly to map. Hence:

$$mapObjectTuple(typeOfObject, numOfObjects) = \\ mapTime(typeOfObject) * numOfObjects \quad (2)$$

The time to map an object depends on the types of the object's attributes, and the cardinalities of collection attributes and relationships. Hence:

$$mapTime(typeOfObject) = \sum_{typeOfAttr \in \{int, \ldots\}} C_{map_{typeOfAttr}} * \\ typeOfObject.numOfAttr(typeOfAttr) \quad (3)$$

Experiments with the mapping of attribute values, such as longs, strings and references, have been obtained from experiments and used as values for $C_{map_{typeOfAttr}}$.

Evaluate predicate over tuple: The cost of evaluating a predicate depends on the number of conditions in the predicate and the average time to evaluate a condition. As in the experimental queries (Section 4), the predicates are conjunctions of conditions, we only describe the formula that applies to this case due to space limitations. We assume that, for a predicate P, on average, half of the conditions are evaluated before the predicate evaluation stops due to a condition evaluating to false. This assumption excepts predicates with only one condition, which have their one condition evaluated. Hence, $1 + ((P_{len} - 1)/2)$ of the conditions are evaluated for each predicate.

$$evalPred(lengthOfPred, numTuples) = ((1 + ((lengthOfPred - 1)/2)) * \mathsf{C_{eval}}) * \\ numTuples \quad (4)$$

IO cost: The IO cost of seq-scan derives from page reads from disk into memory. The number of page reads depends on the number of pages occupied by the extent being scanned, and the cost of reading each page sequentially. Hence:

$$C_{io} = readPagesSeq(extent.Page_{num}) \quad (5)$$

$$readPagesSeq(numOfPages) = \mathsf{C_{seek}} + \mathsf{C_{latency}} + (\mathsf{C_{rotation}} * numOfPages) \quad (6)$$

When two or three other seq-scan operators running in different threads compete for the same disk, the overheads added to the exclusive access time (given by the formula described above) are 1.67 and 2.40 times the exclusive access time, respectively. These multipliers were identified by an experimental assessment of the effects of competition as sequential access times. In general, interference between operators sharing resources is taken into account by adding an overhead time related to shared accesses to the same resource by different operators, when calculating the cost of a particular operator. This overhead may depend on the number of operators accessing the resource and the type of access performed by each operator, e.g., disk random or sequential access.

3.2 Hash-Join

The hash-join operator builds a hash table indexed on the joining attribute(s) of one of its inputs, and probes the hash table using the other input. Hash-join does not perform IO or communication. **Details of the algorithm:**

```
1 for each tuple in the left input
  1.1 hash tuple on the join attribute(s)
2 for each tuple in the right input
  2.1 hash tuple on the join attribute(s)
  2.2 for each tuple in the corresponding hash table bucket
    2.2.1 concatenate tuple in the bucket with right input tuple
    2.2.2 apply predicate over resulting tuple
```

CPU cost: The main CPU operations performed by hash-join are described in lines 1.1, 2.1, 2.2.1 and 2.2.2 of the algorithm. Hence:

$$C_{cpu} = hashTuples(I_{num_{left}} + I_{num_{right}}) + concatTuples(I_{num_{right}} * Bucket_{size}) + evalPred(P_{len}, (I_{num_{right}} * Bucket_{size})) \quad (7)$$

Note that both left and right input tuples are hashed on an OID value. Since all right input tuples get concatenated with each tuple in one of the buckets of the hash table, the number of tuple concatenations and predicate evaluations is approximately the number of right input tuples times the average number of tuples in each bucket in the hash table.

Hash tuples on join attribute(s): When two tuples are joined on an explicit relationship, the join attribute is OID-valued[1]. The cost of hashing thus depends on the cost of hashing one tuple, and the number of tuples to be hashed. Hence:

$$hashTuples(numOfTuples) = \mathsf{C_{hashOnNumber}} * numOfTuples \quad (8)$$

[1] Due to space limitations, we only consider OID-valued join attributes.

Concatenate two tuples: Concatenation of two tuples is done by copying the two tuples into a third tuple. This does not involve copying the contents of the tuples, though, as tuples contain only pointers to objects in memory that are shared between the original tuples and their copies. The model accounts both for the allocation time for the new tuple and for the cost of copying the pointers within the tuple.

$$concatTuples(numOfPairs) = (2 * \mathsf{C_{copy}} + \mathsf{C_{newTuple}}) * numOfPairs \quad (9)$$

The cost of evaluating a predicate is described in formula *(4)*.

3.3 Hash-Loops

The pointer-based hash-loops operator extracts the page number of the OID related to a particular relationship contained in each of its input tuples, hashes each tuple on this page number, and inserts it into a hash table. Each hash table entry contains both the page number and a list of pointers to the input tuples that refer to objects on that page. Once the hash table is built, the hash entries are processed sequentially by reading the corresponding page into memory. Then, each hash table tuple that references the page is joined with the relevant object (i.e. tuple generated from the object) on the page. Although hash-loops is a one-input operator, we refer to its input operand as the left input, and the stored collection to be accessed from disk as its right input.

To avoid building a hash table that is too large to fit in memory, the input tuples can be divided into a number of windows. Each window of tuples is separately loaded into the hash table and processed.

Details of the algorithm:

1 *for each window of the left input*
 1.1 *for each tuple in the window*
  1.1.1 *convert reference to object into a page number*
  1.1.2 *hash tuple on the page number*
 1.2 *for each entry in the hash table*
  1.2.1 *read page*
  1.2.2 *for each tuple in the bucket*
   1.2.2.1 *map referenced object into tuple format*
   1.2.2.2 *concatenate tuples*
   1.2.2.3 *apply predicate over the result*

CPU cost: The main CPU operations performed by hash-loops are described in lines 1.1.1, 1.1.2, 1.2.2.1, 1.2.2.2, and 1.2.2.3 of the algorithm. Hence:

$$\begin{aligned} C_{cpu} = {} & convertOIDpage(I_{num_{left}}) + hashTuples(I_{num_{left}}) + R_{card} * \\ & mapObjectTuple(O_{type}, O_{refnum}) + concatTuples(I_{num_{left}}) + \\ & evalPred(P_{len}, I_{num_{left}}) \quad (10) \end{aligned}$$

Convert OID to referenced object into its page number: As Polar's OIDs are logical, they need to be mapped into the object's physical address. The cost of such mappings depends on the number of OIDs to be mapped (i.e., one for each input tuple) and the cost of converting a single OID. Hence:

$$convertOIDpage(numOfTuples) = \mathsf{C_{conv}} * numOfTuples \quad (11)$$

Map object into tuple format: For hash-loops, the number of times a stored object is mapped into tuple format depends on the number of times the object is referenced by the input tuples. This corresponds, approximately, to the cardinality of the inverse relationship to the one being followed by hash-loops times a factor based on the selectivity of the predicate, R_{card}. This operation is described in formula *(2)*. The CPU operations for evaluation of predicate, hashing of tuples and concatenation of tuples are described in formulae *(4)*, *(8)* and *(9)*, respectively.
IO cost: The IO operations performed by hash-loops relate to the retrieval of stored objects into memory for joining with the input tuples. In pointer-based joins, only pages containing objects referenced within the input tuples are actually read and the type of disk access is random. Hence:

$$C_{io} = readPagesRand(numReadPages) \quad (12)$$

$$readPagesRand(numReadPages) = (\mathsf{C_{seek}} + \mathsf{C_{latency}} + \mathsf{C_{rotation}}) * numReadPages \quad (13)$$

To estimate the number of page reads performed per hash table, we use the Yao's formula [12]. Yao calculates the expected fraction of pages of a collection with cardinality *collectionSize* that must be read to retrieve a subset of this collection with cardinality *numRefObjects*, provided that *numObjPerPage* objects fit on a page. The number of objects that are referenced within the input tuples, *numRefObjects*, can be estimated by a formula proposed in [5], which is described below:

$$numReferencedObjects(windowSize, collectionSize) = \min(windowSize, collectionSize) \quad (14)$$

The number of pages retrieved per window of input is estimated as the fraction of pages containing objects referenced by the input tuples, times the number of pages occupied by the whole collection.

$$numReadPages = Yao(collectionSize, numObjPerPage, numRefObjects) * numPages \quad (15)$$

3.4 Tc-Hash-Loops

The pointer-based tc-hash-loops (tuple-cache hash loops) operator is similar to hash-loops, but seeks to improve on hash-loops by avoiding the mapping of the same object into tuple format multiple times within a window of input. For this purpose, tc-hash-loops builds a table containing the tuples generated from the objects retrieved from the store. So, each retrieved object is mapped once and its tuple is placed into the table of tuples. When the same object is requested a second time, its tuple can be obtained from the table of tuples, without having to map the object a second time.

The main CPU operations performed by tc-hash-loops are the same as for hash-loops, except that tc-hash-loops accesses a table of tuples before mapping an object into tuple format. Therefore, tc-hash-loops differs from hash-loops in the number of object-tuple mappings and the accesses to the table of tuples. As in tc-hash-loops, each object is mapped once per window of input (assuming that the table of tuples is emptied and filled each time the hash table is filled with another window of input), an object referenced within multiple tuples that participate in different windows of input is mapped multiple times. In the worse case, an object will be mapped W_{num} times, if $W_{num} \leq R_{card}$. As the entries of the hash table are processed sequentially, the corresponding disk pages are read into memory and the table of tuples is filled with tuples generated from stored objects. When the first tuple of each entry of the hash table is probed, the referenced object is mapped from scratch, without requiring the table of tuples to be accessed. For the second and subsequent tuples, the table of tuples is always accessed before mapping any stored object from scratch. Therefore, the table of tuples is accessed $W_{size} - H_{size}$ times per window of input. The cost of accessing the table of tuples depends on the time to look for a tuple in the table, and the number of tuples that are to be looked for in the table. Hence, $accessTableOfTuples(numOfTuples) = \mathsf{C}_{\mathsf{look}} * numOfTuples$.

3.5 Unnest

The unnest operator gets each element in a collection attribute or relationship of a tuple, and adds it to a copy of the tuple as a new (single-valued) attribute or relationship. Therefore, the main CPU operations performed by unnest are creating a tuple, copying the contents of a tuple into another tuple, inserting an attribute into a tuple and evaluating a predicate. Hence,

$$C_{cpu} = ((\mathsf{C}_{\mathsf{newTuple}} + \mathsf{C}_{\mathsf{copy}} + \mathsf{C}_{\mathsf{projAttr}}) * Col_{card}) * I_{num_{left}} + evalPred(P_{len}, I_{num_{left}}) \qquad (16)$$

3.6 Apply

The apply operator projects attributes of tuples, discarding attributes that are not relevant to the subsequent steps of execution. It does that by creating a new tuple, and projecting on the tuple only the attributes that are specified in a list of attributes to be projected. Similar to unnest, apply does not perform any IO. The main CPU operations performed by apply are creating a tuple and projecting attributes into a tuple. Hence:

$$C_{cpu} = (\mathsf{C_{newTuple}} + \mathsf{C_{projAttr}} * Proj_{num}) * I_{num_{left}} \quad (17)$$

3.7 Exchange

The exchange operator packs tuples into buffers, sends buffers to other processors, and unpacks tuples from arriving buffers. Hence, the CPU cost of exchange can be defined as follows.

CPU cost:

$$C_{cpu} = (\mathsf{C_{packO_{type}}} * T_{num_{pack}}) + (\mathsf{C_{unpackO_{type}}} * T_{num_{unpack}}) \quad (18)$$

The cost of packing and unpacking tuples depends on the number of tuples to be packed ($T_{num_{pack}}$) and unpacked ($T_{num_{unpack}}$) by exchange, and the cost of packing ($\mathsf{C_{packO_{type}}}$) and unpacking ($\mathsf{C_{unpackO_{type}}}$) a single tuple of a particular type (O_{type}). The number of tuples depends on the data redistribution and the number of consumer and producer operators that exchange communicates with.
Communication cost: The communication cost of exchange relates to the transmission of packets of data through the network. This cost is calculated by dividing the total amount of data to be transmitted in bits (amount of data in bytes times 8) by the network bandwidth in bps ($10^6 * Net_{band}$).

$$C_{comm} = (dataSize(T_{size}, T_{num}) + netOverhead(Pack_{num}) * 8)/(10^6 * Net_{band}) \quad (19)$$

The total amount of data to be transmitted depends on the amount of data related to the tuples contained in the transmission packets and the space overhead imposed by the network per packet, e.g. protocol headers and trailers. The former depends on the average number of bytes contained in the input tuples, and the number of tuples. Hence:

$$dataSize(sizeOfTuple, numOfTuples) = sizeOfTuple * numOfTuples \quad (20)$$

The latter depends on the number of packets to be transmitted and the overhead associated with each packet. Hence:

$$netOverhead(numOfPackets) = Net_{overhead} * numOfPackets \quad (21)$$

The number of packets transmitted by exchange depends on the the number of consumers to which exchange sends packets, and the maximum packet size. Each buffer of tuples to be sent to a particular destination may be divided into a number of packets, if its size exceeds the maximum packet size.

Q1:
select struct(A:a.id,
B:a.partOf.id)
from a in AtomicParts
where a.id ¡= v1
and a.partOf.id ¡= v2;

Q2:
select
struct(A:a.id, B:a.docId,
C:a.partOf.
documentation.id)
from a in AtomicParts
where a.docId !=
a.partOf.
documentation.id;

Q3:
select
struct(A:c.id, B:a.id)
from c in CompositeParts,
a in c.parts
where c.id ¡= v1
and
a.id ¡= v2;

Fig. 1. Experiment Queries

4 Experiments

4.1 Database and Queries

The database used in the experiments is the medium OO7 database [3]. Figure 1 lists the OQL queries used in the experiments. The queries have different levels of complexity, offering different challenges to the query evaluator. Figure 2 shows a PQEP for Q1. In the plan, apply operators are placed before exchange operators, so that attributes that are not relevant to the subsequent steps of execution are discarded, and smaller tuples are transmitted through the network, saving communication costs. The exchange operators send tuples from a producer processor to its consumer(s) using the network and receive the tuples on the consumer processors. Thus exchange defines a partitioning of PQEPs into subplans, as indicated in the figure. The policy used for tuple distribution is chosen at query compile time, e.g. *select_by_oid* or *round_robin*. While the *select_by_oid* policy chooses as destination of a particular tuple the node in which the object referenced within the tuple resides, the *round_robin* policy applies round-robin distribution for choosing the destination of tuples. The exchange that produces data to the print operator is responsible for directing the intermediate results to a single processor (the coordinator) for building the final result and sending it to the user. The print operator simply counts the number of resulting tuples. The plan in the figure uses hash-join for evaluating the join operation. Due to space limitations, corresponding plans using the pointer-based joins are omitted, which differ from the hash-join plan in the absence of seq-scan operators directly linked to the join. For the same reason, query plans for Q2 and Q3 are also omitted.

The hash-loops and tc-hash-loops operators have their tuning parameters set as follows. The hash table size for both operators is set to the first prime number after the number of disk pages occupied by the extent that is being navigated to. This means that there should be few clashes during hash table construction, but that the hash table does not occupy an excessive amount of memory. The window size for both operators is set to the cardinality of the intermediate result which is input to the operator, except where otherwise stated. This decision minimises the number of page accesses carried out by the two operators at the expense of some additional hash table size. In hash-join, the hash table size is set differently for each join, to the value of the first prime number after the number of buckets to be stored in the hash table by the join.

The predicates in the where clauses in Q1 and Q3 are used to vary the selectivity of the queries over the objects of the input extents, which may affect the join operators in different ways. The selectivities are varied to retain 100%, 10%, 1% and 0.1% of the input extents, and this is done by varying the values of *v1* and *v2* in the predicates. None of the experiments use indexes, although the use of explicit relationships with stored OIDs can be seen as analogous to indexes on join attributes in relational databases.

4.2 Results

Elapsed time for queries: Figure 3, 4 and 5 show experimental results using the Polar system and the corresponding cost model estimates for Q1, Q2 and Q3, respectively, using a predicate selectivity of 100%, varying the number of processors, and running the three join algorithms described in Section 3.

The results in figure 3 show that hash-loops is the most costly operator, while hash-join is the fastest for all numbers of processors. Tc-hash-loops stands between the two, but closer to hash-join than to hash-loops. Hash-loops is slower than tc-hash-loops because hash-loops performs 100,000 object-tuple mappings when retrieving *CompositePart* objects (200 mappings for each object), whereas tc-hash-loops only performs 500 (mapping each *CompositePart* once). The numbers of object-tuple mappings coincide for hash-join and tc-hash-loops. However, with hash-join, disk pages containing *CompositeParts* are retrieved sequentially, while in tc-hash-loops the pages are read randomly. The cost model captures the behaviours of the different joins reasonably well, although it is more precise

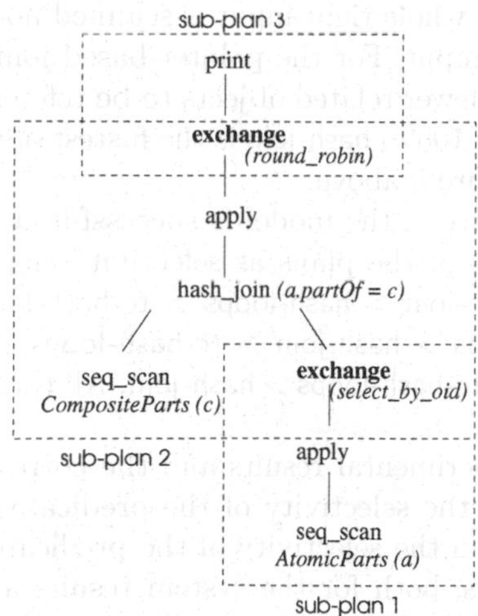

Fig. 2. Execution plan for Q1

for hash-join and tc-hash-loops, as they perform fewer object-tuple mappings for *CompositePart* objects. The model slightly underestimates the mapping cost of *CompositePart* objects compared to the measured times obtained from experimentation with OO7 object mappings – developing a single model for object-tuple mappings (as described in Section 3.1) that works for all shapes and sizes of objects has proved quite challenging.

The results in figure 4 are similar to those in figure 3. The model generally tracks the experimental results for hash-loops very closely, but provides a slightly misleading impression for hash-join and tc-hash-loops. The model predicts hash-join to be cheaper than tc-hash-loops, as for Q1. However, this is not what the system results show for the single processor configuration. We believe that this discrepancy can be explained by mild paging activity for the hash join. In Q2, the two hash-join operators build large hash tables containing substantial *CompositePart* and *Document* tuples. By contrast, the hash tables for tc-hash-loops contain smaller input tuples resulting from the projections that are performed before exchanging data through the network. As a result, there is no paging activity in the evaluation of the plan for tc-hash-loops. Models have been developed that predict the memory usage of different plans, which are not shown here due to lack of space. Overall, the models in this paper assume that the single-pass join algorithms can be evaluated without causing paging.

In figure 5, tc-hash-loops and hash-loops present similar performance, as there is no sharing of *AtomicPart* objects among the objects of *CompositeParts.* This means that tc-hash-loops performs the same number of object-tuple mappings as hash-loops. Hash-join suffers from paging when running Q3 on a single processor.

Varying predicate selectivity: Figures 6 through 8 show experimental results and the corresponding cost model estimates for Q1 and Q3, varying the selectivity of the predicate over the left input to the joins. Both model and experiments show that hash-join is more expensive than the the two pointer-based joins for lower selectivities, as its whole right input is scanned no matter what selectivity is applied over the left input. For the pointer-based joins, a significant filtering on the left input causes fewer related objects to be referenced and retrieved from the store. For selectivity 100%, hash-join is the fastest operator, for reasons given in the discussion of Figure 3 above.

We note that in figure 6, the model is successful at tracking the significant changes to the rankings of the plans as selectivity changes. At 1% selectivity, the cost ranking is hash-join > hash-loops > tc-hash-loops. At 10% selectivity, the ranking is hash-loops > hash-join > tc-hash-loops. At 100% selectivity the ranking is hash-loops > tc-hash-loops > hash-join. All these rankings are correctly predicted by the model.

Figures 7 shows experimental results and the corresponding cost model estimates for Q1 varying the selectivity of the predicate over the right input to the join. The variation in the selectivity of the predicate does not substantially affect the join operators, both for the system results and the cost model estimates. For the pointer-based joins, the predicate on the right input to the join is applied after the join has taken place. For the hash-join, the predicate also

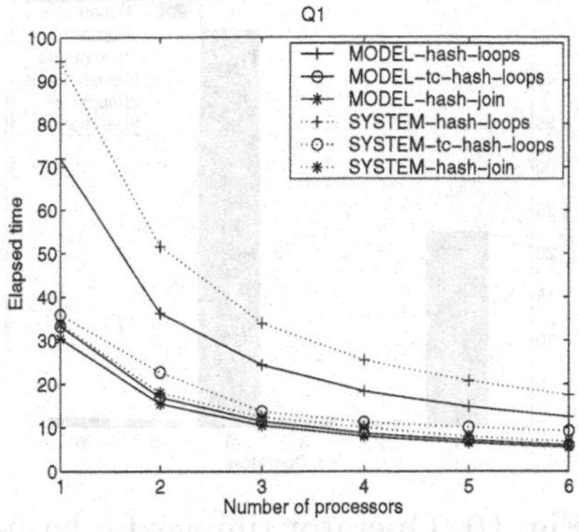

Fig. 3. Elapsed time for Q1

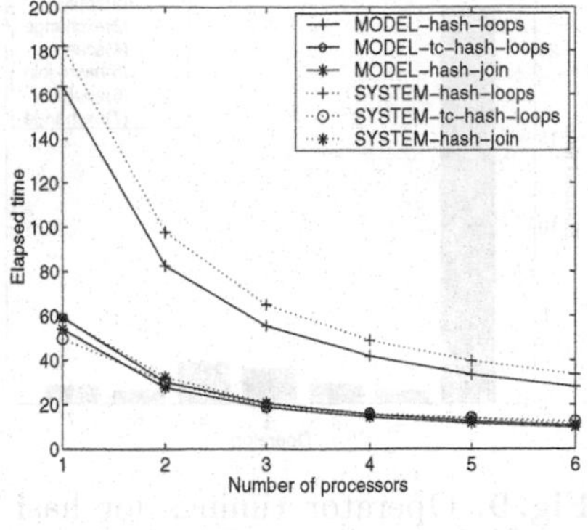

Fig. 4. Elapsed time for Q2

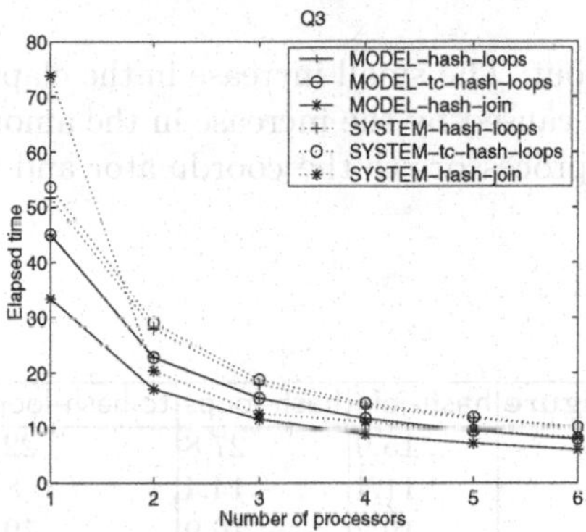

Fig. 5. Elapsed time for Q3

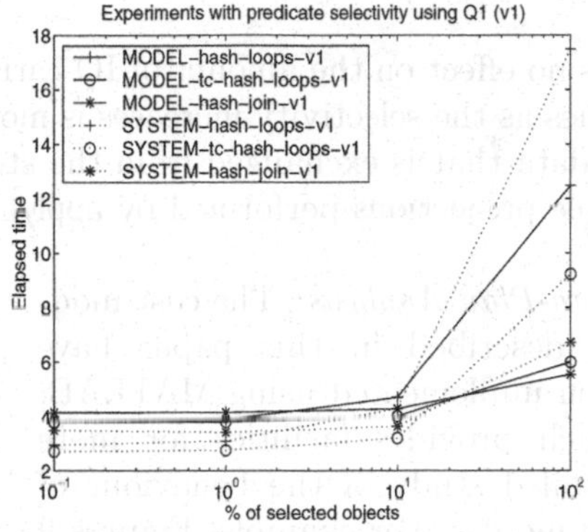

Fig. 6. Selectivity tests for Q1 using v1

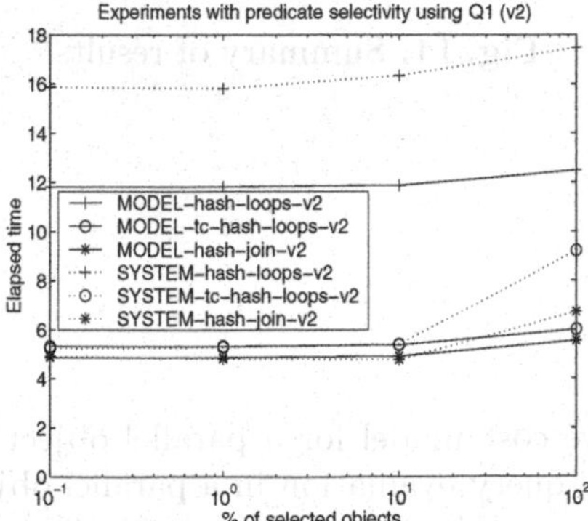

Fig. 7. Selectivity tests for Q1 using v2

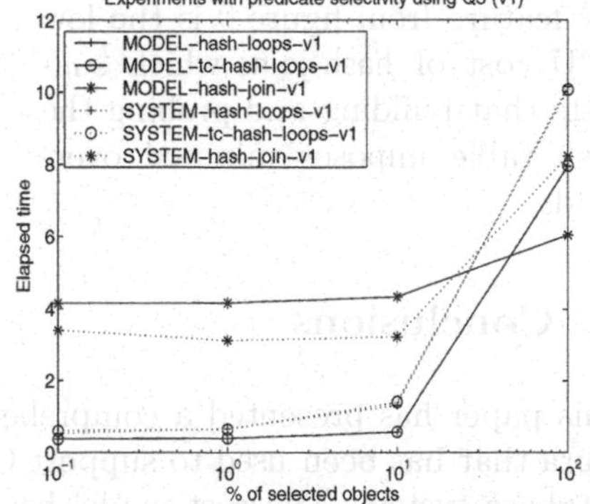

Fig. 8. Selectivity tests for Q3 using v1

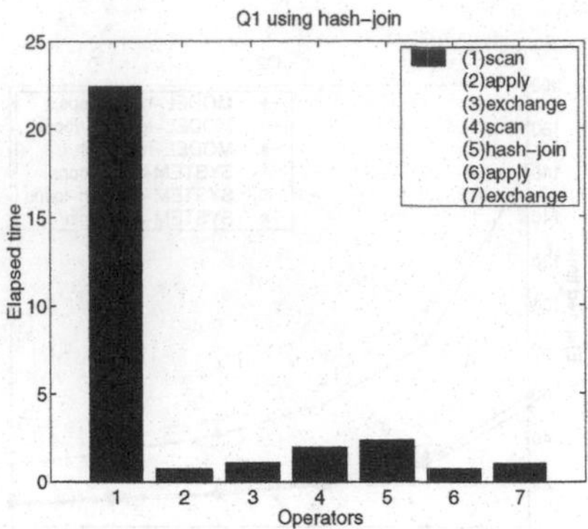

Fig. 9. Operator timings for hash-join

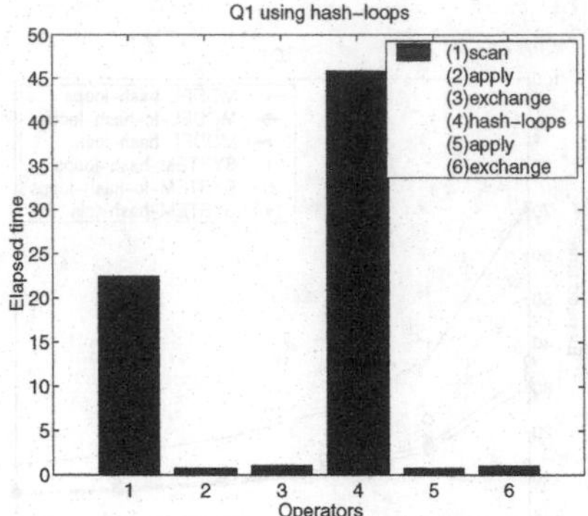

Fig. 10. Operator timings for hash-loops

has no effect on the amount of IO carried out. The small increase in the elapsed times as the selectivity increases is mostly caused by the increase in the amount of data that is exchanged from the store processors to the coordinator and the tuple projections performed by apply.

Intra-Plan Analysis: The cost models described in this paper have been implemented using MATLAB, which provides facilities for more detailed study of the behaviour of the models. For example, Figures 9 and 10 show the contributions of the individual operators to the response times for Q1. One noteworthy feature from figure 9 is the low CPU cost of hash-join, which suggests that building and probing the hash table imposes minimal overheads.

Figure	hash-join	hash-loops	tc-hash-loops
3	15.9	27.8	22.6
4	11.4	14.4	8.6
5	19.2	16.9	19.2
6	18.8	23.3	34.4
7	5.6	26.6	9.4
8	29.0	36.9	38.9

Fig. 11. Summary of results

5 Conclusions

This paper has presented a comprehensive cost model for a parallel object algebra that has been used to support OQL query evaluation in a parallel object database system. The cost model has been validated against empirical results for different join algorithms, selectivities, numbers of processors and relationship cardinalities. As a model of runtime behaviour, the cost model generally both ranks alternative plans appropriately, and provides a useful indication of the response times that can be anticipated from a plan. Table 11 gives average % errors for the results in Figures 3 to 8 for each of the join algorithms.

These average error figures are generally larger than when validation results are reported by others referred to in Section 1, but the scope of both the cost model and the validation is relatively broader here compared to earlier examples of validation in the context of object queries and parallel database systems.

The cost models capture several features of the evaluated system that came as something of a surprise to us as systems developers, such as (i) the substantial contribution of CPU to many of the response times; (ii) the minimal contribution of network costs to response times of parallel queries; and (iii) the significant CPU cost of mapping data from disk format into the intermediate tuple format used by the query evaluator. The identification of (iii) led to the development of the tc-hash-loops algorithm as a variation of hash-loops, which was performing poorly in certain common circumstances.

The MATLAB implementations of the cost models presented in this paper are available from `http://www.ncl.ac.uk/polar/models`.

References

1. R. Braumandl, J. Claussen, A. Kemper, and D. Kossmann. Functional-join processing. *VLDB Journal*, 8(3-4):156–177, 2000. 61
2. P. A. Buhr, A. K. Goel, N. Nishimura, and P. Ragde. Parallel pointer-based join algorithms in memory-mapped environments. In *Proceedings of ICDE*, pages 266–275, 1996. 60
3. M. Carey, D. J. DeWitt, and J. F. Naughton. The OO7 benchmark. In *ACM SIGMOD*, pages 12–21, 1993. 70
4. S. Cluet and C. Delobel. A general framework for the optimization of object-oriented queries. In *Proceedings of the ACM SIGMOD Conference*, page 383, San Diego, CA, June 1992. 61
5. D. J. DeWitt, D. F. Lieuwen, and M. Mehta. Pointer-based join techniques for object-oriented databases. In *Proc. of the 2nd Int. Conference on Parallel and Distributed Information Systems (PDIS)*, pages 172–181. IEEE-CS, 1993. 60, 61, 67
6. G. Graefe. Encapsulation of parallelism in the Volcano query processing system. In *ACM SIGMOD*, pages 102–111, 1990. 61
7. M. Metha and D. J. DeWitt. Data placement in shared-nothing parallel database systems. *VLDB Journal*, 6(1):53–72, 1997. 60
8. S. F. M. Sampaio, N. W. Paton, P. Watson, and J. Smith. A parallel algebra for object databases. In *Proc. 10th DEXA Workshop*, pages 56–60. IEEE Press, 1999. 61, 62
9. E. Shekita and M. J. Carey. A performance evaluation of pointer-based joins. In *Proc. ACM SIGMOD*, pages 300–311, 1990. 61
10. J. Smith, S. F. M. Sampaio, P. Watson, and N. W. Paton. Polar: An architecture for a parallel ODMG compliant object database. In *Proc. ACM CIKM*, pages 352–359. ACM press, 2000. 61
11. A. N. Wilschut, J. Flokstra, and P. M. G. Apers. Parallel evaluation of multi-join queries. In *Proc. ACM SIGMOD*, pages 115–126. ACM Press, 1995. 60

12. S. Bing Yao. Approximating block accesses in database organizations. *Communications of the ACM*, 20(4):260–261, 1977. 67

An Object-Oriented Schema for Querying Audio

José Martinez, Rania Lutfi, and Marc Gelgon

Institut de Recherche en Informatique de Nantes (IRIN / BaDRI)
Ecole polytechnique de l'université de Nantes
La Chantrerie – B.P. 50609 – 44306 Nantes Cedex 3 – France
Tel.: +33 2 40 68 32 56 - Fax: +33 2 40 68 32 32
{firstname.surname}@irin.univ-nantes.fr

Abstract. To be fully usable, digital multimedia contents should be supported by a set of tools to query them, and more generally to manipulate them. This is one of the major goals of an audio database management system (DBMS). Existing work, e.g., radio or television archives, generally tackles the signal processing aspects, often leaving the DBMS question open. In this paper, we lay the foundations for integrating audio into a general purpose DBMS in the form of an object-oriented library. This library provides additional capabilities on top of (MPEG-7) audio descriptions used for mere selections.

1 Introduction and Motivations

Multimedia data is always queried *via meta-data* [10], the only difference with the usual terminology being that part of this meta-data is extracted from the content itself and represents it. Extracting audio meta-data from the raw signal is a difficult and widely investigated research field [6]. Some usual features for speech analysis are *pitch* (reliable determination of the fundamental frequency of vocal cords characterises well the speaker), MFCC (*Mel-scaled Frequency Cepstral Coefficients* are very useful for transcription), and *zero-crossing rate* (the temporal variations of which are a good cue to distinguish speech from music). Encouraging algorithms were demonstrated [4, 11].

However, these works do not address the database issue. We proposed a minimal algebra for manipulating sound tracks [7]. Here, we present the derived object-oriented schema. It does not replace but complement the work that has been done around MPEG-7. We believe that formal querying will be an important access method for audio, especially when signal classification can be made accurate.

The paper is organised as follows. Section 2 describes an object-oriented schema to represent, query, and manipulate audio data at a high level of abstraction. Next, section 3 introduces some examples to illustrate that queries require audio data restructuring in addition to meta-data querying. The proposal is shortly compared to the MPEG-7 proposal in section 4. Finally, the conclusion lists further research issues.

Z. Bellahsène, D. Patel, and C. Rolland (Eds.): OOIS 2002, LNCS 2425, pp. 76-81, 2002.

2 An Object-Oriented Schema

2.1 Analysis of the Problem

At the conceptual level, the two main data types are the *audio recordings* and their *audio segments*. As illustrated in Fig.2, the relationship between them is an aggregation. It translates the syntactical level of MPEG-7 [8, 9]. Other kinds of meta-data are provided by the `Metadata` attribute. We carry out a *temporal segmentation*. The four main classes are "speech", "music", "noise", and "silence". Then, we are able to distinguish between "man", "woman", and "child". Also, thanks to *a priori* training, we can recognise some voices, e.g., the main presenters.

2.2 Modelling Complex Recordings

Sound tracks can be built as a combination of other recordings. This has been formalised as two operators: the *temporal projection* and the *concatenation*. The temporal projection consists in extracting a continuous and non empty part of a recording. Intuitively enough, the concatenation merges a sequence of recordings into a single one. In addition, the most often used operator in set-oriented querying is the generalised temporal projection. It consists in extracting a set of disjoint parts from a sound track and concatenating them in increasing order of start time [7].

As depicted in Fig.1, these two basic operators obey the composite object pattern [3]. Aggregations are weak because recordings can be shared by several excerpts and sequences. Therefore, instances form a directed acyclic graph (DAG), the sinks of which are instances of the `LogicalSoundTrack` class. When necessary, they can be translated into a canonical form, a *concatenation of temporal projections on logical recordings* [7]. Inverse roles are not implemented, as indicated by a question mark.

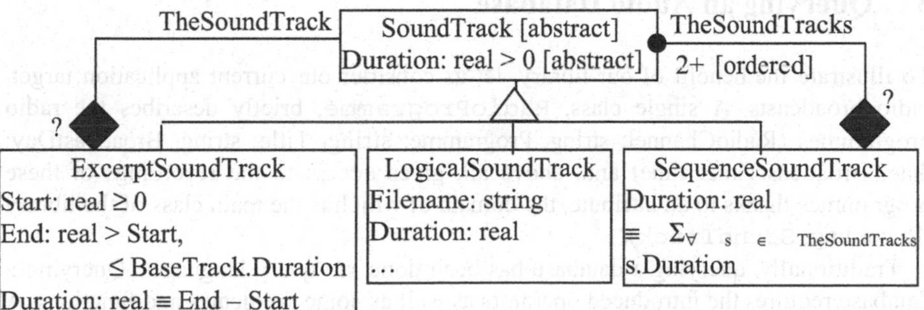

Fig.1. Design schema for supporting temporal projections and concatenations

2.3 Meta-data of Complex Recordings

We have to extend the aggregation relationship to excerpt and sequences. This leads to the whole schema of Fig.2. The logical units are actually indexed in the database.

The generalisation of the role `TheSegments` between the root classes is computed, i.e., indexing of complex recordings is based on the logical recordings that constitute them. For sequences, the computation is simple. The first segments of the sequence are the same as the segments of the first sound track of the sequence, and the others are shifted. Excerpts cause additional difficulty, due to the time interval that can overlap segments, as illustrated in Fig.3. For most segments, there is both a shift and a truncation. In addition to lazy evaluation, the computed results are stored within the corresponding complex sound tracks. This is absolutely necessary, otherwise computations in a DAG with numerous cycles will reach an exponential computation time.

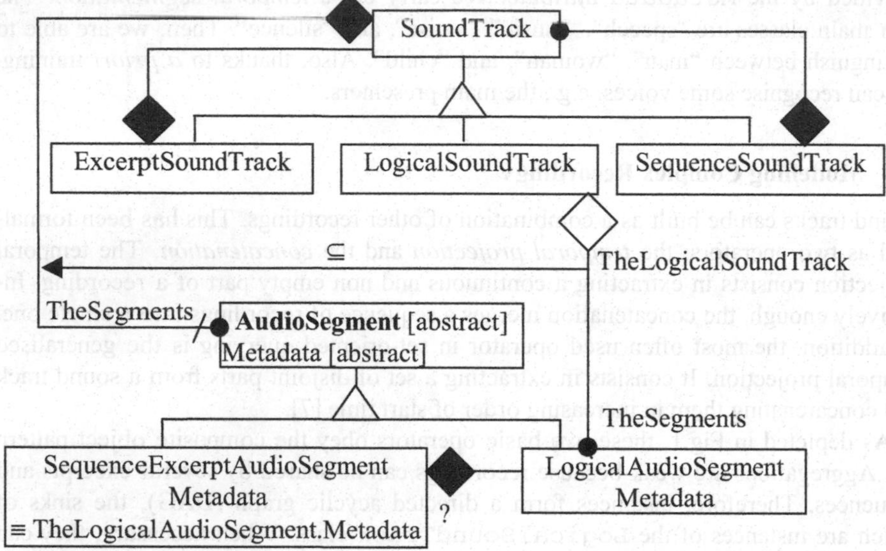

Fig.2. Design schema of the relationships between recordings and segments

3 Querying an Audio Database

To illustrate the benefit of our library, let us consider our current application target, radio broadcasts. A single class, `RadioProgramme`, briefly describes the radio programmes (RadioChannel: string, Programme: string, Title: string, BroadcastDay: date, BroadcastTime: time) and, above all, gives access to the recordings of these programmes thanks to an attribute, the domain of which is the main class of the library (Recording: `SoundTrack`).

Traditionally, querying a database has been done *via* query languages. Querying a database requires the introduced operators as well as some predicates and functions. A set of arbitrary functions and predicates is available for querying the `Metadata` attribute, among which *music*(i), *speech*(i), *man*(i), *samevoice*(i_1, i_2), etc. Because intervals are ubiquitous, set operations are required: union, intersection and difference, which extend to sets of intervals [2]. Besides, the Allen predicates may be used [1]. Equipped with these functions, we are ready to answer queries that require building recordings in their answers.

Because audio recordings are complex objects, the preferred query language is OQL (*Object Query Language*). Nevertheless, queries that directly manipulate audio recordings cannot rely on the basic possibilities of OQL. For instance, let us solve the following query: « list of all the programmes from my favourite radio channel, along with their broadcast time, and *the first two minutes but music* ». Such a query is useful for providing overviews of what the programmes contain. The proposed library allows to answer this query:

```
select struct(Programme: b.Programme,
              Time: b.BroadcastTime,
              Introduction: start)
from b in TheRadioProgrammes
where b.RadioChannel = "MyFavouriteChannel" and
      b.BroadcastDate = Date(4, 4, 2002)
```

where the construction of the *start* value requires the introduced functionality:

```
ExcerptSoundTrack(0, 2 * 60,
   SequenceSoundTrack(
     b.Recording,
     Interval(0, b.Duration)
     -
     (select Interval(seg.Start, seg.End)
      from seg in b.Recording.TheSegments
      where music(seg))))
```

which consist in (i) determining the set of time intervals containing music (i.e., selection on meta-data), (ii) subtracting them from the single interval that corresponds to the complete programme (i.e., set operations on intervals), (iii) using the complemented set of intervals obtained thereby to extract the parts that have to be concatenated (i.e., operations on complex recordings, sequences and excerpts, *via* the constructor of a sequence that takes a list of intervals as a parameter), (iv) concluding by a final extraction of the « first two minutes but music ».

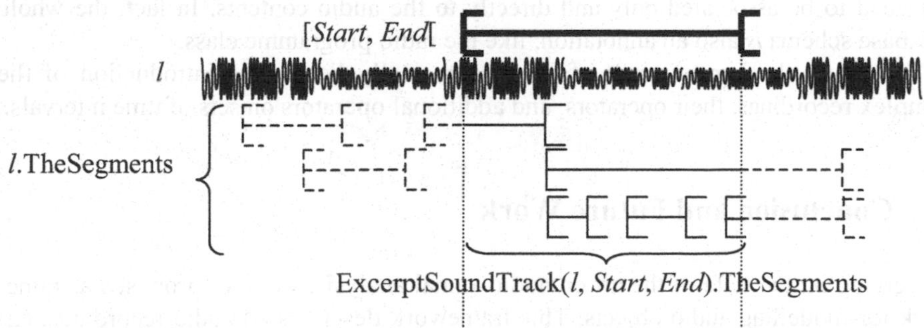

Fig.3. Segments associated to a (logical) recording excerpt

4 A Complement to MPEG-7

MPEG-7 proposes a classification of meta-data into several categories [8, 9]:

Format information: this level associate attributes such as the coding of the content, the duration, mono or stereo for audio, i.e., information that is not related to the content itself;

Physical attributes: these attributes are obtained from various transformations applied to or statistics extracted from the signal [6], like the sound energy or the zero-crossing rate for audio [14];

Perceptual attributes: these attributes are derived from the physical attributes in order to better describe the signal from the semantic point of view, e.g., the pitch is closer to the human ear than the fundamental frequency;

Transcriptions: this is highly semantic information that can be extracted in a limited number of situations, e.g., actual transcription [4] of spoken texts when the model of the speaker is known [13], recognition of specific sounds such as laugher, bells, *etc*.;

Syntactic structures: in the case of audio, this corresponds to a temporal segmentation of the sound track into homogeneous segments, e.g., music, speech, silence;

Annotations: this kind of information is associated to the media by the application, and may consist in an actual database schema in the more general case.

This classification clarifies the role of different kinds of meta-data. It turns out that our proposal leads to almost the same separation, though this has to be pointed out:

Format information: this information is clearly associated to a physical recording, i.e., it is located in the class `LogicalSoundTrack` in Fig.2. Note that the main DBMS providers offer only this kind of meta-data in their products [12].

Physical and *perceptual* attributes, *transcriptions*: these three categories are encapsulated under the `Metadata` attribute of the class `AudioSegment` in Fig.2. There exist candidate proposals [5].

Syntactic structure: this is explicitly translated by the aggregation relationship between sound tracks and audio segments in Fig.2.

Annotations: in the case of a DBMS, we consider that this kind of information does not need to be associated only and directly to the audio contents. In fact, the whole database schema *is* also an annotation, like the radio programme class.

Therefore, the improvement of our library really lies in the introduction of the complex recordings, their operators, and additional operators on sets of time intervals.

5 Conclusion and Future Work

By relying on the state of the art on audio signal analysis, we have proposed a framework for modelling audio objects. This framework describes (i) audio recordings, (ii) their associated segments, and (iii) operators to query them and, above all, to manipulate them, i.e., answers can return complex recordings, not only references to stored recordings It deserves to be integrated into an audio DBMS. From the software engineering point of view, the proposed extension is not trivial to implement and should be factorised for the benefit of all the users.

Research directions are numerous. Firstly, we shall start by applying the framework to a large database. Next, at the meta-data level, we would like to take into account uncertainty on the quality of the meta-data. At the other end, recognising temporal structures and programme types would enhance the quality of the library by offering some classification. Also, it is meaningful to complement querying with browsing.

References

1. Allen, J. F.; Maintaining Knowledge About Temporal Intervals; Communications of the ACM (26):11 (1983) 832–843
2. Fauvet, M.-C., Canavaggio, J.-F., Scholl, P.-C.; Expressions de requêtes temporelles dans un SGBD à objets; Actes des 12èmes Journées Bases de Données Avancées, Cassis, France (1996) 225–250
3. Gamma, E., Helm, R., Johnson, R., Vlissides, J.; Design Patterns: Elements of Reusable Object-Oriented Software; Addison-Wesley (1995)
4. Gauvain, J.-L., Lamel, L., Adda, G.; Partitioning and Transcription of Broadcast News Data; Int'l Conf. on Spoken Language Processing, Sydney, Australia, Vol. 5 (1998) 1335–1338
5. Herrera, P., Serra, X.; A Proposal for the Description of Audio in the Context of MPEG-7; Proc. of the 1st European Workshop on Content-based Multimedia Indexing, Toulouse, France (1999) 81–88
6. Jelinek, F.; Statistical Methods for Speech Recognition; MIT Press (2000)
7. Lutfi, R., Martinez, J., Gelgon, M.; Manipulating Audio into a DBMS; Proceedings of the 8th International Conference on Multimedia Modeling, Amsterdam, The Nertherlands (2001) 91–106
8. Nack, F., Lindsay, A.; Everything you Wanted to Know about MPEG-7: Part 1; IEEE Multimedia, July/September (1999) 65–77
9. Nack, F., Lindsay, A.; Everything you Wanted to Know about MPEG-7: Part 2; IEEE Multimedia, October/December (1999) 64–73
10. Sheth, A., Klas, W. (Eds.); Multimedia Data Management: Using Metadata to Integrate and Apply Digital Media; McGraw-Hill, Series on Data Warehousing and Data Management (1998)
11. Turk, A., Johnson, S. E., Jourlin, P., Spärck-Jones, P., Woodland, P. C.; The Cambridge University Multimedia Document Retrieval Demo System; Proc. of SIGIR 2000, Athens, Greece (2000) 394
12. IBM DB2 Universal Database; Image, Audio, and Video Extenders Administration and Programming; http://itsuite.it.bton.ac.uk/db2/dmba6/dmba6mst.htm
13. Wactlar, H., Hauptmann, A., Witbrock, M.; Informedia: News-on-demand Experiments in Speech Recognition; Proc. of the ARPA Speech Recognition Workshop, Harriman, New York (1996)
14. Zhang, T., Kuo, C.-C. J.; Heuristic Approach for Generic Audio Data Segmentation and Annotation; Proc. of the 7th ACM Int'l Multimedia Conf., Orlando, Florida (1999) 67–76

Supporting Web Development in the OPEN Process: Additional Roles and Techniques

Brendan Haire, David Lowe, and Brian Henderson-Sellers

University of Technology, Sydney
P.O. Box 123 Broadway 2007 NSW Australia
Brendan@staff.usyd.edu.au
david.lowe@uts.edu.au
brian@it.uts.edu.au

Abstract. Effective development of web applications requires process support just as does traditional development. In the context of an established OO/CBD process, OPEN (Object-oriented Process, Environment and Notation), we identify the special requirements of web application development in order to add these elements to the OPEN repository of process components. In particular, we focus on the need for new Techniques to accomplish Tasks and Activities previously identified as well as focussing on the role that individuals need to play in a web development team.

1 Introduction

Web development often appears not to use, nor to require, any formal process. But increasingly it is being realized that a smart idea, a new dot.com company and a blind faith in prototyping and "webtime" development will *not* provide a business environment that can be sustained. For serious software development to support a successful and growing commercial enterprise, the *same* rigour of business and software development process is required in webtime development as for any other commercial-strength information system [1].

A number of design notations have recently emerged, such as WebML [2] (which focuses on information modelling) and work on adapting UML [3] (which focuses on coupling user views with backend functionality). These do not, however, provide any significant guidance for the development process. Similarly, work on methods suited to Web development – such as OOHDM [4] and the more commercially oriented work by IBM on patterns for e-Business [5] – provides some useful approaches to designing Web systems, but largely fail to consider broader process issues. Specifically, they do not take into account a number of the specific characteristics of Web systems such as: increased domain uncertainty; an increased role of design artifacts in supporting client understanding; a complex component-based architecture that couples information elements with functional aspects; an increased emphasis on user inter-

Z. Bellahsène, D. Patel, and C. Rolland (Eds.): OOIS 2002, LNCS 2425, pp. 82-94, 2002.

faces; and diverse Web teams. See [6] for a discussion of some of these issues and problems, and their potential impacts on the development process.

In this paper, we investigate the applicability of (and required adaptations to) an existing object-oriented (OO) process to the support of web development. The process selected is OPEN; which stands for Object-oriented Process, Environment, and Notation. It is a process-focussed methodological approach to software-intensive systems development useful for both OO and CBD (Component-Based Development) systems development (and, indeed, also useful for business modelling). It is the longest established of the third-generation OO approaches and covers the full lifecycle. It is documented in a series of books [7, 8, 9, 10, 11] and in many journal articles, particularly in the journal *JOOP*. Many of these shorter articles are to be found on the OPEN website at http://www.open.org.au.

Here we formulate the necessary extensions for OPEN and, in doing so, create a "dialect" of OPEN to be known as Web OPEN. The extensions are derived primarily from an analysis of documented differences between Web development and conventional development, and justified by results from two case studies [12] undertaken in two web-focussed software development companies, one in the commercial domain and one in the standards domain. Full validation on industry projects is planned.

Finally, it is worth noting that, given the diversity of Web projects, it is impossible to encompass all aspects of the development process that may be appropriate in different circumstances. For example, we have currently largely overlooked issues associated with complex content management. This is, however, one of the strengths of OPEN – that it can be readily extended to incorporate additional aspects as necessary.

2 OPEN's Architecture

OPEN is unique in that it is not a process but rather a configurable family of processes, defined in terms of a metamodel (also known as a process framework): the OPEN Process Framework or OPF. This metamodel contains a number of major elements (Figure 1) that can be multiply instantiated. From these instances of the process fragments (stored in the OPF repository), organizationally-specific processes can be readily constructed.

Although there are many metaclasses in the OPF, they mostly cluster into five groups: Work Units (with major subtypes of Activity, Task and Technique), Work Products and Producers with support from Stages and Languages (Figure 1). Instances of these form a repository of predefined process components (Figure 2). This repository thus contains many examples of each of the (meta)classes defined in the M2[1] process metamodel. For example, at the M2 level there are three major kinds of WorkUnit: Activity, Task and Technique. In the M1 repository, each of these is used to create, for example, a BuildActivity, a RequirementsEngineeringActivity, a ProjectManagementActivity and so on. The OPF defines a useful set of Work Product types, each of which has a number of instantiations in the OPEN library or repository

[1] Using Object Management Group terminology in which M2 is the metalevel and M1 is the model level

(Figure 2). While some are diagrams documented with a modelling language like UML or OML, a large number are textual.

While Activities and Tasks state what needs to be done, tasks are finer grained. They can be accomplished by a single developer or a small development team in a relatively short time and can be adjudged by the project manager to be complete (or not complete). Making these goals achievable requires actions of an individual or a team, referred to as a Producer in the metamodel of the OPF. Producers may be human or non-human, individuals or teams. They utilize one or more Techniques in order to help them complete their Tasks and produce the Work Products.

Outside the main trio, Stages and Languages (Figure 1) provide additional support. There are various kinds of stages, such as phase, life cycle and milestone, which are used to give large-scale organization to the development process. On the other hand, languages, be they natural languages, modelling languages or coding languages, are needed as "tools" by which to help document many of the work products. OPEN supports both the UML notation, the OML notation and any other OO notation of your choice in order to document the work products that the OPEN process produces.

The OPF does not determine an organizational-level process, but rather supplies elements from its process component repository that can be used to construct a process for a particular domain, a specific organization and even a targetted project. This is called process construction. The way in which these elements are put together is the decision of the organization or development team.

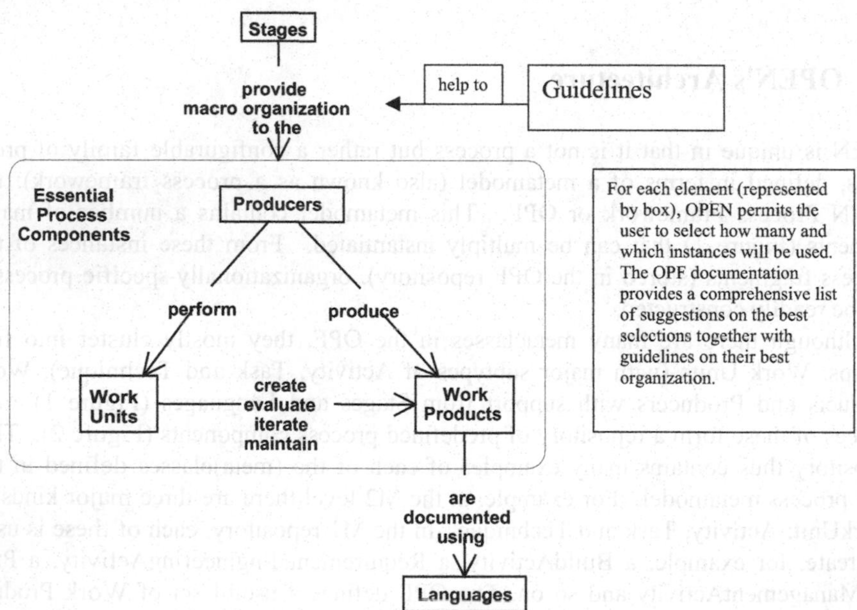

Fig.1. The components of the OPEN Process Framework (based on Firesmith and Henderson-Sellers, 2002)

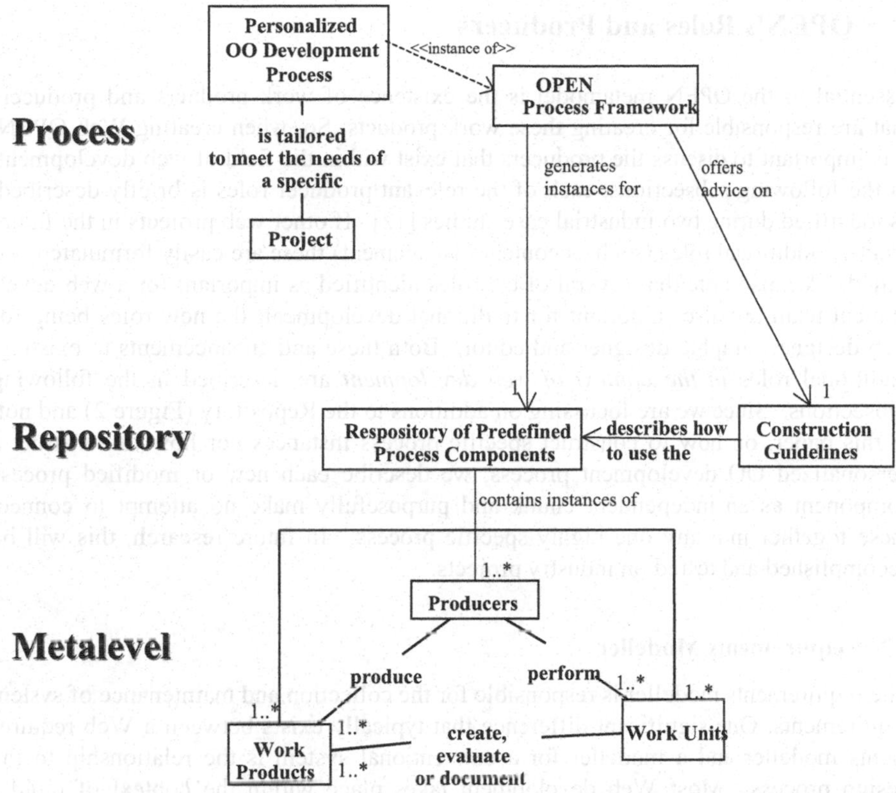

Fig.2. OPEN is a framework defined in terms of a metamodel plus a repository containing instances generated from that metamodel

While there is a wide range of process components predefined (by members of the OPEN Consortium) in the OPF Repository, both users and methodologists can readily add to the Repository with the proviso (an OPF 'rule') that each component thus added *must* be an instance of some existing class in the M2 metamodel. This is the focus of this research project wherein we expand the current repository contents by adding process components needed for web development. Note that there are, of course, many aspects of web development similar to traditional software development. These, of course, are already present in the repository. We thus do not discuss these here; rather we focus only on *new* process components. It is also worth noting at this point that we are not (yet) considering the subsequent issue about how we most effectively combine these process components when instantiating them into an actual process. Rather, we are simply considering what components are typically required.

In this paper, we focus on the new Techniques and the new Roles associated with the Producers. While many of the techniques needed to undertake OPEN's tasks in the web environment already exist in the OPEN literature (e.g. [11]), there are a number of new techniques that need to be introduced here and added to the OPF Repository.

3 OPEN's Roles and Producers

Essential to the OPEN metamodel is the existence of work products and producers that are responsible for creating these work products. So, when creating Web OPEN, it is important to discuss the producers that exist within the field of web development. In the following subsections, each of the relevant producer roles is briefly described, as identified during two industrial case studies [12]. If other web projects in the future identify additional roles (such as content management) these are easily formulated and added. We also note that several of the roles identified as important for a web development team are also important for traditional development; the new roles being for web designer, graphic designer and editor. Both these and enhancements to existing, traditional roles *in the context of web development* are described in the following subsections. Since we are focussing on additions to the Repository (Figure 2) and not, in this paper, on how to construct specific process instances nor how to construct a personalized OO development process, we describe each new or modified process component as an independent chunk and purposefully make no attempt to connect these together into any one highly specific process. In future research, this will be accomplished and tested on industry projects.

3.1 Requirements Modeller

The requirements modeller is responsible for the collection and maintenance of system requirements. One significant difference that typically exists between a Web requirements modeller and a modeller for a conventional system is the relationship to the design process. Most Web development takes place within the context of rapidly evolving technology, a poor client understanding of the consequent changes to their business model and an overall lack of understanding of their own requirements. Typically, the design artifacts, or even partial solutions, are used to drive the elicitation of requirements – leading to an increased need for requirements modellers to understand how to utilise the design activities to facilitate clarification of requirements.

3.2 System Architect

The system architect constructs the structure on which to build the entire web project. Without a good architecture it will be difficult to expand the system in the future. Due to the speed of change on the Internet (few web projects remain unchanged for more than a couple of months), a sound architecture is needed to allow for further system development and can be a key element in the success or failure of a web project. The skills required for this role include excellent modeling skills as well as plenty of experience with various systems and their design.

3.3 System Developer

The system developer fills in holes and connects the framework together. They are responsible for integrating components, developing new components and conducting the detailed design of the system. This is the role that produces most of the final functionality of the system.

3.4 Content Worker

There are several kinds of Content Worker [7]. There is, in web development, often a need for a Content Creator, a Content Approver and a Content Editor, as well as Content Management. A Content Editor is an optional role for many web projects. It is often left as the responsibility of the client to ensure that the content has been correctly edited and reviewed. In many cases, this and other Content Worker roles are not explicitly named but the tasks associated with the role(s) are divided amongst the team. In projects with a large amount of content, someone may be assigned to this role more permanently. Other named roles might be Content Publisher and Content Writer. Defining this role clearly can also be important in terms of clarifying the different client and developer responsibilities.

3.5 Strategist

The role of strategist encompasses technology strategy, business strategy and, of most relevance here, brand strategist. The brand strategist is the most relevant to web design, being the role played when a person develops the digital brand strategy for a customer's business.

3.6 Web Designer

The web designer needs to have a general skill level in a wide variety of areas. Ideally, they have some artistic ability for creating things such as simple graphics as well as general programming experience. The web designer helps to bind thc gap between the artistic world of print media and the programming world of software engineering. They work with the graphic designer as well as system developers to make the proposed content and layout a reality. Skills in web-based technologies are a necessity.

3.7 Graphic Designer

Due to the amount of rich content that goes into many web projects there is a need for this role of a graphic designer. Their responsibility is to help prepare the content and layout for the final system. This can include photographs, music clips, video clips and much more. The graphic designer needs to be artistic and imaginative and possess strong skills in creating and altering computer media.

3.8 Configuration Manager

The role of Configuration Manager is not unique to web development, although it may well have an added significance due to the fine-grained incremental nature of much Web development and the immediate availability of changes. The role is played by a person who is responsible for the configuration management programme including configuration identification, control, auditing and status accounting. Version control may also be under their responsibility or a separate role may be created.

3.9 System Tester

This is another generic role from software development. The system tester is responsible for verifying and validation that all the components of the system meet their requirements. They work closely with the requirement modeller and system developers. The system tester should be methodical and have an eye for detail.

3.10 System/Site Administrator

As web projects gain their strength from their ability to provide up-to-date information, there is a need for constant maintenance of the content (as distinct from maintenance of the system technical components). This role can be completed by the team building the system, in-house by one of the client's team, out-sourced to an external team or some combination of these. The skills required are highly dependent on the system that is to be administered. Skills usually required include a high level of computer literacy, with basic programming skills being an advantage but not a necessity.

3.11 Project Manager

This is a standard role in any project. They are responsible for the organisation and co-ordination of the team, ensuring things get delivered on time and on budget. Skills required are those of any project manager including things like leadership, communication, organisation and so on.

3.12 Prototype Developer

Although the role of prototype developer is useful for application developments, it is included in OPEN with a web focus. This role is filled by the person who is responsible for creating and testing the white site i.e. the prototype website which does not yet have the full rich textual content necessary in the completed website.

3.13 A Quick Analogy

The following analogy portrays the roles and responsibilities of web producers in a more familiar environment. To use an analogy of building a room:

- the requirement modeller decides what type of room you need;
- the system architect provides the foundation and framework;
- the system developer provides the brick walls;
- the web designer provides the plaster over the brick walls;
- the graphics designer paints the plastered walls;
- the system tester makes sure the room will not fall over and that it is the room that was originally asked for;

- the system/site administrator is responsible for changing the pictures hanging on the wall; and finally
- the project manager (a.k.a. foreman) can be thought of as the ceiling that oversees everything and makes sure it comes together in a square (unless of course you are building a round room

4 OPEN Techniques

Techniques in OPEN are ways of doing things, ways of effecting Tasks. In this paper, we try to identify, from the two case studies of [12], Techniques appropriate to web development that are not already part of the OPEN Repository. (The tasks themselves are documented in a previous paper [13]).

Many web development techniques are isomorphic to those used in regular applications development. The new techniques proposed here for addition to the OPEN framework are: "Branding"; “Development Spikes”; “Field Trip”; "Reuse of Graphical Components"; “System Metaphors”; “Web Metrics”; and “Web Templates”. These were all derived from the two case studies (mentioned above) as well as informal information from other organizations and industry journals. In the following subsections, each of these techniques is documented (in alphabetical order since the focus here is at the chunking level of the process component (in the Repository) and not at the constructed process level) following the standard OPEN format seen in [11].

4.1 Branding

Focus: Creation of a brand identity
Typical tasks for which this is needed: Develop and communicate brand identity
Technique description: Web development is increasingly less about software development and more about marketing and developing a market identity or brand. This is a combination of the product and the way that the product is portrayed on the website (and other media – which are of less interest to us here). Brand strategies must be developed, an overall artistic and marketing agreement made as to what constitutes the "brand" and ways to attain widespread brand recognition. An example here in early web commerce was www.amazon.com. A number of high-profile e-commerce failures (such as Boo.com and ValueAmerica) have resulted, at least in part, from a lack of effective branding (see http://www.techwatch.ie/fea/2000_510.htm).
Technique usage: identify the product to be branded; evaluate the website possibilities; investigate new logos or new ways of using old logos; register the website on as many search engines as possible.
Deliverables and outputs (post-condition): Recognition (as demonstrable by media acknowledgement); identified relationships to existing branding strategies and competing brands.

4.2 Development Spikes

Focus: Minimising risk, solving unknowns.
Typical tasks for which this is needed: Develop and implement resource allocation plan, Develop software development context plans and strategies
Technique description: A development spike can be thought of as research. The aim of the technique is to minimize areas of high risk by diving right in and starting development within a certain technology. The idea is that once development has begun, a greater understanding of the problem will be obtained and risk and time assessment will be more accurate. The development done within development spikes can be used as a reference but should never be used in the actual final development of the project. Development spikes are particularly useful in web development due to the rapidly changing nature of technology within this field and the poor client understanding of their own needs.
Technique usage: Areas of high risk are identified and code is quickly created (hacked) to gain better knowledge of a certain technology and/or problem. Development spikes are ideally suited to obtain quick answers regarding specific technologies. A typical development spike might start with the question, "Can I connect to a MySQL database using ASP?" As stated in the description, the work produced within a development spike should not be part of the final solution. eXtreme Programming – or XP [14] – provides a good example of the use of development spikes.
Deliverables and outputs (post-condition): A small working example that demonstrates an answer to the particular question posed.

4.3 Field Trip

Focus: Current business environment and final place of deployment of the system
Typical tasks for which this is needed: requirements engineering tasks.
Technique description: This technique is really quite self-descriptive. It serves the same purpose as school field trips or field trips in the natural sciences or the engineering professions. By actually visiting a site, a greater overall understanding of the problem is gained. This technique is useful in isolating implied (or assumed) user requirements. It is more effective when coupled with techniques such as user focus groups.
Technique usage: A time should be arranged for the development team to go to the physical site of business operations and be given a tour.
Deliverables and outputs (post-condition): Contributions to the user requirements. A list of these may form the post-condition.

4.4 Reuse of Graphical Components

Focus: Generating re-usable graphical components
Typical tasks for which this is needed: Prepare Content, Integrate Content with user interface, Optimize reuse ('with reuse'), Optimize the design
Technique description: This technique is more good practice than an actual technique. It is based around the concept that browsers cache pictures and therefore reus-

ing a number of pictures will improve a site's performance and therefore its quality. This technique also focuses on minimizing the size of graphics without losing a significant amount of picture quality. What signifies a significant amount of picture quality depends on the purpose and use of the graphic.
Technique usage: Identify common graphical components within a system. Focus on re-using these graphical components where possible. Identify large graphical images within the site and experiment with different file formats (GIF, JPG, etc.) as well as picture resolutions to minimize the file size.
Deliverables and outputs (post-condition): A library of optimized graphical components to be used within the user interface.

4.5 System Metaphors

Focus: Conveying the architecture in an understandable non-technical language.
Typical tasks for which this is needed: Identify user requirements, Undertake the architectural design
Technique description: A technique originally used in the Extreme Programming (XP) process [14] for naming classes and methods. It was designed in order to keep the entire team thinking along the same lines when it comes to naming. However, this is also an important technique when discussing the architecture of a system. It is important for the entire development team as well as the client to have an overall understanding of the architecture of the system being produced. As web development teams tend to have a wide range of producers from varying disciplines, the use of a system metaphor is a good tool to communicate across these platforms.

Note that this use of metaphors is different from the way the concept is used in user-interface development. In this latter case, a metaphor is often used as the basis for the design so that users have a known (and consistent) model of interaction. For example, the "supermarket" concept of searching for goods and then adding them to a shopping cart that is then "checked out" is widely used. An alternative metaphor used for e-commerce applications may be an "exclusive boutique" where items are presented to a user for consideration, rather than the user having to search for them.

In effect, the first use of metaphors (the focus of this technique) is to provide a basis for developers to understand the system during development. The second use is to provide a basis for users to understand how to interact with the system.
Technique usage: Choose a system of names for your project that everyone can relate to. Ideally it should be related to the business area for which the system is being designed (i.e. not the system itself); decide on the style of commercial interactions (transaction processing) that is desirable on the website. The example used in the XP process was for the Ford Car Sales system where the naming was structured as a bill of materials. Naming conventions within this system contained metaphors like "production line". There is also a metaphor known as a naïve metaphor that is based on the system itself. A naïve metaphor should not be used unless it is very simple.
Deliverables and outputs (post-condition): A naming scheme for the architecture

4.6 Web Metrics

Focus: Collection of metric data relating to web development
Typical tasks for which this is needed: Evaluate quality; Undertake post-implementation review.
Technique description: One of OPEN's strong characteristics is its attention to metrics. While further work is needed in order to statistically verify what the most appropriate metrics are, an initial proposal should focus on:

- Interface complexity: at a simple level this can be estimated through a page count, though this can be misleading, as a single server-side page may contain scripting that results in many different client-side manifestations. A more effective metric may be interaction counts or something similar, though there has, to date, been little work in this area.
- Performance: this can be estimated initially through number of hits per page per unit time – determines the general usage of a page and indicates where optimization would best be served.
- Access: Total size of pages (including graphics) – a useful quality measure in terms of speed to load.
- Maintenance: Rate of change of content – a metric useful for indicating when a site or page has become stagnant.

Some of the metrics are relevant to the development process and some related to the maintenance aspect of web projects. In addition to these extra metrics supporting web development, the original metric techniques within the OPEN framework (see e.g. [11]) are still relevant.

4.7 Web Templates

Focus: Generating standardised web templates for common user interface pages.
Typical tasks for which this is needed: Prepare Content, Integrate Content with user interface, Optimize reuse ('with reuse'), Optimize the design
Technique description: This technique focuses on isolating common areas of content so they can be displayed in a consistent format. It also assists in the maintenance of a system by providing appropriate templates to use when adding new content to the site. The technology used to implement web templates can vary. Templates generally come with some kind of validation system that verifies that all the appropriate content has been entered. Some commonly used methods include Microsoft Word documents with embedded Visual Basic to validate the content, or online Active Server Pages (ASP) that allow administrators to update and validate new content online.

The main advantage of using web templates is that it allows people with a lower level of technical experience with the system to do the majority of the work to create new content. This reduces the effect of any bottleneck that may occur with the site administrator. Web templates can also ensure that standards are met.
Technique usage: Divide the content into logically grouped areas that are to be displayed in the same style. Determine what aspects of the content need to be validated

and any additional information that needs to be collected (e.g. metadata for search indexing). Design the structure of the web templates and a procedure for using them. Note that this step will be influenced by architectural and design decisions.
Deliverables and outputs (post-condition): A variety of web templates and a procedure for using them.

5 Summary

As part of a research project to extend process support for web development, we have utilized the OO/CBD (Object-Oriented/Component Based Development) process known as OPEN. OPEN is defined by a meta-level architecture or framework that contains several metaclasses (Figure 1). Instances are then created of these metaclasses and, either directly or from the repository (Figure 2), are selected and configured to create an organizationally specific process. As published, there are inadequate instances of several of the metaclasses in the published OPF repository in the context of web development. In this paper, we have identified (based on case study analyses of commercial projects) new and extended definitions for several instances (*in the repository*) of Producer and Role and of Technique. Other Work Unit instances (of Activity and Technique) have been investigated as part of this project [12] but documented separately [13]. All instances were identified from two industry case studies, one in the standards domain and one in the commercial domain, both extensive users of website development approaches.

The approach based on OPEN leverages the benefits of OPEN – it provides a clear framework for constructing customized development processes that are most appropriate to the context of the project under consideration. Specifically, this work has looked at adding to the process repository, to allow the instantiated processes to more directly address Web-specific issues.

It is important to note that we do not claim that the roles and techniques that we have identified in this paper, and the tasks identified elsewhere [13], provide a complete solution. Rather they are necessary pieces of the development process that have heretofore been largely overlooked and/or undocumented. Subsequent work will need to investigate aspects such as heuristics for guiding the most effective instantiation of the process components into actual processes and the nature of these processes themselves. In particular, we shall consider the characteristics of projects and how they affect the particular choice of components, all in the context of industry evaluation.

References

1. Powell, T. A., 1998, *Web Site Engineering*, Prentice-Hall
2. Ceri, S., Fraternali, P., & Bongio, A., 2000, Web Modeling Language (WebML): a modeling language for designing Web sites. *Proceedings of WWW9 Conference*, Amsterdam, May 2000.

3. Conallen, J., 1999, Building Web Applications with UML (1st ed.), Addison-Wesley.
4. Schwabe, D. and Rossi, G., 1995, The object-oriented hypermedia design model, *Communications of the ACM,* **38(8),** 45-46
5. Butler, M., 2000, IBM's Patterns for e-business, White-paper presented at *Object World 2000* (see also http://www.ibm.com/framework/patterns)
6. Lowe, D. and Henderson-Sellers, B., 2001, Impacts on the development process of differences between web systems and conventional software systems, **in** *Procs SSGRR 2001: International Conference on Advances in Infrastructure for Electronic Business, Science, and Education on the Internet*, L'Aquila, Italy, August 2001.
7. Firesmith, D.G. and Henderson-Sellers, B., 2002, *The OPEN Process Framework. An Introduction*, Addison-Wesley, Harlow, UK
8. Firesmith, D.G., Hendley, G., Krutsch, S.A. and Stowe, M., 1998, *Object-Oriented Development Using OPEN: A Complete Java Application,* Addison-Wesley, Harlow, UK, 404pp + CD
9. Graham, I., and Henderson-Sellers, B., and Younessi, H., 1997*, The OPEN Process Specification*, Addison-Wesley, Harlow, UK, 314pp
10. Henderson-Sellers, B. and Unhelkar, B., 2000; *OPEN Modeling with UML*, Addison-Wesley, Harlow, UK, 245pp
11. Henderson-Sellers, B., Simons, A.J.H. and Younessi, H., 1998, *The OPEN Toolbox of Techniques* Addison-Wesley, Harlow, UK, 426pp + CD
12. Haire, B., 2000, Web OPEN: an extension to the OPEN framework, Capstone project, Faculty of Engineering, University of Technology, Sydney, 122pp
13. Haire, B., Henderson-Sellers, B. and Lowe, D., 2001, Supporting web development in the OPEN process: additional tasks, *Procs COMPSAC2001*, IEEE Computer Society Press, Los Alamitos, CA, USA, pp383-389
14. Beck, K., 2000, *Extreme Programming Explained*, Addison-Wesley, Reading, MA, USA, 190pp

Semantic Integration of Heterogeneous XML Data Sources*

Hyon Hee Kim[1,2] and Seung Soo Park[1]

[1]Department of Computer Science and Engineering
Ewha Womans University, Seoul, Korea
(heekim,sspark)@ewha.ac.kr

[2] On leave at Department of Computer Science, IPVR
University of Stuttgart, Stuttgart, Germany
kim@informatik.uni-stuttgart.de

Abstract. As XML is becoming a *de facto* standard data exchange format for web-based business applications, it is imperatively required to integrate semantically heterogeneous XML data sources. In this paper, we study a semantic integration of heterogeneous XML data sources. First, we consider a common data model that is designed to capture semantics of XML data. Second, we define semantic conflicts in the context of XML data, and resolve them using the rule-based method. Third, we develop a semantic integration technique of XML data using XML view mechanism. We describe how our approach has been used to integrate heterogeneous XML data sources providing various object-oriented abstraction facilities such as generalization, specialization and aggregation.

1 Introduction

As XML [8] is becoming rapidly accepted as a standard data exchange format on the Web, most business data that are currently stored in the conventional databases such as relational or object-oriented database are being published as XML documents. However, although the data represented by XML use the same syntax, they have still semantic conflicts. In XML, the meaning of an element is described by the structure of the element (subelements in XML terminology). The same elements can be defined by different structures, and in some cases, different elements can be defined by the same structure. Therefore, it is becoming important to integrate such semantically heterogeneous XML data sources resolving semantic conflicts. In this paper, we study a semantic approach to integrate XML data sources.

First, we introduce a common data model for XML data. Data integration can be done with a common data model that is able to encompass heterogeneous data sources. In particular, the semistructured data models have been introduced to

---

* Supported in part by Brain Korea 21 project of Korean Ministry of Education

Z. Bellahsène, D. Patel, and C. Rolland (Eds.): OOIS 2002, LNCS 2425, pp. 95-107, 2002.

integrate heterogeneous information sources on the Web [2,3,10,23]. Although the semistructured models and XML are very similar [21], the models are not appropriate for representing semantics of XML data. The simplicity of the models can be viewed as a weakness as well as an advantage, because other benefits of the object-oriented data models such as classes, methods, and inheritance suffer a loss. We develop a new data model called the XML Meta Model (XMM). Our data model is different from the semistructured data models in terms of the following two points: One is that the XMM model can describe semantics of XML data. *Semantics* of XML data in this study means meanings of the elements described with nested structures of the elements and relationships between elements such as a *Is-A* relationship and a *Is-Part-Of* relationship. The other is that the XMM model has a simple typing system while the semistructured data models have a weak typing system. That is, the XMM reaches a compromise between type-strong object-oriented data models and type-weak semistructured data models.

Second, we classify semantic conflicts in XML data into the synonym conflicts and the homonym conflicts, and resolve them by using the rule-based approach. In the conventional databases, semantic heterogeneity has been usually classified into naming conflicts and structural conflicts [6,18]. On the other hand, in XML data there is a convergence of naming conflicts and structural conflicts because XML is based on a markup and the markup indicates both structures and semantics. Therefore, a new classification of semantic conflicts is defined in the context of XML data, and a new technique for the resolution of the semantic conflicts is proposed.

Finally, we develop a data integration technique using the XML view mechanism. Although view mechanisms have been studied in the conventional databases and several researches into XML views [4, 20, 22] have been done, to our best knowledge available, there is no work on XML views with data abstraction facilities. In our approach, object-oriented data abstraction facilities such as generalization, specialization and aggregation are added to the XML view mechanism.

To illustrate the problem, let us consider the following application. We plan to build a portal web site to provide an integrated product catalog concerning vehicles. In the first step of automobile purchase, customers will determine the types of cars such as coupes, sedans, vans, etc. and then consider the model of the types, e.g., BMW 3 series or Hyundai Sonata. After choosing the model, they may want to compare the specifications of the car. The specifications include performance, safety, design, etc. Current shopping sites such as yahoo shopping site or lycos shopping site provide users with information from web sites of various companies. However, users should visit the various automobile company sites if they need more detail information of specific models. On the other hand, our system makes the semantic views with the object-oriented data abstraction facilities based on user requirements. Thus it can find the related information more efficiently by using the abstraction facilities.

In Section 2, we explain an overview of the system architecture. In Section 3, we propose a common data model for XML data. Section 4 describes the rule-based resolution method of semantic conflicts in the process of XML integration. In Section 5, we introduce a semantic integration technique using XML views mechanism. Finally, in Section 6, we mention related work and Section 7 give our concluding remarks.

2 System Overview

We provide a multi-agent based architecture that is improved from the mediator architecture [27]. The mediator architecture is extended to multi-layered architecture with multiple intelligent agents [15] as shown in Figure 1. In order to reduce tasks of mediators, we add a facilitation layer on top of the mediation layer. Since we assume that data sources are XML documents, wrappers are omitted. The tasks of each intelligent agent are as follows.

- ***Facilitators*** receive tasks from user agents and make plans for performing the tasks. First, they decompose the tasks, and then generate the subqueries. The subqueries are assigned to the suitable mediator agents. They receive the semantic views and then combine them as integrated views. The integrated views are transferred to the user agents. The facilitators are based on a rule-based expert system, which is composed of the knowledge base and inference engine [13]. Rules for task decomposition and result composition are stored in the knowledge base, and the rules are executed in case that the inference engine matches patterns of the rules.
- ***Mediators*** generate semantic views with object-oriented data abstraction facilities, and resolve the semantic conflicts using the rule-based method. Each mediator has its rule bases for the resolution of the semantic conflicts, and executes the rules when rules are matched.
- ***User Agents*** receive the user query and transfer it to the facilitators. They also provide users with the integrated views as a graphical user interface.

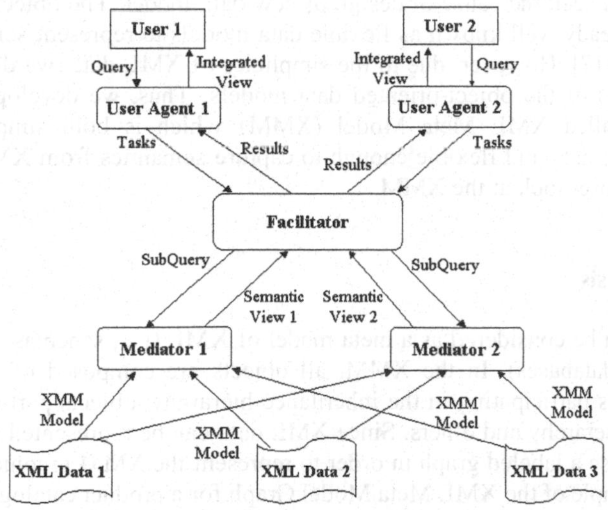

Fig.1. Multi-agent based System Architecture

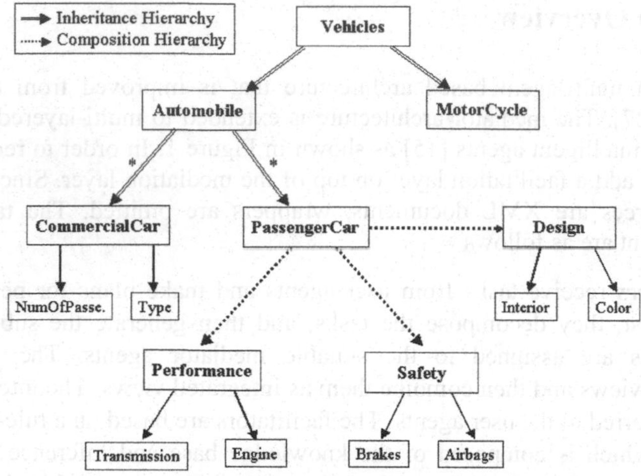

Fig.2. XML Meta Model Graph

3 The XML Meta Model (XMM)

Because of the great similarity of XML with semistructured data [21,23], we started with the OEM model [21] which is one of the first semistructured model. Since our main consideration of designing data model for XML data is how to capture semantics from XML data, the simplicity of the OEM model or other semistructured data model has been the cause of design of new data model. The object-oriented data models are already well known as flexible data models to represent semantics by the class concept [17]. However, due to the simplicity of XML data, we do not need the whole facilities of the object-oriented data models. Thus, we develop a new XML data model called XML Meta Model (XMM) which is both simple enough to represent XML data and flexible enough to capture semantics from XML data. Now, let us take a closer look at the XMM.

The XMM Basis

The XMM can be considered as a meta model of XML (i.e., schemas in terms of the conventional databases). In the XMM, all objects are composed of three types of objects: objects participating in the inheritance hierarchy, objects participating in the composition hierarchy and others. Since XML data can be represented as labeled tree or graph, we use a labeled graph in order to represent the XMM graphically. Figure 2 shows an example of the XML Meta Model Graph for a product catalog.

In Figure 2, `Automobile` object shows common features of `CommercialCar` and `PassengerCar`, and thus `Automobile` is considered as a generalization of `CommercialCar` and `PassengerCar`. Those three objects are the objects participating in the inheritance hierarchy. Objects participating in the composition hierarchy are shown in `PassengerCar` object and its related objects, because `PassengerCar` has `Performance`, `Safety` and `Design` as its parts. Finally, `CommercialCar` and its related objects show the relationship between the element and its subelements in XML data. We use the same symbol as the XML syntax to represent the occurrence of an object in the XMM Graph.

XMM Definition Using XML Schema

In order to define the XMM, we adopt XML Schema [12] among several XML schema [1] definition languages [19], because XML Schema supports supertype/subtype inheritance. Figure 3 shows the part of XML Schema for the example XMM Graph in Figure 2.

```
<schema>
 <element name="Automobile" type="AutomobileType"/>
 <element name="CommercialCar" type="CommercialCarType"/>
  <complexType name="CommercialCarType">
        <complexContent>
                <extension base="AutomobileType">
                        <sequence>
                <element name="Type" type="xs:string"/>
                <element name="NumOfPass" type="xs:integer"/>
                        <sequence>
                <extension>
       <complexContent>
<complexType>
<element name="PassengerCar" type="PassengerCarType"/>
 <complexType name="PassengerCarType">
  <complexContent>
                <extension base="AutomobileType">
                <sequence>
                        <element ref="Design"/>
                        <element ref="Safety"/>
                        <element ref="Performance"/>
                <sequence>
   <extension>
  <complexContent>
 <complexType>
<element name="Design" type="DesignType"/>
<element name="Safety" type="SafetyType"/>
<element name="Performance" type="PerformanceType"/>
</schema>
```

Fig.3. XML Schema

[1] We differentiate two terms: XML schema(s) refers to a general term for a schema for XML, while XML Schema refers to one of XML schema language proposed by W3C.

The inheritance hierarchy is composed of two types of elements, i.e., superclass and subclass elements. A superclass element is an element which contains a generalized concept, and a subclass element is an element which contain specialized concept of the superclass. The subclass `CommercialCar` is defined as the complex type with *extension base* `AutomobileType`. The composition hierarchy is composed of two types of elements, i.e., composite and component elements. A composite element is a root element in the composition hierarchy, and component elements are elements with *Is-Part-Of* semantics of the composite element. The composite element `PassengerCar` is defined by referring component elements instead of using nested subelements, because a composition element does not own the component elements but just refer the component elements. The *ref* attribute is used in the declaration of composite elements. Other elements with the nested structure are defined by the complex type provided by XML Schema.

4 Resolving Semantic Conflicts in XML Data

In this section, we introduce a new definition of semantic conflicts in the context of our data model, and explain the resolution technique of the semantic conflicts.

Definition of Semantic Conflicts

Since the XMM represents the semantic description of the elements with nested structures and relationships between elements, the meaning of an element can be defined using structures of the element. Therefore we only classify all conflicts into the synonym conflict and the homonym conflict by comparing and analyzing the structure of the target elements. The synonym and homonym conflicts are defined as follows.

Definition 1. Synonym Conflict
There will be an element overlap between a pair of participating XML Meta Models XMM_1 and XMM_2. If there are elements E_1 in XMM_1 and E_2 in XMM_2 such that structures S_1 of E_1 and structure S_2 of E_2 are exactly the same; there will be a synonym conflict if $E_1 \neq E_2$.

Definition 2. Homonym Conflict
There will be an element overlap between a pair of participating XML Meta Model XMM_1 and XMM_2. If there are elements E_1 in XMM_1 and E_2 in XMM_2 such that structures S_1 of E_1 and S_2 of E_2 are different; there will be a homonym conflict if $E_1 = E_2$.

Let us explain them with examples in Figure 4. (a) shows an example of the synonym conflict. Since the structures of target elements `Engineering` and `Performance` are the same, there exists the synonym conflict between `Engineering` and `Performance`. (b) and (c) show examples of the homonym conflict.

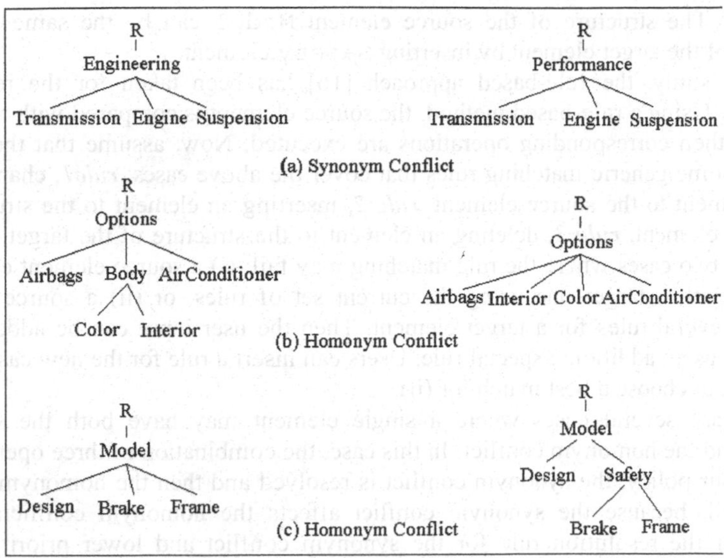

Fig.4. Examples of Semantic Conflicts in XML Data

Target elements are the same, but their structures are different. Sometimes, the synonym conflict and homonym conflict can be occurred in a single element. We have developed the resolution technique covering the above conflicts.

Resolution of Semantic Conflicts

First of all, since XML data represented by the XMM can be represented as ordered labeled trees like other XML documents, we adopt tree comparison algorithm [29]. The algorithm was developed to estimate the distance between two ordered trees using edit operations such as change, delete and insert operations.

- ***Change*** operation of a node *n* changes the label on *n*.
- ***Delete*** operation of a node *n* makes the children of *n* become the children of the parent of *n,* and removes *n*.
- ***Insert*** operation of a node *n* as the child of *n'* makes *n* the parent of a consecutive subsequence of the current children of *n'*.

These three basic operations play a central role in the resolution of semantic conflicts. In order to resolve the synonym conflicts, we change a source element to a target element. Therefore, the change operation is used in the resolution. In the example of Figure 4 (a), `Engineering` is replaced with `Performance` using the change operation. For the resolution of the homonym conflicts, we make different structures of the target elements the same. For this purpose, the delete and insert operations or the combination of them can be used. For example, in Figure 4 (b), the structure of source element `options` can be the same with the structure of target element by deleting the `body` element. Figure 4 (c) shows the use of the insert operation. The structure of the source element `Model` can be the same with the structure of the target element by inserting `Safety` element.

In this study, the rule-based approach [16] has been taken for the resolution technique. Using a rule-based method, the source element is compared with the target one, and then corresponding operations are executed. Now, assume that the system contains some generic matching rules that cover the above cases: *rule1*, changing the target element to the source element. *rule 2*, inserting an element to the structure of the target element. *rule 3*, deleting an element to the structure of the target element. There are two cases where the rule matching may fail: (i) a source element cannot be matched with a target one using the current set of rules, or (ii) a source element matches several rules for a target element. Then the user input can be added to the rule bases as an additional special rule. Users can insert a rule for the new case for (i), and they can choose a best match for (ii).

There are several cases where a single element may have both the synonym conflict and the homonym conflict. In this case, the combination of three operations is used. In our policy, the synonym conflict is resolved and then the homonym conflict is resolved, because the synonym conflict affects the homonym conflict. Higher priority of the resolution rule for the synonym conflict and lower priority of the resolution rule for the homonym conflict are specified in the rule bases. Although there are cases where the differences between the structures require a more complex matching and analysis, e.g., when the elements include deeply nested structures, our

technique. Using a rule-based method, the source element is compared with the target one, and then corresponding operations are executed. Now, assume that the system contains some generic matching rules that cover the above cases: *rule1*, changing the target element to the source element. *rule 2*, inserting an element to the structure of the target element. *rule 3*, deleting an element to the structure of the target element. There are two cases where the rule matching may fail: (i) a source element cannot be matched with a target one using the current set of rules, or (ii) a source element matches several rules for a target element. Then the user input can be added to the rule bases as an additional special rule. Users can insert a rule for the new case for (i), and they can choose a best match for (ii).

There are several cases where a single element may have both the synonym conflict and the homonym conflict. In this case, the combination of three operations is used. In our policy, the synonym conflict is resolved and then the homonym conflict is resolved, because the synonym conflict affects the homonym conflict. Higher priority of the resolution rule for the synonym conflict and lower priority of the resolution rule for the homonym conflict are specified in the rule bases. Although there are cases where the differences between the structures require a more complex matching and analysis, e.g., when the elements include deeply nested structures, our technique. Using a rule-based method, the source element is compared with the target one, and then corresponding operations are executed. Now, assume that the system contains some generic matching rules that cover the above cases: *rule1*, changing the target element to the source element. *rule 2*, inserting an element to the structure of the target element. *rule 3*, deleting an element to the structure of the target element. There are two cases where the rule matching may fail: (i) a source element cannot be matched with a target one using the current set of rules, or (ii) a source element matches several rules for a target element. Then the user input can be added to the rule bases as an additional special rule. Users can insert a rule for the new case for (i), and they can choose a best match for (ii).

There are several cases where a single element may have both the synonym conflict and the homonym conflict. In this case, the combination of three operations is used. In our policy, the synonym conflict is resolved and then the homonym conflict is resolved, because the synonym conflict affects the homonym conflict. Higher

5 Semantic Views and XML Data Integration

Since our data model is based on the object-oriented data models, our view mechanism borrows core concepts from the object database view mechanism. In object-oriented databases, virtual classes are defined by specifying their population [1]. In [1], they provide three facilities such as generalization, specialization and behavioral generalization for populating a virtual class with existing objects. UniSQL/M provides various object-oriented abstraction facilities such as generalization, specialization, aggregation, and method specification and invocation [17]. Our semantic views also provide generalization, specialization, and aggregation. Due to the simplicity of our data model, other object-oriented facilities such as operation and properties like UniSQL/M are omitted. This feature has some benefits in the case of XML data source, because the data structure of XML documents is much simpler than those of object-oriented databases.

The main difference between the conventional view mechanism and our view mechanism lies in the way of generating views. The relational or the object-oriented view mechanism is based on query language, but on the other hand XML view mechanism is based on template rules using XSL/XSLT [28]. Several researches into XML views [4, 20, 22] have been done by using Extensible Stylesheet Language (XSL) which is a language developed by W3C is used [28]. These studies do not mention data abstraction facilities [4,20]. In our approach, object-oriented data abstraction facilities are specified in the template rules, and thus object-oriented XML views called semantic views are generated. Our integration process of XML data follows the three steps. Firstly, source trees are prepared for the integration. XML data sources are parsed and transformed to source trees by using Document Object Model (DOM). Next, instruction trees are specified, which contains object-oriented data abstraction facilities. Finally, result trees are generated by applying the instruction tree to the source trees.

An example of the integrated views with the inheritance hierarchy and the composition hierarchy is shown in Figure 5. `Commercial Car`, `Recreational Vehicle` and `Passengers Car` elements are generalized as `Automobile` element, i.e. a generalization view. `Models` element is generated as a generalization view of `Sedan`, `Coupes` and `Convertible` elements. Finally, `Options` element is generated as aggregation views of `Safety`, `Design` and `Performance` elements. End users can browse the semantic views.

6 Related Work

Much work on the integration of heterogeneous data sources has been done [3, 5, 9,10, 11,14]. The work has focused on resolving schematic heterogeneity based on common data models such as the object-oriented data model [5, 9] or semistructured data model [3, 10, 14]. The strong typing system of the object-oriented data models is not appropriate for integrating data on the Web, because data on the Web are various and changeable and therefore it has some difficulties in defining the classes in advance. On the other hand, due to the simplicity of semistructured data models, the models have become popular middleware models for the integration of heterogeneous data on the Web. However, they also have some difficulties in capturing semantics due to the simplicity. The simple typing system in the XMM model can not only capture rich semantics in XML data different from the semistructured data models but also overcome the disadvantage of strong typing system in the object-oriented data models.

Some work [7, 25] takes the semantic approach and considers the semantic integration of heterogeneous data sources. In MOMIS project [7], they have developed an object-oriented language based on description logics. For the semantic integration, a common thesaurus is generated semi-automatically. Like other ontology-based systems, the main disadvantage of this approach is a lack of interoperability. The other system of semantic integration is the Xylem project in INRIA [25]. In this approach, they do not use a common thesaurus but use DTDs for the semantic integration of XML data sources. In this system, mapping from abstract DTD of real world to instance of XML documents is used, but the main problem is the difficulty of automatic mapping from abstract DTDs to target DTDs. As they mentioned in [25], reasonable mapping results can be achieved when human assistant helps the mapping process.

Recently, researches into the Semantic Web have been active. The Semantic Web is defined as an extension of the current web in which information is given well-defined meaning, better enabling computers and people to work in cooperation [24]. Differently from the above semantic approach [7], the Semantic Web focuses on web-based ontologies with interoperability using Web standard metadata definition language such as Resource Description Framework (RDF) and RDF Schema (RDFS) [27]. The main difference between our approach and the Semantic Web exists in the method of extracting semantics from data sources. In the XMM, data model is used in order to capturing semantics such as generalization and aggregation from XML documents, but in the Semantic Web, ontologies including complicated inference layers are essential in order to define vocabulary, structure and relationships between words about Web resources. Since construction of ontologies needs lots of time and efforts, we believe that development of data model with semantics can be another solution for the semantic-based information integration and retrieval.

7 Conclusions and Future Work

In this paper, we have proposed that semantic integration technique of XML data sources. In order to integrate the semantically heterogeneous XML data sources, a common data model named XML Meta Model (XMM) is used. In the mediation process of XML data, semantic conflicts are resolved. As a result, semantic views with data abstraction facilities of XML data are generated. The key features of our approach are:

- ***Capture of Semantics from XML Data.*** We design a common data model for XML data. It captures the semantics of *Is-A* relationship and *Is-Part-Of* relationships. Since the composite elements are used as a unit of clustering of

XML data elements, a large collection of related objects can be efficiently retrieved from the data sources.

- ***Resolution of Semantic Conflicts in XML Data.*** We develop a rule-based approach in order to resolve semantic conflicts in XML data. We classify semantic conflicts in XML data into synonym conflicts and homonym conflicts using structures of the elements, and resolve them using the generic rules. Users can add new rules to the rule bases or decide the best match in the rule bases.
- ***Semantic View Mechanism.*** We propose a new XML view mechanism based on object-oriented data abstraction facilities. The semantic views provide generalization, specialization and aggregation abstraction. The semantic views can guide users in formulating queries or browsing the data sources, and provide the information reflecting the ever-changing availability of data sources.

There are two directions of further research we are currently pursuing. One issue is extending XML data sources to relational databases. We are considering how to extend the XMM to include relational model preserving semantics. The other is developing view mechanism using a query language. We are also considering how to use XML query language like XQuery in order to generate semantic views.

Acknowledgements

We would like to thank Prof. Bernhard Mitschang for facility supports and useful comments at University of Stuttgart in Germany, without which this paper would not have been possible. We also want to thank anonymous reviewers for their helpful comments. The first author would like to thank Uwe Heinkel for valuable discussion on this work.

References

1. S. Abiteboul, A. Bonner. Objects and Views, In Proceedings of the ACM SIGMOD Conference, Denver, Colorado, 1991.
2. S. Abiteboul, P. Buneman and D. Suciu. Data on the Web, Morgan Kaufmann publishers, 2000.
3. S. Abiteboul, S. Cluet and T. Milo. Correspondence and translation for heterogeneous data. In Proceedings of ICDT, pp. 351-363, 1997.
4. S. Abiteboul, On Views and XML, ACM SIGMOD Record, Vol. 28, No. 4, pp. 30-38, 1999.
5. R. Ahmed, et al., "The Pegasus Heterogeneous Multidatabase System", IEEE Computer, Vol. 24, No. 12, pp. 19-27, 1991.
6. C. Batini, M. Lenzerini and S. B. Navathe. A Comparative Analysis of Methodologies for Database Schema Integration, ACM Computing Surveys, Vol. 18, No. 4, Dec. 1986.

7. S. Bergamaschi, S. Castano and M. Vincini, Semantic Integration of Semistructured and Data Sources. SIGMOD Record Special Issue on Semantic Interoperability in Global Information, Vol. 28, No. 1, March 1999.
8. T. Bray, J. Paoli and C. M. Sperberg-McQueen. Extensible Markup Language (XML) 1.0, http://www.w3c.org/TR/REC-xml.
9. M. J. Carey, et al., Towards Heterogeneous Multimedia Information Systems: The Garlic Approach, In Proceedings of the Fifth International Workshop on Research Issues in Data Engineering, 1995.
10. S. Cluet, C. Delobel, J. Simeon, and K. Sgaga. Your mediator needs data conversion! In Proceedings of ACM SIGMOD Conference, Seattle, Washington, June 1998.
11. A. Elmagarmid and C. Pu, eds., Special Issue on Heterogeneous Databases, ACM Computing Surveys, Vol. 22, No. 3, Sept. 1990.
12. D. C. Fallside, XML Schema Part 0: Primer, http://www.w3c.org/TR /xmlschema-0
13. C. Forgy. Rete: A Fast Algorithm for the Many Pattern/Many Object Pattern Match Problem. Artificial Intelligence, Vol. 19, No. 1, pp. 17-37, 1982.
14. H. Garcia-Molina et al. The TSIMMIS project: Integration of heterogeneous information sources. Journal of Intelligent Information Systems, Vol. 8, No. 2, pp. 117-132, 1997.
15. M. R. Genesereth and S. P. Ketchpel, Software Agent, Communications of the ACM, Vol. 37, No. 7, pp. 48-53, 1994.
16. JESS, The expert system schell for the java platform, http://herzberg.ca.sandia.gov/Jess
17. W. Kim, Modern Database Systems: The Object Model, Interoperability, and Beyond. Addison Wesley, 1995.
18. W. Kim, I. Choi, S. Gala and M. Scheevel, On resolving schematic heterogeneity in multidatabase systems. Distributed and Parallel Databases, Vol. 1, No. 3, pp. 251-279, 1993.
19. D. Lee and W. W. Chu, Comparative Analysis of Six XML Schema Languages, ACM SIGMOD Record, Vol. 29, No. 3, September, 2000.
20. B. Ludascher, Y. Papakonstantinou, P. Velikhov. Navigation-Driven Evaluation of Virtual Mediated View. In Proceedings of EDBT conference, Konstanz, Germany, March 2000.
21. Y. Papakonstantinou, H. Garcia-Molina and J. Widom. Object Exchange Across Heterogeneous Information Sources, In Proceedings of IEEE International Conference on Data Engineering, pp. 251-260, Taiwan, March, 1995.
22. Y. Papakonstantinou and P. Velikhov, Enhancing Semistructured Data Mediators with Document Type Definitions, In proceedings of the IEEE International Conference on Data Engineering, 1999.
23. Y. Papakonstantinou, S. Abiteboul, and H.Garcia-Molina. Object fusion in mediator systems. In Proceedings of VLDB Conference, 1996.
24. Resource Description Framework, http://www.w3.org/RDF/
25. C. Reynaud, J. Sirot and D. Vodislav. Semantic Integration of XML Heterogeneous Data Sources. In Proceedings of the 2001 International Database Engineering & Applications Symposium, Grenoble, France, 2001.
26. Semantic Web Activity, http://www.w3.org/2001/sw/

27. G. Wiederhold. Mediators in the architecture of future information systems. IEEE Computer, Vol. 25, No. 3, pp. 38-49, March, 1992.
28. XSL, http://www.w3c.org/Style/XSL
29. K. Zhang and D. Shasha. Simple fast algorithms for the editing distance between trees and related problems, SIAM Journal of Computing, Vol. 18, No. 6, pp. 1245-1262, Dec. 1989.

F2/XML: Storing XML Documents in Object Databases

Lina Al-Jadir and Fatmé El-Moukaddem

Department of Mathematics and Computer Science
American University of Beirut
P.O. Box 11-0236, Beirut, Lebanon
{lina.al-jadir,fme05}@aub.edu.lb

Abstract. In this paper we propose a new method to store an XML document in an object database (DB). First, the document's DTD is mapped into a DB schema, then the XML document is mapped into a DB instance. Our method stores the element-subelement relationships and the element attributes. It takes into account the order and the cardinality of subelements. It keeps track of the groupings in an element, and alternatives among subelements. Our method allows us also to retrieve back the DTD and the entire document from the database without loss of information. We implemented our method in the F2 database system, and tested it on sample XML documents

1 Introduction

As eXtensible Markup Language (XML) has become an emerging standard for information exchange on the World Wide Web, it has gained attention in database communities to extract information from XML seen as a database model. XML is a textual representation of the hierarchical data model defined by the World Wide Web Consortium (W3C) [6]. An XML document consists of nested elements rooted in a single element. Elements are delimited by user-defined start-tags and end-tags. Elements may have attributes. Elements and attributes are able to contain values. An XML document can be associated with a type specification called Document Type Definition (DTD) which describes the structure of the document.

Recently, researchers have addressed the problem of storing XML data and processing XML queries using database systems. In this paper, we propose a new method to store an XML document in an object database. Our method first maps a document's DTD into an object database schema and then maps the XML document into an object database instance. It stores the element-subelement relationships and the element attributes. It takes into account the order and the cardinality of subelements. It keeps track of the groupings in an element, and alternatives among subelements. Our method allows us also to retrieve back the DTD and the entire document from the database without loss of information. We implemented our method in the F2 object-oriented database system. F2 is a general-purpose database system used to experiment several features such as schema evolution [1] [2], data mining [3], and incremental knowledge acquisition [4]. The paper is organized as follows. In section 2 we review

Z. Bellahsène, D. Patel, and C. Rolland (Eds.): OOIS 2002, LNCS 2425, pp. 108-116, 2002.

related work. In section 3 we describe our F2/XML method. In section 4 we test it on sample XML documents. In section 5 we conclude the paper.

2 Related Work

Several approaches have been proposed to store XML documents in relational databases [14] [8] [13] [10], object-relational databases [15] [11], and object databases [7].

In [14] the authors propose three techniques to generate relational schemas from DTDs. First, the DTD is simplified using transformations. Then a DTD graph is built: its nodes are elements (each element appears once), attributes and operators in the DTD (may appear many times). The *Shared Inlining Technique* is a variation of the *Basic Inlining Technique*. It consists of creating relations for elements that have an in-degree zero (source nodes), that are children below a * operator node, or that have an in-degree greater than one. One of the mutually recursive elements all having in-degree one is made a separate relation. Nodes with in-degree one are *inlined* in their parent node relation. Attributes in a relation are named by the path from the root. An attribute *Id* is added to each relation. An attribute *parentID* is added to relations corresponding to elements having a parent (foreign key). An additional attribute *isRoot* is added to the relations to solve the problem arising when the document is rooted at an element that has been inlined. The *Hybrid Inlining Technique* inlines additional elements.

The approaches in [8] are independent of DTDs. An XML document is represented as an ordered and labeled directed graph. Each XML element is represented by a node labeled with a unique identifier. Element-subelement and element-attribute relationships are represented by edges labeled with the subelement or attribute name. Values are leaves in the graph. In the *Edge approach* all edges are stored in one table *Edge(source node, ordinal, target node, edge label, flag)*. In the *Binary approach* all edges with the same label are grouped in one table. In the *Universal approach* all edges are stored in a single table which is the result of full outer join of all Binary tables. Values of XML document (i.e. strings) can be stored: (a) in separate *Value* tables or (b) together with edges. Both variants can be used with the Edge, Binary, and Universal approaches.

The approach in [13] is independent of DTDs and is based on a complete binary fragmentation of the document syntax tree. The relational Monet XML model is based upon a set of *associations*: associations of type (oid x oid) to represent parent-child relationships between nodes, associations of type (oid x string) to model attribute values of nodes (and character data), and associations of type (oid x int) to preserve the topology of the document (order among nodes). The path to a node in the tree is used to group semantically related associations and to store them as tuples in the same *binary relation*. The authors argue that although a high degree of fragmentation might incur increased efforts to reconstruct the original document, the number of additional joins is fully made up for as they involve only little data volume.

In [10], the authors propose mappings between a DTD and a relational schema according to the characteristics of the XML element (kind of element, if it contains attributes, its cardinality) and the characteristics of the XML attribute (type of attribute, its default declaration). The mappings are not hard-coded within an application, but stored within the meta-schema which has a schema component, a DTD component, and a mapping component.

The approach in [15] is independent of DTDs. First an XML document is represented as a tree, where the nodes are of 3 types: elements, attributes, and text. To each node is associated a path and a pair of positions of the node within the document. Then the tree structure of the XML document is mapped into tuples in 4 relations *Path(pathexp, pathID)*, *Element(docId, pathId, index, pos)*, *Attribute(docId, pathId, attvalue, pos)*, and *Text(docId, pathId, value, wordpos)* in the object-relational database (Postgres).

In [11] the authors first propose straight-forward mappings to transform a DTD into an object-relational schema. Simple elements containing #PCDATA, empty elements, and attributes are mapped into DB attributes. Sequence of elements are translated into *tuple-of* DB attributes. Optional elements result in DB attributes that can have the *NULL* values. Repeatable elements and set-valued attributes (IDREFS) are transformed into *set-of* DB attributes. Then the authors point out mapping problems for alternatives, recursive structures, mixed content, and hyperlinks (ID, IDREF). Since their method results in very large database schemas and sparsely populated databases, the authors propose to use *hybrid databases*, i.e. object-relational databases with data type XML, using statistics. First, the DTD graph is built. Then for each of its nodes a weight is calculated, based on existing XML data, queries and their frequency, and the DTD structure. According to this weight a node will be mapped to a database attribute or to an attribute of type XML.

In [7] the authors store XML data in an object-oriented DB. After building the DTD graph, they use an *inlining technique* similar to the Shared Inlining Technique [14]. Then the authors propose to use *inheritance* in case of alternative and optional elements. Superclasses contain the structural part of an element, i.e. the part which is present in every instance, while subclasses contain the semi-structural part of the element, i.e. the part which may or may not appear in a given instance.

We propose the F2/XML method, based on DTDs, which has the following advantages. First, it uses the object model which allows us to represent element-subelement relationships by direct references (no need to create manually join database attributes and foreign keys as in relational DB), and repetition of subelements by multi-valued database attributes (no need to create separate relations as in relational DB). Note that we use the term *database attributes* for attributes of a class/relation, and *XML attributes* for attributes of an element. Second, it stores alternatives among subelements. The other approaches (except [10]) either do not store the DTD, or remove alternatives by simplifying the DTD, or use inheritance (may lead to an explosion of the number of subclasses due to all combinations). Third, it stores the order among subelements, which is missing in some approaches. Fourth, it keeps track of the groupings in an element, while the other approaches (except [10]) do not. Fifth, it allows us to go backward, i.e. retrieve the DTD from the database and get the same DTD as the original, which is not possible in the other approaches (except [10]). We present the F2/XML method in the next section.

3 F2/XML Method

In this section, we describe the F2/XML method in 3 steps: mapping a DTD into a database schema, extending the F2 meta-schema, and mapping a document into a database instance. Then, we mention how to retrieve the DTD and the entire document from an F2 database.

3.1 Mapping an XML DTD into an F2 Database Schema

```
<!ELEMENT bib (book+)>
<!ELEMENT book (author+, title, publisher?,
      year?, section*)>
<!ATTLIST book isbn CDATA #IMPLIED>
<!ELEMENT author (#PCDATA)>
<!ATTLIST author id ID #REQUIRED>
<!ELEMENT title (#PCDATA)>
<!ELEMENT publisher (#PCDATA)>
<!ELEMENT year (#PCDATA)>
<!ELEMENT section ((title, para+) |
      (title, para*, subsection+))>
<!ELEMENT para (#PCDATA)>
<!ELEMENT subsection (title | (title, para+))>
```

Fig.1. Example of DTD

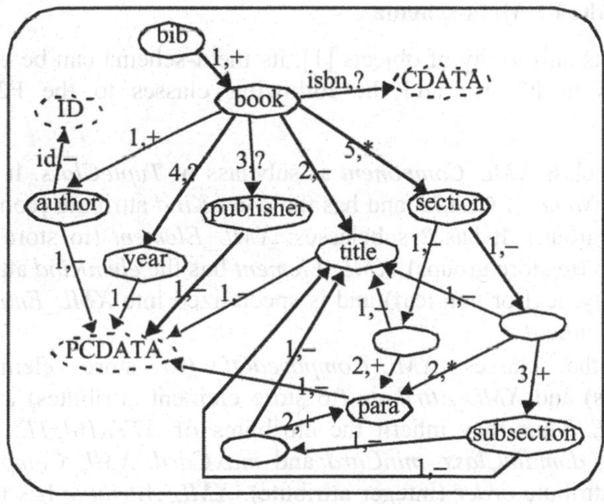

Fig.2. DTD graph (see Fig.1.)

The first step in our method is to build a directed DTD graph as follows. Each element *E* in the DTD is represented as a node labeled *E*. If element *E* is composed of component *C*, this is represented by an edge from node *E* to node *C*. This edge is labeled with an integer indicating the order of the component in the element *E*, and the cardinality (?, –, *, +). The simplest case is when the component is an element. If the component is a group (i.e. between parentheses), an edge is created to link node *E* to an intermediate unlabeled node. To this node are added edges for the components of the group. If the component is #PCDATA (mixed content), or if the element *E* is a leaf, an edge is created to link node *E* to node *PCDATA*. Two alternate components of element *E* take the same order on their corresponding edges. An attribute of element *E* is represented as an edge from node *E* to node *CDATA* or to node *ID* (in case of ID, IDREF, IDREFS. In the last 2 cases, the edge is dashed) or to a new node (in case of enumerated attribute). This edge is labeled with the attribute name and the cardinality ? if IMPLIED or – if REQUIRED (if the attribute is of type IDREFS, the cardinality becomes * or + respectively). An example of DTD [9] and its corresponding DTD graph are shown in figures 1 and 2 respectively.

The second step in our method is to map the DTD graph into an F2 database schema. It is straightforward. Each node labeled *N* is mapped into a class named *N* (classes for unlabeled nodes are named *group1*, *group2*, etc.). Dashed nodes are mapped to predefined classes. Each edge from node *A* to node *B* is mapped into an attribute of class *A*, having domain class *B*, and named *B* (unless the edge has already a name, e.g. for XML attributes). In F2, to each database attribute is associated a pair (minimal cardinality, maximal cardinality). The edge cardinality labels (?, –, *, +) are mapped into (0,1), (1,1), (0,m) and (1,m) pairs respectively. The value of *m* is set by default to 10, and can be changed later by a schema change [1]. To store the edge order label we need to extend the F2 meta-schema. We show how to do it in the next subsection.

1.2 Extending the F2 Meta-schema

Since F2 supports uniformity of objects [1], its meta-schema can be easily extended. To store DTDs in F2, we add the following classes to the F2 meta-schema (see figure 3).

- We add the class *XML_Component* as subclass of *TupleClass*. It inherits the attribute *className* of *CLASS*, and has the *compKind* attribute (component kind is element or group). It has 2 subclasses: *XML_Element* (to store elements) and *XML_Group* (to store groups). *XML_Element* has the *elemKind* attribute (element kind is empty, leaf or non-leaf) and is specialized into *XML_Empty*, *XML_Leaf*, and *XML_NonLeaf*.
- We add the classes *XML_ComposedOf* (to store element-subelement relationships) and *XML_Attribute* (to store element attributes) as subclasses of *ATTRIBUTE*. Thus they inherit the attributes of *ATTRIBUTE*: *attributeName*, *originClass*, *domainClass*, *minCard* and *maxCard*. *XML_ComposedOf* has an additional attribute *order* (integer attribute). *XML_Attribute* has three additional attributes: *attType* (CDATA, enum, ID or IDREF), *defaultValue*, *isFixed* (boolean). We constrain the attribute *originClass* in *XML_ComposedOf* to have *XML_Component* as domain. We constrain also the attribute *originClass* in *XML_Attribute* to have *XML_Element* as domain.

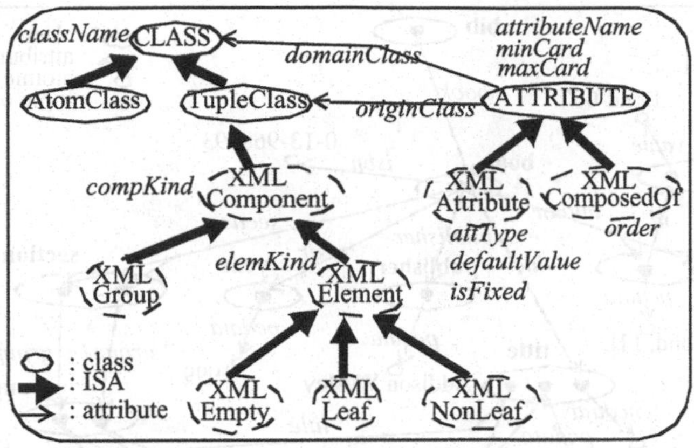

Fig.3. Extending the F2 meta-schema (added classes are dashed)

1.3 Mapping an XML Document into an F2 Database Instance

At this stage, the document's DTD is stored in an F2 database. Our method parses the XML document to get its tree representation. Starting from the root node *R*, it retrieves the children of node *R* and stores them in a string *L1*. It queries the F2 meta-schema to get the attributes of the class corresponding to node *R*, and forms a regular expression *L2* (*L2* corresponds to the definition of the root element in the DTD). It applies then regular expression match between *L1* and *L2*, and creates objects in the corresponding classes in the database. This process is applied recursively. An example of XML document [9] is given in figure 4, and its corresponding F2 database instance is shown in figure 5. Note that classes *PCDATA* and *CDATA* are atomic classes and contain string atomic objects. Class *ID* has a key composed of the attribute *value*, so that two objects in this class can not have the same *value*.

```
<?xml version="1.0">
<!DOCTYPE bib SYSTEM "bib.dtd">
<bib>
    <book isbn= "0-13-968793">
        <author id= "Wilson-001"> Wilson, G.
        </author>
        <author id= "Bond-007"> Bond, J.H.
        </author>
        <title> XML Introduction </title>
        <publisher> Addison Wesley </publisher>
        <year> 1999 </year>
        <section>
            <title> XML Summary </title>
            <para> This section summarizes ...
            </para>
        </section>
        <section>
            <title> XML in Application </title>
            <para> This section presents ...
            </para>
        </section>
    </book>
</bib>
```

Fig.4. XML document conform to the DTD of Fig.1

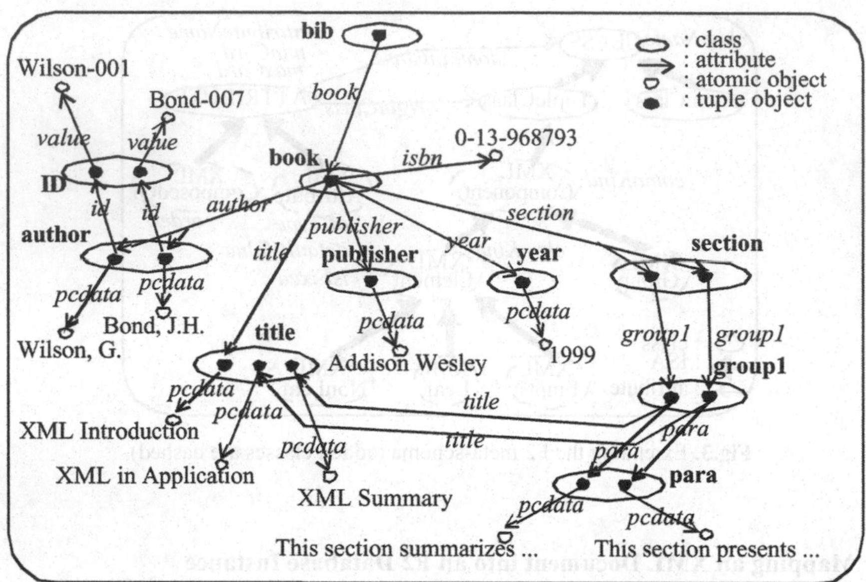

Fig.5. F2 database corresponding to the XML document of Fig.4

1.4 Retrieving an XML Document from an F2 Database

The previous subsections showed how to store an XML document in an object database. It is possible to go backward, i.e. retrieve the DTD and the document stored in the database. By querying the F2 meta-schema in F2-DML, our method retrieves the document's DTD easily. To retrieve the entire document, our method finds first the object representing its root element. Then it navigates through the database by querying the meta-schema and following this object's attribute values. Although the document is fragmented, the object model allows easy navigation (instead of joins as in relational DB) to reconstruct the document.

2 Experiments

To test the F2/XML method we chose readily available XML documents with DTDs: Shakespeare's plays [5] and DBLP bibliography [12]. Shakespeare's DTD contains 21 elements and no XML attributes. The resulting F2 database schema contains 29 classes (21 for elements and 8 for groups) and 53 database attributes. The document hamlet.xml (size: 265 KB) is mapped into a database (size: 1,469 KB) which contains 16,059 objects (belonging to the 29 classes). DBLP's DTD contains 36 elements and 14 XML attributes. The resulting F2 database schema contains 50 classes (36 for elements and 14 for groups) and 242 database attributes (228 for element-subelement relationships and 14 for element attributes). The document bernstein87.xml (size: 21 KB) is mapped into a database (size: 677 KB) which contains 750 objects. In both cases database sizes are much larger than document sizes. However, since the price of disk is sharply decreasing, and since documents are much smaller in size than multimedia data such as video and audio, the increase of data size in storing XML documents is not a big problem [15]. After storing both documents with their DTD in F2, we retrieved them back from F2. We got the same DTDs and documents as the originals (note that the order of XML attributes may be different, but it does not matter).

Table 1. Experimental results of the F2/XML method

	DTD	DB Schema	Document	DB Instance	
Domain	Elem. / Attr.	Classes / Attr.	Size	Size	Tuple Objects
Shalespeare *Hamlet.xml*	21 / 0	29 / 53	265 KB	1,469 KB	16,059
DBLP *bernstein87.xml*	36 / 14	50 / 242	21 KB	677 KB	750

3 Conclusion

We proposed the F2/XML method to store XML documents in object databases. The document's DTD is mapped into a database schema, and the XML document is mapped into a database instance. Our method stores elements as classes, and element-subelement relationships and element attributes as database attributes. It takes into account the order and the cardinality of subelements. It keeps track of the groupings in an element, and alternatives among subelements. Consequently, it allows us to retrieve back the DTD and the document without loss of information. This is not supported by other methods except X-Ray [10]. We implemented our method in the F2 database system and tested it on sample XML documents.

Future work includes enhancement of our method to take into account more features such as entities. Other important issues to address are querying and manipulating XML documents stored in F2 databases.

References

1. Al-Jadir L., Estier T., Falquet G., Léonard M., "Evolution Features of the F2 OODBMS", *Proc. 4th Int. Conf. on Database Systems for Advanced Applications*, DASFAA, Singapore 1995.
2. Al-Jadir L., Léonard M., "Multiobjects to Ease Schema Evolution in an OODBMS", *Proc. 17th Int. Conf. on Conceptual Modeling*, ER, Singapore 1998.
3. Al-Jadir L., "Encapsulating Classification in an OODBMS For Data Mining Applications", *Proc. 7th Int. Conf. on Database Systems for Advanced Applications*, DASFAA, Hong Kong 2001.

4. Al-Jadir L., Beydoun G., "Using the F2 OODBMS to Support Incremental Knowledge Acquisition", *to appear in Proc. 6th Int. Database Engineering and Applications Symposium*, IDEAS, Edmonton 2002.
5. Bosak J., Sample XML documents. shakespeare.1.10.xml.zip available at ftp://sunsite.unc.edu/pub/sun-info/standards/xml/eg/.
6. Bray T., Paoli J., Sperberg-McQueen C.M., Maler E. (eds), "Extensible Markup Language (XML) 1.0 (2nd Edition)", *W3C Recommendation*, http://www.w3.org/TR/2000/REC-xml-20001006, Oct. 2000.
7. Chung T-S., Park S., Han S-Y., Kim H-J., "Extracting Object-Oriented Database Schemas from XML DTDs Using Inheritance", *Proc. 2nd Int. Conf. on Electronic Commerce and Web Technologies*, EC-Web, Munich 2001.
8. Florescu D., Kossmann D., "Storing and Querying XML Data Using an RDBMS", *IEEE Data Eng. Bulletin*, vol. 22, no 3, pp. 27-34, sept. 1999.
9. Hou J., Zhang Y., Kambayashi Y., "Object-Oriented Representation for XML Data", *Proc. 3rd Int. Symposium on Cooperative Database Systems and Applications*, CODAS, Beijing 2001.
10. Kappel G., Kapsammer E., Rausch-Schott S., Retachitzegger W., "X-Ray - Towards Integrating XML and Relational Database Systems", *Proc. 19th Int. Conf. on Conceptual Modeling*, ER, Salt Lake City 2000.
11. Klettke M., Meyer H., "XML and Object-Relational Databases - Enhancing Structural Mappings Based on Statistics", *Proc. 3rd Int. Workshop on the Web and Databases*, WebDB, Dallas 2000.
12. Ley M., DBLP Bibliography. http://www.informatik.uni-trier.de/~ley/db/.
13. Schmidt A., Kersten M., Windhouwer M., Waas F., "Efficient Relational Storage and Retrieval of XML Documents", *Proc. 3rd Int. Workshop on the Web and Databases*, WebDB, Dallas 2000.
14. Shanmugasundaram J., Tufte K., He G., Zhang C., DeWitt D., Naughton J., "Relational Databases for querying XML Documents: Limitations and Opportunities", *Proc. 25th Int. Conf. on Very Large DataBases*, VLDB, Edinburgh 1999.
15. Shimura T., Yoshikawa M., Uemura S., "Storage and Retrieval of XML Documents using Object-Relational Databases", *Proc. 10th Int. Conf. on Database and Expert Systems Applications*, DEXA, Florence 1999.

Customization Policies Need more than Rule Objects

Juan Cappi, Gustavo Rossi, and Andres Fortier

LIFIA-Facultad de Informatica-UNLP
Calle 50 y 115, La Plata (1900) Buenos Aires, Argentina
Tel/Fax: 54 221 4236585
{jcappi,gustavo,andres}@lifia.info.unlp.edu.ar

Abstract. In this paper we analyze the process of mapping business policies into object-oriented software structures. We stress that separation of concerns is a key strategy for obtaining high quality and evolvable implementations. In particular, we show that a naive mapping of business policies into object rules may result in a bad design compromising the overall software stability. We first present our work in the context of customizable of e-commerce applications, and briefly explain why customization functionality should be dealt by separating concerns. We next present our approach for combining object rules with other object-oriented design structures; we show that these modular software constructs allow seamless evolution and maintenance.

1 Introduction and Related Work

Customization has become a very important issue in e-commerce applications. Adapting this kind of applications may mean building different interfaces, (customized to a particular appliance) providing personalized navigation paths, offering different pricing policies, customized checkout procedures, etc. Not only we need to design an application model, but also to design and apply different business policies, manage information about the user and his profile, etc. Furthermore, as we must also cope with constant changes of these policies, the design should be modular enough to make evolution seamless.

So far, little attention has been paid to the modeling and design process of this kind of software. Only recently, some authors have proposed reference design architectures for personalized or customized software [1], [2]. These approaches emphasize a clear separation of concerns among the application objects, the customization rules and the user profile. They follow a widely used strategy for modeling business rules as first-class objects, thus decoupling them from the application-specific code [3], [4].

The user profile is also represented as a set of objects addressing different user preferences (language, location, etc). User profiles are often described as aggregations of objects whose attributes contain plain information such as “English”, “Los Angeles” and the like. Customization and other business rules use this information by checking these attributes and performing corresponding actions.

Z. Bellahsène, D. Patel, and C. Rolland (Eds.): OOIS 2002, LNCS 2425, pp. 117-123, 2002.

The main thesis in this paper is that existing approaches fail to provide a good and modular platform for implementing customization policies.

While the rules paradigm works fine with some kinds of business policies, it may end with a large and flat set of similar rules thus complicating maintenance. Moreover, treating information in the user profile as low-level objects (such as strings or numbers) neglect polymorphism and, as a consequence, makes this kind of software evolution a nightmare. We present an original approach for complementing customization rules with more general customizer objects for building maintainable software.

The structure of the rest of this paper is as follows: We first discuss existing architectural constructs for decoupling concerns in customizable software and introduce an example to illustrate our ideas; we next show that a wise application of objects polymorphism allows us to build composite customizer objects combining different customization policies. Though this paper is based on our previous experience with the OOHDM Method [5], the underlying ideas can be used in a straightforward way with other object-oriented approaches.

2 Customization in Business Applications

While building customizable object-oriented software, it is useful to understand what aspects of an application can be customized. For some years we have mined recurrent patterns in e-commerce applications, focusing on one of the most usual customization types: personalization [6]. These (coarse grained) patterns allow us to focus on *what* can be customized before addressing which concerns are involved in the customization design process. Summarizing we can customize:

- the algorithms and processes described in the application model (e.g. different recommendation strategies, pricing policies or check-out processes for different users, etc).
- the contents and structure of object's interfaces and the link topology in the resulting interface (e.g., building customized home pages such as in my.yahoo.com).
- the look and feel of the interface and the interaction styles (for example according to the interface artifact, e.g. a cellular phone, a PDA, etc).

Most approaches for mapping business rules into object structures have focused on the first kind of customization, i.e. emphasizing on process customization according to different object's values that reflect business states [3]. The main rationale for separating rules from application code is to achieve a better degree of concern separation, thus eliminating spurious if clauses inside object's methods. However when we need to implement customization policies that deal with a user profile, rules are not always the best solution.

3 Reference Architectures for Customizable Software

Existing approaches for building customizable software clearly separate the most important design concerns related with customization, namely the application model, the customization rules and the user profile.

Each module can be considered itself a simple micro-architectural component; the interaction between these components should follow well known patterns in order to keep the software manageable.

In order to make this discussion concrete, we introduce a simple example here. Suppose an electronic store that sells *products* to *customers*. When he decides to buy, the *check-out* process generates an *order* containing products, *paying mechanism, shipping address and price* and *delivering options*. Each customer has an *account* containing his buying history.

While variations in the domain model such as adding new products or paying mechanisms can be solved by sub-classing and composing objects, if we want to introduce some personalization capabilities, we face a new problem: mixing customization code with application logic. Following the previous idea we will have at least two other software modules for dealing with personalization:

- **The user profile**: that contains information about the customer's interests; it will need to interact with some application's objects such as the Customer and Account objects (by the way one may argue that it is debatable whether these classes should be part of the user profile). When software adaptation involves other aspects (such as date or time) a separated context model is also necessary.
- **The rule model**: that encapsulates different kinds of rules, for example for calculating a personalized price, etc; when dealing with event/condition/action rules [2], separated event objects will be used.

However, existing approaches fail to address two key aspects for building this kind of software: how to seamlessly connect application code with customization components and the process of rules engineering and design. We have shown an approach for solving the first problem in [7] by associating customizer objects to each customizable behavior. When an application object receives a message whose answer must be customized, a customizer object is in fact activated; it interacts with the original object, the user profile and the context to generate the correct answer. We will not elaborate the activation of customizer objects in this paper but will focus instead on the engineering of customization policies, which is described in the following section.

4 Mapping Customization Policies into Object Designs

Customization policies express different ways of adapting information and processes to the current context, e.g. the user, date, network connection, etc. It is relatively straightforward to describe policies using a rule-based language, for example event-condition-action (ECA) rules. However it is not so easy to map those "conceptual" structures into good software structures. For example, how should we design a policy such as: "Information should be presented in the user language"? The naive solution would be to map it into a set of rule objects checking the user profile for the user language and acting in consequence. In the same way, we can customize the information the user perceives to the type of interface appliance he is using, by writing a set of rules that according to the artifact (PDA, internet browser, cellular phone) invokes a different method for generating the corresponding information.

In both cases, we end with a flat set of rules checking the type of an object that we have hidden in a string variable. We are thus neglecting polymorphic behaviors.

Meanwhile, it is clear that a policy such as: "Discount a 10% of the regular price to frequent buyers" is easily mapped into a rule object (once we precisely define the meaning of "frequent") in which the corresponding condition checks the user account and the action object calculates the new price. Here, rule objects help us to get rid of malicious if then else clauses.

To make matters worse, it is easy to find applications in which the same aspect of an object (e.g. the product's price) is affected by "hybrid" policies combining the style of the two previously shown examples, e.g. "Customers that live in *x* should receive an additional *y%* discount".

We claim that if we want to achieve stable and modular implementations, we must careful study the nature of each part of the policy (i.e. condition, action) to decide how we map the policy into a good software structure. As said before, we ignore the nature of events (that in fact trigger the customization code) and focus on the pair condition/action.

4.1 Customizer Objects to the Rescue

Even though rule objects represent a good solution for decoupling customization code from base application behaviors, their use should be cautiously evaluated to avoid large sets of flat rules. Treating user profiles or execution contexts (e.g. type of network connection) as data objects with string-based attributes, results in rules that basically query those attributes for specific values in order to decide corresponding actions [2]. Our approach is based on the fundamental idea that rules should replace if clauses but not polymorphic behaviors.

Therefore, when the condition of a customization policy deals with the possible types of an object, we must replace rules with operations that delegate to an object belonging to a class hierarchy of polymorphic classes, each of them providing the corresponding implementation of the policy action. In other words, when a policy condition checks if $T=T_i$ to apply an action A_i , we must build a class hierarchy for different T_i in which each class implements the corresponding A_i behavior. This hierarchy will be usually part of the current profile (describing the user and its context).

In most real applications we have found very easy to identify these situations; for the sake of conciseness we only give some examples related with the previously mentioned e-store.

Suppose that we want to customize the checkout process according to some user attribute such as his address. For example, we may have a policy such as: "if the customer lives in north-America he does not pay for the shipping, if he lives in

Europe he pays a reduced shipping price and if he lives in the rest of the world he pays a regular price". A naive solution is to have some string attribute in the user profile such as continent allowing us to write a condition on this attribute to trigger the corresponding action.

A better solution is obtained by:

- Creating a hierarchy of Continent classes (that may later evolve into a hierarchy of countries if needed). Each class has a behavior for returning the actual discount with respect to the regular price.
- Redefining the user profile by associating a continent object to each user.
- Associating a customizer object to the shipping price behavior (in Class Order); when the order (or the corresponding shipping object) has to inform the shipping price, the customizer object for this behavior is activated. It next delegates into the corresponding continent object in the user profile, which returns the discount.

Notice that the user profile now contains more "intelligence" than in the former solution: it knows which objects it has to invoke to perform the checkout. We have in fact replaced the set of rules that check the continent by a polymorphic behavior activated from the customizer object.

From the point of view of design complexity this solution may seem a bit more complex (in fact rules are easy to engineer) though it may require creating less classes than the rule-based schema, where we need sub-classes for actions and conditions. This resulting approach is easier to maintain.

4.2 Composite Customizers

It usually happens that we need to implement different customization policies for the same application aspect (e.g. the price of products). Some of them may be mapped into rule objects and others into customizers, e.g. the discount policy depends on the customer address and on the number of products he bought before. Even if we implement all of them as rule objects, we need to provide a way to solve conflicts (for example two different discount policies that should not be applied together).

In the most general case we may want to combine different kind of customization policies, independently of the design structure we chose to implement them.

Our approach for solving this problem is treating customizer objects as recursive composites [8]; the leaves of the composite may delegate to a rule object (rules may be also composites), to some user (or context) profile object, or may just provide the customization behavior.

In each composition level there may be a conflict solver (the composed object whose parts may have conflicts). Then, for each customizable aspect in our application we have a customizer object; this object may just initiate the execution of a set of rule objects, may delegate to some "intelligent" profile object (that itself may even delegate in some application object) or may just recursively delegate to other customizers.

4.3 User Profiles and Contexts

As mentioned in section 4.2 our approach requires a significant change in the way in which user profiles and usage contexts are designed. Frequently, existing approaches for modeling the user and the environment (network connection, interface appliance, etc) treat these objects as passive data repositories in which information is described with atomic values such as strings or numbers.

We claim that a better approach is needed; it is necessary to carefully engineer these descriptions with a pure object-oriented view; in particular, possible values of profile or context attributes (such as the user's address, the sports he practices, the kind of connection, etc) should be designed as instances of a class in a hierarchy offering polymorphic behaviors. In this way we simplify evolution and maintenance, as changes related with customization are located in these classes. Moreover, we get a better balance of customization related behaviors, as we don't need to locate all of them in action rule classes (such as action classes in [2]).

5 Conclusions and Further Work

In this paper we have outlined an integrated approach for mapping customization policies into object structures. This approach complements existing work by showing when policies should be implemented as rules, when using polymorphic objects or combination of both types of design solutions.

Our approach is non-intrusive because it provides architectural mechanisms for adding extra functionality (e.g. customization) without re-coding the base business logic. We are now exploring some complementary research directions. First, we are studying how to use UML stereotypes [9] for simplifying class diagrams that involve customizers and rules. We are also working on visual tools for simplifying the personalization process by allowing the designer to plug personalizers to base objects easily.

References

1. N. Koch, M. Wirsing: "The Munich Reference Model for Adaptive Hypermedia Applications", o be presented at 2nd International Conference on Adaptive Hypermedia and Adaptive Web Based Systems
2. G. Kappel, W. Retschitzegger and W. Schwinger. "Modeling Ubiquitous Web Applications: The WUML approach". International Workshop on Data Semantics in Web Information Systems (DASWIS-2001), (ER2001), Yokohama, Japan, November 27-30, 2001
3. http://www.research.ibm.com/rules/commonrules-overview.html
4. The Rule Mark-up Language, in http://www.dfki.uni-kl.de/ruleml/
5. D. Schwabe, G. Rossi: "An object-oriented approach to web-based application design". Theory and Practice of Object Systems (TAPOS), Special Issue on the Internet, v. 4#4, pp.207-225, October 1998

6. G. Rossi, D. Schwabe, J. Danculovic, L. Miaton: "Patterns for Personalized Web Applications", Proceedings of EuroPLoP 01, Germany, July 2001
7. J. Cappi, G. Rossi, A. Fortier, D. Schwabe: "Seamless Personalization of E-Commerce applications" in Proceedings of e-Como 01 (Workshop on Conceptual Modeling in E-Commerce), (ER2001), Japan, December 2001
8. E. Gamma, R. Helm. R. Johnson, J. Vlissides: "Design Patterns. Elements of reusable object-oriented software", Addison Wesley 1995
9. UML reference manual. In www.rational.com/uml.htm

Using Meta-patterns to Construct Patterns

Rébecca Deneckère

Université Paris 1 Panthéon-Sorbonne, Centre de Recherche en Informatique
90 rue de Tolbiac 75013 Paris, France
Tel.: + 33 (0) 1 44 07 86 34, Fax.: + 33 (0) 1 44 07 89 54
denecker@univ-paris1.fr

Abstract. The pattern notion defines techniques allowing the existing knowledge reuse. Usually, the knowledge encapsulated in these patterns is stored in classic library repositories that quickly become overcrowded. To solve this problem, [1] proposes the use of process maps in order to organize and select them. But the completeness of the maps is a very important problem that has to be solved in order to offer a useful guidance to the method engineer. This paper proposes a guideline pattern construction technique guiding engineers when creating the maps.

1 Introduction and State of Art

The pattern notion has been widely used these last years. As a result, the patterns repositories number increases and it is more and more difficult to manage them. A way to solve this problem is the process map technique utilization that helps the method engineer to organize and select patterns. This section described these concepts.

The concept of **pattern** is very present in the literature and in a lot of different domains [2][3][4][5][6][7][8]. In [9] a pattern is described as "*a problem which occurs over an over again in our environment and then describes the core of the solution to that problem, in such a way that you can use this solution a million times over, without ever doing the same twice"*. In Method Engineering, generic patterns aim at proposing a mean for constructing situation specific methods. Such patterns allow to know which are the best processes in a specific situation and they guide the method engineer in the construction of a specific method.

A pattern description must include the *problem* for which the pattern proposes a *solution* and the recurring set of situations in which the pattern applies [10]. We use here the formalism detailed in [11][12]. A pattern contains two parts: the reusable knowledge (the body) and the application aspects of this pattern (the signature). The pattern's *body* encapsulates the process description to apply on the product under modification. The signature is described to represent the situation before the modification, the intention to achieve and the target of that modification. We also call this concept *interface* [12]. It is seen as a triplet <situation, intention, target> associated to a body.

Z. Bellahsène, D. Patel, and C. Rolland (Eds.): OOIS 2002, LNCS 2425, pp. 124-134, 2002.

Following the appearance of a lot of transformation patterns catalogues, we have pointed out in [1] the problems of storing these patterns without order. Firstly, the patterns are stored in a library but this one may rapidly become overcrowded as engineers add new patterns as time goes by, and, secondly, some patterns have precedence relationships and require a way to introduce and execute them in predefined order. [1] has proposed an organizational technique to solve these problems by using **process maps**.

These maps are a formalization of the utilization process of the patterns that help the engineer with a guidance of each transformation. [1] uses the technique of process map [14][15] in order to sort the patterns in a catalogue. It is a labeled graph composed of nodes and edges. Nodes represent intentions that the engineer wants to reach and edges manners for reaching these intentions. The directed nature of the graph shows possible intentions dependencies. An edge enters a node if its manner can be used to achieve its intention. Since there can be multiple edges entering a node, the map is able to represent all the manners that can be used for achieving an intention. An execution path, determined by a map, always starts by the intention *Start* and ends by the intention *Stop*.

In [1], we have defined that a pattern, contextually to a specific map, may be represented by a defined section. Each of these sections (i.e. each of these patterns) represents a specific way to reach a target intention, from a node in the map, by the execution of a particular manner. The next figure shows the equivalence between concepts of *Section* and *Pattern* using the representation of two sections of a map.

This figure illustrates the fact that the applicable pattern between two intentions will be different, according to method engineer's manner choice. Then, we may say that it exists, from a specific source intention to a specific target intention, as many applicable patterns than manners.

The problematic and proposed solution is described in the next section. An application of this technique to the OO method extension approach is done in the section three. We conclude in the fourth and last section.

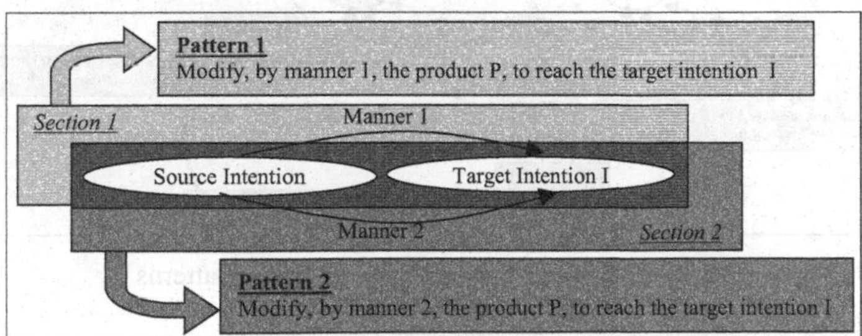

Fig. 1. Sections and patterns

2 Problematic and Proposed Solution

The major problem left was the map completeness. The process maps are perfects if they are complete, so the method engineer knows all the alternatives that are offered to him. However, if some patterns are not present on the map, engineers may come to a dead-end and all the usefulness of this technique is thrown away. In order to construct complete maps, we propose here a specific construction pattern technique using meta-patterns.

Problematic when constructing a map, for a specific application domain, begin with the explicit inventory of all the intentions. For instance, if we want to extend a method, each intention will represent a specific element integration into this specified method. Then, the method engineer makes the inventory of the applicable manners to reach these intentions. Finally, each of these sections has to be described by a pattern. However, manners inventory in a map is a very long, delicate and strategic work and represents the major difficulty of that process. If the method engineer forgets one section and that the extension process of a specific method need this one to reach its goal, this extension can't go farther. To solve that case, this paper proposes to create a set of generic manners specific to the approach used. Apply all generic manners to all map intentions allows map completeness certification.

Furthermore, in order to ease the sections realization of the map (i.e. the description of the associated patterns), all the relative knowledge of the patterns construction is encapsulated in a specific meta-pattern. The method engineer, as soon as the elements to integrate will have been identified, will directly realize the map intentions, by applying all meta-patterns defined. Each meta-pattern application will guide to a pattern construction allowing to reach a target intention, from a source intention, by applying a specific manner on it. This construction process allows to guide the method engineer when identifying the map sections and also when constructing the associated patterns. The next figure shows the instantiation of a meta-pattern using the *specialization* generic manner for the construction of three patterns (i.e. three sections of the map). A complete description of this meta-pattern is done in [11].

To illustrate this paper, we choose to apply this technique to the method extension approach and we will also only focus on the set of patterns that may be used when extending an OO method.

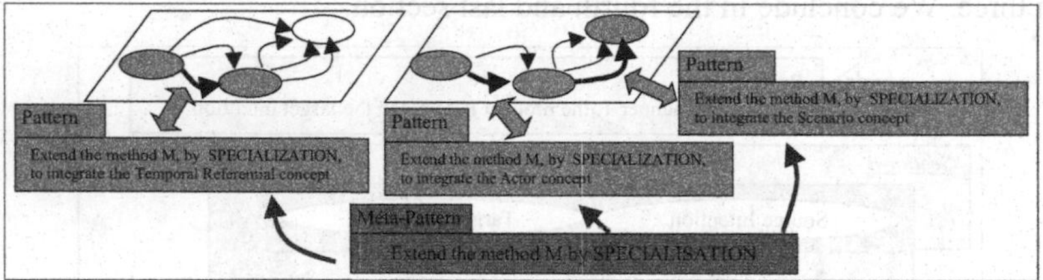

Fig. 2. Meta-pattern instantiation to obtain patterns

3 Application to the OO Method Extension Approach

The method extension approach has been defined in [11]. It is described as a *technique allowing to take into account more things that was in the origin set*. The manners and meta-patterns used here are specific to this particular approach.

The manners studied in this paper allow modifying a method. Three parameters are considered: (a) the method element to modify - [Element X] (this element is a part of the method before the extension), (b) the element that the method engineer wishes to integrate into the method - [Element Y] (this element is a part of the method after the extension) and (c) the element likely to be of no use after the extension – [Element D]: *Manner ([Element X], [Element Y], [Element D])*. Note that the two first arguments are mandatory. The third one – [Element D] – is optional. All extensions don't change the source method to the point of leaving an useless element. In that last case, it is necessary to leave the possibility for deleting this element and guaranty the method coherency.

Lets take the example of a pattern that allows integrating the *Calendar Class* concept into a method that already contains the *Clock Class* concept. In fact, it will be implemented as a replacement of the first one by the second one. The situation before the extension is : *Clock Class = Inherits of (Class), Composition (Temporal Event)*[1]. The manner application is : *REPLACEMENT (Clock Class, Calendar Class, ϕ)*. The situation after the extension is : *Calendar Class = Inherits of (Class), Composition (Temporal Event).*

The knowledge relative to each manner is encapsulated into a specific pattern named *"Meta-pattern"*. As exposed before, the meta-patterns follow the patterns description. They are composed by a signature (Fig. 3) and a body. As for the patterns, the meta-patterns may be differentiated following two specific types: the ones allowing to construct a Product pattern and the ones allowing to build a Process pattern.

The meta-pattern situation represents the Element Y (the additional element we want to integrate into the original method). The meta-pattern intention is to build a pattern that will integrate that element in the method following a specific manner, resulting a target meta-pattern that is a pattern for a specific element and following a specific manner.

The meta-pattern body represents all the operations allowing the construction of the pattern, i.e. the definition of its situation, its intention, its target and its body. This body is constructed by a set of operators corresponding to the manner used. Each manner represents a set of modification operators containing three unknown values : Element X, Element Y and Element D (the three arguments of the manner). Element Y is known when we use the meta-pattern in order to build a pattern. However, Element X and Element D will only be known when instantiating this pattern to a specific method.

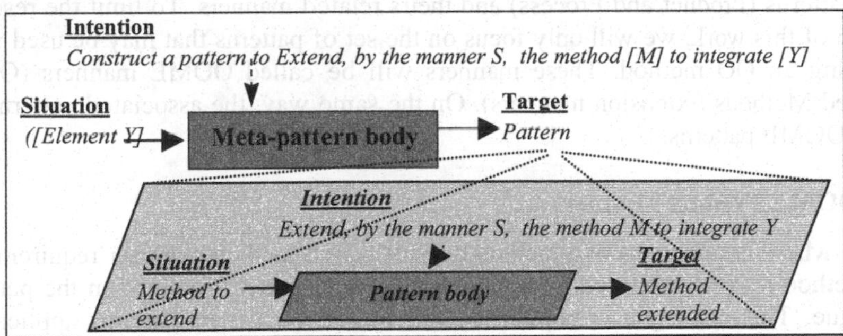

Fig. 3. Meta-pattern interface

[1] This formalism is described in [11].

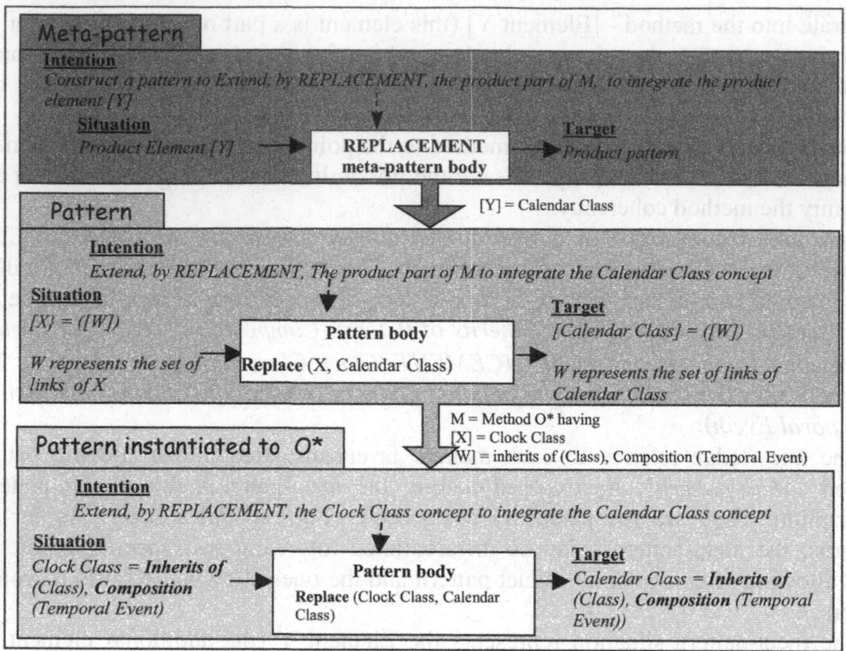

Fig. 4. Example of pattern construction with meta-patterns

Lets illustrate that concept with a sample. The following figure shows the successive instantiations, from a meta-pattern to a pattern (for an integration of a specific element) and to a pattern allowing the extension of a specific method. *Calendar Class* is the concept to integrate in the O* method.

This figure shows the two steps allowing to construct a pattern, given a specific method. The first step represents the meta-pattern instantiation for the *Calendar Class* concept. The second step represents the pattern instantiation to the O* method.

As the objective in this paper is automating patterns building, we will focus on the inventory of all the possible manners to extend a method (the manners set), i.e. all the possible meta-patterns. We will describe here differences between the two types of meta-patterns (Product and Process) and theirs related manners. To limit the research domain of this work, we will only focus on the set of patterns that may be used when extending an OO method. These manners will be called OOME manners (Object Oriented Methods Extension manners). On the same way, the associated patterns are called OOME patterns.

3.1 OOME Product Manners

In case where Product part of a method doesn't match method engineer requirements, that method may be modified by applying a Product pattern defined in the patterns catalogue. This catalogue is populated with the Product meta-patterns application. These specific patterns allow constructing pertinent patterns adapted to the application at hand. They have to be applied on the method in order to modify it. The modified method will then handle a bigger set of concepts to construct a more complete and coherent application.

A Product meta-pattern may be described with its interface. The situation is the Product element to integrate in the method. The intention is the construction of a pattern to extend the method. The target is that pattern, created for a specific product element and following a selected manner. The body is the set of creation operations allowing to create the pattern. The body of the pattern created will be composed of a set of transformation operations (corresponding to the manner chosen).

As a method extension is a *technique allowing to take into account more things that was in the origin set*, a Product part extension will introduce new concepts into an existing model. That merge may be made following two different ways : either the concept to integrate is a new element, or it is a concept already represented in the method but in an incomplete or incorrect way.

Introduction of a New Concept in the Method

The introduction of these new concepts had to be followed by their connection to the rest of the model. A concept is important only if it is linked with other concepts. These grafts are realized by instantiating the different kind of links defined in the Product meta-model of the method. Note that the extension process will be different following these links. As a result, the extensions may be defined according to the link type used to connect the new element to the method model. A generic links set has been defined with the study of several OO methods (OMT[16],OOA&D[17], O*[18], etc) and results in the fact that a new concept may be added in a method product model by connecting it to an other concept with the inheritance, composition or association link.

- *Inheritance Link:* The method engineer may integrate a new concept in the model by connecting it to an existing concept with an inheritance link. The new concept is then inserted as a specialization of an existing or a non-existing concept.

In the first case, the new concept is inserted and the inheritance link between it and the existing concept is added. This technique may be used only if the method already contains a concept that may be viewed as a super-type of the concept to integrate. Lets use an example concerning an extension of the OMT method. Its Product model contains the *Event* concept. The insertion of the *Temporal Event* new concept may be made by a specialization of *Event*. Integrating the *Temporal Event* concept, and connecting it by specialization with the *Event* one, makes the extension.

On the contrary, in the second case, the method does not contain any concept of this kind. However, it contains one with a semantic similar to the concept to integrate. In this case, the extension allows integration of an other element that de facto generalize existing and new concepts. Lets consider again the OMT method. It contains the *Object Class* concept. The insertion of the *Actor Class* may be made with that technique, regarding their semantic similarity. Firstly, the extension of the method will insert a generalization of the *Object Class* that we call the *Class* concept. Next, the *Actor Class* concept is integrated. Finally, this new concept is connected by a specialization link to the *Class* concept.

To insert a concept by an inheritance link may be viewed as two different techniques : inheritance link usage or generalization link usage. Each of these two techniques represents a specific OOME Product manner : SPECIALIZATION and GENERALIZATION.

- *Composition Link:* The method engineer may also integrate a new concept in the model using a composition link. The new designed concept may be inserted as a composed concept or as a component of an existing concept.

In the first case, the concept is added in the target Product model then connected as a composed element of an existing concept. Lets illustrate that with an OMT method case. It contains the designed *Object Class* concept, composed of *Property*, *Event* and *Operation* concepts. The method engineer may extend this method by integrating the *Constraint* concept on the *Object Class*. The best way to integrate this concept is to consider it as a component of the *Object Class*, just as the three others.

In the second case, on the contrary, the new concept doesn't become a *component* of an existing concept but a *composed* concept of an existing one. For instance, a method that contains the concept of *External Event* and where the method engineer wants to integrate the *Actor Class* concept. Then, process first step is the concept *Actor Class* integration in the model. Next, the concept of *External Event* is connected to this new concept using a composition link.

To integrate a concept with this link represents a composition link usage or a decomposition link usage. Each of these two different techniques represents a specific OOME Product manner : COMPOSITION and DECOMPOSITION.

- *Association Link*: An other existing link in the OO methods generic meta-model is association. The method engineer may insert a new element and connect it to the model with this kind of link. In that case, the element is inserted and is connected with an existing concept. Lets take the example of a method containing the *Action* concept. The method engineer wants to integrate the *Agent* concept into that one. This problem may be solved by using an association link (An *Action* is done by an *Agent* and an *Agent* makes one or more *Action*(s)).

This kind of insertion represents the fact that the new concept is related to an existing concept. This is the last OOME product manner : ASSOCIATION.

Introduction of a Concept Incompletely Represented in the Method

It is also possible to extend a model by replacing an existing concept in order to change its description. Lets use the example of a method that contains the *Granule* concept. The method engineer wants to improve this notion of *Granule* by adding the *Calendar* concept. The existing *Granule* concept becomes incomplete according to the method engineer requirements. A way to solve this problem is to replace the existing concept by the new one.

To extend a method with this particular technique is characterized by the application of a concept replacement. This way of working represents a specific OOME product manner : REPLACEMENT.

To resume, we may enumerate the following set of OOME Product manners : Inheritance, Generalization, Composition, Decomposition, Association and Replacement. Each of them will be supported by a Product meta-pattern.

3.2 OOME Process Manners

If the method engineer applies a Product pattern and that the extended method contains a Process part, it is better to also extend this part of the method. It will improve the method completeness. On the same way as we defined Product meta-patterns, it is possible to define some Process meta-patterns.

Like Product meta-patterns, Process meta-patterns may be described with their interface. The situation is the construction concept to integrate in the method. The intention is the construction of a Process pattern in order to extend that method. The target is this Process pattern, created for a specific product element construction, following a certain manner. The body is the set of creation operations allowing to create the pattern (situation, intention, target, body). The created pattern's body will be composed of a set of transformation operations (corresponding to the OOME manner chosen). This section describes OOME process manners.

Extension of a method's Process part is made by grafting new processes in the process tree[2] of the existing method, in order to take into account the new concepts construction. There is two possibilities supplied to the method engineer: either the schema construction step is left untouched and grafts are made on a very controlled way, or the process tree is modified in order to automatically integrate all new processes.

Controlled Integration

Processes allowing the method extensions are grafted in order to leave the existing construction process unchanged. The method engineer will extend the schema elements only when all of them will have been fully defined first. The construction process tree keeps its construction processes („ Construct X “) but is incremented of a new extension process („ Extend X “). These two processes are executed in sequential order. We call that technique a Sequential Extension.

The principle shown on the Fig.5 represents the sequence between the construction process and the extension process of X. However, the *X* term may have a different signification according to the needed granularity. At the lower level, X represents a simple element of the method to extend, i.e. the construction of the *Class*, *Granule* or others concepts. On the contrary, at the highest level, X represents the entire construction schema of that method.

In the first case, the process tree puts into sequence the entire construction of the schema with its extension. In the second case, an extension represents a sequence in the process tree that allows step forward from the construction of a simple element to its extension. As shown in the previous figure, these two possibilities represent two specific Process manners : LOCAL SEQUENTIAL EXTENSION and GLOBAL SEQUENTIAL EXTENSION.

[2] The formalism used to represent the Process part of the methods is the one of the Esprit project „ NATURE “ described in [19][20][21]

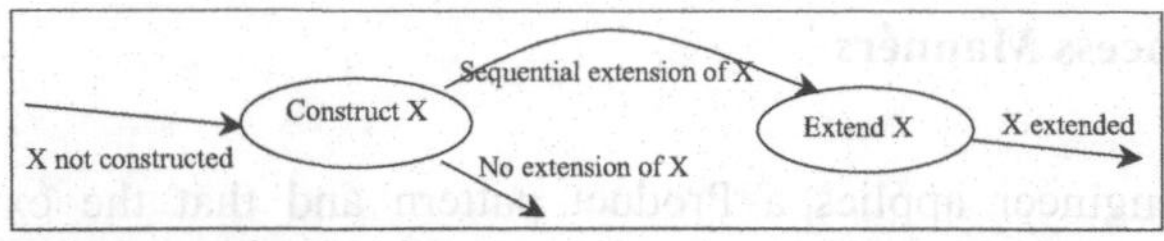

Fig. 5. Global and local sequential extension principles

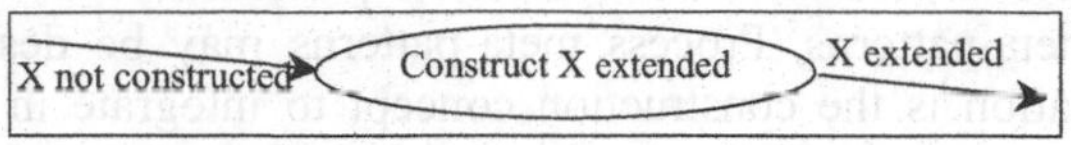

Fig. 6. Integrated extension principle

Transparent Integration

This type of extension doesn't leave the construction process unchanged. On the other hand, the new processes are fully integrated in the existing tree process. Extension doesn't appear as an artificial step but as a more complete step. In consequence, the method engineer doesn't work in a sequence <construction, extension> but simply executes a process tree taking the modifications into account from the beginning. This principle is illustrated in the Fig.6.

That kind of extension represents the specific Process manner INTEGRATED EXTENSION.

A Process part method may be extended by one of these three following process OOME manners : Local sequential extension, Global sequential extension or Integrated extension. Each of these manners will be represented as a Process meta-pattern.

Process OOME Manners *versus* Product OOME Manners

We have to note that an OOME Product manner application will have effects on the OOME Process manners application and induce three possible impacts from it. (1) With a *specialization* or a *generalization*, there will be a modification of the process tree alternatives concerned by the element. It will have an augmentation of the specialized types or an additive step. (2) On the same way, with a *composition* or a *decomposition*, it will guide to a modification of the constructing sequence of a Product element. (3) A *replacement* will leads to a graft of a new branch replacing an old one.

We may also differentiate two cases for the *global sequential extension*. Either the desired extension is the first one to be grafted or it is not the case. If it is the first extension to be realized, the method engineer has to completely reevaluate the precedence graph of the extension sequence in order to guaranty method's coherence and integrity. We call these two types: "First graft" and "Additional graft".

Notice that extensions based on *specialization* and *generalization* will be different according to the specific specialization of the considered element. Then, we may consider two types of specialization: "by type" or "by state". Al thought a type specialization leads to a complete differentiation of all the specialization of a concept, a state specialization will lead to the same description, except the type of the concept that will be different.

Process EM manner / Product EM manner	SEQUENTIAL EXTENSION			INTEGRATED EXTENSION	
	GLOBAL		LOCAL	Element having a type specialization	Element having a state specialization
	First graft	Additional graft			
SPECIALIZATION	GLOBAL SPECIALIZATION (First graft)	GLOBAL SPECIALIZATION (Additional graft)	LOCAL SPECIALIZATION	INTEGRATED SPECIALIZATION (by type)	INTEGRATED SPECIALIZATION (by state)
GENERALIZATION	GLOBAL GENERALIZATION (First graft)	GLOBAL GENERALIZATION (Additional graft)	LOCAL GENERALIZATION	INTEGRATED GENERALIZATION (by type)	INTEGRATED GENERALIZATION (by state)
COMPOSITION	GLOBAL COMPOSITION (First graft)	GLOBAL COMPOSITION (Additional graft)	LOCAL COMPOSITION	INTEGRATED COMPOSITION	
DECOMPOSITION	GLOBAL DECOMPOSITION (First graft)	GLOBAL DECOMPOSITION (Additional graft)	LOCAL DECOMPOSITION	INTEGRATED DECOMPOSITION	
ASSOCIATION	GLOBAL ASSOCIATION (First graft)	GLOBAL ASSOCIATION (Additional graft)	LOCAL ASSOCIATION	INTEGRATED ASSOCIATION	
REPLACEMENT				INTEGRATED REPLACEMENT	

Fig. 7. Process OOME manners *Versus* Product OOEM manners

We defined several Process manners that can be used after the defined Product manners. However, it is not always possible to use them whichever Product manner has been previously used. Moreover, according to the Product manner, the Process modifications will be different. The Fig.7 shows the different possibilities of combinations.

Notice that we didn't allowed to use a *sequential extension* if the OOME Product manner used was a *replacement*. It will not be very useful to construct an element if we have to replace it as soon as we extend the schema.
As a result, we obtain 23 specific OOME Process manners that we may use on an OO method.

4 Conclusion and Future Works

We proposed here a technique to construct patterns with methodical guidelines, guarantying completeness relative to map construction. As a matter of fact, if the process maps aren't complete, it may lead to coherency problem of the modified method. To solve this problem, we defined a set of manners that are encapsulated in specific patterns called meta-patterns. These meta-patterns lead to the construction of all patterns of process maps. As a result, all sections are defined, the method engineer can't reach a dead-end and the map is complete.

We have illustrated this technique with the Extension approach applied on Object Oriented methods. This specific application field leads us to define five Product meta-patterns and twenty-three Process meta-patterns that may be used to integrate new elements (concept and construction) into OO methods.
Despite that technique, following difficulties remain to be solved:

- A larger application field: The application of this technique to other domains than the OO method extension.
- The guidance supported by tools: a first one will help the construction of the map (and its related patterns) with the technique described in this paper and a second one will help its execution.

References

1. Deneckere, R., Souveyet, C. : Organising and Selecting Patterns in Pattern Languages with Process Maps. Proceedings of OOIS'2001 Conference. Springer-Verlag, Calgary (Canada) (2001)
2. Coad, P.: Object-Oriented Patterns. Communications of the ACM, Vol. 35, No. 9 (1992). pp 152-159
3. Beck, K.: Smalltalk, Best Practice Patterns. Volume 1, Coding. Prentice Hall, Englewood Cliffs, NJ. (1997)
4. Buschmann, F., Meunier, R., Rohnert, et al.: Pattern-Oriented Software Architecture - A System of Patterns. John Wiley (1996)
5. Coplien, J.O., and Schmidt, D.O. (ed.) : Pattern Languages of Program Design. Addison-Wesley, Readind, MA. (1995)
6. Gamma, E., Helm, R., Johnson, R., et al.: Design Patterns: Elements of Reusable Object-Oriented Software. Addison Wesley (1994)
7. Hay, D.: Data Model Patterns: Conventions of Thought. Dorset House, NY (1996)
8. Fowler, M.: Analysis Patterns: Reusable Object Models. Addison-Wesley, (1997)
9. Alexander, C., Ishikawa, S., Silverstein, M., et al.: A Pattern Language. Oxford University Press, New York (1977)
10. Software Patterns. Communications of the ACM, Volume 39, No 10, (October 1996)
11. Deneckere, R. : Approche d'extension de méthodes fondée sur l'utilisation de composants génériques. PhD thesis, University of Paris1-Sorbonne (2001)
12. Deneckere, R., Souveyet, C. : Patterns for extending an OO model with temporal features. Proceedings of OOIS'98 conference. Springer-Verlag, Paris (France) (1998)
13. Rolland, C., Plihon, V., Ralyté, J.: Specifying the reuse context of scenario method chunks. Proceedings of the conference CAISE'98, Springer-Verlag, Pisa Italy (1998)
14. Benjamen, A.: Une approche multi-démarches pour la modélisation des démarches méthodologiques. PhD thesis, University of Paris 1, Paris (1999)
15. Rolland, C., Prakash, N., Benjamen, A.: A multi-model view of process modelling. Requirements Engineering Journal, p. 169-187 (1999)
16. Rumbaugh J., Blaha M., Premerlani W., Eddy F., Lorensen W. : Object-Oriented Modeling and Design. P.-H. I. Editions, Eds. (1991)
17. Martin J., Odell J.: Object-Oriented Analysis and Desig.n P.-H. I. Editions, Eds. (1992)
18. Brunet J. : Analyse Conceptuelle orientée-objet. PhD Thesis, University of Paris 6. (1993)
19. Rolland, C., Souveyet, C., Moreno, M.: An Approach for Defining Ways-Of-Working. Information Systems, Vol 20, No4, pp337-359 (1995)
20. Rolland, C., Plihon, V.: Using generic chunks to generate process models fragments. Proceedings of the 2nd IEEE International Conference on Requirements Engineering, ICRE, ICRE'96, Colorado Spring (1996)
21. Jarke, M., Rolland, C., Sutcliffe, A., Dömges, R. (Hsrg.): The NATURE of Requirements Engineering. Shaker Verlag, Aachen (1999)

A Tool and a Formalism to Design and Apply Patterns

Agnès Conte, Mounia Fredj, Ibtissem Hassine,
Jean-Pierre Giraudin, and Dominique Rieu

LSR-IMAG, SIGMA
BP 72, 38402 Saint Martin D'Heres Cedex – France
{Agnes.Conte,Mounia.Fredj,Ibtissem.Hassine,
Jean-Pierre.Giraudin,Dominique.Rieu}@imag.fr

Abstract. Patterns systems are becoming more and more numerous. They offer product patterns or process patterns of varied range and cover (analysis, design or implementation patterns, and general, domain or enterprise patterns). New application development environments have been developed together with these pattern-oriented approaches and should address two kinds of actors: patterns engineers who specify patterns systems, and applications engineers who use these systems to specify information systems. Nevertheless, most of the existing development environments are made for applications engineers; they offer few functionalities allowing definition and organization of patterns systems. This paper presents AGAP, a development environment for defining and using patterns, which distinguishes pattern formalisms from patterns systems. Not only does AGAP address applications engineers, but it also allows patterns engineers to define patterns systems in order to increase the level of reuse. We illustrate the use of AGAP by the presentation of P-Sigma, a common formalism for patterns representation. P-Sigma expresses a semantics common to most of the existing formalisms and standardizes the expression of product patterns and process patterns. It allows to clarify the patterns selection interface and facilitates the organization of patterns systems.

Keywords: Pattern, patterns system, reuse, product pattern, process pattern, pattern formalism, pattern-based development environment.

1 Introduction

A wide variety of reusable component models have already been proposed to integrate reuse in all applications development processes: business objects, generic domain models [18], analysis patterns [10] [12], design patterns [14], frameworks [17], etc. In all cases, a component is considered as a tested and accepted solution to a problem which occurs frequently in information systems development. In this paper, particular interest is given to the pattern approach. Different criteria may be used to compare

Z. Bellahsène, D. Patel, and C. Rolland (Eds.): OOIS 2002, LNCS 2425, pp. 135-146, 2002.

component models [13] [8]. Some of them are particularly interesting to characterize patterns (see figure 1).

- ***Type of knowledge***. A pattern capitalizes ***products*** – a goal to reach - or capitalizes ***processes*** - a way to reach a result.
- ***Coverage***. A pattern coverage may be ***generic*** (resp. ***domain, enterprise***) if it solves a problem frequently occurring in several domains (resp. in an application domain, in a particular enterprise).
- ***Range***. The pattern range may be ***analysis, design*** or ***implementation*** depending on the stage of the engineering process it addresses.

The best known patterns systems (P. Coad [10], E. Gamma [14], etc.) propose ***general product patterns*** dedicated to only one stage of the development process (***analysis*** for P. Coad's patterns, ***design*** for E. Gamma's patterns). S.W. Ambler's patterns [3] are ***general process patterns*** covering all the stages of the engineering process. They provide collections of techniques, actions and/or tasks for software development. Finally, the patterns system proposed by L. Gzara [16] concerns a specific ***domain*** (the Product Information Systems[1] –PIS- or the Product Data Management). In this patterns system, patterns cover the ***analysis*** and the ***design*** of the PIS development and integrate ***product patterns*** and ***process patterns***. Process patterns aim to specify a PIS development process which makes easier the use of product patterns (selection, application, composition, etc.).

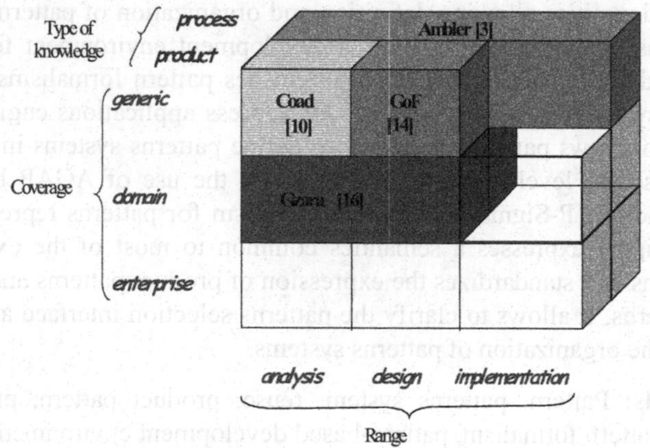

Fig.1. Patterns systems Organization [26]

Patterns are now frequently used in engineering processes. Several works integrate them in application development environments [5] [20]. Different kinds of pattern-based tools exist, research prototypes [19] [15] [21] [7] as well as commercial tools (Rational Rose, Objecteering, etc.). Nevertheless, the majority of existing tools only

---

[1] Product Information Systems (PIS) support all types of engineering data used to define, manufacture and support products. They may include definitions, specifications, CAD drawings, manufacturing process plans and routings, project plans, control records, etc.

integrate E. Gamma's patterns system and don't take into account the patterns engineers needs. Very few tools allow to integrate them in the software life cycle [9]. Section 2 presents AGAP, a development environment which offers solutions to combine the various needs of two kinds of actors: applications engineer who specifies information systems by patterns applications and patterns engineer who specifies patterns and patterns systems by using the same formalism or by reusing items of existing formalisms. Section 3 introduces the P-Sigma formalism. P-Sigma aims to express a common semantics for the majority of existing formalism and to standardize the expression of product patterns and process patterns. Section 3 will show, in particular, that P-Sigma is an instantiation of AGAP's meta-model.

2 AGAP

2.1 Patterns Engineer

The patterns engineer's goal is to define patterns formalisms and patterns systems described according to these formalisms. Several use cases are allocated to him (see figure 2): for example, a patterns engineer must be able to create, modify, validate and visualize a pattern formalism or a patterns system. The validation of a pattern formalism (respectively a patterns system) implies that it is not modifiable, but allows it to be used to create patterns systems (respectively information systems).

The patterns engineer is also authorized to manipulate applications domains and targeted technologies: a patterns system is applied to a given domain (for example banking IS) according to a given technology (for example, relational or object-oriented technology). Finally, AGAP allows a classification of items: the patterns engineer can define, modify and visualize the types of the fields (text, UML diagrams, etc.).

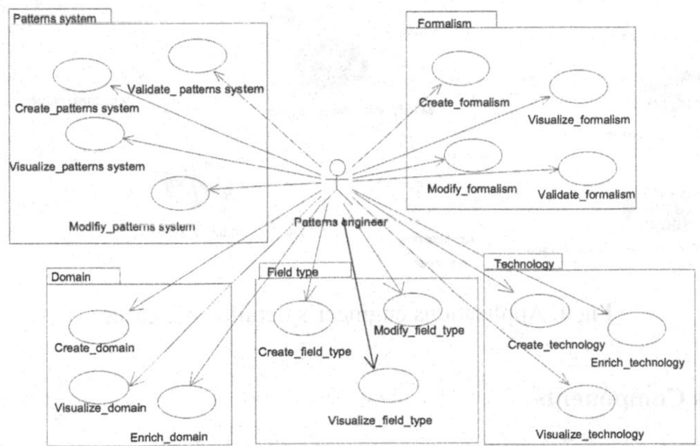

Fig.2. Patterns engineer's use cases

2.2 Applications Engineer

The goal of the applications engineer is to apply patterns in order to model and design information systems. This application is based on one or more patterns systems available in AGAP.

The main needs of the applications engineer can be summarized by UML use cases (see figure 3): an applications engineer must be able to create or modify an information system, to visualize a patterns system and to visualize an information system trace. An information system trace shows patterns selection and patterns application processes by preserving the patterns applications, the patterns from which they result, and the successive integrations of patterns applications. This diagram is enhanced by use-cases used by the basic use cases (see figure 4). For example, the creation of an information system requires the creation of patterns applications.

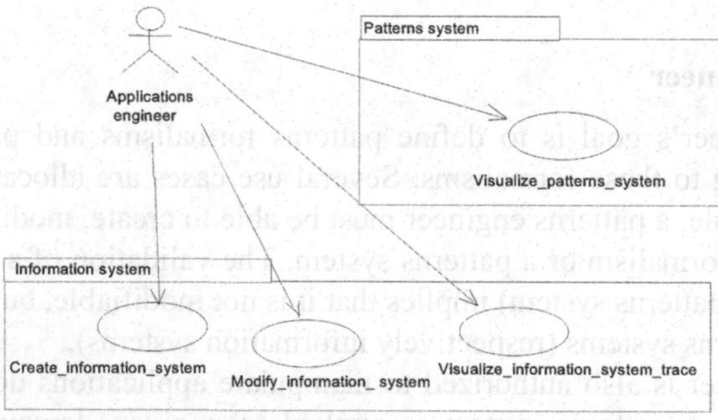

Fig.3. Applications engineer's use cases

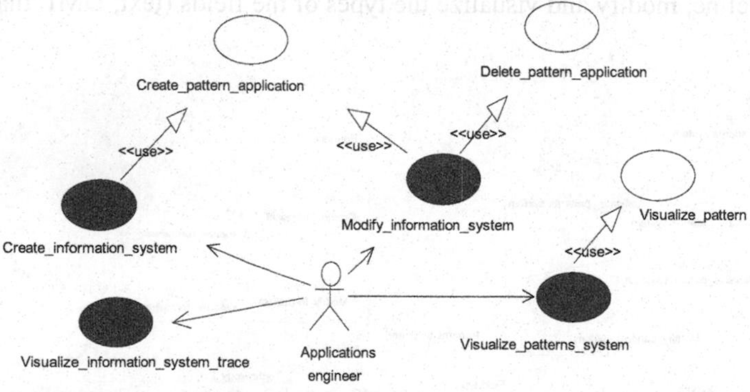

Fig.4. Applications engineer's detailed use cases

2.3 AGAP's Components

AGAP is composed of 7 business components (Tool, Information System, Patterns System, Domain, Technology, Formalism and Field Type) based on a business component model. This model and three business components (Tool, Formalism and Patterns System) are described in this section.

2.3.1 Business Component Model

The structure of each component conforms the business components structuring of the Symphony process. This structuring is inspired by CRC (Class-Responsibility-Collaboration) [25]. According to this method, a business component is modeled by a package composed of three parts (see figure 5): an interface part (*what I can do*), a structural part (*what I am*) and a collaboration part (*what I use*).
The three parts of a component are represented by four object types stereotyped by:

- **Master object**: it is the main object of the component for which the services are carried out. It is identifiable by any external actor.
- **Part object**: the part-object is complementary to the master object. It is identified by its attachment with the master object to which it is linked by a relation of composite type.
- **Role object**: it is an object servant. All the services of the other components are called through this object.
- **Interface**: it represents the component services contract. It supports the operations of the component responsibility.

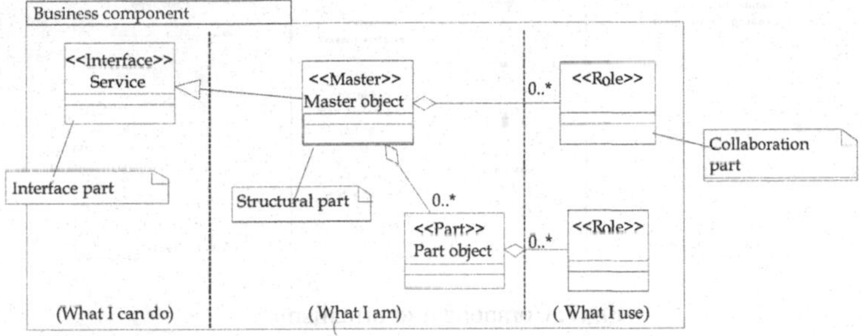

Fig.5. Architecture of a business components in Symphony

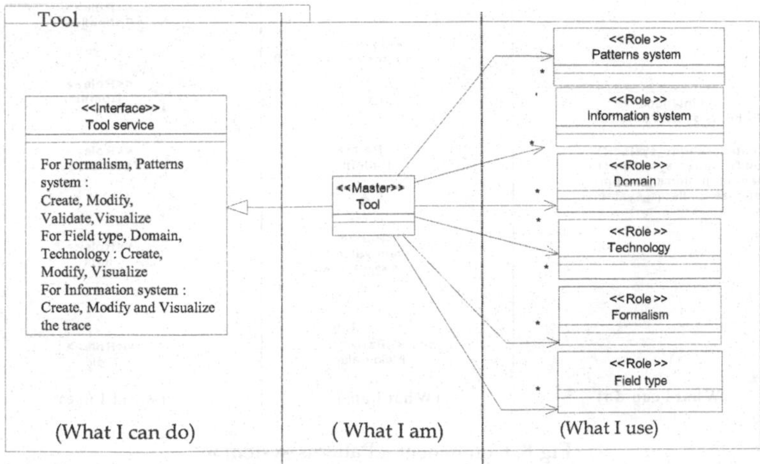

Fig.6. Component « Tool»

2.3.2 Component « Tool »

The component « Tool » is the base component of AGAP. It plays the role of a mediator between the user and the other business components.

2.3.3 Component « Formalism »

A formalism (see figure 7) contains one or more items which can be shared with other formalisms. Some of them are mandatory, and others are optional. Three types of items exist: *Interface item* in order to facilitate patterns sclection, *Realization item* in order to express patterns solution and *Relations item* in order to organize patterns systems. Each item is composed of one or more fields.
A formalism has two states: *"in definition"* and *"validated"*. An "in definition" formalism can be modified, for example by adding or deleting items. A "validated" formalism is not modifiable and can be used to define patterns systems.

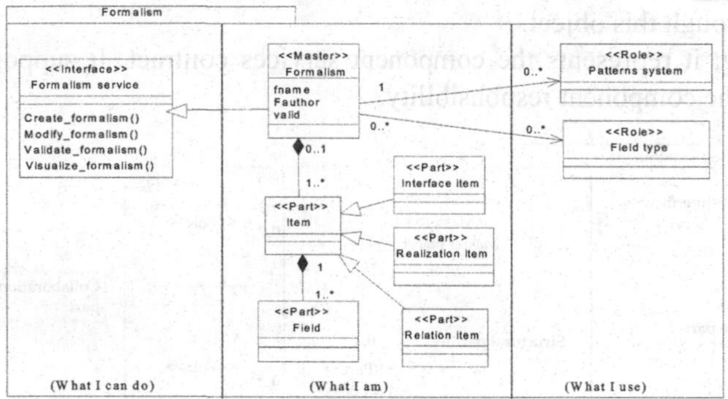

Fig.7. Component «Formalism»

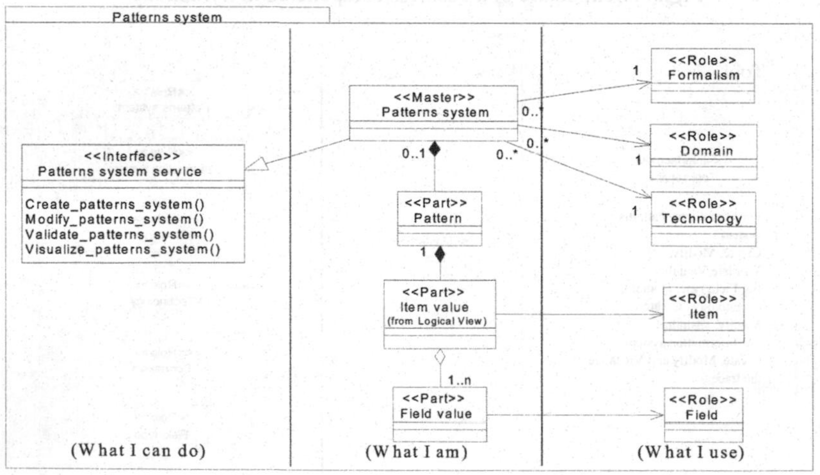

Fig.8. Component « Patterns system »

2.3.4 Component « Patterns System »

A patterns system is composed of patterns. Its representation is described in a given formalism. Each pattern has a given number of items whose fields are defined in the associated formalism. A domain (banking IS, geographic IS, etc.) and a technology (object-oriented, relational, etc.) are associated to each patterns system.

2.4 Meta-model and Implementation of AGAP

Building on the seven business components described above, we propose a model containing the essential information on the patterns managed by AGAP. This model is considered as the meta-model of AGAP (see figure 9).

AGAP is implemented in Java with the RAD JBuilder[2]. The communication between AGAP and Rational Rose is done by Microsoft COM technology. The meta-model is thereafter instantiated to produce patterns systems description formalisms and patterns systems. We present in the next section the formalism P-Sigma, a common patterns representation formalism, instantiation of the meta-model of AGAP.

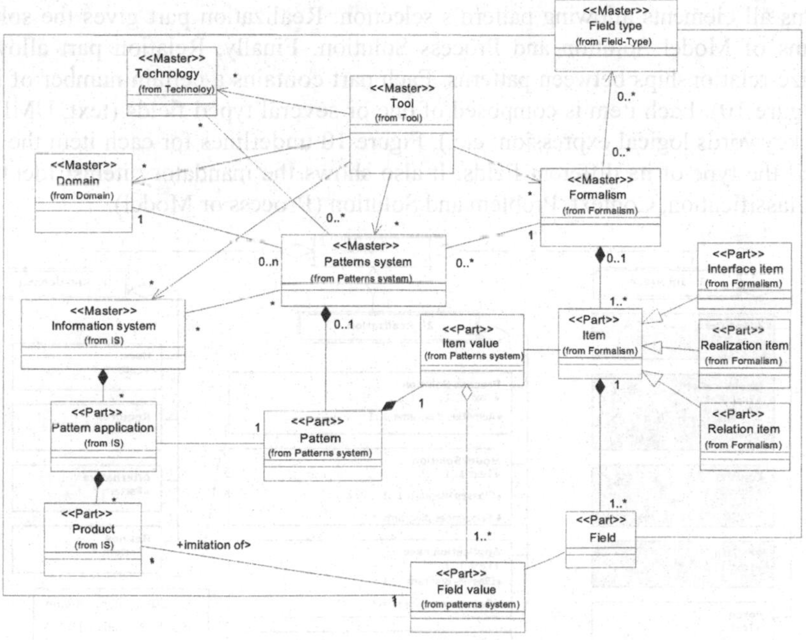

Fig.9. AGAP's meta-model

[2] http://www.borland.fr/produits/jbuilder/

3 The Formalism P-Sigma

P-Sigma is a patterns formalism. Its main objectives are:

- **Standardization of Product and Process Patterns Representation.** A patterns system must integrate product and process patterns and therefore must offer a unique formalism to combine expression of model and process solutions.
- **Better formalization of the Pattern's Selection Interface.** Contrary to the existing representation formalisms, where the items allowing pattern's selection are not explicit, P-Sigma distinguishes five items helping to select patterns.
- **Patterns System Organization.** P-Sigma formalism aims to make explicit the different relations among patterns. The Relation part enables to organize a patterns system thanks to clear relations: uses, requires, alternative, refines, etc.

3.1 General Structure of P-Sigma

P-Sigma is composed of three parts: Interface, Realization and Relation. Interface part contains all elements allowing pattern's selection. Realization part gives the solution in terms of Model Solution and Process Solution. Finally, Relation part allows to organize relationships between patterns. Each part contains a certain number of items (see figure 10). Each item is composed of one or several typed fields (text, UML diagram, keywords logical expression, etc.). Figure 10 underlines for each item the number and the type of its different fields. It also shows the mandatory items: Identification, Classification, Context, Problem and Solution (Process or Model).

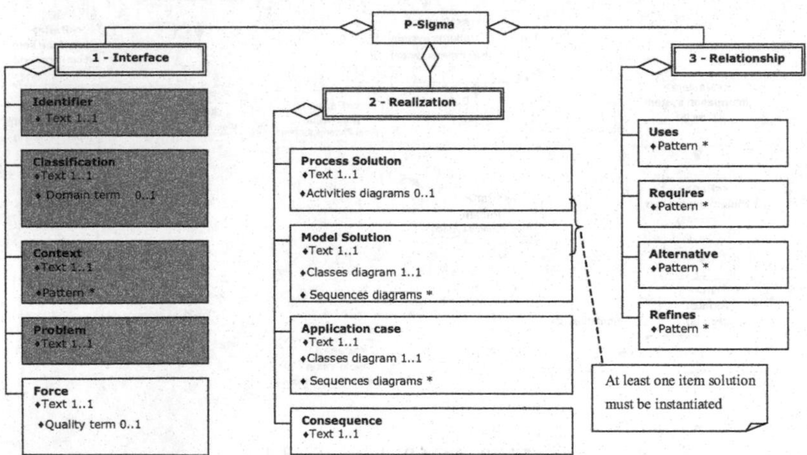

Fig.10. General Structure of P-Sigma formalism

A pattern interface is composed of five items used for pattern selection:

- **Identification:** Defines the couple (problem, solution) that references the pattern.
- **Classification:** Defines the pattern function through a collection of domain keywords (domain terms). Provides an intuitive domain classification.

- **Context:** Describes the pre-condition of pattern application.
- **Problem:** Defines the problem solved by the pattern.
- **Force:** Defines the pattern contributions through a collection of quality criteria associated to a technology.

A pattern realization is composed of four items:

- **Process Solution:** Indicates the problem solution in terms of a process to follow. An activity diagram allows to represent the process.
- **Model Solution:** Describes the solution in terms of the expected products (a class diagram and optionally a set of sequence diagram.
- **Application Case:** Describes application examples of the Model Solution. This item is optional, but recommended in order to facilitate the understanding of the pattern solution.
- **Consequence :** Gives the consequence induced by the pattern application.

The Relation part is composed of four items corresponding to the four types of relationships between patterns: Uses, Refines, Requires and Alternative. In P-Sigma, each relation is expressed by an item giving the patterns linked to the pattern described. The meaning of each relation is based mainly on the items of the Interface part. The Uses relationship is described below.

- If a pattern P1 uses a pattern P2, then: P1's Process Solution must be expressed using P2, P2's Classification may be enriched with respect to P1's one (new keywords may be added in P2's Classification) and in the same way, P2's Context may be enriched with respect to P1's one.

P1 uses P2	**P1**	**P2**
Classification	M1	M1 $\wedge$ M2
Context	C1	C1 $\wedge$ C2
Process Solution	**Apply P2**	

3.2 P-Sigma as Instance of AGAP's Meta-model

Figure 11 partially illustrates the instantiation of AGAP's meta-model for P-Sigma. This instantiation is represented by an object diagram; it only concerns classes of the component Formalism of AGAP (see figure 7). Only realization items are represented. They are instances of the class Realization Item and are linked to instances of the class Field. Let's note the cohabitation between the process solution (Process Sol) and the model solution (Model Sol) whose fields allow to express:

- fragments of process described by a text (Textual Process) and an activity diagram (Formal-Process) ;
- products models described by a text (Textual-Model), a class diagram (Class-Formal-Model) and optionally sequence diagrams (Sequence-Formal-Model).

4 Conclusion

This article presented AGAP, a development environment suited to two types of actors, applications engineers and patterns engineers. AGAP addresses therefore two types of processes:

- a process by reuse allowing the applications engineer to define information systems by selecting, applying and integrating patterns applications,
- a process for reuse allowing the patterns engineer to define and organize patterns systems.

AGAP clearly establishes a distinction between formalisms and patterns systems. It is therefore possible to define several patterns systems by using the same formalism or by reusing items of existing formalisms. An expected improvement of the meta-model consists in managing the synonymies between items having a similar meaning in different formalisms (for example, E. Gamma's Intention item and P-Sigma's Problem item). AGAP was used to specify two formalisms (P-Sigma and E. Gamma's formalism), and two patterns systems written in P-Sigma. These patterns systems result from applied researches on two projects in collaboration with industrial companies. The first one focuses on the engineering of Product Information Systems (PIS) of industrial enterprises [16] and was developed in collaboration with Schneider Electric company (project CNRS PROSPER-POSEIDON). The goal was to propose an engineering process based on reuse of specifications of industrial products. The second patterns system developed in AGAP concerns the specification of Symphony, a development process based on business components proposed by the UMANIS company. UMANIS uses a pragmatic development process for business component oriented information systems. Coupled to this process, UMANIS is developping an environment in which the engineers could be efficiently guided in their design activities, while taking into account specific situations of targeted information systems as well as former expertise.

From these first validated results, other research works were initiated to facilitate reuse in information systems engineering field and to guaranty a traceability between design choices and software products resulting from the design. These works require both improvements of P-Sigma and the definition of a meta-process to combine use of several formalisms. These formalisms would take into account others patterns, architectures and components forms: situational patterns [24] [23], frameworks [6], distributed objects on a CORBA bus, etc.

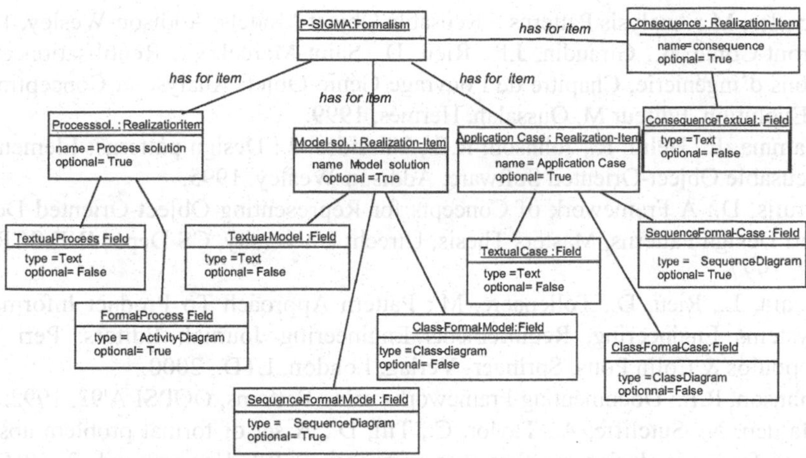

Fig.11. Instantiation in AGAP of Realization items of P-Sigma

References

1. ACM: Software Patterns, Communications of the ACM, vol. 39, n° 10, 1996.
2. Alexander, C.: The Timeless Way of Building, Oxford University Press, 1979.
3. Ambler, S.W.: Process Patterns building Large Scale Systems using Object technology, SIGS Books, Cambridge University Press, December 1998.
4. Berrut, C., Front-Conte, A.: Patterns retrieval system: first attempt, 5th International Conference on Applications of Natural Language to Information Systems (NLDB'2000), Versailles, June 2000.
5. Borne, I., Revault, N. : Comparaison d'outils de mise en oeuvre de design patterns, Object-oriented Patterns, Vol5, num2, 1999.
6. Buschmann, F., Meunier R., & al.: Pattern-Oriented Software Architecture: A System of Patterns, Wiley & Sons, 1996.
7. Casati, C., Castano, S., Fugini, M.G., Mirbel, I., Pernici, B.: WERDE: a pattern-based tool for exception design in workflows, proceedings of SEBD 98, Ancona, 1998.
8. Cauvet, C., Rieu, D., Ramadour, P., Front-Conte, A.: Réutilisation dans l'ingénierie des systèmes d'information, Chapitre de l'ouvrage Ingénierie des systèmes d'information du Traité IC2 – Information – Commande – Communication, Hermès, Février 2001.
9. Chambers, C., Harrison, B., Vlissides, J.: A Debate on Language and Tool Support for Design Patterns, PLOP'00, 2000.
10. Coad, P., North D., Mayfield, M.: Object Models – Strategies, Patterns and Application, Yourdon Press Computing Series, 1995.
11. Eden, A.H.: Precise Specification of Design Patterns and Tool Support in Their Application, PhD Thesis, Department of Computer Science, Tel Aviv University, 2000.

12. Fowler, M.: Analysis Patterns – Reusable Object Models, Addison-Wesley, 1997.
13. Front-Conte, A., Giraudin, J.P., Rieu, D., Saint-Marcel, C.: Réutilisation et patrons d'ingénierie, Chapitre de l'ouvrage Génie Objet: Analyse et Conception de l'Evolution, Editeur M. Oussalah, Hermès, 1999.
14. Gamma, E., Helm, R., Johnson, R.E., Vlissides, J.: Design patterns: Elements of Reusable Object-Oriented Software, Addison-Wesley, 1995.
15. Gruijs, D.: A Framework of Concepts for Representing Object-Oriented Design and Design Patterns, Masters Thesis, Utrecht University, CS Dept., INF-SCR-97-28, 1997.
16. Gzara, L., Rieu, D., Tollenaere, M.: Pattern Approach To Product Information Systems Engineering, Requirements Engineering Journal, Editors: Peri Loucopoulos & Colin Potts, Springer- Verlag, London, LTD., 2000.
17. Johnson, R.E.: Documenting Frameworks using Patterns, OOPSLA'92, 1992.
18. Maiden, N., Sutcliffe, A., Taylor, C., Till, D.: A set of formal problem abstractions for reuse during requirements engineering, ISI, Hermes, vol. 2, n° 6, pp. 679-698, 1994.
19. Meijler, T.D., Demeyer, S., Engel, R.: Making design patterns explicit in face, in European Software Engineering Conference (ESEC/FSE 97), 1997.
20. Rieu, D., Giraudin, J-P. : L'Objet, Numéro spécial Patrons orientés objet, Vol. 5, n° 2, Hermès, 1999.
21. Pagel, B., Winter, M.: Toward pattern-based tools, EuroPLoP'96,1996.
22. Portland: About the Portland Form, http://c2.com/ppr/about/portland.html, 1994.
23. Rolland, C., Prakash, N., Benjamen, A.: A multi-model view of process modeling, Requirements Engineering Journal, pp 169-187, 1999.
24. Welke, R.J., Kumar, K.: Method Engineering: a proposal for Situation-specific Methodology Construction, in Systems Analysis and Design: a Research Agenda, Cotterman and Senn (eds), Wiley, pp 257-268, 1992.
25. Wirfs-Brock, R., Wilkerson, B., Weiner, L.: Designing Object-Oriented Software Prentice-Hall, Englewood Cliffs, New Jersey, 1990.
26. Rieu, D., Giraudin, J.P., Conte A.: Pattern-Based Environments for Information Systems Development, International Conference, The Sciences of Design, 15-16 mars 2002, Lyon, France.

A Support System for Reuse Knowledge Components

Guilaine Talens, Isabelle Dedun, and Danielle Boulanger

MODEME-UMR CNRS 5055, IAE Université Jean Moulin Lyon 3
15, quai Claude Bernard 69007 Lyon France
Tel.: (33) 4.78.78.71.58
Fax.: (33) 4.78.78.77.50
{dedun,talens,db}@univ-lyon3.fr

Abstract. We propose an object oriented support system which suggests solutions in multi-domain problems. It exhibits two reuse levels: (i)during the knowledge acquisition phase, a framework is provided to the experts and allows reusing of other acquisitions, (ii) this framework is given to the end-users for their real cases representation. The system mixes an hybrid approach: object modeling and Case-Based Reasoning paradigm. All the components indexed by specific objects are stored in different libraries. We introduce the concept of version for object types and instances to increase reuse and to manage their evolution.

1 Introduction

We propose a support system dedicated to multi-domain problems[1]. We studied any practical experience involving an error or a fault, leading to situations which entail a damage compensation. In this context, different knowledge domains have to be represented in the same time: medical and legal. We develop an hybrid approach: object modeling and implementation associated with the Case-Based Reasoning paradigm. C.B.R. systems index and retrieve cases to propose whole or part of them as solution(s) to a new problem [1]. Our combination (C.B.R. and object) increases knowledge reuse functionalities through cases and their components and thus, offers new ways to treat C.B.R. system limits. These tools are dedicated to one knowledge domain per time. On the contrary, the proposed object case model, handles several knowledge domains. The object approach structures the cases through two composition levels. Each object component is stored in a specific library organized with object indexes. The lowest composition level references a specific object type: "domain" type. This type covers a large range of informations unknown in advance which correspond to basic knowledge. To propose similar cases to a new problem, the system computes similarities between retrieved domain objects and recompose the cases which contain these domain instances. Thus, the system provides the most similar cases through composition and referencement links defined by the object case model.

[1] Problems which require several knowledge domains for their representation.

Z. Bellahsène, D. Patel, and C. Rolland (Eds.): OOIS 2002, LNCS 2425, pp. 147-152, 2002.

As a result, an original object classification technique is proposed instead of decision trees (usually required in a lot of projects [2]) to manage the knowledge base. To perform the object evolution the version concept is added to our object model. Class versions are used by the experts to store the different phases of the case structure design. Instance versions are employed to store the user's case evolution.

Section 2 details the object case model and the functionalities offered to the different kinds of users: expert/end user. Guidelines are proposed to users. This process differs from classical C.B.R. systems which consider users as experts in the implemented symbolic structure. Section 3 reminds the classification technique of the object case components. The conclusion exhibits the original points of our proposition.

2 The Case Structure

Various approaches for case representation have been developed [3]: attribute-value lists (like records in database) or object-oriented and frame-based approaches [4]. We study the medical errors or faults which entailed damage compensations. Both medical and legal domain knowledge must be represented.

A case structure describes these situations (Figure1). A case is designed through an object modeling [5]. Two concepts composed a case type: task and sub-task types. A task object gathers knowledge of a domain (medical or legal) and structures the reliant problem through sub-task(s) object(s). A domain is represented with one or several sub-tasks which describe the different activities embedded in a task execution. Attributes of each sub-task (context, actor and result) are informed with basic information of the concerned domain. Referencement links connect these attributes to "domain" types. This specific type is not predefined in advance. This case model is a framework proposed to the experts during the knowledge acquisition phase. A prototype stores antitetanus vaccination diseases [6].

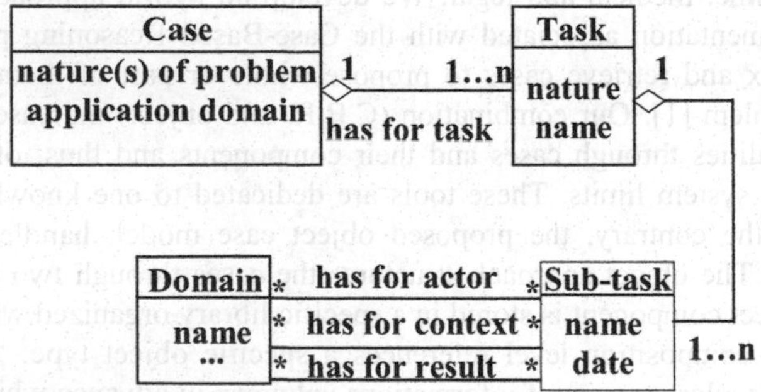

Fig.1. The Object Case Structure

Each "domain" type attribute owns its characteristics (possible values, restrictive values,…) and is implemented by an object to perform a dynamic creation. Moreover, indexation of "domain" types is based on attribute definition, so, their management must be autonomous.

Our prototype is developed with C++ language associated to the OODB POET™. "Domain" types attributes and methods are instances of predefined types which constitute the meta-level of our tool (Meta_Type, Meta_Attribute and Meta_Method).

Relying on this knowledge, the system offers two functionality levels which integrate reuse processes. At first, an expert can reuse the case components of a domain to design a new one or give an other modeling for an existing one (previously represented). The system guides the types creation composing a case with regards to available knowledge elements. In this way, types can be created from existing ones thanks to inheritance mechanism, the new type attributes and methods have to be defined. Moreover, a same attribute can be used through different types (for example, the name attribute can be applied for the doctor and patient "domain" types). Finally, a type can be used through different cases, or several times in the same case. Experts can modify case, task and sub-task types with regards to the following constraint: a type is modified if it is used only once time. Then, the system proposes the expert's framework to the end-users. The end-users perform their case instantiation. A same instance can be reused several times in the same case (for example, the doctor "domain" instance is reused in different sub-task instances (act, check-up or prescription) which compose the same or another consultation task instance). Object case components are stored in libraries to be reused. The classification functionalities are presented in the next section.

3 The Case Component Classification

We combine object design with an object storage method to avoid decision trees [8]. The case base organization associates a specific library at each type of the case object. In this way, a specific library stores respectively case, tasks and sub-tasks. On the contrary, each domain type owns its specific library. Its organization is based on expert's knowledge. Each expert chooses among existing attributes those considered as the relevant properties and specifies a weight for each of them. Then, for each relevant property, and for each value of its definition domain, the expert affects a valuation on a scale between 0 to 1. This valuation expresses the part of the value in the problem context. This process allows index creation also called R.O. (Representative Objects) of the domain type library. The property values positioned on a same point of the scale, constitute a value group. The different combinations of the relevant properties value groups compose the various ROs. Between each domain instance and the concerned index, a semantic distance is computed (Hamming distance [7]). The domain library structure is composed of areas; each area contains an RO and its linked domain instances. An area constituted of too many instances can also be structured into different sub-areas. The system creates automatically the sub-areas when the instance number threshold is obtained in an area [8]. Our indexing method is a kind of semantic VSAM-like technique. Semantic because in a VSAM (Virtual Sequential Access Method) file, index determination does not cope with distance, knowledge reuse and classification concepts.

A same "domain" type can be used in different application domains, so one sub-library per application domain is created. Finally, a "domain" library can be also decomposed in sub-libraries to store the different classifications of a same domain type (eg. the different expert's points of view). Indeed, several experts, for the same application domain, can define other relevant properties and can also change property values. The indexes are different, therefore the instance classifications are different.

4 The Object Evolution Management

We use the version concept [9] to manage the object evolution [10]. Objects are versionable and their versions constitute configurations [11]. Only static configurations are used [12, 13, 14]. During the expert knowledge acquisition process, an existing type can be reused. Added to the inheritance concept, the system allows the creation of "domain" type versions by the expert. This process consists in the adding, deletion or modification of an attribute. A modification on the type structure involves a version creation to avoid consequences on the previous modeling. A fundamental question is to know when, it is necessary to create a sub-type rather than building an object version. Only the expert can explain if it is the same or a new type. The number of created or deleted attributes can be a decision criteria. During the process, the expert is informed about the differences from the original structure until the latest versions. The same possibilities are offered for a sub-task reuse (adding, deleting or modifying "domain" types) and task modifications (deletion or modification of sub-tasks).

For example, a expert derives from the medical consultation task performed in a consulting-room, an task version (hospital consultation : see figure 2).

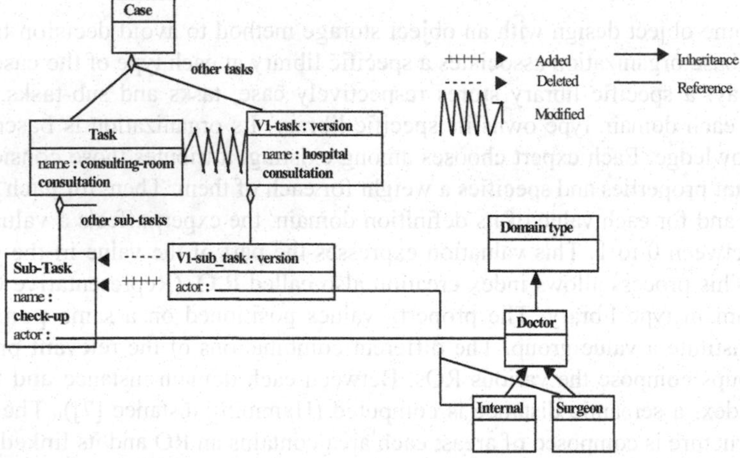

Fig.2. Class Versions

In fact, as the consulting-room consultation is validated, the modification of the check-up sub-task automatically involves the v1-task version creation. Modifications performed in the sub-task (check-up) correspond to a deletion of the doctor (actor of the sub-task) and addition of the internal and surgeon (as actors). The v1-sub-task version is derived by the system from the concerned object. The expert creates two sub-classes from the doctor type; he can also derive versions (*vi* and *vj*) from the doctor type to consider the property differences between doctor, internal and surgeon. The result is the same for the v1-sub-task version, the doctor is deleted and the *vi* and *vj* versions are added.

The consequences on the libraries organization are available during a modification of "domain" types attributes. Instances already stored are re-organized relatively to attribute modifications. The expert can compare the new classification with the existing ones.

The version concept is also implemented on the end-user side for the reuse of a same instance. If its attribute valuation changes, the version concept is applied. For example, the VA attribute value of "patient" instance is modified. The differences between the instance and versions of the "patient" are available.

At the implementation level, the version object references the domain object or the previous versions. The version object only contains attributes which have been modified. VA is a multi-valued attribute and the „ tetanus " value is added. A value modification is possible only if the attribute is mono-valuated. In the other case, it corresponds to the value deletion and the value addition. A double advantage is pointed out: an immediate visualization of the differences between objects without the management of their copies; in the classification step, a version is stored in the same library and area with the corresponding "domain" object.

The end-user chooses his application domain among the expert's cases and he instantiates the framework. The similar cases are searched and extracted. If the result is not appropriate, the end-user can modify his case and the different modifications are stored in the versions of the concerned objects. Thanks to the versions, if the result of the new search is not relevant, the user can get back the previous versions (case, task, sub-task or domain object versions) and make new modifications. He knows all the modifications executed on the objects (modification historical). Thus, he easily measures the impact on the search result.

5 Conclusion

We have proposed a support system for a multi-domain and multi-expert context. The experts are guided in the knowledge acquisition process. Relatively to the object orientation, the parts of case (task, sub-task or "domain" types) can be reused in the same or in other case types. The version concept allows modifications of a reused case component without impact on the other cases. Thus, this concept manages the design and history evolution. The expert can backtrack in the historic. The case type is given to end-user to create his real case. The case is instantiated through an interactive context and each instance is stored in the relevant libraries. The same domain instance can be reused in the case: the version can be applied to manage the instance evolution. The end-user can also create his case not to augment the case libraries (add new instances) but to retrieve similar cases. The version concept can be used to store the case modification and to measure the impact on the retrieved cases.

A perspective concerns the use of the instance evolution to automatically reorganise more precisely the library areas and to adapt the case instances to a new problem.

References

1. Leake D.: Case-Based Reasoning : Experiences, Lessons, and Future Directions. AAAI-Press, 1996.
2. Watson I.: Case-Based Reasoning : an Overview. Progress in CBR, Second United Kingdom Workshop Proceedings, (UKCBR2) April 1996.
3. Althoff K.D., Auriol E., Barletta R., Manago M.: A Review of Industrial Case-Based Reasoning Tools. AI Perspectives Report, pp 106-134, AI Intelligence Oxford United Kingdom, 173p, 1995.
4. Bergmann R.: Engineering Applications of Case-Based Reasoning. Special Issue of International Journal, Volume 12 (6), 1999.
5. OMG : OBJECT MANAGEMENT GROUP, Unified Modelling Language Specifications, Version 1.3., June 1999.
6. Talens G., Boulanger D., Dedun I., Commeau S.: A Proposal of Retrieval and Classification Method for Case Library Reuse. In the 9th IEEE Int' Conference on Software Engineering and Knowledge Engineering (SEKE'97), Madrid, June 1997.
7. Kaufmann A.: Introduction à la Théorie des Sous-Ensembles Flous. Tomes 1 et , Editions MASSON, 1975.
8. Talens G., Boulanger D., Dedun I.: Object Indexes to Implement a Case Base for Reuse in a Multi-Domain Context. In the 13th IEEE Int' Conference on Software Engineering and Knowledge Engineering (SEKE'2001), Buenos Aires, Argentina, June 2001.
9. Katz R.H.: Toward a Unified Framework for Version Modelling in Engineering Databases. In ACM Computing Surveys, Vol. 22, N°4, pp. 375-408, 1990.
10. Estublier J. Casallas R.: Three Dimensional Versioning. In Proceedings of 5th Int'l Workshop of Software Configuration Management, ACM, Software Engineering Notes, Washington, USA, 1995.
11. Moro M.M., Saggiorato S.M., Edelweiss N., Saraiva dos Santos C.: A Temporal Versions Model for Time-Evolving Systems Specifications. In The Thirteenth International Conference on Software Engineering & Knowledge Engineering (SEKE'01), Buenos Aires, Argentina, June 13-15, 2001.
12. Schmerl B.R., Marlin C.D.: Versioning and Consistency for Dynamically composed Configurations. CST, 1997.
13. Cellary W., Jomier G., Koszlajda T.: Formal Model of an Object-Oriented Database with Versioned Objects and Schema. In Proc. DEXA, Berlin, 1991.
14. Zdonik S.B.: Version Management in an Object-Oriented Database. In International Workshop, Tronheim, Ed Reidar Conrad et al., Lecture Notes in Computer Science, N°244, June 1986.

Object Oriented Design Knowledge: Ontology and Measurement of Impact

Javier Garzás[1] and Mario Piattini[2]

[1] ALTRAN SDB Senior Consultant - Projects Engineering Research Group
C/ Ramírez de Arellano, 15. 28043, Madrid - Spain
jgarzas@altransdb.com
[2] Alarcos Research Group
Escuela Superior de Informática - University of Castilla-La Mancha
Ronda de Calatrava, s/n. 13071, Ciudad Real – Spain
Mario.Piattini@uclm.es

Abstract. It has been a long time since appeared of the Object Oriented (OO) paradigm. From that moment, the designers have accumulated much knowledge in design and construction of OO systems. Patterns are the most refined OO Design Knowledge. However, there are many others kinds of knowledge than not yet classified and formalized. We distinguish and classify the following categories: principles, heuristics, patterns and refactorings. In this paper, we propose an Ontology for Object Oriented Design Knowledge and a measure of impact for patterns, two key elements to create a method based in knowledge.

1 Introduction

By the middle of the 90´s the first catalogue of patterns was published (Gamma *et al.*, 1995). The motivation of the authors of the catalogue and of the community that investigates patterns has been to transfer the Object Oriented Design Knowledge (OODK) accumulated during years of experience. However, more knowledge exists apart from that related to patterns and this other knowledge is frequently "hidden". We denominate, distinguish and classify the following categories in OODK: principles, heuristic, patterns and refactorings (Garzás and Piattini, 2001). But there is much uncertainty with the previous elements, and this have never been studied as a whole, neither them compatibility has been studied nor a method based in this knowledge exists.

For principles the main contributions are Liskov and Zilles (1974), Meyer (1988), Gamma *et al.* (1995) and Martin (1995 & 1996), but the study of design principles is limited, leading to them being used in an isolated way or even being ignored. In Garzás and Piattini (2001) a classification and definition of Object Oriented Design Principles (OODP) is shown in a more extensive way, any examples of principles are the Open-Closed Principle (OCP), Dependency Inversion Principle (DIP), Default Abstraction Principle (DAP), Don't Concrete Superclass Principle (DCSP), etc.

Z. Bellahsène, D. Patel, and C. Rolland (Eds.): OOIS 2002, LNCS 2425, pp. 153-159, 2002.

Nevertheless, the work of discovering, formalizing and classifying principles, an activity that we denominate "Principles Mining", is not still finished and it is one of our current investigation lines. With regard to heuristics the only explicit papers to which we can refer are those of Riel (1996) and Booch (1996). Refactoring techniques are characterized by their immaturity, although it is true to say that this topic is rapidly gaining acceptance, the main works in this area are Kent Beck and Fowler's (2000), Tokuda and Batory (2001) and Opdyke (1992). Patterns are, without doubt, the most refined OODK. The application of patterns in OO began in the late eighty and was consolidated by the work of (Coad, 1992), Gamma *et al.* (1994), Buschmann *et al.* (1996), Fowler (1996) and Rising (1998). However, at the present time, when patterns are used several types of problems can occur (Wendorff (2001) and Schmidt (1995)): Difficult application, Difficult learning, Temptation to recast everything as a pattern, Pattern overload, Ignorance, Deficiencies in catalogues, etc.

In this paper, we will show two necessary work lines to create a method based in OODK: we will analyze in more detail the knowledge elements, we will show an OO Design Knowledge Ontology and we will show a measure of Impact of the patterns use.

2 Object Oriented Design Knowledge Ontology

Before beginning an elaborated study, it is necessary to have a definition for each knowledge element. We consider following definitions for Heuristic and Principle (and we consider anyone of the definite in the existent literature for Patterns and Refactorings, for example, Gamma *et al.* (1995) and Tokuda and Batory, (2001)):

- Heuristic: Pertaining to the use of the general knowledge gained by experience, sometimes expressed as "using a rule-of-thumb". Argument derived from experience.
- Principle: a set of proposals or truths based on experience that form the foundation of OOD and whose purpose is to control this process. A principle is a fundamental rule or law that govern a Design in a given situation. Characteristic than desirably the design must not violate and that provide of quality to the design.

We need some way of characterizing the OODK, and we will create an OODK Ontology for it. An ontology describes domain knowledge in a generic way and provides agreed understanding of a domain. In Gruber (1991)'s words: *"I use the term ontology to mean a specification of a conceptualization. That is, an ontology is a description of the concepts and relationships that can exist"*. There are four types of Ontologies (Jurisica *et al.*, 1999): *Static Ontologies* (encompass static aspects of an application), *Dynamic Ontologies* (dynamic aspects within an application), *Intentional Ontologies* (describe the world of things agents) and *Social Ontologies* (describe social settings in terms of social relationships). According to the previous, our OODK Ontology is in the "static" category and we use the UML for expressing this Ontology. The figure 1 shows this OO Design Ontology. The OODK ontology showed on figure is semi-formal, since it is not described in a language with formal semantics, theorems and proofs of such properties as soundness and completeness.

Garzás and Piattini (2001) explicitly detail the possible relationships between principles and patterns. They define three types of relationships:

- *Type 1*, the pattern contributes a good solution to the resulting model of the application of the principle ("from the principle towards the pattern").
- *Type 2*, the pattern completes or contains the principle.
- *Type 3*, the principle can improve a solution to which a pattern has been previously applied ("from the pattern towards the principle").

Previous relations and types are detailed in the figure, in the relation between Principle and Patter entities. We may observe as the entities Principle and Pattern can be introduced in the design for Refactorings (here Refactoring Patterns would be reflected). The entities Principle and Pattern are made out of Heuristics (this are "micro good practices").

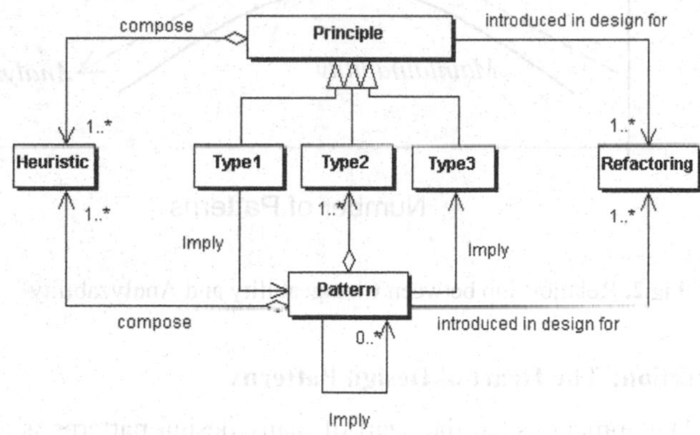

Fig.1. Ontology of Object Oriented Design Knowledge

3 Measure of Impact of the Patterns Use

According to ISO 9126 standard (ISO, 1999), maintainability is subdivided into Analyzability, Changeability, Stability, Testability and Maintainability Compliance. If we obtain a correct OO design, we will obtain a best maintenance, more cheaply and operating. Considering 9126 standard, exist two important parameters for OO Design:

- *Changeability* allows that a design may change easily, important requirement at the time of extend functionality into existing code.
- *Analyzability* allow us understand the design. This is an essential requisite to be able to modify the design in a realist period of time.

When patterns are applied to a software design two opposites forces appear which are related directly with maintainability: we have changeable solutions, but we have the inconvenience that the solution once was obtained can be very complex, and this does that the design be less analyzable. Thus appears a curious relation between Changeability and Analyzability: If we increase the design's Changeability then we will decrease the design's Analyzability, and vice versa.

The figure 2 shows graphically the relationship between Changeability and Analyzability when patterns are applied. The Breaking Point determine the "Optimal Patterns Number", where is the best maintenance in relation to Patterns.

Obviously, we have a problem: how much Changeability can we apply in order not to lose the design's Analyzability? Obtaining a metrics to answer previous question would be a great contribution.

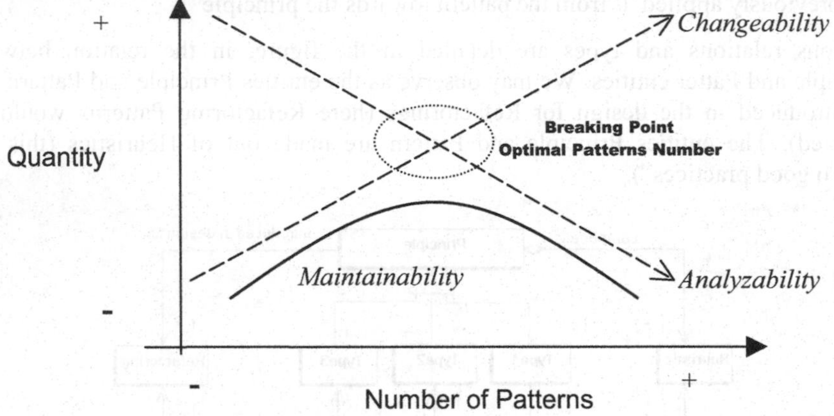

Fig.2. Relationship between Changeability and Analyzability

3.1 The Indirection: The Heart of Design Patterns

Nordberg (2001) comment as "at the heart of many design patterns is an indirection between service provider and service consumer. With objects the indirection is generally via an abstract interface". Unfortunately each level of indirection moves the software farther from the real world or analysis level view of the problem and deeper into relatively artificial mechanism classes that add overhead to both design comprehension and implementation debugging. With respect to the previous, we have observed the following:

- Every time that a pattern gets introduced, at least, an indirection into the design appear and these elements are not of the domain or business logic, such as notifies, observer classes, updates methods, etc.
- Every time that we add an indirection the software moves around further off of the analysis. To the adding indirections or design classes the design becomes less semantic, less comprehensible and less analyzable.
- And every time that an indirection is added this one increases the design changeability or flexibility.

3.2 A Metric for Optimal Patterns Number

With all the previous, we can define a parameter than quantify how of flexible or changeable a design is in relation to indirections:

$$\text{Changeability Number (CN)} = \text{Indirection Classes Number (ICN)} \quad (1)$$

A value that measure design's analyzability must consider the number of design classes introduced. These are of two groups:

- Simplify classes, reusing, such as the subject class into observer pattern.
- Indirection classes, such as the observer class into observer pattern.

Thus:

$$\text{Analyzability Number (AN)} = \text{Domain Classes Number (DCN)} - \text{Indirection Classes Number (ICN)} - \text{Simplify Classes Number (SCN)} \quad (2)$$

We may observe in the last formula, as when we have an analysis diagram its semantics is in the topmost point. When we introduced in the designing phase artifacts on the analysis diagram the model's semantics decrease. We also may observe, as certain patterns will have a larger impact in the semantics than other ones, depending on the classes that the patterns introduce. Now, we may calculate the Optimal Patterns Number (OPN) as follow:

$$\text{Changeability Number (CN)} = \text{Analyzability Number (AN)} \quad (3)$$

$$\text{Indirection Classes Number (ICN)} = [\text{Domain Classes Number (DCN)} - \text{Simplify Classes Number (SCN)}] / 2 \quad (4)$$

Considering in the previous formula that the DCN parameter is a fixed value in design phase. The rest of parameters depend of the kind of pattern or design artifact introduced.

Acknowledges

This research leaves of the DOLMEN project supported by CICYT (TIC 2000-1673-C06-06). We want to thank to ALTRAN SDB the support given to this research.

4 Conclusion and Future Projects

The experts always have used proven ideas. It is in the last years when these ideas, materialized in the pattern concept have reached their biggest popularity and diffusion. Although over recent years different areas of knowledge related to the construction of OO system such as principles, heuristics, patterns and refactoring techniques have been consolidated, but there is a lot of work still to be done in order to systematize and offer this OODK to designers in such a way that it can be easily used in practical cases. However, we still have a considerable amount of work to do.

Our final aim is to offer a detailed systematization of principles, heuristics, patterns and refactoring techniques (together with their respective interrelationships), which will facilitate their application for the designer. Empirical validation of the proposed metrics is also required.

References

1. Booch G. (1996). Managing the Object-Oriented project. Addison-Wesley
2. Buschmann F., Meunier R., Rohnert H., Sommerlad P. and Stal M. (1996). A System of Patterns: Pattern-Oriented Software Architecture, Addison-Wesley.
3. Coad P. (1992, Septiembre). Object-Oriented Patterns. *Comunications ACM,* vol. 35, n 9, pp. 152-159.
4. Fowler M. (1996). Analysis Patterns: Reusable Object Models. Addison-Wesley
5. Fowler M. (2000). Refactoring improving the design of existing code. Addison Wesley
6. Gamma E., Helm R., Johnson R. and Vlissides J. (1995). *Design patterns: Elements of Reusable Object Oriented Software.* Addison-Wesley.
7. Garzás J. and Piattini M. (2001, Agosto). Principles and Patterns in the Object Oriented Design. En Wang Y., Patel S. and Johnston R.H. (Eds.), *OOIS 2001, 7th International Conference on Object-Oriented Information Systems* (pp. 15-24). University of Calgary, Calgary, Canada: Springer.
8. Gruber, T. (1991). The Role of a Common Ontology in Achieving Sharable, Reusable Knowledge Bases. *Proceedings of the Second International Conference on Principles of Knowledge Representation and Reasoning*. Cambridge.
9. ISO (1999). ISO 9126 – Software Product Quality.
10. Jurisica I., Mylopoulos J. and Yu E. (1999, Octubre). Using Ontologies for Knowledge Management: An Information Systems Perspective Knowledge: Creation, Organization and Use. *Proceedings of the 62nd Annual Meeting of the American Society for Information Science (ASIS'99).* Washington, D.C. pp. 482-296.
11. Liskov B. H. and Zilles S. N. (1974). Programming with Abstract Data Types., *Computation Structures Group*, n 99, MIT, Project MAC, Cambridge Mass.
12. Martin R. C. Engineering Notebook. C++ Report 1996; Aug-Dec (published in four parts)
13. Martin R. C. Object Oriented Design Quality Metrics: An analysis of dependencies. ROAD 1995; Vol. 2, Nº 3
14. Meyer B. (1988). Object Oriented Software Construction. Prentice Hall.
15. Nordberg M. E. (2001, October). Aspect-Oriented Indirection – Beyond OO Design Patterns. *OOPSLA 2001, Workshop Beyond Design: Patterns (mis)used.* Bahía Tampa, Florida, EEUU.
16. Opdyke W. (1992). Refactoring OO frameworks. PhD Thesis, Department of Computer Science. University of Illinois.
17. Riel A. J. (1996). *Object-Oriented Design Heuristics*. Addison-Wesley.
18. Rising L. (1998). The Patterns Handbook: Techniques, Strategies, and Applications, Cambridge University Press.

19. Schmidt D. C. (1995, Octubre). Experience Using Design Patterns to Develop Reusable Object-Oriented Communication Software. *Communications of the ACM,* 38,10, pp 65-74.
20. Tokuda L. and Batory D. (2001). Evolving Object-Oriented Designs with Refactorings. *Kluwer Academic Publishers - Automated Software Engineering,* vol8, N°1, pp 89-120
21. Wendorff P. (2001). Assessment of Design Patterns during Software Reengineering: Lessons Learned from a Large Commercial Project., *CSMR 2001 - European Conference On Software Maintenance And Reengineering,* pp 77-84.

Generating Domain Models from Ontologies

Ludwik Kuzniarz and Miroslaw Staron

Department of Software Engineering and Computer Science
Blekinge Institute of Technology
S-372 25 Ronneby, Sweden
{lku,mst}@bth.se

Abstract. The paper presents and elaborates on the idea of automatic acquisition of knowledge about domain structure from ontologies into an object-oriented software development process. The information required to be included in the domain model produced during the development process is identified. The existence of the knowledge in ontologies is investigated. Requirements for ontology description languages are formulated followed by brief evaluation of existing languages against these requirements. A schema for domain knowledge acquisition is outlined. A realization of the schema is sketched in the paper while the implementation details can be found in the technical report.

1 Introduction and Motivation

A vision of using the existing information, and more general, knowledge by different users or agents for specific application was presented in [1]. This vision was partially realized by the introduction of Semantic Web [2, 20] where knowledge is expressed in *ontologies*. In general ontologies provide a shared and common understanding of a domain that can be communicated between people and heterogeneous and distributed application systems [13]. It is also a formal specification of a conceptualization or an abstract model for some phenomenon in the world which identifies relevant concepts of the phenomenon [14,18]. Software development process is an activity where producing an abstract model for a phenomenon in the real world called domain model is also an important issue. The domain model is constructed at a very early stage of the development process and usually is done manually from scratch based on the investigation in the problem domain [4]. But the required knowledge may already and in many cases does exist and is stored as an ontology. So the question is if this knowledge can be automatically acquired to the development process. Formally such acquisition should be a transformation from an ontology specification language to a language used to expressed artefacts produced throughout the development process. This paper elaborates on the general idea of automatic acquisition of the knowledge from ontologies into software development. The information used in domain models is identified, and it is shown that the information can be acquired from ontology. Requirements for ontology description language are imposed to make it possible to

Z. Bellahsène, D. Patel, and C. Rolland (Eds.): OOIS 2002, LNCS 2425, pp. 160-166, 2002.

extract the structural knowledge about the domain from the ontology describing the domain. The most widely used languages for describing ontologies are proved that they fulfill the requirements. Based on that the schema of domain knowledge acquisition process is outlined and its practical realization is sketched. The process is a general description of a concrete knowledge acquisition method from ontologies expressed in DAML+OIL into domain model expressed in Unified Modeling Language [22] presented in [11].

The paper contains a short description of domain models and ontologies, which is followed by a description of knowledge acquisition process. Based on this an automatic knowledge acquisition process from DAML+OIL encoded ontologies into UML domain model is sketched. The paper ends with a short evaluation of a proposed knowledge acquisition process.

2 Domain Models

Domain model is an artefact produced at the early stage of software development process and illustrates meaningful (to the modelers) conceptual classes in a problem domain. According to [16,17] the domain model is a set of class diagrams that show:

- domain objects or conceptual classes,
- associations between conceptual classes,
- attributes of conceptual classes,

Although there are more elements that can be expressed by languages used for domain model, the elements above are crucial for object-oriented analysis. They form a knowledge about the domain, and helt the modelers to understand the problem area. One of the most widely used language for object oriented modelling is the Unified Modeling Language (UML). It has a rich set of elements used for modeling software, but only few of them are actually used for domain models. The useful elements are classes, their attributes, associations between them, and inheritance. A sample domain model expressed in UML for a part of reality describing relationships between such concepts as Person, Man and Woman is presented on figure 4. The key rationale behind domain models is that they are a kind of visual dictionaries of *abstractions*. They depict abstractions of conceptual classes. Despite the description of phenomenons like man and woman is very rich, only some concepts are of interest from the given domain perspective. The domain model displays a partial view, or abstraction and ignores uninteresting (to the modelers) details. Usually identification of the meaningful abstractions is performed manually by the analyst, who identifies the concepts and relationships among them. However, the concepts may already be described, they may already be a part of a knowledge that is used in different areas. One of such areas is the Semantic Web, where knowledge is expressed by means of ontologies.

3 Ontologies

The term Ontology comes from philosophy, where it was used to characterize a science about the nature of things, what types of things exist and what are the relationships among them. It was adopted for computer science where it describes the concepts of some phenomenon that exists in real world and how it is connected to other phenomenons [10]. Ontologies are widely used for describing resources that exist on the Web, and for adding some semantics to these resources. They are a knowledge about the domains, which can also be used by mobile agents, which need information not only about the knowledge they encounter, but also about its structure.

There are several languages used to describe ontologies. Some of them are based on first order logic and provide a programming language-like syntax (like Knowledge Interchange Format [18]). Other are dedicated for use with ontologies, like Ontology Interchange Language (OIL) [9] or dedicated for use with agents, like DARPA Agent Markup Language (DAML) [7]. The latter two are similar in the design and concept, and as they are designed to serve for the describing ontologies, the unifying activity has been performed and a joint specification has been introduced for ontology description language. The language is called DAML+OIL [21]. It is a markup language based on XML. It is build on top of resource Description Framework (RDF) and its schema (RDFS) [19]. DAML+OIL contains elements and mechanisms which allow to express not only the knowledge, but also its structure in the same document. The structure of the knowledge is described by a set of classes, attributes and relationships between classes. Knowledge that belongs to the described domain consists of objects that have concrete values of the attributes and are connected to other concrete objects. DAML+OIL is the emerging standard for ontology description language. It is used not only by research communities across academia, but also industry. It can express the concepts identifies in paragraph 2, for instance, a sample class defined in DAML+OIL can be expressed by the following set of tags (from [21]):

```
<daml:Class rdf:ID="Man">
          <rdfs:label>Man</rdfs:label>
          <rdfs:SubclassOf rdfs:Resource="#Person">
</daml:Class>
```

A sample ontology describing the same domain as in paragraph 2 expressed in DAML+OIL is visually presented on figure 2. Elements required for domain models are identified in paragraph 2. Based on that, there are some requirements that need to be imposed on language used to describe ontologies. If the requirements are fulfilled, then the domain knowledge can be acquired from the ontology. The requirements that the language must allow to:

- express classes - concepts significant for the domain,
- express attributes of classes - properties of the concepts,
- express relationships between classes - both is-kind-of relationships and associations between concepts,

Languages presented in this paper fulfill the above requirements. DAML+OIL is the emerging standard for the ontology description language, thus it is used as a base for the practical realization of the domain acquisition process described in [11]

4 Domain Knowledge Acquisition Process

Acquisition of knowledge is a translation from ontology description language to language used for domain modelling. Figure 1 outlines the process. Because there is more knowledge in ontologies than is needed in domain models, some of the knowledge must be filtered out. It is possible to acquire the knowledge directly from ontology (depicted by a dashed line), but it is advisable to introduce additional, intermediate step. It is a filtration of elements of ontologies identified in paragraphs 2 and 3. The result of this step is an ontology, which contains only these meaningful concepts, which are transformed into language used for domain modelling. The filtration skips out the elements of ontology which are not meaningful from domain modeling perspective. If the ontology description language could express only the concepts required (identified in paragraph 2), then the ontology of meaningful concepts and the original ontology would be identical. But since ontology description languages can express more than its required, then the ontology presented on gray background on figure 1 is a subset of the original ontology. The transition from the ontology to domain modelling language is a translation between the languages. In case of DAML+OIL as ontology

description language and UML as language for domain modelling, the translation is a transformation. Since UML can be represented by an intermediate language Extensible Metadata Interchange (XMI) [23], which is a dialect of XML, the transformation can be performed automatically with use of technologies dedicated for XML transformations. The details of the transformation and filtration processes are described in [11].

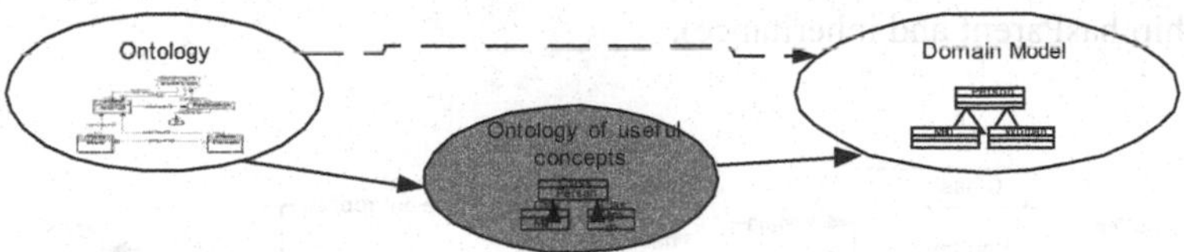

Fig.1. Knoweldge acquisition process schema

5 Automatization of the Process

It is desirable that the acquisition process is automated. The automated process and technology used for it depends on the language used for ontologies and the language used for domain modeling. If the languages are respectively DAML+OIL and UML, then the process can be performed with use of Extensible Stylesheet Language for Transformations - XSLT [12]. The reason for using XSLT is that UML can be represented with use of XMI. Therefore, the process of acquiring the knowledge is a filtration and a subsequent translation, both performed by XSLT. The filtration is an XSLT transformation from DAML+OIL encoded ontology into DAML+OIL encoded ontology with only meaningful concepts. The translation is an XSLT transformation, which changes the representation of the same concepts from DAML+OIL encoded ontology to XMI encoded UML domain model. The details of both the filtration and the transformation are described in [11]. As DAML+OIL is built on top of RDF and RDFS, the translation is described only for those elements that are expressed with use of DAML+OIL. The relationship and mapping between RDFS constructs and UML are presented in [4].

To illustrate how the acquisition process can be performed in practice, a small example is presented,. It shows how the knowledge about a domain is introduced into domain model. DAML+OIL is used to describe the ontology of the domain, and UML is used to express domain model. An ontology describing the domain is presented on figure 2.

The knowledge contains such concepts as Person, Man and Woman. It also describes a relationship hasParent, between two instances of class Person and shows that class Man is a subclass of class Person (is-kind-of relationship). The ontology also contains information that is not required from the domain model perspective, which is the information that each instance of class Person is either a man or a woman (disjointUnionOf relationship on figure 2). Since DAML+OIL encoded ontology contains some additional information about the domain than is required, the filtration produces a new ontology, which contains only the meaningful information from domain modeling perspective. The filtered ontology is presented on figure 3. In this example the resulting ontology does not contain the information that each person is either a man or a woman. It is a semantic information, which is not relevant for domain modeling. The next step is a transformation which changes the representation from DAML+OIL to UML. The domain model, which is the result of the acquisition process is presented on figure 4. It contains all classes that were in the original ontology (Person, Man and Woman), and some relationships between them (the relationship hasParent and inheritance).

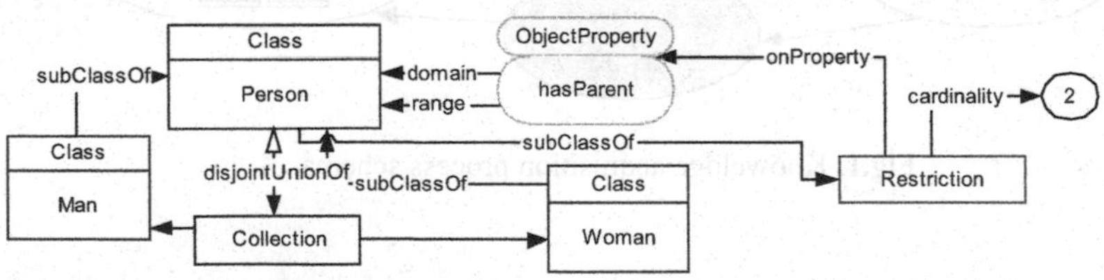

Fig.2. Domain knowledge expressed as DAML+OIL encoded ontology

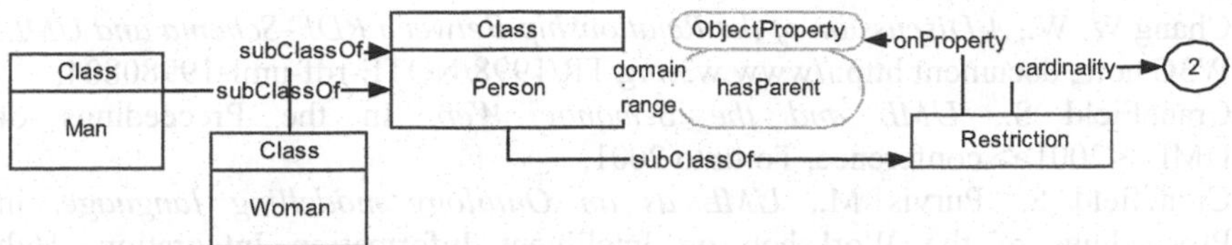

Fig.3. DAML+OIL encoded filtered ontology

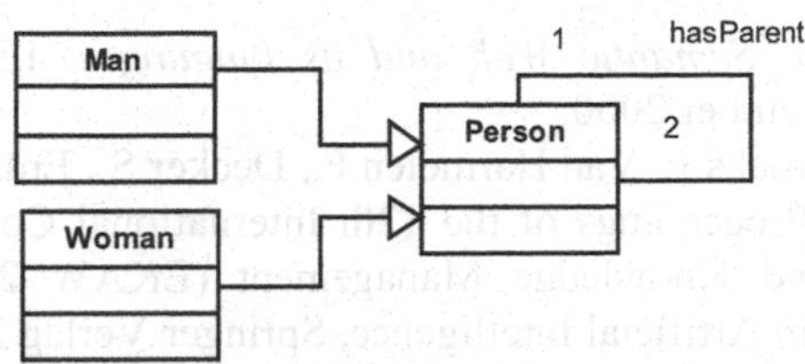

Fig.4. Domain knowledge expressed as UML domain model

6 Conclusion

The paper deals with a general problem of knowledge sharing and reuse. It presents and elaborates on the process of automatic acquisition of domain knowledge from ontologies into domain models used in software development process. The elements that are required for domain models were identified, and from this perspective requirements for ontology description languages were imposed. Some of the available languages were investigated. It was also shown that some of the most commonly used languages for describing ontologies fulfill the requirements. A general method of acquiring the knowledge from ontologies into software development process was described. The practical acquisition process for DAML+OIL as ontology description language and UML as object-oriented modelling language was outlined. The details and practical realization of the method for these languages can be found in [11]. An important feature of the acquisition process is that it ensures consistency of the obtained domain model with the existing knowledge.

As it is possible to use the UML as ontology description language [5,6], the idea is not used in this paper. The main feature of the acquisition process presented in this paper is that is provides a mean to reuse the existing domain knowledge, thus incorporating it into newly build software.

References

1. Barners-Lee T., Hendler J., Lasilla O., *The Semantic Web,* Scientific American, May 2001,
2. Barners-Lee T., *Semantic Web Road map,* WWW Consortium September 1998, http://www.w3c.org/DesignIssues/Semantic.html,
3. Booch G., Unified Software Development Process, Addison-Wesley, 1998,

4. Chang W. W., *A Discussion of the Relationship Between RDF-Schema and UML*, W3C note, document http://www.w3.org/TR/1998/NOTE-rdf-uml-19980804,
5. CraneField S., *UML and the Semantic Web,* In the Preceedings of UML<<2001>> conference, Toronto 2001,
6. Cranefield S., Purvis M., *UML as an Ontology modelling language,* in Proceedings of the Workshop on Intelligent Information Integration, 16th International Joint Conference on Artificial Intelligence (IJCAI-99), 1999,
7. DAML language specification, http://www.daml.org/2000/10/daml-ont.html, 2000,
8. Fenzel D., *The Semantic Web and its languages,* IEEE Inteligent Systems, November/December 2000,
9. Fensel D., Horrocks I., Van Harmelen F., Decker S., Erdmann M., Klein M., *OIL in a nutshell,* Proceedings of the 12th International Conference on Knowledge Engineering and Knowledge Management (EKAW 2000), volume 1937 of Lecture Notes in Artificial Intelligence, Springer Verlag 2000,
10. Gruber T. R., A Translation approach to portable ontology specification, Knowledge acquision 5(2), October 2000,
11. Hellman E., Kuzniarz L., Staron M., *Translation from DAML+OIL encoded Ontologies to UML domain models,* Internal technical report, Blekinge Institute of Technology,
12. Kay M., XSLT, Programmer's reference, Wrox press, 2000,
13. Klein M., Fensel D., Van Harmelen F., Horrocks I., *The Relation between Ontologies and Schema-languages: Translating OIL-specifications in XML-Schema,*Proceedings of the Workshop on Applications of Ontologies and Problem-solving Methods, 14th European Conference on Artificial Intelligence ECAI-00, Berlin, Germany August 20-25, 2000,
14. Klein M., Broekstra J., Decker S., Fensel D., Harmelen F., Horrocks I., *Enabling knowledge representation on the Web by extending RDF Schema,* http://www.ontoknowledge.org/
15. Klempe A., Warmer J., Object Constraint Language: Precise modeling with UML, Addison-Wesley, 1999,
16. Kruchten P. The Rational Unified Process, An Introduction, Addison-Wesley, 2000,
17. Larman C., Applying UML and Patterns, An introduction to Object-Oriented Analisys and design and The Unified Process 2nd edition, Prentice Hall, 2001,
18. National Comitee for Information Technology standards, Technical Comitee T2 (Information Interchange and Interpretation), http://logic.stanford.edu/kif/dpans.html, 1998,
19. *Resource Description Framework (RDF) Model and Syntax Specification,* WWW Consortium, 1999, http://www.w3c.org/TR/1999/REC-rdf-syntax-19990222,
20. Schwartz A., *The Semanic Web In Breadth*, http://logicerror.com semanticWeb-long,
21. *Annotated DAML+OIL (March 2001) Ontology Markup,* http://www.daml.org/2001/03/daml+oil-walkthru.html,
22. *UML Specification version 1.4,* OMG 2001, www.omg.org,
23. XMI Specification version 1.1, OMG 2000, www.omg.org

A Framework to Review Complex Experimental Knowledge

Michel Sala, Pierre Pompidor, and Danièle Hérin

LIRMM – Univ. Montpellier II / CNRS, [2]LASER – Univ. Montpellier I
161, rue Ada 34 392 - Montpellier cedex 5 – France
{sala,pompidor,dh}@lirmm.fr

Abstract. The aim of our work is to provide researchers in experimental sciences means to review their knowledge in a given domain, while confronting it to experimentation data or to calculation tool results. To set up this environment and a methodology, we described the researcher's knowledge as an oriented object framework and we make use of a format of exchange facilitating the comparison of the results generated by the different tools. Besides, our tool is able to provide researchers the useful information which is extracted from the domain databases. In this article, we present the architecture of our approach and its components. Finally, we will illustrate our framework by an acquisition/revision cycle argued by an example in immunogenetics.

Keywords: modeling of knowledge, exchange of data, aid to the discovery, explanation.

1 Introduction

Currently the researcher in the field of experimental sciences has a knowledge of his domain. For all experimentation wether achieved in his laboratory or contained in the databases of the available domain on the web, he must check that theses experimentations match with his knowledge of the domain. The researcher is confronted to a mass of experimentation data coming from his laboratory or his international colleagues that he must retrieve, select, process and analyse. Currently, the big data banks on the genome double every eighteen months and this phenomenon tends to accelerate. Besides, the researcher must use some computer calculation tools to process these data, tools that he sometimes manipulates without initial training, without knowledge of the underlying heurisms or of the parameters used.

A researcher in experimental sciences gets some representation of his domain that can be represented using object oriented modeling and by a global ontology. For all experimentation data, the researcher compares it with his representation of the domain. If there is a problem, he must assess the experimentation data in relation to the different world data contained in the databases and if necessary, he must be able to review his knowledge.

Z. Bellahsène, D. Patel, and C. Rolland (Eds.): OOIS 2002, LNCS 2425, pp. 167-172, 2002.

To be able to implement this reviewing, the researcher is confronted to problems of data homogenization. Indeed, the information contained in the databases available on the web have different formats. Besides, the modeling of the global ontology of the domain rests on structural knowledge on the data as well as on treatments on this same data in relation to other data. This representation leads us therefore to conceptualize this modeling while using the object formalism that is going to permit to represent the attributes, the operations and the links on these data (generalization, association and aggregation). In this article, we are going to present the different modules necessary to the architecture of our environment in the first place. We will present our methodology and the framework that we propose. Then, we will then conclude and present our future work.

2 Environment Architecture

2.1 Experimentation Data

We consider that the experimentation data is the information collected after all experiments. This basic information must be modelised while taking into account an object oriented formalism.

To this experimentation data, we associate a global ontology that represents the semantics of this data. Concerning the previous work on the construction of the ontologies, we can note that there exist two types : those based on logical approaches Classic [1], KIF [2], Cyc [3] and those based on the object-oriented representation of knowledge OIL [4]). After having worked using the language of Classic description [5], we decided to use the XML representation to describe the ontologies. In fact, nowadays, XML (eXtensible Markup Language) is the standard format for exchange and representation of data. We use a schema that enables us to define a common vocabulary to represent the semantics of the global ontology and the local ontologies.

This description permits to describe the semantics of the domain and to exchange these descriptions under a standard format over the web. Our parser captures the semantics in the educational resources and the XML format allows us to exchange these structures of data. Precisely, we direct ourselves towards an ontology based on XML like XOL [6]. XOL is an XML-based ontology-exchange language. Although XOL was designed for exchange of bioinformatics ontologies, it can be used for ontologies in any domain.

2.2 Calculation Tools

Calculation tools permit to get a calculation result from experimentation data. Depending on the publisher of the software, it uses the different heuristics and different formats. Besides, this software can run in local on the researcher's station or on a web site. The problem is to use a format of exchange between the different sites and the researcher's environment to be able to retrieve the calculation results. XML is very appropriate since it is now the standard of data exchange on the web and it makes easy to parse data. Besides it while permitting to visualize, publish and maintain then with tools of standard word processors. Finally, its use is natural insofar as an important industrial community develops it so that it is at the basis of the next generation of application linked to internet.

2.3 The Researcher's Knowledge Basis

The knowledge of the researcher's domain is described by constraints on the experimentation data and constraints on the calculation tools results. All these constraints are represented in the object oriented diagram of the experimentation data as operations.

2.3.1 Constraints on the Experimentation Data

The constraints on the experimentation data concern the structure of the data, that i.e.:

domain constraints : taking into account the constraints on the format of the data and the values of the attributes, and inter-attribute constraints and/or on an attribute : that can be represented by the methods.

Example: The biologist's knowledge on a sequence of immunoglobulin is described by the existence of two key amino acids (named points of anchorage), Cytosine (noted C) and Tryptophane (noted W). These two amino acids are functional and determine the physical structure of the immunoglobulin (cf. fig1).

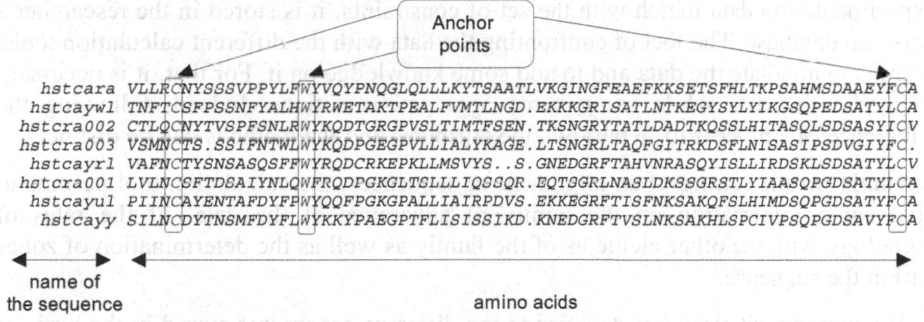

Fig.1. Representation of an alignment with three points of anchorage

2.3.2 The Constraints on the Tool Results

The constraints on the tool results are represented by methods, which, from experimentation data, enable to send back a normalized result that uses a format of exchange described previously.

2.3.3 The Databases of the Domain

If, during the analysis of experimentation data, a violation of a constraint occurs, the researcher wishes to know the different information that are contained in the international databases of the domain being connected to this experimentation data. For that, we must represent the databases of the domain in the same formalism as the experimentation data.

As well as for the results of the calculation tools, the chosen exchange format is XML. Many tools of conversion exist such as gb2xml [7] (conversion of Genbank toward XML), or as Boulder [8]. In fact, the Boulder data interchange format is an easily parseable hierarchical tag/value format suitable for applications that need to pipe the output of one program into the input of another. It was originally developed for use in the human genome project at the Whitehead Institute/MIT Center for Genome Research, but has since found use in many other areas including system administration and Web software development.

3 The Methodology

The proposed environment makes interact a base of knowledge representing the researcher's knowledge, the calculation tool and the databases storing the knowledge of the other biologists. This work follows a collaboration with the L.I.G.M. (Laboratoire d'ImmunoGénétique Moléculaire de Montpellier) , on the alignment of protein sequences of immunoglobulins and gave birth to the SIGALE system [9].

3.1 The Adopted Principle

The process set up is incremental. The goal of this methodology is to confront all new experimentation data with the base of knowledge. In the case where the experimentation data match with the set of constraints, it is stored in the researcher's personal database. The fact of confronting the data with the different calculation tools, permits to annotate the data and to add some knowledge on it. For that, it is necessary to model the data while using some aggregation notions. Indeed, following the adherence of a process to "a part of", the attributes and the methods can be distinct.

Example: In the setting of an alignment of sequences, the calculation tool permits to give some information on the family of adherence of the data, of the rates of homology with the other elements of the family as well as the determination of zones within the sequence.

If a experimentation data satisfies to the different constraints stored in the basis of knowledge, there is not any problem and it can be stored directly without human intervention. On the other hand, in the case where one or several constraints are violated, an explanation is provided to the researcher who decides either to rejet the data (for example mistake of manipulation), or to initiate a process of revision. This explanation comes from the methods contained in the structure of the experimentation data. The explanation provided by the environment comes from the analysis of the researcher's needs in experimental sciences. More precisely, the terms and the semantics chosen used come from the researcher himself or from the knowledge of the domain.

Example: We have a new SVH data that violates a constraint on the experimentation data and on the calculation tool resultss. We get a set of explanations:

- explanations on the data:

- access number : SVH, species : shar, the sequence of the amino acids: *VVLTQPEAETAKPGGSLTLTCKTSGFTLSSYYMYLVRQVPGQGLEWLLTYHASSSTKYFAPGIESRF* *TPSTDNSNNIFTVIARNLKIEDTAVYYCARDQGGADYPLDYWGGGTMLTVTN*

-explanations on the constraint of the knowledge basis on the experimentation data:

"The anchorage point W (in a distance of 10 to 17 amino acids in relation to the anchorage point C) is absent."

-explanations on the calculation of the constraint on the experimentation data, i.e. on the alignment of the SVH sequence with the previous set :

```
SVH
LTCKTSGFTLSSYYMYLVRQVPGQGLEWLLTYHASSSTKYFAPGIESRFTPSTDNSNNIFTVIARNLKIEDTAVYYCA
  tcara
LRCNYSSSVPPYLFWY..VQYPNQGLQLLLKYTSAATL....VKGINGFEAEFKKSETSFHLTKPSAHMSDAAEYFCA
  tcayl
FTCSFPSSNFYALHWY..RWETAKTPEALFVMTLNGD.....EKKKGRISATLNTKEGYSYLYIKGSQPEDSATYLCA
  tcaul
INCAYENTAFDYFPWY..QQFPGKGPALLIAIRPDVS.....EKKEGRFTISFNKSAKQFSLHIMDSQPGDSATYFCA
  tcayy
LNCDYTNSMFDYFLWY..KKYPAEGPTFLISISSIKD.....KNEDGRFTVSLNKSAKHLSPCIVPSQPGDSAVYFCA
              ⇧<------12------> ⇧<-------------------------------62-------------------------------> ⇧
```

-explanations on the constraint of the knowledge basis on the results of the tools :

"Overtaking of the number of authorized subfamilies, four instead of three."

-explanations on the results of every calculation tool

Visualization of the set of the calculation tools results (different trees or dendrograms)

3.2 The Phase of Revision

The proposed methodology allows the researcher to focus only on the experimentation data that raise a problem in relation to his mental model. The incremental process allows the researcher to get for every "problem" data a set of explanations in his specific vocabulary. While using these explanations, it is able to determine if the non consistency with a constraint comes from a flagrant mistake or a deeper problem. In that case, he has the possibility to ask for further information on the databases of the domain. As a standard exchange format has been created between all the databases of the domain, it is possible to make some requests and to process the results.

Example : explanations on Kaba's [10] database, that provides the set of the immunoglobulin sequences of the species given. The sequences found are the following :

RE20, HXIA, RE10, RE12 et RE11.

To assess the result better, the researcher aligns the sequences found in Kabat with the SVH sequence :

```
  RE20
TCVTSGFSLSSSNVHWVKQVPGKGLEWVAIMWYDD...DKDYAPAFSGRFTVSRDS.SNVYLQ.MTNLSLADTATYYCAA
  HXIA
TCKTSGFSLGSYYMTWVRQVPGQGLEWLV..SYHSS.SYQYYAPEIKDRFTASKDTSNNIFALDMKSLKTGDTAMYYCAR
  RE10
TCKVSGFALSSYAMHLVRQAPGQGLEWLL..RYFSS.SNKQFAPGIESRFTPSTDHSTNIFTVIARNLKIGDTAVYYCAR
  SVH
TCKTSGFTLSSYYMYLVRQVPGQGLEWLL..TYHASSSTKYFAPGIESRFTPSTDNSNNIFTVIARNLKIEDTAVYYCAR
  RE12
TCKTSGFTLSSYYMYLIRQVPGQGLEWLL..AYHAP.TTVYFAPGIESRFTPSTDNSNNIFTVIARNLKIEDTAVYYCAR
             ⇧<--------------- ⇧-----------------------------------------------------------------------------------> ⇧
```

From this information (if it exists), the researcher can make the decision to review his model. As he knows the constraints that have been violated, he can ask for a modification of them or of others, corresponding to his mental model. Following the degree of generalization, this modification can be achieved on the method of a super-class, a class or a subclass.

4 Conclusion and Future Work

Our generic environment has been tested experimentally with the SIGALE system dedicated to immuno-genetics. Our system permitted to make advances in this domain such as the setting up of annotations in the immunoglobulin superfamily. We proved that in the domain of the experimental sciences it was possible, to put a system of explanations in place. It helps the researcher in his phase of aid towards the discovery to review his knowledge on the domain. This model was based on a representation of knowledge with the help of production rules. Our new environment uses the object formalism, the use of standard exchange formats and the aspects of web semantic.

Our perspective is to experiment our environment on a more important data set to clear some inconsistencies on the researcher's hypotheses rather than to define other shapes of knowledge representation. Indeed, in the domain of immunogenetics and more generally in the domain of genetics, the majority of the present hypotheses should be reviewed. The researcher is confronted to a bigger and bigger flow of experimentation data and with the world sequencing programs, this phenomenon is going to accelerate.

Soon, we wish to create a data warehouse that will allow the researcher to have access to aggregated numerous data (in our example of the notions of families, of point of anchorage…), to tools of data mining and why not to a visualization of MOLAP type.

References

1. A. Borgida, R. Brachman, D. McGuiness, L. Resnick : Classic, a structural data model for objets, in procedings of ACM SIGMOD, 1989
2. M. Genesereth, R. Fikes : Knowledge Interchange Format, version 3.0 reference manual, technical report Logic-92-1, Computer Science Departement, Stanford University, Palo Alto, California, 1992
3. www.cyc.com
4. D. Fensel, I. Horrocks, F. van Harmelen, D. McGuinness, P. F. Patel-Schneider : OIL An Ontology Infrastructure for Semantic Web In IEEE Intelligent Systems, Vol 16, N° 2, 2001
5. M.-S. Segret, P. Pompidor, D. Herin, M. Sala : Use of ontologies to integrate some information semi-structured exits of pages web, INFORSID'2000, Lyon pp 37-55
6. P.D. Karp, K.V. Chaudhri, J. Thomere : XOL: An XML-Based Ontology Exchange Language Technical Note 559, AI Center, SRI Internationnal,1999
7. gb2xml ftp://ftp.pasteur.fr/pub/GenSoft/unix/db_soft/gb2xml
8. Boulder : http://stein.cshl.org/software/boulder/
9. M. Sala "Environnement pour le transfert de connaissances d'Agents Artificiel vers un agent humain - Application à la classification automatique de séquences protéiques" III ème Rencontres des Jeunes Chercheurs en I.A., Luminy, 1994
10. E.A. Kabat, T.T Wu, H.M. Perry, K.S. Gottesman, C. Foeller Sequences of proteins of immunological interest - Public Health Service National Institutes of Health - US Departement of Health and Human Services, 1991

A Framework to Translate UML Class Generalization into Java Code*

Pedro Sánchez[1], Patricio Letelier[2], Juan A. Pastor[1], and Juan A. Ortega[3]

[1]Universidad Politécnica de Cartagena, Spain
{pedro.sanchez,juanangel.pastor}@upct.es
[2]Universidad Politécnica de Valencia. Spain
letelier@dsic.upv.es
[3]Universidad de Sevilla. Spain
ortega@lsi.us.es

Abstract. The concept of generalization used during analysis when building a class diagram has a close relationship with the notion of inheritance included in object-oriented programming languages. However, from the point of view of programming, inheritance is a useful mechanism but not especially conceived to implement the generalization specified in analysis. Thus, generalization should be treated suitably in order to obtain sounded design and code from analysis specifications. In addition, it is known that it does not exist concensus about the interpretation and use of inheritance and each programming language provides its particular vision. Hence, when moving from analysis to design and/or implementation (and normally without using a formal approach) the generalization relationships are prone to misinterpretation. OASIS is a formal approach to specify object-oriented conceptual models. In OASIS generalization is included as a language construct that allows specifying generalization patterns with precise semantic and sintaxis. Although OASIS is a textual formal language, the main aspects of one OASIS specification can be mapped and represented using the UML notation, in particular generalization relationships among classes. In this paper we present OASIS generalization patterns and we show how they can be implemented in Java. We also propose other ways to carry out this implementation.

1 Introduction

Generalization is a specification mechanism that allows introducing taxonomic information in the model of a system. Generalization improves the reusability and extensibility of specifications. Class generalization establishes an ordering between classes, *parent classes* and *child classes*. Child classes inherit structure and behavior

* This work has been supported by CICYT (Project DOLMEN-SIGLO) TIC2000-1673-C06-01.

Z. Bellahsène, D. Patel, and C. Rolland (Eds.): OOIS 2002, LNCS 2425, pp. 173-185, 2002.

from parent classes. In UML[1] [1], as in other previous modeling notations, class generalization[2] has been roughly defined, mainly because there is no wide consensus about its interpretation and usage [2]. The inheritance mechanism behind the generalization relationship has two points of view: it is a modelling tool and it is a code reuse tool, these visions are usually at odds [3]. Due to the lack of precise semantics for generalization at the conceptual level, usually when building analysis models[3] it is implicitly assumed the interpretation of the target object-oriented language which normally it is not the most suitable perspective. In these circumstances the analyst can specify generalization relationships at implementation level which is obviously a contradiction respect to the level of abstraction of analysis. Usually, the solution is to leave generalization relationships loosely defined, which has the risk of possible misinterpretation in design and implementation. In addition, when using semi-formal methods and notations the transition from models to its sounded implementations is even more difficult.

As far as generalization is concerned, UML establishes that "the more specific element is fully consistent with the more general element (it has all its properties, members, and relationships) and may contain additional information". Wegner proposed four levels of compatibility between the child class and the parent class, in a descending order of compatibility they are [4]: behavior compatibility, signature compatibility (the same signature for the same operations), name compatibility (the same names for the same operations) and cancelation (some parent class operations are not available in the child class). At the implementation stage, inheritance between classes (the implementation of generalization) means adding, redefining or canceling the inherited features and associations in the child class. This wide definition has different interpretations in distinct programming languages. Thus, in general, it depends on the programmer to maintain the correspondences between the implementation of the child class and its corresponding parent class.

OASIS (Open and Active Specification of Information Systems) [5] is a formal approach to conceptual modeling following the object-oriented paradigm. Generalization in OASIS is included as a language constructor which allows specifying the different aspects characterizing a generalization relationship between classes. Thus several common patterns of generalization can be directly represented with OASIS. Although OASIS is a textual language, most parts of a specification can be represented using UML, in particular generalization relationships. The aim of this paper is to show how to use the OASIS generalization as the intended semantic for class generalization in UML models. Thus analysis specifications with generalization

[1] In this work we have used the UML specification version 1.4.

[2] Previously to UML this term was commonly referred as class specialization. Both generalization and specialization are abstraction mechanism, used to establish inheritance relationships between classes. The nuance between generalization and specialization is whether, taking the parent classes we establish the child classes (specialization), or taking the child classes we establish the parent class (generalization). But in the end, the result is the same: there will exist inheritance from the parent class to the child class.

[3] We have preferred using "analysis" to "conceptual modeling" (and "analysis model" to "conceptual model") to follow the UML terminology.

can have a seamless and sounded translation to design and implementation. To illustrate the implementation aspects we will use Java.

The organization of this article is as follows. After this introduction section, we briefly introduce the OASIS formal framework for generalization. Next, we give a description of the equivalences between the UML generalization and the Java programming language. Then, we comment some related works and finally, we present the conclusions and future work.

2 Generalization in OASIS

Through generalization a new class specification can be partially defined establishing a relationship with others already defined classes. The new class can summarize or extend the previous classes. The generalization incorporated in OASIS is based on the work by Wieringa et Al. [6]. In a generalization relationship one class play the role of *parent class* and the others are *child classes*. A child class inherits the features defined in the parent class. A child class can be at the same time parent class, and in this form, a hierarchy of classes is created (it is a directed acyclic graph). The features that are common to all child classes are specified in the parent class, and the specific child class features are defined in the corresponding child classes. In OASIS we distinguish three orthogonal kinds of generalizations: *static classification*, *dynamic classification* and *role group*.

Each of these kinds of generalization with its associated characteristics represents a different conceptual modeling pattern of generalization, offered directly as OASIS constructs. With this expressiveness the modeling task can focus on specifying the problem rather than on its solution in a specific programming language. At the same time these patterns of generalization impose a disciplined usage of inheritance [7], constraining its utilization only to specify relevant aspects at the level of analysis.

Although different aspects of OASIS are normally presented using several convenient and more expressive formalisms, Dynamic Logic constitutes the basic and uniform formal support. In this article we present the generalization in OASIS using set theory and process algebra. However, we have established the corresponding mappings to Dynamic Logic [8].

In this paper we will focus only on static and dynamic classifications due to the fact that these are the only kinds of generalization defined in UML. Role groups are a more specific kind of generalization useful when a inheritance relationship is necessary but the object in the child class is a role of the object in the parent class (the player), they are thus different objects. Though not so directly, role groups can be modeled using association relationships.

2.1 Classification Hierarchies

A classification hierarchy establishes an inheritance relationship among one parent class and child classes whose populations are subsets of the parent class instances. For each class C, two aspects can be distinguish:

- The class **intention**, int(C), is the set formed by all the class features and associations. It represents the class type.
- Given any instant t, the class **extension** (population), $ext_t(C)$, is the set of instances of the class in that instant.

Let C_1 and C_2 be two classes, if $ext_t(C_1) \subseteq ext_t(C_2)\ \forall t$, then C_1 is child class of a classification of C_2. When this occurs, a inverse inclusion relationship between the intensions of C_1 and C_2, that is, $int(C_2) \subseteq int(C_1)$.

A classification hierarchy divides[4] the population of the parent class in **disjoint** subsets. That is, let $C_1,\ldots, C_n$ be child classes of the parent class C_0. Then

$$ext_t(C_0) = \cup\ ext_t(C_i)\ .$$
$$ext_t(C_i) \cap ext_t(C_j) = \varnothing,\ i \neq j \neq 0\ . \tag{1}$$

Demanding that each classification hierarchy be complete and disjoint solves several ambiguities and contradictions. Let us consider the example where the class `student` is child class of `person`. A person object can be or not a student object in one instant of its existence. The operation `become_student` should occur in the life of a `person` object and not in the life of a `student` object[5], but class `student` inherits this operation, thus this is contradictory. This problem is solved by having complete classifications, for example in this case specifying the child class `not_student` and instead of putting the operation `become_student` in the class `person`, put it in the class `not_student`.

In a classification hierarchy each object is an instance of the parent class and at the same time of one (and only one) of the child classes, that is, it is the same object (the same Oid). This dictates the following semantic:

- There must exist behavior compatibility between the child class and the parent class, that is, the Substitution Principle [9] must be accomplished. Thus, every object instance of the child class could be used as an object instance in the context of the parent class.
- When the object in the parent class is destroyed, this also means its destruction in the child class, and vice versa too.

2.2 Static Classification

In a static classification the object instances of the child classes are associated to them during their whole lives. That is, suppose t_1 and t_2 any two instants, C_i and C_j ($i \neq j$) child classes of a static classification. Then:

$$ext_{t1}(C_i) \cap ext_{t2}(C_j) = \varnothing\ . \tag{2}$$

Fig. 1 shows two static classifications of the class vehicle. The discriminators "by fuel" and "by purpose" allow us to distinguish two different hierarchies with the same parent class.

---

[4] Although this does not mean that in UML we are obliged to specify all the child classes. The constraint *incomplete* can be attached to the classification hierarchy indicating that there is an implicit child class "others".

[5] Except if we want to specify an OASIS role group hierarchy which does not exist in UML.

2.3 Dynamic Classification

In a dynamic classification hierarchy the instances of one child class can migrate to another child class in the hierarchy. Thus the intersection presented in formula 2 can be different from the empty set. There are at least two ways of specifying the migratory process: on the one hand based on the occurrence of certain actions, on the second hand based on the state of the object (the values of its attributes).

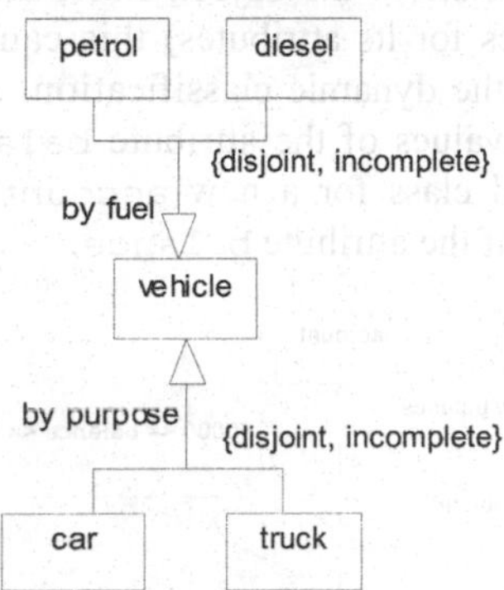

Fig. 1. Two static classifications of `vehicle`

An important difference between static classification and dynamic classification is that in the later the extension of one of its child classes can change without changing the extension of the parent class. It is not allowed specifying a static classification by taking as a parent class a class that is child class in a dynamic classification. This constraint eliminates unnecessary complexity in the model, without decreasing the expressiveness of the language.

Dynamic Classification based on event occurrence. In this case the migratory process is defined by means of a process specification[6]. The operations involved in the process specification belong to the child class where the migration step takes place. The agent constants (or states in a state diagram) are the names of the child classes. By default, the starting state receive the name of the parent class and the new event establishes the first transition to the suitable child class. A dynamic classification of `car` determined according the occurrence of events `new_car`, `be_repaired` and `break_down` is shown in Fig. 2.

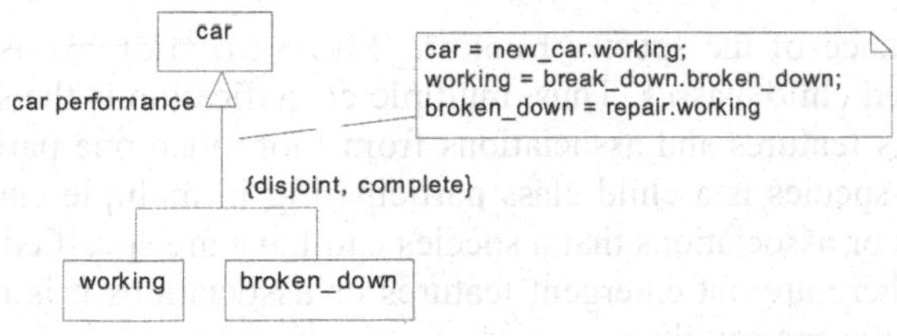

Fig. 2. A dynamic classification of `car` based on action occurrence

[6] In OASIS we use a simple process algebra. It would be a state diagram in UML.

The creation of one instance of `car` class implies that its life starts belonging to the child class `working`. While it belongs to the class `working` it can be affected by events of the parent class `car` or child class `working`, for example, the event `break_down`. If this event occurs, then the instance migrates from the child class `working` to the child class `broken_down`.

Dynamic Classification based on the state of the object. In this case the migratory process is determined by the state of the object. Each time that the object reaches a new state (a new set of values for its attributes) this can involve its migration from one child class to another in the dynamic classification. A dynamic classification of class `account` based on the values of the attribute `balance` is shown in Fig. 3. In this example, the initial child class for a new `account` object will be established according to the initial value of the attribute `balance`.

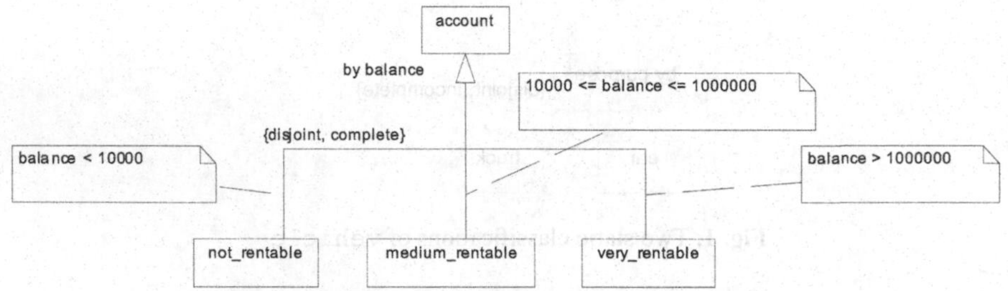

Fig. 3. A dynamic classification of `account` based on the state of the object

2.4 Species and Multiple Classification

A species is basically a class whose type is obtained combining the types of the child classes in the lower levels of a hierarchy of classes, taking each child class from a different classification. Each species involves the notion of multiple inheritance of the features and associations belonging to each child class selected. Species cannot be child class of any parent class what is normally allowed in UML and programming languages. Thus, this concept of species involves a disciplined use of multiple classification which has methodological advantages due to the fact that the model is clearer and prevents mistakes [6]. In example, the class (species) `truck*diesel` can have as an emergent property the attribute representing the date of the latest revision. Thus we specify this class in the same way as a non-species class, defining the emergent attribute.

An object instance of the species `broken_down*car*petrol` is an instance of each of the selected child classes. Thus, multiple classification is the situation when a child class inherits features and associations from more than one parent class. In the OASIS context a species is a child class participating in multiple classification. The emergent features or associations that a species can have are specified in a usual class specification. If there are not emergent features or associations it is not necessary to explicitly specify the species class.

3 Java Implementation

Regarding the implementation in Java language, the class generalization framework of OASIS demands four features that are not offered directly or imposed in Jav

1. There must be supported dynamic classification.
2. It might be more than one static or dynamic classifications (distinct classification hierarchies) with the same parent class.
3. Every classification must have at least two child classes.
4. Method implementation in child classes must accomplish behavior compatibility with the method implementation in the parent class.

Instead of giving a general implementation pattern we have developed implementation solutions for representative situations and it should be easy to extrapolate to other more specific cases. We will call *simple* the situation in which for the same parent class exists only one classification (static or dynamic), otherwise we will call it *complex* (where multiple inheritance by means of *species*).

3.1 Static Classification (Simple)

Let us consider the next dynamic classification where class C is the parent class[7]:

```
C1, C2 static specialization of C;
C11, C12 static specialization of C1;
```

In static classifications objects are created at the lowest class in the hierarchy (leaf classes). In the example these classes are C11, C12 and C2. The Java implementation would be:

```
public abstract class C {…}
public abstract class C1 extends C {…}
public class C2 extends C {…}
public class C11 extends C1 {…}
public class C12 extends C2 {…}
```

The classes C and C1 are labeled abstract. Thus, it is not possible to create objects directly on them. The following object creations are allowed:

```
C11 objC11 = new C11(…);
C12 objC12 = new C12(…);
C2 objC2 = new C2(…);
```

3.2 Dynamic Classification (Simple)

Regarding dynamic classification, Barbara Liskov suggests in [9] a Java implementation using the "state pattern" of Gamma et Al. This proposal separates the type being implemented from the type used to implement it. Although this

---

[7] In the next examples we will use OASIS syntax although, as it has been showed in previous examples, there exist a direct correspondence with generalization in UML class diagrams.

implementation pattern provides a better modularity it only takes into account the trivial situation: one dynamic classification partition but no other classifications of the parent class at the same time. In this situation a more general solution is needed which can be extended to allow implementing all cases. Let us consider the next dynamic classification of the C class:

```
C1 where {atr < 10},
C2 where {atr >= 10} dynamic specialization of C;
```

For each child class belonging to the dynamic classification an inner class is written:

```
public class C
 {int atr;
 // subclass instances
 C1 c1; C2 c2;
 Public C (int v)
   {setAtr(v);}
 public void setAtr(int v)
   {atr=v; setDyn();}
 // migration engine
 private void setDyn()
   {if (atr<10)
    {c1=new C1(…); c2= null;
    else {c2=new C2(…);
    c1=null;}
   }
// C1 perspective
public C.C1 asC1()
  {if (c1!=null) return c1;
   else throw new
   NullPointerException();}
// C2 perspective
public C.C2 asC2()
  {if (c2!=null) return c2;
   else throw new
   NullPointerException();}}
private class C1
  {… //C1 is an inner class}
private class C2
  {// C2 is an inner class}
}
```

The child classes `C1` and `C2` have full visibility of `C` features or associations. The method `setDyn()` implements the corresponding child object creation. The methods `asC1()` and `asC2()` of `C` return the respective objects of the defined inner classes. This is necessary when we need to refer to emergent features or associations of child classes. An exception is triggered if the object does not belong to the child class and a request is made for child class features or associations. This exception is a `NullPointerException` what needs to be caught in the client object. The object creation of `C` instances follows the usual Java syntaxis: `C myObj = new C(...)`. The child classes features and associations of `myObj` object are available in `myObj.asC1()` and `myObj.asC2()`. Another implementation alternative is to specify child classes out of the parent class, solving features and association visibility by means of the *delegation* mechanism. The drawback in this case is the bidirectional communication needed: (1) child classes need to see inherited features and associations; and (2) the parent class needs to maintain references to the objects which are in the child classes, and any feature or association demanded at the parent class needs to be routed. We have chosen the inner class alternative because one way of communication is easily solved.

3.3 Static Classification (Complex)

When there are more than one static classification from the same parent class the situation is more complex because it is potentially possible to create an object in any case given by the possible species. An important matter is to know which is the most frequent child class in where the objects should be created. Because the event "new" must be specified with concrete information (available at the lowest level) we have discarded the object creation at the parent class. It is impossible to design a good architecture which facilitates the object creation from any species. For this reason we have decided to choose one classification and we will refer to it as the *primary classification*. The idea is to implement an inheritance schema which involves the primary classification and which makes use of the *extends* Java language mechanism. For example, let us consider the following static classifications:

```
B1, B2 static specialization of C;
C1, C2 static specialization of C;
```

Where B1 and B2 are child classes of the primary classification. A first approximation in Java language would be the next one:

```
public abstract class C {...}
public class B1 extends C {...}
public class B2 extends C {...}
```

Then, the creation of objects is made as before at the leaf classes:

```
B1 objB1 = new B1{…};              B2 objB2 = new B2{…}
```

The next step is to complete the description of the class C including those child classes of non-primary classifications. The class C implementation adds the rest of child classes as inner classes:

```
public abstract class C
{public class C1 {…}
 public class C2 {…}…}
```

The object creation begins as `B1 objB1 = new B1(…);`. Once an object has been created then we need to specialize it in each of the non-primary classifications. In our example we would write `C.c1 objB1xC1 = objB1.new C1(…);`. That is, the object objB1xC1 represents the specialization perspective in that non-primary classification and all the new or overwritten requested features or associations need to be routed to it. The programmer has the responsibility of assuring the atomicity of these two creations.

3.4 Dynamic Partitions (Complex)

Now let us see the situation in which there is more than one dynamic classification from the same parent class. In the next example, we have two dynamic classifications with the class C as parent class:

```
C1 where {atr<10},
C2 where {atr>=10} dynamic specialization of C;
D1,D2 dynamic specialization of C migration relation is
C = new().D1;   D1 = m2().D2; D2 = m3().D1 + m4().D1();
```

In this example, when the object has just been created it begins as a D1 instance. When m2() occurs then the object migrates to the child class D2. Afterwards, occurrences of m3() or m4() produce the migration to the child class D1. When using

UML a state chart diagram need to be used to represent the migration relatioship. The simplified Java code for this case is:

```
public class C
 {
 int atr;
  C1 c1; C2 c2;
  D1 d1; D2 d2;
  public C (int v)
   {atr=v; setDyn();
    d1 = new D1(…);}
  public void m2()
   {d2 = new D2(…);
    d1 = null;}
 public void m3()
   {d1=new D1(…);d2=null;}
```

```
public void m4()
    {d1=new D1(…);d2=null;}
private void setDyn(){…}
public void setAtr(int v){…}
private class C1 {…}
private class C2 {…}
private class D1 {…}
private class D2 {…}
public C.C1 asC1() {…}
public C.C2 asC2() {…}
public C.D1 asD1() {…}
public C.D2 asD2() {…}
}
```

The implementation is similar to the simple situation, that is, in the dynamic classification child classes are implemented as inner classes of the parent class. The parent class implements the migration process.

4 Other Implementations

In this section we describe two other possible implementations using interfaces and design patterns. Choosing interfaces, in order to establish the semantics we could use Java Modeling Language (JML). JML [10] is a behavioral interface specification language that can be used to specify the behavior of Java modules. It combines the approaches of Eiffel and Larch, with some elements of the refinement calculus. Eiffel and Larch are well known, and the refinement calculus is a formalization of the stepwise refinement method of program construction. The required behavior of the program is specified as an abstract, possibly non-executable, program which is then refined by a series of correctness-preserving transformations into an efficient, executable program. JML allows including constraints when the interface is specified. However, when a class implements such an interface its contract forces it only to accomplish with the syntaxis, because the constraints imposed by JML are exclusively syntaxis constraints. Another approach would be using the Role Object [11] design pattern. This design pattern adapts an object to the different needs of the clients through transparently attached role objects, each one representing a role that the object has to play in that context of the client. The object manages its role set dynamically. By representing roles as individual objects, different contexts are kept separate and system configuration is simplified. Generalization from the point of view of this design pattern is based on the fact that the definition of a class changes according to the semantic demands on it. Therefore, this pattern is appropriated because in the generalization it is necessary to handle the available roles dynamically, thus they can be attached and removed on demand, that is, at run-time rather than statically at design-time.

5 Related Work

Although generalization is a key concept in the object-oriented approach, the UML specification only dedicates a few pages to its definition, leaving many aspects open to interpretation. Few works has been reported in order to give a more precise semantic for UML class generalization and we have not found references of works translating UML class generalization of analysis models into implementation. Some details are given in [12] and [13] about what a static and a dynamic classifications should be. However, many books and CASE tools claim that they establish or include code generation from UML models, and particularly considering class generalization. Unfortunately, after having a look at what they offer we usually find out that they consider only a simplified version of static classification, Furthermore, they do not distinguish more than one classification having the same parent class. Maybe the work by Gamma et Al. [14], and especially their state pattern is the more popular approach when there is some concern about translating dynamic classification into inheritance in a programming language. However, firstly, the state pattern is a design pattern, that is, useful in the design level (when an abstraction of the implementation must be established) and it is not comparable to the more abstract dynamic classification patterns offered in OASIS (they are patterns at the analysis level). Secondly, the state pattern does not establish the treatment of several orthogonal classifications with the same parent class, or other considerations like migration by means of events.

6 Conclusions

When considering only one static classification with the same parent class there would be no problems in translating UML class generalization into an object oriented programming code. However, classifications can also be dynamic and several classifications can have the same parent class. In addition, the translation encloses a number of considerations and decisions regarding the semantic associated to the classifications. This semantic is left open enough in UML, what makes necessary to take some more precise framework. In this work we have used OASIS generalization as an intended semantic for UML class generalization. When inheritance is seen only from an implementation perspective then those theoretical and conceptual features (such as behavior compatibility) are ignored and others are more relevant, such as reuse of coding, performance, etc. Most programmers see inheritance as a mechanism of incremental modification which allows programs to be extended or refined without changing the original code. The discussed implementation patterns in Java use *inner* classes and the *extend* mechanism. Before choosing the pattern for static classification we put the constructor method at the parent class level. Then we have looked for a way in which any object could be created (from the parent perspective) but we have not found an alternative solution due to the possible existence of several classifications from the same parent class. When we offer dynamic classification we increment the expressiveness although the structural clarity is reduced because it is not easy (neither formal) to deduce child class properties from the parent class. The class generalization cases analyzed in this paper are not all the possible situations. Nevertheless, the solutions provided should be easy enough to extend to more specific modeling scenarios. Although OASIS is a formal language used to specify analysis models, from its origins there has been interest in using it as a support for industrial environments for software development. Thus, around OASIS three aspects have always been present : software development process, tool support, and automatic code generation from models oriented to model validation or to obtain final code[8].

References

1. Object Managment Group. OMG Unified Modeling Language Specification (v. 1.4), 2001
2. Taivalsaari A. *On the Notion of Inheritance*. ACM Comp. Surv., Vol. 28(3) (1996) 438-478
3. Al-Ahamad W. and Steegmans E. *Integrating Extension and Specialization Inheritance*. Journal of Object-Oriented Programming, December (2001)
4. Wegner P. and Zdonik S. *Inheritance as an Incremental Modification Mechanism or What Like Is and Isn't Like*. In Proc. of the 7th. European Conference on Object Oriented Programming, LNCS 322, ECOOP'88 (1988) 55-77
5. Letelier P., Ramos I., Sánchez P. and Pastor O. *OASIS 3.0: A Formal Approach for the Object Oriented Conceptual Modeling*. Technical University of Valencia, ISBN 84-7721-663-0, Spain, http://www.dsic.upv.es/users/oom/books.html. (in Spanish) (1998)
6. Wieringa R., Jonge W. and Spruit P. *Using Dynamic Classes and Role Classes to Model Object Migration*. Theory and Practice of Object Systems, Vol. 1(1) (1995) 61-83
7. Letelier P., Sánchez P., Troyano J. and Crespo Y., *Specialization in Conceptual Modeling: A rigurous use of Inheritance*. Actas del 3er Workshop Iberoamericano de Ingeniería de Requisitos y Ambientes Software (IDEAS), Cancún, Méjico (in Spanish) (2000)
8. Sánchez P., Letelier P. and Ramos I. *Animating Formal Specifications with Inheritance in a DL-Framework*. Requirements Eng. Journal, Vol.4, Springer-Verlag (2000) 198-209
9. Liskov B., Guttag J. Program Development in Java: Abstraction, Specification and Object-Oriented Design. Addison-Wesley (2001)
10. Leavens G., Rustan K., Leino M., Poll E., Ruby C. and Jacobs B. *JML: notations and tools supporting detailed design in Java*. In OOPSLA '00 Companion, Minneapolis, Minnesota, Copyright ACM (2000) 105-106
11. Bäumer D., Riehle D., Siberski W. and Wulf M. *Role Object*. In Pattern Languages of Program Design 4. Edited by Neil Harrison, et Al. Addison-Wesley, Chapter 2 (2000) 15-32
12. Martin J. and Odell J. *Object-Oriented Methods: A Foundation*. Prentice Hall (1998)

[8] Information about these lines of works at www.dsic.upv.es/users/oom.

13. Fowler M. and Kendall S. UML Distilled: Applying the Standard Object Modeling Language. Addison-Wesley (1997)
14. Gamma E., Helm R., Johnson R. and Vlissides J. *Design Patterns: Elements of Reusable Object-Oriented Software*. Professional Computing Series. Addison-Wesley, MA (1994)

UML Aspect Specification Using Role Models

Geri Georg[1] and Robert France[2]

[1]Agilent Laboratories, Agilent Technologies
Fort Collins, USA
geri_georg@agilent.com
[2]Department of Computer Science, Colorado State University
Fort Collins, USA
france@cs.colostate.edu

Abstract. We demonstrate a flexible technique for aspect specification using the UML. The technique uses Role Models to specify design aspects. Roles allow greater flexibility in an aspect over other template-based techniques (e.g. profile extensions). While Role Models do allow us to create templates, they also allow us to create flexible specifications that can be applied by identifying existing model elements that can play aspect roles either as is, or with augmentation based on the aspect specification. This additional capability means that our aspect designs can be applied to specific system designs with fewer constraints on the designer and the initial system models.
We demonstrate this flexibility by applying a design aspect developed for one problem domain to a problem in a different domain. No changes are needed in the aspect models, although not all portions of the aspect specification are used in the second problem. In addition, there is no need to constrain the problem in the new application of the aspect; the specification technique is flexible enough that we can apply the aspect without change. We are also able to use the same set of weaving rules to compose the aspect with models of the new problem.

1 Introduction

Many authors are extending the ideas of aspect-oriented programming (AOP; e.g. [2, 3, 11, 11, 12, 15, 19] to the architecture and design of complex systems, creating new applications of separation of concerns and aspect-oriented design (AOD; e.g. [1, 9, 13, 16-18]). Some AOD researchers use the Unified Modeling Language (UML; [14]) to specify aspects as well as the models resulting from weaving aspects and other system models (e.g. [4, 5, 8, 10, 20]). Aspect specifications can be viewed as template models, and they are generally woven by using regular expression to match existing model elements and aspect elements. Many aspect compositions essentially result in wrapping additional functionality around an existing model. The proper model factoring must already exist to apply the aspect, so it is conceivable that effort

Z. Bellahsène, D. Patel, and C. Rolland (Eds.): OOIS 2002, LNCS 2425, pp. 186-191, 2002.

must be applied to re-factor existing models to correctly compose them with aspect models.

Our approach uses Role Models to specify design-level aspects using the UML. Roles are property-oriented specifications, and for a model element to play a particular role it must exhibit the specified properties (e.g. attributes, operation signatures, operation behaviors, and association multiplicities). (See [6, 7] for a complete description of Role Models.) We use UML static diagrams as well as behavioral diagrams to describe aspects. We use the Object Constraint Language (OCL; [14, 21]) to express constraints. We develop weaving rules that allow us to identify model elements in existing system models that can play the required roles in an aspect. The weaving rules also allow us to use aspect roles as either templates (in which case they are added to existing system models), or as extensions that need to be added to existing model elements so that these elements can play the aspect roles. As we discuss in a previous paper [8], our role specifications are based on a more precise and rigorous approach than other AOD methods (e.g. [4, 20]).

The ability to act as a template, or to extend existing model elements, means that our aspects are flexible and therefore fewer constraints need to be placed on their use than if they were strictly templates. We demonstrate this flexibility by applying an example of our aspects (a replicated repositories fault tolerance mechanism developed for a simple order entry system) to a different problem domain (a road traffic pricing system). Section 2 of this paper introduces the fault tolerant aspect. Section 3 demonstrates applying the aspect to a portion of the road traffic pricing system. We conclude in Section 4 with plans for continued work in this area.

2 Fault Tolerance Aspect – Replicated Repositories

We use Static Role Models (SRMs) and Interaction Role Models (IRMs) to specify replicated repositories. SRMs characterize the static structure of our aspect. IRMs characterize interaction diagrams such as collaboration diagrams. This paper only discusses the SRM model of replicated repositories. (We develop and use replicated repository IRMs in [8].) Figure 1 shows the SRM specification of the replicated repository aspect we developed for an Order Entry System (see [8]). In the next section we will see that the form of the aspect facilitates reuse in another application domains.

An SRM consists of roles, and each role has a base type. The base must be either a classifier type (e.g. Class or Interface) or a relationship type (e.g. Association or Generalization). The base indicates the type of UML construct that can play the role. The SRM in Figure 1 consists of two types of roles: class roles (roles with base *Class*) and association roles (roles with base *Association*). The class roles are connected via association roles. Since the role RepositoryCollection shown in Figure 1 has a base Class, only UML class constructs can play this role. The behavioral roles specified in RepositoryCollection determine the additional behavioral properties that must be present in any UML class that plays this role.

A role can consist of two types of properties, metamodel-level constraints and feature roles. Feature roles are further defined as either structural roles (e.g.properties that can be played by class attributes) or behavioral role (e.g. properties that can be played by methods). Feature roles are only associated with classifier roles in our aspect work. While RepositoryCollection does have behavioral roles, neither it nor any of the other classifier roles in Figure 1 have structural roles.

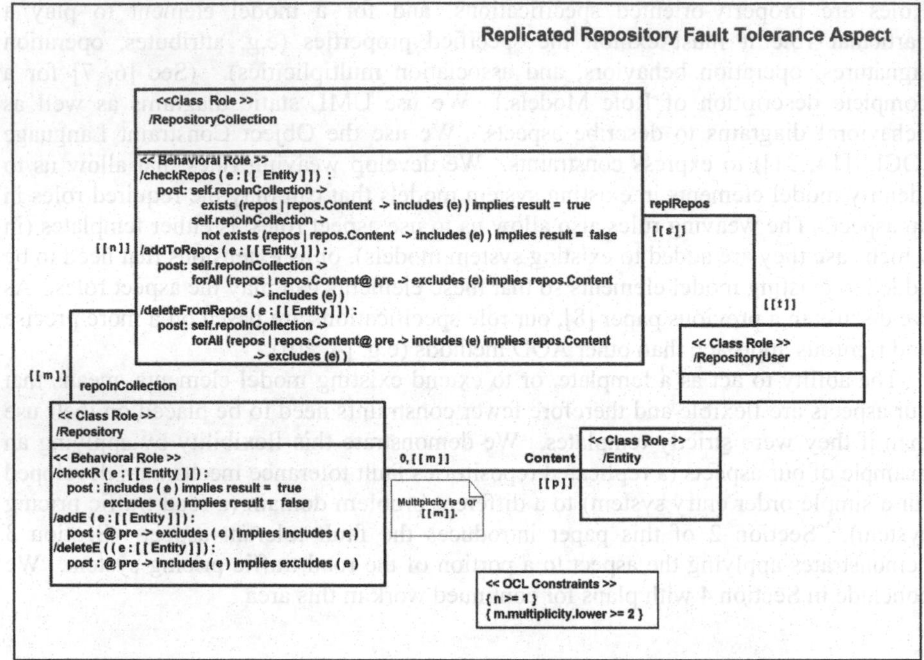

Fig. 1. Static role model specification of a replicated repository aspect

The association roles shown in Figure 1 are templates; conforming associations can be created by substituting a set of ranges for *m*, *n*, *p*, *s*, and *t* that satisfy the OCL constraints shown in the *OCL Constraints* box.

As in our previous paper (see [8]), a model element conforms to a role if it satisfies the metamodel-level constraint and if the constraints associated with its features imply the constraints that would be obtained by instantiating the role as a template. We use a stereotype notation (e.g. <<RepositoryCollection>>) in a woven model to indicate that the model element realizes that role. Stereotypes used in this manner can result in UML model elements with more than one stereotype.

Figure 1 shows four class roles in the replicated repository fault tolerant aspect. RepositoryUser represents the role played by the user of a repository. This user can interact with a replicated repository (an object of a class that plays the RepositoryCollection role) in order to access individual repositories (an object of a class that plays the Repository role) . A replicated repository consists of two or more individual repositories. These repositories contain some replicated content, or entities. Since repositories are replicated, entities are related to more than one repository. Methods that access the repositories in the non-fault tolerant version of the design must be changed (during the weaving process) to access the repository collection in the fault tolerant version. Method post conditions are shown in OCL.

There are three access methods, one to check for the existence of an entity in the repositories, one to add an entity to the repositories, and one to delete an entity from the repositories. The first method returns either true or false, depending on whether there is a repository that contains the entity. The second method adds the entity to each repository in the collection, and the third method removes the entity from all repositories in the collection.

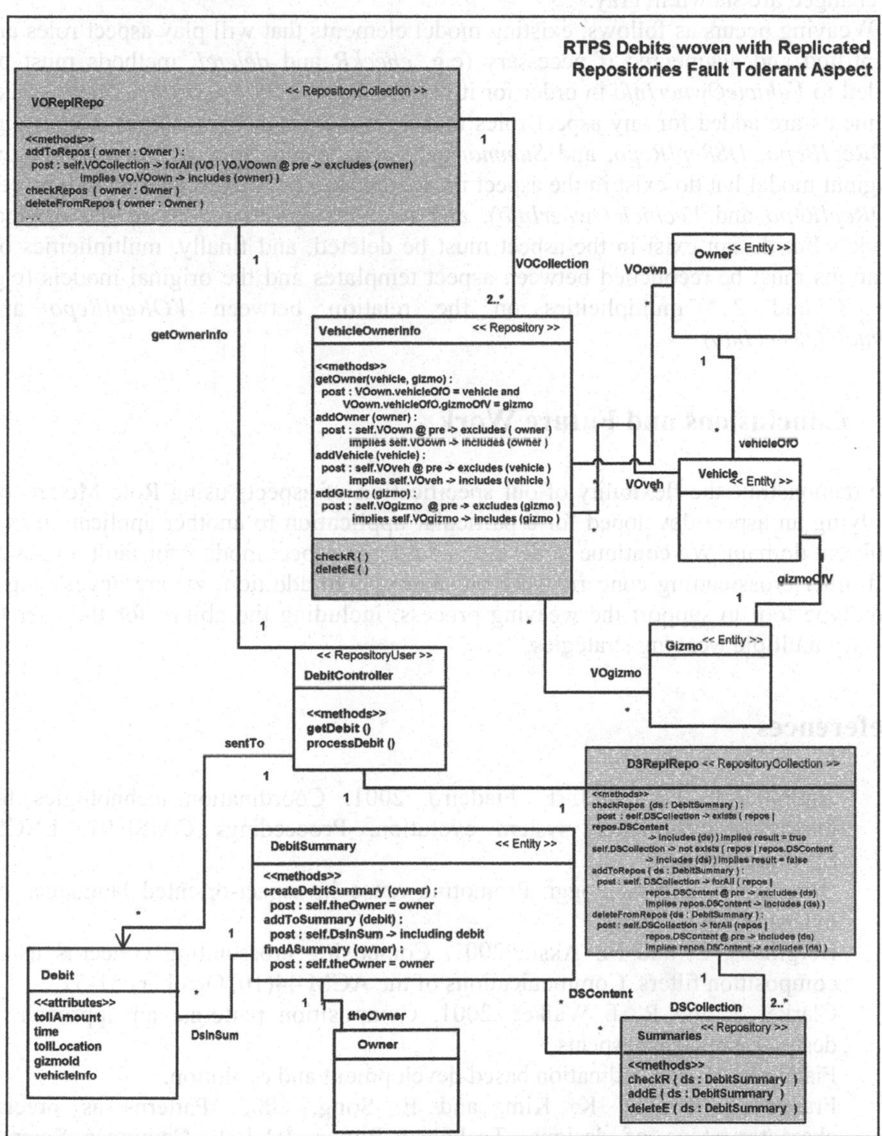

Fig. 2. Road Traffic Pricing System static diagram with replicated repositories

3 Adding the Fault Tolerant Aspect to a Road Traffic Pricing System

Figure 2 shows changes that are made when weaving Replicated Repositories into the core functionality of a portion of a road traffic pricing system. Classes that are added or changed are shown in gray.

Weaving occurs as follows: existing model elements that will play aspect roles are identified and augmented if necessary (e.g. *checkR* and *deleteE* methods must be added to *VehicleOwnerInfo* in order for it to play the role of *Repository*), new model elements are added for any aspect roles that do not exist in the original model (e.g. *VOReplRepo*, *DSReplRepo*, and *Summaries*), relationships that do not exist in the original model but do exist in the aspect must be added (e.g. the relationship between *VOReplRepo* and *VechicleOwnerInfo*), and relationships that exist in the original models but do not exist in the aspect must be deleted, and finally, multiplicities on relations must be reconciled between aspect templates and the original models (e.g. the *1* and *2..** multiplicities on the relation between *VOReplRepo* and *VehicleOwnerInfo*).

4 Conclusions and Future Work

We demonstrate the flexibility of our specification of aspects using Role Models by applying an aspect developed for a particular application to another application in a different domain. We continue to develop additional aspect models for fault tolerance and other cross-cutting concerns such as security. In addition, we are developing a prototype tool to support the weaving process, including the ability for the user to specify multiple weaving strategies.

References

1. Andrade, L. F. and J. L. Fiadeiro. 2001. Coordination technologies for managing information system evolution. Proceedings CAISE'01. LNCS, Springer-Verlag.
2. Bergenti, F. and A. Poggi. Promoting reuse in aspect-oriented languages by means of aspect views.
3. Bergmans, L. and M. Aksit. 2001. Composing crosscutting concerns using composition filters. Communications of the ACM 44(10, October):51-57.
4. Clarke, S. and R. J. Walker. 2001. Composition patterns: an approach to designing reusable aspects.
5. Fiadeiro, J. L. Co-ordination based development and evolution.
6. France, R. B., D. K. Kim, and E. Song. 2002. Patterns as precise characterizatons of designs. Technical Report 02-101, Computer Science Department, Colorado State University.
7. France, R., D. K. Kim, E. Song, and S. Ghosh. 2001. Using roles to characterize model families. Proceedings of the Tenth OOPSLA Workshop on Behavioral Semantics: Back to the Basics.

8. France, R. and G. Georg. 2002. Modeling fault tolerant concerns using aspects. submitted to ISSRE 2002.
9. Gray, J., T. Bapty, S. Neema, and J. Tuck. 2001. handling crosscutting constraints in domain-specific modeling. Communications of the ACM 44(10, October):87-93.
10. Jurjens, J. 2001. Towards development of secure systems using UMLsec. 4th International Conference on Fundamental Approaches to Software Engineering (FASE 2001):187-200.
11. Kiczales, G., E. Hilsdale, J. Hugunin, M. Kersten, J. Palm, and W. G. Griswold. 2001. Getting started with AspectJ. Communications of the ACM 44(10, October):59-65.
12. Lieberherr, K., D. Orleans, and J. Ovlinger. 2001. Aspect-oriented programming with adaptive methods. Communications of the ACM 44(10, October):39-41.
13. Netinant, P., T. Elrad, and M. E. Fayad. 2001. A layered apporach to building open aspect-oriented systems. Communications of the ACM 44(10, October):83-85.
14. Object Management Group. 2001. Unified Modeling Language V. 1.4. http://www.omg.org, September.
15. Ossher, H. and p. Tarr. 2001. Using multidimensional separation of concerns to (re)shape evolving software. Communications of the ACM 44(10, October):43-50.
16. Pace, J. A. D. and M. R. Campo. 2001. Analyzing the role of aspects in software design. Communications of the ACM 44(10, October).
17. Silva, A. R. Separation and composition of overlapping and interacting concerns.
18. Silva, A. R. 1999. Separation and composition of overlapping and interacting concerns. In OOPSLA '99, Multi-Dimensional Separation of Concerns in Object-Oriented Systems. http://www.esw.inesc.pt/dasco/.
19. Sullivan, G. T. 2001. Aspect-oriented programming using reflection and metaobject protocols. Communications of the ACM 44(10, October):95-97.
20. Suzuki, J. and Y. Yamamoto. 1999. Extending UML with aspects: Aspect support in the design phase. Proceedings of the third ECOOP Aspect-Oriented Programming Workshop.
21. Warmer, J. and A. Kleppe. 1999. The Object Constraint Language, Addison Wesley Longman, Inc.

Generic XMI-Based UML Model Transformations

Jernej Kovse and Theo Härder

Department of Computer Science, University of Kaiserslautern
P.O. Box 3049, D-67653 Kaiserslautern, Germany
{kovse,haerder}@informatik.uni-kl.de

Abstract. XML-based Metadata Interchange (XMI) is an interchange format for metadata defined in terms of the MOF standard. In addition to supporting the exchange of complete models, XMI supports the exchange of models in differential form. Our paper builds on this feature to examine the possibility of XMI-based generic transformations of UML models. A generic transformation can be configured to generate (via XSLT) a specialized transformation that will be used to transform a UML model. The approach promotes model reuse, speeds up the modeling process and can be used to assure that only predefined semantics (as specialized by an agent) is included in the transformed model.

1 Motivation

The XML-based Metadata Interchange (XMI) [11] is an interchange format for metadata that is defined in terms of the Meta Object Facility (MOF) [8] standard. Since the adopted UML specification [10] defines the UML meta-model as a MOF meta-model, XMI can be used as a model interchange format for UML. This allows UML modeling tools or repositories from different vendors to use XMI to exchange UML models. In addition to supporting the export or import of complete models or model fragments, XMI allows the exchange of models in differential form, i.e. in case a modeling tool is used to extend a UML model m_1 with new model constructs to produce model m_2, XMI supports the exchange of differences between the two models. An important consequence of this feature is that XMI can be used to describe model transformations.

This paper[1] builds on this feature of XMI to examine an infrastructure needed for semi-automatic transformations of UML models in a UML repository. A general usage scenario for such transformations looks like this: A UML model m_i is given and stored in a UML repository. A human or a software agent wants to transform m_i, i.e. add, remove, or modify model elements to obtain a model m_{i+1} which expresses the new (extended, deprived or modified) semantics. However, suppose completely manual model transformation by an agent is unacceptable - we would like to assure that the semantics contained in m_{i+1} is understood by a UML model-driven compiler (e.g.

[1] The research is part of Sonderforschungsbereich (SFB) 501, funded by the Deutsche Forschungsgemeinschaft (DFG).

Z. Bellahsène, D. Patel, and C. Rolland (Eds.): OOIS 2002, LNCS 2425, pp. 192-198, 2002.

a model-based software generator [2]) or interpreter (e.g. a workflow engine based on UML activity graphs [4]). As a solution to this problem, we half-fabricate a model part (the difference between m_{i+1} and m_i) and represent it as a generic transformation. Generic transformations are stored in a database that allows the agent to query them and select the one matching its design requirements. By configuring a generic transformation, the agent produces an XMI document describing the transformation that has to be applied to obtain the model m_{i+1}. The process of selecting different generic transformations, configuring them and transforming the model can be iterated to meet different requirements that have to be present in the final model. Generic transformations promote model reuse, speed up the modeling process and assure that only predefined semantics (as specialized by the agent) is integrated in the final UML model.

Section 2 of this paper focuses on the required infrastructure supporting the application of XMI-based generic transformations in detail. Section 3 gives a brief overview of related work. In Section 4, we make a conclusion and present some ideas for the future work related to the approach.

2 An Infrastructure for Generic XMI-Based Transformations

2.1 XMI-Supported Model Transformations

XMI defines four elements (we refer to them as differential elements) used to support differential description of UML models: `XMI.difference` is the parent element used to describe differences from the base (initial) model; it may contain zero or more differences, expressed through the elements `XMI.difference`, `XMI.delete`, `XMI.add` and `XMI.replace`. `XMI.delete` represents a deletion from the base model, `XMI.add` represents an addition to the base model and `XMI.replace` represents a replacement of a model construct with another model construct in a base model.

2.2 Generic Transformations

Suppose a set of transformations $\{T_k; k\in[1,n]\}$, which may all be derived (specialized) from a common transformation blueprint. We call such a blueprint a generic transformation T. T gives a generic view on a modular part of a UML model whereas each T_k represents a full specialization of this part and allows its integration with an existing base model m_i. T_k can be generated from T by configuring T's parameter values. To allow a direct application of T_k to m_i, T_k is expressed as a series of XMI's differential elements. The configuration parameters (specified by an agent) define how a transformation generator generates T_k from T using the following three mechanisms (Fig. 1 illustrates an example of two specialized transformations generated from the same generic transformation where `Z` is the class added in each transformation):

- *Static parameterization*: Parameters of T are used to generate concrete properties of differential elements used in T_k, e.g. class names, association names, role names, multiplicities, visibility kinds, definitions of OCL constraints, etc. The designer of T defines places (templates) in T that are used as placeholders for pa-

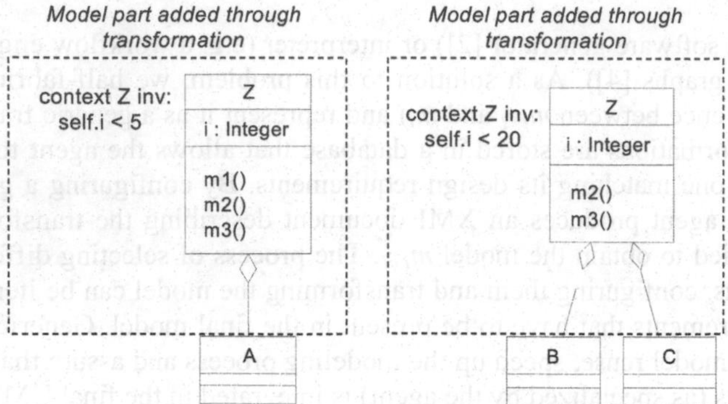

Fig. 1. A pair of specialized transformations

rameter values. For example, an invariant limits the values of `i` to two different ranges in Figs. 1a and 1b.

- *Iteration*: Parameters of T allow the agent to influence how many times a segment of T will be used in T_k. For example, in Fig. 1a, `Z` acts as a container for `A` whereas in Fig. 1b, it acts as a container for classes `B` and `C` meaning that two aggregation associations had to be created.
- *Conditional include*: Parameters of T allow the agent to decide whether a segment of T will be used in T_k. For example, in Fig. 1b, we have omitted the method `m1` from class `Z`.

It is the responsibility of the designer of T to carefully consider how to combine the above mechanisms so that T_k could be generated and applied in a meaningful (consistent) form. To achieve this, the designer always has to specify parameter guidelines (described in Section 2.3) used to limit the set of specialized transformations that can be derived from the same generic transformation T.

T_k is generated as an XMI document (referred to as `Tk.xml`) using two sources: A definition of T (provided by the designer of T) and a list of parameter values for T (provided by the agent). We suggest that both sources should be provided as XML documents, referred to as `T.xml` and `parameters.xml`, respectively. In this case, XSLT (Extensible Stylesheet Language Transformations) [14] can be used by the transformation generator to process `T.xml` and `parameters.xml` to generate `Tk.xml`. XSLT is a language for transforming XML documents (source trees) into other XML documents (result trees). An XSLT transformation, expressed as an XSLT stylesheet (referred to as `generate.xslt`), specifies rules used by the transformation generator to generate `Tk.xml` from `T.xml` and `parameters.xml`. `generate.xslt` is used to support the identified three mechanisms in XSLT.

- Static parameterization is supported using XSLT template rules (element `xsl:template`) [14].
- Iteration (see example in Fig. 2) can be supported either by XSLT template rules or XSLT repetition (element `xsl:for-each`) [14].
- Conditional include is supported using XSLT conditional processing (`xsl:if` and `xsl:choose`) [14].

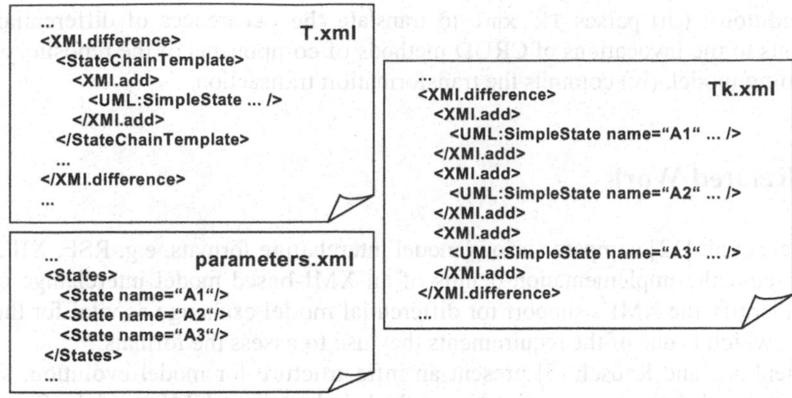

Fig. 2. Iteration (supported via XSLT template rules or repetition)

2.3 Constraints

We cannot always rely on the agent to make the appropriate judgment on whether T_k can be consistently applied to m_i. For this reason, the designer of T defines two sets of constraints for each generic transformation: *parameter guidelines* define valid configurations of parameter values in `parameters.xml` and are thereby used to limit the set of transformations that can be derived from T. *Transformation preconditions* define constraints that apply to m_i and assure that the constructs it contains allow a consistent application of T_k. Since they apply to a UML model, transformation preconditions are expressed as OCL constraints [10].

2.4 Applying Transformations

As `Tk.xml` is generated, the model transformer attempts to apply it to the model m_i. The infrastructure includes a UML repository [6] that stores UML models. A repository [1] offers several benefits for the process of applying transformations. Since it supports version control, the models obtained by applying consecutive transformations can be represented as versions. This allows an agent to revert to a previous version of the model even after a transformation has committed. Since a repository supports configuration control, it allows multiple model segments that have been transformed independently to be combined into configurations. Notification services allow UML-model driven compilers or interpreters (see Section 1) to be notified whenever a model change (that they have as listeners registered to) occurs.

The UML repository offers the access to stored UML models via a programming model [1], which is a mapping of the UML metamodel [10] to enterprise components. The components expose the core Create-Read-Update-Delete (CRUD) methods for the UML model elements. A programming model based on enterprise components delivers persistence, scalability (to leverage the performance of complex model transformations) and programming level transactions. The model transformer is implemented as a session component that performs a transformation T_k in the following order: (i) it initiates a transformation transaction, (ii) checks m_i for transformation preconditions, (iii) parses `Tk.xml` to translate the occurences of differential XMI elements to the invocations of CRUD methods of components of the repository's programming model, (iv) commits the transformation transaction.

3 Related Work

St-Denis et al. [12] compare various model interchange formats, e.g. RSF, XIF, XMI, and discuss the implementation details of an XMI-based model interchange engine. They identify the XMI's support for differential model exchange as vital for the scalability, which is one of the requirements they use to assess the formats.

Keienburg and Rausch [5] present an infrastructure for model evolution, schema migration and data instance migration, which is based on UML models. Successive differences on the evolution path are represented using the XMI's differential elements.

Yoda [15] presents an approach to developing applications using parameterized frameworks. The approach applies to the OMG's Model Driven Architecture (MDA) [9]. He recognizes model transformations as a way to customize predefined and parameterized frameworks. The parameterized UML diagrams he presents can be compared to the mechanism of static parameterization we identified in Section 2.2. Yoda classifies the parameterized frameworks as attribute- or operation-centric.

Demuth et al. [3] outline XMI-based scenarios in the forward and reverse engineering of different applications. As an example, they show how XSLT can be used to generate a SQL schema from a UML model.

Schema transformations are extensively discussed by McBrien and Poulovassilis [7]. In case an evolving UML model has to be consecutively mapped to an (object-)relational database schema, issues related to schema evolution, discussed by Türker [13], become highly relevant to the proposed approach.

4 Conclusion and Future Work

This paper presented our work on generic XMI-based transformations of UML models. The proposed infrastructure allows agents that want to transform UML models to select a predefined generic XMI-based transformation and configure it via parameter values. A specialized XMI transformation is generated by using XSLT as a mechanism for transforming XML documents. The generated transformation is applied in a UML repository that allows versioning of successively transformed models and formation of model configurations from independently transformed model parts.

The target applications of the proposed approach are UML model-driven compilers and interpreters that can understand the UML-specified semantics only in predefined ways. Thus, agents using them can apply generic transformations to build UML models that conform to their requirements. The approach also promotes model reuse, speeds up the modeling process and assures that only predefined semantics is included in the final models.

As future work, we intend to examine whether automatic identification of generic XMI-based transformations is feasible: Given a base UML model m_i and a set of transformed UML models, $\{n_j, j \in [1,l]\}$, what are the possibilities to automatically extract a generic transformation that would allow any model from the set to be generated from m_i.

Second, we are interested in the extension of the proposed infrastructure that would support model-based generative software development. This paper has handled semi-automatic transformations of UML models. In our future work, we will try to identify how the current concepts of generative programming, e.g. feature modeling, template metaprogramming, aspect-oriented programming [2] fit into the proposed infrastructure that would support semi-automatized implementation of software parts from the UML models that have been successively enhanced using generic XMI-based transformations.

References

1. Bernstein, P.A.: Repositories and Object Oriented Databases, Proc. Conf. BTW'97, Ulm, March 1997, Springer-Verlag, pp. 34-46.
2. Czarnecki, K., Eisenecker, U.W.: Generative Programming: Methods, Tools and Applications, Addison-Wesley, 2000.
3. Demuth, B., Hussmann, H., Obermaier, S.: Experiments with XMI-based Transformations of Software Models, in: Online Proc. WTUML: Workshop on Transformations in UML (ETAPS 2001 Satellite Event), Genova, Apr. 2001, http://ase.arc.nasa.gov/wtuml01/
4. Dumas, M., ter Hofstede, A.H.M.: UML Activity Diagrams as a Workflow Specification Language, in: Proc. Int. Conf. UML 2001, Toronto, Oct. 2001, Springer-Verlag, pp. 76-90.
5. Keienburg, F., Rausch, A.: Using XML/XMI for Tool Supported Evolution of UML Models, in: Proc. Int. Conf. HICSS'01, Maui, Jan. 2001, IEEE, 2001.
6. Mahnke, W., Ritter, N., Steiert, H.-P.: Towards Generating Object-Relational Software Engineering Repositories, in: Proc. BTW'99, Freiburg, March 1999, Springer-Verlag, pp. 251-270.
7. McBrien, P., Poulovassilis, A. : A Formal Framework for ER Schema Transformation, in: Proc. ER'1997, Los Angeles, Nov. 1997, Springer-Verlag, pp. 408-421.
8. OMG: Meta Object Facility Specification, version 1.3.1, OMG document 01-11-02.
9. OMG: Model Driven Architecture - A Technical Perspective (Draft), OMG document 01-07-01.
10. OMG: Unified Modeling Language Specification, version 1.4, OMG document 01-09-67.
11. OMG: XML Metadata Interchange Specification, version 1.2, OMG document 02-01-01.
12. Saint-Denis, G., Schauer, R., Keller, R.K.: Selecting a Model Interchange Format. The SPOOL Case Study, in: Proc. Int. Conf. HICSS'00, Maui, Jan. 2000, IEEE, 2000.

13. Türker, C.: Schema Evolution in SQL-99 and Commercial (Object-)Relational DBMS, in: Proc. 9th Int. Workshop on Foundations of Models and Languages for Data and Objects (FoMLaDO 2000), Dagstuhl, Sep. 2000, Springer-Verlag, pp. 1-32.
14. W3C, XSL Transformations (XSLT), version 2.0 (Working draft), http://www.w3.org/TR/xslt20/
15. Yoda, T.: Creating Applications Using Parameterized Frameworks: Quickly developed and highly customized, presentation at OMG's 2nd Workshop: UML for Enterprise Applications: Model Driven Solutions for the Enterprise, Burlingame, Dec. 2001.

A UML Variant for Modeling System Searchability

Axel Uhl[1] and Horst Lichter[2]

[1] Interactive Objects Software GmbH
Freiburg, Germany
uhl@io-software.com

[2] Aachen Technical University
Aachen, Germany
lichter@informatik.rwth-aachen.de

Abstract. Internet search engines today are facing problems in keeping up with the pace of web growth. Two facts are responsible: bandwidth bottlenecks due to central indexing; *deep web* (or *invisible web*) contents that are inaccessible for search engines. Powerful and flexibly extensible object-oriented frameworks are available that assist in the implementation of distributed search infrastructures, thus addressing the first problem. In order to address the second problem, searchability has to be designed into the online applications constituting the deep web, and integrations to the distributed search infrastructures have to be implemented. A model-driven approach to software construction can be used to specify an application's searchability. This paper presents an extension to the UML that can be used to specify an application's searchability in an efficient way. The resulting models can be used to generate large parts of the searchability implementation automatically.

1 Introduction

A fast growing share of the publicly available web content is no longer being served from static HTML documents but rather from online applications that are often database-driven. Given this trend it turns out that more and more highly relevant web content [1] appears in the so-called "deep web" that is not amenable to search engines' crawlers which are still based on a paradigm that assumes a static web.

Existing search infrastructures, e.g. [17,13], many of them leveraging the benefits of object technology and thus by far exceeding simple low-end protocols like HTTP / HTML in functionality and extensibility, can be used to make deep web contents searchable. The content providers have to contribute by means of providing an implementation that adapts their content to the search infrastructure, making their specific information searchable in the ways they want it to be.

An architecturally solid approach is to make *searchability* an integral part of the overall application architecture like it has become common for persistence, distribution, and transactionality. Using a model-driven approach to application

Z. Bellahsène, D. Patel, and C. Rolland (Eds.): OOIS 2002, LNCS 2425, pp. 199–210, 2002.

development, searchability can be integrated into application models, as is already done today for the other architectural aspects mentioned above [8]. Not only will this enable automatic integration with object-oriented, global Internet search infrastructures as will be shown in this paper, but also it will become possible to utilize this model information for automating the implementation of information retrieval support within the application.

We have organized this paper as follows. First we explain the concept of searchability in the context of Internet applications. We describe the New Wave Searchables framework offering an object-oriented infrastructure for distributed Internet search. Section 3 gives an overview on model-driven development and lists its benefits for application development. In section 4 we show how to combine both approaches: model-driven development and modeling searchability. Section 5 exemplifies these concepts by sketching the model-driven development of J2EE systems and then adding searchability support for a selected search infrastructure. After presenting existing and related work we finally evaluate our approach, summarize the main ideas and findings, and give an outlook on issues for future research.

2 Searchability

2.1 Definition and Problem Statement

The *searchability* of data and applications can formally be defined as a function taking a query as argument and producing a (potentially empty) set of results. Different searchability definitions may accept different kinds of queries and may relate the results to the queries in different ways, even for equal kinds of queries.

Something is said to be *globally searchable* if it can be searched by submitting a query to a general search engine that claims to search the whole Internet.

The largest share of web content today is brought online by complex, database-driven applications exhibiting a web front-end. Many of these applications are comparable in their functionality and complexity to usual desktop applications.

These web application architectures break the assumptions of typical web search engines of a statically linked and crawlable web. For example, URLs, which were used to identify *documents*, are abused by attaching information about the application's state, like a session identifier. HTML is no longer used only to represent documents containing the requested information, but instead is overloaded with presentation issues like frame layout, popup window instructions, JavaScript animations for menu or tree displays and input validation, etc. Instead of providing hyperlinks to all information that the application makes available online, in many cases HTML forms are used that, when submitted, dynamically produce HTML documents.

Therefore, search engines are usually unable to index the contents of these types of Internet applications. Instead, Internet applications have to define explicitly which data are searchable in which ways, and they have to implement their specified searchability.

2.2 Approach to Improved Application Searchability

It is specific to each application which types of queries the application may answer and how these queries are applied to the content and processes that are brought online through the application. Regarding the architecture of the search infrastructure, centralized approaches to Internet search have repeatedly been reported to fail regarding scalability issues [10,18]. Instead, architectures that distribute index information and query processing can be implemented in much more scalable and efficient ways.

Such architectures consist of protocol and interface specifications that govern how queries are transmitted, received, and routed to the searchable sources, how results are retrieved, ranked, and merged, how queries can be transformed, and how query capabilities of searchable sources are formally described. Several different such architectures have been conceived and implemented over the course of various research and industry projects. Section 2.3 will present one that will be used as example for the remainder of this paper.

2.3 The New Wave Searchables Framework

In [17,16] the *New Wave Searchables* framework for object-oriented, distributed Internet search has been presented. It combines best practices from many research projects in the field of distributed search technology and implements them using Java technology which lends itself well to the implementation of a distributed object-oriented infrastructure. It constitutes a search architecture in the above sense.

Its key abstraction is the interaction between four object types: *Searchable*, *Query*, *Production*, and *SearchResult* (see figure 1). Searchables specify their query capabilities using Production objects. Productions can tell if they match a Query object. Query objects that are understood by a Searchable are sent to it, and the Searchable can produce zero or more SearchResult instances.

Using inheritance, new *Query* subtypes as well as specialized *Searchable* and *Production* implementations can be plugged into the framework in intuitive

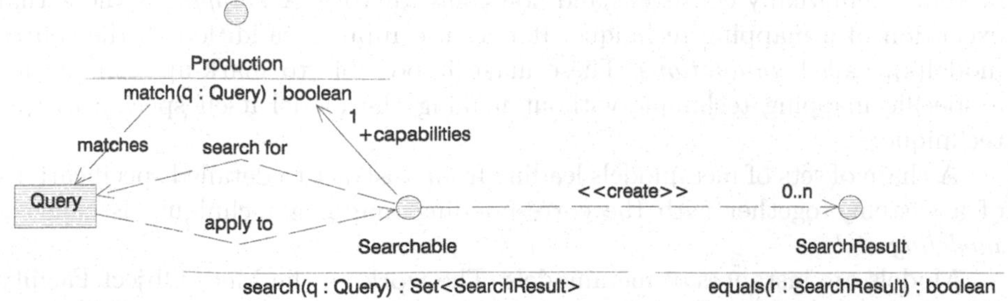

Fig. 1. UML model of the top-level abstractions of the *New Wave Searchables* framework

ways. This allows developers to integrate new ways of searching information and searching new types of media at any time. Java's RMI subsystem transparently manages all relevant issues regarding polymorphic remote method calls and even the transmission of implementation byte code for specialized value-type classes over the network.

The framework supports query transformation. Each query type may implement transformation algorithms that receive as input a *Production* instance describing the search capabilities of a searchable source to which to apply the query. The query can tell whether or not it may transform itself such that the resulting query or queries can be processed by the searchable source.

Query routing, result ranking and merging is implemented in the New Wave Searchables framework by so-called *Traders*. A trader implements a *Composite* pattern on searchables.

At `http://www.NewWaveSearchables.com` a prototypical implementation is online that demonstrates how the concepts can be integrated with existing web technologies. Queries can be created and submitted using a web frontend, searchable web sources are presented as wrapped New Wave Searchables objects, and search results are displayed in HTML documents. The New Wave Searchable framework is also maintained as an active open source project on SourceForge (`http://search.sourceforge.com`).

3 Model Driven Development

In 2001 the Object Management Group (OMG) started an initiative named *Model-Driven Architecture* (MDA) [14,9]. It suggests using *models* to describe software systems at various levels of abstractions, where the models are always held consistent with each other. The software development process benefits from the easier specification at appropriate abstraction levels (see figure 2, left), the increased portability of system specifications, and the improved readability of specifications that serve as additional up-to-date documentation of the system. Figure 2, right, illustrates the increase in portability.

Precise specifications of *mapping techniques* that describe how to transform models between the different abstraction layers ensure that all models for one system are mutually consistent and non-contradictory. A *mapping* is the actual execution of a mapping technique. It may use input in addition to the source model(s), called *annotations*. These make it possible to mark-up a model for a specific mapping technique without making the model itself specific to this technique.

A chain of sets of metamodels leading from abstract to detailed specifications of a system, together with the corresponding mapping techniques is called a *modeling style*.

Models are instances of metamodels. The work on the Meta Object Facility (MOF) [5] provides definitions of models, metamodels, and their mutual relations. Metamodels may be arranged along abstraction and refinement relations and describe aspects of a platform. For example, the Java programming language

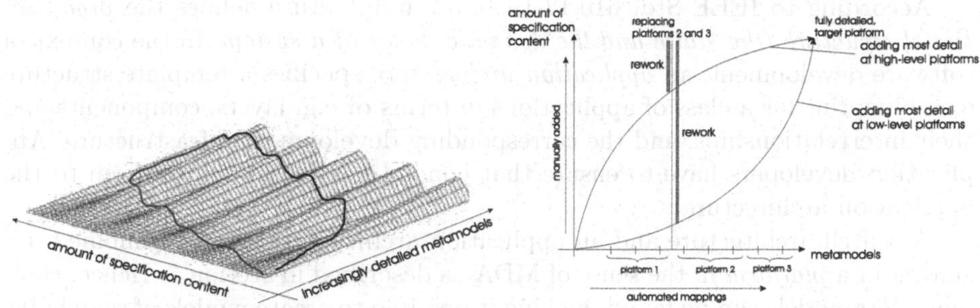

Fig. 2. Left: Development efficiency. The same amount of specification content usually can be provided much easier at higher levels of abstraction while transformations into more detailed levels can be automated, working in favor of the left path, "crossing the hills where they are lower". Right: Specifying as abstract as possible (above curve) increases portability and reduces the amount of rework in case of changing a platform decision or developing for multiple platforms. Too much too detailed specifications (lower curve) result in increased porting effort

specification together with the set of standardized APIs form the metamodel for the Java platform.

It is an important achievement of the MDA initiative to abstract from existing automated model transformations like programming language compilers, and extend this notion into the realm of more abstract models of a system, like Unified Modeling Language (UML) [12] models or Class-Responsibility-Collaboration (CRC) card models [19]. Within MDA, generation of source code and other text-based artifacts of a software system becomes merely a special case of more general transformations between arbitrary models. However, text-based documents can themselves be regarded a model in the context of MDA, and hence can be used as input or output of model transformations.

4 Combining Search Architecture and Application Architecture

Distributed search infrastructures define a technical architecture for parts of a software system: the *search architecture*. It defines the protocols, interfaces, and semantics that can be used to implement an application's *searchability* (see again section 2). For example, the New Wave Searchables framework defines a search architecture by means of its top-level types and interfaces *Searchable*, *Query*, *SearchResult*, and *Production* and the protocol it uses for communication between the distributed components (Java RMI).

Typically, a search architecture cannot stand alone but needs to be integrated with the architecture that an application is built with: the *application architecture*. The application architecture defines the nature of the entities that are to be made searchable using the search architecture.

According to IEEE Std. 610.12-1990, an architecture defines the *organizational structure (the static and the dynamic view) of a system*. In the context of software development, an *application architecture* specifies a template structure or a blueprint for a class of applications in terms of e.g. layers, components and their interrelationships, and the corresponding development infrastructure. Application developers have to ensure that concrete architectures conform to the application architecture.

A search architecture and an application architecture can be combined, resulting in a *platform* in the sense of MDA as described in section 3. Hence, common metamodels can be found, making it possible to create models of searchable applications, serving as specification of both the core application *and* its searchability.

A technology platform supporting searchability with a given search infrastructure typically consists of the *core application* implemented in the application architecture, e.g. a component-based J2EE or .NET environment, that is extended by an adaptation layer that mediates between the core application and the search infrastructure. Figure 3 illustrates this setup. The adaptors access the application's core and adapt it to the search infrastructure.

The combination of the application architecture, the search architecture and the *search adaptor micro-architecture* form the platform on which the search-enabled application gets deployed. The benefit in having specified this platform is that it becomes possible to define MDA support for it. This includes the definition of metamodels that allow for the creation of models for this platform at appropriate levels of abstraction and corresponding mapping techniques that can be automated. By being able to use appropriate abstraction levels for specifying an application's searchability and having automated mapping techniques handle the transformation into source code, the search-related functionality can be developed much more efficiently.

5 Defining a Modeling Style for Searchability

In this section, excerpts from an existing modeling style for J2EE systems are presented. It is then shown how this modeling style can be extended to support modeling searchability in such a way that an adaptor layer for the New Wave Searchable framework can be generated mostly automatically from the models.

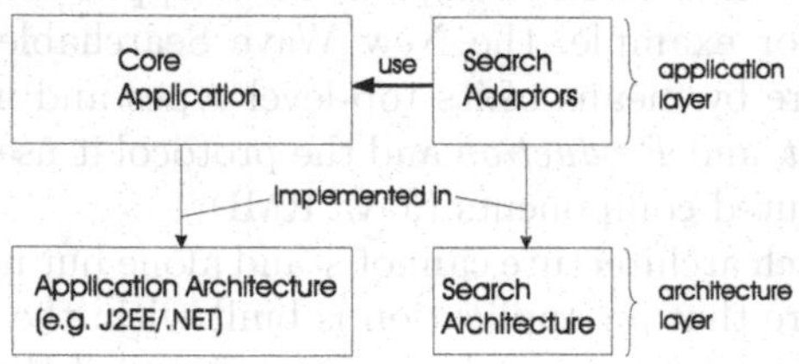

Fig. 3. Extending an application architecture by searchability

5.1 A Modeling Style for J2EE Systems

The modeling style for developing J2EE systems described here is a small subset of the style used by *ArcStyler* [4], limited to those aspects that are required to demonstrate the integration of searchability support with this style.

At the most abstract level, the system is described using CRC cards with responsibilities [19] which, due to space limitations, is not described in any more detail here.

An automated mapping technique transforms the responsibility-driven models into technical UML models. Each card becomes a UML class, and the generalization relationships between the CRC cards are mapped to UML generalizations. Responsibilities and collaborations are, based on model annotations, mapped to one or more of the following UML metamodel elements: attributes, operations, and association ends (roles).

In the UML model several technical properties of these model elements can be specified, for example the multiplicities and navigability of association ends or solely technically motivated inheritance relationships.

Next, the UML model is annotated for a mapping technique transforming it into a set of Java source files, deployment descriptors, Java IDE project files, ANT (see `http://jakarta.apache.org/ant/`) build support scripts, and SQL scripts. This includes the specification of a component's transactional behavior.

Eventually, the annotated model is used as input to a mapping technique producing all of the abovementioned output. The generated Java IDE project files can be used to modify the generated source code in order to insert "if-then-else" logic in marked areas.

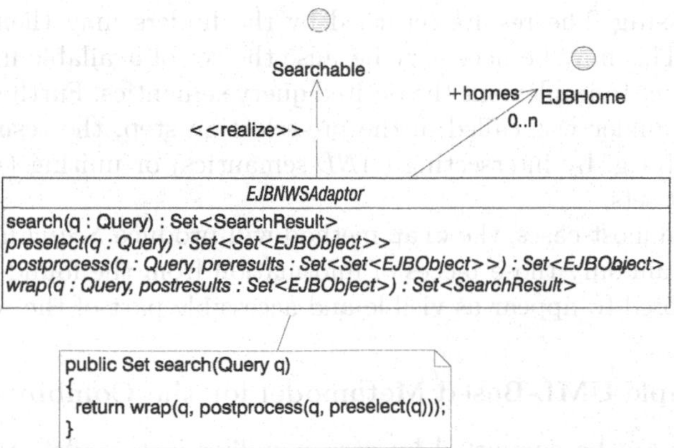

Fig. 4. Adaptor between New Wave Searchables *Searchable* interface and J2EE/EJB architecture. Angle brackets denote parameterized type instantiations

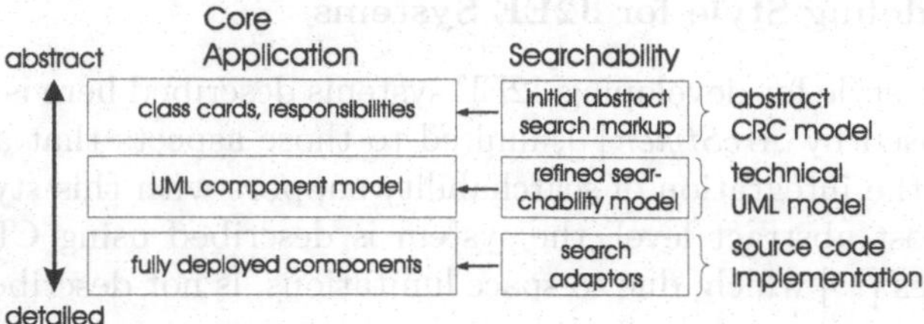

Fig. 5. Modeling a searchable system at different levels of abstraction

5.2 Combining J2EE and New Wave Searchables Architectures

For clarity and brevity of this example, a simple micro-architecture is chosen for the adaptors that mediate between the New Wave Searchables and the J2EE architectures, shown in figure 4. The abstract class *EJBNWSAdaptor* implements the *Searchable* interface provided by the New Wave Searchables framework. At the same time it references one or more *home interfaces* of EJB components that it makes searchable.

The default implementation of the `search` operation performs the search in three steps:

pre-selection Zero or more finders on any of the home interfaces that the adaptor references are called (basically a query on the corresponding component's extent, exposed as an operation of the life-cycle-managing home interface). The parameters for the finder calls are retrieved from the passed query object. The collections of EJB remote references that each finder call produced are returned.

post-processing The results returned by the finders may then be processed further. This may be necessary because the set of available finders may not be sufficient to implement the desired query semantics. Furthermore, if more than one finder was called in the pre-selection step, the results have to be combined, e.g. by intersecting (*AND*-semantics) or uniting (*OR*-semantics) the result sets.

wrapping In most cases, the `wrap` method will produce *SearchResult* instances that contain only those pieces of information from the found instances that are supposed to appear as visible and accessible part of the results.

5.3 A Simple UML-Based Metamodel for the Combined Platform

Searchability can be supported by corresponding metamodel extensions at all levels of abstraction provided by the J2EE modeling style, as depicted in figure 5. The extensions for the UML level are provided as an example.

Figure 6 shows the extensions to the UML-based metamodel used for specifying the system at the technical level. *SearchableClass* is a metaclass whose instances model a single search adaptor, each. For each adaptor a single query type must be specified. Furthermore, a set of finders to be called when receiving

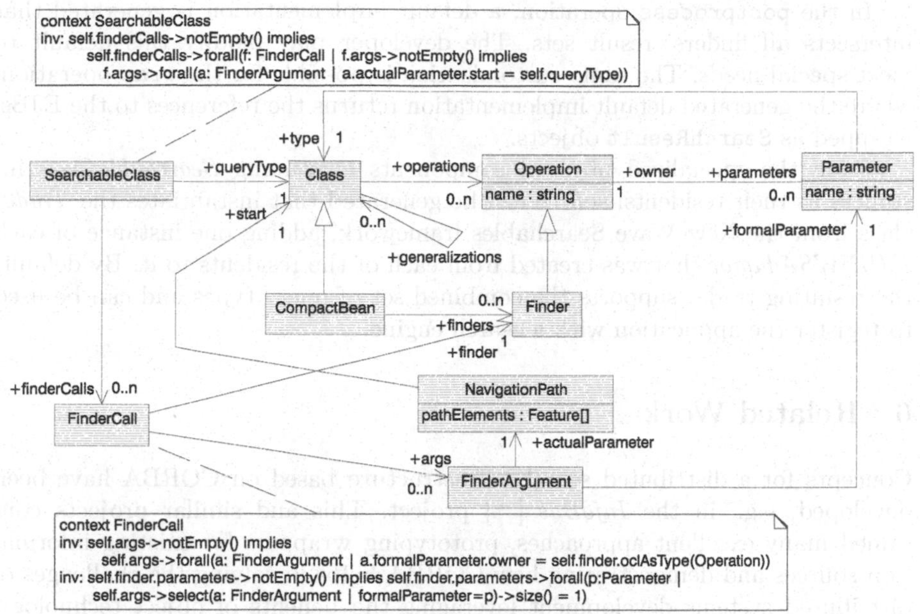
context SearchableClass
inv: self.finderCalls->notEmpty() implies
self.finderCalls->forall(f: FinderCall | f.args->notEmpty() implies
f.args->forall(a: FinderArgument | a.actualParameter.start = self.queryType))
SearchableClass
+queryType
+type 1
Class
+start
+operations
Operation
name : string
+owner
+parameters
Parameter
name : string
+formalParameter
+generalizations
CompactBean
Finder
+finders
+finder
+finderCalls
FinderCall
NavigationPath
pathElements : Feature[]
+actualParameter
+args
FinderArgument
context FinderCall
inv: self.args->notEmpty() implies
self.args->forall(a: FinderArgument | a.formalParameter.owner = self.finder.oclAsType(Operation))
inv: self.finder.parameters->notEmpty() implies self.finder.parameters->forall(p:Parameter |
self.args->select(a: FinderArgument | formalParameter=p)->size() = 1)

Fig. 6. Example: metamodel for describing searchability of a J2EE architecture

a query of the specified type has to be associated with the adaptor. For each finder the model must specify how the finder arguments are retrieved from the query. It does so by providing *NavigationPath* instances that describe how to retrieve the value to be used as finder argument, starting on the query object, and navigating along features (attribute, associations, operations) of the query.

Specialized physical components can be used to group multiple *SearchableClass* instances together that are assigned as residents of the component.

5.4 Source Code Level

An instance of the extended UML metamodel sketched in section 5.3 can be used to generate corresponding source code that provides sections where the developer has to add more detail. Each *SearchableClass* instance is transformed into a Java class extending the *EJBNWSAdaptor* class (see again figure 4). An implementation of the `getSupportedQueryTypes` operation is generated that returns a *Production* that matches queries of the query type specified in the model for the *SearchableClass*.

In the constructor of the generated class, the home interfaces of those EJBs whose finders are used by the *SearchableClass* are resolved and stored in the `homes` role. An implementation for the `preselect` method is generated that calls the finders on the homes as specified by the model, retrieving the arguments from the passed query and returning the results returned by the finders.

In the `postprocess` operation, a default implementation is generated that intersects all finders' result sets. The developer may modify this default to meet special needs. The same customization is possible for the `wrap` operation, where the generated default implementation returns the references to the EJBs, wrapped as `SearchResult` objects.

From the specialized physical components containing *SearchableClass* instances as their residents, source can be generated that instantiates the *Trader* class from the New Wave Searchables framework, adding one instance of each *EJBNWSAdaptor* that was created from each of the residents to it. By default, the resulting trader supports the combined set of query types and can be used to register the application with a search engine.

6 Related Work

Concepts for a distributed search infrastructure based on CORBA have been developed, e.g., in the *InfoBus* [13] project. This and similar projects contained many excellent approaches, prototyping wrappers for existing information sources and demonstrating how CORBA helps in solving the challenges of distributed systems development leveraging the benefits of object technology. However, they have not addressed other important aspects like showing how different query types can be applied in the presence of heterogeneous data sources that support different sets of query types.

Garlic [3] is a project that has conducted research in the area of information retrieval on heterogeneous multi-media data sources. Garlic uses an object-oriented model to represent data and queries. One task was query rewriting in the context of an extensible query type set [7], using search capability descriptions and query execution cost models for the participating searchable data sources. Given these descriptions and models a query could be mapped to a cost-optimal execution plan using standard planning algorithms. Garlic does not address issues like integerating the query type framework with web frontends and the problem of handling large numbers of searchable collections.

Another approach to heterogeneous and distributed search has been researched in the *DISCO* project [15]. In DISCO the search capabilities of the data sources are described as grammars for the queries. All DISCO-enabled sources have to be capable of delivering *all* their retrievable instances which can be prohibitive for huge data collections. DISCO, like Garlic, also uses a cost model for query execution. A special feature of DISCO is that it can reasonably deal with temporary unavailability of data sources. Web integration of the framework was not discussed.

Other existing approaches that define distributed search infrastructures, and that cannot be discussed in detail due to space limitations are *Lexibot* (`http://www.lexibot.com`), Apple's *Sherlock* [11], and *Grub* (`http://www.grub.org`).

The general ideas of model-driven software construction are combined in the OMG's work on MDA [14,9]. Many application- or domain-specific modeling styles have been created, e.g. for multimedia or real-time applications. [2] provides an overview. Examples can also be found in [6].

7 Conclusions and Future Work

In this paper we have presented a model-driven approach for search-enabling Internet applications that constitute parts of the deep web. This was achieved by combining an application architecture and an object-oriented search architecture into a platform that can then be supported by the Model-Driven Architecture (MDA). A chain of metamodels and corresponding mapping techniques have been presented that enable developers to specify an application's searchability in convenient and portable ways.

The automation of mapping techniques reduces the implementation effort to a minimum. As a result, making deep web applications searchable using a powerful search infrastructure that leverages the benefits of distributed object technology becomes straightforward, easy, and intuitive, which in turn gives rise to hopes that an increasing share of deep web information will be globally searchable in the future.

Future research will have to focus on improving the metamodels with regard to their applicability to a wide range of combinations of application and search architectures. The example presented here assumed that a set of query functions (*finders* in the case of EJB) are available that the model can refer to. Intelligent target-technology-aware mappings may be found that create default sets of such query operations. We will investigate to what extent portable specifications of search logic details are possible by defining mapping techniques to other object-oriented search infrastructures.

References

1. Michael K. Bergman. The deep web: Surfacing hidden value. July 2000. URL `http://128.121.227.57/download/deepwebwhitepaper.pdf`. 199
2. Margaret Burnett. Visual language research bibliography. URL `http://www.cs.orst.edu/~burnett/vpl.html`. 209
3. M. J. Carey, L. M. Haas, P. M. Schwarz, M. Arya, W. F. Cody, R. Fagin, M. Flickner, A. W. Luniewski, W. Niblack, D. Petkovic, J. Thomas, J. H. Williams, and E. L. Wimmers. Towards heterogeneous multimedia information systems: The garlic approach. In *Research Issues in Data Engineering,* pages 124-131. IEEE Computer Society Press, Los Alamitos, Ca., USA, March 1995. ISBN 0-8186-7056-8. URL `http://www.almaden.ibm.com/cs/garlic/ride-dom95.html`. 208
4. Interactive Objects Software GmbH. ArcStyler User's Guide. URL `http://www.io-software.com/products/docu/Users-Guide.pdf`. 205
5. The Object Management Group. The MOF specification version 1.3, March 2000. URL `http://www.omg.org/cgi-bin/doc?formal/00-04-03`. 202
6. John C. Grundy and John Hosking. High-level static and dynamic visualisation of software architectures. In *IEEE Symposium an Visual Languages, Seattle, WA,* USA, September 2000. URL `http://www.cs.auckland.ac.nz/~john-g/papers/vl00.ps.gz`. 209

7. Laura M. Haas, Donald Kossmann, Edward L. Wimmers, and Jun Yang. Optimizing querfies across diverse data sources. In *Proceedings of the Twenty-third International Conference an Very Large Databases,* pages 276-285. VLDB Endowment, Saratoga, Calif., Athens, Greece, August 1997. URL `http://www.almaden.ibm.com/cs/garlic/vldb97opt.ps`. 208
8. Richard Hubert. White Paper: Convergent Architecture & The ArcStyler Tool Suite, 2000. URL `http://www.io-software.com/products/docu/iO_CA_ArcStyler_Whitepaper.pdf`. 200
9. Thomas Koch, Axel Uhl, and Dirk Weise. Model-Driven Architecture, January 2002. URL `http://cgi.omg.org/cgi-bin/doc?ormsc/02-01-04.pdf`. 202, 208
10. Steve Lawrence and C. Lee Giles. Searching the World Wide Web. *Science,* 280(5360):98, 1998. URL `http://www.neci.nj.nec.com/~lawrence/science98.html`. 201
11. John Montbriand. Extending and controlling sherlock. November 1999. URL `http://developer.apple.com/technotes/tn/tn1141.html`. 208
12. The Object Management Group (OMG). The unified modeling language, version 1.4, September 2001. URL `http://www.omg.org/cgi-bin/doc?formal/01-09-67.pdf`. 203
13. M. Roscheisen, M. Baldonado, C.-C. K. Chang, L. Gravano, S. Ketchpel, and A. Paepcke. The stanford infobus and its service layers: Augmenting the internet with higher-level information management protocols. In *Digital Libraries in Computer Science: The McDoc Approach, LNCS,* volume 1392. Springer, 1998. URL `http://www-diglib.stanford.edu/diglib/WP/PUBLIC/DOC148.pdf`. 199, 208
14. The Object Management Group (OMG). Model Driven Architecture: The Architecture of Choice for a Changing World, 2001. URL `http://cgi.omg.org/cgibin/doc?ormsc/01-07-01`. 202, 208
15. A. Tomasic, Louiqa Raschid, and Patrick Valduriez. A data model and query processing technique for scaling access to distributed heterogeneous databases in DISCO. *IEEE Transactions an Computers, special issue an Distributed Computing Systems,* 1997. URL `ftp://ftp.umiacs.umd.edu/pub/ONRrept/IeeeTOCS96.ps`. 208
16. Axel Uhl and Horst Lichter. New Wave Searchables: Changing the paradigm of Internet scale search. In *International Conference an Advances in Infrastructure for Electronic Business, Science, and Education an the Internet.* SSGRR, L'Aquila, Italy, August 2001. ISBN 88-85280-61-7. URL `http://shipping.accesscable.net/uhl/SSGRR.PDF`. 201
17. Axel Uhl. The future of Internet search. In Roberto Baldoni, editor, *DOA'01 International Symposium an Distributed Objects and Applications, Short Papers,* September 2001. ISBN 888665811-7. URL `http://shipping.accesscable.net/uhl/DOA2001Short.PDF`. 199, 201
18. Axel Uhl. A bandwidth model for internet search. In *Proceedings of the 28th International Conference an Very Large Data Bases (VLDB '02).* Morgan Kaufmann, Orlando, September 2002. URL `http://www.vldb.org/conf/2002/P687.pdf`. 201
19. Rebecca Wirfs-Brock, Brian Wilkerson, and Lauren Wiener. *Designing ObjectOriented Software.* Prentice-Hall, Englewood Cliffs, NJ 07632, 1990. 203, 205

A Methodological Framework for Understanding IS Adaptation through Enterprise Change[1]

Camille Salinesi and Jaana Wäyrynen

Centre de Recherche en Informatique, Université Paris 1 – Sorbonne
90, rue de Tolbiac, 75013 Paris – France
Camille@univ-paris1.fr

Abstract. In both academy and practice, BP (Business Process) modelling and re-engineering are used to enlighten the IS adaptations required when enterprises change. However, industrial scale BP models are large and complex, and analysing the current and the required BPs at the same time is difficult. We believe this issue can be dealt with by abstracting BP models. This paper proposes a methodological framework organising this analysis into several levels. At the highest level an abstract formalism, called MAP, is used to synthesise BP goals and strategies. Our expectation is that MAP facilitates analysis of change with traditional BP models. A process starting with MAP is also proposed to conduct BP change and IS adaptation analysis. The resulting method was applied in an industrial case study. The paper reports the framework, case study and lessons learned by observation and critics made during the case study.

1 Introduction

According to [1], 50% of the Information Systems (IS) lifecycle costs are incurred after initial development, including for adaptation. Several methods exists to analyse the *adaptations* required on IS in the context of enterprise change [2] [3] [4]. These methods have some common characteristics: (i) they assume the rationale for IS adaptation is to be found in contextual forces relating to the enterprise change, (ii) they differentiate the current situation from the future one, (iii) they exploit different modelling techniques to describe the required business models and IS, and (iv) they assume a limited scale of the studied change or adaptation. In such methods, BP models are used to define the IS context of use. Understanding the future BPs helps eliciting the requirements for the future IS, and thus guide its design. However, BP models tend to be complex [5]: they are often very detailed, and non-standard BPs usually make their structure even more complex. Experience shows that this is in part the reason why understanding the transition to the future BPs and IS is long and difficult [6].

---

[1] This paper was partly funded by France Télécom R&D

Z. Bellahsène, D. Patel, and C. Rolland (Eds.): OOIS 2002, LNCS 2425, pp. 211-222, 2002.

We propose to facilitate this activity by focusing on BP goals rather than on details. This is achieved with MAP, a goal-oriented modelling technique integrating the concept of strategy. Based on our experience with MAP, a methodological framework was developed to provide an organised picture of the models used in an IS adaptation project. According to the framework:

- Specific modelling techniques can be used to understand change at multiple levels. The framework uses MAP to model the enterprise's business goals and to indicate how these goals are achieved.
- Change is studied under the form of gaps between models specifying on the same level the current and future situations. Three collections of models are thus used: *As-Is* models for current phenomena, *To-Be* models for the future situations, and *gap* models to specify changes. No assumption is made on how gaps are implemented (although it could affect the successfulness of a project [7], this issue is out of the scope of this paper).
- The justification of a gap at some level stands in change forces resulting from an upper level. Therefore, the approach uses a *top-down* strategy. In this paper, change forces are assimilated to gaps specified at an upper level [8]. Other kinds of change forces such as market tension, enterprise merges or take-overs, technology evolution, etc, can also be considered, but this paper provides no systematic way to handle them.

The improvements expected from such an approach are globally: more synthetic models of the BPs, facilitated identification of the gaps between As-Is and To-Be BP models, and better organisation of the models.

This paper reports the observations made during the application of the framework on a case study dealing with the re-organisation of SCS, a Swedish repair workshop. The purpose is to draw from this qualitative evaluation lessons on the approach effectiveness and to raise efficiency issues. The actual efficiency of the approach will be evaluated later on in a series of quantitative evaluations.

The next section, presents an overview of the proposed methodological framework, and introduces how observations and critics were made during the SCS case study. Section 3 reports the process followed. Section 4 presents the critics and lessons learned. On-going research activities are synthesised in the concluding section.

2 The Methodological Framework for Enterprise Change Based IS Adaptation

This section presents an overview of the methodological framework, presents the MAP meta-model and the BP modelling technique used during the case study, namely EBML. The last subsection defines the approach taken to evaluate the framework.

2.1 Overview of the Methodological Framework

The purpose of the framework is to provide an integrated understanding of the complementary roles played by IS analysis and design, BP modelling, and enterprise goal modelling in a change project. Its theoretical foundation lies in Lewis's three-step model of change [9]. According to Lewis, change creates a movement from an existing situation to a new one. The model indicates that change is about 'de-freezing' the current situation of the enterprise, implementing change, then 're-freezing' the enterprise in a stabilised situation consistent with its desired form. While change is being implemented, the enterprise passes through a collection of different 'liquefied' or 'transient' states [10] [7].

In a similar way, our change framework assumes a discontinuous perception of change. The enterprise and IS are not considered as perpetually changing, but seen as in a sequence of stable situations alternated by change achievements. This is shown in Figure 1 by *As-Is*, *To-Be* and *Liquefied* models.

As-Is and To-Be models can be specified using the same concepts or meta-models [11]. However, whereas As-Is models describe indicative properties, i.e. perceived phenomena of the current situation (before de-freezing), the purpose of To-Be models is to describe optative properties of phenomena as they are foreseen in a future situation (as desired after re-freezing).

To ensure a correct transition from the current situation to the future situation [7] it is necessary to understand the difference between As-Is and To-Be models. This is done by specifying *Gap* models that define transformations to apply to As-Is models and obtain the corresponding To-Be models. A typology of gaps is presented in [8] to guide the specification of such models.

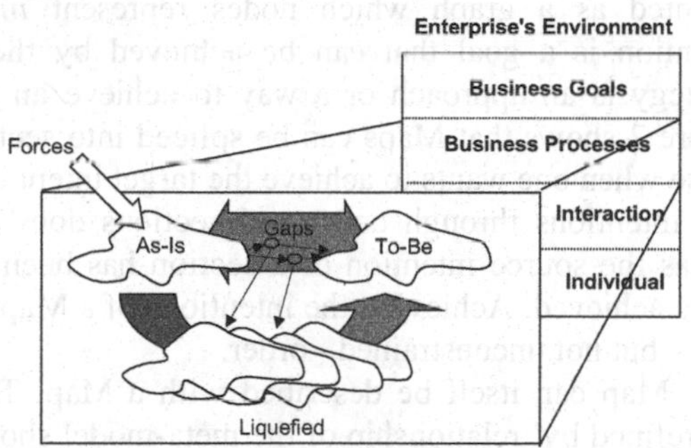

Fig. 1. Basic building block of the change framework

There is a wide range of levels at which specify the As-Is models, To-Be models and Gap models. Depending on the concern, one can for instance differentiate the individual level to study the internal properties of the enterprise's actors, from the interaction level at which the primary concern is the interface between actors. The BP level can be tackled to focus on the flows and organisation of activities and differentiated from the business goal level at which the enterprise's goal implemented in BPs can be analysed. Different formalisms can be used to focus on each level. For example, Entity/Relationship models, Object Oriented diagrams, State-Transition diagrams, are often used to specify individually the internal properties of an IS and other kinds of actors at the corresponding level. The interface between actors can be modelled at the interaction level with Message Sequence Charts, Use Cases, or Scenarios. As Figure 1 shows, the framework's basic building block applies at any of these levels.

The literature quotes different reasons for undertaking enterprise change and IS adaptation: 'aspirations' [12], 'motors of change' [13], 'opportunities' [14], 'sources of change' [15], etc. These *change forces* result from 'abnormal' situations (issues, problems) resulting from a mismatch between the enterprise's goals, its BPs, its IS and/or its environment. Change forces are a source for new requirements calling for change facilitators. Gap modelling is proposed as one of these.

To summarise, the framework has six main characteristics: (i) it integrates multiple perspectives provided by different modelling techniques, (ii) it organises analysis according to levels of abstraction, (iii) it proposes to use MAP at the enterprise goal level, (iv) it uses a discrete definition of time and differentiates As-Is, To-Be and liquefied situations, (v) it uses gap models to specify the difference between As-Is and To-Be, and (vi) it defines change forces as driving change.
In the remainder, we focus on two 'upper' levels of the framework, namely the *BP* level, and the *business goal* level. At the BP level, models define the sequencing of events occurring in a business. The business goal level focuses on the purpose and rationale of BPs. The framework suggests to use MAP at the former level, whereas it should be possible to use any BP meta-model - EBML in our case study. The next two sub-sections respectively introduce the concepts used in MAP and EBML.

2.2 MAP

A Map is represented as a graph which nodes represent *intentions* and edges *strategies*. An intention is a goal that can be achieved by the performance of a process, and a strategy is an approach or a way to achieve an intention. The Map meta-model in Figure 2 shows that Maps can be spliced into sections. These identify which strategy to use when one wants to achieve the target intention.

The ordering of intentions through connected sections does not identify a strict sequence. As long as the source intention of a section has been achieved, its target intention can also be achieved. Achieving the intentions of a Map is therefore done in a non-deterministic – but not unconstrained - order.

Any section in a Map can itself be described with a Map. This is done through refinement, as the 'refined by' relationship of the meta-model shows. This results in a net of refinement links between Maps. For consistency reasons, this net should not contain any loop.

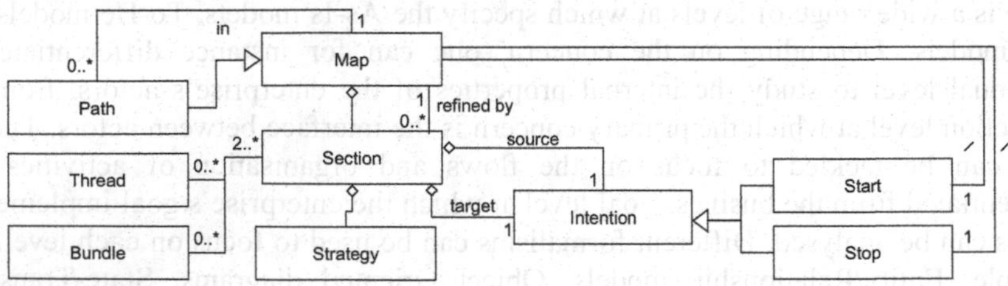

Fig. 2. The MAP meta-model defines the key concepts and their inter-relationships in UML

A *path* is a subset of a Map's sections respecting the Map definition (i.e. a complete graph of sections including one *start* intention and a *stop* intention). Sections can thus be refined by Map paths.

Two or more sections can identify exclusive or complementary strategies to achieve a single intention. In the former case they are grouped in a *bundle*, in the latter case they are in a *thread*. Thread sections can have different source intentions whereas bundled sections have the same source intention. However, in both case all the sections of the group have the same target intention.

2.3 EBML

EBML is a method for describing BP models with the aim of defining IS system requirements. The EBML key concepts and their inter-relationships are shown in the meta-model presented in Figure 3. The meta-model is defined in standard UML.

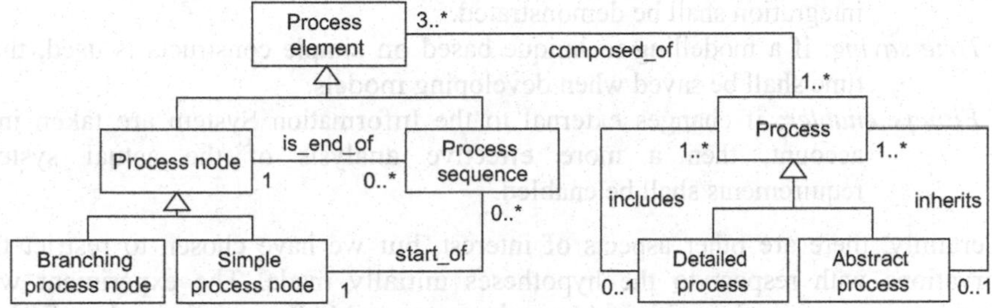

Fig. 3. The EBML BP meta-model in standard UML

An EBML model contains processes describing the sequencing of events that occur in a business. *EBML processes* are either abstract or detailed. They are composed by a set of process elements ordered with sequences and branching positioned between start nodes and end nodes.

Abstract processes cannot be instantiated, i.e. they do not exist in reality but are useful to define inheritance hierarchies. Indeed, the elements of an abstract process also belong to all its sub-processes. Process elements in a process can be abstract, in which case the process can be abstract itself.

A *detailed process* can inherit its contents from an abstract process. This holds for sequence, branching, as well as for simple process nodes such as: message sending or reception, manual or automated activities performed by actors, waiting states, and timer start or expiration.

2.4 Approach Taken to Evaluate the Framework

Several approaches have been developed to provide a basis for studying, analysing and comparing different modelling techniques. For example, the four process perspectives by [16], and the framework for evaluating BPM and ISM techniques proposed by [6]. These were adapted to define criteria for the evaluation of three main hypotheses:

H1: the proposed methodological framework is effective,

H2: the understanding and organisation of BP models can be facilitated by the usage of the more abstract MAP modelling technique,

H3: modelling with MAP helps making more complete BP models.

Six criteria were defined to evaluate our three hypotheses:

C1. *Perspective enlargement*: if the introduction of a high level business modelling technique makes the business intentions explicit, then it shall enlarge the process view.

C2. *Facilitation*: if a model with a simple semantic is used as a starting point, then it shall make it easier to understand the other models.

C3. *Model management*: if a top-down way of working provides the business rationale for the BPs, then the intentional elements shall be associated to their corresponding operational elements.

C4. *Integration*: if the modelling techniques used integrate common information elements, such as aspects of why and how, then some level of integration shall be demonstrated.

C5. *Time saving*: if a modelling technique based on simple constructs is used, then time shall be saved when developing models.

C6. *Fitness enabler*: if changes external to the Information System are taken into account, then a more effective analysis of the actual system requirements shall be enabled.

Certainly, there are other aspects of interest, but we have chosen to restrict the observations with respect to the hypotheses initially made. The experiment was undertaken in co-operation with two experimenters: a MAP specialist and an EBML specialist. At each step of the case study, the list of criteria was used to trigger discussion about the validity of the framework. The evaluation was qualitative and subjective. The lessons learned from the case study introduced in the next section take this into account. In particular they identify specific ways of further investigating the observations made.

3 The Stockholm Central Service (SCS) Case Study

3.1 Overview of the SCS Company

Stockholm Central Service (SCS) is a Swedish company offering overhaul and reparation services of home electronics. In 2001 a decision to re-organise was made in order to solve a number of issues relating to the company's productivity. The project to change SCS business was undertaken with the aim of improving competitiveness, suppress insufficient response times to customers, and find an appropriate organisation of the work structure. The approach initially taken was based on BP modelling. BP models were developed with EBML [17] to understand the current business, situate the issues, identify opportunities for change, design the BP models to implement in the future, and locate the impact on the company's IS design.

Once the aforementioned activities completed, specifying new requirements for the future IS from BP models was rather straightforward. However, several difficulties were encountered during this initial experience: process models were large and complex, they contained many details making their reading difficult. This was also an obstacle to the search of changes to report on the EBML specifications. Besides, it was difficult to emphasise the gaps between the EBML specifications for the current and future BPs. This was not only due to the complexity of the models, but also because the models didn't differentiate the stable elements of the business (such as important business intentions), from elements more likely to change (such as the different way of working of business actors).

3.2 Process Applied During the Case Study

A re-play was undertaken based on a combined usage of MAP and EBML as prescribed by the framework. The process chosen had three objectives: (i) make the business intentions explicit with Maps, (ii) facilitate the organisation of the models by relating Maps to BPs , and (iii) facilitate the identification gaps between the As-Is and To-Be models. As Figure 4 shows, a spiral model [18] was developed. At each of the two levels the process is incremental: each spiral turn in the process complements the output resulting of previous turns. The angular dimension of the spiral represents the stage of process completeness whereas the radial dimension of the spiral indicates the progress in the production of increments.

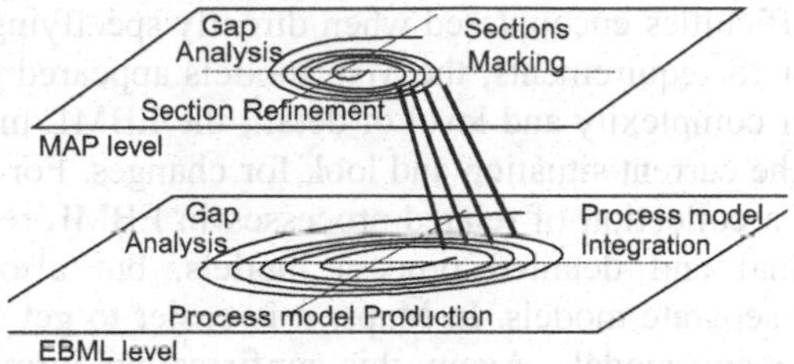

Fig. 4. Overview of the process applied during the case study

Figure 4 shows that a turn of the spiral at the MAP level is due to section refinement. It is only when no further refinement is needed that movement from the MAP to the lower EBML level occurred. In other words, the movement between levels resulted from a decision related to every section in a Map: either the To-Be section was understood enough to move to the EBML level or it required further intention-driven analysis at the MAP level. The latter necessitated a new intentional turn to refine sections whereas the former generated a spiral turn at the lower level of the hierarchy. Thus this movement established a dynamic link between sections at the MAP level and the corresponding fragments at the EBML level.

A detailed description of SCS and the initial EBML change project, of the gap analysis process, and of the SCS Map models can respectively be found in [17], and [19].

While analysing gaps and looking for their impact on SCS BPs, observations and critics were made. The next sections sums up our findings in terms of lessons learned about the framework validity, and need for further investigation.

4 Lessons Learned from the Case Study

The analysis is based on the evaluation criteria used to criticise the application of the framework during the case study. The conclusion made for each of the six chosen criteria is reported in the corresponding subsection below.

4.1 Perspective Enlargement

The comparison of the represented level of abstraction reveals that Maps are adequate for reasoning about the business level. They help exploring the business space and making the business vision explicit. In SCS, Maps helped understanding the business intentions, which were recognised in EBML but were not as clearly stated. By clearly defining the objectives, the Maps helped completing the BPs. As a result, the initial focus on stocking apparatus enlarged to a wider vision of the entire order process. In other words, reasoning about the higher business level widened the focus, helped stating the SCS business objectives, strengthened the process view [20], and helped making the EBML processes more complete. The same was observed in a former industrial project, in which the Map/gap approach was applied to understand required IS adaptations [8].

4.2 Facilitation

In contrast to the difficulties encountered when directly specifying the To-Be EBML models to search for IS requirements, the Map models appeared easy to read and to analyse. Due to their complexity and level of detail, the EBML models made it more difficult to analyse the current situation and look for changes. For example, analysing the "big picture" of a collection of related processes in EBML required not only the analysis of individual and detailed process models, but also the analysis and structuring of many separate models. In Maps, it is easier to get a general overview, without developing many models. Again, this confirms our former observations. To give an order of magnitude, the models and schemas representing the information system, composed 2000 screens and 150 relational tables with about 40 attributes per table. In contrast, the top-level Map included 5 intentions and 13 strategies [8].

4.3 Model Management

The case study showed that a top-down way of working where the business goal level is considered first provides a better rationale for BP models. For example, using the refinement mechanism proposed permitted to associate the section *<Receive an apparatus; Repair an apparatus; by prerequisite quotation>* with fragments in the corresponding EBML process *Reparation*. Thus, the framework seems to facilitate the management of models on different levels. However, one can argue that model management was made easier because the As-Is EBML process models already existed and that the use of MAP with another process modelling language could not be as effective as with EBML. Besides, managing Maps in addition to the other existing models, could become more difficult. We believe that this difficulty can be overcome by a careful management of the links between models.

4.4 Integration

Maps define business intentions and the ways to achieve them. Different ways of working can be represented by associating strategies to each intention. On the contrary, in EBML the modelling objective is to describe the dynamics of businesses in processes. This include different ways of working represented by interleaved fragments of BPs. Once again, the level of complexity may have increased because more models had to be connected. However, the intentions in Maps and process names could naturally be assimilated, and strategies could be linked to process fragments. These two elements of integration facilitated the analysis of BPs based on the selection of well identified business intentions and strategies. A more effective "synergy effect" [21] is however expected from a tighter integration of the models of the different levels.

4.5 Time Saving

The time taken to construct and develop Maps was considerably shorter than for EBML modelling. This observation is based on the modelling of a set of high-level Maps, including a maximum of three levels of refinement. All together this took about five workdays. To model the corresponding BPs originally took about double the time. The case study showed that although time consuming, Map modelling was significantly faster than BP modelling. Besides, in terms of the amount of knowledge and understanding of the business gained, Maps appeared to be superior to the EBML expert. Therefore, BP modelling time could be saved if Maps are developed first. We believe this observation needs further quantitative evaluation. In particular, the overall amount of time and knowledge gained by the combined use of Map and EBML could be evaluated in an empirical study.

4.6 Fitness Enabler

The case study showed that, compared to a pure BP modelling approach, Maps support more rationale and creative design decisions by helping to initially avoid unnecessary details, such as technical details of the IS, as proposed by the framework. This finding coincides with Giaglis's argument [6] that one way to achieve IS fitness for use, is to guide high-level IS design by BP modelling and leave the technical details of IS design and implementation as consequences of BP change decisions. Giaglis shows that this approach has two advantages:

- it ensures that the focus on the alignment of organisational and IS structures is always maintained, thereby allowing business managers to assess the organisational impact of structural and informational changes in an integrated fashion, and
- it drives the complexity of designing detailed IS structures out of the process change endeavour, thereby allowing decision-makers to concentrate on organisational rather than technical factors when designing and evaluating changes[6].

4.7 Summary of the Lessons Learned

The lessons learned from the SCS case study can be summed up as follows:

- the proposed methodological framework is effective, although some aspects must be improved; for example a collection of relationships between levels might help guiding gap analysis,
- the understanding and organisation of BP models is facilitated by the usage of the more abstract Map models focusing on business intentions; the time saved and amount of knowledge gained must however be demonstrated by a series of empirical evaluations,
- modelling with Map helps making more complete BP models, but the efficiency of Map modelling for BP models completion should however be compared to other approaches.

The approach taken for the case study contains some inherent drawbacks that must be made explicit to put our lessons learned in perspective. First, the case study was based on known facts about SCS. The company did not take part in the Map modelling phase. This, of course, impacts our findings regarding the amount of knowledge gained and time spared by using Maps before modelling BPs. We believe our claims can be, at least in part, substantiated by an experiment in which our approach is applied independently from the traditional BP modelling approach. As to the methodological framework itself, the definition of the As-Is, Liquefied and To-Be models are still only grounded on theory, even though it is a traditional approach to perceive change (even in the industry). The question of whether these situations are met in real life might however be raised. To this point in our research program, we have not been able to find a suitable alternative definition of enterprise change and IS adaptation.

Contradictions to the hypotheses were also found during the case study. For example, the framework assumes a top-down analysis strategy. However, the experimenters found it difficult to put in practice the idealistic view of a fully top-down process. They started by describing Maps at an intermediate level before going onto a higher level. Different levels of refinement were treated in parallel, making the consistency between level sometimes difficult to maintain. This issue should be solved by more guidance of the initial Map development, for example, our experiences with industrial project showed re-occurring patterns in high level Maps.

5 Conclusions

The challenge of the enterprise change–based IS adaptation framework is to bring business intention design, BP design and IS design together without adding to the already high complexity of each individual approach. The approach taken is the one of a decomposition of the problems into levels of analysis. At each level, two time horizons are considered, and the gaps between models specifying these looked for. Such an approach has two main advantages:

- it ensures that a focus on the alignment of business intentions and strategies, business processes, and IS structures is always maintained, thereby allowing business managers to assess the organisational impact of structural and informational changes in an integrated fashion, and

- it drives the complexity of designing detailed IS structures out of the process change endeavour, thereby allowing decision-makers to concentrate on organisational rather than technical factors when designing and evaluating changes.

A method based on the proposed framework was experimented with the re-organisation of Stockholm Central Service (SCS), a Swedish company offering overhaul and reparation services for home electronics. The need to change the company was caused by competitiveness issues, insufficient response times to customers, and an inappropriate working organisation. The approach adopted was based on MAP models, EBML BP modelling, and gap analysis. The originality of the approach stands in the abstraction of business intentions and strategies prior to detailed BP modelling. While achieving the activities of modelling the business intentions, the current BPs, and the gaps with the corresponding To-Be models, observations were made to criticise the proposed framework. The critics related to six criteria chosen to confirm, invalidate and put in perspective issues about the hypotheses made on the framework.

The case study gave some interesting clues about the effectiveness of the framework. For example, it showed that a better knowledge of the problem domain could be gained by modelling at the goal level, and that the resulting BPs could be more complete, hence the designed IS more adequate to its future use. These findings are however still very subjective and need to be confirmed, for example by empirical experiments comparing intention modelling with MAP and other approaches.

Besides, several difficulties were encountered during the SCS experiment: the integration between multiple models is not clear, reasoning about intentions and strategies is less easy than reasoning about sequential processes, adopting at once a top-down attitude is not as easy as the framework and process used might let the user think. Several threads have been undertaken in our research program to better consider these issues. They include in particular the development of a typology of links between MAP and BP modelling techniques, and the creation of training material to guide the process and undertake further experiments.

References

1. Nosek J.T and Palvia P.: Software Maintenance Management: Changes in the Last Decade. In: Journal of Software Maintenance, Vol. 2, No. 3, p. 157-174, 1990.
2. Bubenko J., Brash D., Stirna J.: *EKD User Guide, Elektra Electrical Enterprise Knowledge*. Department of Systems and Computer Science, University of Stockholm/Royal Institute of Technology, Sweden 1998.
3. Jacobson, I., Ericsson, M., Jacobson, A: *The Object Advantage: BP Reengineering With Object Technology*. Addison Wesley, Wokingham, 1994.
4. Freeman M., Layzell P.: *A Meta-Model of Information Systems to Support Reverse Engineering*. Information and Software Technology, 36 (5), pp. 238-294. 1991.

5. Fathee M.M., Redd R., Gorgas D., Modarres B.. *The Effect of Complexity on BP Reegineering: Values and Limitations of Modeling and Simulation Technologies*. Proc. of the 1998 Winter Simulation Conference. D.J. Meideros, E.F. Watson, J.S. Carson, M.S. Manivannan (eds). 1998.
6. Giaglis G. M.: *On the integrated Design and Evaluation of BPs and Information Systems*. Communications of the Association for Information Systems, Volume 1, Article. Department of Information Systems and Computing, Brunel University, UK, June 1999.
7. Nanda A.: *Implementing Organizational Change*. Internal Report. Harvard Business School. USA 1996.
8. Salinesi C., Presso M.J.: *A Method to Analyse Changes in the Realisation of Business Intentions and Strategies for Information System Adaptation*.Proc. of EDOC'02, 6th IEEE International Enterprise Distributed Object Computing Conference, Lausanne, Switzerland, 2002.
9. Lewis P., Goodman S., Fandt P.: *Challenges in the 21st Century Management*. South-Western, 1998.
10. Conradi R., Fernstrom C., Fuggetta A. : *Concepts for evolving software processes*. In A. Finkelstein, J. Kramer, and B. Nuseibeh, editors, Software Process Modeling and Technology, pages 9--31. 1994
11. Jackson M.: Software Requirements and Specifications. Addison-Wesley, 1995.
12. Lodin S.: *Intrusion Detection Product Evaluation Criteria*. http://citeseer.nj.nec.com/16intrusion.html, 1998.
13. van de Ven A., Poole M.S.: *Explaining Development and Change in Organizations*. Academy of Management Review (20:3), 1995, pp. 510-540.
14. Yu E.: *Strategic Modeling for Enterprise Integration*. Proceedings 14 th World Congress of the International Federation of Automatic Control, July 5-9, 1999, Beijing, China.
15. Weinrich, H. & Koontz, H. : *Management: A Global Perspective*, McGraw-Hill, 1993.
16. Curtis W., Kellner M. I., Over J.: *Process Modeling*. Communications of the ACM, 35, 9, USA 1992.
17. Pettersson P. and Wäyrynen J.: *Verksamhetsmodellering med EBML*. Department of Computer and Systems Science, University of Stockholm/Royal Institute of Technology, Master Thesis, Sweden 2001.
18. Boehm, B.: *Software Engineering*. In IEEE Transactions on Computers, Vol. C-25, No. 12, 1976.
19. Salinesi C. and Wäyrynen J.: *Business Maps Presentation of Concepts and Illustration with the Stockholm Central Service (SCS) Case Study*. FTR&D internal report, project "Objectifs d'Entreprise et Système d'Information – Réflexion Conceptuelle et Cadre Méthodologique pour l'Analyse de Changement", France 2001.
20. Hammer, M. *Beyond Reengineering*. Harper Collins Publishers, USA 1996.
21. Warboys B.: *Reflections on the relationship between BPR and Software Process Modeling*. Informatics Process Group (IPG), Department of Computer Science, University of Manchester, UK 1994.

Adapting Analysis and Design to Software Context: The JECKO Approach

Isabelle Mirbel[1] and Violaine de Rivieres[2]

[1] Laboratoire I3S
Route des Lucioles - BP 121, 06903 Sophia Antipolis Cedex, France
[2] Amadeus sas
485 Route du Pin Montard, B.P. 69, 06902 Sophia Antipolis Cedex, France

Abstract. New object-oriented technologies have been developed in order to manage complexity inherent in new information system development. But developments are very different one from the others, and a given technique, notation or mechanism is used differently depending an the Software under consideration. Flexibility is required from the methodology with regards to the Software context.
We propose JECKO, a flexible approach to analysis and design rohere flexibility is handled through a fragmentation mechanism. In order to adapt the analysis and design activities, fragments are selected with regards to Software context. The chosen fragments constitute the route map built for the Software specificity.

1 Introduction

New object-oriented technologies have been developed in order to manage complexity inherent to new information system development. Adapted methodologies have also been developed to support and take advantage of these techniques and mechanisms [1,2]. Moreover, developments are very different one from the others, and a given technique, notation or mechanism may be used in a different way depending on the development under consideration. There is no universal methodology [4]. Therefore it seems to be a need for flexible processes, adaptable to different kinds of software development [6,4].

In this paper, we propose JECKO, a flexible approach to analysis and design: Flexibility is handled through a `fragmentation` mechanism. In order to adapt the analysis and design activities, `fragments` are selected with regards to software context, specified through four predefined basic criteria.

A fragment embodied modeling rules and guidelines to help through the analysis and design activities (A&D-Ac).

The chosen `fragments` constitute the route map built for the software specificity.

2 The Software Context

Software development success requires initially the advised selection of modeling concepts (model elements, diagrams, artifacts, etc.) in order to deal efficiently

Z. Bellahsène, D. Patel, and C. Rolland (Eds.): OOIS 2002, LNCS 2425, pp. 223–228, 2002.

with A&D-Ac. In this section, we present four criterias to specify the software context. Thanks to these criterias, the Analysis and Design Process (A&D-Pr) can be better adapted by selecting tasks to do and artifacts to use for getting accurate outcomes.

Dealing with Running Software: Most of the softwares are now built on top of running software. In this context, it is required to specify precisely what has to be kept from what has to be replaced or enhanced. Different aspects of running software may be taken into consideration: the `code`, the expertise about the `functional domain`, the `interfaces` describing the relationships the running software has with other systems. A&D-Ac will be different with regards to the preservation kind. Different diagrams and modeling concepts may be more or less suitable to highlight different reuse aspects. The three preservation aspects (functionalities, interfaces, code) should be modulated in order to be better exploited during the development phase. We qualify each of them by : (i) *strong* when no modification is allowed, (ii)*medium* when modifications are allowed inside given boundaries, and (iii) *weak* when modifications are allowed with few limits. Preservation specification and qualification help to tailor the A&D-Pr to manage it more efficiently. In [3], the authors propose a profile to deal with such context through the UML notation.

Dealing with Graphical User Interface (GUI): Lot of tools and techniques are currently available on the market and propose generic frameworks to facilitate GUI development, reducing the design activity for this aspect. In consequence, to fully benefit from such tools and techniques, the A&D-Pr has to be adapted by isolating the GUI specification from the business one; this is not so easy for end-users who are usually enclined to describe the software business only through its GUI.

Dealing with Database: Dealing with database requires to organize data in such way that specific database rules (as the normal form decomposition) can be followed. Traditional A&D-Pr propose efficient ways for dealing with database design. Moreover, dedicated concepts are required to built effective database: primary key, index, etc. To fully manage these concepts, additional information has to be captured through the analysis activity. And finally, if the project under development includes the choice of one database management system, the analysis outcome must be one key input for this choice. For these reasons, the A&D-Pr has to be adapted with regards to database aspect.

Dealing with Distributed Software: Distributed softwares are more complex to apprehend. Most of the time, they require particular organization of the A&D-Ac to fully handle the distribution aspects. Moreover, specific problems and requirements may be encountered with distributed software (link feature, response time, network security aspects, ...). The A&D-Pr has to be adapted to handle correctly and at the right time such specificity.

The four criterias we have presented are simple and concrete. They only require an answer by *yes* or *no* to allow the A&D-Pr adaptation and to improve its outcomes. The software context is evaluated *a priori* with regards to these criterias.

3 The JECKO Framework

In order to be used by anyone without fundamentally changing his main A&D-Pr phases, the JECKO framework supports a decomposition into standard phases.

3.1 Facing Problems through Different Points of View: JECKO Phases

The `Requirement Analysis` deals with the requirement formalization: explicit requirements, expressed by the end-user, as well as implicit ones, deduced by the analyst. Then, the `Domain and Business Object Analysis` focuses on the specification of the business covered by the software to be developed. *Requirement Analysis* and *Domain and Business Object Analysis* may be processed in parallel. The third phase concentrates on the `Software and System Architecture`. Then, the forth phase, `Component Specification`, copes with the integration of the different components mainly through the identification of the interfaces among them. *Software and System Architecture* and *Component Specification* phases may be processed in parallel. They provide two complementary and essential view points on the software to be developed. Finally, through the *Internal Design* phase, the specification of each element (mainly component) previously defined is refined to allow the implementation.

3.2 Organizing Analysis and Design Work: JECKO Steps

Each phase reassembles related A&D-Ac dedicated to a given aspect of the A&D-Pr. The different phases have been decomposed into `steps`, which allow to better organize the activities associated with the current phase. We provide the same decomposition into four main steps, in each phase to help in having a coherent and systematic approach.

- The first step, `Introduction` step, copes with preliminary tasks to enhance the forthcoming step progress.
- The second step, `Core` step, encompasses the main tasks of the current phase. These tasks concentrate on the elaboration of the phase outcome.
- The third step, `Refinement` step, focuses on organizing and refining the various diagrams and concepts built through the previous steps.
- The last step, `Investigation` step, concerns specific tasks required to better handle additional aspects crucial for the A&D-Pr success.

3.3 JECKO Backbone: The Fragment

The JECKO methodology proposes in each step a set of `guidelines`, expressed with the UML notation. To help in applying the guidelines, they are provided with additional information in what we call a `fragment`, which allows to handle flexibility of the A&D-Pr with regards to the software context. A fragment is defined with the following elements:

- **Name:** to identify the fragment;
- **Situation:** to position the fragment with regard to the software context;
- **Intention:** to present the fragment purpose;
- **Guidelines:** to explain how to proceed for answering the intention.
- **Associated fragments:** to point out related fragments which have to be considered because they share some aspects with the current fragment.

Whatever is the software context, A&D-Ac include unavoidable tasks: specification of the system boundaries, business description, etc; but they have to be handled slightly differently depending on the software context. Furthermore, context-related additional tasks may also be suitable through the A&D-Pr. Therefore, in JECKO, we distinguish *context-dependent* fragments from *context-independent* ones. They are respectively named `dedicated fragments` and `prime fragments`.

3.4 JECKO Framework Instanciation: The Route Map

By situating the software with regards to the four predefined criteria, the framework is tailored: suitable fragments (mandatory *prime fragment* and dedicated *specific fragment*) are selected to drive the A&D-Ac. These fragments, sequentially organized in time, constitute the `route map` associated with the software specificity.

4 Handling Flexibility through the JECKO Approach

Flexibility is handled by selecting the fragments dedicated to the software under development. In this section we present, as an example, the different fragments provided through the `Domain & Business Object Analysis` phase. They are summarized in figure 1 and detailed in the following. A presentation of the whole process may be found in [5].

Prime Fragments: This phase of the A&D-Pr is dedicated to the study of the business objects, mainly supported by the `Business Object` fragment. Most of the time, objects are described in a static way through classes, attributes and relationship among classes. Sometimes it may be interesting to investigate the specification by a dynamic point of view (`Object State` fragment - *Investigation* step). Functional tests are handled through the `Tests` fragment.

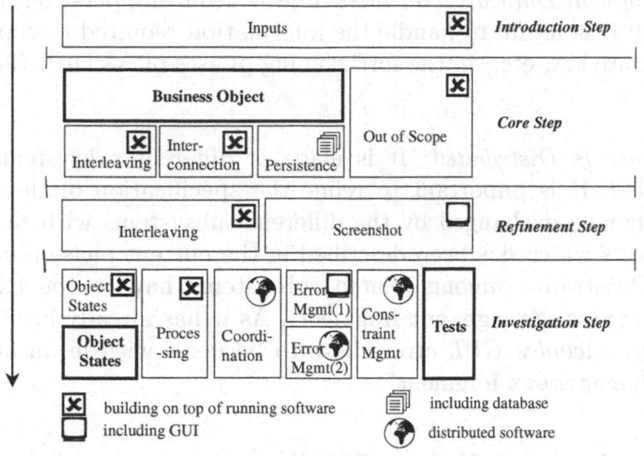

Fig. 1. The JECKO Framework - Domain and Business Object Analysis

When Dealing with Running Software: Information about business object may have to be taken from the running part of the software (`Inputs` fragment). It is crucial to document the interleaving between existing and new aspects of the software (`Interleaving` fragments - *core* and *refinement* steps). In the same way, business objects from the running software, which are not directly related to the new development, may be of interest to help to understand what is or not provided through the new development (`Out of scope` fragment). Communications with the running software are represented in terms of actors interacting with the software under development. Actors may represent constraints on the way the new software will be working (`Interconnection` fragment).

The description of business objects specified through the development may be completed by a dynamic point of view through state diagrams, as it has been explained above. To be coherent, if business object from the running software are statically described through the A&D-Pr, they also have to be described from a dynamic point of view (`Object states` fragment).

When developing on top of existing softwares, some services provided by the whole software may indeed be supported by both the new and the existing part of the software. In this case, it is important to explain what is the process flow associated with the service (`Processing` fragment).

When Dealing with GUI: The screen shots elaborated through the *Requirement Analysis* phase have to be refined through the *Domain and Business Object Analysis* with regards to the object specification (`Screen shoot` fragment). In the same way, errors which have been used through the functionality specification have to be summarized in a class diagram. It will ensure coherence and consistency in error management (`Error Management` fragment).

When Dealing with Database: Business objects requiring persistence have to be distinguished: it is useful to handle the information required to support persistence (candidate key, etc.) in the forthcoming phases of A&D-Pr (`Persistence` fragment).

When Software Is Distributed: It is made of different subsystems communicating together. It is important to refine the specification of the information (messages, signals) exchanged by the different subsystems with regards to the business objects which has been described in the current phase (`Coordination` fragment). Constraints among related subsystems have to be clearly established (`Constraint-Management` fragment). As it has already been highlighted when *software includes GUI*, errors have to be dealt with in an homogeneous way(`Error Management` fragment).

5 Conclusion and Future Work

In this paper, we have presented JECKO, a flexible approach to analysis and design. A&D-Ac are adapted with regards to software *context*, specified through four predefined basic *criteria*. Thanks to this context, suitable fragments may be selected to better deal with the specificity of the software being considered. The main purpose of a fragment is to propose modeling rules and guidelines to help through the A&D-Ac. The chosen *fragments* constitute the *route map* built for the software, to focus on the critical aspects of the development and to better handle its complexity.

In the future, we would like to improve the context specification with information related to the project (i.e. time pressure, dependency with other projects). And we would also like to weight the fragments with regards to the designer expertise to provide end-users adapted route maps.

References

1. Rochefeld A. Bouzeghoub M. *OOM, la conception objet des systemes d'information.* Hermes Sciences, 2000. 223
2. D'Souza D. *Catalysis: Objects, Components, and Frameworks with UML.* Object Technology Series. Addison-Wesley, 1998. 223
3. Mirbel I. and de Rivieres V. Towards a UML profile for building on top of an existing application. In *Information Resources Management Association International Conference*, Seattle, USA, May 2002. 224
4. Ralyte J. *Ingenierie des methodes a base de composants.* PhD thesis, Universite Paris I - Sorbonne, January 2001. 223
5. De Rivieres V. Mirbel I. Adapting Analysis and Design to Software Context: the JECKO Approach. Technical Report I3S/RR-2002-14-FR, I3S Laboratory, April 2002. 226
6. Glass R.L. Vessey I. Applications-based methodologies. *Information System Management*, pages 53–57, Fall 1994. 223

Organizational Transition to Object Technology: Theory and Practice

M.K. Serour[1], B. Henderson-Sellers[1], J. Hughes[1], D. Winder[2], and L. Chow[2]

[1]University of Technology, Sydney
P.O. Box 123 Broadway 2007 NSW Australia
{mserour,brian,hughes}@it.uts.edu.au
[2]Thomson Legal and Regulatory Group Asia Pacific Ltd.
Level 5, 100 Harris Street, Pyrmont, NSW 1009, Australia
{darryl.winder,lynette.chow}@thomson.com.au

Abstract. The use of object technology (OT) has been highly successful for many software development companies, yet there are still a large number of organizations who have not yet adopted OT. For those companies currently adopting object technology, the transition from traditional procedurally-oriented technologies remains a challenge. Indeed, there is sparse empirical evidence to suggest the best ways to undertake this culture change. Here, we reports on action research results of two case studies within the software development arm of a large multinational professional information solutions provider. The company used the Trans-OPEN process for their transition process. This transition process has seven major activities: initiation, planning, technology insertion, deployment, the use of a retrospective for evaluation, improvement planning and further improvement – the process is incremental and iterative. Furthermore, the case studies underline the need for a more formal approach to culture change in the context of the adoption of object technology.

1 Introduction: Company Transition to Object Technology

While it is clear that the use of object technology (OT) has been highly successful for many companies e.g. [1,2], there are still a large number of organizations who have not yet adopted OT. This is a reflection of the traditional bell shaped adoption curve in which 50% of companies are "followers" or "laggards" in the adoption of any new information technology. These more conservative organizations seem now to be the focus of a "second wave" of interest in the adoption of object technology (the first wave being many of the financial and telecommunications organizations for whom OT is now "old hat" and mainstream).

However, the adoption of OT implies a number of problems, commonly including resistance to the necessary organizational culture change. It has to be made very clear from the beginning to both developers and managers that OT is not a magic wand or a

Z. Bellahsène, D. Patel, and C. Rolland (Eds.): OOIS 2002, LNCS 2425, pp. 229-241, 2002.

silver bullet to make the entire organization's dreams come true but, rather, is simply today's best technology option [3]. Nonetheless, it is also important that managers appreciate not only the benefits of OT, but also become aware of all the pitfalls [4] and consequences of new technology adoption.

Since OT contains elements relevant to all stages of the development lifecycle (not only coding) and includes models for requirements engineering, project management, team building and so on, adopting OT, often supplemented by a Component-Based Development (CBD) approach[1], requires a combination of learning about technical issues as well as larger scale sociological and process issues [6]. Here we focus on those process issues in the context of a case study undertaken with a professional information solutions provider in Sydney, Australia to evaluate the efficacy of the Trans-OPEN approach [7] for the introduction of an OO software process into an industrial site.

2 The Need for a Process

A software development project team uses a methodology/process to assist them in their efforts to create a software-intensive system as effectively and efficiently as possible. Team dynamics play a major role [8], as do individual skills. While playing second fiddle to the peopleware, the use of a process is seen by many as part of a successful recipe. Processes range in "size" from lightweight e.g. [9] to "high ceremony" e.g. [10] and must be compatible with the level of process formality within the organization. For instance, a highly bureaucratic organization will prefer a more rigid, high ceremony process whereas a free thinking "cowboy coding" shop will prefer minimal process (for details of organizational cultural stereotypes, see [11]). Process capability assessment is also increasing in visibility, through the work of the Capability Maturity Model (CMM) [12] and the more recent CMMi as well as ISO15504 [13], which resulted from the SPICE (Software Process Improvement and Capability dEtermination) initiative. Both of these "hold up a mirror" to the organization in order that they might assess their maturity, particularly in their use of process and metrics.

3 Process Diffusion

While methodologies/processes offer good advice on the processes for software development, they offer no support for the necessary pre-condition: that the organization (or team) become familiar with the use of the object-oriented paradigm itself, through the adoption of one of the currently available OO methods/processes. For a team about to embark on its first OO project, there is an additional need for guidelines

[1] Whilst OT and CBD are orthogonal "technologies", most component-based systems developed today use OT as, at least, their underpinning implementation technology. Current work in the OOSPICE project [5] beings together components and objects in the context of capability assessment.

describing the transition from a traditional organizational culture to one in which the object paradigm is dominant.

With the increasing demand from organizations to transition to OT/CBD, project managers find it hard to proceed when there is (still) very little guidance available from real world experience besides the existence of a large number of methodologies and tools for software development. Transitioning to OT/CBD requires its own special guidance and specific methodological support during the different stages of transition. Making a decision to move the organization from where they are to what they are aiming at is a very serious managerial and technical matter since it can have a strong impact on the entire organization. Management level sponsorship is another people-focussed constituent for successful transition. In other words, everyone, from senior managers and decision-makers through project managers to developers must endorse the idea of a transition to OT/CBD. If any key individual offers resistance, it is all too easy for that resistance to be manifested in project failure.

The best guidance that could be offered would be a means by which the technology insertion (of OT/CBD) would be accomplished. In other words, a *process* needs to be used and followed to support the transition to OT. While companies have successfully transitioned to OT/CBD, the process they followed has never been either written down, published or otherwise disseminated. It is likely that the technology insertion processes followed have been ad hoc and are unlikely ever to be formalized. In this paper, we describe the use in industry of a process which can be used to "insert the technology". The full description of this insertion process, a process based on the well-known OO process OPEN [14,15], is to be found in [7]. We use an instance of the OPEN Process Framework (or OPF), augmented with a few new activities and tasks and called Trans-OPEN, to assist in bringing the full OO method/process into full acceptance within an organization. The first case study (of a professional information solutions provider) commenced in August 2000 and the second case study began in February 2001. These are described in detail in Section 5.

4 Trans-OPEN in Theory

Trans-OPEN is a specially constructed process generated from the process components of the OPEN Process Framework's (OPF) repository (Figure 1). The OPF consists of a process metamodel that provides a set of definitions from which can be created a large number of instances. These are process components, stored in the repository. From this set of components, a number are selected and put together to form a highly customized process/ methodology – here one targetted at supporting the organizational transition (Trans-OPEN). A process instance (bottom box of Figure 1) is an enactment of this customized process for one particular project. In other words, while many instantiations from the OPF are designed to support software development, Trans-OPEN is a process used to assist a company in its introduction of a software development process into the organization. Process introduction requires social as well as technical and financial commitment so that the company culture moves from (usually) a "cowboy coding" culture to one in which a process is followed and even improved as the organization starts to climb the "SPICE or CMM ladder".

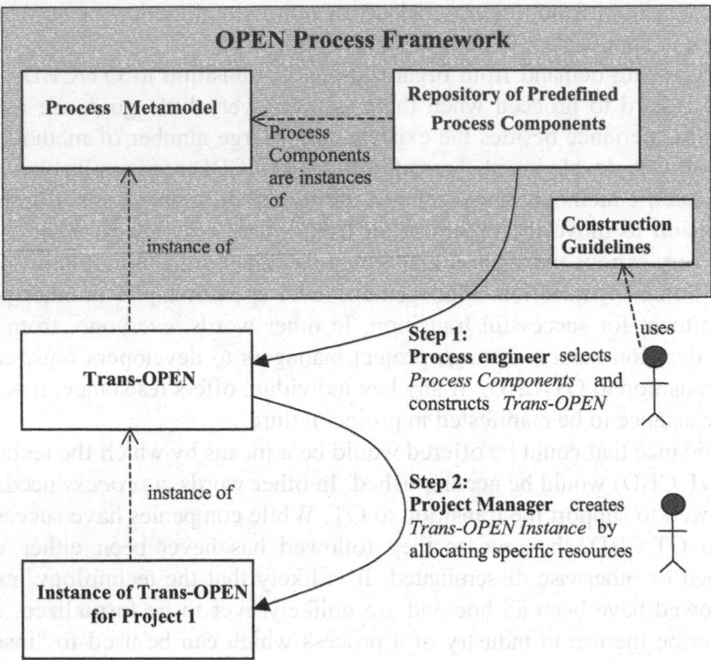

Fig. 1. Creation of Trans-OPEN from the OPEN Process Framework. Components are selected from the repository by the process engineer. This customized process is then used, either for software development or, as here, for supporting the process of organizational transition (adapted from [16])

The Trans-OPEN process [7] uses process components already existing in the OPEN Process Framework (OPF) and also identified a number of identified process components necessary to support process introduction that were not already described. These were then added to the OPF repository and are listed in Table 1. The enhanced suite of process components now provides the source material for the construction of a process to insert a process i.e. Trans-OPEN (Figure 2). This process can itself be constructed in such a way as to optimize the support it offers for the particular organization about to undergo the (cultural) transition to the use of a standardized process (and possibly object technology at the same time).

Based on the theory for Trans-OPEN, expounded in [7] and summarized here, we now report on the results of its application at a major professional information solutions provider operating in Sydney and Canberra (Australia) who chose to transition their IT teams from a non-OO, non-process focus to a process-focussed development environment using, incidentally, the OPEN process as its software development process and introducing UML to support its new object-oriented directions which had commenced earlier with their adoption of Java as their coding language of preference.

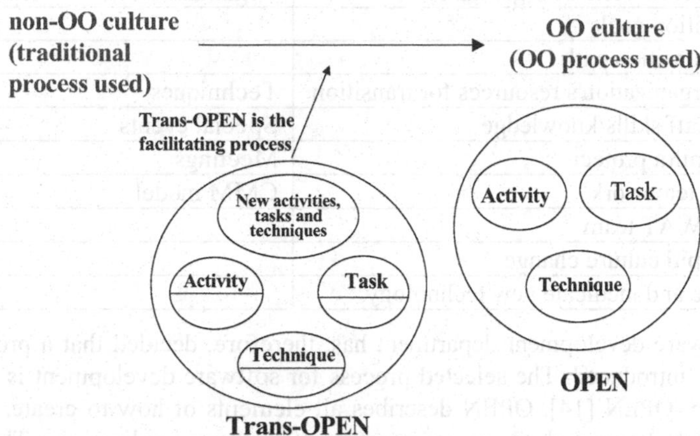

Fig. 2. Moving from a non-OO culture to an OO culture, including the use of an OO process, requires the use of a transition process. Here, Trans-OPEN [7] – an instance of the OPF – is used to accomplish this culture change. The end result is the adoption of OT and the use of the OPEN process in a form suitable for supporting software development

Using an action research methodology, we investigate the suitability of this transitioning approach in terms of a research hypothesis, which can be stated as

> In the context of moving to the new technologies of OO/CBD, following a transition process specifically constructed to help organizations in planning and managing their move to OT can have a positive impact on the success of their adoption of a well-defined software engineering process.

5 Trans-OPEN in Practice

Trans-OPEN supports all the necessary aspects of a process by which an OO process can be introduced into a software development organization. The two case studies relate to a Sydney professional information solutions provider: Thomson Legal and Regulatory - Asia Pacific. Thomson currently has a fairly small development team made up of a mixture of experienced and inexperienced permanent staff and a number of contractors. All software development is done in a fairly ad hoc way depending on the experience of the developers, which has caused major problems especially with contractors. These problems manifest themselves in a number of different ways: mismatches in communications when discussing different aspects of the system, time wasted due to ad hoc/informal on-the-job training and inconsistencies in the final design.

Table 1. Activities, Tasks and Techniques added to the OPF repository to create Trans-OPEN

Tasks	Activities
Assess current state of organization	Organization Assessment
Set transition goals	
Assess transition path	
Assess organization's resources for transition	Techniques
Assess staff skills/knowledge	Special events
Identify pilot project	Meetings
Enhance teamwork	CMM model
Create SWAT team	
Effect rapid culture change	
Introduce and inculcate new technology	

The software development department has, therefore, decided that a process must be officially introduced. The selected process for software development is an object-oriented one: OPEN [14]. OPEN describes all elements of how to create, tailor and use an OO/CBD approach to the construction of software applications. The research reported here targets the creation and testing of a process for the insertion of OPEN. Rather than using an incompatible insertion/diffusion process, we have created a totally aligned insertion process, itself created from the metamodel underpinning OPEN. This insertion process is the Trans-OPEN process described above.

5.1 Case Study 1 (August 2000 – February 2001)

The first case study revolved around the proposition of introducing OT and OPEN into the organization. The research hypothesis was the testing of the already pre-configured Trans-OPEN process for process insertion (described above) together with the opportunity to further improve this Trans-OPEN process. The research methodology was action research e.g. [17] in which the first author (MKS) worked on site with the professional information solutions provider and, incidentally, the second author (BH-S) provided training on basic object technology, OPEN and project management to various groups within the organization. In addition, training on UML together with the company's selected CASE tool was given by an external consultant.

This first case study commenced in mid-August 2000. The focus of this first pilot project was the introduction and establishment of a Software Engineering Process (SEP) into the organization to replace the existing ad-hoc process then in use. For this first pilot project, the organization selected one of its existing software applications (Search Engine) to be re-developed. Prior to the authors' involvement, it had been proposed to introduce RUP [10]. However, it was soon realized that this process was much too "heavyweight" for a pilot project. Before the commencement of this first project, the organization was assessed at level 1 of the SPICE scale (Table 2). The organization declared an aim of achieving level 3 of the SPICE scale (equivalent to CMM Level 3) by the end of the transition project.

Table 2. Results of the SPICE assessment undertaken prior to commencement of the two pilot projects

Process to be assessed	SPICE Level achieved
Requirements elicitation	1
Software development	1
Configuration management	0
Quality assurance	0
Problem resolution	0
Project management	1
Risk management	0
Process establishment	0

By early 2001, it was becoming evident that the commitment to the project was not total. Team members found they had other commitments; middle management, while being fully committed with a (reasonable) budget was unable to identify and commit the necessary (human) resources. In February 2001, it was decided to terminate this first pilot project – the organization's management stated that an enormous amount had been learned and thus overall the project had been very successful. However, from the point of view of an action researcher, the project was not successful since it was prematurely terminated and the end result was not the anticipated widespread use of a software development process. Rather than being part of the culture the idea of using a process was still somewhat of an anachronism within the company.

Nevertheless, what had been learned was that, with appropriate financial and resource commitment, this was clearly the right direction. Consequently a larger budget was sought for a second pilot project (see below). In February 2001, the mindset was still epitomized by the phrase "I haven't got time to sharpen my axe; I am too busy chopping trees". In fact, the team was experiencing the low productivity that necessarily follows a few months after the initial introduction of a new technology (Figure 3). They therefore looked for "excuses" including

- lack of proper planning, introduction of OT to the developers, provision of education/training and general preparation for the transition to OT
- lack of time and resources to instantiate an organizational SEP from the OPF
- misinterpretation of the business objectives
- wrong selection criteria for choosing the pilot project (probably a realistic and important conclusion)
- need for new resources necessarily removed from other, existing projects
- changing company policies
- lack of resources despite having a budget for the project (a second important conclusion)
- changing customer requirements
- poor estimation of tasks required in new technology (not surprisingly)
- slower learning curve than originally anticipated
- slower than anticipated progress
- low importance of pilot project

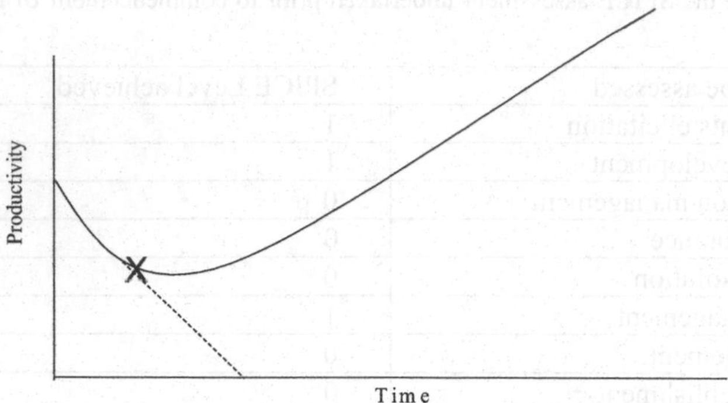

Fig. 3. The schematic plot of productivity against time when adopting a new technology. As a result of the inevitable learning curve, productivity initially drops, before rising later to levels greater than those achieved initially (i.e. with the old technology). Many projects are cancelled at the low productivity point (X) since the pessimism of the extrapolated line (dashed) is accepted rather than the non-linear increase that is observed by successful (and tenacious) companies

In addition, it soon became clear that the wrong project had been selected since it had little visibility and insufficient importance within the organization (few would care whether it failed or succeeded) and, finally, that the involvement of end users was too low.

From the researchers' viewpoint, while the above list is understandable, we would highlight the limited resources and lack of commitment, often imposed because of the need to retain involvement of the transition project team members in existing (older) projects.

We also observed (as is often the case) resistance from several participants in this pilot project. There was often frustration about the slowness of the adoption of this (potentially exciting) new technology – the initial excitement soon waned. For some, the encouragement of any process to create more documentation than a coder often finds satisfying (often none!) was thought to be detrimental to progress. A final problem that was unearthed was the considerable challenge of a monolithic or "big bang" process adoption. This turned out to be a major stumbling block.

5.2 Case Study 2 (February 2001 – February 2002)

The conclusion of the first case study was that if sufficient resources could be made available (especially people and time) and that the process ideas could be introduced incrementally, then a much higher profile (within the company) second pilot project could be introduced and could succeed. This was more successful.

The second pilot project was a new set of web-based software applications urgently needed for the organization to offer their products on-line – a direct response to their competitors' actions. In contrast with the first project, this pilot project was not focussed on the rewriting (in OO) of an existing piece of software, a software development unlikely to impact anyone in the organization significantly, whether it succeeded or not. Senior management did not justify the enormous cost associated with the introduction of a new technology when this first pilot project was selected. On the other hand and for the second project, senior management was willing to meet any cost to get the new software developed since they way the project not simply in terms of a potentially successful or unsuccessful outcome but rather one that was critical to the future viability of the group. The organization was thus willing to do everything possible in order to ensure the project's success, emphasizing the important and compelling reasons for transition as identified in early 2001.

The observations of the researchers during March and April 2001 were more favourable. The manager had been promoted which gave him the ability to sponsor the project more effectively and thus the budget was significantly expanded. The learning of the team continued and a more realistic understanding of iterative and incremental delivery was gained.

By April 2001, a first draft document of the OPEN/Thomson process had been constructed and reviewed. The terminology was now beginning to be the lingua franca across the two groups (management and technical teams in Sydney and Canberra). One important observation from one particular management meeting was that individuals were being (unfairly) criticized rather than the products. This harmed the team building exercise that was otherwise very successful. The members of the transition team, charged with leading the culture change, were increasingly being seen as some sort of "champions" within the organization. Thoroughness was becoming the norm e.g. in using consistent terminology, in ensuring everyone understood any acronyms used, undertaking regular reviews and creating a supportive environment for the team rather than a punitive one.

During the first review meeting, the transition team "champions" documented everyone's comments and feedback regarding all the changes and/or modifications that needed to be applied to OPEN/Thomson process. A transition discussion list and a special email address were created on the Thomson Intranet for people to discuss and send further feedback. The transition team enhanced the new process by applying all the appropriate changes and also updated the associated documents and created new ones to support the whole transition. These documents included:

- Software Engineering Process – User Guide
- Software Engineering Process – Reference Manual
- Software Engineering Process – Glossary
- Software Engineering Process – Quick Reference Card

By June 2001, the second draft documents of the OPEN/Thomson process were reviewed by a group of senior and programme managers, project leaders and system developers. Two weeks prior to the review meeting, all documents were made available to everyone on Thomson's Intranet for reviewing. The main discussion issues were related to the process support level and creating new support documents. The OPEN/Thomson process was configured from the OPF to support software engineering at the organizational level. This process will be instantiated for different projects within the organization. Managers and project leaders suggested modifying the OPEN/Thomson process to support and guide system developers at the project level.

The senior manager commented that they needed to solve problems of day to day operations first before worrying about the organizational level.

New process support documents were recommended including:

- Policy and Procedure Manual – to provide base details about the Thomson IT infrastructure in terms of databases, languages, tools and so on.
- Software Engineering Process Work Book – to give a walkthrough of the whole process using a case study from Thomson domain. This document can be used by new people joining Thomson to get familiar with the process in operation.

At the same time, an external consultant was called in to undertake a thorough analysis of available CASE/drawing tools for UML. Based on his recommendation, the TogetherSoft tool was selected and purchased and the consultant then provided training in UML in the context of this selected tool.

Later, another meeting was conducted by the researcher to meet with the organization culture change manager to discuss some related issues regarding the organizational management changes. During this meeting, the researcher suggested setting up a reward system for the people working on the transition process in order to encourage them to "keep up the good work". This could be a pleasant letter or a certificate or even a quick email message to show them that their work is greatly appreciated. The manager welcomed and accepted the idea and promised that prompt action would be taken soon.

By October 2001, the final documents were constructed and a full process presentation was designed to introduce and launch the new process in Sydney and Canberra. The process launch in Sydney was performed in two separate sessions with around 25 people in each session. The whole presentation was very successful and the transition team effort was greatly appreciated by everyone. The transition team members received a number of greeting and thank you messages from most of the audience. Two days later, one of the transition team member went to the Canberra office with the senior manager to launch and present the new process to all managers and developers. With great success again, the Canberra launch went very well and everyone was so excited to start using their new process on real projects.

The Software Engineering Process Group (SEPG). After the successful launch of the OPEN/Thomson software engineering process, a special group was voluntarily established to facilitate evaluation and improvement of the software engineering process. The SEPG was established to:

- Assist project managers and business managers in incorporating the new SEP into all projects
- Continuously improve the existing SEP
- Provide support to managers in changing the present culture of software development from being 'ad hoc' to one of formal process

By November 2001, the transition team began to evaluate two different projects prior to finally selecting their first pilot project. A final decision is expected to be made in March 2002.

6 Discussion and Summary

The elements of the previously proposed Trans-OPEN process for process insertion were able to be evaluated and refined. Based on observations from the two pilot projects, using the action research methodology, together with reflection on these observations, we have been able to provide empirical evidence for the transition process as shown in Figure 4. This process has seven major activities: initiation, planning, technology insertion, deployment, the use of a retrospective for evaluation, improvement planning and further improvement. Thus the process is incremental and iterative – some of the iterative feedback paths are shown in Figure 4.

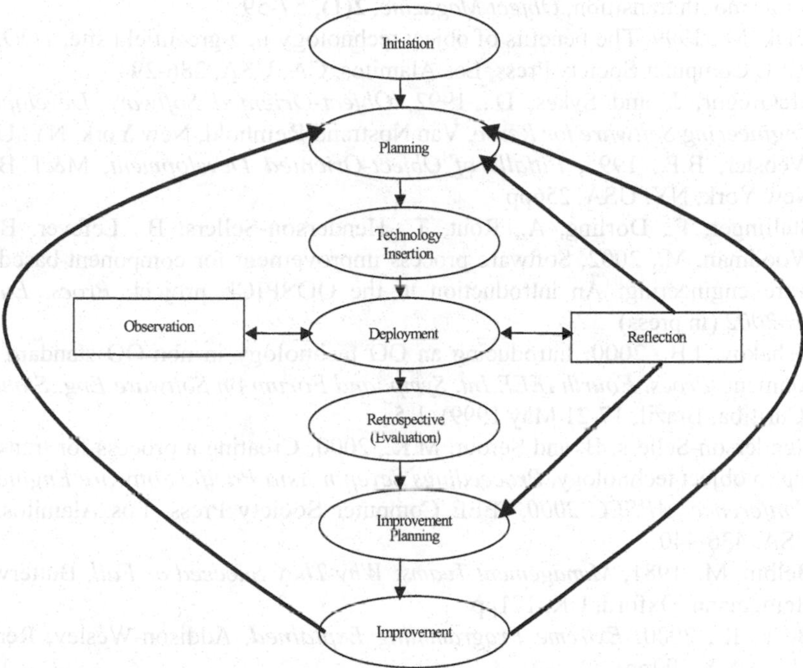

Fig. 4. The SEP for process transition as configured from the OPF and evaluated in the two case studies at Thomson, as described in this paper

The case studies underline the need for a more formal approach to culture change in the context of the adoption of object technology, together with a process improvement strategy leading the organization under study to being a migration from SPICE level 0/1 towards level 3. Planning is a vital component, both pre-planning and mid-process re-planning as necessary. The final stages of the company's transition are now assured and will be completed by the undertaking of a second SPICE assessment later in 2002.

Acknowledgements

This research was funded in part by grants from the Australian Research Council. This is Contribution Number 02/06 of the Centre for Object Technology Applications and Research (COTAR).

References

1. Parkhill, D., 1992, Object-oriented technology transfer: techniques and guidelines for a smooth transition, *Object Magazine*, **2(1)**, 57-59
2. Dick, M., 1999, The benefits of object technology in a greenfield site, *TOOLS32*, IEEE Computer Society Press, Los Alamitos, CA, USA, 286-294
3. McGregor, J. and Sykes, D., 1992, *Object-Oriented Software Development: Engineering Software for Reuse*, Van Nostrand Reinhold, New York, NY, USA
4. Webster, B.F., 1995, *Pitfalls of Object-Oriented Development*, M&T Books, New York, NY, USA, 256pp
5. Stallinger, F., Dorling, A., Rout, T., Henderson-Sellers, B., Lefever, B. and Woodman, M., 2002, Software process improvement for component-based software engineering: An introduction to the OOSPICE project, *Procs. Euromicro2002* (in press)
6. Ushakov, I.B., 2000, Introducing an OO technology in non-OO standard environment, *Procs. Fourth IEEE Int. Symp. and Forum on Software Eng. Standards* (Curitiba, Brazil, 17-21 May 1999), 1-5
7. Henderson-Sellers, B. and Serour, M.K., 2000, Creating a process for transitioning to object technology, *Proceedings Seventh Asia Pacific Software Engineering Conference. APSEC 2000*, IEEE Computer Society Press, Los Alamitos, CA, USA, 436-440
8. Belbin, M., 1981, *Management Teams: Why They Succeed or Fail,* Butterworth-Heinemann, Oxford, UK, 171pp
9. Beck, K., 2000, *Extreme Programming Explained*, Addison-Wesley, Reading, MA, USA, 190pp
10. Kruchten, Ph., 1999, *The Rational Unified Process. An Introduction,* Addison Wesley Longman Inc., Reading, MA, USA, 255pp
11. Constantine, L.L. and Lockwood, L.A.D., 1994, Fitting practices to the people, *American Programmer*, **7(12)**, 21-27
12. Paulk, C., Weber, C.V., Garcia, S., Chrissis, M.B. and Bush, M., 1993, Key Practices of the Capability Maturity Model, Version 1.1, CMU/SEI?93?TR?25, Software Engineering Institute, Carnegie Mellon University, Pittsburgh, PA, USA (February 1993)
13. ISO/IEC, 1998, *TR15504, Information technology – software process assessment*, in 9 parts, International Standards Organization, Geneva, Switzerland
14. Graham, I., Henderson-Sellers, B. and Younessi, H., 1997, *The OPEN Process Specification,* Addison-Wesley, Harlow, UK, 314pp

15. Henderson-Sellers, B., Simons, A.J.H. and Younessi, H., 1998, *The OPEN Toolbox of Techniques*, Addison-Wesley, Harlow, UK, 426pp + CD
16. Henderson-Sellers, B., Bohling, J. and Rout, T., 2002, Creating the OOSPICE model architecture - a case of reuse, *Procs. SPICE 2002,* Palazzo Papafava, Venice, 13-15 March 2002 (ed. T. Rout), Qualital, Italy, 171-181
17. Mumford, E., 2001, Advice for an action researcher, *Information Technology & People*, **14(1)**, 12-27

Reflective Analysis and Design for Adapting Object Run-Time Behavior

Walter Cazzola[1], Ahmed Ghoneim[2], and Gunter Saake[2]

[1] Department of Informatics and Computer Science, Università degli Studi di Genova
Via Dodecaneso 35, 16146, Genova, Italy
cazzola@disi.unige.it

[2] Institute für Technische und Betriebliche Informationssysteme
Otto-von-Guericke-Universität Magdeburg
Postfach 4120, D-39016 Magdeburg, Germany
{ghoneim,saake}@iti.cs.uni-magdeburg.de

Abstract. Today, complex information systems need a simple way for changing the object behavior according with changes that occur in its running environment. We present a reflective architecture which provides the ability to change object behavior at run-time by using design-time information. By integrating reflection with design patterns we get a flexible and easily adaptable architecture. A reflective approach that describes object model, scenarios and statecharts helps to dynamically adapt the software system to environmental changes. The object model, system scenario and many other design information are reified by special meta-objects, named *evolutionary meta-objects*. Evolutionary meta-objects deal with two types of run-time evolution. Structural evolution is carried out by causal connection between evolutionary meta-objects and its referents through changing the structure of these referents by adding or removing objects or relations. Behavioral evolution allows the system to dynamically adapt its behavior to environment changes by itself. Evolutionary meta-objects react to environment changes for adapting the information they have reified and steering the system evolution. They provide a natural liaison between design information and the system based on such information. This paper describes how this liaison can be built and how it can be used for adapting a running system to environment changes.

Keywords: Reflection, Meta-Objects, Design Pattern, UML, Software Evolution.

1 Introduction

Nowadays a topical issue in the software engineering research area consists of producing software systems able to adapt themselves to environment changes by adding new and/or modifying existing functionalities. There are a number of mechanisms for obtaining adaptability. One of these mechanisms are the design patterns [10,2]. Another mechanism for obtaining adaptability is *reflection* [16,3].

Z. Bellahsène, D. Patel, and C. Rolland (Eds.): OOIS 2002, LNCS 2425, pp. 242–254, 2002.

A non-stopping software system with long life span, has to be able to dynamically adapt itself to changes to its environment. Two aspects control the evolution of a system of objects: *behavior*, and *dependencies*. Both of them can be involved in system evolution to comply with changes to system requirements.

We present a novel design approach that provides a system with the ability to change object behavior at run-time. This approach integrates reflection and design patterns, by reifying object model, scenario, and statechart of the system. This paper explores how to design a dynamically self-adapting system extending the idea of shifting reflection from linguistic to methodological, that has been presented by Cazzola et al. in [4].

Object oriented methodologies like Objectory [13], and UML [1] statically describe the system's behavior during the design phase: all functions in the system are captured by a use-case model. The dynamic behavior of each use case is described by scenario, and interaction diagrams. Models in the *unified modeling language* (UML) [1] are classified in structural (e.g., class diagram) and behavioral (sequence diagrams and statecharts). Behavioral models deal with the representation of the behavior of the system. Class diagrams show how the system is structured, i.e., the classes composing the system and their relationship. Sequence diagrams and use cases describe the interactions between objects, whereas statecharts [12,11] describe, as a state machine, the behavior of every object in the system. UML provides a special key, named stereotype, to deal with concepts not well-defined or difficult to model by using only class diagrams. Cazzola et al. [4] adopt a special stereotype, named "`causal-connection`", to model with class diagrams a reflective system. This one has been the basic approach to reflective object-oriented analysis (ROOA).

All these methodologies provide a way to adapt software system to requirement changes as long as the system is under design/development. By subsequent refinement of a prototypal system up to reach its final version. These methodologies don't foresee a way to adapt the system when it is running without stopping it and modifying its design. Hence they are not enough to model a non-stoppable and adaptable software system.

Our approach gets two types of dynamic evolution: *structure*, and *behavior evolution*. To comply with this achievement the system is structured in two levels: base- and meta-level. In the base-level we have the system we want to render self-adapting, whereas in the meta-level there are some meta-objects, called *evolutionary meta-objects*, reifying all the design information related to the base-level. Evolutionary meta-objects deal with both structure and behavior evolution modifying these information. The causal connection is the mechanism which really realizes the dynamic self-adaption reflecting the changes performed by the evolutionary meta-objects in the base-level. The causal connection is achieved by using the pattern *adapter* [10], which allows base-objects to delegate the execution to their meta-objects, and by acting on inter- and intra-object connections through changing systems sequence and collaboration diagrams and applying such a change by using the *state design* pattern [10,9], which allows an object to change its behavior when its internal state changes.

Saake et al. [17] have proposed a specification framework for modeling evolving objects as basic building blocks of information systems. This is done by dividing object behavior into rigid and dynamic parts at the specification phase, thus we will extend this idea to the design phase.

The rest of the paper is organized as follows: section 2, outlines run-time adaptation approaches. Section 3, illustrates the proposed approach for object behavior evolution. Section 4, briefly points at related works in the discipline of building adaptable software system. Section 5 briefly describes our approach on modeling a banking system. Finally section 6 concludes with an outline of our ongoing research in adapting object behavior.

2 Run-Time Software Engineering Adaptation Techniques

The main motivation for using *reflection* and *design patterns* in software engineering is to build applications able to adapt themselves to environmental changes. The continuous evolution in information technologies forces the designer to deal with more and more ambitious requirements. Adaptability is the fundamental property that software systems must have to satisfy their evolution. A system can be considered to be adaptable when it can be modified to satisfy new requirements.

2.1 Design Patterns

The use of patterns is essentially the reuse of well-established good ideas. A pattern is a named, well-understood good solution to a common problem in a specific context.

Collections of design patterns were described in [10,2]. Patterns are used for changing structure and behavior of a software system. Design patterns have been classified into *structural* and *behavioral* patterns. *Strategy* patterns, in [10] on page 315, have been used in the design of dynamically adaptable systems. The design principle underlying the strategy pattern is to delegate the implementation of exported operations of the buffer manager to a replaceable strategy object. Multiple strategies can be derived from an abstract strategy class and compiled into the system.

In this work we will use two type of design patterns: *adapter*, in [10] on page 139, and *state* patterns, in [10] on page 305. An adapter class implements an interface known to its clients and provides access to an instance of a class not known to its clients. Hence it delegates the execution of a method to another object. A state pattern allows an object to change its behavior when its internal state changes.

2.2 Reflection

Reflection is the ability of a system to observe and to modify its computation [16]. An object-oriented reflective system is logically structured in two or

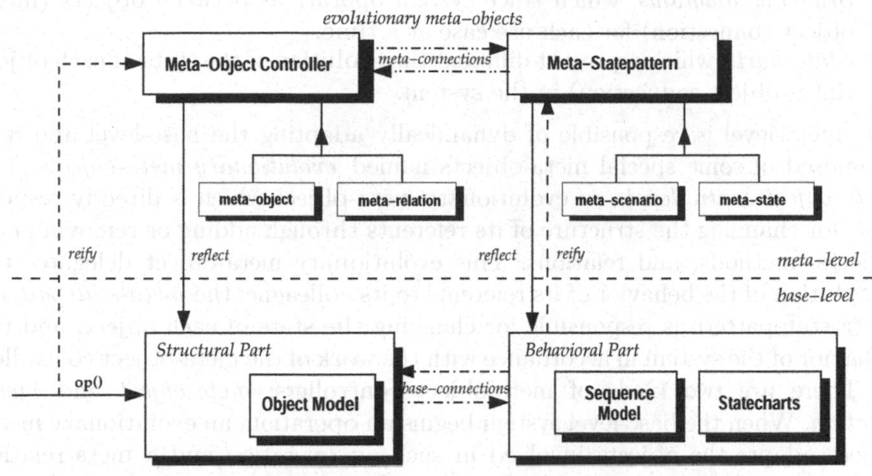

Fig. 1. Structure of an Adaptable System

more levels, constituting a *reflective tower* [16]. The first level is the *base-level* and describes the computations that the system is supposed to do. The second one is the *meta-level* and describes how the base-level computations have to be carried out. Objects working in the base-level are called *base-objects*, whereas objects working in the other levels (meta-levels) are called *meta-objects*. Each level is *causally connected* to adjacent levels, i.e. objects working into a level have data structures reifying the activities and the structures of the objects working into the underlying level and their actions are reflected into such data structures. Meta-objects supervise the activity of their *referents*, i.e., the base-objects. Trap mechanism explains how supervision takes place. Each base-object action is trapped by a meta-objects, which performs a meta-computation, then it allows its referent to perform the action.

3 Reflective Dynamic Adaptation of Software Systems

The main purpose of our approach consists of adapting the object behavior at run-time, by using its design information. To do this we are going to apply to the dynamic objects structure offered by Saake et al. [17], a reflective approach as explained by Cazzola et. al. [4].

In our approach the system is divided into its structure (described by its object model) and its behavior (described by statechart and sequence diagrams). Similarly an application is divided into two levels, as shown in Fig. 1: a base-level and a meta-level. The base-level, which implements the real system, is described by three models:

– *Object model*, which describes objects and their relations. This model represents the structural part of the system.

- *Sequence diagrams*, which trace system operations between objects (inter-object connection) for each use case at a time.
- *Statecharts*, which represent different the evolution of the state of each object (intra-object connection) in the system.

The meta-level is responsible of dynamically adapting the base-level and it is composed of some special meta-objects named *evolutionary meta-objects.* The *meta-object controller*, is an evolutionary meta-object which is directly responsible for changing the structure of its referents through adding or removing new objects, methods, and relations. This evolutionary meta-object delegates the adaptation of the behavior of its referents to its colleague: the *meta-statepattern.* Meta-statepattern is responsible for changing the state of each object, and the behavior of the system in accordance with the work of the meta-object controller.

There are two kinds of meta-object controllers: *meta-object* and *meta-relation.* When the base-level system begins an operation, an evolutionary meta-object adapts the objects involved in such an operation and a meta-relation adapts their behavior in accordance with the preconditions to that operation. After that, we need to determine the states for each referent involved in the execution of that operation. This is done by delegating the control to the meta-statepattern which detects the states of the involved referents. The relationship among the evolutionary meta-objects and its referents is specified by means of a meta-object protocol (MOP) [15]. The MOP works as follows: when an object asks for an operation, the operation and all objects involved in its execution are reified by the evolutionary meta-object controller. Then, it adapts the reified objects and reflect the changes on the base-level. Figure 2 shows, through a sequence diagram, the protocol steering the interactions between base- and meta-level. Basically we have:

- When an object asks for an operation, the meta-object controller sends this operation to the evolutionary meta-object. The evolutionary meta-object reifies the involved base-objects. At the meta-level some meta-computations involving the reified objects occur. Base-objects evolution is carried out by these meta-computations. Evolutionary meta-objects return the result to meta-controller through meta-connection.
- Meta-object controller entrusts the meta-statepattern, to determine the state of each object and the behavior for the system. There are two kinds of meta-statepatterns: the *meta-scenario* which traces the execution of the trapped operation, and the *meta-state* which determines the state of each object involved in the its execution.
- Verified the feasibility of the evolution, the changes are reflected on the base-system via the causal connection relationship among meta-statepattern, meta-object controller and their counterpart in the base-level (the behavioral and structural part).

3.1 Adaptation by Causal Connection and Design Patterns

In the just described architecture the meta-level is causally connected to the base-level, i.e., each event that occur in the base-level is implicitly reified by

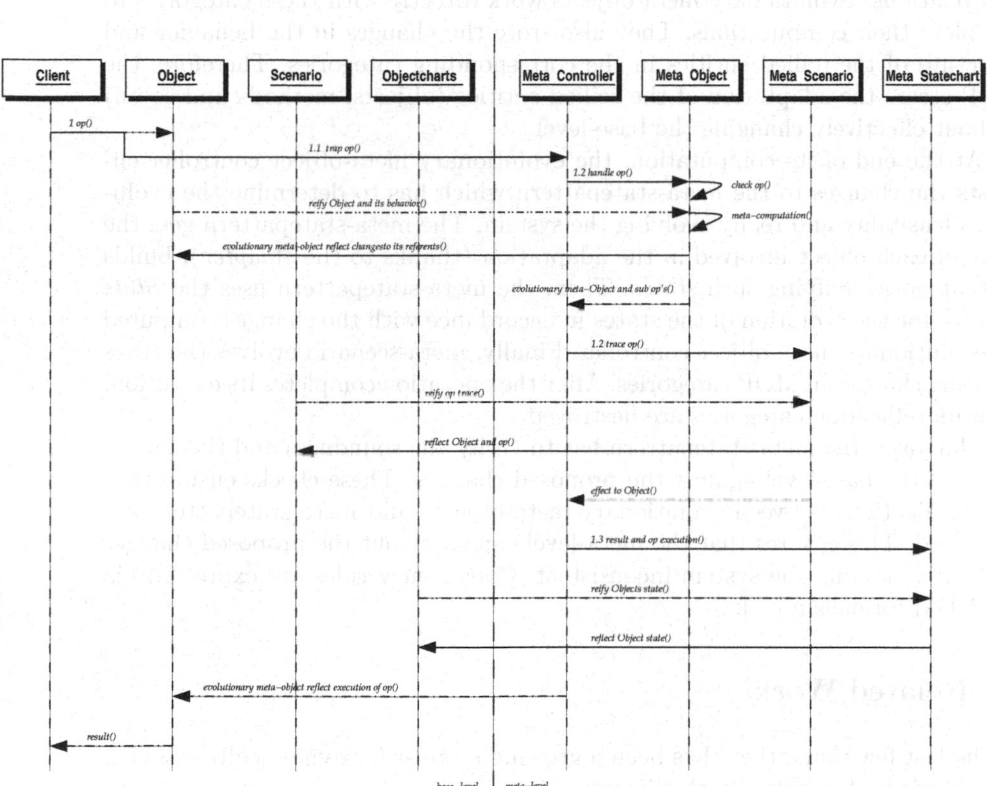

Fig. 2. Reflection interaction system protocol

the meta-level and every action carried out by the meta-level is automatically reflected on the base-level [16]. A system (the base-level) causally connected to another (an active engine supervising the adaptation) is the key to get a system that can evolve.

Evolutionary meta-objects are responsible for supervising and controlling their referents in the base-level. They use the pattern *Adapter* for reifying all objects, and their behavior involved in the execution of an operation. The implicit mechanism that is responsible for changing the behavior of the objects is realized by the evolutionary meta-objects and its MOP. MOP contains *reification categories*, these categories are entities representing objects, methods, and relations. Evolutionary meta-objects work directly with these categories to complete their computations. They also store the changes in the behavior and structure of the reified entities in the corresponding categories. Therefore, the MOP steers the adaptation of the reified entities (objects, methods and so on) without effectively changing the base-level.

At the end of its computation, the evolutionary meta-object controller entrusts the changes to the meta-statepattern which has to determine the evolution's feasibility and really evolving the system. The meta-statepattern gets the state of each object involved in the adaptation (thanks to the *Adapter*), builds the categories reifying such states. Then, the meta-statepattern uses the *State* pattern for the evolution of the states in accordance with the changes computed by evolutionary meta-object controller. Finally, meta-scenario evolves the trace by using changes in MOP categories. After the operation completes its execution, then its reification categories are destroyed.

Moreover, the meta-statepattern has to verify the soundness and the consistency of the base-level against the proposed changes. These checks ensure that the implications between evolutionary meta-objects and meta-statepattern are respected. This ensures that the meta-level can carry out the proposed changes without rendering the system inconsistent. Consistency rules are expressed via the VDM formalism [14].

4 Related Work

In the last few years, there has been a growing interest for dynamically evolving object-oriented systems. In the literature there are several approaches related to building adaptive software systems that allow system behavior to evolve after design time.

Dowling and Cahill [8] have proposed a meta-model framework named *K-components*, that realizes a dynamic, self-adaptive architecture. It reifies the features of the system architecture, e.g., configuration graph, components and connectors. This model presents a mechanism for integrating the adaptation code in the system, and a way to deal with system integrity and consistency during dynamic reconfiguration.

Another approach consists of building a reflective architecture by using cooperative object-oriented style [19]. Structural elements of this approach are

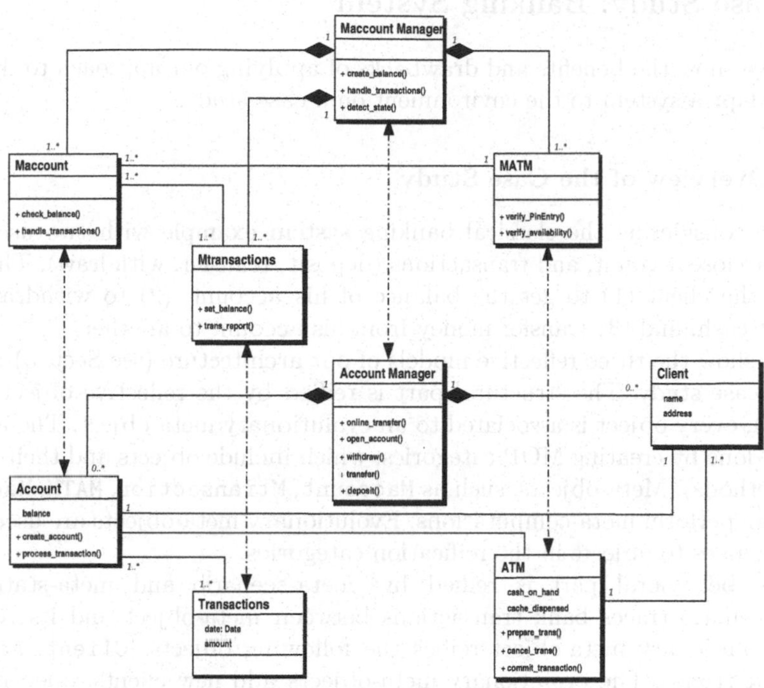

Fig. 3. Reflective object model

classes as the basic components, and *CO actions* (*cooperative actions* represent the interactions among objects characterizing the collaborative behavior [7]) as the basic connectors. This approach achieves adaptability by (1) dynamically extending objects behavior using roles, and (2) by selecting at run-time the objects and roles participating in a cooperation.

Seiter et al. [18] have proposed a new relation between classes, named *context relation*. The context relation is meaningful at analysis, design, and implementation levels. It may also impact software testing. As inheritance and dynamic binding modify traditional program flow and subsequent testing models, the context relation may modify them as well.

In the above approaches, the adaptation is achieved in three ways. First, by controlling components and connectors through a reflective architecture. Second, by separating the objects from their interactions and by entrusting their adaptation to meta-objects. Finally, by using design patterns to define a new relation, or providing a mapping between interfaces which are not possible to dynamically change. Our approach exploits all these techniques: we have a reflective architecture, with meta-objects dealing with design information and adapting the system by using design patterns.

5 Case Study: Banking System

Now, we show the benefits and drawbacks of applying our approach to dynamically adapt a system to the environment on a case study.

5.1 Overview of the Case Study

We are considering the classical banking system example with two use cases: open or close account, and transactions (deposit, transfer, withdraw). The bank allows the client (1) to get the balance of his account, (2) to withdraw, and deposit cash, and (3) transfer money from his account to another.

We show the three reflective models of our architecture (see Sect. 3) applied to the case study. The structural part is reified by the reflective object model (Fig. 3), every object is associated to an evolutionary meta-object. The adaptation is done by creating MOP categories, which include objects and their behavior (methods). Meta-objects, such as `Maccount`, `Mtransaction`, `MATM`, `Maccount manager` perform meta-computations. Evolutionary meta-objects are used to reflect changes to objects in the reification categories.

The behavioral part is reified by: meta-scenario and meta-state. The meta-scenario traces bank transactions between meta-object and its referent. The evolutionary meta-object reifies the following objects (`Client`, `Account`, `Transactions`). The evolutionary meta-objects add new clients, open new accounts and add these instances in the base-level, initialize the balance, and so on.

Moreover, evolutionary meta-objects add transactions such as deposit, transfer, withdraw and so on, to client objects. The purpose of all these transactions consists of adding (or subtracting) money to (from) balance of the client account. Hence, we need only two meta-scenarios for describing the whole system's behavior. The former for describing the open and close operation, the latter for dealing with money movements (Fig. 5). The adaptation of the state of every object is done by delegating it to the meta-statepattern which is responsible for detecting and notifying every change to their state during transactions.

Finally, Meta-statecharts control the state of base-level objects (Fig. 4). Evolutionary meta-object and its MOP categories have the rules to dynamically change the objects. The object states change at run-time by reifying the object states from base-level to state category. Meta-statepattern uses evolutionary meta-objects and its MOP to determine the changes to object states. After that, meta-statepattern reflects the changes to base-state for every object. We use the logic of partial functions from VDM [14], for representing a postcondition for transactions between object states. The transactions of account objects in the bank system are:

- →(suspense):(balance closed no effects)(time=t)
- (suspense)→(suspense):(balance closed no effects)(settime)(time=$\overleftarrow{t}$+t)
- (suspense)→(non-suspense):(true)(balance opened for any transactions)
- →(debit):(true)(open client account)(setbalance)(balance=0)

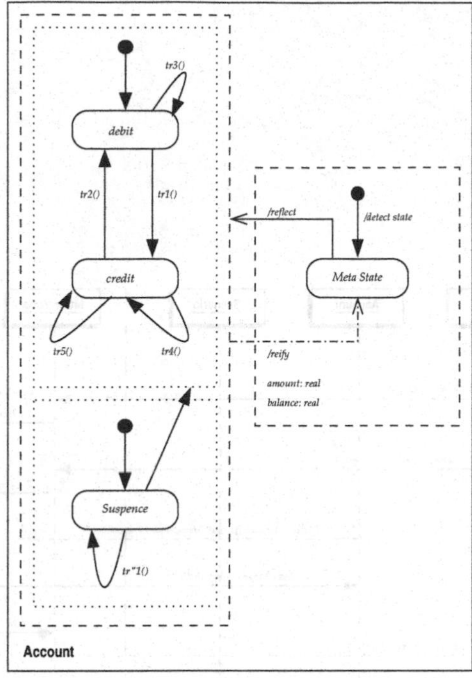

Fig. 4. Reflective objectcharts

- (debit)→(credit):(true)[tr1=deposit(amount)](amount>-balance) (setbalance)(balance=$\overleftarrow{balance}$+amount-charge)
- (credit)→(debit):(true)[tr2=withdraw(amount)][amount>balance] (setbalance)(balance=$\overleftarrow{balance}$-amount)
- (debit)→(debit):(true)[tr3=deposit(amount)][amount≤-balance] (setbalance)(balance=$\overleftarrow{balance}$+amount-charge)
- (credit)→(credit):(true)[tr4=withdraw(amount)][amount≤balance] (setbalance)(balance=$\overleftarrow{balance}$-amount)
- (credit)→(credit):(true)[tr5=deposit(amount)](setbalance) (balance=$\overleftarrow{balance}$+amount)

6 Conclusion

In this paper we addressed the problem of dynamically adapting the behavior of a running system. This has been done by building a reflective architecture, which integrates reflection (meta-object) and design pattern (Adapter and State). The proposed reflective architecture was implemented by two levels: meta- and base-level. In the meta-level, we defined new meta-objects named *evolutionary meta-objects*, which are responsible for reifying objects of the base-level and their

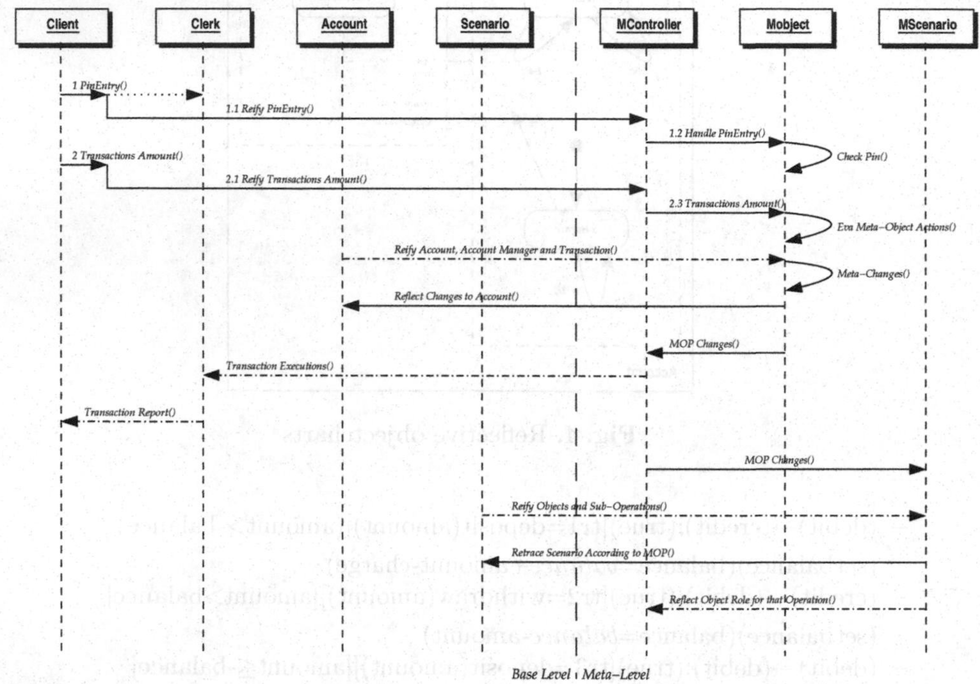

Fig. 5. The sequence diagram describing money movements

behavior at run-time. Also, they reflect changes to their referents. The architecture consists of three reflective models: *reflective object model*, *reflective scenario*, *reflective state*. This reflective approach provides a self adaptable information system that extends the initial trial [4] to move reflection from linguistic to methodological.

As future works, we are planning to put this approach on a firm semantic foundation by using object-Z as formal object-oriented language. In our approach, control flow is shifted from base-level to meta-level. So, we can validate the adaptation of objects and their behavior by using *animation*. Finally, we will implement the approach by using a reflective language, like OpenC++ [5] or OpenJava [6].

References

1. Grady Booch, James Rumbaugh, and Ivar Jacobson. *The Unified Modeling Language User Guide*. Object Technology Series. Addison-Wesley, third edition, February 1999. 243
2. Frank Buschmann, Regine Meunier, Hans Rohnert, Peter Sommerlad, and Michael Stal. *Pattern-Oriented Software Architecture: A System of Patterns*. John Wiley and Sons Ltd, 1996. 242, 244
3. Walter Cazzola. Evaluation of Object-Oriented Reflective Models. In *Proceedings of ECOOP Workshop on Reflective Object-Oriented Programming and Systems (EWROOPS'98)*, in 12th European Conference on Object-Oriented Programming (ECOOP'98), Brussels, Belgium, on 20th-24th July 1998. Extended Abstract also published on ECOOP'98 Workshop Readers, S. Demeyer and J. Bosch editors, LNCS 1543, ISBN 3-540-65460-7 pages 386-387. 242
4. Walter Cazzola, Andrea Sosio, and Francesco Tisato. Shifting Up Reflection from the Implementation to the Analysis Level. In Walter Cazzola, Robert J. Stroud, and Francesco Tisato, editors, *Reflection and Software Engineering*, Lecture Notes in Computer Science 1826, pages 1–20. Springer-Verlag, Heidelberg, Germany, June 2000. 243, 245, 253
5. Shigeru Chiba. A Meta-Object Protocol for C++. In *Proceedings of the 10th Annual Conference on Object-Oriented Programming Systems, Languages, and Applications (OOPSLA'95)*, volume 30 of *Sigplan Notices*, pages 285–299, Austin, Texas, USA, October 1995. ACM. 253
6. Shigeru Chiba, Michiaki Tatsubori, Marc-Olivier Killijian, and Kozo Itano. OpenJava: A Class-based Macro System for Java. In Walter Cazzola, Robert J. Stroud, and Francesco Tisato, editors, *Reflection and Software Engineering*, Lecture Notes in Computer Science 1826, pages 119–135. Springer-Verlag, Heidelberg, Germany, June 2000. 253
7. Roger de Lemos and Alexander Romanovsky. Coordinated Atomic Actions in Modelling Object Cooperation. In *Proceedings of the 1st IEEE International Symposium on Object-Oriented Real-Time Distributed Computing*, volume 30 of *Sigplan Notices*, pages 152–161, Kyoto, Japan, April 1995. 249
8. Jim Dowling and Vinny Cahill. The K-Component Architecture Meta-Model for Self-Adaptive Software. In Akinori Yonezawa and Satoshi Matsuoka, editors, *Proceedings of 3rd International Conference on Metalevel Architectures and Separation of Crosscutting Concerns (Reflection'2001)*, LNCS 2192, pages 81–88, Kyoto, Japan, September 2001. Springer-Verlag. 248

9. Luciance Lamour Ferreira and Cecilia M. F. Rubira. The Reflective State Pattern. In Steve Berczuk and Joe Yoder, editors, *Proceedings of the Pattern Languages of Program Design, TR-WUCS-98-25, Monticello, Illinois-USA*, August 1998. 243
10. Erich Gamma, Richard Helm, Ralph Johnson, and John Vlissides. *Design Patterns: Elements of Reusable Object-Oriented Software.* Professional Computing Series. Addison-Wesley, 1995. 242, 243, 244
11. David Harel and Eran Gery. Executable Object Modeling with Statecharts. In *Proceedings of 18th International Conference on Software Engineering*, pages 246–257. IEEE Press, March 1996. 243
12. David Harel and Michael Politi. *Modeling Reactive Systems with Statecharts: The STATEMATE Approach.* McGraw-Hill, 1998. 243
13. Ivar Jacobson, Magnus Christerson, Patrick Jonsson, and Gunnar Overgaard. *Object-Oriented Software Engineering: A use Case Driven Approach.* Addison Wesley, 1992. 243
14. Cliff B. Jones. *Systematic Software Development Using VDM.* Englewood Cliffs, NJ: Prentice-Hall, second edition, 1990. 248, 250
15. Gregor Kiczales, Jim des Rivières, and Daniel G. Bobrow. *The Art of the Metaobject Protocol.* MIT Press, Cambridge, Massachusetts, 1991. 246
16. Pattie Maes. Concepts and Experiments in Computational Reflection. In Norman K. Meyrowitz, editor, *Proceedings of the 2nd Conference on Object-Oriented Programming Systems, Languages, and Applications (OOPSLA'87)*, volume 22 of *Sigplan Notices*, pages 147–156, Orlando, Florida, USA, October 1987. ACM. 242, 244, 245, 248
17. Gunter Saake, Can Türker, and Stefan Conrad. Evolving Objects: Conceptual Description of Adaptive Information Systems. In H. Balsters, B. de Brock, and S. Conrad, editors, *FoMLaDO/DEMM2000, LNCS 2065*, pages 163–181. Springer-Verlag Berlin Heidelberg, 2001. 244, 245
18. Linda M. Seiter, Jens Palsberg, and Karl J. Lieberherr. Evolution of Object Behavior Using Context Relations. *IEEE Transactions on Software Engineering*, 24(1):79–92, 1998. 249
19. Emiliano Tramontana. Reflective Architecture for Changing Objects. In Walter Cazzola, Shigeru Chiba, and Thomas Ledoux, editors, *On-Line Proceedings of ECOOP'2000 Workshop on Reflection and Metalevel Architectures*, June 2000. Available at `http://www.disi.unige.it/RMA2000`. 248

Generation of Object Models for Information Systems from Business System Models

Ying Liang

Division of Computing and Information Systems
School of Information and Communication Technology
University of Paisley, Paisley, U.K
lian-ci0@paisley.ac.uk

Abstract. There exists a gap between business system modelling and object-oriented information system modelling as organization structures and business processes are not explicitly modelled in object models by current object modelling techniques and methods. Organization structures are considered as the outside of the system boundary and business processes are implied by sequences of messages among objects. This gap has caused a difficulty of building object models for information systems that are suited not only to information systems but also to organizations. This paper suggests a new object modelling approach that aims to bridge the gap by building a business system model for organizations and using it as a vehicle for generating an object model for information systems. Three primary business elements (i.e., business processes, organization structures, and resources) are focused and explicitly modelled in the business system model, using business concepts and terms. They are then translated into classes in the object model, using object concepts and terms. Three types of classes (i.e. user interface classes, control classes, and entity classes) are particularly generated by the translation.

1 Introduction

Many object modelling methods focus and model two primary business elements, i.e., business processes and resources, with classes in object-oriented information system (OOIS) modelling and design. They do not model another primary business element, organization structures explicitly. Our experiences on teaching and using them showed the following problems with such modelling:

- Organization structures such as departments and sections cannot be explicitly modelled although they are owners of business processes in the organization.
- Business elements are modelled by object concepts and terms that may not have the meaning same as business terms and may be difficult for the user to understand and check in requirements analysis.

Z. Bellahsène, D. Patel, and C. Rolland (Eds.): OOIS 2002, LNCS 2425, pp. 255-266, 2002.

- It is very difficult to identify business classes and their structures from the unstructured business elements in the organization such as a problem statement.
- Some classes in the object model do not make sense to the user as they are created for the implementation purpose in software engineering

Similar problems have been also indicated in other work. Taylor [1] said: "Although the fundamentals of convergent engineering bring business and software engineering much closer than they have been historically, there can still be a significant gap between business design and object modelling. For example, business system typically requires the explicit representation of high-level organizational process, whereas these processes are represented implicitly in object models as sequences of messages, among business entities." He introduced an object modelling approach to bridging the gap by modelling three primary business elements (i.e., organization structure, business processes, and resources) of an organization explicitly into an object model. This object model however can show the elements only separately but not show the collaboration between them.

Jacobson *at al.* [2] suggested another approach to bridging the gap. This approach used a use case model to show high-level business processes explicitly using use cases and then identified resources from the use cases in the model. It classified classes into three types of business classes (i.e., user interface classes, control classes, and entity classes) that they thought any OOIS could consist of, and used entity classes to represent the resources involved in business processes. User interface classes and control classes are however created for OOIS to implement business processes. The use case model therefore cannot fill the gap completely as it only model business processes but not model the other two primary business elements, i.e., organization structures and resources. Such lack in the object model makes it difficult to address the business needs in system analysis.

Information passing between stakeholders and the organization, and the thread of business processes are also important in business systems as they mean how the organization operates the business system. Both Taylor and Jacobson approaches however did not model them in the object model or the use case model.

The other object-oriented methods such as [3], [4], [5], [6] that were created in the early of 1990s focused on technical solutions with OO system elements rather than on business needs with business system elements. They cannot be used to bridge the gap completely between the two systems in OOIS development.

To help bridge the gap more completely, we developed a different approach whose objective is to build a business system model for the organization before building an object model for OOIS so that three primary business elements can be considered and explicitly shown with business concepts and terms such as "stakeholder" in requirements analysis and then the object model can be generated from it. We chose to use the business system model as a vehicle for building the object model as it can help requirements analysis by directing focus towards meeting business needs rather than purely technical solutions [7]. For example, high-level business processes such as "sell product" in the organization are modelled by activities in the business system model and interfaces in the object model. The owners of the processes such as "sales department" are modelled by units in the first model and by control classes in the second model. In general, the business system model describes an organization and a problem; the object model specifies OOIS and a solution to the problem.

This paper introduces this approach in details. It will define the business system model in the second section and the object model in the third section. An example of the two models will be shown in the fourth section. The conclusions and future work will be discussed in the final section.

2 The Business System Model for Organizations

The business system model shows an organization including organization structure, business processes, and resources. Business processes can be interpreted differently in different views. From the outside, a business process is viewed as 'a structured, measured set of activities designed to produce a specified output for a particular customer or market [8]. From the inside, it is viewed as internal process that produces a value that may be beneficial to other internal processes [9]. The both of views are important, we think, in modelling a business system and should be considered explicitly in the business system model. The model therefore includes information passing between the stakeholder and the organization.

2.1 Business System Model

A business system model is a graph of business elements and connections in an organization (see Fig. 1). It uses *unit* figures to show organization structures, *unit service* and *resource action* ovals to represent business processes, and *resource* rectangles to show resources. The unit services are collaborated with the resource actions in the model. In addition, it uses *stakeholder* figures to show stakeholders and *form* parallelograms to illustrate information passing between the stakeholders and the business system.

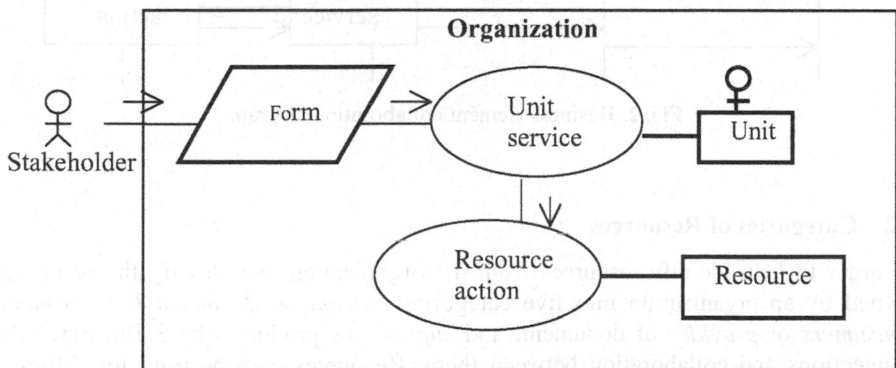

Fig. 1. Business system model

The modelling constructs used by the business system model are defined in the following:

- *Stakeholder*: A stakeholder is a customer or a vendor of the organization, or a supplier who communicates with and has impact on the organization.
- *Form*: A form is information passing from the stakeholder to the unit or vice verse in a business process. It may be a physical form, sound, graphics, or image and so on that can be suited to the organization.
- *Unit*: A unit is a department, or a section, or a team, or an agent of the organization. It carries out one or more business processes in the organization.
- *Unit service*: A unit service is a business process carried out by the unit as the owner. Unit services show the roles and responsibilities of the unit in the organization.
- *Resource*: A resource is a document or a file that is produced and maintained by the organization for storing information about a thing, a person, a device, or a form, and so on, that is involved in the business processes.
- *Resource action*: A resource action represents what a unit service expects a resource to collaborate in achieving the service, for example, producing a specified output for a stakeholder or a value benefit to other unit services.
- *Connection* (the dark line): A connection is used to link a unit service or a resource action with its owner (i.e., unit or resource).
- *Thread* (the line with an arrow): a thread represents collaboration of two business elements in a business process. They can be shown by a business element collaboration diagram in Fig. 2 that focuses the collaboration of business elements in the realization of a business process in the organization.

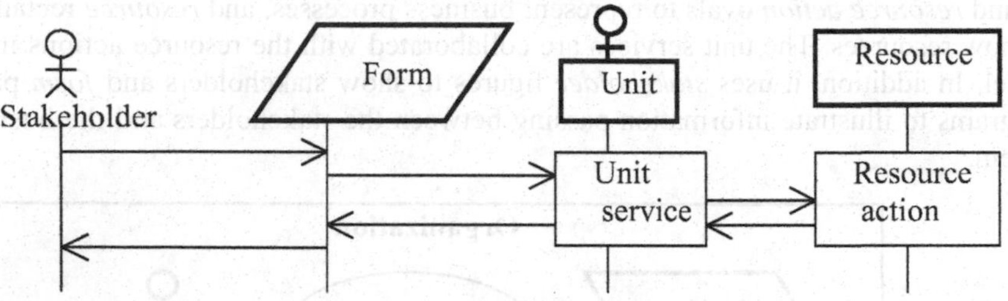

Fig. 2. Business element collaboration diagram

2.2 Categories of Resources

In order to help identify resources from the organization, we classify the resources owned by an organization into five categories: *document*, *document line*, *product*, *consumers* or *provider* of document, and *supplier* of product. Fig. 3 illustrates the connections and collaboration between them. Resources may be used for different purposes and therefore they may belong to more than one category in business processes. For example, "order" is a document as well as a provider of another document "invoice" in the "sell product" business process.

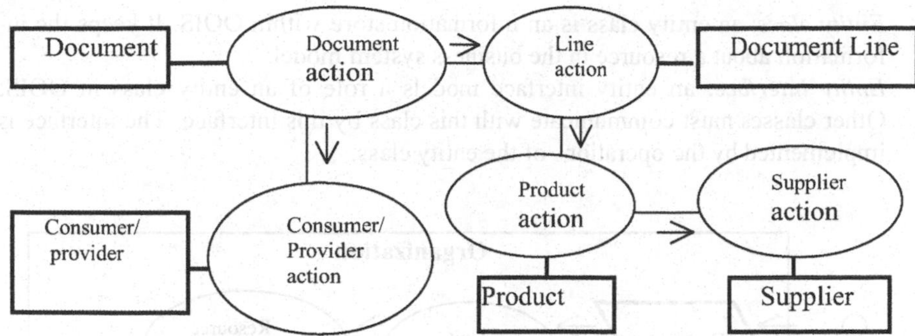

Fig. 3. Five categories of resources and their collaborations

3 The Object Model for OO Information Systems

Jacobson *el al.* [2, 10] classified business classes in OOIS into three categories: user interface or boundary classes, control classes, and entity classes. We adopted and used them as modelling constructs in our object model as the business elements in the business system model can be translated into these classes straightforward.

3.1 Object Model

The object model (see Fig. 4) is a graph of classes and collaborations between classes by their interfaces. The business system model is used to generate the object model for OOIS. Forms, units, and resources in the former are translated into *user interface classes*, *control classes*, and *entity classes* in the latter, respectively. In addition, in order to separate specifications and implementations of unit activities and resource actions in the object model, they are modelled by interfaces (i.e., specifications) and operations (i.e., implementations) of control classes and entity classes. Interfaces mean the roles of classes in the system [11].

The modelling constructs in the object model are defined as follows:

- *User interface class*: a user interface (UI) class is a view of OOIS by which the user communicates with the system. The way of communication is modelled by a set of dialogues defined as the operations of that class. A UI class represents an abstraction of forms in the business system model. It is often modelled by a window class or a form class in OOIS.
- *Control class*: a control class is a coordinator of entity classes within OOIS. It decides and controls the entity classes that are needed to participate in realising a business process. A control class represents an abstraction of units in the business system model.
- *Control interface*: a control interface models a role of a control class in OOIS. Other classes must communicate with this class by this interface. The interface is implemented by the operations of the control class.

- *Entity class*: an entity class is an information store within OOIS. It keeps the information about a resource in the business system model.
- *Entity interface*: an entity interface models a role of an entity class in OOIS. Other classes must communicate with this class by this interface. The interface is implemented by the operations of the entity class.

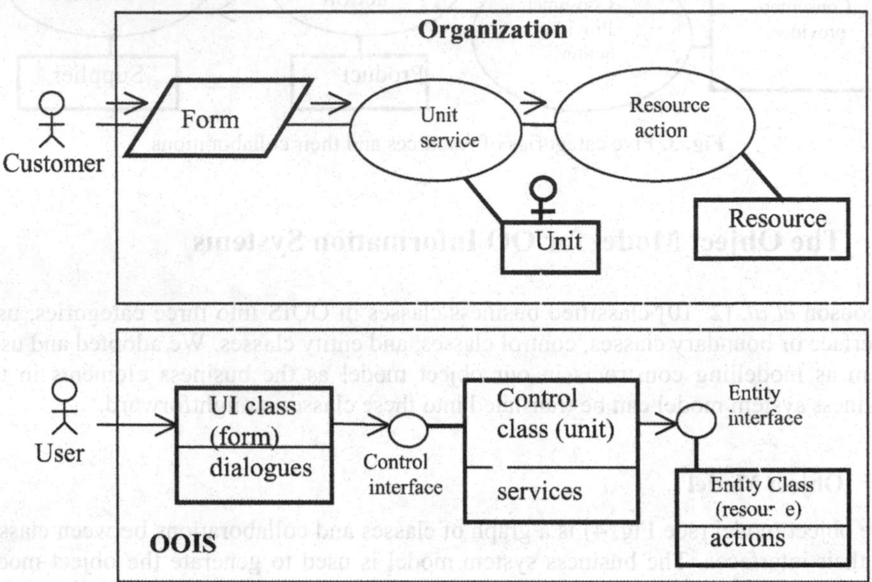

Fig. 4. Object model generated from the business model

The collaboration of classes in business processes can be also represented by a class collaboration diagram in Fig. 5 that emphasizes which operations within a class are used to implement the interface of a class for that role in collaboration. A thread may be attached by an event such as a signal that triggers the collaboration.

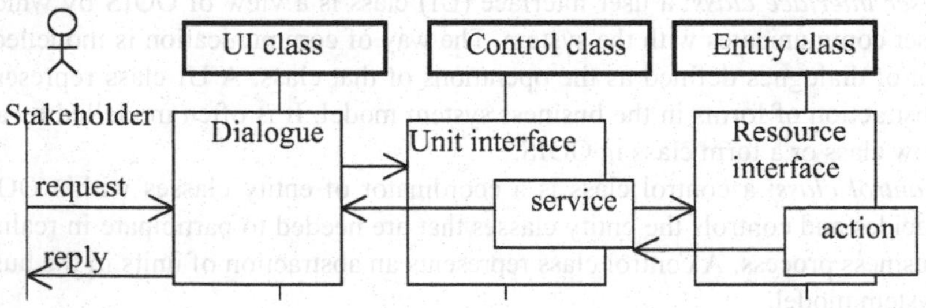

Fig. 5. Class collaboration diagram

3.2 Categories of Entity Classes

Also the five categories of resources in the business system model are translated into five types of entity classes: *document classes*, *document line classes*, *product classes*, *consumer classes*, and *supplier classes*. Fig. 6 shows them and their collaboration.

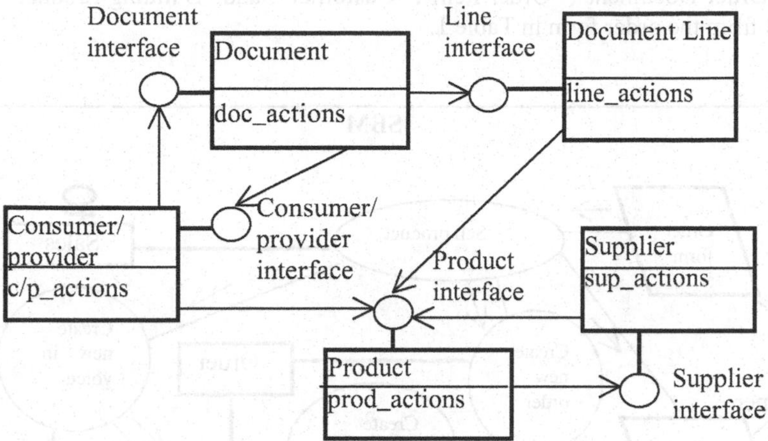

Fig. 6. Five types of entity classes in the object model

4 An Example

The Superior Builders Merchants (SBM) is a company that sells building products to its customers. A customer buys the product by sending an order form shown in Table 1 [12] to the sales department. The sales department generates and sends an invoice to the customer. The customer then sends the payment to the account department that will process payments and produce a receipt.

Table 1. Order form

SUPERIOR BUILDERS MERCHANTS

123 Renfrew
Glasgow
Scotland

Order No	Customer No	Date
017321	0324	15/10/88

Item	Product Code	Product Description	Unit of Measure	Quantity
01	PA129	Paint - royal blue	5 Ltr	100
02	MH005		1	15

4.1 The Business System Model for SBM

The business system model for SBM shown in Fig. 7 was developed by this approach. As the information passing between the stakeholder and the business system is usually made up of the resources, different types of resources can be identified from the forms in the business system model in terms of the five categories. For example, resources "Order Document", "Order Item", "Customer", and "Building Product" were identified from the order form in Table 1.

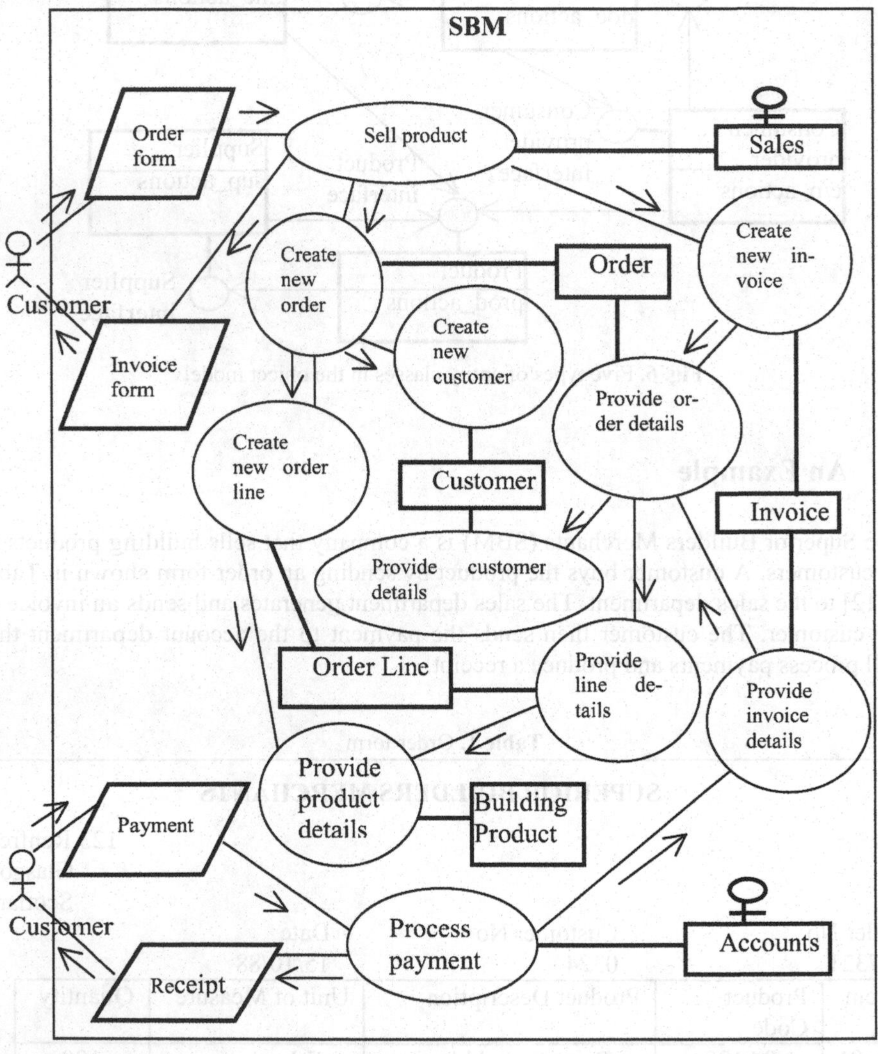

Fig. 7. The business system model for Superior Builders Merchants

4.2 The Object Model for OOIS of SBM

The business system model of SBM has been used to generate the object model for its OOIS that is shown in Fig. 8. A class may have more than one interface if it plays different roles in OOIS. For example, Order, Customer, Order line, and Invoice in the object model have two interfaces: "creation" with which the classes are a generator of new objects and "view" with which they are a provider of information about an object of them.

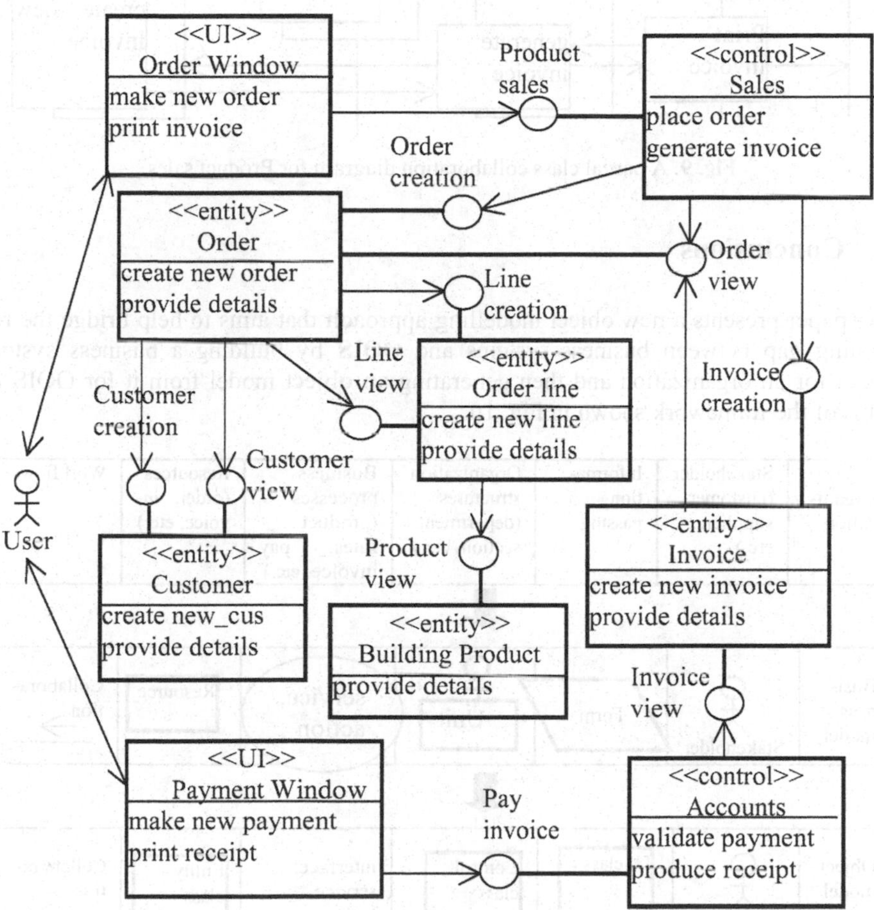

Fig. 8. An object model for OOIS of the Superior Builders Merchants

Fig. 9 is a partial class collaboration diagram for the "product sales" business process, as an example.

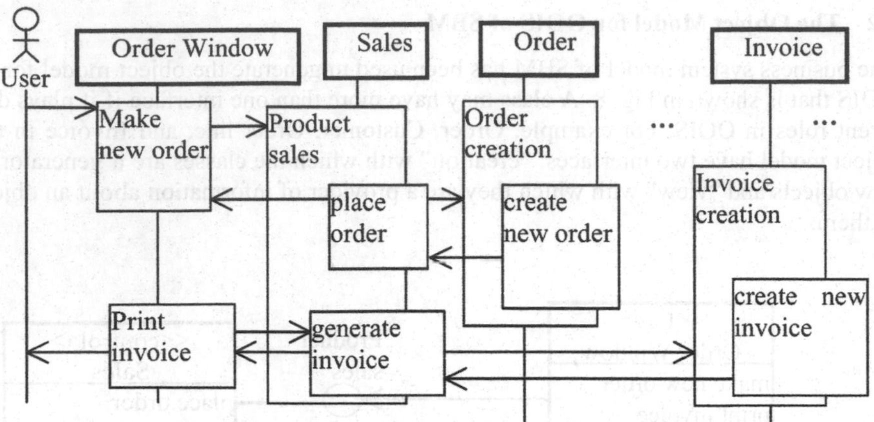

Fig. 9. A partial class collaboration diagram for Product sales

5 Conclusions

This paper presents a new object modelling approach that aims to help bridge the remaining gap between business systems and OOIS by building a business system model for an organization and then generating an object model from it for OOIS in terms of the framework shown in Fig. 10.

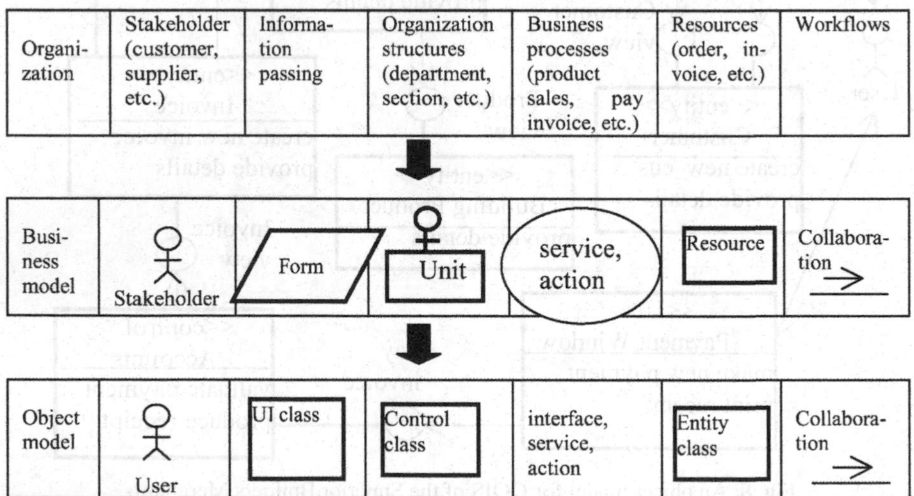

Fig. 10. The framework for generating object model from business model

In comparison with other object-oriented methods [3], [4], [5], [6] that build the object model as the first model in OOIS development, our approach is to build the business system model as the first model instead. This change helps focus on organization details and business needs instead of ignoring them in OOIS development.

At present, UML [13] is industry standard modelling language. A unified process [10] has been provided as an approach (see Fig. 11) to developing object-oriented systems with UML. In comparison with this approach, our approach has a stronger focus on the organization structures and business processes by building separate business system model and object model in OOIS development. It generates the object model by translating business concepts in a business system to object concepts in OOIS more smoothly and directly.

We hope that the approach helps solve the problem that business processes are implied by sequences of messages among objects and are not explicitly modelled by current object models. It is expected to make the object model more close to the business system run by an organization and more understandable to the user than other object models built by [3], [4], [5], [14]. By applying the approach in case studies, we found that business classes were identified from the business system model easier than from a problem statement. This may be helpful in building and validating the object model. The approach also enables us to allocate business processes into classes by considering and explicitly modelling the roles and responsibilities of the classes in terms of interfaces. Improvements of business processes in an organization with new OOIS can be explicitly described and discussed with the user in terms of these two models. This may help manage the changes of organizations as well as the maintenance of OOIS.

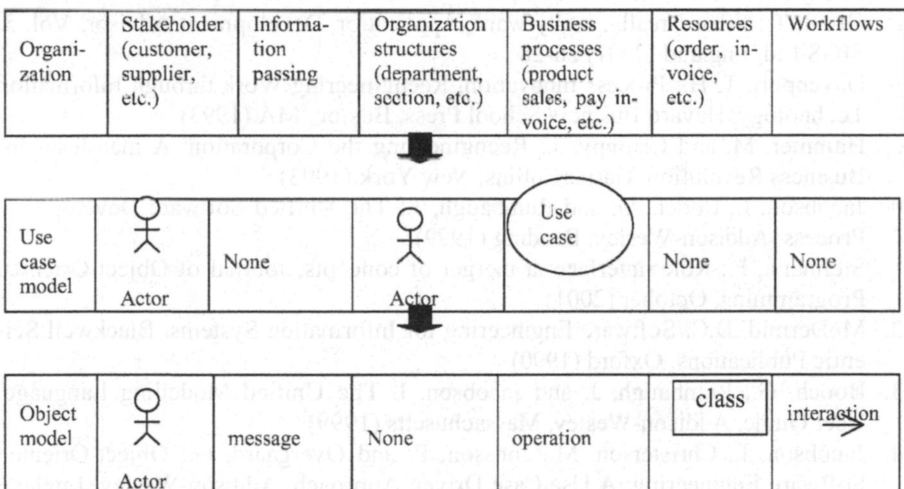

Fig. 11. The framework for building object model from use case model

The approach shown in this paper can be regarded as the completeness of the approach suggested by us [15] that generated the object model by focusing on actors and goals of use cases of OOIS. These two approaches together provide a complete way of developing object models for OOIS with different views and focuses. At next stage, we will merge them into one object modelling method with the framework shown in our paper [16]. The integrated method is hoped to enable the user to be involved in requirements analysis and object modelling more than before and the analyst to build the object model for OOIS in a systematic way from a business system to an OOIS. We will also consider, in future, the link of them with component-based software engineering based on class interfaces as the interface in component design and implementation is thought an extension to object technology [17].

References

1. Taylor, D.A.: Business Engineering with Object Technology. John Wiley & Sons, New York (1995)
2. Jacobson, I., Ericsson, M. and Jacobson A.: The Object Advantage: Business Process Reengineering with Object technology. Addison-Wesley, Massachusetts (1995)
3. Booch, G.: Object-Oriented Analysis and Design with Applications. 2nd edn. Benjamin/Cummings, California (1994)
4. Rumbaugh, J., Premerlani, J., Eddy, M. and Lorensen, W.: Object-Oriented Modeling and Design. Prentice Hall, New Jersey (1991)
5. Shlaer, S. and Mellor, S. J. :Object Lifecycle: Modeling the World in States. Prentice Hall, New Jersey (1992)
6. Coad, P. and Yourdon, E.: Object-Oriented Analysis. 2nd edn. Prentice Hall, New Jersey (1991)
7. Grout, T.: What I really, really want, Application Development Advisor, Vol. 5. SIGS Ltd, England (2001) 26-28
8. Davenport, T. H.: Process Innovation, Reengineering Work through Information Technology. Havard Business School Press, Boston, MA (1993)
9. Hammer, M. and Champy, J.: Reengineering the Corporation: A manifesto for Business Revolution. HarperCollins, New York (1993)
10. Jacobson, I., Booch, G. and Rumbaugh, J.: The Unified Software Development Process. Addison-Wesley, Reading (1999)
11. Steimann, F.: Role=interface: a merger of concepts, Journal of Object-Oriented Programming, October (2001)
12. MeDermid, D.C. Software Engineering for Information Systems. Blackwell Scientic Publications, Oxford (1990)
13. Booch, G., Rumbaugh, J. and Jacobson, I. The Unified Modelling Language: User Guide. Addison-Wesley, Massachusetts (1999)
14. Jacobson, I., Christerson, M., Jonsson, P. and Overgaard, G.: Object-Oriented Software Engineering: A Use Case Driven Approach. Addison-Wesley, England (1992)
15. Liang, Y.: Actor-led object modelling for requirements and systems analysis. In Wany, Y., Patel, S. and Johnston, R.H. (eds.): Proceedings of the 7th International Conference on OOIS, Springer-Verlag, London, August (2001) 37-46
16. Liang, Y. Establishing the framework for business object analysis and design models. In Patel, D., Choudhury, S., Patel, S. and de Cesare, S. (eds.): Proceedings of the 6th International Conference on OOIS. Springer-Verlag, London, December (2000) 155-162
17. Cheesman, J. and Daniels, J.: UML Components-A Simple Process for Specifying Component-Based Software. Addison-Wesley, England (2001)

Requirements Capture Workflow in Global Information Systems

M.J. Escalona, J. Torres, and M. Mejías

Department of Computer Languages and Systems, University of Seville
Avda. Reina Mercedes S/N, 41012 Seville
Fax: 95 455 71 39. Phone: 95 455 71 39
{escalona,risoto,jtorres}@lsi.us.es

Abstract. The development of information systems has changed a lot in the last years. Nowadays, applications are often developed in distributed environment. It is quite common, they are distributed via Internet and they usually have hypermedia and multimedia elements in huge databases. They are characterized by having complex functional and security requirements, many and undefined users who have different degree of knowledge. These systems are named *Global Information Systems*. The development of these complex global information systems must be like a software project, based on a development methodology, to get the application suitable to the client's requirements. This methodology must offer a right treatment of all its aspects. Nowadays, there is no standard methodology which covers all these characteristics. On the one hand, there are some traditional propositions, like the Unified Process [11]. This is a good proposition to work with storage and functional requirements. On the other hand, there are propositions that have come from the multimedia environment, like OOHDM [18], Hyper-UML [14], WSDM [4], etc. which, although give more importance to the interface and navigation, don't cover all the phases of the whole life cycle. After doing a comparative study of the most relevant methodologies for hypermedia and Web development published in the last few years [7], we have made a methodology proposition to develop global information systems. This methodology is based on the Unified Process, but it adds new models and aspects to treat correctly the navigation, the hypermedia and the interface. In this paper, we present a global vision of our methodology and we focus on the proposition to get requirements from the user. To present the results, we apply the proposition to a real problem in a public company in Seville.

Keywords: Global Information System, development methodology, requirements, navigation, global interface.

Z. Bellahsène, D. Patel, and C. Rolland (Eds.): OOIS 2002, LNCS 2425, pp. 267-279, 2002.

1 Introduction

Nowadays, if a developer wants to apply a methodology to develop his global information system, he has a lot of possibilities. Global information systems are similar to classic management systems because both must deal with complex storage and functional requirements. So, the developer could use an object-oriented methodology like RUP [2]. However, global information systems have some characteristics like navigation, interface or hypermedia, which need a special treatment. In this sense, the developer could use a proposition to hypermedia applications, like OOHDM, EORM, etc. But these propositions don't cover the complete life cycle. They are often focused on design and they forget other phases like requirements capture or analysis. We have studied the actual possibilities that a developer has to apply to his global information system. In table 1, we offer an abstract of this study [7]. In this table, we can read the name of the methodology, its reference and a short description. Also, we show what life cycle phases it treats (R: Requirements capture; A: Analysis; D: Design; I: Implementation; T: Tests) and the aspects which it covers (S: Storage; F: Functional; N: Navigation; I: Interface; M: Multimedia)

In this table, we can observe that there isn't any proposition which cover the whole life cycle and deal with all global information system characteristics. However, these propositions offer models and techniques that can be applied successfully.

We have studied all these models and techniques to decide which are the most suitable. Therefore, we are developing a new methodological proposition to global systems [6]. This proposition takes some of these models and techniques and proposes others. The life cycle of our methodology is quite simple. Our methodology proposes that the project life is divided into five workflows: requirements capture, analysis, design, implementation and test. In each workflow, our methodology proposes different activities and tasks to treat correctly the classic aspects (storage, functionality, security, etc.), as well as the multimedia aspects (interface, navigation, hypermedia, etc.). The first workflow to do is the capture and the definition of requirements. In this paper, we would like to present this workflow, namely, the activities to do, the techniques that we have to apply and the structure of the workflow results.

2 Getting Requirements

In global information systems, the requirements capture is a critical workflow because the rest of the process is based on it. In this workflow, users and developers must decide what the system must offer. We have said that global information systems have some special characteristics: complex storage and functionality, navigation, interface and hypermedia. These special characteristics must be defined in the first workflow. Therefore, it's necessary that the methodology offer a mechanism to define all these aspects. However, this mechanism must be simple enough to be understood by the user as well as complete enough to be useful to the developer.

Table 1. Abstract of the actual methodology

Methodology	Description	Phases					Aspects				
		R	A	D	I	T	S	F	N	I	M
HDM [8]	It proposes a model to design hypermedia systems. It's based on ERD.			X			X		X		X
RMM [9]	It's a methodology to design hypermedia system. It is based on HDM.			X	X						X
EORM [12]	It's a methodology to design hypermedia system. It has a tool to help the developer.			X	X		X		X		
OOHDM [18][19][20]	It's a methodology to design hypermedia system. It offers new models and quite interesting techniques.			X	X		X		X	X	X
WSDM [4]	It's a methodology to design kiosk web. Its design is based on the user		X	X	X		X				X
OO-Method [17]	It's an environment to develop information systems.			X	X	X	X	X		X	
SOHDM [12][21]	It's a methodology that uses OOHDM, but that adds the scenario technique to capture requirements to it.	X		X	X		X	X	X	X	X
RNA [1]	It's a proposition to do the analysis in web information systems.	X				X	X			X	
HFPM [16]	It's a proposition that describes what process must be used to develop web systems.	X	X	X	X	X	X		X	X	
RUP [2]	It's the methodology proposed by the authors of UML	X	X	X	X	X	X	X			
Building Web Applications with UML [3]	It's a proposition which add some stereotypes to UML to design web information systems.			X					X	X	X

Our proposition is based on getting the system objectives. Starting from them, the developer has to define the information storage requirements, that is, what information the system has to store. Afterwards, actors, which are going to interact with the system, must be defined, as well as the functionality the system offers them, defining the functional requirements. When the designer knows what actors can do with the system, who can work with it and what will be stored by the system, the interaction requirements must be identified and described. The interaction requirements capture how the information will be presented to the user and how actors will be able to use the system functionality and to do queries to the system. Finally, in this workflow, non-functional requirements, like security, communication aspects, etc., must be defined. In figure 1, a diagram of requirements capture workflow is shown.

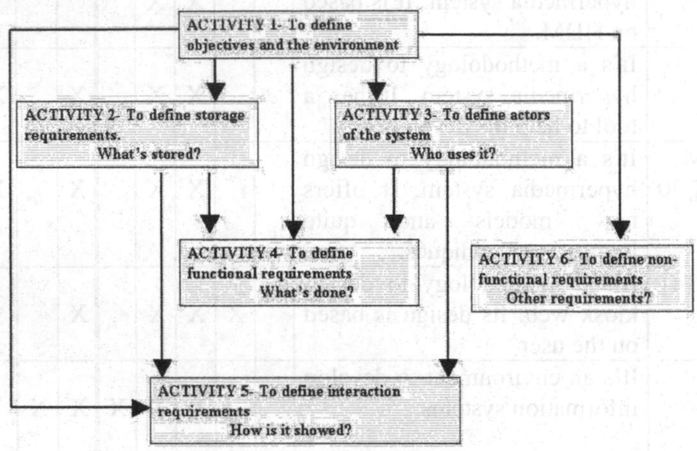

Fig. 1. Requirement capture squema

In our methodology, in order to present the result to the client, patterns have been defined. These patterns offer a structured and complete technique, but also easy to be interpreted by the client. To present the different activities, we will use a real example. A global information system to spread out and manage information about historic heritage.

2.1 Activity 1- To Define Objectives and the Environment

In this activity, the developer must:

- Study the environment and the company. To get that, it's necessary to get brochures and to study old systems. This study isn't necessary when the developer knows the company well.
- Do interviews with final users in order to get their necessities. Some interview techniques (JAD, Brainstorming, etc.) could be applied [5].
- Define the objectives. When the developer knows the necessities, he must define the objectives. In order to describe them, a pattern is used. In our example, the principal system objective is to manage the information of monuments. In table 2, this objective description is made using the pattern.

Table 2. An objective pattern to our example

OBJ-01	To manage the information of monuments
Description	The system must let manage patrimonial information. This information is divided into: Identification information, which lets identify each monument Description information, which describes each monument Graphical information, which is a set of images of each monument

An identifier names each objective. This identifier starts with OBJ, followed by a unique number. A description of the objective must be offered.

2.2 Activity 2- To Define Storage Requirements

When we know what we want to get, it's necessary to define what information is stored by the system. To describe this information, we propose to use another pattern. So, our example must store the information of monuments. The user needs the name and the address of the monument, its chronology, namely when it was built; its authors, that is who did it; its styles, such as baroque, gothic, etc.; its typology: a church, a square, etc; and a list of images where the monument appears. These are its specific data. In the pattern in table 3, we can read the description of this storage requirement. An identifier names each storage requirement, which starts with "SR", and a unique number follows it. In the 'associated objectives' row, the developer must enumerate which objectives are gotten (or are partial gotten) with this storage requirement. So, storing information about monuments we get a partial solution to manage the information of monuments.

Table 3. A storage requirement description

SR-01	Information of the monument	
Associated objectives	OBJ-01: To manage the information of monuments	
Description	The system must store information about monuments. Specifically:	
Specific data	Name and description	Nature
	Name: It's the name of the monument.	String
	Address: It's the address of the monument.	String
	Chronology: It's the date when the monument was built	Chronology
	Author: It's a set of authors or creators, who did the monument or contributed in its building.	String Cardinality: 0..n
	Style: It's the set of the monument styles.	String Cardinality: 0..n
	Typology: It's the set of the monument typologies.	String Cardinaly:0..n
	Image: It's a set of images where the monument appears.	Image Cardinality: 0..n

In the next row, a description is required. After that, the specific data are described. Each piece of specific data has a unique name, a description and a nature. The nature is the abstract type of each piece: integer, string, sound, image, etc. In our methodology, there are some predefined nature, but a mechanism to define new natures is given. In this example, there are some specific data with predefined nature: string, images, etc. But there is a new nature, namely the chronology. Each new nature must be described by another pattern, in order to clarify its meaning. In table 4, the Chronology structure is described. In this pattern, we describe the structure of the nature, its rank and its restrictions.

Table 4. A new nature description

NA-01	Chronology	
Structure	Field	Nature
	Beginning year: It's the year when the monument was started to build.	Date Format: yyyy
	Finished year: It's the year when the monument was finished.	Date Format: yyyy
Rank	Years can be positive (a. D.) or negative (b. C).	

In table 3, we can observe that some specific data can have a cardinality. When a storage requirement can have multiple values for a piece of specific data, we show the number of values in the cardinality. So, a monument can have 0 or an indeterminate number of styles or typologies.

2.3 Activity 3- To Define Actors

When the developer knows what the system has to store, he must define who can use the application. Therefore, he must define actors. An actor is a person, an external system or an external process that works with the system.

In this activity, the developer has to start defining basic actors. A basic actor is a simple role, which is identified with a specific criterion. In our system, we can classify according to two criteria. On the one hand, we can classify the actor according to his investigation area. So we have: Archaeologist (table 5) or Artistic. On the other hand, we can classify according to the actor's use in the system. So we have: Administrator or General User. An administrator is the person who can update and consult information. A general user can only consult.

In order to define basic actors, the developer has to do a pattern. We present the Archaeologist description in table 5. This actor has a unique identifier: AC-01. In the second row, objectives that are associated with this actor must be enumerated. Afterwards, the used criterion to classify this actor must be described. Finally, the developer has to describe the basic actor.

Table 5. A basic actor definition

AC-01	Archaeologist
Associated objectives	OBJ-01: To manage the information of monuments
Criterion	This is a possible actor in the system when we classify users according to his investigation area
Description	The system must offer a mechanism to work with archaeologists. An archaeologist is a person who is interested in archaeologist monuments.

After defining basic actors, we must study the incompatibility between them. Two basic actors are incompatible when a user can't use the system playing like both of them. Therefore, in our system, the same user can't be an administrator and a general user, but he could be an administrator and an Archaeologist at the same time.

In order to define actors' incompatibility, a matrix must be used. In table 6, we present our system incompatibility matrix.

Table 6. An incompatibility matrix

Basic Actor	Archaeologist	Artist	Administrator	General user
Archaeologist	-			
Artist		-		
Administrator			-	X
General user			X	-

'X' represents the incompatibility between two actors. So Administrator and General user are incompatible. Sometimes, there are other very important actors in the systems, which are complex actors. A complex actor is a role, which is composed of two or more actors (basic or complex). So, in our system we must have an artistic-archaeologist. It's an actor who is an archaeologist and an artist at the same time.

To define complex actors, we use a matrix. In table 7, we show the complex actor matrix of our system.

Table 7. Complex actor definition

	Actor				
Complex Actor	Archaeologist	Artist	Archaeologist-Artist	Administrator	General user
Archaeologist-Artist	∧	∧			
Archaeologist-Administrator	∧			∧	
Archaeologist-Artist-Administrator	∧	∧	∧	∧	
Artist-Administrator		∧		∧	

'∧' represents that the complex actor in the row takes the same role as the actor in the column.

2.4 Activity 4- To Define Functional Requirements

When the developer knows what the system stores and who can use it, he must define the system functionality. To define functional requirements, we propose to use the standard use cases [10]. It's not necessary to explain what it is. In our example, we have a lot of use cases. One of these is the use case which describes how a user can introduce a new monument into the system. A use case is composed of a diagram and a description. In figure 2 we show a use case diagram for this example.

Table 8. A functional requirement definition

FR-01	Introducing a new monument	
Associated objectives	OBJ-01: To manage the information of monuments	
Description	The system has to do this use case when the user wants to introduce a new monument into the database	
Precondition	The user has to be an available user in the system	
Actors	AC-04: Administrator	
Normal sequence	Step	Action
	1	Execute the option "New".
	2	The system accepts the user.
	3	The user introduces the address of the monument.
	4	The system asks for the name of the monument.
	5	The user introduces the name.
	6	The system introduces the new monument in the database and the user is allowed to introduce the information of the monument (images, chronology, etc.).
	7	The user introduces the rest of the information.
	8	The systems goes back to the main menu.
Postcondition	Nothing	
Exceptions	Step	Action
	1	The user is not an available user in the system, so the system doesn't let introduce a new monument
	5	The monument is already in the system. So an error message is showed
Approximate frequency	10 times a month	

Each use case has to be described using a pattern. In table 8, we describe use case diagram in figure 2. In this pattern we must identify the use case with a unique identifier (FR-01). We must justify why this use case is defined, therefore it's necessary indicate associated objectives. Afterwards, it's necessary to do a description and indicate the functional requirement precondition. In the 'Actors' row, the developer has to enumerate actors who can execute this use case. To complete the use case description, normal execution sequence, postcondition and exceptions of this use case must be described. Eventually, if it's possible, the developer has to give an approximate frequency.

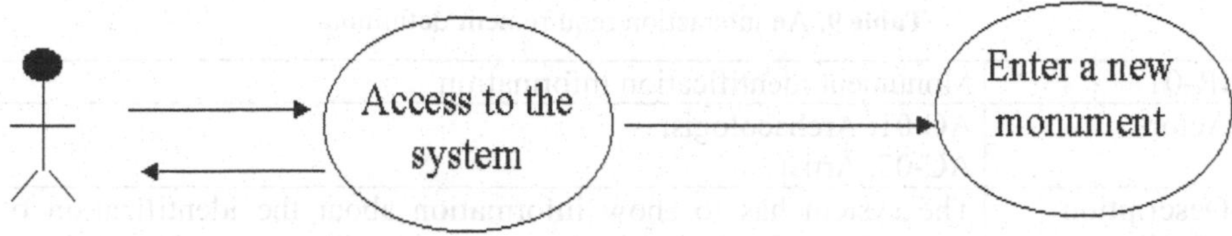

Fig. 2. A use case diagram

2.5 Activity 5- To Define Interaction Requirements

At this point, the developer knows what the system has to store, who can use it and what can be done with it, but it isn't enough. In global information systems, interface and navigation are critical aspects, so we have to define how the information will be presented to the user. In order to define this, the developer has to define interaction requirements using patterns again. Each interaction requirement is a node, in which specific information is showed. Information in a node is about a specific subject. Therefore, in our system we can define a node, which shows information about the identification of monuments. In this node, we must show information, which identifies the monument: its name, its address and its images.

A unique identifier names each interaction requirement. In the pattern of table 9 is IR-01. For each interaction requirement, the developer has to enumerate the actors who can interactuate with it. Moreover, a description must be defined. If some entry parameters are necessary in order to show this requirement, they will be described in the fourth row. In the 'associated functionality' row, the developer must enumerate functional requirements, which can be executed in this interaction requirement. Afterwards, the developer has to mention specific data of storage requirements in order to detail the information showed by the node. An interaction requirement can show specific data of different storage requirements and a piece of specific data can be showed in different interaction requirements. So, in this row, we must indicate the storage requirement identifier and the names of each piece of specific data.

Eventually, we must indicate navigation. From this information requirement, the user will be able to navigate to other information requirements, so the developer must enumerate them in the 'Exit' row. As the same time, from other information requirements, the user can navigate to this information requirement. Those are enumerated in the 'Entry' row. In our example, the user can get IR-01 information requirement from IR-03 and can navigate from IR-01 to IR-02 too.

2.6 Activity 6- To Define Non-functional Requirements

To conclude, it could be possible that there are other requirements which aren't storage, functional or interaction requirements. These are non-functional requirements. In the last workflow activity, the developer has to describe other requirements like security, efficiency, etc. To describe these requirements, we propose another pattern.

For instance, in our system we can indicate that it must offer a mechanism to do automatically backups. In table 10, we describe this requirement.

Table 9. An interaction requirement definition

IR-01	Monument identification information
Actors	AC-01: Archaeologist AC-02: Artist
Description	The system has to show information about the identification of monuments.
Entry parameters	The user must introduce the name of the monument.
Associated functionality	FR-01: Introducing a new monument
Showed information	SR-01.Name SR-01.Address SR-01.Image
Exit	IR-02
Entry	IR-03

Table 10. A non-functional requirement definition

NFR-01	Backups
Associated objectives	OBJ-05: Get a safe system to manage monuments
Description	The system must offer an automatic mechanism to do backups and to recover the information when it is necessary.
Commentary	This is a very important requirement because in this system there is very important information

Again, we must identify each non-functional requirement with a unique identifier: NFR-01, in this case. Moreover, we must indicate its associated objectives and give a short description. In addition, we can indicate other commentaries about the requirement.

3 Requirements Capture Document

To present results of the requirements capture workflow, the developer must do the requirements capture document. Our methodology proposes a structure to this document.

The first page of the requirements capture document must be a cover. The cover must include the version, the name of the document and the date. If the organization has a predefined cover, it can be assumed. Afterwards, an index, a figure index and a table index must be include.

Table 11. Searching matrix structure

	OBJ-01	OBJ-02	...	OBJ-0n
IR-01	X	X		
IR-02				X
...				
AC-01	X			X
AC-02		X		
...				
FR-01	X	X		X
FR-02		X		
...				
IR-01	X	X		
IR-02				X
...				
NFR-01	X			
NFR-02		X		
...				

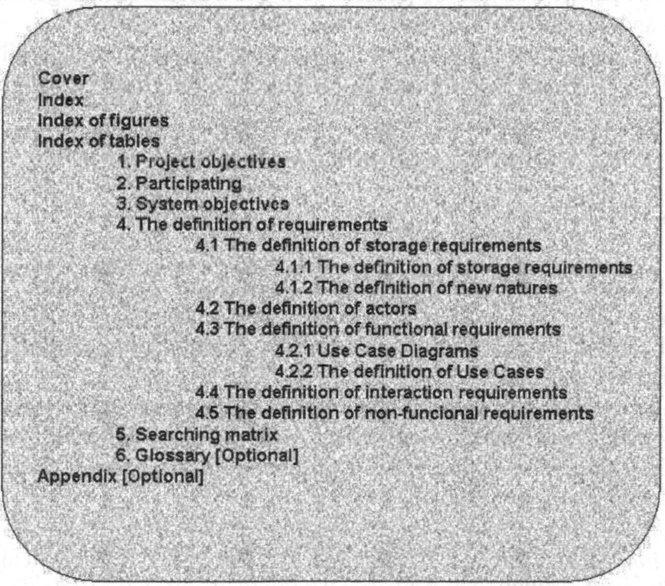

Cover
Index
Index of figures
Index of tables
1. Project objectives
2. Participating
3. System objectives
4. The definition of requirements
4.1 The definition of storage requirements
4.1.1 The definition of storage requirements
4.1.2 The definition of new natures
4.2 The definition of actors
4.3 The definition of functional requirements
4.2.1 Use Case Diagrams
4.2.2 The definition of Use Cases
4.4 The definition of interaction requirements
4.5 The definition of non-funcional requirements
5. Searching matrix
6. Glossary [Optional]
Appendix [Optional]

Fig. 3. The structure of the Requirements capture document

After these pages, the developer must include definitions of objectives and requirements. Therefore, the developer has to write patterns of objectives, defined in activity 1, patterns of storage requirements and new natures (activity 2). After these patterns, patterns of actors and functional requirements (defined in activity 3 and 4) must be included.

Afterwards, the developer has to describe interaction and non-functional requirements, using patterns defined in activity 5 and 6. To finalize, the developer must design a matrix. This matrix shows what objectives are associated to a specific requirement. In table 11, we show the structure of this matrix.

To finalize, in figure 3 we show the structure of the requirement documents following our proposition.

4 Conclusions

In this paper, we have presented our proposition to do the requirements capture applying our idea to a real information global system in a public company.

This proposition has been applied to several real global information systems, giving very good results. Using patterns to define system requirements and objectives is a very interesting idea. Users who are not expert in computer science, understand patterns easily. But patterns present complete and non-ambiguous information to the developer, who can use them in analysis and design.

Nowadays, we are developing a proposition to do the analysis workflow in global information systems. This analysis proposition is based on the requirements capture presented in this paper. The use of patterns is a good technique to get the analysis class diagram and interface prototypes cuasi-automatically.

Moreover, we are developing a tool which lets generate the patterns easily. Patterns are structured, so it's quite easy to introduce their information in a database, which produce the requirements capture document automatically.

References

1. M.Bieber, R.Galnares And Q. Lu. *Web engineering and flexible hypermedia.* The 2nd Workshop on Adaptative Hypertext and Hypermedia, Hypertext 1998.
2. G. Booch, J. Rumbaugh, I. Jacobson. *Unified Modeling Language User Guide.* Ed. Addison-Wesley, 1999.
3. J. Conallen. *UML Extension for Web Applications 0.91.* Available in http://www.conallen.com/technologyCorner/webextension/WebExtension091.htm .
4. O.M.F. De Troyer, C.J. Leune. *WSDM: A User Centered Design Method for Web Sites.* Tilburg University, Infolab. 1997
5. Durán. *Un Entorno Metodológico de Ingeniería de Requisitos para Sistemas de Información.* Department of Language and Computer Science. University of Seville. September 2000. Available in http://www.lsi.us.es/~amador .
6. M.J. Escalona, J.Torres, M.Mejías. *Propuesta de metodología para el desarrollo de sistemas para el tratamiento de bibliotecas digitales.* Internal Report, 2-2000. Department of Language and Computer Science. University of Seville. Seville, June 2000. Available in http://www.lsi.us.es/~informes .

7. M.J. Escalona. *Metodología para el desarrollo de sistemas de información global: análisis comparativo y propuesta*. Department of Language and Computer Science. University of Seville. Seville, January 2002. Available in http://www.lsi.us.es/~informes .
8. F. Garzoto, D.Schwabe and P.Paolini *HDM-A Model Based Approach to Hypermedia Application Design*. ACM Transactions on Information System, 11 (1), Jan 1993, pp 1-26.
9. T.Izakowitz, E.Stohr, P. Balasubramaniam: *RMM:A methodology for structured hypermedia design*. Comm. Of ACM, October 1995, pp.34-35.
10. Jacobson. *Modeling with use cases-Formalizing use-case modelling*. Journal of Object-Oriented Programming, June 1995.
11. Jacobson, G. Booch, J. Rumbaugh. *The Unified Software Development Process*. Ed. Addison-Wesley, 1999.
12. D.B. Lange. *An Object-Oriented Design Approach for Developing Hipermedia Information Systems*. Research Report RT00112, IBM Research, Tokyo Research Laboratory, Japan, 1995.
13. H. Lee, C. Lee & C. Yoo. *A Scenario-based object-oriented methodology for developing hypermedia information systems*. Processing of 31st Annual Conference on Systems Science. Eds. Sprague R.
14. L. Mandel, A.Helmerich, L.A. Olsina, G.Rossi, M.Wirsing, N.Koch. Hyper-UML. Specification and modeling of multimedia an Hypermedia Applications in Distributed systems. August 2000.
15. J. Nanard, M. Nanard. *Hypertext design environments and the hypertext design process*. Communication of the ACM, August 1995. Vol 38(8), 49-56. 1995.
16. L. Olsina. Building a Web-based information system applying the hypermedia flexible process modeling strategy. 1st International workshop on Hypermedia Development, Hypertext 1998.
17. O. Pastor, E.Insfran, V. Pelechano, J.Romero and J. Merseguer. OO-METHOD: *An OO Software Production Environment Combining Conventional and Forma Methods*. CAiSE'97. International Conference on Advanced Information Systems, 1997.
18. G. Rossi. *An Object Oriented Method for Designing Hipermedia Applications*. PHD Thesis, Departamento de Informática, PUC-Rio, Brazil, 1996.
19. Schwabe, D., Rossi, G.. *An Object Oriented Approach to Web-Based Applications Design*. TAPOS – Theory and Practice of Object Systemss, vol. 4, 1998.
20. Schwabe, D. Rossi, G. *A Conference Review System with OOHDM*. 1st International Workshop on Web-Oriented Software Technology. Valencia, Junio 2001.
21. W. Suh, and H. Lee, *A Methodology for Building Content-oriented hypermedia systems* The Journal of Systems and Software, Vol. 56, 2001, pp. 115-131.

Supporting Development of Enterprise JavaBeans through Declarative Meta Programming

Johan Fabry*

Programming Technology Lab, Vrije Universiteit Brussel
Pleinlaan 2, 1050 Brussel, Belgium
Johan.Fabry@vub.ac.be

Abstract. Enterprise JavaBeans is a successful component model for the development of distributed business applications. Enterprise JavaBeans have to adhere to a set of rules and guidelines which, amongst others, require that a significant amount of glue code between the components is written. By using Declarative Meta Programming (DMP) we can codify these rules and guidelines as a logic program which operates on the Java code. Our DMP development tool can not only generate Java code, but can also verify compliance of developer code.

1 Introduction

Building the back-end servers of Internet information systems is a daunting task. The business application logic of the system is intertwined with services such as concurrency, transaction management, persistence and so on. To ease development of these servers, middleware technology such as Sun's Enterprise JavaBeans (EJB) component model[5, 6] has been developed.

In this model business logic is encapsulated into a number of Beans, while additional tasks, such as network communication, concurrency and transaction management, are performed by the EJB server. Beans cooperate to respond to network requests originating from the user interface, using data which is stored in the database.

The EJB specification defines two kinds of Beans: entity Beans and session Beans. Entity Beans are an objectified representation of data in a database and are therefore persistent. Session Beans encapsulate the business logic of the application and are not persistent.

To be considered a Bean, a business object must conform to a number of requirements, as given in the EJB specification. This ensures correct cooperation between the EJB server and the Bean. To satisfy these requirements a certain amount of repetitive tasks, which can be automated, have to be performed by the programmer.

* Author funded by a doctoral grant of the Flemish Institute for the advancement of scientific-technological research in the industry (IWT)

Z. Bellahsène, D. Patel, and C. Rolland (Eds.): OOIS 2002, LNCS 2425, pp. 280–285, 2002.

So, although EJB is a significant step forward, it is still non-trivial for a developer to develop using this component model. Development support for building EJB's enhances the process by, for example, decreasing the amount of code that should be written by the developer. We propose the use of Declarative Meta Programming (DMP) to provide such development support. DMP has the added value of being able to reason about the code being written by the developer, which makes it possible to firstly extend the code generation capabilities beyond what is offered by current-day tools. Secondly, we can verify code compliance with regard to the EJB specifications, which allows us, for example, to detect possible runtime exceptions at coding time.

We will now give an introduction of DMP before showing how we use DMP to provide advanced development support.

2 Declarative Meta Programming

Checking whether a piece of source code matches some requirements, detecting violations of these requirements, and generating code according to the requirements are activities eminently suited to Declarative Meta Programming (DMP).

DMP[8, 4, 3] is a technique where a declarative meta language is merged with a standard OO base language. Base level programs are reified as logic facts at the meta level. This allows the logic interpreter to reason about the base program. Using DMP, we can specify requirements of the base program in logic code, query the interpreter for code that does not comply to these rules and we can generate base code.

For our experiments we extended the tool SOUL[9], to provide a version, named SOULJava, which reasons about base programs written in Java.

Working with SOULJava entails first parsing the Java code, which adds a parse tree representation of it to a Java code repository. The logic interpreter reasons about the code in this repository, and is able to add and modify it. To compile the code, the parse trees are exported to java source code format, and are compiled with the standard Java compiler.

Basic use of the EJB support only requires coding in Java, and providing a few logic facts to the interpreter. This does only require minimal knowledge of the logic language, as will be shown later.

3 Development Support

Using DMP we have built an EJB, named SJB (SoulJava ejBtool). In this section we first show how code generation similar to that done by existing tools[1, 7, 2] is done. Next we introduce the more advanced features of SJB in code generation and code verification.

3.1 Basic Code Generation

Basic usage of SJB consists of specifying properties of a Bean and letting SJB generate the required code. Indeed, we can generate fully functional entity Beans solely by specifying their properties. Consider the following specification for a Room EJB used in a computer room booking system:

```
ejbClass(Room, entity).
primaryKey(Room, number).
field(Room, number, String, <persistent>).
field(Room, numcomputers, int, <persistent,property>).
field(Room, computertype, String, <persistent,property>).
```

This specification consists of 6 logic facts written in SOULJava. We declare "Room" an entity bean, with "number" as primary key, followed by the instance variables of the bean. The arguments of the "field" declarations are, in order, the Bean to which it belongs, its name, type, and a list of attributes of the field. At this time, fields may have two attributes: whether it should be "persistent", and whether it is a "property", i.e. accessible to clients[1].

SJB contains a number of logic rules that transform this specification to a parse tree for the equivalent Java program. We illustrate this by examining the rules for fields. Consider first the rule for the instance variable declarations as given below:

```
fieldDeclaration(?class, ?field, ?tree) if
  field(?class, ?field, ?type, ?attrib),
  javaInstVarDecl(?class, public, ?type, ?field, ?tree).
```

This rule introduces new syntax: words prefixed with "?" are logic variables, "if" separates the signature from the body of a rule, and a comma in the body signifies a logical "AND". "field" is used to verify if the field exists for that class, and to obtain the type and attribute list. "javaInstVarDecl" is a logic rule which we will not discuss in detail here; it unifies its last argument with a parse tree according to the previous three arguments. In the rest of the text we adopt as convention that logic variables with the name "?tree" contain parse trees.

Note that due to the multi-way reasoning capability of SOULJava, the "fieldDeclaration" rule can be called with any variable unbound, and the results will contain all possible bindings for the unbound variables.

As we have seen above, if a field has the "property" attribute, clients must be able to access and modify it. The EJB specification states that this is done by using getter and setter methods which also have to be declared in a specific interface of the Bean. The names of the methods should be "getFieldName" and "setFieldName", where "FieldName" is the capitalized name of the field. We show the rule for a getter (the rules for setters and the interface declarations are similar, therefore we omit them):

```
ejbGetter(?class, ?field, ?tree) if
  field(?class, ?field, ?type, ?attrib),
```

[1] We use the term "clients" of a Bean to refer to all objects that use services offered by the Bean. Clients can be other Beans or user interface software.

```
   member(property, ?attrib),
   javaReturnStatementBody(?field, ?bdtree),
   capitalize(?field, ?capfd),
   javaMethodDecl(public, ?type, get+?capfd, <>, ?bdtree, ?tree).
```

Four new elements are introduced. Firstly, the "member" predicate verifies if "property" is contained in the attribute list. Secondly, a parse tree for a method body containing a "return" of the field is generated. Thirdly we capitalize the name of the field, and fourthly we create the getter method. In this last statement, "+" signifies concatenation and an empty list "<>" is given for the arguments.

Usage of this rule is analogous to "fieldDeclaration": if only "?class" is bound to a class name, it returns a list of all property fields of that class, and a list of the parse trees for the getters of that class.

When exporting code the above rules will be called at given times, and their results will be integrated into the Bean package.

3.2 Advanced Code Generation

Because DMP allows us to reason about Java code written by the developer, we can extract this information to generate additional code and configuration information.

Beans cooperate to implement the business logic by calling methods on other Beans. To be able to refer to another, external, Bean, some configuration issues need to be resolved. For example, at compile time and at runtime the interfaces of the external reference must be available. SJB also takes care of this by detecting all occurrences of external references, as shown in the following rules, and including the interface definitions where needed.

```
usesEJB(?used, ?methodtree) if
   ejbClass(?used, ?beantype),
   traverseMethodParseTree(?methodtree, <?msg, ?type>,
      messageSend, collectReturnType),
   or(equals(?type, ?used+Home), equals(?type, ?used+Remote)).

collectReturnType(messageSend(?msg), <?msg, ?type>) if
   messageReturnType(?msg, ?type).

usesEJB(?used, ?methodtree) if
   ejbClass(?used, ?beantype),
   traverseMethodParseTree(?methodtree, <?msg, ?type>,
      castExpression, collectCastType),
   or(equals(?type, ?used+Home), equals(?type, ?used+Remote)).

collectCastType(castExpression(?msg),<?msg, ?type>) if
   castType(?msg, ?type).
```

We use a generic parse tree traversal rule "traverseMethodParseTree" here, which will traverse the method parse tree, respectively find message sends and cast expressions, and collect the resulting type. ("messageSend" and "castExpression" are logic representations of parse tree elements.) "usesEJB" is called on all methods at code generation time, and will return a list of used Beans. This list is then used to ensure that all needed interfaces are available.

3.3 Validating Code

When the developer starts adding non-generated code to the Bean, we can verify that this code complies to the specifications. It has been shown that DMP is eminently suited for verifying code, for example when regarding coding conventions and adherence to design patterns[4].

Detecting violations early in the development process shortens the development cycle. Using SJB we can perform code verification at the moment a method definition has been completed by the developer.

Consider cooperation between Beans: this is performed by method calls, however there are some restrictions on these method calls. For example: return and parameter types must be either primitives or Strings or serializable types or implement the Remote interface. The correct definition of serializable types can be quite complex, however in the most cases, Serializable types implement the Serializable interface.

Due to this complex definition, compliance cannot be fully checked at compile time, and the compiler can be quite forgiving. This allows that, at runtime, a type will not comply to this rule. In such cases a runtime exception is thrown and the operation is aborted. We want stronger compliance checking, and at least have a warning if there is ambiguity. This is achieved by calling the "beanMethodParametersCompliance" rule, shown below:

```
beanMethodParametersCompliance(?mtree) if
   findall(?typelist,
      traverseMethodParseTree(?mtree, <?msg, ?typelist>,
         messageSend, collectMessageTypes), ?typelistcoll).
   forall(member(?typeslist, ?typelistcoll), bmpComp(?typeslist)).

collectMessageTypes(messageSend(?msg), <?msg, ?typelist>) if
   messageArgumentTypes(?msg, ?typelist).

bmpComp(?typeslist) if
   forall(member(?type, ?typeslist), bmpTypeComp(?type)).

bmpTypeComp(?type) if primitive(?type).
bmpTypeComp(String).
bmpTypeComp(?type) if classOrSupersImplement(?type, Serializable).
bmpTypeComp(?type) if classOrSupersImplement(?type, Remote).
```

We first find the lists of argument types for all method calls on other Beans and collect them in "?typelistcoll". Then, for each member of the collection, we verify if all the elements of that type list conform to the specification as given above.

This section detailed how we can use DMP to provide development support for building Beans. We have shown how our tool, SJB, can generate more code than traditional tools due to the ability to reason about the Java code. Furthermore we illustrated how this ability allows us to verify developer code compliance early in the development cycle.

4 Conclusions

We have shown here that DMP's ability to reason about code allows it to extract information from the developers' Java code, and use this to aid in development. This is done first by generating a larger amount of "support" code, required for EJB compliance, than other tools. Repetitive and labor-intensive tasks are significantly automated. Second, developer code is verified for compliance, as it is being written, so to speak. This allows us, for example, to detect possible runtime exceptions at the start of the implementation phase.

It is clear that making the programmer write less code, and verifying the code for compliance, lowers the chance for errors in the code, and therefore significantly supports the development cycle.

Acknowledgments

Thanks to Tom Mens, Werner Van Belle and Dirk van Deun for proofreading this paper.

References

[1] Cedric Beust. EJBGen. http://www.beust.com/cedric/ejbgen. 281
[2] Borland. JBuilder. http://www.borland.com/jbuilder/. 281
[3] Programming Technology Lab. Declarative meta programming pages. http://prog.vub.ac.be/research/DMP/. 281
[4] Kim Mens, Isabel Michiels, and Roel Wuyts. Supporting software development through declaratively codified programming patterns. *Expert Systems with Applications*, 2002. 281, 284
[5] Sun Microsystems. Enterprise JavaBeans specification. http://java.sun.com/products/ejb/docs.html. 280
[6] Richard Monson-Haefel. *Enterprise JavaBeans*. O'Reilly, 2001. 280
[7] Pramati Technologies. Pramati studio 3.0. http://www.pramati.com/product/studio30. 281
[8] R. Wuyts. Declarative reasoning about the structure of object-oriented systems. In *Proc. Int'l Conf. TOOLS USA'98*, pages 112–124. IEEE Computer Society Press, 1998. 281
[9] R. Wuyts and S. Ducasse. Symbiotic reflection between an object-oriented and a logic programming language. *Multiparadigm Programming with Object-Oriented languages*, 7, 2001. 281

Evaluating the DSMIO Cache-Coherence Algorithm in Cluster-Based Parallel ODBMS*

Carla Osthoff[1], Cristiana Bentes[2], Daniel Ariosto[3], Marta Mattoso[3], and Claudio L. Amorim[3]

[1] Computer Science Department - LNCC
{osthoff}@lncc.br

[2] Systems Engineering Department - UERJ
{cris}@eng.uerj.br

[3] Computer Science Department - COPPE/UFRJ
{marta,amorim}@cos.ufrj.br

Abstract. In this paper, we assess the performance of DSMIO cache-coherence algorithm implemented in a parallel object-based database management system (ODBMS). The distinguishing feature of DSMIO is its use of the lazy release memory consistency model and multiple-writer protocol to reduce both the number and size of coherence messages required to keep coherent a distributed ODBMS across a cluster of PC servers. Using a large distributed database and several application workloads we evaluate DSMIO performance and also compare it against that of the well-known Call-Back Locking (CBL) algorithm. Our results show that both algorithms perform very well for read operations whereas DSMIO outperforms significantly CBL for write operations with DSMIO speed-ups attaining as much as 5.4 while CBL speed-ups reach at most 1.4 for an 8-node cluster. Overall, these results suggest that designers of cluster-based ODBMS should consider DSMIO as an efficient option for developing future projects in the field.

1 Introduction

Cache coherence issues arise in many types of parallel and distributed systems, including Distributed Shared-Memory (DSM) systems ([1]). In fact, there are many similarities between the cache coherence techniques available in parallel database and DSM systems [8]. Furthermore, the study of database cache coherence is very tightly coupled with the study of concurrency control, since cached data can be concurrently accessed by multiple clients and locks can be cached along with data at clients. Our work is based on the observation that the techniques developed to improve software DSM systems can be exploited to improve parallel database systems that apply client caching. In particular, well-established techniques to reduce false-sharing in page-based software DSM systems, such as relaxed memory consistency models and multiple-writer protocols, can be very useful for parallel database systems.

* This work was supported in part by the Brazilian Agencies: FINEP and CNPq.

Z. Bellahsène, D. Patel, and C. Rolland (Eds.): OOIS 2002, LNCS 2425, pp. 286–297, 2002.

Bearing these ideas in mind, in a previous work [4] we proposed a new approach to cache coherence in parallel ODBMS, called **DSMIO**, that uses the Lazy Release memory Consistency model and multiple-writer protocol to limit the number and size of coherence messages in cluster-based parallel ODBMS. Although DSMIO's preliminary results were encouraging the small-size (100 MBytes) database we used limited the scope of experiments and the performance issues that could be addressed for a sound evaluation of DSMIO. For instance, without submitting DSMIO to a large enough database we were not able to assess the impact of cache overflow on DSMIO performance. Cache overflow does not only exacerbate the cache coherence problem in DSMIO but also demands efficient page replacement policies to prevent DSMIO performance to degrade further. Moreover, the results we obtained were based on an (outdated) IBM SP2 multicomputer with a high communication/computation ratio (320 Mb/s switch and 66 MHz Power2 processor), which raised the question whether DSMIO performance would scale on modern high-performance cluster technology.

In this work, we examine **DSMIO** benefits to the performance of a parallel ODBMS system implemented in a cluster of 8 (dual-pentium 650 MHz, 512 MB) PC servers connected by a low-latency high-bandwidth (1.8 Gb/s) Myrinet switch. We evaluate DSMIO using a 3 GBytes distributed database over an wide range of application workloads, enabling us to assess cache overflow while increasing substantially (up to two orders of magnitude) the amount of read and write operations as well as the cache coherence traffic that degrade performance. We assess DSMIO performance in isolation as well as in comparison with that of the well-known CallBack Locking (CBL) cache-coherence algorithm [6]. Our results show that both algorithms perform very well for read operations whereas DSMIO outperforms significantly CBL for write operations with DSMIO speedups attaining as much as 5.4 while CBL speedups reach at most 1.4 for an 8-node cluster. Overall, these results suggest that designers of cluster-based ODBMS should consider DSMIO as an efficient option for developing future projects in the field.

The contributions of this papers are as follows: 1) we describe a new improved version of DSMIO that implements an efficient cache replacement policy to support large-size databases; 2) we evaluate the impact of DSMIO on the performance of a cluster-based parallel ODBMS for various application workloads, and 3) we report results of a performance comparison between DSMIO and CBL.

This paper is structured as follows. Section 2 treats the DBMS cache coherence problem. In section 3, we discuss related works. In section 4 through 6 we describe and compare two proposed solutions: DSMIO approach and the **CBL** algorithm. Section 7 describes our experimental methodology. In section 8, we evaluate DSMIO performance under several application workloads. In section 9 we present a performance comparison between DSMIO and CBL. Finally, in section 10, we draw our conclusion and outline future works.

2 Cache-Coherence Algorithms for Parallel ODBMS

Current parallel ODBMS employ disk caching at client and server nodes so as to access local data as much as possible and to reduce costly disk accesses. However, keeping coherent the distributed caches is a challenging task since the coherence traffic causes communication overheads that degrade ODBMS performance.

Usually, ODBMS cache coherence algorithms are classified as either avoidance-based or detection-based. Detection-based algorithms allow accesses to stale data in cache but detect and resolve them at commit time whereas avoidance-based algorithms prevent access to stale data within a transaction. Stale data refer to data in cache that are outdated due to committed updates issued by concurrent clients. Avoidance-based algorithms increase the amount of messages while detection-based algorithms cause high transaction abort rate. For further comparison between cache-coherence algorithms refer to [17].

In this paper we are interested in avoidance-based algorithms since our focus is on applications that do not allow transaction abortion. In particular, we implemented and used the CBL as a reference for comparison. CBL is a synchronous page-based avoidance-based algorithm in which clients cache both data and read locks across transaction boundaries. Also, CBL like DSMIO does not adapt to fine-grain sharing thus CBL provides an adequate basis for comparison purposes.

We evaluate DSMIO performance in the context of a parallel ODBMS client-server architecture, where each machine acts as both server and client. Typically, ODBMS client/server architecture employs the data-shipping model in which clients fetch data from the server into their caches and perform some database processing locally. Again, given that both DSMIO and CBL are page-based algorithms we consider the page-based server architecture as an appropriate architectural platform for our studies.

3 Related Work

Several works in distributed object and object-relational DBMS addressed the problem of client cache consistency. Although the CBL algorithm [6] is the most popular one, an adaptive version of CBL, called ACBL[5], has been proposed to tackle the problem of false sharing. ACBL is now commonly accepted as the leading algorithm of its class. Differently from CBL, ACBL can adapt to both page and object level locks according to the granularity of the access. Nevertheless, we choose to use CBL to compare against DSMIO because both algorithms are page-based and can be submitted to application workloads that have the same access granularity. Also, object servers and page servers are the two competing data-shipping architectures employed by existing ODBMS. Recent works propose hybrid adaptive server architectures [18] that can adapt between page and object server according to the application behavior. In a future work, we plan to implement and compare ACBL against that of an adaptive version of DSMIO.

In the area of SDSM systems, although many research efforts have been made on improving SDSM systems performance for scientific applications, relatively few works[15, 16] concentrate on applying SDSM techniques to parallel DBMS designs. The work [15] uses TreadMarks as a platform for supporting Postgres DBMS. In contrast to our work they do not intend to change the DBMS design but to add support to deal with some application characteristics. The work[16] runs queries from TPC-D on a commercial database (Oracle) over a cluster with a fine-grain SDSM called Shasta. The main difference between our work and theirs is that Shasta uses compiler support to rewrite application binaries.

4 Overview of DSMIO

The DSMIO approach to cache coherence exploits two basic features often found in current software Distributed Shared Memory (DSM) Systems: relaxed memory consistency models and multiple-writer protocols.

4.1 Relaxed Memory Consistency Models

Release Consistency (RC) and Lazy Release Consistency (LRC) are two well-established relaxed memory consistency models [11]. In these two models, accesses to shared data are protected by acquire and release operations on locks. Lock acquire (e.g., lock operation) is used to gain access to shared data and lock release (e.g., unlock operation) to give such access away.

In the RC model, modifications made to shared data by a client that acquired a lock need to become globally visible at other clients at the time of lock release. In contrast, in LRC only the processor that acquires a lock will see the modifications that precede the lock acquire. To know which modifications precede the lock acquire, LRC divides the program execution into intervals in such a way that the intervals can be partially ordered by synchronization accesses. So, on lock acquire, the acquiring processor asks the last releaser of the lock for the information about the modifications made to shared data during the intervals that precede the acquiring processor's current interval.

Several software DSM systems (SDSM) implemented the LRC model of which TreadMarks[12] is a well-known page-based SDSM and forms the base of our DSMIO System. TreadMarks is an invalidation-based protocol in that modifications to shared data take the form of write-notices that are transferred on lock acquire operations. A write-notice informs that a virtual memory page has been modified during a particular interval, but does not contain the new data written to the page. The new data is only requested and later received by the acquiring processor on a subsequent access to the page.

4.2 Multiple-Writer Protocol

TreadMarks can potentially suffer from false sharing since it uses the page as the coherence unit. To alleviate this problem, TreadMarks implements a multiple-writer protocol that allows multiple processors to write concurrently on different objects of the same page. TreadMarks utilizes the twinning and diffing mechanism to detect the actual modifications made by each processor. Each concurrent writer maintains a twin copy with the original version of the page (before the modifications are done). A comparison of the twin and the later version of the page is used to create a *diff*, which is a run-length encoding of the differences between the two versions. The diff can then be applied to update the page. When all the diffs are merged on the page, a new up-to-date version of the page can be built.

4.3 The DSMIO Cache Coherence Algorithm

DSMIO integrates a disk cache structure with SDSM mechanisms as provided by TreadMarks, as follows. First, DSMIO uses a shared memory region established by TreadMarks as a shared disk cache to store data transferred between disk and memory. In contrast, modifications made to the shared-memory pages are kept separately in the local memory as diffs. Second, DSMIO keeps coherent the shared disk cache by adapting TreadMarks' implementation of the LRC model. More specifically, DSMIO implements statically a server node for each page transferred from disk to memory so that each server node is the manager of only a fraction of pages that form the shared disk cache.

In addition, DSMIO supports three basic disk operations: read, write, and flush. Let us illustrate how these operations work in simple cases; the operations are described in detail in [4]. On a **DSMIO** read operation, the client requests the page to the server, which reads the page from the disk, stores it in the **DSMIO** shared cache and sends a copy of it to the client. When the requested page arrives the client looks up the list of write notices to find out whether it needs diffs from other clients. If so, the client sends diff requests to remote clients and waits for their replies. After receiving all the requested diffs, the client apply them in turn to bring its copy of the page up-to-date.

On a DSMIO write operation, the client first starts a read operation to obtain a fresh copy of the page. After that, it creates a twin copy of the page and copies a private up-to-date version of the page on top of it. At this point, the **DSMIO** algorithm generates a diff for the page, comparing the modified version with its twin. The diff is stored in the client's local memory and a write notice is incorporated to its current interval so that TreadMarks' interval structure remains unmodified.

Flush operations in DSMIO are executed in two cases: 1) when the application finishes, and 2) the disk cache overflows and the server node has to remove pages to free cache space. In the latter, the server node uses a FIFO policy to select pages to discard. To remove valid pages that are also shared the server node needs to multicast an invalidation message to the sharing nodes of each page. On receiving an invalidation message a node sets its page copy as unavailable locally. For every selected page, after receiving all the acknowledgments back the server node writes the page to the disk and clear the corresponding cache page.

5 The CBL Cache Coherence Algorithm

In **CBL**, clients access a virtual memory page by acquiring either a write or a read lock for the page. When a client C_i tries to acquire a read or a write lock for a page P, it sends a lock request message to the server of the page and blocks until it gets a response from the server. If there is no one else caching page P, the server immediately grants the read or write lock page P to client C_i. If there is another client, C_j, caching page P, the server takes different actions depending on the type (R/W) of lock C_i is requesting and the type (R/W) of lock C_j is holding. More details can be found in [7].

Note that in **CBL**, before a lock is acquired, the previous writes to the page must be observed at the server and at all the clients that cache the page, so CBL follows the Release Consistency model.

Our CBL' cache server implements flush operations in a way similar to that of **DSMIO**, and differs only by the fact that CBL is a single-writer protocol, which requires no diffing mechanism.

6 CBL versus DSMIO

It is worth to point out the basic differences between **DSMIO** and **CBL**. First, **DSMIO** allows multiple concurrent writers, while **CBL** is a single-writer protocol. As a result, the **CBL** algorithm suffers from two main sources of overheads: callback delay and false sharing. The callback delay is due to the fact that the server has to wait for a callback reply from each client that has a page copy, before sending a write lock to a client. Furthermore, increasing the number of clients dilates the callback delay, which can hurt CBL performance further. In contrast, DSMIO's multiple-writer protocol triggers coherence operations at lock acquires where only the lock releaser and acquirer exchange coherence messages. As a result, DSMIO is expected to be less negatively affected by coherence overheads than CBL, which at (write) lock releases sends coherence messages to all nodes that cache the page even if they do not access the lock shortly. False sharing occurs when two clients write to different objects allocated to the same page. Given that **CBL** uses the page as its coherence unit and a page if often much larger than an object then many objects can fit in a page and false sharing is likely to occur.

Second, cache overflow cost much less in CBL because it keeps pages single-writer and thus they need no coherence actions at flushing time and can be sent to disk immediately. In contrast, DSMIO's flush operations often cause execution of synchronization operations to collect diffs from remote nodes and apply them to bring pages up-to-date, before sending them back to disk. Given that increasing the number of processors DSMIO tends to execute more flush operations, it is more susceptible to cache overflow than CBL.

7 Methodology and Workload

7.1 Hardware Platform

We implemented both DSMIO and CBL on a Linux cluster of 8 x Dual-Pentium III (650 MHz, 512 MB) interconnected by a low-latency (9us) high-bandwidth (1.8 Gb/s) Myrinet switch. We used the UDP communication protocol and the 007 database [6] as our reference ODBMS.

7.2 Application Workloads

Basically, the 007 database structure consists of a three-level tree formed by *assembly parts, composite parts, and atomic parts.* We defined a 3 Gbytes 007 database for our experiments.

Besides the definition of database sizes, we specified T3 traversal operations with and without updates on the database taking into account data sharing patterns we wanted for performance analysis purposes. We refer to these two variations of T3 as the *update* and *read applications*, respectively.

We also varied the percentage of data sharing in each of these applications. We did so by dividing the database into a set of private regions and a common shared region, and defining three different workloads: *private*, *shared*, and *high contention*. There is no data contention in the private workload, while data contention increases when we move from shared to high-contention workload. In the experiments, lock-based synchronization is used in the update applications and applied to objects individually.

The whole database is distributed among the disks of all processing nodes, and data are distributed in round-robin fashion. We implemented a balanced distribution in such a way that 75% of the data are accessed locally and the other 25% are accessed remotely.

7.3 ODBMS

To evaluate the performance of **DSMIO** and **CBL** we incorporated them into an ODBMS called GOA, developed at COPPE/UFRJ [9], that implements a client/server architecture. The client contains the application code, while the server executes the database persistence services and query processing. The GOA client requests objects from the GOA server. The GOA data model is based to the ODMG standard [3], and thus ODL is used to create a database schema and OQL is used to query stored collections of objects.

We built two parallel GOA systems, which only differ in terms of their ODBMS's cache architecture. The **CBL**-based system, implements concurrency and transaction management according to the **CBL** algorithm. The **DSMIO**-based system alters the original GOA cache architecture in order to both the clients and the server access a single cache This system implements concurrency and transaction management according to the **DSMIO** algorithm. Also read locks have the same implementation in both systems.

8 Experimental Results

In this section we evaluate DSMIO performance on executing read and update applications for basic workloads. Next, we compare DSMIO performance against that of CBL.

8.1 DSMIO Performance

Due to limited space we concentrate our analysis on shared workload although our findings are also valid to the other workloads. To evaluate DSMIO performance we consider the shared workload and three applications with increasingly update rates. More specifically, we evaluate read applications (R) and two update applications (U10 and U50) with update rates of 0%, 10%, and 50%, accordingly.

DSMIO Speed-Up Figure 2 shows DSMIO speed-ups for R, U10, and U50 executions of the shared workload. As can be seen in the figure, read applications scale very well with speed-ups as much as 6 out 8 processors. Also, both update applications perform quite well, with U10 and U50 speed-ups reaching 4.3 and 5 out of 8, respectively. Most importantly, the small performance difference (9%) between U50 and U10 is remarkable since U50 writes five times more than U10. These results suggest that DSMIO performance scales well for our cluster-based ODBMS prototype, as increasing the update rate does not degrade DSMIO performance significantly. In the next section, we explain these results by examining the potential sources of DSMIO overheads and its impact on parallel ODBMS performance.

8.2 Detailed Analysis

For reasons of space we limit our analysis to the U50 application although we obtained similar performance results for the other applications. Figure 1 divides DSMIO's overheads for U50 running the shared workload into four main categories: *lock, flush, read, and write. Lock* and *flush* categories represent the percentage of execution time U50 spent in lock synchronizations and performing flush operations, respectively. The latter overhead category includes communication costs due to synchronization operations that are executed inside cache flushes. The *read and write* categories account for the percentage of execution time spent by U50 on read and write accesses to data, respectively. The figure shows that U50 execution time reduced from 166 s for 1 processor to 31 s for 8 processors. The reasons were that both read and write overheads decreased as much as 92%, confirming DSMIO's cache effectiveness on reducing disk accesses. However, Lock and flush overheads doubled for 8 processors. Therefore, DSMIO successfully trades off disk accesses for less costly lock and flush overheads. Note that, disk I/O operations practically did not affect DSMIO performance, thanks to the efficient Linux prefetching mechanism. More specifically, since each database server stores 1/8 (376 MB) of the entire database (3 GB) in our 8-node cluster, and that the memory size for each processor is 512 MB then the Linux's prefetching system could anticipate and hide most of disk I/O operations.

Communication Overhead Communication overhead for each of the three applications correspond to the amount of messages that U10, U50, and R applications generate for the shared workload as we increase the number of database servers.

The read application presents a relatively low communication traffic even for an 8-node cluster; in this application, messages contain either requests to remote data or server replies. The number of messages goes from over 30,000 for 2 processors up to over 90,000 for 8 processors.

As expected, DSMIO generates considerably more messages for update applications than that for the read application. U10 goes from over 75,000 messages for 2 processors up to 150,000 for 8 processors and U50 goes from over 280,000 messages for 2 processors upd to 620,000 for 8 processors. Over 90% of messages that DSMIO generates for U10 and U50 occur at synchronization points according to the lazy release consistency model. At these points, update applications use lock/unlock operations to gain access to shared data. Due to the LRC model, coherence communication occurs between only the lock acquirer and the last lock owner, which explains the low coherence overhead in DSMIO. As a result, the number of messages per processor approximately halves when the number of nodes vary from 2 to 8. For instance, U10's msg/node reduces from

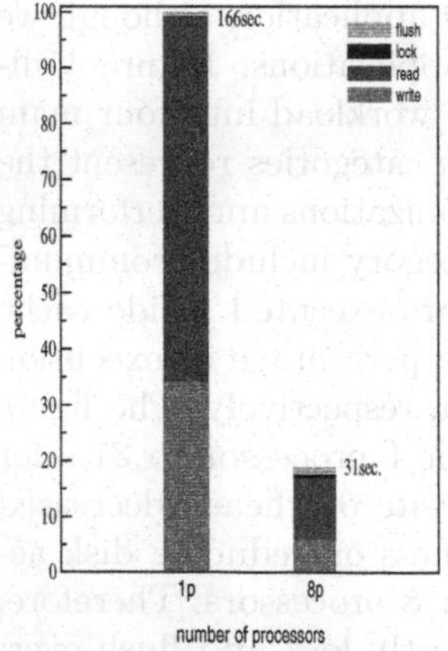

Fig. 1. DSMIO overheads for U50 (shared workload)

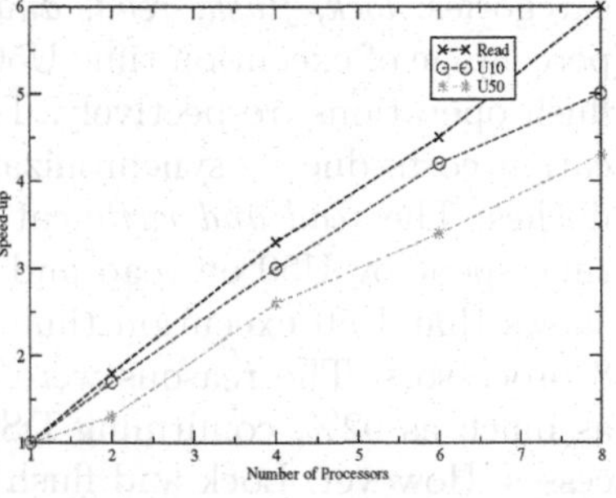

Fig. 2. DSMIO speed-ups for R, U10, and U50 (shared workload)

approximately 40000 for two nodes to less than 20000 for eight nodes, whereas U50's msg/node reduces from 140000 for two nodes to less than 78000 for eight nodes.

The remaining communication overhead (10%) corresponds to data requests for pages and diffs. Such a low data communication overhead is due to both DSMIO multiple-writer protocol and the use of a diffing mechanism. A multiple-writer protocol alleviates false-sharing by allowing multiple concurrent writers to the same page whereas the diffing mechanism reduces the size of data request messages, which decreases both sender and receiver messaging overheads.

Finally, Myrinet switch provides a low-latency communication network that helps the messaging overhead to have little impact on DSMIO performance.

Cache Overflow Cache overflow could be particularly harmful to DSMIO performance as increasing the number of processors DSMIO tends to flush its cache more frequently. The problem with flush operations in DSMIO is that they require costly synchronization operations before pages can be discarded otherwise they may become inconsistent. Figure 1 confirms that each processor generates relatively more flushes for 8 processors because each processor's cache share diminishes. Also, some processors receive more data requests than the average due to workload imbalance therefore causing extra flush operations. Overall, the speed-up gain indicates that although *flush* overheads are considerable, they do not affect significantly the DSMIO performance even in the case of high-contention workload as the experiments in the next section will demonstrate.

9 DSMIO versus CBL

First, we found that CBL (figure ommited) like DSMIO performs very well for read applications and both algorithms achieve similar speed-ups.

The main difference appears for update applications, since CBL slows down for both U10 and U50. For a closer examination, we used instead the U5 application that modifies only 5% of atomic part objects and compared algorithm performance using only the high-contention workload since this illustrates the performance differences better.

We found that DSMIO speed-up (figure ommited) reaches 4.8 out 8 while CBL slows down. To explain such a large difference in performance we present in figure 3 the overhead profile for both algorithms. The figure reveals that DSMIO execution time for 1 processor is higher than that for CBL. The reason is that TreadMarks pays a high overhead even for 1 processor due to its use of the virtual memory protect system. In this workload, true sharing dominates, and the coherence overhead involved in their different consistency models becomes critical to performance. Furthermore, although both algorithms execute the same amount of synchronizations in CBL lock operations cost considerably more due to its consistency model. As a result, in CBL the Lock overhead accounts for nearly 90% of execution time for 8 processors while for DSMIO the same overhead is responsible only for 25% of execution time. In addition, both algorithms reduced drastically the read overhead whereas only DSMIO practically succeeded in eliminating the write overhead but at the expense of increasing the flush overhead from 9% to 37% of execution time for 8 processors.

Therefore for update applications, DSMIO successfully trades off disk accesses for less costly lock operations, while CBL does not. Also, in previous work [4], DSMIO performance gains over CBL for update operations are even greater due to higher latency of SP2 network switch.

10 Conclusion and Future Works

In this paper, we evaluated the **DSMIO** cache-coherence approach to efficiently implement a parallel object-oriented database system in a cluster of PC servers. Our results show that DSMIO performance scales very well and also that it outperforms significantly the CBL algorithm for a wide range of workload applications running on an 8-node cluster. Most importantly, our experiments reveal that the lazy release model and multiple-writer protocol, in this order, are the key enabling mechanisms for DSMIO' superior performance. These results allows us to conclude that DSMIO can be an effective option to improve performance of parallel cluster-based ODBMS systems.

In the near future, we intend to implement and compare adaptive versions of DSMIO to those of adaptive CBL-based systems. In addition, we plan to address fault tolerance issues on DSMIO inspired on previous works in Recoverable **DSM** systems [14] and also to evaluate DSMIO-based parallel servers for e-commerce in the context of the NCP3 project under development at COPPE/UFRJ.

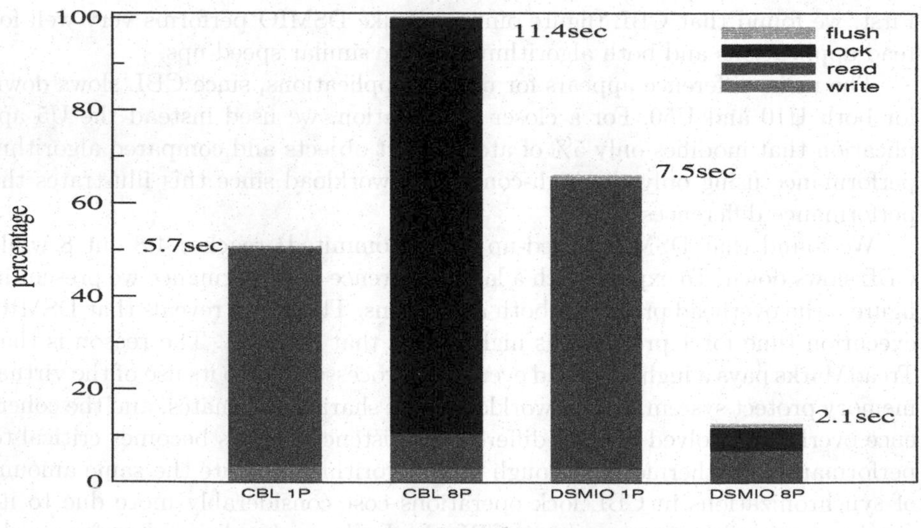

Fig. 3. DSMIO and CBL overheads for U5

References

[1] S. V. Adve and K. Gharachorloo. Shared Memory Consistency Models: A Tutorial. *IEEE Computer, December 1996.* 286

[2] Y.Breibart, R. Komondoor, R. Rastogi, S.Seshdri. Update Propagation Protocols for Replicated Databases. In Bell Labs Technichal Reports.

[3] R. Cattell The Object Database Standard: ODMG-3.0 In *Morgan Kaufmann Publisher, 2000.* 292

[4] C.Osthoff,C.Bentes,R.Bianchini,M.Mattoso, C.Amorim. Evaluating Cache Coherence in the DSMIO System. In Proceedings of the 12th Symposium on Computer Architecture and High Performance Computing, Sao Pedro, Brazil, 2000. 287, 290, 296

[5] M. J. Carey, M. J. Franklin, and M. Zaharioudakis. Fine-Grained Sharing in a Page Server OODBMS. In *Proceedings ACM SIGMOD Conference, 1990.* 288

[6] M. J. Carey, D. J. DeWitt, and J. F. Naughton. The 007 Benchmark. In *Proceedings of the ACM SIGMOD International Conference on Management of Data, pp.12-21, 1993.* 287, 288, 292

[7] M. J. Franklin and M. J. Carey. Client-Server Caching Revisited. In *Technical Report 1089, Computer Science Department, University of Wisconsin-Madison, May 1992.* 291

[8] M. J. Franklin, M. J. Carey, and M. Livny. Transactional Client-Server Cache Consistency: Alternatives and Performance. In *ACM Transactions On DataBase Systems, Sept. 1997.* 286

[9] GOA http:://www.cos.ufrj.br/ goa 292

[10] B.Kemme, G.Alonso. Don't be lazy, be consistent: Postgres-R, a new way to implement Database Replication. In *Proceedings of th 26th VLDB Conference, Cairo, Egypt,2000.*

[11] P. Keleher, A. L. Cox, and W. Zwaenepoel. Lazy Release Consistency for Software Distributed Shared Memory. In *Proceedings of the 19th International Symposium on Computer Architecture, May 1992.* 289

[12] P. Keleher, S. Dwarkadas, A. L. Cox, and W. Zwaenepoel. Treadmarks: Distributed Shared Memory on Standard Workstations and Operating Systems. In *Proceedings of the 1994 Winter USENIX Conference, January 1994.* 289

[13] ncp3 http://www.cos.ufrj.br

[14] C. Morin and I. Puaut. A Survey of Recoverable Distributed Shared Virtual Memory Systems. In *IEEE Transactions on Parallel and Distributed Systems, sept.1997.* 296

[15] T. Parker, and A. Cox I/O-Oriented Applications on a Software Distributed-Shared Memory System. Master of Science Thesis - Computer Science Dept- Rice university, 1999. 289

[16] D.Scales, K. Gharachorloo and C. Thekkath. Shasta: A low overhead,software-only approach for supporting fine-grain shared memory. In *Technical Report 96/2, Western Research Laboratory, Compaq Corporation,1996.* 289

[17] M. Ozsu, K. Voruganti, and R. Unrau. An Asynchronous Avoidance-Based Cache Consistency Algorithm for Client Caching DBMSs. In *Proceedings of the 24th Very Large DataBases Conference, 1998.* 288

[18] K. Voruganti, M. Ozsu, and R. Unrau. An Adaptative Hybrid Server Architecture for Client-Caching Object DBMS. In *Proceedings of the 25th Very Large DataBases Conference, 1999.* 288

A Retrieval Technique for Software Components Using Directed Replaceability Similarity

Hironori Washizaki and Yoshiaki Fukazawa

Department of Information and Computer Science, Waseda University
3-4-1 Okubo, Shinjuku-ku, Tokyo 169-8555, Japan
{washi, fukazawa}@fuka.info.waseda.ac.jp

Abstract. A mechanism of retrieving software components is indispensable for component-based software development. However, conventional retrieval techniques require an additional description, and cannot evaluate the total characteristics of a component. In this paper, we propose a new similarity metric, "directed replaceability similarity" (DRS), which represents how two components differ in terms of structure, behavior, and granularity. We developed a retrieval system that automatically measures DRS between a user's prototype component and components stored in a repository, without any source codes or additional information. As a result of evaluation experiments, it is found that the retrieval performance of our system is higher than those of conventional techniques.

1 Introduction

Recently, software component technology, which is based on building software systems from reusable components, has attracted attention because it is capable of reducing developmental costs. In a narrow sense, a software component is defined as a unit of composition, and can be independently exchanged in the form of an object code without source codes. The internal structure of the component is not available to the public. Since it is natural to model and implement components in an object-oriented paradigm/language[1], we limit this study to the use of OO language for the implementation of components.

The reuse of components over the Internet is emerging, but a technique for retrieving a component that satisfies a given requirement has not yet been established[2]. Important characteristics of components are the following[3]:
(1) Structure: internal participants and how they collaborate
(2) Behavior: stateless behavior and behavior which relates to states
(3) Granularity: the component size and the classification
(4) Encapsulation: to what degree are design/implementation decisions hidden
(5) Nature: main stage used in the development process
(6) Accessibility to Source Code: the modifiability of the component

We aim to reuse components in the form of the object code, and at the implementation stage. Moreover, users retrieve a component generally on the basis of its functionality, and it is possible to verify the encapsulation after retrieval. Therefore, "structure", "behavior" and "granularity" can be considered to be important characteristics of the component in terms of retrieval.

Z. Bellahsène, D. Patel, and C. Rolland (Eds.): OOIS 2002, LNCS 2425, pp. 298–310, 2002.

2 Component Retrieval

Conventional retrieval approaches for software components can be classified into four types: automatic extraction approach, specification-based approach, similarity-based approach and type-based approach.

The automatic extraction approach is based on the automatic extraction of structural information from components[4]. When source codes are not available, the extracted information is insufficient for the retrieval[5].

The semi-formal specification-based approach is based on catalog information of components[2]. In addition, the formal specification-based approach, which uses a semantic description of the component's behavior, has been proposed[6]. The preparation costs of both approaches become large because additional descriptions are necessary.

The similarity-based approach is based on the similarity between a user's query and the component stored in the repository[5, 7]. User's queries are given as a prototype of the component that satisfies the user's requirement.

The type-based approach is based on the component type and the method type[8]. Search results are classified according to adaptability, for example, exact match and generalized match, but more detailed ranking within each match set cannot be obtained. There is another type-based approach by which detailed ranking can be obtained[9], but it requires source codes of components.

These approaches consider a single characteristic of the component, and cannot evaluate the total semantic adaptability of the component[2]. The retrieval mechanism should be able to consider two or more characteristics simultaneously. In addition, not all components available over the Internet have additional specification descriptions[5]. The retrieval mechanism should not require any additional information other than the components themselves.

3 Directed Replaceability Similarity

We propose directed replaceability similarity (DRS) as a metric to represent semantically the degree of difference between two components. In a situation in which the component c_q is used and system requirements are the same before and after the replacement, when c_q is replaced with another component c_s, parts which use c_q must be modified. $DRS(c_q, c_s)$ indicates the necessary adaptation cost in such a situation. It is assumed that all methods of c_q are uniformly used.

DRS is composed of three primitive similarities corresponding to considered characteristics: the structural similarity DRS_S, the behavioral similarity DRS_B and the granularity similarity DRS_G. All primitive similarities are normalized between 0 and 1. DRS is defined as a dynamically weighted linear combination of primitive similarities. The weight values can be adjusted by users to reflect their own perspectives on the importance of three characteristics. $DRS(c_q, c_s)$ is defined as follows, where $\sum_{i=1}^{3} w_i = 1$ and $w_i \geq 0$:
$DRS(c_q, c_s) ::= w_1 DRS_S(c_q, c_s) + w_2 DRS_B(c_q, c_s) + w_3 DRS_G(c_q, c_s)$.

We first define a similarity function, $d(x, y, z)$, which is commonly used while defining primitive similarities. In this paper, "type" means the classification of any attributes of the component. It is assumed that the binary relation $\preceq$ is defined on the set τ composed of instances of the type t, and $\langle \tau, \preceq \rangle$ is a partially ordered set. We call the least element of $\langle \tau, \preceq \rangle$ "the least instance"($root_t$). The transformation to obtain the immediate predecessor of a certain instance is assumed to be f. The type instance's position is defined as the value by which 1 is added to the number of transformation (f) times necessary for the instance to arrive at $root_t$ in $\langle \tau, \preceq \rangle$.

$d(x, y, z)$ represents how an instance Y differs from an instance X from the viewpoint of X using positions x, y and z corresponding to X, Y and Z; Z is a common deepest ancestor instance between X and Y. Z satisfies the following expression: $M = \{Z' : t \mid Z' \preceq X \wedge Z' \preceq Y : Z'\}$, $Z \in M \wedge (\forall Z'' : t \mid Z'' \in M : Z'' \preceq Z)$. M is the set of small or equal instances from X and Y about $\preceq$.

The requirements defining d are the following:

(r1) The similarity is always normalized between 0 and 1.
(r2) The similarity between equivalent instances is always 0.
(r3) When the position of X is smaller than that of Y, the similarity between X and Y seen from X is smaller than that seen from Y.
(r4) If relative positions among instances X, Y, Z are fixed, the similarity between X and Y becomes small as the position of Z becomes deep.

We define $d(x, y, z)$ as follows based on the above-mentioned requirements.

$$x, y, z \in \text{(Positive Integer Set)}, \quad 0 < z \leq x, y$$
$$d(x, y, z) ::= \int_{1+y\frac{2z}{x+y}}^{1+y} \frac{1}{t^2} dt = \frac{y(x+y-2z)}{(y+1)(x+y+2yz)}$$

$d(x, y, z)$ satisfies the following features corresponding to the requirements. In the following, a, b, c, e are all positive integer values.

(f1) $c \leq a, b \Rightarrow \lim_{b \to \infty} \int_1^{1+b} \frac{1}{t^2} dt = 1 \Rightarrow d(a, b, c) < 1$
(f2) $a = b = c \Rightarrow d(a, b, c) = d(b, a, c) = 0$
(f3) $c < a < b \Rightarrow 0 < d(a, b, c) < d(b, a, c) < 1$
(f4) $c \leq a, b \Rightarrow d(a + e, b + e, c + e) < d(a, b, c)$

3.1 Structural Similarity

The component's name and the component's method structures (signatures) can be enumerated as attributes that compose the structural characteristic of the component.

For example, there are four components, $C_1 \sim C_4$, shown in Figure 1 and C_1's calc1 is assumed to be used. These components have only one method and one member field respectively. Parts which use calc1 need not be modified when calc1 is replaced with a method where the value range of the argument's type is the same or greater than int, and the value range of the return value's type is the same or less than int. The relation among value ranges of types is as follows: $\{x : \text{short}| : x\} \subset \{x : \text{int}| : x\} \subset \{x : \text{long}| : x\}$. Therefore, the order of easiness

Component	Field	Signature	Body
C_1	int data = 0;	int calc1(int x)	{ data = x; return x; }
C_2	long data = 0;	short calc2(int x)	{ data = (long) x; return 0; }
C_3	long data = 0;	short calc3(long x)	{ data = (long) x; return x; }
C_4	int data = 0;	long calc4(short x)	{ return 0; }

Fig. 1. Examples of methods with different structures/behaviors

to replace with calc1 is as follows in terms of the structure: calc2 < calc3 < calc4. DRS_S is calculated from sets of such method structural difference and the difference between components' names which components have before and after replacement.

DRS_S is defined as follows, using the string similarity dw for names of components and the instance set similarity dr for sets of method structures.

Structure of component C_S, Method structure M_S
$C_S ::= \{name : \text{String}, methods : \{m_1 : M_S, ..., m_n : M_S\}\}$ $c_q, c_s : C_S$
$c_q = \{name = n_q, methods = ms_q\}$ $c_s = \{name = n_s, methods = ms_s\}$
$DRS_S(c_q, c_s) ::= \frac{dw(n_q, n_s) + 2dr(ms_q, ms_s)}{3}$

The string similarity $dw(w_q, w_s)$ between w_q and w_s is defined as follows using the longest common substring w_p of two strings and the function d.

$$w_q, w_s, w_p \text{: String } \#w_q = (\text{length of } w_q) \;\; dw(w_q, w_s) ::= \begin{cases} d(\#w_q, \#w_s, \#w_p) \\ 1 \; (w_p \text{ does not exist}) \end{cases}$$

The instance set means the set of the same type's instances. The instance set similarity $dr(R_q, R_s)$ of two instance sets R_q and R_s of the type x can be calculated by averaging the total of dx of all pairs in $R_q \times R_s$ without any duplications of instances. dx means the similarity of two instances of the type x. We call dx "the internal similarity". However, the instance set similarity should reflect the difference of the number of instances. Here, $\#R$ is the number of instances in R.

First, at $f_1(R_q, R_s)$, $dx(q, s)$ are calculated for all pairs of (q, s), which consist of the instance q in R_q and the instance s in R_s. From all pairs of (q, s), pairs are selected in order from the smallest of $dx(q, s)$ so that instances in the pair may not overlap with instances in already selected pairs. The set of these selected pairs is defined as S_f. Second, if $\#R_q > \#R_s$, for all q in the remainder of R_q after calculating f_1, new pairs (q, root_x) are created using the root_x, which is the least instance of the type x, at $f_2(R_q, R_s)$. On the other hand, if $\#R_q < \#R_s$, for all s in the remainder of R_s, new pairs (root_x, s) are created at $f_3(R_q, R_s)$. Finally, $dr(R_q, R_s)$ is defined as an average value of the total of f_1, f_2, f_3.

$$f_1(R_q, R_s) ::= \sum_{(q,s)\in S_f} dx(q, s)$$
$$f_2(R_q, R_s) ::= \sum_{q\in R_q - \{q':x|q'\in S_f:q'\}} dx(q, \mathrm{root}_x) \quad (\text{if } \#R_q > \#R_s)$$
$$f_3(R_q, R_s) ::= \sum_{s\in R_s - \{s':x|s'\in S_f:s'\}} dx(\mathrm{root}_x, s) \quad (\text{if } \#R_q < \#R_s)$$
$$dr(R_q, R_s) ::= \frac{f_1(R_q,R_s)+f_2(R_q,R_s)+f_3(R_q,R_s)}{max(\#R_q,\#R_s)}$$

The method structure M_S is composed of the method name and the functional type of the signature. The method structural similarity $dms(m_q, m_s)$ between method structures m_q and m_s is defined as follows, using the string similarity between method names and the functional similarity *df* between signatures.

$$M_S ::= \{name : \text{String}, signature : F\} \quad m_q, m_s : M_S$$
$$m_q = \{name{=}name_q, signature{=}sig_q\} \;\; m_s{=}\{name{=}name_s, signature{=}sig_s\}$$
$$dms(m_q, m_s) ::= \frac{dw(name_q, name_s)+2df(sig_q, sig_s)}{3}$$

When the instance set similarity between instance sets of the method structure is calculated at DRS_S, *dms* is used as the internal similarity and the following root_{ms} is used as the least instance of the method structure: $\mathrm{root}_{ms} = \{name = \text{" "}, signature = \{params = \{\} \rightarrow return = \mathrm{root}_T\}\}$.

The functional similarity $df(f_q, f_s)$ between functional types f_q and f_s uses the instance set similarity for arguments and the normal type similarity *dt* for the return value. Since arguments of the functional type in an object-oriented type system follow a contravariance rule in terms of subtyping[10], arguments after replacement (p_s) are compared with those before replacement (p_q). In the following, T denotes the power type of normal types. Each instance of T is the normal type itself.

$$\text{Functional type } F ::= \{params : \{t_1 : T, ..., t_n : T\} \rightarrow return : T\} \quad f_q, f_s : F$$
$$f_q = \{params = p_q \rightarrow return = r_q\} \quad f_s = \{params = p_s \rightarrow return = r_s\}$$
$$df(f_q, f_s) ::= \frac{dr(p_s, p_q)+dt(r_q, r_s)}{2}$$

The value type (int etc.), the object type (Object etc.), and the value-wrapper type (Integer etc.) are enumerated as the normal type. By introducing the least instance of T (root_T) as the super type of all normal types, normal types form a single partially ordered Is-a graph. We use the subclass relation as the subtyping relation of the object type. Since value-wrapper types have primitive values (instances of value types), we use the subset subtyping of these primitive values as the subtyping relation of the value-wrapper type. Figure 2 shows a standard Is-a graph in Java language.

The subtyping relation is described as *subtype* <: *supertype*. When $t_s <: t_q$, the necessary cost for the replacement of t_q with t_s seems to be lower than that for the replacement of t_s with t_q. Therefore, $dt(t_q, t_s) \leq dt(t_s, t_q)$ should be satisfied if $t_s <: t_q$. When the common deepest supertype of t_q and t_s is t_p, the normal type similarity $dt(t_q, t_s)$ is defined as follows, using the function d.

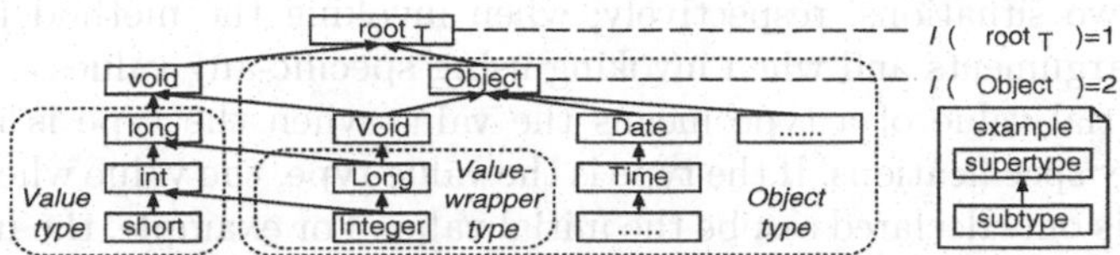

Fig. 2. Is-a graph of normal types

$$\mathrm{root}_T, t, t_q, t_s, t_p : T \quad l(t_q : T) ::= (\text{depth of type } t_q \text{ from } \mathrm{root}_T) \quad l(\mathrm{root}_T) = 1$$
$$M = \{t : T \mid t_q <: t \wedge t_s <: t : t\} \quad t_p \in M \wedge (\forall t : T \mid t \in M : l(t) \le l(t_p))$$
$$dt(t_q, t_s) ::= d(l(t_q), l(t_s), l(t_p))$$
$$1 \le l(t_p) < l(t_q) < l(t_s) \Rightarrow 0 < dt(t_q, t_s) < dt(t_s, t_q) < 1$$

When the instance set similarity between instance sets of the normal type is calculated at df, dt is used as the internal similarity and root_T is used as the least instance of the normal type.

3.2 Behavioral Similarity

Component's method execution results and the value changes of component's readable properties along with method executions can be enumerated as attributes which compose the behavioral characteristic of the component. The readable property means the component's member field whose value can be obtained from the outside. ActiveX and JavaBeans[11] are component systems that support the readable/writable property mechanism using the IDL definition or the introspection mechanism.

For example, C_1's calc1 (Figure 1) is assumed to be used. "data" is a readable property, and has been initialized by the initial value corresponding to the member field's type. When calc1 is invoked using specific-any value (defined later) of int for the argument, the value change of the property whose type is int can be observed, and the value of the return value is not the initial value. In cases of calc2 and calc3, the type of the changed property is long. long is similar to int as numeric types. The invocation of calc4 does not bring about any changes in readable properties. In addition, values of the return value of calc2 and calc4 are always initial values regardless of the kind of argument value. Therefore, the order of easiness to replace with calc1 is as follows in terms of the behavior: calc3 < calc2 < calc4. DRS_B can be calculated from sets of such method behavioral differences which components have before and after replacement.

The behavioral similarity is defined as follows, using the instance set similarity for sets of method behaviors.

Behavior of component C_B, Method behavior M_B
$$C_B ::= \{methods : \{m_1 : M_B, ..., m_n : M_B\}\} \quad c_q, c_s : C_B$$
$$c_q = \{methods{=}ms_q\} \quad c_s = \{methods{=}ms_s\} \quad DRS_B(c_q, c_s) ::= dr(ms_q, ms_s)$$

The method behavior M_B is composed of return values and sets of changed properties. Return values and sets of changed properties are composed of two values in two situations, respectively; when invoking the method using initial values for arguments and when invoking using specific-any values.

The initial value of a type means the value when the type is instantiated without any specifications. If the type is the value type, the value when a variable of its type is only declared can be the initial value. For example, the initial values of int and boolean are 0 and false in Java language. If the target type is the value-wrapper type or object type, the value when a default constructor (the constructor without any arguments) of its type is only used for instantiation can be the initial value. If the default constructor is not available, the initial value can be obtained by inputting initial values corresponding to constructor arguments' types for constructor's arguments recursively.

The specific-any value means an identical value other than the initial value. For a uniform comparison, specific-any values of value types are decided statically. For example, we decided that specific-any values of int and boolean are 1 and true. If the target type is the value-wrapper type or object type, the specific-any value can be obtained by inputting specific-any values for constructor's arguments recursively.

The return value is represented by the typed value type (Value). The changed property is represented by the changed property type (Property). The method behavioral similarity *dmb* between two methods is defined as follows, using the typed value similarity *dv* and the instance set similarity for sets of changed properties. m_q and m_s are instances of M_B.

$$M_B ::= \{returns : \{rinit : \text{Value}, rany : \text{Value}\}, changes :$$
$$\{cinit : \{p_1{:}\text{Property}, ..., p_m{:}\text{Property}\}, cany{:}\{p_1{:}\text{Property}, ..., p_n{:}\text{Property}\}\}\}$$
$$m_q = \{returns = \{rinit{=}ri_q, rany{=}ra_q\}, changes = \{cinit{=}ci_q, cany{=}ca_q\}\}$$
$$m_s = \{returns = \{rinit{=}ri_s, rany{=}ra_s\}, changes = \{cinit{=}ci_s, cany{=}ca_s\}\}$$
$$dmb(m_q, m_s) ::= \frac{dv(ri_q,ri_s)+dv(ra_q,ra_s)+dr(ci_q,ci_s)+dr(ca_q,ca_s)}{4}$$

When the instance set similarity between instance sets of the method behavior is calculated at DRS_B, *dmb* is used as the internal similarity and the following root_{mb} is used as the least instance of the method behavior: $\text{root}_{mb} = \{returns = \{rinit = \{type = \text{root}_T, init = \text{false}\}, rany = \{type = \text{root}_T, init = \text{false}\}\}, changes = \{cinit = \{\}, cany = \{\}\}\}$.

The typed value type is composed of the normal type and the boolean type which represents whether its value is an initial value. The typed value similarity *dv* between two typed value types is defined as follows, using the normal type similarity and the boolean similarity *db*.

$$\text{Value} ::= \{type : T, init : \text{boolean}\} \quad v_q, v_s : \text{Value} \quad v_q = \{type = t_q, init = in_q\}$$
$$v_s = \{type = t_s, init = in_s\} \quad dv(v_q, v_s) ::= \frac{dt(t_q,t_s)+db(in_q,in_s)}{2}$$

The changed property type is composed of the property name, the normal type, and two boolean types which represent whether its values are initial values before and after value changing. The changed property similarity *dp* between two changed properties is defined as follows, using the string similarity, the normal type similarity, and the boolean similarity.

$$\text{Property} ::= \{name\text{:String}, type\text{:}T, bef\text{:boolean}, aft\text{:boolean}\} \quad p_q, p_s\text{:Property}$$
$$p_q = \{name = n_q, type = t_q, bef = b_q, aft = a_q\}$$
$$p_s = \{name = n_s, type = t_s, bef = b_s, aft = a_s\}$$
$$dp(p_q, p_s) ::= \frac{dw(n_q,n_s)+dt(t_q,t_s)+db(b_q,b_s)+db(a_q,a_s)}{4}$$

When the instance set similarity between instance sets of the changed property type is calculated at *dmb*, *dp* is used as the internal similarity and the following root_p is used as the least instance of the changed property type: $\text{root}_p = \{name = \text{“ “}, type = \text{root}_T, bef = \text{false}, aft = \text{false}\}$.

The boolean similarity *db* between two boolean values is defined as follows, using the function *d*. b_q and b_s are instances of boolean.

$$g(x : \text{boolean}) ::= \begin{cases} 1 & (x \equiv \text{false}) \\ 2 & (\text{otherwise}) \end{cases} \quad db(b_q, b_s) ::= d(g(b_q), g(b_s), g(b_q \wedge b_s))$$

3.3 Granularity Similarity

The component's static size seen from the outside and the component's internal complexity can be enumerated as attributes which compose the granularity characteristic of the component. We measure the internal complexity indirectly using the execution time of each component's method under the same environment. Using both initial values and specific-any values for method arguments, it is thought that the execution time can reflect the component's granularity.

For example, there are three components, C_1 (size: 10kbytes, total method execution time: 10msec), C_2 (15kbytes, 20msec) and C_3 (100kbytes, 150msec). C_1 is assumed to be used. The component size and total execution time for C_3 are large compared with those for C_1 and C_2. Therefore, the replacement of C_1 with C_3 is more difficult than its replacement with C_2. DRS_G can be calculated from such components' size difference and sets of method granularity differences.

The granularity similarity is defined as follows, using the integral number similarity *dn* for component sizes and the instance set similarity for sets of method granularities.

Granularity of component C_G, Method granularity M_G
$$C_G ::= \{size\text{: int}, methods : \{m_1\text{:}M_G, ..., m_n\text{:}M_G\}\} \quad c_q, c_s : C_G$$
$$c_q = \{size = size_q, methods = ms_q\} \quad c_s = \{size = size_s, methods = ms_s\}$$
$$DRS_G(c_q, c_s) ::= \frac{dn(size_q,size_s)+dr(ms_q,ms_s)}{2}$$

The method granularity M_G is composed of the execution time using initial values for arguments (*init*) and an execution time using specific-any values (*any*). The method granularity similarity *dmg* between two methods is defined as follows, using the integral number similarity for execution times.

$$M_G ::= \{init : \text{int}, any : \text{int}\} \quad m_q, m_s : M_G \quad m_q = \{init = in_q, any = an_q\}$$
$$m_s = \{init = in_s, any = an_s\} \quad dmg(m_q, m_s) ::= \frac{dn(in_q,in_s)+dn(an_q,an_s)}{2}$$

When the instance set similarity between instance sets of the method granularity is calculated at DRS_G, dmg is used as the internal similarity and the following root_{mg} is used as the least instance of the method granularity: $\mathrm{root}_{mg} = \{init = 0, any = 0\}$.

For the integral number value of 0 or higher, the integral number similarity is defined as follows, using the function d.

$$n_q, n_s : \mathrm{int} \quad dn(n_q, n_s) ::= d(n_q + 1, n_s + 1, min(n_q, n_s) + 1)$$

4 Component Retrieval System

$DRS(c_q, c_s)$ reflects the degree of adaptability of c_s to the specification of c_q. Therefore, when retrieving components from the repository, if a prototype component which satisfies a user's requirement specification is given, DRS between the prototype and one of the components stored in the repository can be used as the index for search ranking. This mechanism does not require any source codes or additional information other than the component itself. We have developed a retrieval system called RetrievalJ, in Java language, using the DRS technique. JavaBeans is the target component system. The repository is composed of description files that contain automatically analyzed component information.

Retrieval sequences are described as follows according to Figure 3.

(1) The user prepares a prototype component, which has the methods and readable properties to realize the required specification. However, the prototype does not need to actually function.

(2) The user inputs the prototype as the query.

(3) RetrievalJ analyzes the input component statically and dynamically.

– In the static analysis, RetrievalJ collects the component name, size, and structural information on methods by introspecting a BeanInfo object as the meta information of the JavaBeans component.

– In the dynamic analysis, RetrievalJ records execution times, execution results of methods, and information on value changes of readable properties by instantiating the component and invoking all of the methods using initial/specific-any values for arguments. By acquiring all readable properties' values and comparing before and after invocation of each method, RetrievalJ detects value changes of readable properties. Since initial/specific-any values are decided statically corresponding to each type, this dynamic analysis is performed automatically.

(4) RetrievalJ generates the report object based on analyzed information.

(5) RetrievalJ restores report objects from description files in the repository.

(6) RetrievalJ calculates all DRS between the query report object and each of the restored report objects.

(7) RetrievalJ outputs the search result in a list form and an individual form. At this time, the user can set weight values corresponding to three primitive similarities. In the list form, all components are ranked in order from the smallest of each DRS. In the individual form, primitive similarities are displayed in detail.

(8) The user downloads the arbitrary component from search results.

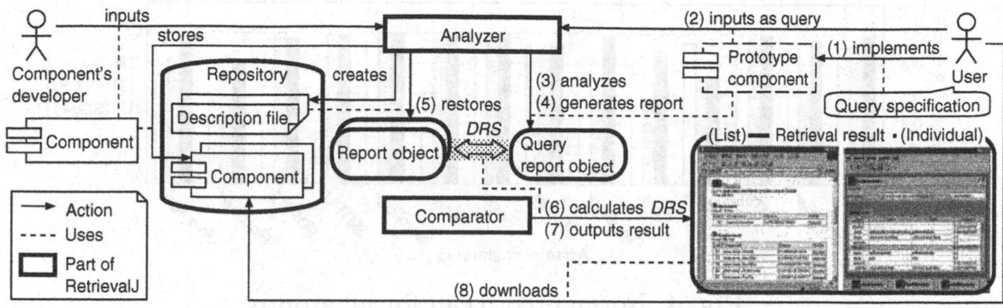

Fig. 3. Mechanism of RetrievalJ

5 Evaluation

We have clarified that the structure is the most important characteristic. Moreover, because the component system has been currently limited to JavaBeans, the importance of granularity is lowered in relation to the behavior. Therefore, we use the following DRS' as our technique: $DRS'(c_q, c_s) ::= 0.5DRS_S(c_q, c_s) + 0.3DRS_B(c_q, c_s) + 0.2DRS_G(c_q, c_s)$.

As conventional techniques, we use Spanoudakis's similarity technique ([SC94][7]) and Michail's similarity technique ([MN99][5]). Both techniques are similar to our technique in that their preparation costs are extremely low. In [SC94], components are ranked high whose positions in the class inheritance hierarchy are closest to the user's query component. In [MN99], components are ranked high whose similarities in the set of terms to the user's query component are large with respect to the term frequency.

We use 257 components provided in [11, 12, 13, 14, 15, 16, 17, 18, 19, 20] as evaluation samples. From among all of the samples, we set 13 agreement groups, in which all components functionally resemble each other based on documents attached to components: Calendar(number of components : 5), ProgressBar(3), SMTP(3), POP3(3), Clock (3), Calculator(2), Gauge(2), Finger(2), Stock(2), ScrollBar(2), GUI for SMTP (2), GUI for POP3(2), PlotChart(2). When the component is given as the user's query from a certain group, the retrieval performance is high if components in the same group as the query are ranked high.

5.1 Normalized Recall

We mesured the normalized recall as an evaluation of the retrieval result. R_{norm} (G) about a group G when one component c_g in G is given as the user's query is defined as follows. $rank(c)$ is the rank of the component c when retrieving from 256 components. $\#G$ is the number of components in G.

$$\text{Normalized recall } R_{norm}(G) ::= 1 - \frac{2\sum_{c \in G-\{c_g\}} rank(c) - \#G(\#G-1)}{2(\#G-1)(257-\#G)}$$

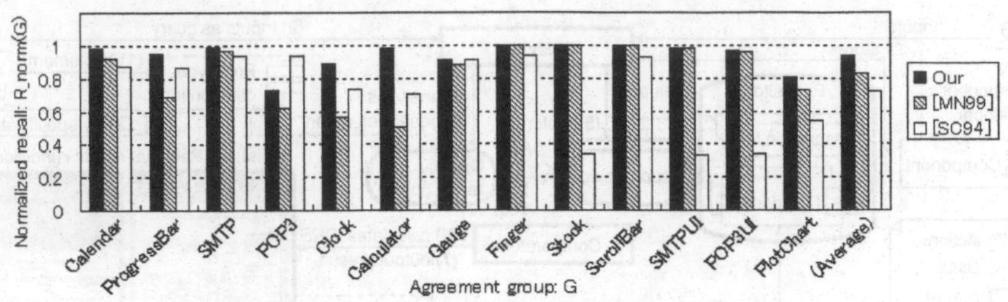

Fig. 4. Normalized recall for all groups

Figure 4 shows normalized recalls for all groups obtained using three techniques. The average value of our technique (0.938) exceeds those of [SC94](0.722) and [MN99](0.832). Therefore, the retrieval performance of our technique is higher than those of [SC94] and [MN99], regardless of the kind of user's query.

This result originates in that components in the same group have interfaces that provide a common function concerning the target domain, and those interfaces are similar, particularly with respect to the structure. For example, about the Calendar group, Table 1 shows method structural similarities (*dms*) between the selected date acquisition methods which are found to be in common using our technique. Table 1 also shows ranks of components obtained using three techniques when Calendar[16] is used as the user's query. These methods are similar in terms of names and types of return. In our technique, because consideration is given to the structural similarity of methods, components in the Calendar group are ranked high.

Even if functions are the same, if two components' developers are different, positions of components in the class inheritance hierarchy are generally different. Therefore, the retrieval performance of [SC94] is low. [MN99] considers the difference between methods, but the consideration is limited to the name; the type of method is not considered.

Table 1. Comparison of method structures and ranking result

Component	Method	Return	*dms*	Our	[SC94]	[MN99]
Calendar[16]	getResultSelectedDateAsString	String	–	–	–	–
SSCalendar[18]	getAllSelectedDates	Message	0.067	1	19	4
CalendarBean[15]	getSelectedDate	String	0.011	2	76	14
CalPanel[18]	getDate	int	0.071	5	20	5
CalendarViewer[12]	(none)	(none)	0.187	12	21	63

Table 2. Obtained similarities (result ranks in repository)

	[SC94]: similarity	[MN99]: similarity	Our: DRS'	Our: $1.0DRS_S$
Bean1 (rank)	0.3935 (2)	1362.1 (3)	0.0238 (1)	0.0399 (1)
Bean2 (rank)	0.3935 (2)	1362.1 (3)	0.0304 (5)	0.0399 (1)

5.2 Consideration of Total Characteristics

We prepared two components that are the same for all method structures: Bean1 functions as a GUI label, and Bean2 does not function at all. As our technique, we use DRS' and the structural similarity $1.0DRS_S$. When retrieving from 259 (257 + Bean1, Bean2) using the java.awt.Label component as the user's query, each measurement value of two components, as obtained using our techniques, [SC94] and [MN99], is shown in Table 2. [SC94] and [MN99] cannot clarify the difference between Bean1 and Bean2, because these techniques do not consider the component behavior. RetrievalJ can detect the behavioral difference. For example, RetrievalJ detects the value changing of the property when invoking methods of Bean1, and does not detect in Bean2. Therefore, with our technique, a user can recognize that Bean1 satisfies the query more closely than Bean2 using DRS' which can consider the total characteristics of the component.

6 Conclusion

We have presented a new similarity metric, DRS, and realized a retrieval system that can be applied for components without source codes. Our approach is excellent regarding the preparation cost because additional information is not necessary. The retrieval performance of our system is high because of the consideration of the total component characteristics. RetrievalJ is available from http://www.fuka.info.waseda.ac.jp/Project/CBSE/. We will verify the possibility of using RetrievalJ together with other retrieval techniques.

References

[1] Hopkins, J.: Component Primer, Communications of the ACM, Vol.43, No.10 (2000) 298

[2] Meiling, R., et al.: Storing and Retrieving Software Components: A Component Description Manager, Australian Computer Science Conference (2000) 298, 299

[3] Yacoub, S., et al.: Characterizing a Software Component, International Workshop on Component-Based Software Engineering (1999) 298

[4] Seacord, R., et al.: Agora: A Search Engine for Software Components, IEEE Internet Computing, Vol.2, No.6 (1998) 299

[5] Michail, A., et al.: Assessing Software Libraries by Browsing Similar Classes, Functions and Relationships, International Conference on Software Engineering (1999) 299, 307

[6] Penix, J. and Alexander, P.: Efficient Specification-Based Component Retrieval, Automated Software Engineering, Vol.6, No.2 (1996) 299
[7] Spanoudakis, G., et al.: Measuring Similarity Between Software Artifacts, International Conference on Software Engineering & Knowledge Engineering (1994) 299, 307
[8] Zaremski, A. and Wing, J.: Signature Matching: a Tool for Using Software Libraries, ACM Transactions on Software Engineering and Methodology, Vol.4, No.2 (1995) 299
[9] Ye, Y. and Fischer, G.: Promoting Reuse with Active Reuse Repository Systems, International Conference on Software Reuse (2000) 299
[10] Cardelli, L.: Type Systems, Handbook of Computer Science and Engineering, CRC Press (1997) 302
[11] Watson, M.: Creating JavaBeans: Components for Distributed Applications, Morgan Kaufman (1997) 303, 307
[12] Neil, J.: JavaBeans Programming from the Ground Up, McGraw-Hill (1998) 307, 308
[13] Harold, E.: JavaBeans: Developing Component Software in Java, IDG Books (1998) 307
[14] Englander, R.: Developing JavaBeans, O'Reilly (1997) 307
[15] http://www.jars.com/ 307, 308
[16] http://www.alphaworks.ibm.com/alphabeans/ 307, 308
[17] http://www.javacats.com/ 307
[18] http://www.sjug.org/showcase/ 307, 308
[19] http://openlab.ring.gr.jp/kyasu/ 307
[20] http://www.bekkoame.ne.jp/~sakamo_m/ 307

Evaluating Information Systems Development Methods: A New Framework

Peter Bielkowicz, Preeti Patel and Thein Than Tun

Dept. Computing, Information Systems and Mathematics
London Guildhall University
100 Minories, London EC3N 1JY, UK
{bielkowi,patelp,thein}@lgu.ac.uk

Abstract. Our detailed investigation into various approaches to evaluate Information Systems Development methods has shown that numerous attempts to assess these methods only yield inconclusive and questionable results. There are two general trends as to how various criteria for evaluation are organised. There are relatively ad hoc lists of criteria for evaluation, and systematically organised frameworks, which generally provide more authoritative assessment results. However, the frameworks investigated are too generic and disproportionate in their emphases on certain parts of a method. Our initial motivation was the development of a framework for assessment of Component-based Software Development methods. However, in response to the shortcomings in existing approaches to method evaluation, a more generic framework that can be used to evaluate various types of Information Systems Development methods such as object-oriented methods, structured methods etc, is presented in this paper. The proposed framework defines three major elements of a method, namely, System Models, System Development Process and Software Architecture. This paper discusses the technique for evaluation of System Models and due to limitations on length of the paper, discussions on the evaluation of the other two elements are not included.

1 Introduction

The primary purpose of this paper is to present some interesting aspects of our current work on a new approach to evaluation of Information Systems Development methods. The authors are involved in an academic research project to critically evaluate published Component-based Development methods in order to create a holistic approach to Component-based development. As part of our research, we first set out to establish a theoretical framework for evaluation of Component-based Development methods, e.g. [2]. However, our investigation into several existing approaches to evaluation and comparison of different kinds of methods reveal that most attempts to evaluate methods do not yield decisive answers.

Z. Bellahsène, D. Patel, and C. Rolland (Eds.): OOIS 2002, LNCS 2425, pp. 311-322, 2002.

Due to these weaknesses in existing approaches, we decided to shift our focus a little and present certain aspects of our framework that is applicable not only to Component-based Development methods, but also to other types of Information Systems Development methods such as object-oriented and structured methods.

Selected approaches and our criticism of each of them are summarised in the following section. Section 3 presents our framework that deals with three major elements of a method, namely, System Models, System Development Process and Software Architecture. In this paper, only the technique for evaluation of System Models is discussed due to shortage of space. Conclusions and references can be found in Section 4 and 5 respectively.

2 A Survey of Existing Approaches to Method Comparison and Evaluation

In order to provide some indications of the state of the art, this section presents a summary of selected existing method evaluation approaches we investigated.

2.1 Wieringa's Approach: A Framework for Surveying Methods and Techniques

Wieringa [11] suggests an evaluation framework that is based upon the concept of system, in particular, a system that interacts with its environment. These interactions can be grouped into meaningful units called 'functions'. Interactions are 'by nature always communications'. Functions, when ordered in time, become behaviour.

This approach regards functions, communication and behaviour as 'system properties'. These properties can be described at various levels of abstraction. System interaction at the top level can be termed the 'mission' of the system. At a more detailed level, are functions, and at the bottom level, there are 'atomic transactions'. Also, behaviour of the system can be described at various levels and they are shown in the 'refinement hierarchy'. Systems are composed of parts, and the composition of the system is shown in an aggregation hierarchy. Hierarchies of aggregation and refinement are also intrinsic, which can be represented in a magic square. Finally, the mapping between system interactions and system components is shown in Function Decomposition Table.

Based upon these concepts, Wieringa concluded that a method should offer techniques for four properties. They are:

1. function specification techniques,
2. behaviour specification techniques,
3. communication specification techniques, and
4. decomposition specification techniques.

Since decomposed system parts are regarded as systems in their own right, the approach states that the techniques for the specifications of function, behaviour and communication are divided into 'external' specifications, i.e. specifications for the entire system, and 'internal' specifications, i.e. specifications for system components.

2.1.1 Comments

The framework does explain what kind of models one should expect from a method and why. However, there are some weaknesses in the framework. For instance there is an overemphasis on system interaction, which is described from three different perspectives. The framework does not highlight the importance of information that is being communicated, and information that needs to be stored inside the system.

Also, when references to 'system' are made, it seems that only the 'process of the system' is implied. This is evident from the assessment of the Entity Relationship model, which is regarded as a system decomposition model. However, the concepts of communication, function and behaviour cannot be applied to entities in the ER model and the idea that decomposed units of a system should be regarded as 'systems in their own right' appears to be invalid in this sense.

We also believe that decomposition of the system and refinement of system interaction is mutual, contrary to the suggestion made by the approach that it is possible to decompose a system without detailed knowledge of its interactions and vice versa.

Finally, there does not seem to be much need for communication, which for most purposes is similar to function.

2.2 Jayaratna's Approach: NIMSAD

Jayaratna [7] proposed the Normative Information Model-based Systems Analysis and Design (NIMSAD) framework, which is a generic framework for the evaluation of 'any' method[1], including Information Systems Development methods. The framework suggests that effective application of a method depends on three elements: the method itself, the person who applies the method, and the context in which the method is applied.

Evaluation of the three elements, namely, the problem-solving process, the problem solver, and the problem situation will be carried out at three stages: 'before intervention in order to minimise our efforts and effectiveness; during intervention because of the dynamic nature of the elements; and after intervention so that lessons can be learned about the three elements' [7].

2.2.1 Comments

The NIMSAD framework is rather unique in many regards. First, it highlights the fact that, practically speaking, effective problem-solving not only depends on the method used, but also on the situation to which the method is applied and the person who uses the method. The NIMSAD framework also treats the evaluation of a method as a dynamic activity that is carried out before, during and after the application of the method. This treatment is also a very original feature of the NIMSAD framework.

[1] Jayaratna uses the term methodology. Some authors prefer 'method' to 'methodology', and others use the two interchangeably. We opted for the term method and for the limited purpose of the discussion, it can also be read as 'methodology'.

The framework appears to be too generic in some areas. For instance, the framework assumes that a method is a 'problem-solving process'. However, the framework does not attempt to define specifically what constitutes a method and how to compare elements of a method. The lack of which makes the framework less efficient for the technical and theoretical evaluation of very specific kinds of methods, e.g. Component-based Development methods.

2.3 Other Approaches

Other approaches are also of interest and were therefore investigated. Some are briefly described here.

Avison and Fitzgerald [3] provide a list of criteria which includes philosophy, model, techniques and tools, scope, outputs, practice and product. The criteria however suggest only what to compare in general terms, but not how to carry out the comparison. How can one compare different philosophies of methods? Also some criteria are too generic. For example, what exactly needs to be compared in models?

As mentioned in [3], Catchpole, Land, and Bjorn-Andersen, compile extensive lists of criteria (see [3] for references). We believe that comparison criteria should not be a never-ending list of randomly collected questions, but they should rather focus on important features of methods that affect the overall quality of the methods.

Hong et al [6] describe the following two-phased approach to compare object-oriented methods. Phase One consists of building meta-process and meta-data models whilst Phase Two is concerned with the comparison of analysis and design steps, concepts and techniques. Hong et al made some attempt to quantify the quality attributes, but as Jayaratna [7] pointed out, if one can create a supermethodology, would we still be needing to compare imperfect methods?

2.4 General Findings of the Investigation

We believe that many attempts to compare or evaluate methods using lists of criteria are unsuccessful because they tend to deploy criteria that are too subjective, ill-defined, and narrowly-focused. For instance, criteria such as 'simplicity', 'symbols', and 'reusability' are rather common across many catalogues of criteria. Some of these criteria are, of course, important. The clear weakness of criteria lists is that they tend to be rather ad hoc and incomprehensive due to lack of congruent fundamental principles. Therefore, assessment results produced by these criteria are often inconclusive. For example, if a method is not simple, does it necessarily make it a bad method? Some of the quality criteria are also hard to gauge let alone compare them. How does one confidently measure the simplicity of a method?

A good alternative to such fragmented lists of criteria is assessment frameworks. Frameworks such as [7] and [11] are based upon rather sound logical reasoning, and they provide some fairly objective and systematic ways to question the quality of methods. However, a potential drawback is that since the frameworks can be too generic, there can be areas for subjectivity to creep in. The proposed framework will draw from the fundamental rules on which these frameworks are built, but will also supplement them with specific mechanisms to gauge various quality attributes.

3 The Proposed Framework

As our investigation has shown, there are a number of weaknesses in the existing approaches, which leads to the proposal of our framework. Frameworks such as [7] and [11], and 'systems thinking' [10] in general have some bearing on this framework but it also sheds new light on other important areas of method evaluation such as categorising systems models, mapping their correlations etc. that are not explored by existing approaches. Hence the proposed framework does not overturn these approaches, but rather synthesises and enhances them by providing more concrete guidelines.

Elements of Evaluation

At a very generic level, this framework agrees with the NIMSAD framework that successful evaluation of a method requires assessment of not just the method, but also the context in which the method is applied and various personal qualities of the person who applies the method. This framework also agrees with NIMSAD that the evaluation of the three elements should be done at three stages, before intervention, during intervention and after intervention. Since NIMSAD is designed for the evaluation of a wide range of methods, its definition of method is very generic. The framework regards a method as 'a problem-solving process'. It is very process-focused and for most Information Systems Development methods, it is a rather simplistic description. In modern methods, such as Component-based Software Development methods, there are specific issues such as modelling techniques that are too important to be ignored.

Authors such as Song [9] have made various proposals on what constitute a method. Based on these proposals and our observations of modern methods, the proposed framework suggests that a method has three major elements.

Three Major Elements of a Method

This framework proposes that a method has three main elements namely, System Models, System Development Process and Software Architecture (see Figure 1).

In fact these three elements are not totally independent of each other. For instance, in a good method, process stages can be expressed in terms of models produced. Deliverables from the process stages can be mapped to the elements defined in the architecture and (especially design) models should have some correspondence with the software architecture.

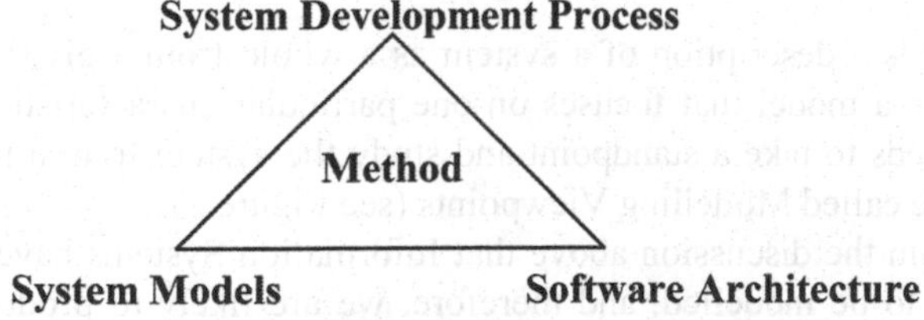

Fig. 1. Three major elements of a method

Now we will look at the evaluation of System Models.

3.1 System Models

In order to understand the aspects of the system that need to be modelled, this framework has applied the principles of 'systems thinking' to Information Systems.

Main Characteristics of Information Systems

Authors such as Waring [10], Wieringa [11] discuss various characteristics of systems. Based on such discussions, we argue that there are, among others, three main characteristics of Information Systems: Information, Process/Functionality and Interaction.

Information: Perhaps the most distinguishing feature of Information Systems is that they provide information to their users. In order to provide useful information, Information Systems have to carry out some tasks such as gathering, storing and manipulating information, which leads to the second characteristic Process/Functionality.

Process/Functionality: Information Systems perform actions such as storing, retrieving, manipulating, presenting data etc. Some of these actions require the system to communicate (to obtain or transmit information) with the outside world (users, other systems etc) through system interactions.

Interaction: Information Systems communicate with the outside world by means of Interaction. In a broad sense, Interaction means conveying of information from a source to a destination.

These three characteristics are by no means the only characteristics of Information Systems. Properties such as emergence, control, and others also apply to Information Systems. We believe that the three characteristics are the most defining characteristics of Information Systems. Therefore, when modelling Information Systems, paramount attention should be paid to capture these three characteristics.

Two Types of Models

Methods provide various system models to express the method-users' reflection of the 'situation of concern'. In terms of coverage, there are two types of models: Global Models and Contextual Models. Global models are the descriptions of the system in its entirety from a modelling viewpoint. Contextual models are the descriptions of the contexts in which system components operate. The following sections examine both models in detail.

3.1.1 Global Models

A global model is a description of a system as a whole from a given perspective. In order to produce a model that focuses on one particular characteristic of the system, the modeller needs to take a standpoint and study the system from a particular angle. These angles are called Modelling Viewpoints (see Figure 2).

It is clear from the discussion above that Information Systems have three main aspects that need to be modelled, and therefore, we are likely to produce three global models that capture these three characteristics. In general, one can practically have a global model for each major characteristic of the type of system that one is dealing with.

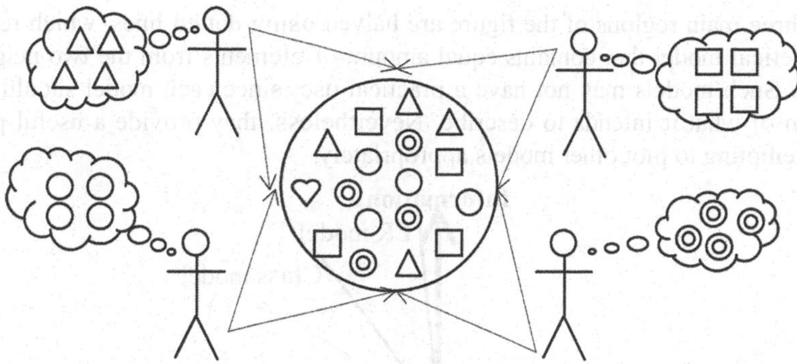

Fig. 2. Modelling Viewpoint: A perspective from which a modeller perceives the system

In this framework, these characteristics are represented as three axes as in the following IPI (Information, Process/Functionality & Interaction) Matrix, and we can map global models suggested by methods onto the matrix (Figure 3). A line is drawn near the Process/Functionality axis to represent a process/functionality model that provides an overall view of the system's functionality. Similarly, lines are drawn near the Information and Interaction axes to represent an information model that provides a representation of (or information about) interesting things in the real world, and an interaction model that provides a high-level description of the system's communication with the outside world respectively.

Models from every method may not neatly fit into these three categories. For instance, it is possible that a model that depicts the process/functionality view of the system also contains elements of system interactions. Such models can be accommodated in the matrix by tilting the lines towards the appropriate axis or shading an angular area.

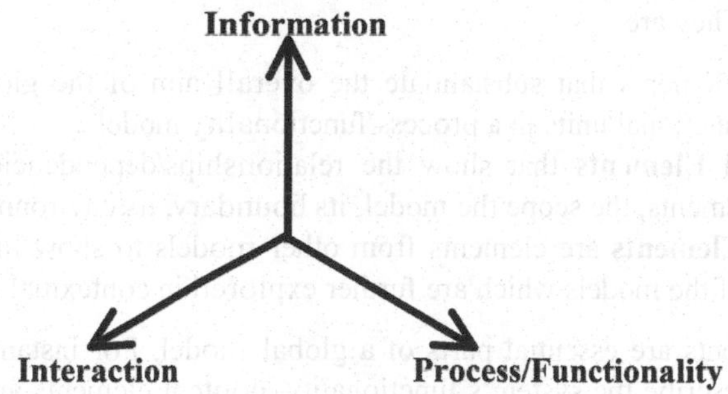

Fig. 3. IPI Matrix for Global Models of Information Systems

In Figure 4, ER model is drawn very close to the Information axis because ER models only deal with the information aspect of the system. On the other hand, Class model has elements of processing: class operations. Therefore, it is aligned towards the Process/Functionality axis. DFD is essentially a process/functionality model but also contains elements of interaction and information, and therefore it is shown as an angular area.

The three main regions of the figure are halved using dotted lines, which represent a hypothetical model that contains equal amount of elements from the two neighbouring axes. Such models may not have a practical use, since each model should have a clear aim of what it intends to describe. Nevertheless, they provide a useful purpose when attempting to plot other models appropriately.

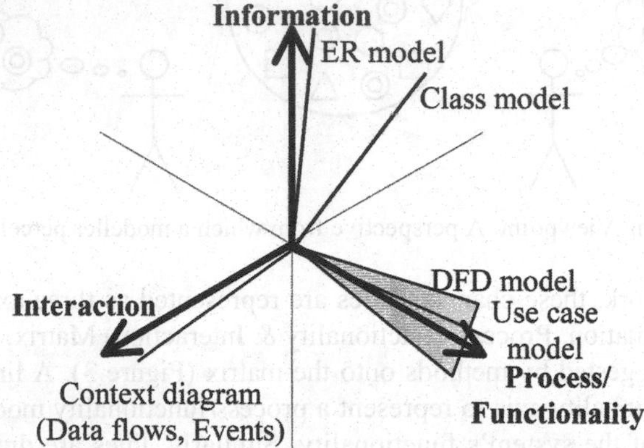

Fig. 4. Global Models of various methods

Elements of a Global Model

These global models can be broken down into basic meaningful units. Basic units of a Process/Functionality Model are processing units, basic units of an Information Model are logical groups of data items, and basic units of an Interaction Model are events (an event is an abstraction of some data flows/messages).

Model elements mentioned above are one of the three notable kinds of elements in a global model. They are:

1. **Content** Elements that substantiate the overall aim of the global model. For example functional units in a process/functionality model.
2. **Structural Elements** that show the relationships/dependencies between the content elements, the scope the model, its boundary, its environment etc. and
3. **Overlap Elements** are elements from other models to show linkages between elements of the models which are further explored in contextual models.

Content elements are essential parts of a global model. For instance if the global model aims to describe the system's functionality, content elements are units of processing. If the global model is to depict the Interaction of the system, content elements are units of interaction, such as data flows and events. Structural elements provide ways to interconnect these content elements, e.g. class relationships. They also are used to add other information such as the boundary, limitations of the model etc. Because of a need for traceability between models, most global models also contain elements from other global models called overlap elements. (Alternatively, some methods use extra models to show such overlaps e.g. Entity Event Model in SSADM [5].)

3.1.2 Contextual Models

Contextual models take each of these basic major units of global models and show how these units take part in the running of the system. For instance, a contextual model can show how a unit of Process/Functionality uses Information units and Interaction units to perform a specific task. In this regard, the use case realisation model in the UML can be regarded as a contextual model [1] and [8].

Contextual models are shown as arrow-headed arches. There are two kinds of contextual model. One is abstract (a direct relationship) and the other detailed. Direct relationships are represented by arches with dash lines, and the detailed relationships are represented by arches with thick full lines as shown in Figure 5.

The direct relationship is to represent a model or part of a model that shows an abstract correlation between one unit of the global model at the bottom end of the arrow with one or many units of the global model at the pointed end. The other arrow represents a model that details the abstract relationship. For example, a row in Entity Event Matrix is a contextual relationship showing in abstract terms how an event affects one or many entities, and Effect Correspondence Diagram details exactly how the effects are realised.

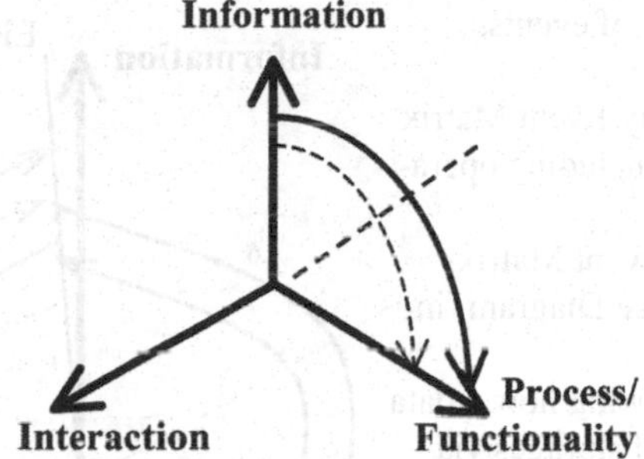

Fig. 5. Contextual Models show abstract and detailed relationships between elements of global models

Contextual models describe the system view from individual component's perspective, contrast with global models that portray the entire system from outside. Global models tend to be static, i.e. time-independent. It is largely because of the sheer amount information that needs to be presented in a highly abstract form. Contextual models, on the other hand, deal only with a small portion of the system, and hence they are better suited to show the dynamics of various components of the system.

Contextual models present a good opportunity to check the validity of the global models since time-dependent modelling is good for checking certain assumptions taken in the global models by unrolling them.

Figure 6 shows complete examples of the IPI Matrices showing SSADM and UML models.

3.1.3 Evaluation of Models

When evaluating a given method, in addition to the assessment of the coverage of the global models and how they are strengthened by various contextual models, this framework also provides mechanisms to measure the rigour of various modelling techniqes. This paper however, does not deal in detail with the second part of the assessment, which is discussed at length in [4].

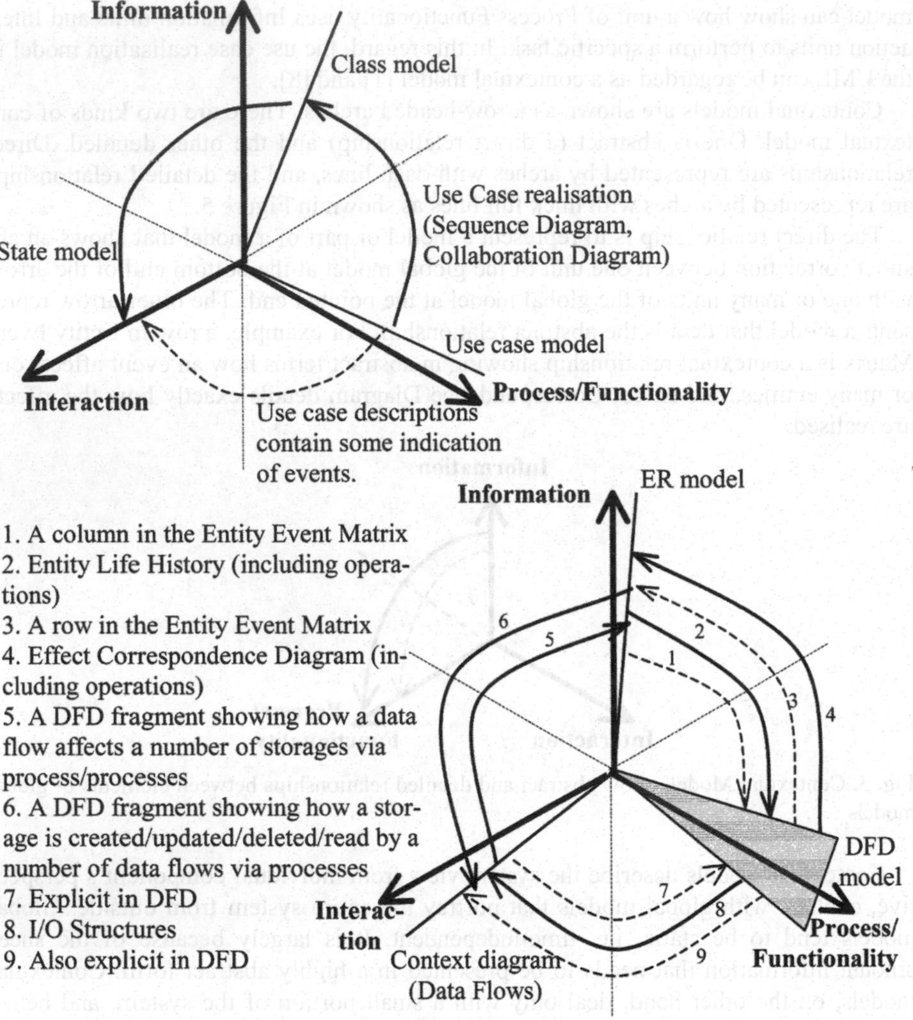

Fig. 6. IPI Matrices showing all major UML and SSADM models

As we can see clearly, the UML does not have a global interaction model that shows interactions with the outside world. There also seems to be too few contextual models in the UML. It means that crosschecking between models will be less rigorous in the UML, compared with SSADM which provide numerous contextual models.

What and How to Evaluate in Global and Contextual Models

In order to evaluate models of a given method, we need to complete the IPI matrix by drawing appropriate lines and arches for global and contextual models provided by the method. Then from the matrix, one can ascertain the following:

1. Ideally, there should be three global models in an Information Systems Development method, one for each major characteristic of the system. Each global model should have a clear aim of what it intends to describe and the components of the models should reflect that.
2. As far as contextual models are concerned, ideally there should be four arches (two direct and two detailed) for each pair of global models. This will guarantee that models have a good coverage and they are tightly knitted.

Evaluation of Modelling Techniques

Our previous paper [4] deals with a detailed approach to measure and compare techniques to specify what we called 'data requirements', which in the context of this discussion means information models. In the paper, when assessing techniques to specify data requirements, we first identified the desirable quality attributes of data requirement specifications, and various elements of data requirement specifications. By applying all the quality attributes to each of the elements of a data requirement specification, we came up with a detailed list of criteria. We then identified the data specification techniques and found out the sort of quality that one can achieve in data requirement specifications using these techniques. There we used 0, 1, and 2 rigour scales. These criteria are recommended for the assessment of techniques used by global information models. Similar detailed criteria for other global modelling techniques are still under development.

4 Conclusions

The use of random lists of assessment criteria to evaluate methods does not tend to provide conclusive answers. Frameworks, which are based upon more rigorous logical foundations, deploy a more systematic questioning approach. The existing approaches we investigated are theoretically sound, but there are deficiencies in pragmatics. NIMSAD, for instance, is too generic and does not tell us, say, how to evaluate modelling techniques. Wieringa's work is indeed very interesting but we believe that certain aspects of the framework can be enhanced. In our proposed framework, we have attempted to show how methods can be evaluated by looking at three major elements. To evaluate models, we provided a new assessment technique that is not founded on trivia, such as symbols, simplicity etc, but on wider issues such as coverage models, rigour of their techniques etc. The framework proposed the diagrammatic IPI matrix, onto which various models of a method can be mapped, and qualities of the models at a high level can be ascertained from it. Many assessment approaches only concentrate on what we call 'global models', and very little attention is paid to the importance of 'contextual models'. These contextual models are equally important because they deal with very detailed analysis of the system and serve as crosschecks between global models. Our framework emphasises that without these contextual models, it would be almost impossible to validate the global models. The framework also deals with the other two elements of a method, System Development Process Model and Software Architecture, by providing mechanisms for evaluation (which we were not able to present in this paper). These mechanisms can be used to select an appropriate development process and architectural model for a given application development. We believe that this framework provides a comprehensive and rigorous approach to the evaluation of Information Systems Development methods.

Acknowledgement

We would like to thank our colleague Islam Choudhury for comments on the UML.

References

1. Booch G., Rumbaugh J., and Jacobson I. (1999). The Unified Modeling Language User Guide, Addison-Wesley.
2. Allen P., and S. Frost. (1998). Component-Based Development for Enterprise Systems: Applying the SELECT Perspective. Cambridge University Press/SIGS Books.
3. Avison D. E. and Fitzgerald G. (1995). Information Systems Development: Methodologies, Techniques and Tools (2nd Edition). Berkshire, England: McGraw-Hill.
4. Bielkowicz P. and Tun T.T. (2001) A Comparison and Evaluation of Data Requirement Specification Techniques in SSADM and the Unified Process. In Proceedings of CAiSE 2001, Interlaken, Switzerland, pp.46-59.
5. Goodland M. and Slater C. (1995) SSADM Version 4: A Practical Approach McGraw-Hill, London
6. Hong S., Goor G. van den and Brinkkemper S. (1993). A formal approach to the comparison of object-oriented analysis and design methodologies. In Proceedings of the 26th Hawaii International Conference on System Sciences, January, pp. 689-698.
7. Jayaratna N. (1994). Understanding and evaluating methodologies: NIMSAD A Systemic Framework. Berkshire, England: McGraw-Hill.
8. Rumbaugh J., Jacobson I., and Booch G. (1999) The Unified Modeling Language Reference Manual, Addison-Wesley, Reading, Mass.
9. Song X. (1995). A Framework for Understanding the Integration of Design Methodologies. ACM SIGSOFT Software Engineering Notes 20(1) pp. 46-54.
10. Waring A. (1996). Practical Systems Thinking. London, UK: International Thompson Business Press
11. Wieringa R. J. (1999). A Survey of Structured and Object-oriented Software Specification Methods and Techniques. ACM Computing Survey, 30(4), pp 459-527.

Non-functional Capability-Based Access Control in the Java Environment*

Daniel Hagimont[1] and Noël De Palma[2]

[1] INRIA Rhône-Alpes
655 avenue de l'Europe, 38334 Saint-Ismier Cedex, France
Daniel.Hagimont@inrialpes.fr

[2] France Telecom R&D
28 chemin du vieux chêne, BP98, 38243 Meylan Cedex, France
Noel.Depalma@rd.francetelecom.com

Abstract. This paper describes a capability-based access control mechanism implemented on a Java environment. In this scheme, access to objects is controlled by means of software capabilities that can be exchanged between mutually suspicious interacting applications. Each application defines the access control rules that must be enforced when interacting with other applications. The definition of access right is managed as a non-functional aspect in the sense it is completely separated from the application code, thus enforcing modularity and ease of expression. It is described in an extended Interface Definition Language (IDL) at the interface level. We have experimented with two prototypes that show how this access control mechanism can be efficiently implemented on a standard Java environment.

1 Introduction

With the development of the Internet, distributed applications often rely on mobile software components which can be downloaded from a remote location or moved to a server machine in order to perform a given task. Examples of such mobile components are Sun's applets [6] which may be downloaded in a Web browser or mobile agents systems [3] which allow computation units to migrate and visit Internet locations.

In this context, protection is a crucial aspect. It is a prerequisite to the deployment of applications distributed over the Internet: the Internet connection should not be a trap-door for the local host.

Java [6] is probably the best known runtime environment which provides facilities for the development of mobile applications. Java was specifically designed to provide features for managing portable and mobile objects. The code generated by the Java compiler is interpreted by the Java virtual machine, thus enabling code transfer between heterogeneous sites. From a protection point of view, the main advantage of

* This work is supported by the Réseau National des Technologies Logicielles (RNTL Arcad).

Z. Bellahsène, D. Patel, and C. Rolland (Eds.): OOIS 2002, LNCS 2425, pp. 323-335, 2002.

Java is that the Java language is type-safe (the language is interpreted and does not allow the use of virtual addresses). Type-safety is the key-technique used to achieve protection, but this is not sufficient to allow interacting applications to control access rights in a flexible way.

In this paper, we propose a protection scheme for managing access control in the Java environment. This protection model is based on software capabilities [8] and it allows mutually suspicious applications to dynamically exchange access rights according to their execution context. This protection scheme has the following advantages:

- Evolution: since it is based on capabilities, access rights can be dynamically exchanged between applications during execution.
- Mutual suspicion and decentralization: each application is responsible for the definition of its own protection policy, which is linked with code of the application. There's no need for registering protection policies in a third party protection sub-system.
- Modularity: the protection scheme enforces modularity since the definition of protection is totally separated from the application code. Access control is therefore managed as a non-functional aspect.

We describe the design of this access control model on top of the Java virtual machine and we describe two prototypes that show how it can be efficiently implemented.

The rest of the paper is structured as follows. Section 2 presents the access control model that we designed. Section 3 presents a first implementation which relies on proxies (or indirection objects). In section 4, a second implementation is described, which avoids any indirection object and therefore performs much better. Section 5 presents the results of our measurements, showing the cost of access control with both prototypes. After a brief description of the related works in section 6, we conclude in section 7.

2 Access Control Model

2.1 A Capability-Based Protection Model

The protection model we propose is based on software capabilities.

A capability is a token that identifies an object and contains access rights, i.e. the subset of the object's methods whose invocation is allowed. In order to access an object, an application must own a capability to that object with the required access rights. When an object is created, a capability is returned to the creator application, that usually contains all rights on the object. The capability can thus be used to access the object, but can also be copied and passed to another application, providing it with access rights on that object. When a capability is copied, the rights associated with the copy can be restricted, in order to limit the rights given to the receiving application.

Therefore, each application executes in a protection environment in which it is granted access to the objects it owns. This application can obtain additional access rights upon method invocation. When an object reference is passed as parameter of an invocation, a capability on that object can be passed with the parameter in order to provide the receiving application enough access rights to use the reference.

In order to illustrate capability based protection, let us consider the example of a *Printer* object, exported by a print server, that allows a client to print a text (Fig. 1).

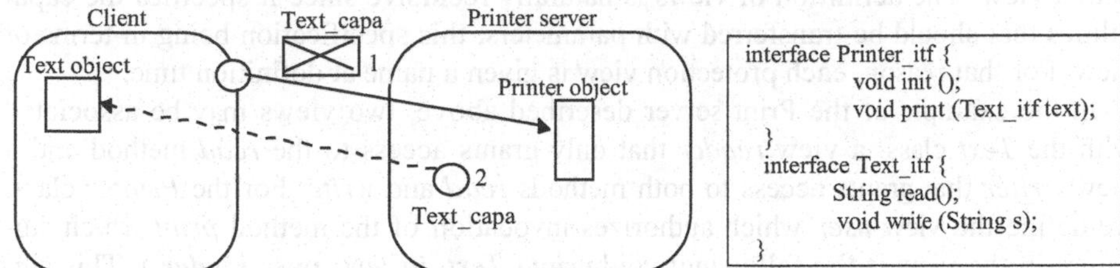

Fig. 1. Print server example

A capability on the *Printer* object is given to the client applications providing them with the right to print texts. When a client wants to print a text (*Text* object), the *Printer* object needs to get read rights for this text; therefore the client will pass, at invocation time (1), a read-only capability on the text (*text_capa*) to the callee application. This capability allows the *Printer* object to read the contents of the text (2).

2.2 Exchanging Capabilities

As explained in the previous section, software capabilities provide a model in which access right can be dynamically exchanged between applications. The issue is then to provide application programmers with a means for controlling rights exchanges with other applications.

One strong motivation for our protection model is modularity. Indeed, we don't want to provide extensions to the programming language that allow expressing capability parameter passing when another application's object is invoked. This would overload programs and make them much more difficult to maintain. Our goal is to separate protection definition from application code, i.e. to manage access control as a non functional aspect. To achieve this goal, our idea is to define capability exchanges between interacting applications using an interface definition language (IDL). Since an interface can be described independently from any implementation, describing capability exchanges at the level of the interface allows the protection definition to be clearly separated from the code of the application.

Therefore, an IDL has been defined that allows the application programmer to express the capabilities that should be transferred along with parameters in a method invocation. This IDL allows the definition of *views*. A view is an interface that includes the definition of an access control policy. A view is associated with a capability and describes:

- the methods that are authorized by the access rights associated with the capability,
- the capabilities that must be transferred between the caller and the callee along with the parameters of the methods authorized by the view. These transferred capabilities are expressed in terms of views.

Therefore, a capability is a structure which includes the identifier of the object, the access rights that the capability provides to its owner and the capability exchange policy which defines what capabilities must be passed along with parameters when the object is invoked. The access rights and the capability exchange policy are defined with a view. The definition of views is naturally recursive since it specifies the capabilities that should be transferred with parameters, this specification being in terms of view. For that reason, each protection view is given a name at definition time.

In the example of the Print server described above, two views may be associated with the *Text* class: a view *reader* that only grants access to the *read* method and a view *writer* that grants access to both methods *read* and *write*. For the *Printer* class, we define the view *user* which authorizes invocation of the method *print* which signature in the view is the following: void *print* (*Text_itf text* **pass *reader***). This signature expresses that a capability with the *reader* view must be passed to the callee along with the reference to a text object passed as parameter of *print*.

Such a protection policy, defined only on the callee side, would be sufficient if we were considering a client/server architecture where protection is only there to protect the server against its clients. Instead, we are considering an architecture where applications are mutually suspicious. Each application must have full control over the capabilities it exports to other applications (both the caller and the callee). Moreover, we want to ensure applications independence. More precisely, it is not possible for an application programmer to verify the protection policy defined by an application that exports a service since at programming time, the programmer may not yet know which applications it is going to interact with. This is particularly important when interacting applications are mobile, for instance in a mobile agents system [3].

For these reasons, each application can define its own view of the protection policy to apply when interacting with other applications. Therefore, two views are associated with a capability: the view of the caller application and the view of the callee application.

The view defined by the callee application *A* describes:

- The methods that are authorized.
- For each input parameter of a method (reference *R* received by *A*), the view describes the capabilities that are given by *A* when the reference *R* is used for method invocation. This view describes, from the callee point of view, the capabilities that the application accepts to export.
- For each output parameter of a method (reference *R* given by *A*), the view describes the capability returned with the reference *R*.

and similarly the view defined by the caller application *A* describes:

- For each input parameter of a method (reference *R* given by *A*), the view describes the capability given with the reference *R*.
- For each output parameter of a method (reference *R* received by *A*), the view describes the capabilities that are given by *A* when the reference *R* is used for method invocation. This view describes, from the caller point of view, the capabilities that the application accepts to export.

This symmetric scheme is the answer to mutual suspicion and applications independence. Both the caller and the callee specify their protection views for their objects. They are taken into account as follows.

When an application exports an object reference through the name server (similar to *rmiregistry*, but on a local machine), it defines the view associated with the reference, i.e. the capability which is exported for this exported reference. This way, the application also defines the capabilities that may be exported subsequently to an invocation of that object. When an application fetches the reference from the name server, it also defines the view associated (on its side) with the reference it obtained. This way, the application defines the capabilities that may be exported subsequently to an invocation of the object. Any invocation that derives from an invocation on that object will take into account the view definitions from both applications.

2.3 Example

In order to illustrate the expression scheme of our protection model, let's consider again the print server example. The Java interfaces of the *Printer* application were given in Fig 1. These interfaces are shared between the caller and the callee. In order to make the print service available to the clients, the *Printer* application exports an instance of class *Printer* through the name server. The *Printer* class is an implementation of the *Printer_itf* interface. On its side, the client application fetches this instance from the name server and can invoke a method (*init* or *print*) on this instance, using the *Printer_itf* interface. When the client wants to print a text, it invokes the method *print* and passes a reference to an instance of class *Text* which implements interface *Text_itf*. In the example, the definition of protection aims at avoiding the following protection problems:

- the printer doesn't want the client to invoke the *init* method on its printer objet (and to initialize the printer),
- the client doesn't want the printer to invoke the *write* method on its text object (and to modify the text of the client).

In our protection scheme, the client and the server will define the views presented in Fig. 2.

<table>
<tr><th><u>Client</u></th><th><u>Server</u></th></tr>
<tr><td>view client implements Printer_itf {
    void init ();
    void print (Text_itf text pass reader);
}
view reader implements Text_itf {
    String read();
    void not write (String s);
}</td><td>view server implements Printer_itf {
    void not init ();
    void print (Text_itf text);
}</td></tr>
</table>

Fig. 2. Protection views in the *Printer* application

Each application defines a set of views that define its protection policy. Each view „ implements " the Java interface that corresponds to the type of the objects it protects. A **not** before a method name means that the method is not permitted. When an object reference is passed as parameter in a view, the programmer can specify the view to be passed with the reference using the key-word **pass**. If no view is specified, this means that no restriction is applied to this reference.

In this example, the print server defines the view *server* which prevents clients from invoking method *init*. No restriction is applied to the parameters of method *print*. The client defines the view *client* which says that, when a reference to a text is passed as a parameter of method *print*, the view *reader* must be passed, which prevents the print server from invoking method *write*. Notice that the client doesn't have any reason to prevent itself from invoking method *init*; this is a decision to be taken by the print server.

When the print server registers an instance of class *Printer* in the name server, it associates view *server* with it. When the client obtains this reference from the name server, it associates the view *client* with it. These two views and the nested ones (*reader*) define the access control policy of the two applications.

To sum up, each application defines its own protection policy independently from any other application or server and this policy specification is defined separately from the application implementation using views, thus enhancing modularity.

In the following, we describe two implementations of this model, respectively relying on proxies [9] and on bytecode injection [1].

3 Proxy-Based Implementation

For the implementation of this protection model, we used the fact that Java object references are almost capabilities (Java is strongly typed). Indeed, since Java is a safe language, it does not allow object references to be forged. This implies that if an object *O1* creates an object *O2*, object *O2* will not be accessible from other objects of the Java runtime, as long as *O1* does not explicitly export a reference to object *O2* towards other objects. The reference to *O2* can be exported (as a parameter) when an object invokes *O1* or when *O1* invokes another object. Therefore, as long as an application does not export a reference to one of its objects, these objects are protected against other applications. Thus, a Java object reference can be seen as a capability. However, they are all-or-nothing capabilities since it is not possible to restrict the set of methods that can be invoked using this reference. In order to implement our capabilities, we implemented a mechanism inspired from the notion of proxy [9], which allows access rights associated with a reference to be restricted.

Our implementation relies on the management of *filters* that are inserted between the caller and the callee. For each view defined by an application, a filter class is generated (by a pre-processor) and an instance of that class is inserted to protect the application.

When a reference to an object is passed as input parameter of a method call, instead of the real object, we pass a reference to an instance of the filter class generated from the view defined by the application providing the reference. This filter class implements all the methods declared in the interface of the view. It defines an instance variable that points to the actual object and which is used to forward the authorized method calls. If a forbidden method is invoked on an instance of a filter class, then the method raises an exception. The reference to the filter instance, which is passed instead of the reference parameter, is inserted by the caller application. In fact, this filter instance is inserted by the filter used for the current invocation. In Fig. 3a, the invocation of *O2* performed by *App1* passes a reference to *O1* as parameter. The filter *F1(O2)*, which corresponds to the protection policy of *App1* for invocations of *02*, inserts filter *F1(O1)* before the parameter *O1*. Therefore, filters that are associated with reference parameters are installed by filters that are used upon method invocations.

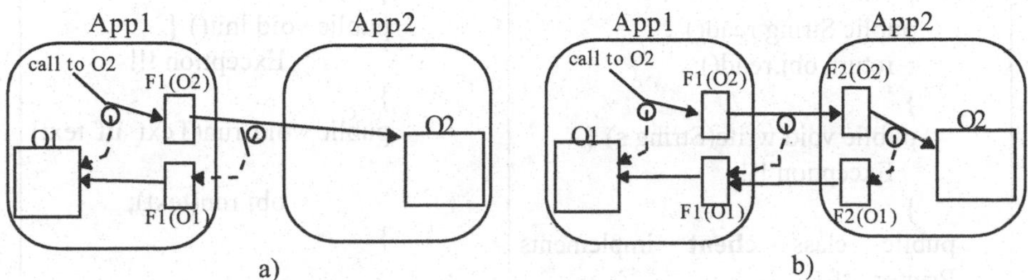

Fig. 3. Management of filters

Conversely, when a reference is received by an application, a reference to a filter instance is passed instead of the received parameter, which class is generated from the view specified by the application that receives the parameter. In Fig. 3b, the filter *F2(O2)*, which corresponds to the protection policy of *App2* for invocations of *02*, inserts filter *F2(O1)* before the received parameter. Therefore, two filter objects (*F1(O1)* et *F2(O1)*) are inserted between the caller and the callee for the parameter *O1* passed from *App1* to *App2*. These two filters behave as follows:

- *F1(O1)*: it enforces that only authorized methods can be invoked by *App2* and it inserts filters on the account of *App1* for the parameters of invocations on *O1* performed by *App2*.
- *F2(O1)*: it inserts filters on the account of *App2* for the parameters of invocations on *O1* performed by *App2*.

The code of the filter classes for the print server example is shown in Fig. 4.

In the next section, we present a second prototype implementation which avoid using indirection objects (filters) to manage capabilities.

4 Injection-Based Implementation

The general idea that we apply in this second implementation is to inject the protection related code (which was previously integrated in indirection objects) within the functional code of the application (Fig. 5). This way at runtime, we avoid two costly indirections. This code injection can be performed at compile time or at load time. We use a bytecode transformation tool (BCEL [1]) to inject in the application code, the code which implements capability management. In order to present this approach and for clarity in the rest of the paper, we will describe the transformed code in Java.

Client

```
public class reader implements
        Text_itf {
  Text_itf obj;
  public reader(Text_itf o) {
    obj = o;
  }
  public String read() {
    return obj.read();
  }
  public void write(String s) {
    Exception !!!
  }
public class client implements
Printer_itf {
  Printer_itf obj;
  public Printer_stub(Printer_itf o)
  {
    obj = o;
  }
  public void init() {
    obj.init();
  }
  public void print(Text_itf text) {
    reader stub = new reader(text);
    obj.run(stub);
  }
}
```

Server

```
class server implements Printer_itf {
  Printer_itf obj;
  public
Printer_stub(Printer_itf o) {

  }
  public void init() {
      Exception !!!
  }
  public void run(Text_itf text)
{
      obj.run(text);
  }
```

Fig. 4. Code of the filter classes for the print server

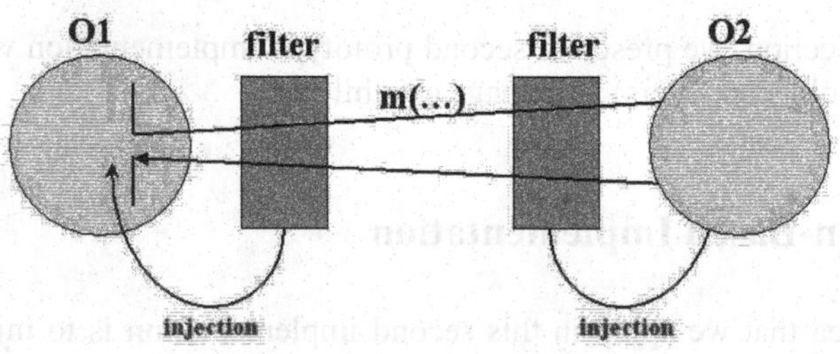

Fig. 5. Code injection technique

The protection code injection proceeds as follows:

- For each reference variable (field or local variable) pointing to a protected object, we have to inject the declaration of two new variables which represent the two views associated with the capability: the view specified by the object owner (the callee view) and the view specified by the owner of the capability (the caller view). These two variables are view identifiers (integers). They are assigned when the reference variable is assigned (we inject the code that does it).
- For each protected method invocation using a reference, we add the callee view associated with this reference (the above integer which identifies this view), as parameter of the method. We inject at the beginning of the invoked method the code which checks whether this invocation is authorized in the definition of this callee view.
- When a reference to a protected object is passed as a method parameter, we inject the code which will initialize the caller view and callee view variables on the parameter receiver side. This initialization depends on the definitions of the views (caller and callee) associated with the capability used for the method invocation. This is further clarified on the printer example.

In the case of our printer example, when a client receives a reference to the printer (from a name server), it also receives the capability's caller and callee views (the integer identifiers). The method invocation to the printer takes two additional parameters, the callee view of the reference to the printer which allows checking access rights on the printer side, and the callee view for the text parameter which specifies the access rights that are granted to the printer on the text object (this callee view to pass with the text is defined in the view identified by *pr_caller* in the code in Fig. 6).

```
public class ClientMain {
    public static void main(String args[]) {
        Printer_itf pr; // ref to the printer
        short pr_caller; // printer caller view
        short pr_callee; // printer callee view
        Text text = new Text();
        // pr_callee : passed for checking
        //    the capability on the callee side
        // view_reader_id : the view passed with
        //   the text, depends on the (local)
        //   definition of pr_caller
        switch (pr_caller) {
            ...
            pr.print(pr_callee, text, view_reader_id);
        }}}
```

Fig. 6. Code of the client after protection code injection

On the server side (Fig. 7), the printer checks that the access rights, associated with the view received as parameter, grant access to the method (for *init()* and *print()*).

In the *print()* method, the injected code initializes the view variables associated with the text received parameter. The callee view is received as parameter. The caller view for the text is defined in the callee view for the printer (depending on *pr_callee*).

```
class Printer implements Printer_itf {
  public void print (short pr_callee, Text_itf text, int text_view)
{
        short text_caller; // text caller view
        short text_callee; // text callee view
        // checking the capability … based on
        // the (local) definition of pr_callee
        if (pr_callee != … ) {
            Exception !!!
        }
        // initialize the views for the text
        text_callee = text_view;
        switch (pr_callee) {
            …
            text_caller = …
        }
        text.read(text_callee);
        return;
    }}
```

Fig. 7. Code of the print server after protection code injection

With this code injection technique, it is possible to manage implement our capability-based access control mechanism without requiring (paying for) indirection objects.

5 Evaluation

In this section, we provide performance measurements for the two prototypes that we implemented. This performance evaluation shows the cost of capability management in our protection scheme. It also shows that this cost can be significantly reduced with the implementation based on code injection. For the second prototype, the implementation of the bytecode translator is in progress. The evaluation presented in this section is based on hand-written code, i.e. the code injection was performed at the application source level, applying our transformation patterns by hand.

For this performance evaluation, we consider a basic scheme where an object *o1* invokes an empty method *m()* on an object *o2*. We consider the case where method *m()* does not take any parameter and the case where it takes a reference to another object *o3* as parameter. These measurements have been done under three conditions:

- on Java without integration if any access control policy,
- with the prototype implementation based on proxy object (filters),
- with the prototype implementation based on code injection.

Here are the resulting performance figures using a 1GHz Pentium processor with 256 Mo of RAM. These results are given for 10^8 iterations over the method call.

Table 1. Performance results

Operation	Straight call	Proxy-based	Injection-based
m()	1552 ms	6458 ms	3354 ms
m(o3)	1713 ms	14400 ms	3565 ms

Compared to a direct method invocation, a method call with access control is quite costly in the proxy-based implementation, due to object indirections and proxy instantiations. In the case of a single method call with no parameter, the injection-based implementation performs 48% faster than the proxy-based implementation. This is explained because we avoid two indirection calls. In the case of a method call with a reference parameter, the improvement is of 75%. In the proxy-based implementation, when we transmit a protected object reference (to *o3*) as parameter, *o2_stub* has to instantiate *o3_skel* to protect *o3*. In a worth case, *o2_skel* could have to instantiate *o3_stub* to implement the protection policy associated with object *o3*. In the code injection version, we don't have to instantiate any stub since the protection code is embedded in the caller and callee objects (however we have to pass new parameters to implement the capability transfer).

6 Related Work

Early attempts to manage protection by means of capabilities were based on specific hardware. Several capability-based hardware addressing systems [5][12] were built for the management of protected shared objects. These machine and system architectures were very popular in the 70s, but the standardization of the hardware and the widespread use of Unix systems stopped the trend towards capability based architectures.

In a second step, software capability based systems were designed on standard hardware, capabilities being protected by encryption. In these systems, the standard addressing mechanism of the underlying hardware (i.e. virtual addresses) is used for addressing objects, and capabilities are only used for object protection and access control. Examples of software capability based systems are the Amoeba system [11] based on the client-server paradigm and the Opal single address space system [2]. However, in these systems, capabilities are made available at the programming language level through capability variables that are used explicitly for accessing objects and exchanging access rights. In this paper, we propose to manage a capability-based access control mechanism as a non-functional aspect. The definition of an access control policy is completely separated from the functional code of the application, thus enforcing modularity and ease of expression.

Our first prototype implementation of the protection model relies on proxy objects [9]. Proxies (or indirection objects) are often used to implement non-functional aspects, as in the EJB [10] or CCM [4] component-based middleware systems. Our second prototype implementation relies on code injection, which has been often used as a foundation technique to manage aspects [7]. To our knowledge, the experiment described in this paper is the unique attempt to manage a capability-based access control model as a non functional aspect.

7 Conclusion

In this paper, we presented an access control model which allows the definition of the access control policy of an application which interoperates which other applications. Access control is managed as a non-functional aspect in the sense it is defined at the level of the application interface, thus enhancing modularity and making this definition easier and clearer. The model is based on software capabilities and allows access rights to be dynamically exchanged between mutually suspicious applications. In this model, each application defines its protection policy independently from any other machine or application. This policy is enforced dynamically during execution.

Our protection scheme has been prototyped on the Java runtime environment. We actually implemented two prototypes. The first relies on object indirection to plug the access control policy of an application. The second relies on code injection to directly insert the access control policy of an application within that application's functional code, thus avoiding the overhead of object indirections.

We are currently experimenting with different non-functional aspects. The ultimate objective is to provide a generic framework which would allow to easily describe and integrate new non-functional aspects.

References

1. BCEL, http://bcel.sourceforge.net/
2. J. Chase, H. Levy, M. Feeley, E. Lazowska, Sharing and Protection in a Single-Address-Space Operating System, ACM Transactions on Computer Systems, 12(4), November 1994.
3. D. Chess, C. Harrison, A. Kershenbaum, Mobile Agents: Are They a Good Idea?, IBM Research Division, T.J. Watson Research Center, New York, March 1995.
4. Corba Components – Volume I, OMG TC Document orbos/99-07-01
5. D. England, Capability, Concept, Mechanism and Structure in System 250, RAIRO-Informatique (AFCET), Vol 9, September 1975.

6. J. Gosling and H. McGilton, The Java Language Environment: a White Paper, Sun Microsystems Inc., 1996.
7. G. Kiczales, C. Lopes, Aspect-Oriented Programming with AspectJ, Technical Report, Xerox PARC, 1998.
8. H. Levy, Capability-Based Computer Systems, Digital Press, 1984.
9. M. Shapiro, Structure and Encapsulation in Distributed Systems: The Proxy Principle, 6th International Conference on Distributed Computing Systems, 1986.
10. Sun Microsystems, Inc. Enterprise Java Beans Specification, Sun Microsystems, 2000.
11. A. Tanenbaum, S. Mullender, R. Van Renesse, Using Sparse Capabilities in a Distributed Operating System, 6th International Conference on Distributed Computing Systems, 1986.
12. M. Wilkes, R. Needham, The Cambridge CAP Computer and its Operating System, North Holland, 1979.

A European COTS Architecture with Built-in Tests

Yingxu Wang [1] and Graham King [2]

[1] Theoretical and Empirical Software Engineering Research Centre (TESERC)
Dept. of Electrical and Computer Engineering, University of Calgary
2500 Univ. Dr., NW, Calgary, AB, Canada T2N 1N4
Tel: +1 403 220 6141, Fax: (403) 282 6855
wangyx@enel.ucalgary.ca

[2] Research Centre for Systems Engineering, Southampton Institute
Southampton, UK
graham.king@solent.ac.uk

Abstract. This paper presents a European approach to the development of a new industrial architecture of commercial off-the-shelf (COTS) software components, and a practical technology for design and implementation of test-reusable COTS. This work, known as the European COMPONENT+ project, is supported by the European 5th Framework programme and by a number of leading industrial partners in component-based software engineering.

Existing COTS architectural technologies were focused on code reuse. The following fundamental problems inherited in conventional COTS technologies have been identified: a) Low testability for end-users; b) Low maintainability for end-users; c) No support for run-time testing; and d) Separated software code and test cases.

Being oriented to the problems and challenges as identified above, this paper presents new solutions and techniques for testable COTS architecture developed in the European Component+ project, such as: a) A new technology for implementing BIT-based COTS; b) A new approach to COTS test; c) An extension of OO technology from code reuse to test reuse in COTS development; and d) A new approach to enabling COTS test at run-time. BIT components can be embedded in any conventional COTS for enabling test reuse as well as code reuse. The BIT + COST technologies have been found a wide range of applications in component-based software engineering.

Keywords. Software engineering, component, COTS, architecture, OO, built-in tests, test reuse, run-time testing, real-time software, industrial practices.

Z. Bellahsène, D. Patel, and C. Rolland (Eds.): OOIS 2002, LNCS 2425, pp. 336-347, 2002.

1 Introduction

Component-based software engineering is a new approach to software development. Software components are adopted in order to improve software development and maintenance efficiency and quality, and to increase reuse rate of existing software in multiple applications. Viewing software architectures as being composed of components is helpful for enabling software development, test, and maintenance to be carried out at a higher level than that of language statements.

Component-based software engineering studies methods and techniques for building, acquiring, maintaining, and managing software systems consisting of commercial off-the-shelf (COTS) and in-house software components. The following problems inherited in conventional COTS technologies have been identified in the software industry [1-3]:

- Low testability for end-users
- Low maintainability for end-users
- No support for run-time testing
- Separated software code and test cases

Being oriented to the current problems and challenges identified above, this paper presents new solutions and techniques for COTS testing, as shown below, on the basis of a recent European 5th Framework research project – Component+ [4, 5]:

- A new architecture for implementing BIT-based COTS
- A new approach to COTS test
- An extension of OO technology from code reuse to test reuse in COTS development
- A new approach to enabling run-time COTS test

A BIT-based COTS is a new kind of software component where tests are explicitly described in the component source code as special functions. BIT technologies [1, 3, 4] are considered to be a significant extension of OO technology to self-testable and test-reusable COTS in component-based software engineering. A wide range of applications of COTS with BITs has been identified, *inter alia*, as follows: BIT-based COTS test, COTS test reuse, BIT-based COTS maintenance, run-time testable COTS with BITs, BIT-based COTS for safety critical systems, and real-time system fault-tolerance with BIT-based COTS.

2 COTS Test: Challenges and Solutions

Along with the emergence of software component providers, and inspired by the hardware engineering experience, a new approach to software engineering, component-based software engineering, has been emerged and been widely accepted in the software industry. The component-based software engineering approach is based on the composition-enabled software framework architecture, and the broad availability of COTS components. This section analyses architectural problems and challenges for

COTS design and applications, and presents a new type of COTS for enabling test reuse as well as code reuse in component-based software engineering.

2.1 Problems Identified in COST Test

The foundations of component-based software engineering are based on technologies of OO, reuse, COTS, middleware, patterns and frameworks. However, current COTS technologies are focused on code reuse. The following problems inherited in conventional COTS technologies have been identified as analyzed below.

Low Testability for End-Users

Because of much closer encapsulation and distribution with only executable code, end-users of COTS components have found it was very difficult to test a purchased and adopted COTS component. As a result, quality and reliability of software based on COTS and in-house components are largely affected by the limitation of testability.

Low Maintainability for End-Users

For the same reasons described above, the maintainability of COTS and in-house software components has been tied up with the original component developers. As a result the maintainability of a purchased or adopted COTS component has been found to be lower than that of conventional technologies.

No Support for Run-Time Testing

Run-time testing comprises special test requirements for COTS and systems. In component-based software engineering, as well as in conventional programming, run-time test is very much in demand because almost all crucial software faults, such as code corruption, hardware platform faults, random faults caused by external interferences, dynamic memory allocation faults, etc, can only be detected and tested at run-time. However, run-time test for COTS is extremely hard to implement because of lack of internal design information and unpredictable run-time environments for COTS.

Separated Software Code and Test Cases

Conventionally, software tests are regarded as extra artefacts other than functional code. The source code of COTS is usually separated from its tests, and the tests are only available for the original developers or vendors, rather than end-users as required in component-based software engineering. This convention has been found cost-intensive and energy-wasting in programming, especially in component-based software development, because almost all the tests have to be regenerated by the end-users in the phases of system integration and maintenance.

To avoid the above problems, this paper provides a new solution that incorporates software source code and tests within a single piece of coherent software documentation, and within the same executable code. This is also considered to be a new evolution of programming style to meet the requirements for component-based software engineering.

2.2 Solutions for COTS Test

Being oriented to solve the current problems identified in COTS architecture and test as analyzed in Section 2.1, this paper describes the built-in-test (BIT) method that enables tests be embedded and reused as that of code in COTS and in-house software components. The BIT-based COTS possesses a set of novelty in component-based software engineering, as described below.

A New Technology for Implementing BIT-Based COTS

As analyzed in Section 2.1, software tests were regarded as extra artefacts separated from code in conventional programming technologies. The expression equivalency between code and its tests is found recently by the authors [3, 4]. By this philosophy, built-in tests can be embedded into COTS and systems as special code. The explicitly programmed BITs in a COTS are special functions for test and maintenance of the component. In this way the BIT components use the same syntax and semantics as that of pure functional code. Therefore, the BIT components can be seen as a combination of conventional code and its test cases in a unified COTS architecture. This provides a novel type of software encapsulation and documentation.

An Extension of OO Technology from Code Reuse to Test Reuse

By adopting BITs, tests can be reused for the first time just as is the code for COTS. As a result, the reusability of OO technology can be extended from code to test. When a BIT component is inherited, both functions and tests of the component are reusable. This adds value significantly to the emerging new technologies of component-based software engineering. All COTS components can benefit from this advantage. As a result, reuse software engineers and end-users of COTS need no longer to worry about the testing and maintaining of a component being as a black box.

A New Approach to OO Software Test in Component-Based Software Engineering

As analyzed in Section 2.1, COTS test techniques were mainly the same as those of non-OO software. Tests designed and used during development are hardly ever available for end-users and maintainers. This is one of the major barriers for component-based software engineering. Therefore, the BIT and reusable tests for COTS provided in this paper are a significant progress toward component-based software engineering.

A New Approach to Enabling Run-Time Software Test

In Section 2.1 we have identified that run-time tests for COTS are a hard problem, but this is in high demand for dealing with dynamic faults such as code corruption, hardware platform faults, random faults caused by external interferences, and dynamic memory allocation faults, etc.

The BIT-based COTS components are self testable so that dynamic faults may be detected at run-time, whenever the BITs are periodically executed and/or manually triggered. Run-time testable COTS by using BITs is considered to be another significant technological advance for improving software reliability and fault-tolerant capability in component-based software engineering.

A New Style of Programming: Software = Functional Code + Testing Code

Conventionally, software development technologies were focused on implementation of normal functionality. Therefore, what the end-users of COTS purchased are purely functional code packaged in a component as a black box. However, during system integration and maintenance, it is found that COTS users need more than just the executable code.

From this scenario it can be deduced that COTS users in component-based software engineering need a new style of programming documentation – a combination of source code and the built-in test code. By adopting the BIT technologies, the combinatorial software code and tests within the same COTS can be implemented in a practical way.

3 A New Architecture of BIT-Based COTS

This section describes new architectural methodologies for BITs and BIT-based COTS. It is noteworthy that a good technology is not necessarily complicated. The BIT technologies can be implemented much easier and be used in a wide range of applications.

3.1 The Architecture of a BIT Component

The fundamental attributes that can be commonly identified in OO-based COTS technologies are encapsulation, inheritance, reusability and polymorphism. A conventional COTS consists of two structural parts: an interface and an implementation. The 'interface' of the COTS is the only means of external access to the functions packaged in the component; The 'implementation' of the COTS is the description of codes for all internal functions. A COTS component is reusable because of its natural encapsulation and inheritability.

There are two basic findings in the project on testable software component architectures. They are: a) the tests of COTS components are code too; and b) tests and code can be integrated into a unified encapsulation of software components. Based on these principles, a BIT-based COTS can be described as shown in Fig. 1.

In Fig. 1, the BITs for the COTS are declared in the test interface of the component and are implemented in the body of the component. In this way, the BITs can be naturally inherited and reused in the same way as that of code in the COTS. The BITs adopt the same syntax and semantics as those of the conventional functions in the COTS component. Thus, the BITs can be well fit into an OO components supported by any OO languages.

The BIT-based COTS has the same behaviors as that of conventional COTS when normal functions of the component are executed. Whilst if the *i*th BIT is called as a special built-in function of the COTS, e.g.:

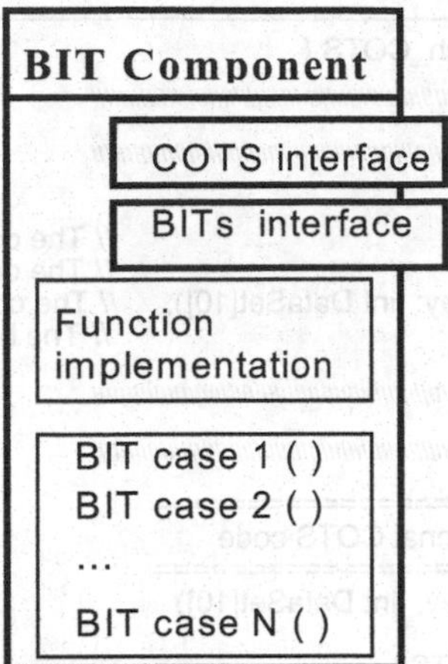

Fig. 1. The architecture of a BIT-based COTS

```
BIT-COTS . BITCase1;
BIT-COTS . BITCase2;
      ......
BIT-COTS . BITCaseI;
      ......
BIT-COTS . BITCaseN;
```

the component can be automatically tested by the BITs in static environment and at run-time. This provides a new capability for enabling self-testable, test-reusable, run-time testable, and end-user-testable COTS components to be developed and implemented at the same technical platform of conventional OO components.

3.2 Example of a COTS with BITs

Methods for design and implementation of BIT-based COTS components are developed that treats tests as special code in the COTS. The explicitly programmed BITs in a COTS are special functions for test and maintenance of the component. Therefore, the BIT components may be seen as a combination of conventional code and its test cases in a unified COTS architecture and a new type of software documentation.

A case study on implementing BIT-based COTS is provided in Figs. 2 and 3. A typical example, a binary search COTS, is taken in the case to show how the BIT method is used to develop built-in-test COTS. The BIT-based COTS of binary search is implemented in two parts: the conventional functions (Fig.2) and the BIT functions (Fig.3).

For the binary search COTS listed in Fig. 2, a set of test cases may be generated by using equivalent partitioning or other test generation techniques. Only one of the test cases is built-in to show the method of BITs in Fig.3. It is significant that the BIT method can incorporate any test cases generated by the black-box (functional) and/or white-box (structural) testing methods as the BITs.

```
Class BITsBinarySearch_COTS {
//////////////////////////////////////////////////////////////////////////////////
// Interface
//////////////////////////////////////////////////////////////////////////////////

// Member functions
BITsBinarySearch();                              // The constructor
~BITsBinarySearch();                             // The destructor
int BinarySearch (int Key; int DataSet[10]);    // The conventional object
void BIT1();                                     // The built-in-test

//////////////////////////////////////////////////////////////////////////////////
// Implementation
//////////////////////////////////////////////////////////////////////////////////

// ===================================
// Part 1: The conventional COTS code
// ===================================
int BinarySearch (int Key, int DataSet[10])
{
// The conventional COTS
// Assume: DataSet is ordered
//          LastElement -FirstElement >=0
//          and FirstElement >=0
// Input:   Key to be found in the DataSet
// Output:  TestElemIndex

Private:
int bott, top, i;
int found;

found = false;
Bott = 1;
Top = ArraySize (DataSet);  // The last element in DataSet
while (bott <= top) && (not found)
      {
        i = floor ((bott + top)/2));
        if DataSet[i] == Key
           found = true;
           else if DataSet[i] < Key
                bott = i +1
                else Top = i +1;
      }
if found == true
   return i;          // The index of the element
   else return 0;     // An indicator of not existence
}
// ====================================
// Part 2: The BITs
// ====================================

See Fig. 3
}
```

Fig. 2. A COTS of binary search with BIT

Inheritance and reuse of the BIT components in development and maintenance of BIT-based COTS are useful in two ways: a) to activate the BIT components for self-test, maintenance and/or fault diagnosis; and b) to derive a new COTS that inherits the existing BITs in the parent components. Applying the BIT technology for COTS, what the programmer, tester, maintainer, and end-user inherited are instant and self testable. Assuming that existing software systems are reengineered using the BIT-based COTS technologies, future software production, testing and maintenance will benefit strongly from reuse of the BITs in COTS components.

```
// =====================================
//  Part 2: The BITs
// =====================================

// BIT case 1
void BIT1()
{
// BIT case 1: Test for odd array size, and key not in array
private:
int DataSet[7] = {16,18,21,23,29,33,38};
int Key =  25;
int StdElemIndex = 0;
int TestElemIndex;

char TestResult1 [5];
// Test implementation
TestElemIndex = BinarySearch (Key, DataSet);
// Test analysis
cout  << "StdElemIndex1 =  "  <<  StdElemIndex  <<  "\n";
cout  << "TestElemIndex1 =  "  <<  TestElemIndex  <<  "\n";
if TestElemIndex == StdElemIndex
   TestResult1 = "OK";
   else  TestResult1 = "FALSE";
cout << "TestResult1: " << TestResult1 << "\n";
}
```

Fig. 3. A BIT for the COTS of binary search

4 Test-Reusable COTS with BITs

The methods for developing BIT-based COTS have been developed in Section 3. Corresponding to the design of the BIT-based COTS, reuse of the BITs can be implemented systematically in an object-oriented environment.

4.1 Reuse Mechanisms of BIT-Based COTS

One of the major barriers for component-based software engineering is that tests for conventional COTS are hardly ever available for maintainers and end-users. This subsection develops practical technologies for built-in test reuse in a COTS, including inherence and invocation technologies for BITs.

Functions of a BIT-based COTS can be categorised into normal mode and test mode. The former is applied for code reuse and the latter for test reuse. In the *normal mode*, a BIT-based COTS component has the same functions as that of conventional COTS. Its static and dynamic behaviors are the same as those of the conventional ones. The application-specific functional code can be called by: ClassName . FunctionName, such as:

BITsBinarySearch_COTS .
BinarySearch(int Key, int DataSet[10])

and the BITs are stand-by and without any effect to run-time behaviors.

In the *test mode*, the test-built-in COTS can be activated by calling the test cases as member functions: ClassName . TestCaseI, I ∈ 1 .. N, such as:

BITsBinarySearch_COTS . BIT1();

Each TestCaseI consists of a BIT driver and test cases for the specific object. Test results can be automatically reported by the BIT driver.

A BIT-based COTS has testing mechanisms ready as well as functional code. This enables end-users of an applied test-built-in COTS to call and reuse all BITs as special functions in the test mode.

4.2 Example of BIT Reuse in COTS

The approach to reuse BIT-based COTS components in software testing and maintenance is shown in Fig. 4. For instance, when a new COTS, DatabaseQuery, is needed, the BIT components (Fig. 3) developed in the BITsBinarySearch_COTS can be inherited and reused directly as that of the conventional functions (Part 2, Fig. 4). Also, additional BITs can be incorporated into the new COTS as shown in Part 3 of Fig. 4.

In the new object DatabaseQuery as listed in Fig. 4, the inherited BITs developed in the BITsBinarySearch_COTS object can be activated by calling:

DatabaseQuery . BIT1();
// equivalent to BITsBinarySearch_COTS . BIT1

and the new BITs supplemented in the DatabaseQuery object can be activated in the same way:

DatabaseQuery . BIT2();
// new BITs only in class DatabaseQuery

It is interesting to note that in the BIT approach, software tests themselves are software too. As shown in Figs. 2 to 4, the effort for implementing BITs in the COTS "BITsBinarySearch_COTS" has been repaid by the ideal inheritability and reusability of tests in the case shown in Fig. 4 and all the subsequent reuse of the BITs in any future applications. Assuming that the existing COTS components and systems can be reengineered using the BITs architecture, the future software production will benefit strongly from the reuse of BITs in new COTS development, testing and maintenance.

In the BIT approach, what the developer, end-user and maintainer of COTS inherit, is instant and self testable. It is a kind of ideal COTS architecture with complete design messages and high testability, reusability, and reliability.

4.3 Run-Time Testable COTS with BITs

The BIT-based COTS technology enables real-time detection, diagnosis and handling of OO software faults at component and system levels. For ensuring real-time system reliability and depend-ability, run-time test, self-diagnosis, and automatic fault handling were common technologies. With the BIT-based COTS architecture, faults of a COTS can be detected, diagnosed, and handled at run-time [6].

```
Class DatabaseQuery: public BITsBinarySearch_COTS
{
////////////////////////////////////////////////////////////////////////////////
// Part 1: The inherited conventional functions
////////////////////////////////////////////////////////////////////////////////

int DatabaseQueryBinarySearch (int Key,  int DataSet[10]) :
    BITsBinarySearch_COTS::BinarySearch(int Key;  int DataSet[10]);
...
////////////////////////////////////////////////////////////////////////////////
// Part 2: The inherited BIT functions
////////////////////////////////////////////////////////////////////////////////
void BIT1() : BITsBinarySearch_COTS::BIT1();
...
////////////////////////////////////////////////////////////////////////////////
// Part 3: The newly developed BITs
////////////////////////////////////////////////////////////////////////////////
//
// -----------------------------------------------------------
// BIT case 2
// ------------------------------------------------------------------------
void BIT2()
{
// BIT case 2: Test for even array size, key in array, and key is not first or last
private:
   int DataSet[6] = {16,18,21,23,29,33};
   int Key =  23;
   int StdElemIndex = 4;
   int TestElemIndex;
   char TestResult2 [5];
// Test implementation
   TestElemIndex = BinarySearch (Key, DataSet);
// Test analysis
   cout << "StdElemIndex2 = "  << StdElemIndex  << "\n";
   cout << "TestElemIndex2 =  "  << TestElemIndex  << "\n";
   if TestElemIndex == StdElemIndex
     TestResult2 = "OK";
     else TestResult2 = "FALSE";
   cout << "TestResult2: "  << TestResult2  << "\n";
}
}
```

Fig. 4. Inheritability and reusability of BITs in BIT-based COTS

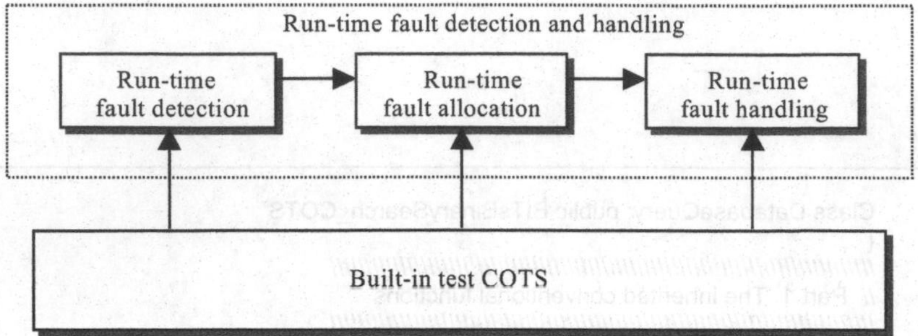

Fig. 5. BIT methods and classes for run-time fault detection and handling

In case a fault in the COTS is detected at run-time, source and type of the fault can be diagnosed and allocated by special BITs deployed in the COTS as shown in Fig. 5. By this approach, detailed causes of faults in the COTS can be allocated by the corresponding BITs at run-time. After the detection and allocation of any faults in a BIT class in an OO software system at run-time, an appropriate fault handling BIT at system level can be invoked according to a pre-designed fault processing strategy. Typical fault handling strategies are measures such as to alarm, log, report, reset system, reload objects, reload data, reconfiguration, switch to stand-by system, replace hardware, etc. A decision table of BIT class fault handling for a real-time software system, for instance, is provided in [6]. Thus, the BIT class provides a practical approach to improve OO software and information systems' reliability, maintainability, test-reusability, and run-time testability.

5 Conclusions

This paper has developed a new type of COTS architecture incorporating built-in tests and functional code into an integrated encapsulation – BIT-based COTS. The BIT-based COTS components have enabled tests be reused at both debugging phase and run-time. The BIT method has not only extended inheritability and reusability of conventional COTS from code to tests, but also significantly improved COTS run-time testability. More significantly, the BIT-based COTS technology presents a new programming style and COTS architecture.

The BIT-based COTS technologies provide a number of significant advantages for programmers and system designers in component-based software engineering, such as:

- Self-testable COTS and in-house components
- Test-reusable COTS and in-house components
- Run-time testable COTS and in-house components
- End-user testable COTS and in-house components
- Easy maintainable COTS and in-house components
- Built-in run-time fault handling capability for COTS and in-house components
- Higher quality and more reliable COTS and in-house components

The BIT-based COTS architecture and technologies have found a wide range of applications in the software industry. These include, *inter alia*: BIT-based COTS test, COTS test reuse, BIT-based COTS maintenance, run-time testable COTS, COTS for safety critical systems, and real-time system fault-tolerance with BIT-based COTS. The BIT-based COTS technology presented in this paper has been well received by the industrial user groups of Component+ in the European software industry [4, 5].

Acknowledgements

This work is supported by the EU 5th Framework Project IST-1999-20162. The authors would like to acknowledge the funding organization for its support, and all partners and industrial users-group members for their contributions to the project.

References

[1] Binder, R.V.: Design for Testability in Object-Oriented Systems, *Communications of the ACM,* Vol. 37, No. 9, Sept. (1994), 87-101.

[2] Wang Y., King, G., Fayad, M., Patel, D., Court, I., Staples, G., and Ross, M.: On Built-in Tests Reuse in Object-Oriented Framework Design, *ACM Journal on Computing Surveys,* **32, 1**es, March (200) 7-12.

[3] Wang Y., Wickberg, H. and King, G.: A Method for Built-in Tests in Component-based Software Maintenance, *Proceedings of 3rd IEEE International Conference on Software Maintenance and Reengineering (IEEE CSMR'99),* IEEE CS Press, Amsterdam, March (1999) 186-189.

[4] Wang, Y., et al.: *A New Approach to Extend OO Technology with BITs in CBSE*, Technical Report D2.1, The Component+ project, EU IST-1999-20162, (2001) 1-23.

[5] Wang, Y., et al. (2001), *Design Principles of BIT Components in CBSE*, Technical Report D2.2, The Component+ project, EU IST-1999-20162, (2001) 1-53.

[6] Wang, Y., King, G., Patel, D., Patel, S. and Dorling, A.: On Coping with Software Dynamic Inconsistency at Real-Time by the Built-in Tests, *International Journal of Annals of Software Engineering,* Baltzer Science Publishers, Oxford, 7, (1999) 283-296.

Active Objects for Coordination in Distributed Testing

Mohammed Benattou[1] and Jean-Michel Bruel[2]

[1] ESSI
École Supérieure d'Ingénierie Informatique
33700 Mérignac, France
[2] LIUPPA
Université de Pau et des Pays de l'Adour
64000 Pau, France,
{Jean-Michel.Bruel}@univ-pau.fr

Abstract. In practice, the development of distributed systems is complex as the design process must take into account the mechanisms and functions required to support interaction, communication and coordination between distributed components. In the context of distributed testing, we illustrate how we can use the concept of active object including the concepts of multi-threading, object and process to solve the problem of the coordination.

Keywords: CORBA, ODP, Active objects, Computational object, Coordination, Communication channel.

1 Introduction

The evolution of midlleware products, models, architecture and frameworks suggest several key issues that will contribute to the success of open distributed systems. The ODP (Open Distributed Processing) [5] provides a generic architecture for designing and building open distributed systems based on viewpoints specification.

With similar objectives to those of ODP and with a more implementation-oriented architecture, the OMA (Object Management Architecture [1]) provides a decisive support to create distributed applications and to relieve the software developer from all the details concerning the access to remote objects, the encoding of data and the localization of the objects. Defined by the OMG, the CORBA (Common Object Request Broker Architecture) [9] provides an object-oriented framework for distributed computing and mechanisms that support the transparent interaction of objects in a distributed environment.

A distributed system may be viewed as a system providing standardized distributed interfaces for interacting with other systems. The ODP configuration aspects of distributed system appear in the computational, engineering and technology. Based on the object oriented paradigm, the computational viewpoint

[1] `http://www.omg.org/oma/`

Z. Bellahsène, D. Patel, and C. Rolland (Eds.): OOIS 2002, LNCS 2425, pp. 348–357, 2002.

focuses on the functional decomposition of the system into objects with well-defined interfaces. The interaction between computational objects is described in terms of communication objects. The engineering viewpoint focuses on the infrastructure required to support distribution in terms of communication objects and channels. The technology viewpoint of an ODP system focuses on the choice of technology to support the system. The technology specification defines how the system is structured in terms of software components by selecting standard solutions for a basic components and communication mechanisms.

However, in practice the development of distributed systems is more complex, as the design process must take into account the mechanisms and functions required to support interaction as long as communication and coordination between distributed components. Examples of such applications are systems comprising a set of components that broadcast commands among themselves, multicast controllers that coordinate messages between components, the systems using the alarm signals in non deterministic order, network and application systems, event queues, etc. [13]. The typical reaction of such systems is the generation of sets of errors: time-outs, locks, channels and network failures. The programming models most often used to implement these environments rely on an event loop with callbacks, or using the CORBA services. In the CORBA event services, the system decouples the communication between objects by defining two objects roles: suppliers and consumers. The event service objects can be used to provide automated notification. When a supplier produces an event, the generated event is propaged to all interested consumers. Our preliminary experiences in the use of the event CORBA service for the implementation of the broadcast and multicast channels of distributed testing applications [2], have shown that the distributed testers arise many time-outs problems influencing fault detection during the testing process.

Object-oriented based, the development of such applications using the "classical" objects is very difficult as there are many possible ways of activating or deactivating event sources and to dispatch the callbacks. The concept of active objects extends the paradigm of object by defining the conditions under which objects methods can be executed and thus provides a precise definition of the behavior of the object interactions.

In this paper, we show how we can use active objects to implement the coordination of distributed testers in a distributed testing application prototype that we have developed. We have used the sC++ [10] as language to implement the coordination of distributed active tester objects. The sC++ is an object oriented language based on a limited extension of C++, that merges the concepts of object and the one of process.

The paper is structured as follows. Section 2 describes the architecture and modeling concept of distributed testing application. Section 3 raises some issues in the implementation of the communication channels of the distributed testing prototype using the CORBA notification events service. Section 4 raises some problems of the coordination. Section 5 describes the way active objects are used in our prototype. Section 6 gives some conclusions and identifies future works.

2 Distributed Testing Specification

The principle of testing is to apply input events to an implementation under test (IUT) and to compare the observed output events with the expected results. A set of input events and the expected results is generally called a *test case* and it is generated from the IUT specification. Conformance testing may be seen as a mean to executing an IUT by carrying out test cases, in order to observe whether the behavior of the implementation is conform to its specification. In the context of open distributed system, the IUT may be viewed as a system providing standardized interfaces for interacting with other systems. As illustrated in [8], the local interfaces can be defined as ODP conformance points in which the behavior of interactions can be observed.

2.1 Architecture

The basic idea of the proposed work [2] is to coordinate the testers by using a communication service parallel to the IUT through a multicast channel. Each tester interacts with the IUT only through the port to which it is attached and communicates with the other testers through the multicast channel. On a high level abstraction, we can distinguish three actors allowing the organizational requirements of the distributed testing environment to be captured:
IUT. It represents the executable implementation of the distributed software system to be tested. It can be seen as a black-box with points of control and observation (PCO) at which the test system can apply the input events and observe the output results during the testing process.
Management system. It generates local test sequences according to the behavior described in [2, 12], dispatches these sequences to related testers, starts and stops the execution of the testers, and provides a global verdict for the test process. The global verdict is deduced from the local test verdicts given by testers. *Management system* has the obligation to stop the execution of the test process if at least one *Tester* object provides a *Fail* verdict.
Tester. Each *Tester* object executes its local test sequence. The execution process of a *Tester* object consists of:

- to apply input events to the IUT interface related to it,
- to observe the output results, and
- to provide its local verdict to the *Management system*.

In order to coordinate the test execution process, *Testers* exchange coordination messages during their execution. *Tester* objects process together but independently [15].

2.2 Modeling Concepts

In order to be able to reason about the testing process in a formal setting, the specification and IUT must be modeled by using the same concepts. Therefore, conformance of an IUT to its specification may be defined by means of relations between the IUT model and specification model [6].

I/O FSM (Input/Output Finite State Machines) are widely used in the communication protocol area [6], and may be easily adapted with some extensions for modeling distributed systems. In a communication protocol, a protocol entity communicating with a peer entity, is described by an I/O FSM with one input queue and one output queue. Distributed applications are supposed however to communicate with multiple partners. This leads to the notion of a multi-port FSM [11] which may use several input/output queues called ports.

A *multi-port FSM with n ports* (np-FSM) $\mathcal{A}$ is a 6-tuple $(Q, \Sigma, \Gamma, \delta, \lambda, q_0)$, where: $\mathcal{A}$; Σ is a n-tuple $(\Sigma_1, \Sigma_2, \ldots, \Sigma_n)$ where Σ_k is the *input alphabet of port k*, and $\Sigma_i \cap \Sigma_j = \emptyset$ for $i \neq j$. We write $\bar{\Sigma}$ for the *input alphabet* $\Sigma_1 \cup \Sigma_2 \cup \cdots \cup \Sigma_n$ of $\mathcal{A}$; Γ is a n-tuple $(\Gamma_1, \Gamma_2, \ldots, \Gamma_n)$ where Γ_k is the *output alphabet of port k*, and $\Gamma_i \cap \Gamma_j = \emptyset$ if $i \neq j$. We write $\boldsymbol{\Gamma}$ for the *output alphabet* $(\Gamma_1 \cup \{\}) \times (\Gamma_2 \cup \{\}) \times \cdots \times (\Gamma_n \cup \{\})$ of $\mathcal{A}$; δ is the *transition function*, it is a partial function $Q \times \bar{\Sigma} \to Q$; λ is the *output function*, it is a partial function $Q \times \bar{\Sigma} \to \boldsymbol{\Gamma}$. Moreover, $\lambda(q, \alpha)$ is defined if and only if $\delta(q, \alpha)$ is.

A *transition* of np-FSM $\mathcal{A}$ is a 4-tuple $\mathbf{t} = (q, \alpha, \gamma, q')$ where $q, q' \in Q$, $\alpha \in \bar{\Sigma}$ and $\gamma \in \boldsymbol{\Gamma}$ are such that $\delta(q, \alpha) = q'$ and $\lambda(q, \alpha) = \gamma$.

A *test sequence* of np-FSM $\mathcal{A}$ is a sequence in the form: $!x_1?y_1!x_2?y_2 \cdots !x_t?y_t$ where, for $i = 1, 2, \ldots, t$, $x_i \in \bar{\Sigma}$ and $y_i \subset \bigcup_{k=1}^{n} \Gamma_k$ is such that, for each port k, $|y_i \cap \Gamma_k| \leq 1$, i.e. y_i contains at most one symbol from the output alphabet of each port of $\mathcal{A}$. $!x_i$ means sending message x_i to the IUT and $?y_i$ means receiving the messages belonging to y_i from the IUT.

An example of 3p-FSM with set state as long as a corresponding test sequence can be found in [1]. Test sequences are generally generated from the IUT specification and characterized by their fault coverage (output faults and transfer faults [11]). In order to synchronize the test execution, testers exchange coordination messages. These messages encapsulate the information that allows the test system to solve controllability and observability problems. As pointed out in [2] each local test sequence executed by a given tester includes the coordination messages to be sent or to be received from other testers.

In the distributed test method, each tester executes a local test sequence constructed from the complete test sequence of the IUT. A *local test sequence* is in the form $\alpha_1\alpha_2 \cdots \alpha_t$, where each α_i is either:

- $!x$, sending of message $x \in \Sigma_k$ to the IUT,
- $?y$, receiving of message $y \in \Gamma_k$ from the IUT,
- $!c_{h_1,\ldots,h_r}$, sending of coordination message c to testers $h_1, \ldots, h_r$,
- $?c_h$, receiving of coordination message c from tester h.

For each α_i, if it is a sending, either of a message to the IUT or of a coordination message, the tester sends it. If α_i is a receiving, either of an output from IUT or of a coordination message, then the tester waits for a message. If no message is received, or if the received message is not the expected one, the tester gives a fail verdict. If the tester reaches the end of its sequence, then it gives a pass verdict. If all testers give a pass verdict, then the test system ends the test by giving a global pass verdict. If the IUT has n ports, the algorithm [2] is dedicated to compute the n related local test sequences from a complete test sequence of IUT.

3 CORBA Prototype

The ODP configuration aspects of distributed system appear in the computational, engineering and technology viewpoint. Object based, they are focusing on the functional decomposition of the system into objects with well-defined interfaces. After describing the configuration of the distributed testing prototype in terms of computational and communication objects, this section presents some basic CORBA elements used in the implementation prototype of distributed testing object.

3.1 Communication Objects

A computational specification viewpoint of an ODP application is the functional decomposition of the system into a collection of interacting data processing objects in distribution-transparent manner [5]. It defines the computational objects within an ODP application, the activities within those objects, and the interaction that occur among them. Computational objects can interact, if the interfaces to be involved have been associated by creating a binding [5]. The required rules associated with the interactions to be performed are then expressed by the behavior of the binding objects. Object based, the computational specification describes the computational objects, their interface signatures, and the binding objects. The computational viewpoint of a distributed testing application contains two types of object: computational objects (*Management system*, *Tester*, and *Interface IUT*) and binding objects (*Broadcast link* and *Multicast link*) which are detailed below.

Management system. Its behavior can be described by a set of ordered actions. The generation of local test sequences and the analysis of a global verdict constitute the principal actions that compose its internal activity. The distribution of test sequences and commands to start and to end the test were considered as the actions allowing the *Management system* to interact with testers using the *Management Interface* and external objects (user of testing system) using the *Result Interface*.

Tester. Based on the object oriented approach, each tester used in the distributed testing application is considered as an instance of the computational object *Tester*. The principal internal activity of a *Tester* object is the execution of its local test sequence. Its behavior is defined by three interfaces:

- *Coordination interface* allows a *Tester* to exchange coordination messages with other *Testers*.
- *Control interface* allows a *Tester* to receive its local test sequence and the command to start and to end the test given by the *Management system*. On

the other hand, it allows a *Tester* to send its verdict to the *Management system.*
- *Invocation interface* allows a *Tester* to apply input actions by the invocation method principle and to receive the results provided by the IUT.
- The *Broadcast* binding object is used to link the *Management interface* of the *Management system* to *Control interfaces* of all *Testers.* It encapsulates the rules allowing the signals start and stop from the *Management system* to be delivered to all *testers.*
- The *Multicast* binding object is used to link the *Coordinate interface* of the tester that submits a coordination message to the *Control interface* of the testers to which coordination messages must be delivered.

3.2 CORBA Implementation

CORBA mainly defines the interface between an application and the package that encapsulates all the functions needed to handle network access. This package transforms the network into a bus on which the objects of an application can be hooked to prempty uniform communication between these objects [9, 13].

The OMA object model defines how objects distributed across an heterogeneous environment can be described, while the reference architecture deals with interactions between those objects. CORBA specification details the interfaces and characteristics of an ORB that conveys requests for invocation of objects operations from CORBA client to CORBA object implementation. The key feature of an ORB is transparency. Usually, an ORB hides the following characteristics of objects by using object references: object location, object implementation, object execution state, and object communication mechanisms. Due to page limitation, we invite interested reader to consult the full version of this paper [1] for more details about the implementation itself.

4 Coordination Problems

Our preliminary experiences in the use of the event CORBA service for the implementation of the broadcast and multicast channels of distributed testing applications have shown that in the distributed testers arise many time-outs problems influencing fault detection during the testing process. Here is an example (onather one can be found in [1]).

Example 1: Lets a given general test sequence ω and local test sequences ω_1, ω_2 and ω_3, generated from ω = !a?{x,y}!b?{x,y}!c{z}

$$\begin{cases} \omega_1 = !a?x?x?C_3 \\ \omega_2 = ?y!b?y \\ \omega_3 = !C_1!c?z \end{cases} \tag{1}$$

The conform execution of local test sequences ω_1, ω_2 and ω_3 must give the result shown in figure 1 (a), but the execution of our prototypes gives the failed

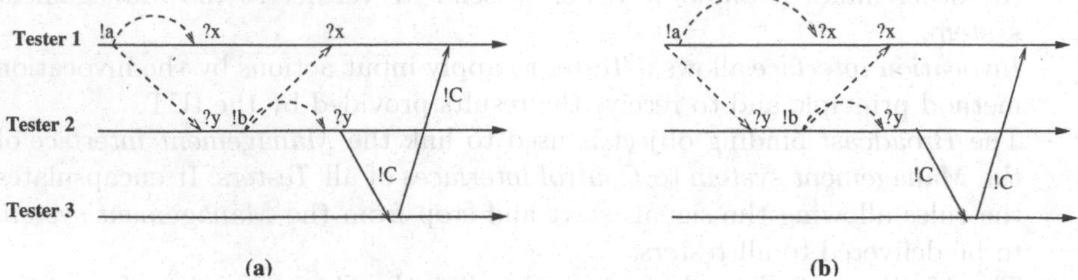

Fig. 1. Example 1 of prototype execution

result shown in figure 1 (b). Indeed, in figure 1 (b) the tester 2 sends the message b to the IUT before the tester 1 receives the output message x from the IUT, and thus the execution of the local sequences is not conform to the specification of ω where the message b must be sent to the IUT after all output messages caused by the sending of the message a by tester 1 has been received.

The execution example illustrate that the coordination between testers objects allows some failed errors, that can be solved by blocking the sending of the message b as long as all outputs caused by the last message have been received by all testers.

5 Active Object

The concept of active objects extends the object oriented paradigm to control the conditions under which such objects can execute their method. It provides a very precise definition of the behavior of the object interaction. This section present the sC++ language that includes the concept of active objects and the prototype implementation of the object testers using the sC++ we have performed.

5.1 sC++

sC++ is a limited extension of C++, that adds parallelism to C++ by integrating active object with threads. The sC++ syntax for the definition of object (instantiation, reference, call), inheritance and deletion is identical to standard C++, but an active object can delay the execution of its methods, when they are called from outside, until it is ready to accept one or some of them [13, 10]. The internal activity of an active object is carried out by a special method, called the body, that has the same name as the class pressed by the @ sign. The execution of this body is started at the end of the constructor of the class on a separate thread. The execution of the methods in an active object is synchronized with the execution of the body. Such method can be executed only if active body terminates or suspends its execution on one or several *accept* statements that contain the names of the methods that can be called.

```
active class Communication_Interface {
....
public:
 void send_message(...)
 void receive_message(...)

@Communication_Interface {
 while(1) {
          select {
                   accept send_message
                   ||
                   accept receive_message
                   ||
                   accept~Communication_Interface
                 }
          ||
         accept~Communication_Interface
          }
                            }
                                     }
```

Fig. 2. Example of active object on sC++

The example given in figure 2 shown the declaration of an active object *Communication_Interface* with two methods *send_message* and *receive_message*. If an outside object calls one of the two above methods before *Communication_Interface* accepts the called method, the call is blocked until it is accepted. Conversely, if the *Communication_Interface* object executes the statement *accept method* (*send_message* or *receive_message*) before an outside object call the corresponding method, the *Communication_Interface* is blocked until an object calls one of the two methods.

5.2 Implementation

As we have shown in section 4, the main problem in the distributed testing prototype is the coordination between the testers. The message sent or received can be treated at any time. The main reason for this problem is the fact that there is no specification of delay, time-out or locks explicitly used. The active objects with sC++ give an appropriate concept to manage this particular problem.

As we have shown above, *Tester* object has tree interfaces allowing it to communicate with *Management System*, IUT, and other *Testers* object. Such interface is presented in sC++ by the TCPSocket, as illustrated in figure 3.

The body of *Tester* active object is executed from line 14, on separate thread, after the constructor of the *Tester* has terminated, and its execution on line 16, waiting for one of the events (sending message to IUT, sending coordination message to one or some testers, receiving output message from IUT, receiving coordination message from other tester, deletion of itself) on lines 17, 19, 21, 23, and 25 that occurs self.

```
active class Tester {
....
/*TCP interfaces with Manager, and IUT*/
TCPSocket *Manager, *IUT ;
/*TCP interface with other Testers */
TCPSocket *Testers ;

public:
// constructor
.....
  void send_message_to_IUT(...)
  void send_Coordination_to_Testers(...)
  void receive_message_from_IUT(...)
  void receive_Coordination_from_Tester(...)
 @Tester{
  while(1) {
          select {
                  accept send_message_to_IUT(...)
                  ||
                  accept send_Coordination_to_Testers(...)
                  ||
                  accept  receive_message_from_IUT(...)
                  ||
                  accept receive_Coordination_from_Tester(...)
                  ||
                  accept~Communication_Interface
              }
       ||
        accept~tester
      }
  }
}
```

Fig. 3. Testers of active object on sC++

6 Conclusion and Future Works

Not only ODP and CORBA are both object based, but their objectives are quite similar. They aim to describe distributed systems implemented in terms of the configuration of distributed objects. However, in practice the development of distributed systems is more complex, and especially where the implementation must take into account some synchronization rules, and the coordination of distributed components, as it is often the case in complex information systems. In this paper, we have described how we can use active objects to implement the coordination of distributed testers in distributed testing using the sC++ language. Our work is now oriented toward the development of an environment, which take into consideration the functional requirements of time constraints in this context.

References

[1] M. Benattou and J.-M. Bruel: *Active Objects for Coordination in Distributed Testing*; Internal Research Report R2I-02-02, available at **http://www.univ-pau.fr/%7Emessine/R2I.html**. 351, 353

[2] M. Benattou, L. Cacciari, R. Pasini, and O. Rafiq: *Principles and Tools For testing Open distributed Systems*; Proceeding of the IFIP International Workshop on Testing of Communicating Systems (IWTCS'99), Budapest, Hungary, 1999, pp. 77-92. 349, 350, 351, 352

[3] M. Born, A. Hoffmann, M. Li, and I. Schieferdeck: *Combining Design Methods For Service Development*; Proceeding of the IFIP International Conference on Formal Methods for Open Object Distributed Systems (FMOODS'99), Italy, 1999, pp 281-291.

[4] CCITT/ITU-T:*Message Sequence Charts*; Z.120, Genf, 1996.

[5] ISO/IEC, *Open distributed processing, Reference model*, 10746, Parts 1-4, 1995. 348, 352

[6] ISO/IEC, *Information retrieval, transfer and managment for OSI, Framework: formal methods in conformance testing*, CD 13345-1, 1996. 351

[7] ITU/IEC 9646: *Information Technology -Open Systems interconnection - Conformance testing methodology* ; International Standard, Geneva, 1991.

[8] P. F. Linington, J. Derrick, and H. Bowman: *The specification and Testing of Conformance In ODP systems*; Proceeding of the IFIP International Workshop on Testing of Communicating Systems, (IWTCS'96), Germany, 1996, pp. 93-114 350

[9] OMG:*The common object request broker: architecture and specification*, Version 2.2, 1998. 348, 353

[10] C. Petitpierre, *Synchronous C++, a Language for Interactive Applications*, IEEE Computer, September 1998, pp 65-72. 349, 354

[11] A. Petrenko, G. v. Bochmann and M. Yayo, On fault coverage of tests for finite state specification, Computer Network and ISDN Systems 29, 1996, pp. 81-106. 351

[12] O. Rafiq, L. Cacciari, M. Benattou: *Coordination Issues in Distributed Testing*; Proceeding of the International Conference on Parallel and Distributed Processing Techniques and Applications (PDPTA'99), Las Vegas (Nevada), USA, 1999, CSREA Press. 350

[13] A. J. Restrepo-Zea, C. Petitpierre: *A Simple, Modeling prone CORBA Architecture* 349, 353, 354

[14] TINA-C: *Overall concepts and principles of TINA*, version 1.0, Document Label: TB_MDC.018_1.0_94, 1995.

[15] A. Ulrich, H. Konig:*Architectures For Testing Distributed Systems*; Proceeding of the IFIP International Workshop on Testing of Communicating Systems (IWTCS'99), Hungary, 1999, pp. 93-107. 350

[16] T. Vassiliou-Gioles, I. Schieferdeck, M. Born, M. Winkler and M. Li:*Configuration and Execution Support For Distributed Tests*; Proceeding of the IFIP International Workshop on Testing of Communicating Systems (IWTCS'99), Budapest, Hungary, 1999, pp. 61-76.

[17] T. Walter, I. Schieferdeck, and J. Grabowwski: *Test architecture for distributed systems: state of the art and beyond*; Proceeding of the IFIP International Workshop on Testing of Communicating Systems (IWTCS'98), Russia, 1998, pp. 149-173.

Associative Modeling and Programming

Bent Bruun Kristensen

Maersk Mc-Kinney Moller Institute
University of Southern Denmark
bbkristensen@mip.sdu.dk

Abstract. The notion of associations is motivated and presented. This kind of association is seen as first class a concept in notations at both modeling and programming level. Among others the association support evolution of systems by adding descriptions and instantiations of associations to executing systems.

1 Motivation

We briefly motivate our introduction of the notion of association by the problems with object-centric modeling and programming and exemplify non object-centric abstractions by the relation from [18]. Next we briefly introduce concepts from pervasive and ubiquitous computing and motivate associations by the very dynamic nature of such systems—illustrated by an intuitive example system. Finally we give a schematic outline of our notion of associations.

1.1 Object-Centric Modeling

The notion of associations is already available in object-oriented modeling. In object-oriented programming associations are implemented by means of references. We discuss an extension of the existing notion of associations in both modeling and programming. We make the association a first class concept in our modeling and programming notation. In a later section we return to the background for our work including a brief overview of related work on relations and associations.

In classical object-centric modeling and programming the fundamental problem is that "no object is an island" [2]. In object-oriented systems

- The object supports encapsulation
- The object is self-contained
- The focus is on structure instead of function
- The focus is on methods instead of processes

These characteristics are all seen as appreciated properties of object-oriented systems, but they also form essential problems because they all emphasize an object-centric point of view.

Z. Bellahsène, D. Patel, and C. Rolland (Eds.): OOIS 2002, LNCS 2425, pp. 358-371, 2002.

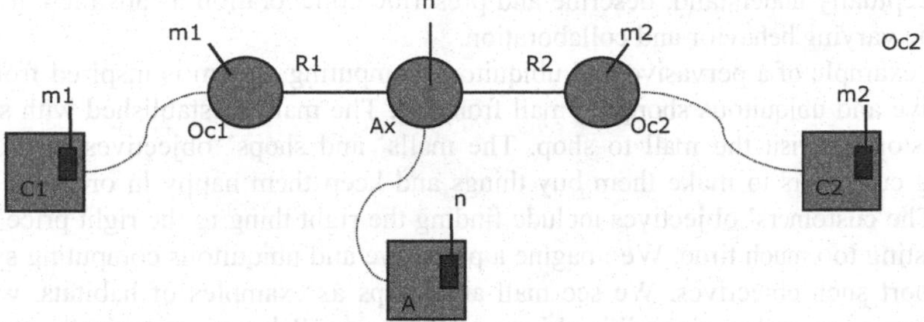

Fig. 1. Illustration of relations from [18]

In [18] relations are introduced as non object-centric abstractions. In Fig. 1 we illustrate a relation A with property n. An instance Ax of relation class A is instantiated to relate two objects Oc1 and Oc2 of classes C1 and C2 respectively. Ci has the property mi. Oci and plays the role Ri of relation Ax. In an illustrative example from [18] a relation A=Employment with property n=Salary is defined between objects of classes C1=Person and C2=Company. Objects of class Person play the role of R1=Employe and objects of class Company play the role of R2=Employer. The relation Employment captures an abstraction, which we do not want to place at neither Person nor Company—the relation is between these and therefore in conflict with the appreciated properties of the object-centric approach.

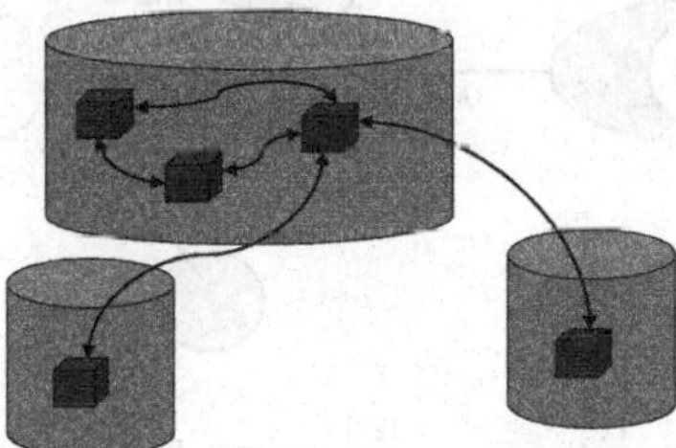

Fig. 2. Illustration of associations (arrows), tangible objects (boxes) and habitats (cylinders)

1.2 Pervasive and Ubiquitous Computing

The more general understanding of an association is motivated by a conceptual model for understanding systems known as pervasive and ubiquitous computing systems. In such systems we face a much more dynamic situation with respect to collaboration among the entities in the system cf. Fig. 2 from [17]. We imagine tangible objects existing in habitats and collaborating with other tangible objects inside or outside the habitat—and we imagine that tangible objects enter and leave habitats as very basic operations in such systems. As part of this very dynamic picture tangible objects engage in collaboration with other tangible objects—either simple, short collaborations or long, complex ones. We see the notion of associations as the means of capturing these planned or spontaneous collaborations between two or more tangible objects—

to conceptually understand, describe and prescribe collaboration as abstractions over dynamic varying behavior and collaboration.

Our example of a pervasive and ubiquitous computing system is inspired from the pervasive and ubiquitous shopping mall from [4]. The mall is established with shops, and customers visit the mall to shop. The malls' and shops' objectives include attracting customers to make them buy things and keep them happy in order to come back. The customers' objectives include finding the right thing to the right price without wasting too much time. We imagine a pervasive and ubiquitous computing system to support such objectives. We see mall and shops as examples of habitats, we see customers as examples of tangible objects and we see collaborations between mall and customer, shop and customer, customer and customer as examples of associations. We imagine that a customer is wearing some kind of communication device, not specified further, but with audio, visual etc interaction possibilities to support the various needs to operate in the mall and shops appropriately.

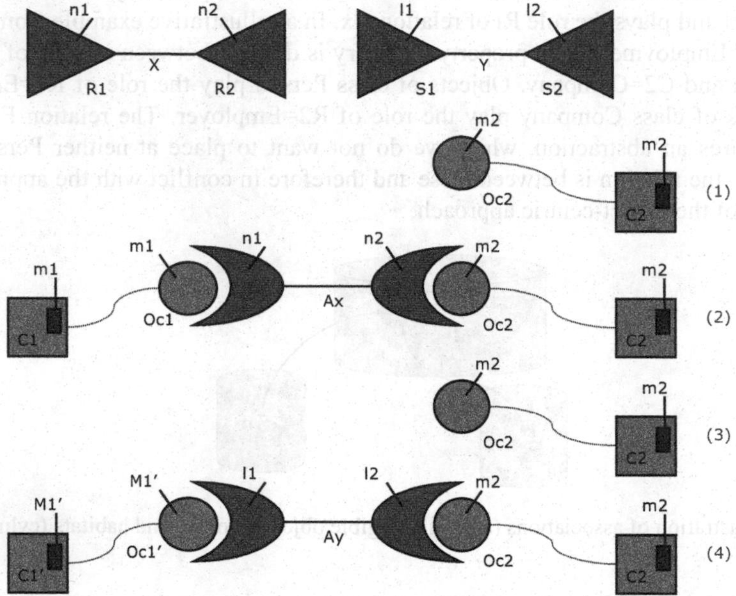

Fig. 3. Illustration of the notion of a generalized powerful association

1.3 Associative Modeling and Programming

The kind of associations we introduce in this article represents an alternative to object-centric modeling and programming. Our associations may be seen as an objectification of relations between objects—associations support not only structural relationship, but also interaction as well as collaboration between objects. An association is described, it may be instantiated, and it has identity. Dynamic changing associations are supported—descriptions may be added to executing systems and instances of these may be added to objects of the existing executing system.

The notion of associations appears to be very useful and expressive in our conceptual understanding. Classical object-oriented modeling and programming is still supported on its own, and can be seen as a special case of associative modeling and programming. Fig. 3 illustrates descriptions and instances of associations. Topmost we see graphical illustrations of associations X and Y. X defines roles R1 and R2 (with properties respectively nl and n2) while Y defines roles S1 and S2 (with properties respectively l1 and l2). Below the illustrations of X and Y we see four snapshots illustrating the dynamic creation and deletion of (2) an instance Ax from X and later (4) an instance Ay from Y. In the right hand side the object Oc2 of class C2 function as one participant in the associations. In snapshot (1) no associations exist for Oc2. In (2) Oc2 is associated by means of Ax with object Oc1 of class C1. OC2 plays the role R2 while Oc1 plays the role R1. In (3) the association Ax no longer exists. In (4) Oc2 is associated by means of Ay with object Oc1' of class C1', where Oc1 play roles S2 and Oc1 plays role S1.

2 Modeling with Associations

We briefly introduce our underlying understanding of conceptual modeling where we distinguish between target, referent and model system. Next we discuss our notion of associations for modeling, where we briefly mention association classes and sequence and collaboration diagrams as known from UML [3]. Finally we outline the potentials of our associations as abstractions over collaboration through generalization and aggregation hierarchies of these abstractions.

2.1 Abstraction: Conceptual Modeling

Fig. 4 illustrates target, referent and model system, relations (modeling and interpreting) between these systems, specifically the use of the model system in relation to the target system. The user observes the target system, thinks about it as the referent system, and constructs it as the model system. A perspective is always applied (implicitly or explicitly) in order to focus on certain properties of the phenomena observed in the target system.

The introduction of our notion of associations influences the possibilities in the referent and model systems. Conceptually we use the associations in the abstraction process of the referent system. We identify collaborations in the target system and form mental models of these through classification. Furthermore we may organize the identified association concepts in generalization and aggregation hierarchies. Similarly we build models based on our notion of concepts in the model system. In this article our intention is to make a notation available for expressing these associations—both at modeling and programming level. In this way we obtain the essential correspondence between the universe for our conceptual abstraction in the referent system and the concrete expression of this mental model as the model system.

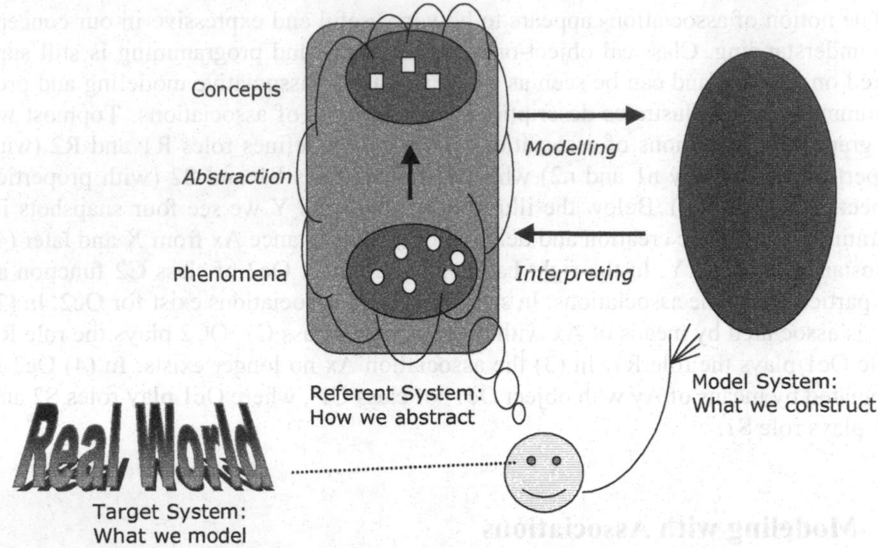

Fig. 4. Conceptual Modeling: We model a target system by abstracting the referent system and constructing the model system [6]

2.2 Associations in Modeling

In UML [3] models we typically find class diagrams supplied with association classes as the fundamental model structures—the main concepts are captured through these diagrams. In addition we find sequence and collaboration diagrams, where the interaction of objects in the system is modeled in terms of method invocations. This description is separated from classes and associations, and neither sequence nor collaboration diagrams are conceptualized as abstractions over interaction. Our notion of association is seen as abstraction over interaction and collaboration and the actual method invocations between objects are modeled as integrated elements of the association. In addition the roles played by the participating objects in an association are also modeled as extensions of the objects integrated in the association.

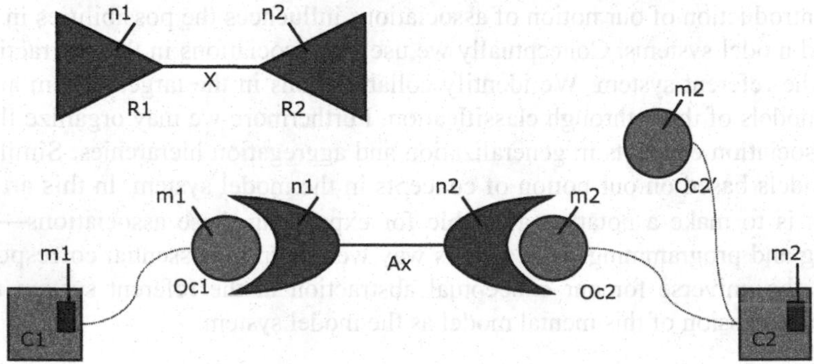

Fig. 5. Illustration of our notion of association

In Fig. 5 the association X has two participants R1 and R2 qualified by respectively classes C1 and C2. The descriptions of R1 and R2 may utilize each other's description, i.e. for example the description of n1 may utilize n2. The descriptions of R1 and R2 may utilize descriptions of respectively C1 and C2, i.e. for example the description of n1 may utilize the existence of m1.

We identify the following characteristics of this schematic example from associative modeling: The association is a description from which instances may be dynamically created (and deleted) and associated with objects. The association is qualified by a class, which determines which types of objects may be associated with instances of the association. The association captures a collection of collaborative purposes between its participants.

In our example of a pervasive and ubiquitous system we imagine that a "well-come" association is established between the mall and the customer when the customer enters the mall. The purpose of the "well-come" association is for the mall to present offers of the day to the customer and for the customer to announce his/her requests to the mall. The association may continue to exist throughout the customer's entire visit to the mall, but the actual collaboration through the association may be reduced. When the customer finds his/her way through the mall new "shopping" associations are instantiated between the customer and relevant shops to support the collaboration between the shop and the customer in order for the customer to find the right thing and possibly buy the thing. In addition the mall may offer services for customers to establish contact and eventually meet physically in a restaurant—a "talk" association may be established between customers to support communication while in the mall.

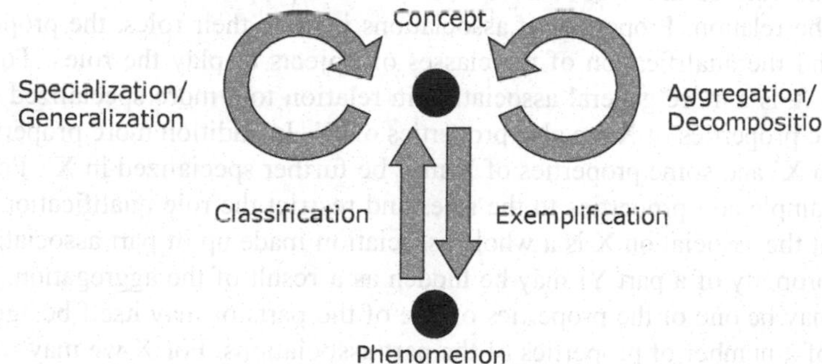

Fig. 6. Conceptual abstraction by the so-called OVARY model [13]

2.3 Conceptual Abstraction

Our notion of association is seen as an additional abstraction possibility during conceptual modeling. In conceptual modeling we find different forms of abstraction in terms of concepts and phenomena, namely

- classification and exemplification (a concept classifies a number of phenomena, which themselves exemplify the concept),

- specialization and generalization (a more general concept generalizes a more specific concept, which itself specializes the general concept), and
- aggregation and decomposition (a whole concept describes the aggregated phenomenon of several part phenomena of part concepts, which themselves can be decomposed from the phenomenon of the whole concept).

Fig. 6 illustrates the different forms of abstraction and how they relate to the notion of concept and phenomenon. This model of conceptual abstraction has been named the ovary model.

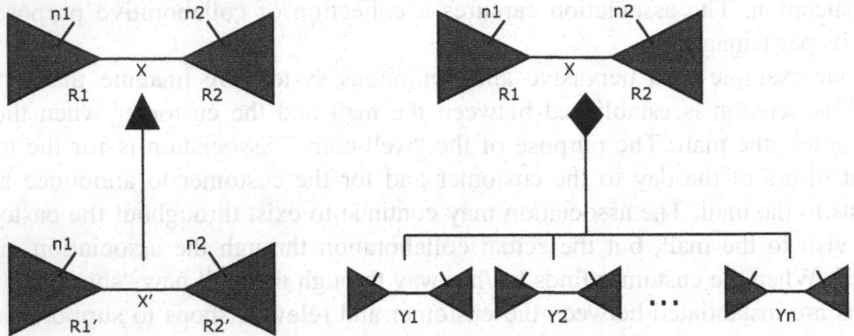

Fig. 7. Illustration of generalization and aggregation hierarchies for association concepts

Fig. 7 illustrate to the left a generalization relation between X and X' and to the right an aggregation relation between X and Y1, … Yn. The kind of relation is determined by the various kinds of relations between the properties of the association involved in the relation. Properties of associations include their roles, the properties of the roles and the qualification of the classes of objects to play the roles. To the left association X is a more general association in relation to a more specialized association X'. The properties of X are also properties of X'. In addition more properties may be added to X' and some properties of X may be further specialized in X'. For X' we may for example add properties to the roles and restrict the role qualification further. To the right the association X is a whole association made up of part associations Y1, … Yn. A property of a part Yi may be hidden as a result of the aggregation. A property of X may be one of the properties of one of the parts or may itself be aggregated by means of a number of properties of the part associations. For X we may for example specify properties of its roles by combining properties of the roles of the parts appropriately.

3 Programming with Associations

We characterize the difference between our notion of association and the notion of a reference as known from object-oriented programming. Next we briefly discuss a textual format for the description of an association and various applications. Finally we describe how to make associations active by adding life cycle aspects to its roles.

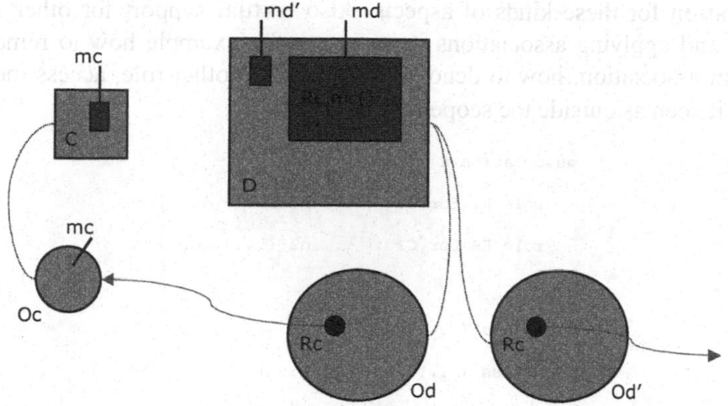

Fig. 8. Illustration of class, object, reference and method invocation

3.1 References

References support the relations between objects in object-oriented programming languages (for example JAVA [1]). In Fig. 8 we illustrate classical notions of class, object, reference and method invocation. Class C has method mc and object Oc is an instance of C. Class D has method md and a reference Rc qualified by C. Object Od is an instance of D and reference Rc has the value Oc. Method md of Od can invoke method mc of Oc by Rc.mc().

We observe the following characteristics of this schematic example from object-oriented programming: The reference is statically bound to the class (and any object of the class) whereas the value of the reference vary dynamically. The reference is qualified by a class, which determines which types of objects may be referenced by the reference. The reference is used for different purposes (invocations of different methods from different methods). The use of a reference for a given purpose is separated from the reference and distributed over several method bodies.

In comparison (with the characterization following Fig. 4) we notice that our notion of the association supports dynamical relations between objects, an integration of the relation with the purpose of the relation as well as the properties relevant for the relation.

3.2 Associations in Programming

The following code sequence illustrates a description of an association in a JAVA-like [1] textual format. The association X is described with its roles R1 and R2 for objects with qualification respectively C1 and C2. Also an instantiation of X as Ax is included, where objects Oc1 and Oc2 of classes C1 and C2 respectively participate in the association. Attributes like n1, n2, m1 and m2 are shown only in schematic form.

Associations can be of any order (only binary associations are illustrated in the article, but also ternary or higher order associations are possible). The multiplicity of objects associated with a role of the association may be specified including for example exactly one, one or zero, one or more and zero or more. It is straightforward to supply notation for these kinds of aspects. Also textual support for other aspects of describing and applying associations is necessary for example how to remove an instance of an association, how to denote attributes in another role, access multiple objects—but it seen as outside the scope of this article.

```
association X  {
    role R1 for C1  { ... n1:(...) ... }
    role R2 for C2  { ... n2:(...) ... }
}
C1: class ( ... m1:(...) ... )
C2: class ( ... m2:(...) ... )
C1 Oc1 = new C1();
C2 Oc2 = new C2();
X Ax = new X(Oc1, Oc2);
```

Fig. 9. Illustration of associations in textual form

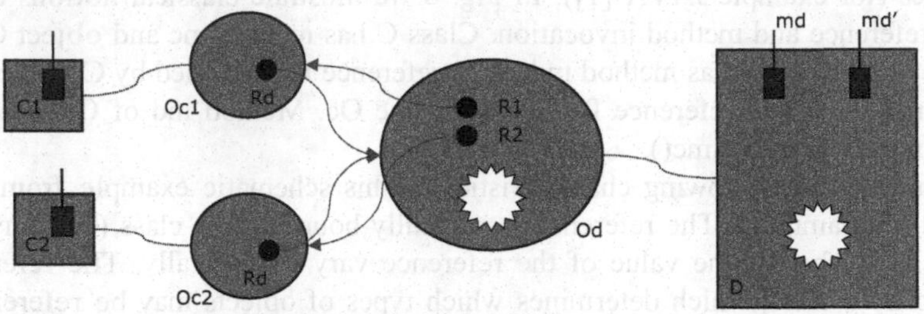

Fig. 10. Illustration of active objects

3.3 Active Objects and Associations

In Fig. 10 we illustrate an example with autonomous objects (objects with an active and self-initiating lifecycle (a reactive object is a special case of the autonomous object). The white stars in the class D and object Od symbolize the life cycle. Typically the life cycle is used for specifying method invocations in other objects like Oc1 and Oc2 through references R1 and R2 respectively. Or the life cycle is used for specifying acceptance of method invocations from outside from objects like Oc1 and Oc2 through references Rd of the methods like md and md' of the object itself. A system of active objects may be alive, and not just be sleeping to once in a while react on some kind of user interaction. The roles of an association may be active similarly to active objects as illustrated in Fig. 11. We assume that the object itself is active and that participation in various roles of associations simply adds activity to the basic life cycle. The interplay between the life cycle of the object and the life cycle of a role for the object is per interleaving—the life cycles take turn and leave the initiative to others at well-defined language specific interleaving points. The life cycle of the object

Oc1 itself only takes care of the object itself including for example attributes as m1. The life cycle of a role of the object R1 takes care of object interactions including mainly its own attribute n1 and the other role R2's attribute n2, but could also involve attributes m1 and m2 of the basic objects respectively Oc1 and Oc2. By including life cycles in the roles of the association the description of the actual collaboration is integrated in the description of the association.

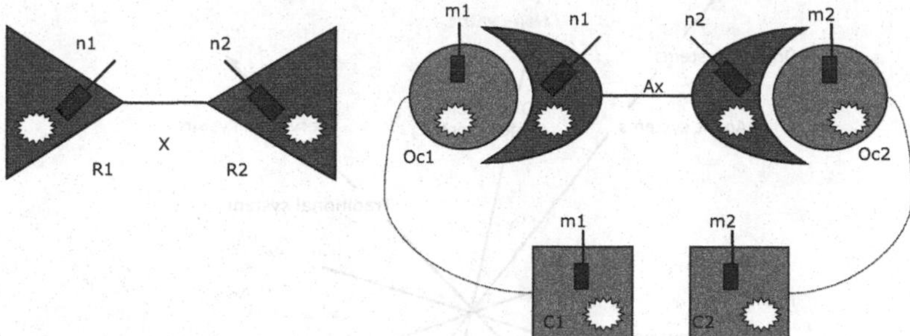

Fig. 11. Illustration of active (roles of) associations

In our example of a pervasive and ubiquitous system we imagine that a customer visiting the mall is engaged in several associations simultaneously. The "well-come" association with the mall may be activated occasionally throughout the visit according to the needs of the customer or new information from the mall. As an example the customer may need to find a toilet or other assistance from the mall. At the same time the customer may be engaged in associations with one or more shops as well as with friends and family also visiting the mall. Individual associations are supporting these engagements but must be potentially active whenever necessary. By executing the life cycles of all these associations interleaved we support their coexistence.

4 Conclusion

We briefly discuss the positioning of our notion in an appropriate universe. Then we summarize the identified characteristics of our notion of associations and we comment on other approaches to non object-centric modeling and programming. Finally we enumerate a number of identified challenges and problems to be addressed.

4.1 Approach

As illustrated in Fig. 12 our approach is inspired by a development from more traditional systems including information systems among others towards pervasive and ubiquitous systems with additional challenging elements. Pervasive and ubiquitous systems also illustrate the tendency to move away form the development of systems towards an understanding where systems are grown through evolution (intentionally or not). We see our notion of associations as a move away from object-centric technology towards non-centric technology. There seems to be similarities with this tendency and related technologies such as for example agent technology and organic systems. We still distinguish between a more abstract, informal and conceptual modeling level and a more concrete, formal and executable programming level.

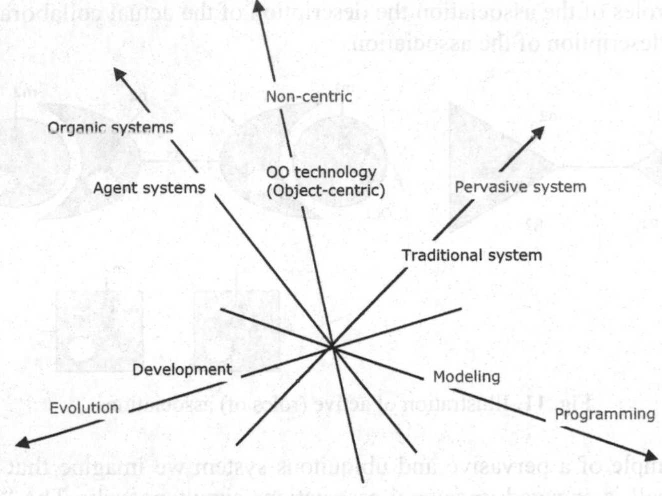

Fig. 12. Illustration of universe of associations

4.2 Related Work

We characterize our notion of association by

- Abstraction: Associations are abstractions over collaboration
- Subjectivity: Associations support roleification of objects
- Evolution: Dynamic changing descriptions and instantiation of associations

Abstractions over certain aspects of an object—as for example the collaboration of the object with other objects or the objects' role towards other objects—are also seen as objectification of such aspects. In this sense our notion of association can also be seen as an integrated objectification of collaboration and role aspects.

Other approaches to non object-centric modeling and programming exist—we briefly list and comment on various selected approaches:

- Relations [18] and the corresponding associations in OMT [19], [3] are object-external abstractions but these relations/associations only cover structural aspects, not collaboration.
- Sequence and collaboration diagrams in UML [3] support the description of object interaction by means of method invocation, but not as abstractions and not integrated with the relations/associations of objects.
- Complex associations [12] are object-external abstractions and support only complex structural relationships between structured objects.

- Subject-oriented programming [5] and subjective behavior [8], [7] support different views on objects respectively from an external and internal perspective, but not relationships between objects.
- Activities [10], [14], [15] are abstractions over collaborations of objects, but include no support of roleification of objects integrated into the collaboration.
- Roles [9], [11] are abstractions over roleification of objects for various relationships of objects, but no explicit collaboration is included.

4.3 Challenges

Various challenges exist for our notion of associations, including

- Associations of associations: Associations could be associated through the roles of the association (as illustrated in Fig. 13)
- Creation and deletion of association instances: Specific form and meaning of modeling and programming support for creation and deletion of instances
- Dynamic enter and leave of association: Dynamic (versus only static) participation of objects in associations could be supported
- Life cycle combination: Similarities and differences to inheritance anomaly[1] [16]
- Association from an object to itself only: What is the relation to subjectivity and roles?
- Access from R1 of properties of C1: Restrictions on this access
- Objects of associations: The objects to be part of the association must be known
- Description of collaboration: How is the collaboration defined in the life cycle part? How does an object interact with objects of its associations?

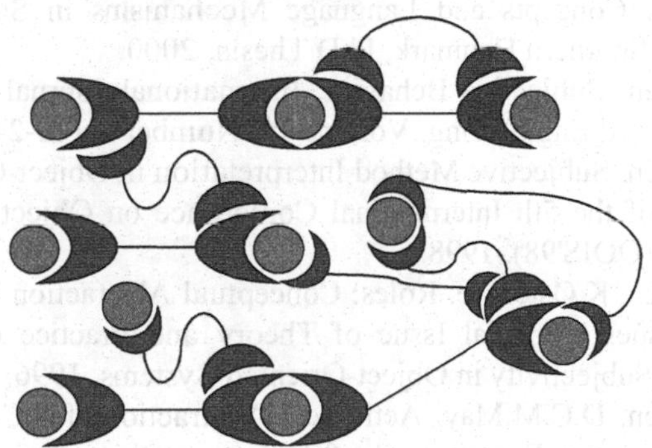

Fig. 13. Illustration of (associations of) (roles in) associations

[1] Inheritance anomaly refers to the serious difficulty in combining inheritance and concurrency in a simple and satisfactory way within a concurrent object-oriented language. The problem is caused by synchronization constraints imposed on the acceptance of a message by an object. Synchronization code is often hard to inherit and tends to require extensive redefinitions.

Acknowledgments

This research was supported in part by the Danish National Center for IT Research, Center for Pervasive Computing Project No. 212, Flexible Inter Processing (FLIP) and the A. P. Møller and Chastine Mc-Kinney Møller Foundation. We thank the SWEAT group at the Maersk Mc-Kinney Moller Institute for collaboration and contributions to this article.

References

1. K.Arnold, J.Gosling. The JAVA Programming Language. Addison Wesley, 1999.
2. K.Beck, W.Cunningham. A Laboratory For Teaching Object-Oriented Thinking. Proceedings of the Object-Oriented Systems, Languages and Applications Conference (OOPSLA'89), 1989.
3. G.Booch, J.Rumbaugh, I.Jacobson. The Unified Modeling Language User Guide. Addison Wesley, 1998.
4. K.Hallenborg, B.B.Kristensen. Pervasive Computing: Mapping TangO Model onto Jini Technology. Proceedings of the 6th World Multiconference on Systemics, Cybernetics and Informatics (SCI 2002), Orlando, Florida, 2002.
5. W.Harrison, H.Ossher. Subject-Oriented Programming (A Critique of Pure Objects). Proceedings of the Object-Oriented Programming Systems, Languages and Applications Conference (OOPSLA'93), 1993.
6. E.E.Jacobsen. Concepts and Language Mechanisms in Software Modelling. University of Southern Denmark, PhD Thesis, 2000.
7. B.B.Kristensen. Subjective Behavior. International Journal of Computer Systems Science and Engineering, Volume 16, Number 1, (13-24), January, 2001.
8. B.B.Kristensen. Subjective Method Interpretation in Object-Oriented Modeling. Proceedings of the 5th International Conference on Object-Oriented Information Systems (OOIS'98), 1998.
9. B.B.Kristensen, K.Østerbye. Roles: Conceptual Abstraction Theory & Practical Language Issues. Special Issue of Theory and Practice of Object Systems (TAPOS) on Subjectivity in Object-Oriented Systems, 1996.
10. B.B.Kristensen, D.C.M.May. Activities: Abstractions for Collective Behavior. Proceedings of the European Conference on Object-Oriented Programming (ECOOP'96), 1996.
11. B.B.Kristensen. Object-Oriented Modeling with Roles. Proceedings of the 2nd International Conference on Object-Oriented Information Systems (OOIS'95), 1995.
12. B.B.Kristensen. Complex Associations: Abstractions in Object-Oriented Modeling. Proceedings of Conference on Object-Oriented Programming Systems, Languages, and Applications (OOPSLA'94), 1994.
13. B.B.Kristensen, K.Østerbye. Conceptual Modeling and Programming Languages. Sigplan Notices, 29 (9), 1994.

14. B.B.Kristensen. Transverse Activities: Abstractions in Object-Oriented Programming. Proceedings of International Symposium on Object Technologies for Advanced Software (ISOTAS'93), 1993.
15. B.B.Kristensen. Transverse Classes & Objects in Object-Oriented Analysis, Design and Implementation. Journal of Object-Oriented Programming, 1993.
16. S.Matsuoka, A.Yonezawa. Analysis of Inheritance Anomaly in Object-Oriented Concurrent Languages. In G. Agha, P. Wegner, and A. Yonezawa, editors, Research Directions in Object-Based Concurrency. MIT Press, 1993.
17. D.C-M.May, B.B.Kristensen, P.Nowack. TangO: Modeling In Style. Proceedings of the Second International Conference on Generative Systems in the Electronic Arts (Second Iteration—Emergence), Melbourne, Australia, 2001.
18. J.Rumbaugh. Relations as Semantic Constructs in an Object-Oriented Language. Proceedings of the Object-Oriented Systems, Languages and Applications Conference (OOPSLA'87), 1987.
19. J.Rumbaugh, M.Blaha, W.Premerlani, F.Eddy, W.Lorensen. Object-Oriented Modeling and Design. Prentice Hall 1991.

A Controlled Experiment for Validating Class Diagram Structural Complexity Metrics

Marcela Genero, Luis Jiménez, and Mario Piattini

Department of Computer Science, University of Castilla-La Mancha
Paseo de la Universidad, 4, 13071, Ciudad Real, Spain
{marcela.genero,luis.jimenez,mario.piattini}@uclm.es

Abstract. Measuring quality is the key to developing high-quality software, and it is widely recognised that quality assurance of software products must be assessed focusing on early artifacts, such as class diagrams. After having thoroughly reviewed existing OO measures applicable to class diagrams at a high-level design stage, a set of metrics for the structural complexity of class diagrams obtained using Unified Modeling Language (UML) was defined. This paper describes a controlled experiment carried out in order to corroborate whether the metrics are closely related to UML class diagram modifiability. Based on data collected in the experiment, a prediction model for class diagram modifiability using a method for induction of fuzzy rules was built. The results of this experiment indicate that the metrics related to aggregation and generalization relationships are the determinant of class diagram modifiability. These findings are in the line with the conclusions drawn from two other similar controlled experiments.

Keywords: UML class diagram structural complexity, UML class diagram modifiability, structural complexity metrics, empirical validation, prediction model, fuzzy rule system

1 Introduction

Nowadays, the idea that "measuring quality is the key to developing high-quality OO software", is gaining relevance [30]. This can be seen from the great effort that has been made to achieve better quality OO software products [14],[19],[25], [37]. Even though most of these works pursue the goal of evaluating -by means of quantitative measures- the quality of the code or the advanced design, it is widely recognised that in order to obtain better OO software products the focus should be on measuring the quality characteristics of early artifacts, such as class diagrams.

In response to the great demand for measures of class diagram quality characteristics, such as modifiability, and after a review of some of the existing OO measures, applicable to class diagrams at high-level design stage [10],[12],[23], [24] we proposed a set of measures for UML class diagram structural complexity related to the use of UML relationships, such as associations, generalizations, aggregations and

Z. Bellahsène, D. Patel, and C. Rolland (Eds.): OOIS 2002, LNCS 2425, pp. 372-383, 2002.

dependencies [15], [18]. We also put them through theoretical validation following Briand et al.'s [6] and Poels and Dedene's framework [28], discovering that they are complexity metrics characterised by a ratio scale and are constructively valid [15]. This last point gains relevance when the measures have to be used in empirical studies, which is our case.

Even though our purpose is to measure UML class diagram modifiability, this is an external quality characteristic [20] that can be evaluated once a product is finished or nearly finished, so our work focuses on measuring an internal quality characteristic, the structural complexity of class diagrams. Our idea is to use these measures to predict class diagram modifiability in the early development stages of the OO software life cycle.

However, the proposal of metrics is of no value if their practical use is not empirically demonstrated [3],[14],[21],[31], either by means of case studies taken from real projects or by controlled experiments. Therefore, our main motivation is to investigate, through experimentation, if the metrics we proposed in [15], [18] are related to class diagram modifiability. If such a relationship exists and is confirmed by empirical studies, we will have obtained real early indicators of class diagram modifiability. These indicators will allow OO software designers to make better decisions early in the OO software life cycle, thus contributing to the development of better quality OO software.

Previously, we performed other two controlled experiments [16], [17], pursuing a similar objective. In both of them, as in the current one, the independent variable is the UML class diagram structural complexity. In the first of the experiments mentioned, the dependent variables were three maintainability sub-characteristics (understandability, analysability and modifiability) measured by means of user ratings on a scale composed of seven linguistic labels. Even though the results obtained in that previous experiment reflect that the metrics we proposed were highly related to class diagram maintainability, we are aware that the way we chose to measure the dependent variable was subjective and relied solely on judgment of the users, which may have biased the results. Therefore, we decided to carry out a second experiment, measuring the dependent variable in a more objective way. In the latter experiment the class diagram maintainability was measured by the time spent in modification tasks, called maintenance time (time is the time taken to comprehend the class diagram, analyse the required changes and to implement them). After performing the second experiment we found that the maintenance tasks required for each diagram were not similar. This fact could bias the results, and consequently threatens the validity of that experiment. This lead us to carry out a third experiment, in which we undertook similar modification tasks for each diagram.

This paper is organised in the following way: Section 2 present a set of metrics we defined in [15],[18]. Section 3 shows a controlled experiment we have carried out in order to evaluate if there is empirical evidence that UML class diagram structural complexity metrics are related to UML class diagram modifiability. Section 3 also shows how we used the empirical data collected in the experiment to build a prediction model for class diagram modifiability. For building that predict model we use a method for induction of fuzzy rules (see section 3). Lastly, section 4 summarises the paper, draws our conclusions, and presents future trends in metrics for OO early artefacts using UML.

2 Metrics for UML Class Diagram Structural Complexity

Table 1 presents the metrics defined in [15], [18] which can be applied at class diagram level as a whole. We also consider traditional metrics like, the number of classes, the number of attributes and the number of methods.

Table 1. Metrics for UML class diagram structural complexity

Metric name	Metric definition
Number of Classes (NC)	The total number of classes.
Number of Attributes (NA)	The total number of attributes.
Number of Methods (NM)	The total number of methods.
Number of Associations (NAssoc)	The total number of associations.
Number of Aggregation (NAgg)	The total number of aggregation relationships within a class diagram (each whole-part pair in an aggregation relationship).
Number of Dependencies (NDep)	The total number of dependency relationships.
Number of Generalisations (NGen)	The total number of generalisation relationships within a class diagram (each parent-child pair in a generalisation relationship).
Number of Aggregations hierarchies (NAggH)	The total number of aggregation hierarchies (whole-part structures) within a class diagram.
Number of Generalisations hierarchies (NGenH)	The total number of generalisation hierarchies within a class diagram.
Maximum DIT (MaxDIT)	It is the maximum of the DIT (Depth of Inheritance Tree) values obtained for each class of the class diagram. The DIT value for a class within a generalisation hierarchy is the longest path from the class to the root of the hierarchy.
Maximum Hagg (MaxHAgg)	It is the maximum of the HAgg values obtained for each class of the class diagram. The HAgg value for a class within an aggregation hierarchy is the longest path from the class to the leaves.

3 Empirical Validation of the Proposed Metrics through a Controlled Experiment

In this section we describe an experiment we have carried out to empirically validate the proposed measures as early modifiability indicators, following some suggestions provided in [4],[26],[33].

Definition. Using the GQM template [1], [2] for goal definition, the experiment goal is defined as fit is shown in table 2.

Table 2. Experiment goal

Analyse	UML class diagram structural complexity metrics
For the purpose of	Evaluating
With respect to	their capability of being used as class diagram modifiability indicators
From the point of view of	OO software designers
In the context of	Undergraduate Computer Science students at the Department of Computer Science in the University of Seville[1].

- **Context Selection.** The context of the experiment is a group of fifty two undergraduate students, enrolled in the final-year of Computer Science at the Department of Computer Science of the University of Seville in Spain. The experiment is specific since it focuses on UML class diagram structural complexity metrics. The ability to generalize from this specific context is further elaborated below when we discuss threats to the external validity of the experiment. The experiment addresses a real problem, i.e., which indicators can be used to assess the modifiability of class diagrams? To this end, it investigates the correlation between metrics and modifiability.
- **Selection of Subjects.** The subjects were chosen for convenience, i.e., the subjects are undergraduate students that have enough experience in the design of OOIS using UML, to do the tasks required in the experiment.
- **Variables Selection.** The independent variable is the UML class diagram structural complexity. The dependent variable is UML class diagram modifiability.
- **Instrumentation.** The objects were UML class diagrams. The independent variable was measured by the metrics (NC, NA, NM, NAssoc, NAgg, NDep, NGen, NAggH, NGenH, MaxHAgg, MaxDIT). As we knew what modifications were required for each of the nine class diagrams we could then assess the accuracy of completing the maintenance tasks. To this end we used the following measures, proposed in [5], [27], as indicators of modifiability:

$$Correctness = \frac{Number\ Of\ Correct\ Modifications}{Number\ Of\ Modifications\ Applied}$$

$$Completeness = \frac{Number\ Of\ Correct\ Modifications}{Number\ Of\ Modifications\ \mathrm{Re}quired}$$

1 Even though we belong to the Department of Computer Science of the University of Castilla-La Mancha, we carried out the experiment with subjects which belong to the University of Seville, to avoid the persistence effect, because our students have already done a similar experiment.

- **Hypothesis Formulation.** We wish to test the hypothesis "A close relationship exists between structural complexity metrics (NC, NA, NM, NAssoc, NAgg, NDep, NGen, NAggH, NGenH, MaxHAgg, MaxDIT) and UML class diagram modifiability".
- **Experiment Design.** We selected a within-subject design experiment, i.e., all the tests (experimental tasks) had to be solved by each of the subjects. The subjects were given the tests in different order.
- **Preparation**. At the time the experiments were carried out, the subjects had taken two Software Engineering courses. In these courses they learnt how to design OO software using UML. Moreover, the subjects were given an intensive training session before the experiment took place. However, the subjects were not aware of what aspects we intended to study. Neither were they informed of the hypothesis stated.

  The material we gave the subjects, consisted of a guide explaining UML notation and nine UML class diagrams of different application domains, that were easy enough to be understood by each of the subjects. The diagrams have different structural complexity, covering a broad range of metric values. Each diagram had an enclosed test that included a brief description of what the diagram represented and four new requirements for the class diagram. Each subject had to modify the class diagrams according to the new requirements. The modifications to each class diagram were similar, including adding or deleting attributes, methods, classes, etc.
- **Execution.** The subjects were given all the materials described in the previous paragraph. We explained how to do the tests, and allowed one week to carry out the experiment, i.e., each subject had to do the test alone, and could use unlimited time to solve it. We collected all the data including the modified class diagrams with the maintenance time obtained from the responses of the tests and the metrics values automatically calculated by means of a metric tool we designed.
- **Data Validation.** Once the data was collected, we controlled the tests. We discarded the tests of three subjects, which included all the incomplete required modifications for a class diagram . Therefore, we took into account the responses of 49 subjects.
- **Analysis and Interpretation.** We used the data collected in order to test the hypotheses formulated in section 3.2. As we have said before, our goal is to ascertain if any relationship exists between each of the proposed metrics (see section 2) and the correctness and completeness.

  Due to the nature of the software development process and products, one cannot expect to use in Software Engineering the same measurement data analysis techniques that are used in "exact" sciences, e.g., Physics, Chemistry, nor obtain the same degree of precision and accuracy. Therefore, we need other techniques, like machine learning techniques that allow us to build prediction models with two characteristics: they must be highly qualitative and more straightforward and intelligible to human beings.

  In this work we have used a data analysis technique based on a method for induction of fuzzy rules [35], [36]. This approach, as a method of supervised

learning, provides models that allow us to discover the most relevant conceptual relationships between the data we are analysing, where the accuracy of those models is sacrificed in favour of its simplicity and ease of understanding.
Due to space constraints we can not give an explanation of the whole method for induction of fuzzy rule systems, we used for analysing the data obtained in the experiments. More details about it can be found in [13],[16],[17],[22].
Hereafter we show the results obtained by the application of the induction method we propose. We established a fuzzy rule system for correctness and completeness. We used a learning set with X={set of our metrics} and Y={the values of the correctness and completeness in our experiment}. We have obtained 441 values (9 class diagrams and 49 subjects) of this unknown function:

F1(NC,NA,NM,NAssoc,NAgg,NDep,NGen,NAggH,NGenH,MaxHAgg,MaxDIT) =Correctness
F2(NC,NA,NM,NAssoc,NAgg,NDep,NGen,NAggH,NGenH,MaxHAgg,MaxDIT) =Completeness

By means of the induction method we have obtained a prediction model composed of fuzzy rules. A fuzzy rule is formed by the antecedent part (left part of the rule) and the consequent part (right part of the rule) to reflect a cause-effect relation. The antecedent part is formed by aggregation of fuzzy statements such as " X is A", where X is a metric value and A is a fuzzy set over metric domain.
In this example we have used a trapezoidal function for fuzzy sets, which are defined by four numbers. The fuzzy set [a,b,c,d] has the following members:

$$A(x,a,b,c,d) = \begin{cases} 0 & x <= a \\ \dfrac{x-a}{b-a} & a < x < b \\ 1 & b \le x \le c \\ \dfrac{d-x}{d-c} & c < x < d \\ 0 & x \ge d \end{cases}$$

Applying our method to the data collected in the experiment we have obtained the fuzzy rules shown in table 3 which represents a correctness fuzzy model, where MIN is the minimum value of the metrics, MAX is the maximum value of the metrics and [-] represents the whole domain of the metrics.

The rows represent the rules. We can read rule 18 as "IF NAgg is in the fuzzy set [MIN;MIN;0;1] and NAggH is in the fuzzy set [MIN;MIN;0;1] and MaxHAgg is in the fuzzy set [MIN;MIN;0;1] and MaxDIT is in the fuzzy set [MIN;MIN;0;1] THEN Correctness is 0,8754" . This rule has a 0.004 error and has a data coverage percentage of 21.73%.

Table 4 shows the set of fuzzy rules of completeness. This table could be read in the same manner as the previous table.

Table 3. Correctness fuzzy model

	NAgg	NaggH	MaxHAgg	MaxDIT	CORRECTNESS	ERROR	COV%
1	[MIN;MIN;0;1]	[1;2;MAX;MAX]	[-]	[-]	0.9216	0.0002	1.10%
2	[MIN;MIN;0;1]	[0;1;1;2]	[-]	[-]	0.8933	0.0001	0.23%
3	[MIN;MIN;0;1]	[MIN;MIN;0;1]	[-]	[1;2;MAX;MAX]	0.6027	0.0039	10.86%
4	[1;3;MAX;MAX]	[MIN;MIN;1;2]	[-]	[-]	0.896	0.003	13.97%
5	[1;3;MAX;MAX]	[1;2;MAX;MAX]	[-]	[MIN;MIN;1;2]	0.9292	0.0014	8.74%
6	[0;1;1;3]	[1;2;MAX;MAX]	[-]	[-]	0.9377	0.0006	3.81%
7	[MIN;MIN;0;1]	[MIN;MIN;0;1]	[-]	[0;1;1;2]	0.5993	0.0001	0.39%
8	[1;3;MAX;MAX]	[1;2;MAX;MAX]	[-]	[1;2;2;3]	0.9694	0.0005	8.46%
9	[1;3;MAX;MAX]	[1;2;MAX;MAX]	[-]	[2;3;MAX;MAX]	0.8867	0.0035	19.64%
10	[0;1;1;3]	[MIN;MIN;0;1]	[-]	[-]	0.9277	0	0.03%
15	[0;1;1;3]	[0;1;1;2]	[-]	[1;2;MAX;MAX]	0.854	0.0004	0.96%
16	[0;1;1;3]	[0;1;1;2]	[-]	[MIN;MIN;1;2]	0.8557	0.0037	9.69%
17	[MIN;MIN;0;1]	[MIN;MIN;0;1]	[1;2;MAX;MAX]	[MIN;MIN;0;1]	0.8755	0.0001	0.31%
18	[MIN;MIN;0;1]	[MIN;MIN;0;1]	[MIN;MIN;0;1]	[MIN;MIN;0;1]	0.8754	0.004	21.73%
19	[MIN;MIN;0;1]	[MIN;MIN;0;1]	[0;1;1;2]	[MIN;MIN;0;1]	0.9304	0	0.01%

Where: each row is one of the obtained rules; the columns **NAgg, NAggH, MaxHAgg, MaxDIT** are the fuzzy sets associated with each metric name; the column Correctness is the output or the consequent of the rules.; the column **ERROR** is the error produced when the rule is generated and the column **COV%** is the data coverage percentage taking into account the sample data.

Table 4. Completeness fuzzy model

	NA	NM	NGen	MaxDIT	COMPLETENESS	ERROR	COV%
1	[12;16;19;30]	[-]	[MIN;MIN;0;1]	[MIN;MIN;0;1]	0.8331	0.0064	21.47%
2	[-]	[-]	[-]	[0;1;1;2]	0.8314	0.0076	21.17%
3	[19;30;MAX;MAX]	[31;65;MAX;MAX]	[5;14;MAX;MAX]	[2;3;MAX;MAX]	0.7419	0.0079	20.76%
4	[MIN;MIN;12;16]	[-]	[MIN;MIN;0;1]	[MIN;MIN;0;1]	0.8296	0.0032	11.59%
5	[-]	[-]	[1;3;3;5]	[1;2;2;3]	0.9104	0.0026	10.57%
6	[-]	[-]	[3;5;5;14]	[1;2;2;3]	0.6373	0.0073	9.90%
7	[-]	[-]	[MIN;MIN;1;3]	[1;2;2;3]	0.8261	0.0009	2.01%
8	[MIN;MIN;19;30]	[-]	[5;14;MAX;MAX]	[2;3;MAX;MAX]	0.8203	0.0004	0.91%
9	[-]	[-]	[5;14;MAX;MAX]	[1;2;2;3]	0.6535	0.0005	0.65%
10	[-]	[-]	[MIN;MIN;5;14]	[2;3;MAX;MAX]	0.8286	0.0001	0.29%
11	[-]	[-]	[1;3;5;14]	[MIN;MIN;0;1]	0.8005	0.0001	0.19%
12	[-]	[-]	[5;14;MAX;MAX]	[MIN;MIN;0;1]	0.7878	0.0001	0.14%
13	[19;30;MAX;MAX]	[-]	[MIN;MIN;0;1]	[MIN;MIN;0;1]	0.8509	0	0.09%
14	[19;30;MAX;MAX]	[MIN;MIN;31;65]	[5;14;MAX;MAX]	[2;3;MAX;MAX]	0.7743	0	0.04%
15	[-]	[-]	[0;1;1;3]	[MIN;MIN;0;1]	0.7884	0	0.00%

Where: each row is one of the obtained rules; the columns **NA, NM, NGen, MaxDIT** are the fuzzy sets associated with each metric name; the column Completeness is the output or the consequent of the rules.; the column **ERROR** is the error produced when the rule is generated and the column **COV%** is the data coverage percentage taking into account the sample data.

Now we will analyse the content of table 3 and 4 in order to corroborate our hypothesis "A close relationship exists between the presented metrics and UML class diagram modifiability measured by the correctness and completeness ". First of all we can point out that not all of the 11 metrics presented in section 2 are related with correctness and completeness.
Seeing table 3 we can conclude that:

- The accuracy of the correctness fuzzy model is put forth in the error column, which is close to 0. This fact means that the model we obtained is a good approximation of the real model.
- The values of the metrics NAgg, NAggH, MaxDIT, MaxHAgg (in this order) influence the correctness. The values of the rest of metrics have nothing to do with respect to the correctness values.
- Most of correctness values are close to 1, which means that "the accuracy" is high, i.e., that most of the performed modifications were correctly done.

Seeing table 4 we can conclude that:

- The accuracy of the completeness fuzzy model is put forth in the error column, which is close to 0. Therefore, the model we obtained is a good approximation of the real model.
- The values of the metrics MaxDIT, NGen, NA, NM (in this order) influence on the completeness. The values of the rest of metrics have nothing to do with respect to the completeness values.
- Most of completeness values are close to 1, which means that most of the required tasks were done, in other words the number of modifications not done are minimum.

As can be seen from tables 3 and 4, correctness can be determined by the metrics related to aggregation relationships, and completeness by metrics related to generalisation relationships.

The correctness and completeness values (very close to 1) also put forth that the subjects had enough experience to perform the tasks required by the experiment, which adds value to the results obtained.

The fuzzy rules system shown in table 3 and table 4 could be also used as prediction models for correctness and completeness. By means of an example we will demonstrate how the correctness of the modifiability of a class diagram can be predicted using the model presented in table 3. Suppose that we want to answer the following question, **"What is the value of Correctness, if we know that NAgg is 10, NAggH is 2, MaxHAgg is 3 and MaxDIT is 2?".** This question, can be answered by inference using approximate reasoning [32] and with a simplified consequent, detailed in table 3. We obtained the value of Correctness as 0.9694, by taking a weighted average of the output (correctness) of each rule with its degree of membership. Even though this is a very simple example, it illustrates that it is possible to predict the class diagram correctness from the metrics values, early in the development of OO software (analogously, the completeness value can be inferred).

- **Validity Evaluation.** We will discuss the various issues that threaten the validity of the empirical study and how we attempted to alleviate them:

- Threats to Construct Validity. The construct validity is the degree to which the independent and the dependent variables are accurately measured by the measurement instruments used in the study. The measure we used for the dependent variable are correctness and completeness. They are objective measures so we consider these measures constructively valid. The construct validity of the measures used for the independent variables is guaranteed by Poels and Dedene´s framework [28], used for their theoretical validation [].
- Threats to Internal Validity. The internal validity defines the degree of confidence in a cause-effect relationship between factors of interest and the observed results. The following issues have been dealt with: Differences among subjects, Knowledge of the universe of discourse among class diagrams, Precision in the time values, Learning effects, Fatigue effects, Persistence effects, Subject motivation, Plagiarism and influence between students.
- Threats to External Validity. External validity is the degree to which the research results can be generalised to the population under study (UML diagrams used as design artefacts for developing OO software) and to other research settings. The greater the external validity, the more the results of an empirical study can be generalised to actual software engineering practice. Two threats to validity have been identified which limit the ability to apply any such generalisation: Materials and tasks used and Selection of subjects.

- Presentation and package. As the diffusion of the experimental data is important to the external replication [11] of the experiments we have put all the material of this experiment on our web site http:\\alarcos.inf-cr.uclm.es.

4 Conclusions and Future Work

It is widely accepted that the more complex an UML class diagram, the more complex the OO software which is finally implemented, and therefore more effort is needed to develop and maintain it. So that the metrics we proposed [15], [18] could be very fruitful, because they will allow OO software designers to assess the complexity of their designs, and compare between design alternatives, from the early phases of OO software life cycle.

In this paper, we have presented a controlled experiment for assessing if the metrics we proposed are closely related with class diagram modifiability, measured by means of the level of correctness and completeness of the modification tasks.

From the structural complexity metrics values we have built a prediction model for class diagram maintainability using a method for induction of fuzzy rules. The data used to build those prediction models was collected through a controlled experiment.

This experiment reveals that not all the metrics are related with class diagram modifiability. Metrics regarded to aggregation relationships are highly related with correctness, whereas, metrics regarded to generalisation relationships are closely to completeness. From a practical point of view these findings mean that when class diagram modification tasks are required, looking at the values of aggregation metrics can be useful to predict the level of correctness of those tasks, and looking at values of generalisation metrics can predict how complete the modifications can be done. These findings could be very valuable when maintaining OO software products, as maintainability has become one of the software product quality characteristics that software development organisations are more worried about.

Despite the encouraging results obtained we are aware that we need to do more metric validation in order to assess if the presented metrics could be really used as early quality indicators. Also, data of "real projects" on UML class diagram maintainability efforts would be useful, as well as time spent on maintenance tasks in order to predict data that can be highly fruitful to software designers and developers. However, as the scarcity of such data continues to be a great problem we must find other ways to tackle validating metrics. Several experts [7],[8],[9] suggested the necessity of a public repository of measurement experiences, which we think would be a good step towards the success of all the work done on software measurement.

Pending further research we have the definition of measures for other quality factors like those proposed in the ISO 9126 [20], which not only tackles class diagrams, but also evaluates other UML dynamic diagrams, such as use-case diagrams, state diagrams, etc. To our knowledge, little work has been done towards measuring dynamic and functional models [29], [34]. Therefore, this is an area which needs further investigation.

Acknowledgements

This research is part of the DOLMEN project (TIC 2000-1673-C06-06) and the CIPRESES project (TIC 2000-1362-C02-02), both supported by the Ministry of Science and Technology.

We would like to express our gratitude, specially to Isabel Ramos, of the Department of Computer Science of the University of Seville for having permitted us to use her students for the experiment presented in this paper.

References

1. Basili V. and Rombach H. The TAME project: towards improvement-oriented software environments, IEEE Transactions on Software Engineering, 14(6) (1988) 728-738
2. Basili V. and Weiss D. A Methodology for Collecting Valid Software Engineering Data., IEEE Transactions on Software Engineering, 10 (1984) 728-738
3. Basili V., Shull F. and Lanubile F. Building Knowledge through Families of Experiments. IEEE Transactions on Software Engineering, 25(4) (1999) 435-437

4. Briand L., Arisholm S., Counsell F., Houdek F. and Thévenod-Fosse P. Empirical Studies of Object-Oriented Artefacts, Methods, and Processes: State of the Art and Future Directions. Empirical Software Engineering, 4(4) (1999) 387-404
5. Briand L., Bunse C. and Daly J. A Controlled Experiment for evaluating Quality Guidelines on the Maintainability of Object-Oriented Designs. IEEE Transactions on Software Engineering, 27(6) (2001) 513-530
6. Briand L., Morasca S. and Basili V. Property-Based Software Engineering Measurement. IEEE Transactions on Software Engineering, 22(1) (1996) 68-86
7. Brito e Abreu F., Zuse H., Sahraoui H. and Melo W. Quantitative Approaches in Object-Oriented Software Engineering. Object-Oriented technology: ECOOP´99 Workshop Reader, Lecture Notes in Computer Science, 1743, Springer-Verlag, (1999) 326-337
8. Brito e Abreu F., Poels G., Sahraoui H. and Zuse H. Quantitative Approaches in Object-Oriented Software Engineering. Object-Oriented technology: ECOOP´00 Workshop Reader, Lecture Notes in Computer Science, 1964, Springer-Verlag, (2000) 93-103
9. Brito e Abreu F., Henderson-Sellers B., Piattini M., Poels G. and Sahraoui H. Quantitative Approaches in Object-Oriented Software Engineering. Object-Oriented technology: ECOOP´01 Workshop Reader, Lecture Notes in Computer Science, Springer-Verlag, (2001) (to appear)
10. Brito e Abreu, F. and Carapaçua, R. Object-Oriented Software Engineering: Measuring and controlling the development process. 4th Int Conference on Software Quality, Mc Lean, Va, USA, (1994)
11. Brooks A., Daly J., Miller J., Roper M., Wood M. Replication of experimental results in software engineering. Technical report ISERN-96-10, International Software Engineering Research Network, (1996)
12. Chidamber, S. and Kemerer, C. A Metrics Suite for Object Oriented Design. IEEE Transactions on Software Engineering, 20(6) (1994) 476-493
13. Delgado, M., Gómez Skarmeta, A. and Jiménez, L. (2001). International Journal of Intelligent Systems, 16 (2001) 169-190
14. Fenton, N. and Pfleeger, S. Software Metrics: A Rigorous Approach. 2nd. edition. London, Chapman & Hall, (1997)
15. Genero M. Defining and Validating Metrics for Conceptual Models, Ph.D. thesis, University of Castilla-La Mancha, (2002)
16. Genero M., Jiménez, L. and Piattini M. Empirical Validation of Class Diagram Complexity Metrics. SCCC 2001, November, Chile, IEEE Computer Society Press, (2001) 95-104
17. Genero, M., Jiménez, L., Piattini, M. A prediction model for OO information system quality based on early indicators. ADBIS 2001, Vilnius, Lithuania, (2001) 211-224
18. Genero, M., Piattini, M. and Calero, C. Early Measures For UML class diagrams. L´Objet. 6(4), Hermes Science Publications, (2000) 489-515
19. Henderson-Sellers, B. Object-Oriented Metrics - Measures of complexity. Prentice-Hall, Upper Saddle River, New Jersey, (1996)
20. ISO/IEC 9126-1.2. Information technology- Software product quality – Part 1: Quality model, (1999)

21. Kitchenham, B., Pflegger, S. and Fenton, N. Towards a Framework for Software Measurement Validation. IEEE Transactions of Software Engineering, 21(12) (1995) 929-943
22. Linares, L. J., Delgado, M. and Skarmeta, A. Regression by fuzzy knowledge bases. Proceedings of the 4th European Congress on Intelligent Techniques and Soft Computing. Aachen, Germany, September, (1996) 1170-1176
23. Lorenz, M. and Kidd, J. Object-Oriented Software Metrics: A Practical Guide. Prentice Hall, Englewood Cliffs, New Jersey, (1994)
24. Marchesi, M. OOA Metrics for the Unified Modeling Language. Proceedings of the 2nd Euromicro Conference on Software Maintenance and Reengineering, (1998) 67-73
25. Melton , A. (ed.). Software Measurement. London, International Thomson Computer Press, (1996)
26. Perry, D., Porter, A. and Votta, L. Empirical Studies on Software Engineering: A Roadmap. Future of Software Engineering. Ed:Anthony Finkelstein, ACM, (2000) 345-355
27. Poels G. and Dedene G. Evaluating the Effect of Inheritance on the Modifiability of Object-Oriented Business Domain Models. 5th European Conference on Software Maintenance and Reengineering (CSMR 2001), Lisbon, Portugal, (2001)
28. Poels G. and Dedene G. Distance-based software measurement: necessary and sufficient properties for software measures, Information and Software Technology, 42(1) (2000) 35-46
29. Poels, G. and Dedene, G. Measures for Assessing Dynamic Complexity Aspects of Object-Oriented Conceptual Schemes. 19th International Conference on Conceptual Modeling (ER 2000), Salt Lake City, Lecture Notes in Computer Science, 1920, Springer-Verlag, (2000) 499-512
30. Schneidewind, N. Body of Knowledge for Software Quality Measurement. IEEE Computer, 35(2) (2002) 77-83
31. Schneidewind, N. Methodology For Validating Software Metrics. IEEE Transactions of Software Engineering, 18(5) (1992) 410-422
32. Sugeno, M. An Introductory Survey of Fuzzy Control. Information Sciences, 36 (1985) 59-83
33. Wohlin C., Runeson P., Höst M., Ohlson M., Regnell B. and Wesslén A. Experimentation in Software Engineering: An Introduction, Kluwer Academic Publishers (2000)
34. Yacoub, S., Ammar, H., Robinson, T.. Dynamic Metrics for Object Oriented Designs Sixth IEEE International Symposium on Software Metrics (1998)
35. Zadeh, L. Fuzzy sets. Information and control, (1965), 338-353
36. Zadeh, L. The Concept of Linguistic Variable and its Applications to Approximate Reasoning Part I. Information Sciences, 8 (1973) 199-249
37. Zuse, H. A Framework of Software Measurement. Berlin, Walter de Gruyter (1998)

Domain-Specific Runtime Variability in Product Line Architectures

Michael Goedicke, Klaus Pohl, and Uwe Zdun

Institute for Computer Science, University of Essen, Germany
{goedicke,pohl,uzdun}@cs.uni-essen.de

Abstract. A software product line primarily structures the software architecture around the commonalities of a set of products within a specific organization. Commonalities can be implemented in prefabricated components, and product differences are typically treated by well-defined variation points that are actualized later on. Dynamic, domain-specific aspects, such as ad hoc customization by domian experts, are hard to model with static extension techniques. In this paper, we will discuss open issues for dynamic and domain-specific customizations of product line architectures. We will also present an indirection architecture based on Component Wrapper objects and message redirection for dynamically composing and customizing generic components for the use in concrete products. As a case study, we will discuss two designs from a Multimedia Home Platform product line: end-user personalization across different new media platforms and customization of interactive applications by content editors.

1 Introduction

Software product lines or system families structure a set of products of a specific organization into a product line architecture that contains a set of more or less generic components. Each individual product architecture is derived from the product line architecture. Each product uses a set of generic components and introduces product-specific code as well. Generic components provide well-defined interfaces. In the products-specific code those generic components are configured for the use in the product's architecture.

The typical process of adopting and/or using the product line approach concentrates on reducing structural complexity by finding and extracting commonalities. The system is primarily built from a common set of assets [1]. Often these common assets are desinged as black-box components. In the industrial practice such building blocks may have a substantially different form than in an ideal academic view [2]. Industrial components are usually very large and have a complex internal structure with no enforced encapsulation boundaries. Often there is no explicit difference between interface entities and non-interface entities.

In software product line approaches, component configuration is usually handled by well-defined variation points, implemented with appropriate variability

Z. Bellahsène, D. Patel, and C. Rolland (Eds.): OOIS 2002, LNCS 2425, pp. 384–396, 2002.

mechanisms. Common (traditional) variability mechanisms are parameterization, specialization, or replacement of entities in the reusable component. The designer decides for variability mechanisms and architectural styles. Once a design and implementation is based on a certain variability mechanism, in traditional approaches, it is often quite hard to exchange them with other mechanisms.

One of the main contributions of the product-line approach is its focus on domain-specific architectures. A product-line should provide a systematic derivation of a tailored approach suited to an organization's capabilities and objectives [4]. Therefore, the approach pays special attention to the traceability between architectural decisions and functional and non-functional requirements. However, many domains impose requirements for domain-specific customizations that can hardly be implemented with variation points that are bound before runtime. In this paper, we will concentrate on techniques that can be applied to introduce domain-specific ad hoc customizability, e.g. for domain experts. To reach that goal in a large product-line, it is important for domain experts to be able to understand a product's variabilities without requiring to learn about other parts of the architecture.

We have studied these issues theoretically and practically in three larger industry projects: TPMHP (focusing on a generic product line architecture for development of digital business television applications on top of the MHP (Multimedia Home Platform) [5]), ESAPS and CAFÉ [6,11] (aiming at engineering software architectures, processes, and platforms for system-families), and a document archive system [10]. In these projects, late-bound flexibility is not only a useful feature, but a requirement for using a product line approach at all. For instance, domains like web engineering are characterized by constant *domain changes*. For rapid incorporation of these changes it is impractical to hand-code the changes in long development and deployment cycles. In some product lines customer-specific *customization requirements* are foreseeable, and then rapid customizability, ideally even by non-programmers, is required. Sometimes variations are dependent on the *runtime context*, and thus, such product lines require runtime variability. Many *24×7 server applications*, such as custom web servers and application servers, usually cannot simply be stopped for deploying new components. Thus in such domains a dynamic component exchange mechanism is required.

In this paper, at first, we will outline open issues in designing variation points in Section 2 that are a prerequisite to practically implement domain-specific variation points. For resolving these open issues, we will present an object-oriented runtime indirection architecture for encapsulating variation points in Section 3. For implementing the architecture we require runtime variability mechanisms, and different runtime variability mechanisms have different consequences. As a case study, in Section 4, we will introduce practical runtime customization requirements from the TPMHP project, and discuss solutions based on the architecture presented beforehand.

2 Open Issues in Designing Variation Points

In this section we will discuss a set of open issues during design of runtime variation points for domain-specific concerns in product line architectures. Variation points are implemented using a variability mechanism. Typical traditional examples for variability mechanisms are association of an object in Decorator style [7], delegating to a Strategy [7], using inheritance for specialization, exchanging a runtime entity (such as an object), parameterization, and preprocessor directives. Obviously all these variability mechanisms have quite different properties. For instance, the binding time differs: some mechanisms have to be bound at design time, some at compile time, some at startup of the program, some at runtime. In general, the later we bind a variation point, the more flexible the solution is. However, we have to deal with certain drawbacks as well, for instance, by binding at runtime, the performance, memory consumption, and runtime complexity may be influenced negatively.

When we build complex design dependencies or architectural artifacts, such as variation points, on top of traditional variability mechanisms we face a set of potential problems if domain-specific customizations have to be rapidly incorporated (some of these issues are also identified in [3]):

- *First-class representation:* An architectural artifact does not have a first-class representation in design and programming languages. Thus the recurring use of the artifact has to be built with certain syntactic conventions. The resulting designs and programs are harder to read. Moreover, the constructs used to implement the architectural artifact cannot be easily reused. For a domain expert, who is not a technical expert for the product line design and implementation, this means the design and implementation are impenetrable because her/his task-specific idioms do not map well to the design and programming language elements.
- *Traceability:* Without a first-class representation in the program code or design, the architectural artifact is not recognizable ad hoc as an entity. Therefore, the artifact as a whole is hard to trace; that is, (complex) variation points are hard to locate for a client of the component. At runtime, traceability can be provided using reflection or introspection mechanisms. Without such functionality, it is hard to extend a given product without intimate knowledge of the product line architecture's internals. A domain expert usually does not have an intimate knowledge of the internal implementation; thus, the system can only be customized by qualified programmers.
- *Implicit dependencies:* Dependencies between architectural elements and features are often only implicit. As a result it is not clear what parts of the product line architecture are needed for a specific product. For a domain expert that means that all dependent components have to be understood to understand a given component.
- *Scattering variation points:* Variability at the requirements level often does not map nicely onto programming language code. Thus, in naive implementations, features are simply scattered across system parts, and multiple features

are tangled within system part. Scattered variation points heavily reduce understandability of the design and code, especially for non-technical people.

If the issues discussed above are not resolved, it may become hard to use, extended, and customize products that require rapid changeability. For each customization a larger, non-trivial programming effort is required. Often, initially found abstractions for variation points do not match the reality or the implementation well. Thus it is important that we are able to rapidly exchange variation point implementations and variability mechanisms during software maintenance.

3 Encapsulating Variation Points

In this section, we will present an architecture for indirecting component interactions, so that we can encapsulate variation points. Then we will discuss some choices for runtime variability mechanisms in the indirection architecture as well as its consequences.

3.1 Indirecting Component Interactions with Component Wrapper Objects

In this section we discuss an indirection architecture that enables us to treat different variability fields in a product line separately, but yet let the product line offer an integrating extension architecture. In general, we propose that each component is divided into three parts: a component implementation, an explicit export interface, and an explicit import interface. Export and import relationships are first-class entities of the programming (and design) language. For instance, export and import can be modeled as first-class objects, but they can also be modeled with runtime constructs specifically designed for component wrapping and interface adaptation, such as interception techniques for component composition [8]. Usually we provide explicit relationship introspection options for these export and import entities, so that we can trace at runtime which components are connected to which other components. Thus, we can trace the architectural construction of a product at runtime.

Note that there is only a single design and implementation step necessary to transform a given (industrial) component into a component fulfilling these conventions. That means, the industrial reality of large-scale components with no enforced boundaries [2] is not ignored. Moreover, the former interfaces do not have to be changed; that is, backwards compatibility can be ensured. Both issues are crucial to acceptance of the proposed architecture in industrial practice.

In Figure 1 we can see that the generic component parts, implementing the component's tasks, do not directly access the used components but use a central Message Redirector [9]. The Message Redirector is usually not implemented for each component but derived from the product line's extension architecture. It is used as a simple indirection mechanism: no external component is accessed directly but only with the redirector. A symbolic call is mapped to the correct

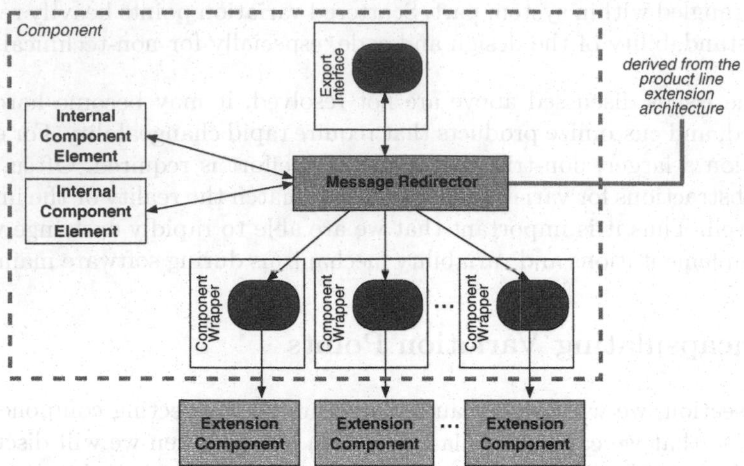

Fig. 1. Variant encapsulation in a component-oriented indirection architecture (illustrated for an individual component)

interface in the Component Wrapper object [14] that defines the expected import from a component. The used component, in turn, provides the same structure. Thus it provides an explicit export interface as well. This provided interface is configured in the Component Wrapper to fulfill the expected interface. Thus, we can deal with slight interface changes and other necessary adaptations on the Component Wrapper. Concerns cross-cutting multiple components can be handled by the Message Redirector.

There are different ways to implement the architecture for component-oriented runtime variability sketched above. For different products and product lines different variability mechanisms are useful. To implement the architecture we require runtime variability mechanisms, and in most cases more than one variability mechanism is used, including traditional mechanisms such as inheritance and parameterization.

In contrast to solely using traditional variability mechanisms, in an architecture, as described above, it is quite easy to exchange the used variability mechanisms or adapt their inherent properties to new requirements. This is mainly due to the central Message Redirector that allows for adaptations of the extension process of one or more components. This way the variability mechanism hidden by a symbolic Message Redirector call can be adapted without interfering with the component's internals.

As we can see, there are no impositions on how the component is implemented internally or which variability mechanisms are used. As a requirement, each component has to implement one or more component export interfaces as Facades to the component, and one or more component import interfaces as Component Wrappers to wrap the used components. Each arrow in Figure 1 indicates an explicit component connection that is traceable and dynamic at runtime.

Component connections are handled via the Message Redirector; therefore, they expose runtime variability. The Message Redirector is an abstraction for the process of component composition; thus, variations in this process can be applied here. The extensional components, included in the component import, can be derived from the product line architecture or they can be part of the specific product. An interesting aspect is that product-line specific implementations of variability mechanisms are usually integrated as components as well.

3.2 Runtime Variability Techniques

Using the product line extension architecture presented, we can individually make the choice for a runtime variability mechanism for each element in the product line. We are able to use the most appropriate technique for introducing variability in each individual part of the product line. If necessary, it is also possible to change the choice in a component-oriented fashion during product or product line evolution. There are different techniques that we use for introducing runtime variability in our product lines, with different benefits and liabilities. There are different runtime variability approaches that operate at different abstraction levels and have different properties. In different customization situations, different domain expert participation requirements have to be mapped to these properties to find the best alternative. A few examples are:

- The most simple technique is to simply *design and program the variation point by hand* using traditional variability mechanisms. However, this strategy can lead to significant problems, including higher complexity, more maintenance efforts, etc.
- *Scripting* languages, such as Tcl, XOTcl, Python, or Perl, are widely used and accepted in industry for configuration, customization, test automation, and component glueing. In many projects scripting languages are used as languages for domain-specific customization. The scripting language commands can be used as symbolic indirections in the Message Redirector. However, if system languages are used as well, two or more languages have to learned by developers and the language models have to be integrated.
- Our *pattern language for flexible component architectures* [14] can be used for implementing the indirection architecture, sketched in Section 3.1. A benefit of the pattern approach is that the required expertise is rather low: a design with patterns can rather easily be understood by non-technical stakeholders. Thus patterns are a good means to convey and discuss design decisions in early phases without (a) having to specify the concrete variability mechanism used for implementation and (b) being too vague in the technical realm. As a drawback, the patterns have to be implemented before they can be used. This may be too large an effort for very small projects. For larger product lines often this is not problematic. Here, the patterns are used as a conceptual guidance for designing variation points by hand.
- Using *markup languages for customization* is a simple technique for implementing limited dynamic customizations of applications, as discussed in [13].

A markup languages such as XML is used to describe the customizable elements of an application, and application parts are dynamically generated from these XML files. XML tags are used as symbols in the Message Redirector, and the information architecture follows the hierarchical structure of the XML texts in form of a Composite pattern implementation. This technique, is simple and reliable, but of course, it has its limitations as it is only a powerful form of parameterization.

3.3 Consequences of Runtime Variability in the Indirection Architecture

In this section we discuss the contribution of the architecture to resolve the open issues in designing variation points, identified in Section 2, as benefits and potential liabilities of the architecture. There are the following benefits:

- In conventional implementations of our indirection architecture, for each architectural fragment there is a conceptual entity in design and implementation that is also an entity in the Message Redirector. As the target language itself is not extended, a *first-class representations* is only partially archived. Some languages, as for instance Tcl, XOTcl, Smalltalk, and Lisp, do allow for language extension with components so that these components are actually *first-class representations* of architectural fragments in the language. Nonetheless, in all approaches domain-specific indirections can be provided to represent the idioms and structures of the domain.
- On the Message Redirector we provide a symbolic identifier for each component and for all imported and exported functionality. If we provide introspection options as well, we can ensure runtime *traceability* of architectural fragments in the product line.
- Avoiding *implicit dependencies* is a primary goal of the architecture. The components do not directly refer to each other but use the central Message Redirector. Features are usually encapsulated in architectural fragments. Therefore, dependencies among fragments and to the design-/requirements-level can be made explicit at runtime.
- Since variation points are encapsulated and only accessed through the Message Redirector, *scattering variation points* across the code can be avoided. However, in conventional implementations this is only a convention, and developers are able to violate the convention, when they use direct component accesses that bypass the Message Redirector.

As our indirection architecture relies on runtime variability, we also have to consider the following potential liabilities:

- *Runtime resources:* Performance, memory, and other runtime resources, may be negatively influenced by mechanisms such as reflection, dynamic linking, dynamic invocation, and interpretation.

- *Runtime complexity:* Additional runtime structures do also add more complexity to the runtime environment; thus, understandability and maintainability may be negatively affected. Moreover, if the variation points are hard to trace, it is hard to understand the (complex) interfaces of the product line.
- *Variation point management:* Adding and binding variants at a late moment in time implies extra work for managing, implementing, and documenting variation points.
- *Predictability:* A large amount of variability may make it virtually impossible to test all combinations during development. Mechanisms may be needed that allow testing at a late moment in time and that ensure the consistency of the products. Thus a certain amount of discipline among developers is required to create an extensive regression test suite.
- *Adjusting to product specifics:* The idea of one explicit interface used for multiple implementations implies the problem that products are reduced to their common denominator. In extreme cases, when a workaround is virtually impossible, it may be necessary to re-implement parts of the common product line implementation in concrete products. Usually, adaptations and extensions on the export and import interface objects let us avoid such problems.

A product line designer has to care for these issues in a very early stage of development. Often it cannot even be predicted which concrete requirements a product has, say, because they are not yet known or the impact of a change can only be found out by runtime testing. Usually the issues named above are highly context-specific and domain-specific, thus they can only be adjusted per product line, or sometimes only per product. The techniques, discussed in Section 3.2, entail the consequences named above to a different degree. Therefore, in each architectural fragment of the product line we should use the most appropriate approach for implementing runtime variability.

4 Domain-Specific Customization in an MHP Product Line

In this section we will discuss the problem of domain-specific customization in the context of the EU project "Technological Perspectives of the Multimedia Home Platform (TPMHP)" aiming at a product line architecture for the Multimedia Home Platform (MHP) [5]. The MHP specification is a generic set of APIs for a client-side software layer for digital content broadcast applications, interaction via a return channel, and internet access on an MHP terminal, such as digital set-top boxes, integrated digital TV sets, and multimedia PCs. The MHP standard defines a client-side technical specification for MHP terminal implementations, including the platform architecture, an embedded Java virtual machine implementation running DVB-J applications, broadcast channel protocols, interaction channel protocols, content formats, application management, security aspects, a graphics model, and a GUI framework.

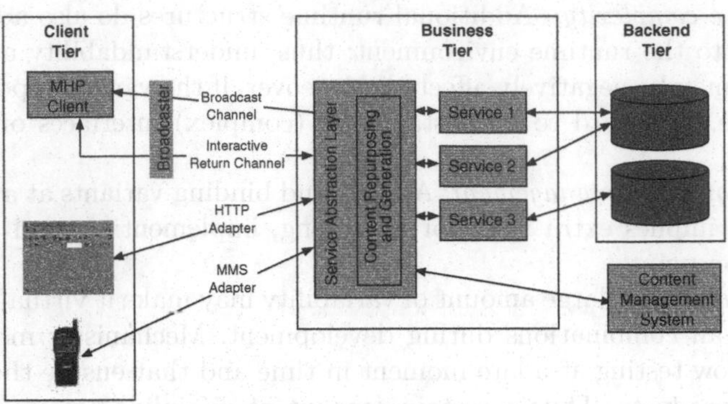

Fig. 2. Service abstraction for MHP terminals, mobiles, and web browsers

In the project, we considered the situation of a large German warehousing company with multiple different stores as a content provider for the MHP. Different new media shop types, including web shops, MHP-based interactive television shops, and m-commerce shops (e.g. based on MMS) should be supported. The basic architecture is a Service Abstraction Layer [12], as depicted in Figure 2. Each of the customizable shopping applications is realized by one or more services. In this context we face multiple different requirements for runtime variability:

- *User Personalization:* On client-side, users can personalize their user experience. Customization happens on client-side with a simple (e.g. form-based or grapical) interface. The personalization information are stored on the server. The server generates personalized pages for different content formats, such as DVB-J Java classes, HTML pages, MMS pages, etc.
- *Shop Branding:* For the customer relationship it is important that each individual store has its own unique brand identity, including logos, layouts, banners, colors, etc. Such properties should to be visible for each of the platforms supported. Shop branding is handled by content editors, and it requires rather complex behavior that is not solely expressible by providing a CSS-like style sheet a priori. The customer should not experience the common product line realization during shopping, but should have the impression that each shop has an individual appearance. Thus, shop branding requires writing custom code for layout of the shop sites.
- *Customizing Interactive Applications:* Interactive applications are customized by domain experts and content providers. That is, simple interfaces for customization by these non-programmers are required. Other representations of user interaction such as web forms or applets are also generated from these information.

In the indirection architecture presented, each individual variability requirement can be implemented in a separate component. The locality gained by abstracting details of other components also reduces the knowledge that a domain expert has to have to perform a customization step. In the remainder of this section, we will present two examples of customizing MHP-based applications: first, we present an integration architecture for tracking client-side consumer customizations on server-side, and, secondly, we will discuss behavioral customization by domain experts.

4.1 Personalization on Client- and Server-Side

As usual in web portals, consumers have to be able to personalize their shopping environment. Usually, form-based pages or tools are provided for this task. However, as different platforms are supported, personalizations on the settop-box should also appear on the other platforms, such as the web and mobile devices, and vice versa.

As a solution for the MHP client, the personalization page implementation sends commands to a lightweight client-side Message Redirector (written in Java). The Message Redirector indirects the consumer's customization commands to DVB-J Java implementations for the MHP platform. Moreover, if required, it sends them with the interaction channel to the server as well. Another Message Redirector on server-side understands the same symbolic instruction set (and also other instructions) but maps the instructions to different components implementing server-side building, publishing, and caching of pages for the platforms on which personalization is handled on server side such as the web. This way, the same client-side customization do also appear on other platforms such as web browsers.

For integrated client-side and server-side customizations the following steps are performed, if the consumer performs a customization on the MHP client:

1. The consumer uses a form-based customization page or tool to customize or personalize the application logic. The tool creates little scripts entirely composed out of commands that can be understood by the client-side Message Redirector.
2. The client-side Message Redirector maps the customization commands to Java implementations and applies the customizations directly on the MHP client platform. The personalization components are used by different shop products, and so cross-cutting personalizations are applied to all shops. As the personalization component only exhibits the abstract shop product interface, consumers are not confronted with complex product and component interdependencies.
3. The personalization script is send to the server via the return channel.
4. The next server-side request, say, by a web browser, causes cached customized pages to be invalidated and recalculated with the new customization script. As the server-side Message Redirector understands a super-set of the client-side Message Redirector, it can map all provided commands to implementations for HTML content creation. Note that these implementation do not have to be DVB Java classes, but can be implemented in any programming language.
5. The same customization is visible on all supported platforms.

In this example we have seen that the Message Redirector's personalization commands abstract the different components and products. The commands only have to conform to the interfaces offered by the Message Redirector. Different products running on one platform (as for instance different shops) and also components for other platforms can be customized in an integrated way. Qualified programmers are only necessary to define the "personalization language," and implement it for each product and each platform.

4.2 Shop Branding by Content Editors

Different shops of the warehousing company should have an unique appearance, but should share the same information architecture. Content editors should be able to perform simple interactive behavior customizations such as shop branding across different platforms and channels. Here, we use XML based customization files for shop branding and simple domain-specific customizations on top of the indirection architecture. For each page there are one or more associated classes, called page templates [13]. A page template is a class defining the customization of a page with program behavior, but the class is largely constructed from an XML file stored in the content cache. The XML file contains the customizations. As program code is dynamically generated, we can specify behavioral extensions in the XML file. Each XML tags maps to an instruction in the Message Redirector. Only for new customization styles programming efforts are required: all other customizations can be done in the XML file. For extending the application with a new customization, we simply have to register a new command with the Messages Redirector.

In Figure 3 this architecture is visualized for one product that is able to display and handle different interactive warehousing pages for different platforms. Here, separated concerns for domain-specific customization, such as shop layout in the figure's example, are implemented independently of the warehousing product, but yet incorporated in the product-line architecture. Domain experts and content editors can simply edit the XML files, then new shop layout classes are generated, and the Message Redirector switches dynamically to these new implementations. The product's business logic is not affected by the changes at all. Similarly, other aspects such as format styles, channel specifics, etc. can also be implemented.

5 Conclusion

In this paper we have discussed a set of open issues in designing variation points that we have identified in three larger product line architecture projects. An object-oriented indirection architecture was presented with the aim to reduce the dependency of concrete product implementations and domain-specific variability requirements. This way we can treat domain-specific customizations of products separately from the product-line implementation. We can choose the appropriate variability mechanism for each functionality and encapsulate variation points.

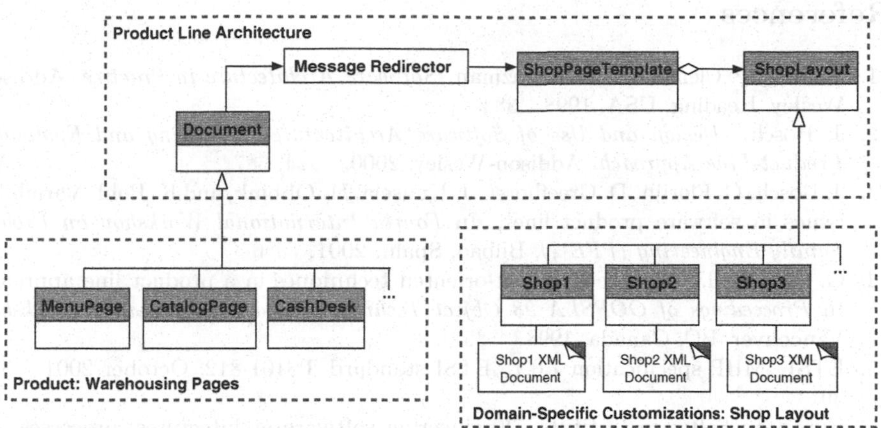

Fig. 3. Customizing shop layout with XML files independently from the generic product implementation

As a consequence, we are able to cope with the identified open issues, such as traceability, avoiding implicit dependencies, and scattering variation points.

These issues are especially important for introducing domain-specific customizability, e.g. for domain experts. Customizations should be possible without an intimate knowledge of the whole product-line. The domain experts should only see the task-specific elements of the product and the interfaces of used components. The symbolic calls in the Message Redirector enable us to define a "little" customization language that hides issues that are not relevant for a task-specific view. The indirection architecture presented requires runtime variability resources. In many cases it is beneficial that we can bind every variation point at runtime, but there are also some problematic consequences, such as a negative influence on runtime efficiency and memory consumption. Moreover, for different stakeholders different techniques are appropriate to enable customizations. Therefore, we have to choose the right variability mechanism for each design situation.

Acknowledgements

The work described in this paper has partially be founded by the "Technological Perspectives of the Multimedia Home Platform (TPMHP)" EU project, an industry cooperation with the company BetaBusiness TV, and the BMBF, Project CAFÉ, "From Concept to Application in System Family Engineering"; Förderkennzeichen 01 IS 002 C; Eureka $\sum$! 2023 Programme, ITEA Projekt ip00004.

References

1. L. Bass, P. Clement, and R. Kazman. *Software Architecture in Practice.* Addison-Wesley, Reading, USA, 1998. 384
2. J. Bosch. *Design and Use of Software Architectures: Adopting and Evolving a Product-Line Approach.* Addison-Wesley, 2000. 384, 387
3. J. Bosch, G. Florijn, D. Greefhorst, J. Kuusela, H. Obbink, and K. Pohl. Variability issues in software product lines. In *Fourth International Workshop on Product Family Engineering (PFE-4)*, Bilbao, Spain, 2001. 386
4. G. Campbell. The role of object-oriented techniques in a product line approach. In *Proceedings of OOPSLA 98 Object Technology and Product Lines Workshop*, Vancouver, BC, Canada, 1998. 385
5. ETSI. MHP specification 1.0.1. ETSI standard TS101-812, October 2001. 385, 391
6. European Software Institute. Engineering software architectures, processes and platforms for system-families. www.esi.es/esaps, 2001. 385
7. E. Gamma, R. Helm, R. Johnson, and J. Vlissides. *Design Patterns: Elements of Reusable Object-Oriented Software.* Addison-Wesley, 1994. 386
8. M. Goedicke, G. Neumann, and U. Zdun. Design and implementation constructs for the development of flexible, component-oriented software architectures. In *Proceedings of 2nd International Symposium on Generative and Component-Based Software Engineering (GCSE'00)*, Erfurt, Germany, Oct 2000. 387
9. M. Goedicke, G. Neumann, and U. Zdun. Message redirector. In *Proceedings of EuroPlop 2001*, Irsee, Germany, July 2001. 387
10. M. Goedicke and U. Zdun. Piecemeal legacy migrating with an architectural pattern language: A case study. *Journal of Software Maintenance and Evolution: Research and Practice*, 14(1):1–30, 2002. 385
11. K. Pohl, M. Brandenburg, and A. Gülich. Scenario-based change integration in product family development. In *2nd ICSE Workshop on Software Product Lines: Economics, Arch-tecture and Implications*, Toronto, Canada, May 2001. 385
12. O. Vogel. Service abstraction layer. In *Proceeding of EuroPlop 2001*, Irsee, Germany, July 2001. 392
13. U. Zdun. Dynamically generating web application fragments from page templates. In *Proceedings of Symposium of Applied Computing (SAC 2002)*, Madrid, Spain, March 2002. 389, 394
14. U. Zdun. *Language Support for Dynamic and Evolving Software Architectures.* PhD thesis, University of Essen, Germany, January 2002. 388, 389

Methodological Approach to Software Quality Assurance through High-Level Object-Oriented Metrics

José Romero, Oscar Pastor, and Jorge Belenguer

DSIC, Valencia University of Technology, Camino de vera s/n , Valencia, Spain
{jromero,opastor}@dsic.upv.es

Abstract. Traditionally, quality software development has been based on the study of lines of implemented code. Software is usually evaluated by means of metrics coming from programming languages.
On the one hand, regarding the great importance of the early stages of development, metrics must be defined from higher level of abstraction. Consequently, high-level metrics to be defined and validated in this work, come from specification languages.
On the other hand, the concept of quality has subjective aspects leading to numerous proposals for its assurance. Typically, thcy can bc classified in process-centric and product-centric methods. This classification establishes a gap among existing methods. This paper is an attempt to bridge this gap by means of unifying part of the most relevant work about the quality issue, under one umbrella framework. This framework is a methodological approach to software quality assurance based on an object-oriented conceptual modeling method including automatic code generation. It also combines a formal specification language with standard notation.
Due to the particular concepts included in our method, the core of this work is to define and validate a specific set of high-level metrics. They assess the quality of an Information System from the Conceptual Model designed with this method.
The originality of the paper is the way that high-level metrics are obtained. Using practical experiences modeling real systems, the Quality Hypotheses are established. Metrics involved in them are chosen as candidates to be incorporated in the set which is being defined. The final step is to describe the strategy for their formal and empirical validation.
Summing up our methodological approach, software quality assurance consists of: modeling a problem, evaluating the set of metrics, and automatically generating the code of the final software application for a target environment.
In future works, the generalization of these ideas to other object-oriented methods will be studied.

Z. Bellahsène, D. Patel, and C. Rolland (Eds.): OOIS 2002, LNCS 2425, pp. 397-408, 2002.

1 Introduction

Nowadays, there are multiple approaches concerning the software quality assurance issue. On the one hand, the academic point of view, is more centered in obtaining a valid set of metrics about program code[1]. On the other hand, the industry point of view, more centered in the research of excellence in business processes of software development[9].

These different visions of software quality assurance come from the discussion of the essence of the concept "software quality". Traditionally, there has been two dual points of view when talking about this concept:

- the quality regarding the developed products
- the quality regarding the process of software development

Talking in general, the academic branch of research has put more emphasis than industry on adapting software quality metrics to be compliant with the new paradigms of software development such as the object-oriented paradigm. Therefore, the type of metrics to be applied to measure a program has changed; for instance, from function points to object-oriented metrics. Simultaneously, the empirical and formal validation of the obtained metrics is also a must in a quality framework.

The industrial branch of research is strongly focused on standardization. The goal to achieve seems to be the merge of the two main existing proposals about process quality: the ISO9000[5] and the CMM[9] ones. The SPICE[4] project has held a status of a standardization proposal generating the ISO/IEC 15504[5] after several years of studies, reviews and refinements.

Alternatively, there are also intermediate positions, combining academic with industrial points of view, such as the one of the Unified Software Development Process-USDP-[6]. It defines a process of software development during which, who and how get things done is always controlled. USDP is based on the standard notation UML[2] and can guide the software development process from analysis to implementation.

In our opinion, all the mentioned proposals share a common problem underneath; there is still a gap to bridge between the process-centric and the product-centric points of view. Implicitly, they focus on one aspect but they forget the other one.

In this paper, a global framework is defined based on a methodological approach. It is close to the USDP ideas, but the originality is the use of a specific method called the OO-Method[8]. This method is an object-oriented development method that combines formal aspects with standard notation, and incorporates automatic application generation.

OO-Method provides the required formalisms in a transparent way in order to make robust our proposed quality framework. In addition, this framework integrates treatment of process excellence achievement coming from the ISO/IEC 15504 theories. In this way, the meeting point between the academia and the industry is efficiently found. Software companies can benefit of applying the two different classic points of views in software quality at the same level. This framework can be customized for any kind of architectures without losing of generality to our framework; for instance, web solution development.

This paper is structured beginning with a definition of the quality framework, and enumerating the different types of quality provided by our methodological approach. Thereafter, the idea of Quality Hypothesis is presented as a way to justify the need of defining high-level object-oriented metrics. Finally, both the formal and empirical validation of the set of metrics are described. The final goal is the reader to have a global vision of the framework used to develop quality solutions based on a methodological point of view.

2 Methodological Framework for Quality Assurance

From the very beginning of our research there has always been the goal of generating quality software. Following the previously commented classification of process and product, the research leads to broaden the gap between two. Our approach is to narrow that gap by means of studying software quality based on conceptual modeling techniques and methods. A detailed description of our methodological proposal, the OO-Method, can be reviewed at [8], but here we introduce the main idea of the method in order to describe later how it interacts with the quality framework.

OO-Method consists of two essential parts:

- **The Conceptual Model**: gathers the information about the problem to solve using a standard modeling language (UML), and stores it into a high level repository. This repository is structured based on a formal object-oriented specification language called OASIS[7] which uses a well defined semantic. The use of the repository produces a decoupling between what problem to solve is and how to solve it. In addition, the repository is a key element which allows to check certain properties about the quality of the problem specification.
- **The Execution Model**: retrieves the stored information from the repository and generates the code that implements the previously specified problem. This is achieved by translating conceptual patterns identified in the Conceptual Model and building software components for a particular design and implementation language. Due to the independence with the Conceptual Model introduced by the repository, several solutions can be generated from the same specified problem for different programming environments (including either imperative or declarative ones).

Our work is centered on imperative environments because of their spread influence in industrial environments. Consequently, the repository is implemented over a Relational Database Management System. It must be also mentioned that the OO-Method is currently supported by a CASE tool[10]. This method constitutes the core of the proposed quality framework. Therefore, software quality will be greatly influenced by the developed technology.

Additionally, coming from the application of this technology to an industrial context, two new factors emerge regarding software development quality: the organizational issues and the people who are entitled to implement the software project. As a result of combining all these factors, the quality framework handles both academic and industrial aspects; resulting in a quality triangle composed of: technology, organization (a company) and people. So, the quality framework has three main types of quality: technological, organizational and personal.

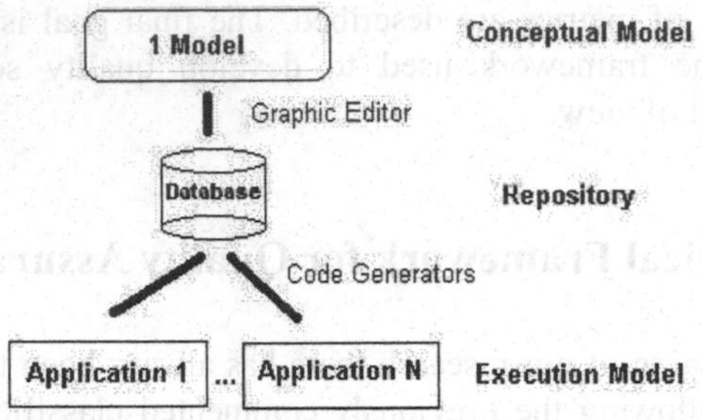

Fig. 1. The OO-Method phases

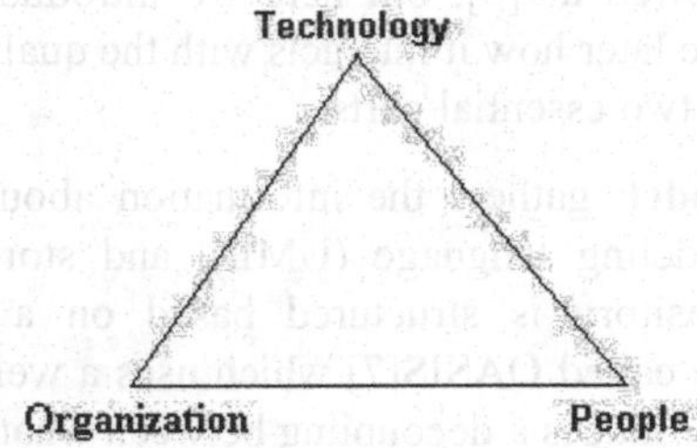

Fig. 2. Quality factors

- **Technological Quality**: is the one inherent to the method used (OO-Method) and it is derived from their models. This technological quality can be divided even more into four types of quality coming from the matching of the OO-Method phases and the classic treatment of quality (process versus product quality).
- **Modeling Language Quality**: evaluating Conceptual Model and process quality.
- **Modeled System Quality**: evaluating Conceptual Model and product quality.
- **Code Generation Quality**: evaluating Execution Model and process quality.
- **Generated Application Quality**: evaluating Execution Model and product quality.
- **Organizational Quality**: is the one linked to the definition of the necessary processes in the company for producing software in an efficient way. For instance: planning, documentation and control of existing processes, and management configuration changes control. It is crucial the search for excellence in organizational processes if we want to cope with optimal response time in software development even in stress situations. When a stressful situation appears in a company having bad quality processes, solutions are developed based on craftsmanship of developers, leading to take ad-hoc, and usually incorrect, decisions.

- **Personal Quality**: is the one centered on relationships between the company and the persons involved in a project. It can determine even the success or failure of a software project. For example, training, time management and resources (hardware and software) must be controlled and combined with the expectations of the progress of a personal career inside the company. It is crucial to define roles and tasks to be performed by every person involved in a software project.

Technological Quality	Conceptual Model	Execution Model
Process View	*Modeling Language Quality*	*Generation Quality*
Product View	*Modeled System Quality*	*Final Application Quality*

Fig. 3. Types of Technological Quality

Once described the types of quality, and in order to assist software quality assurance in industrial environments, the quality framework includes the implementation of the idea of a library (documental database). This library is a repository of all the information generated when developing software projects (from analysis to implementation). It is intended to be a refinement and superset of the OO-Method repository. The information introduced in the library is structured matching with the three types of quality introduced before: technological (for instance, conceptual models or generated components), organizational (for example, documentation of business processes), and personal (for example, skills and training of the persons developing a software project).

The union of this library and the corresponding tools, required to retrieve stored information and reuse it, is called The Quality Library. When it is implemented in a web architecture, it becomes a portal to share information among the development teams independent from the location of the different nodes which a company can have.

This paper is focused on assuring technological quality (on its product perspective) through the definition of a set of metrics that allow the modeler to build a quality Conceptual Model. Therefore, these metrics assure the modeled system quality; that is directly connected to the generated application quality due to the automatic code generation process. Using the OO-Method, assuring the first one, implies a quality software product. It is possible because of its formal basis, and a well defined translation model from conceptual elements to software components.

Assuring the other types of quality is equally important in our methodological approach to software quality, but is out of the scope of this paper. So, the next point is to define the set of conceptual metrics for the OO-Method.

3 Defining the Set of High-Level Metrics

An obvious question arises when defining a new set of metrics: why not using existing ones? The answer is that we are working at the conceptual level and using a particular method that has its own elements for modeling a solution.

However, there is no intention to re-invent the wheel. The existing proposals of metrics definition (including those ones at implementation level) are considered for defining the high-level OO-Method's metrics.

The strategy followed in the definition is to start from the experience of the projects that have been develop with the OO-Method; thanks to an agreement between the University of Technology of Valencia and a Spanish-based company called Computer Aided Requirements Engineering Technologies.

Consequently, the first step is deriving from the industrial experience of solving real cases. A series of Quality Hypotheses are stated to summarize the results based on comparing them with the existing attributes of quality and guides of modeling existing in the scientific literature.

The following step is to extract the metrics involved in the Quality Hypotheses to be considered the relevant ones for the OO-Method.

Finally, the metrics are to be validated from the theoretical and empirical points of view.

In order to facilitate the understanding of the high-level metrics and the Quality Hypotheses, the OO-Method's Conceptual Model is described briefly.

There are three fundamental models which allow a problem to be specified in terms of a **Conceptual Schema**:

- **The Object Model**: gathers the static structure of the problem by means of classes and relations among classes. The most important relationships are: inheritance ("is-a") relationships and aggregation ("part-of") relationships. There are other kinds of relationships that are also specified such as the synchronized event execution ("event sharing"). Classes can be visually organized using Clusters. Views selecting a subset of classes can also be specified. A class has the typical structural properties components of the object paradigm: attributes (constant, variable, derived from another ones) and methods (also named as events). Moreover, a class can specify: restrictions over the state of the object as a mean of declaring invariants, interfaces with respect to other classes, and even transactions that execute several events under an all-or-nothing policy.
- **The Dynamic Model**: captures the behavioral vision of the problem. In this model, life cycles of the objects are represented through the use of: state charts, activity rules called Triggers (event-condition-action rules), and transactions among objects from different classes named as Global Interactions.
- **The Functional Model**: represents the link between the structural and the behavioral visions. It consists on a set of well formed formulas that declare the change of state of an object when an event occurs. These formulas are called evaluations. They are categorized depending on the type of change of state that is produced in the object (increment of an attribute, reset of an attribute value, etc.).

Next, the twelve Quality Hypotheses are presented. They are structured in two groups. On the one hand, those ones related with the attributes of quality [5]. On the other hand, those related with the Guidelines of Modeling[11].

i) Quality Hypotheses based on the Guidelines of Modeling:

Hypothesis 1 (construction adequacy): When the ratio of use of an element is approximately zero, a problem of construction adequacy in the OO-Method can exist. The no use of a element can indicate that its semantics are not well defined in the Method, and consequently, modelers do not use it.

Hypothesis 2 (language adequacy): The ratio of validation errors divided into the number of classes is, can be used as a flexibility indicator of the method. The more modeling flexibility, the less adequacy of the modeling language, because of the more number of inconsistencies in the specified models. An example of flexibility is whether a formula is validated as entered or all the formulas are validated on-demand when the modeler thinks the model is finished.

Hypothesis 3 (systematic design): An absolute value of the number of validation errors greater than zero indicates a lack of systematic design in the system. The number of validation errors should always be zero.

Hypothesis 4 (comparability): Comparability between OO-Method models is determined by counting the elements (classes and relationships) used when constructing a Conceptual Schema. In order to compare an OO-Method model with a model constructed using other method, both semantics of the models has to be compared as a previous step. If they have different semantics, it is not possible perform the desired comparison. The number of elements of a model is not determinant, but it can be used as an indication of the more or less complexity of a Conceptual Schema.

Hypothesis 5 (clarity): A high rate of relationships per class has a negative impact on the clarity property of a model. Clarity is connected with complexity. Using a ratio of number of classes divided into the total of elements can also be used to evaluate the complexity of a model. A complex model tends to be less clear, and actions to handle visual complexity must be taken into account.

Hypothesis 6 (economic efficiency): The economic efficiency guideline can be determined based on the control of the software project plan. That is to say that the condition of accepting a certain degree of refinement on a model can be derived from the ratio of variation of the problem specifications. The more variability of the specifications (usually, because of incorporating new functionality not previously stated), less emphasis should be applied to the refinement of the modeled solution (at least, while the client is not capable of specify what the problem to solve is).

ii) Quality Hypotheses based on quality attributes from ISO9126:

Hypothesis 7 (functionality): The number of inconsistencies comparing requirements in the inception phase with the evaluation formulas of the OO-Method's Functional Model, determine the correct or incorrect functionality of the system. It is a problem to calculate this number of inconsistencies, if not including scenario descriptions (for instance, using UML use cases) in the OO-Method basis (and implementation). When including scenario descriptions, we can add the number of inconsistencies as a metric. The higher ratio of inconsistencies, the less degree of functionality accomplished by the implemented system.

Hypothesis 8 (reliability): The number of relational operators introduced in the formulas of transactions, is a factor with a direct influence on the reliability of a model developed using the OO-Method.

Hypothesis 9 (usability): The number of classes related with one particular class (this is also called "visible classes" from one class to another) can be used as an indicator of the usability of a model. The more class visibility, the less usability of a model because the classes are more coupled. Coupling among classes results on less flexibility to reuse parts of a model.

Hypothesis 10 (efficiency): The number of inserted or deleted classes in one development iteration can be useful to determine whether the solution is leading to the specified model in an efficient way. The less variation in the number of classes inserted or deleted, the more close to the final solution the modeler is. A high variation rate, usually indicates a bad requirement collecting phase.

Hypothesis 11 (maintainability): The maintainability of an application is a function of the complexity of a model. The more complexity (for instance, number of visible classes), the more effort to maintain the model when a change of requirements is produced.

Hypothesis 12 (portability): Portability of as model is determined by the number of elements not represented with the UML standard notation. A ratio can be established dividing the number of non-represented elements by the total number of elements in the standard. This ratio is the level of compliance with the standard. The goal is to achieve a value equal to zero.

Now, the candidate metrics to define the set of OO-Method's metrics are introduced:

- **Conceptual Schema Metrics**: Number of Clusters, number of Views, number of Shared Events, number of Global Interactions, use of Inheritance Ratio, number of State Transition Diagrams, total number of Triggers, number of schema validation errors, total number of Classes, number of relationships among classes, number of visible classes (those which are related directly or indirectly) from one class.
- **Object Model Metrics**: Number of attributes (constant, variable, derived), number of services -methods- components of a transaction, number of server classes -which offer services to the rest of classes-, number of active classes -which can invoke methods in objects-, number of agent relationships -possible invoked methods from a class-, number of classes that have modified its default interface, number of static constraints of a class, number of dynamic constraints of a class.

- **Dynamic Model Metrics**: Number of states in a class, number of transitions, maximum number of transitions per state, number of triggers per class, number of inherited state charts.
- **Functional Model Metrics**: Number of evaluations of a class, number of non-inherited evaluations, number of inherited evaluations, number of overridden evaluations.

Once established the high-level set of metrics, it is a must to validate them empirically and formally. The strategy to follow in order to perform this validation is described in the following point.

4 Validation Framework for High-Level Metrics

The validation of the metrics must be carried out from two points of views. On the one hand, the empirical validation of the metrics. On the other hand, the formal validation of them completes the process.

As it can be rather tedious to validate every metric included in the OO-Method's set of metrics, the global strategy of validation is described. However, that explanation is illustrated with examples to give the idea of how to validate the rest of them.

Empirical Validation

The empirical validation of the metrics is based in designing experiments for statistically testing the Quality Hypotheses; similar to the idea of [1] but with different objectives. This is the way to demonstrate that the involved metrics are relevant.

In order to perform the experiments some considerations must be taken:

- Establish a study case to be solved by different modelers.
- Select the persons involved in the experiment. They must be classified by their experience in analyzing information systems. This information can be obtained by means of questionnaires. The final goal is to randomly assign the most qualified modelers to different groups.
- Determine the deliverables after an iteration of modeling. That means the type of documentation to deliver: analyzed model and the values of its metrics.
- Test the deliverables to check that they really model the requirements of the problem to solve.

After experiments are performed, is time to statistically analyze the results to give them an interpretation. Statistical values of: mean, maximum, minimum, median and standard deviation are required. Then, a correlation analysis is carried out to prove that the metrics involved in the hypotheses are independent variables. Finally, a univariate logistic regression model is established to determine the probability of a incorrect requirement modeling.

For instance, in order to validate the reliability hypothesis (that establishes a relation between the use of relational operators in transaction formulas and the reliability of the system), the actions to be performed are the described next.

The user evaluates in a range from cero to ten the reliability of the automatic generated system. It is done contrasting the requirements and the resultant implementation. In doing so, both variables (reliability and number of relational operators) are in a continuous form. Now, the regression model can be established and an analysis of the relation between them can be derived from a residual analysis, and observing the regression of one variable on another or the statistical residual plot. The assessment determines whether the metrics can be used as useful predictors of a quality Conceptual Model.

It is also possible to study the effect of several metrics simultaneously. It can be obtained through a multivariate logistic regression model.

Theoretical Validation

In order to validate the OO-Method's metrics formally, the framework defined by Briand et al. is used[3]. This theoretical framework defines which mathematic properties characterize the concepts in software measurement. This framework can be applied to any software artifact. It is based on the concepts of size, length, complexity, cohesion and coupling.

In the case of its application to the OO-Method, the Schema represents the concept of the System described in this framework. A System S is represented as a pair <E,R> where E represents the set of elements of S, and R is a binary relation on E. So, relationships between elements of the system are represented as (R ⊆ExE).

A module (a class talking in OO-Method's concepts) is defined from a system. Given a system <E,R> , a system m=<E_m, R_m> is a module of S if and only if E_m ⊆ E, R_m ⊆ E_m x E_m and R_m ⊆ R.

Incoming or Intra-modules relationships (intra-class) are defined as

InputR(m) = { <e_1,e_2> in R | e_2 in E_m and e_1 in E-E_m}.

Outgoing or Inter-modules relationships (among classes) are defined as

OutputR(m)= {<e_1,e_2> in R | e_1 in E_m and e_2 in E-E_m}.

Measurement characterization is done on the basis of well defined properties. For example, for a length metric, the following properties will be checked: non-negativity, existence of null value, non-increasing monotonicity for connected components (NIM), non-decreasing monotonicity for non-connected components (NDM), and the disjoint modules property.

As a practical example of applying this framework, and in order to validate the number of agent relationships (NAR) of a class, the following rules must be accomplished:

- **Non-negativity**: The number of services (methods) that a class can invoke must be always equal or greater than zero. That is to say that the negativity of this metric results in a non-sense.
- **Null value**: If there are not agent relationships, then NAR = 0.
- **NIM**: If two related classes A, B are merged in one C then NAR(A) + NAR(B) = NAR(C).

- **NDM**: If two non-related classes A, B are merged in one C then NAR(A) + NAR(B) = NAR(C).
- **Disjoint modules**: If two classes A, B are merged in one C then the length of the system is maximum(NAR(C)) = maximum(NAR(A), NAR(B)).

In a similar way, the rest of the size metrics in the OO-Method set of metrics are validated (or not). For the rest of length, cohesion, and coupling metrics, the steps of the Briand framework are followed.

5 Conclusions

This paper has studied the way to achieve quality software by means of measuring the quality of conceptual models. This measurement is based on the definition of a set of high-level metrics and the use of an object-oriented method which includes automatic code generation (called the OO-Method).

The way to define the set of high-level metrics begins with the establishment of a series of Quality Hypotheses that come from the experience of using the method in real industrial contexts. The following step is to contrast them with the traditional metrics (focused on code evaluation) and derive a new set of metrics adapted to the conceptual elements supported in the OO-Method. In a final step, the formal and empirical validation process of the high-level metrics is overviewed.

The benefit of using this methodological approach is the simplicity of evaluating technological quality. The only thing to do is to compare the values of the metrics for a particular conceptual model with the thresholds determined by the experience of using the Quality Hypotheses.

In future works, the Quality Hypotheses must be refined to adjust these threshold based on the accumulative experience of solving real cases. Additionally, this strategy to cope with the problem of assuring software quality must be completed dealing with the other types of quality defined in this work. Finally, the idea of this quality framework will be generalized to be usable in the context of other object-oriented methods.

References

1. V.R. Basili, L.C. Brian, and W.L. Melo, A validation of object-oriented design metrics as quality indicators, IEEE Transactions on Software Engineering 22 (1996), no. 10.
2. G. Booch, I. Jacobson, and J. Rumbaugh, OMG Unified Modeling Language specification, June 1999, version 1.3.
3. L.C. Brian, S. Morasca, and V.R. Basili, Property-based software engineering measurement, IEEE Transactions on Software Engineering 22 (1996), no. 1.
4. The SPICE User Group, The software process improvement and capability determination project, October 2001, [online] from World Wide Web http://wwwsel.iit.nrc.ca.

5. ISO, International organization for standardization, online, October 2001, [online] from World Wide Web http://www.iso.ch/iso/en/ISOOnline.frontpage.
6. I. Jacobson, G. Booch, and J. Rumbaugh, The unified software development process, The Addison-Wesley Object Technology Series, Addison-Wesley Publishers Corporation, January 1999.
7. O. Pastor, F. Hayes, and S. Bear, Oasis:an oo specification language, CAiSE-92Conference, Lecture Notes in Computer Science, Vol. 1250, Springer, 1992, pp. 348–363.
8. O. Pastor, E. Insfran, V. Pelechano, J. Romcro, and J. Merseguer, OO-METHOD: An OO software production environment combining conventional and formal methods, Advanced Information Systems Engineering, 9th International Confer-ence CAiSE'97 (Barcelona, Catalonia, Spain), Antoni Olive, Joan Antoni Pastor (Eds.). Lecture Notes in Computer Science, Vol. 1250, Springer, June 1997, pp. 145–159.
9. M.C. Paulk, C.V. Weber, and B. Curtis, The capability maturity model: Guidelines for improving the software process, The SEI Series, Addison-Wesley Publishers Corporation, August 1999, Carnegie Mellon University. Software Engineering Institute.
10. J. Romero, J. Merseguer, J. Barber′ a, and O. Pastor, An automatic software generation tool, SW Engineering Workshop IDEAS'98, Universidade Federal do Rio Grande do Sul, Porto Alegre, Brazil, 1998.
11. R. Schuette and T. Rotthowe, The guidelines of modeling - an approach to enhance the quality in information models, International Conference on the Entity Relationship Approach (ER) (Singapore), 1998.

Sizing Use Cases: How to Create a Standard Metrical Approach

B. Henderson-Sellers, D. Zowghi, T. Klemola, and S. Parasuram

University of Technology, Sydney
P.O. Box 123 Broadway 2007 NSW Australia
{brian,didar}@it.uts.edu.au,
{tklemola,sparasuram}@yahoo.com

Abstract. Use-case modelling provides a means of specifying external features of a system during requirements elicitation. In principle, use cases can be used to size the system about to be built but, for that, a standard format for their documentation is required. Furthermore, gathering use-case metrics requires a software development process that produces complete use-case descriptions in a repeatable way. Here, we set out the requirements for such a standardization so that use cases can be metricated. Once accomplished, it is possible to evaluate the important research questions of whether use-case attributes such as size and complexity can be controlled and whether use-case metrics are sufficiently rigorous for estimating effort. Finally, we note that this added rigour applied to use cases should improve the consistency and quality of communication between client and developer, helping to ensure that the right system is built.

1 Introduction

The success of a software development project is measured by many factors. Among them are how close the final product meets the requirements of the client, how close the delivery date is to the scheduled date and how close the final cost is to original budget forecasts. Improving any of these project success attributes involves changing something about the existing software development process. Getting the correct user requirements is known to be challenging [1], yet improvements made in the early stages of a software development process can have significant benefits compared to changes in later stages of the process [2].

In this paper, we examine the use of use cases for requirements engineering and propose a framework for developing use-case metrics appropriate to the requirements phase of the software development life cycle. In order to undertake a quantitative comparison of use cases between projects, or possibly to use them as a basis for a future prognostic model for effort, it is necessary to ensure that use cases are constructed in such a way that they are consistent and to a standardized format both within the project and from project to project.

Z. Bellahsène, D. Patel, and C. Rolland (Eds.): OOIS 2002, LNCS 2425, pp. 409-421, 2002.

Use cases are an old technique manifested in many guises – most recently in Ivar Jacobson's work in OOSE [3]. What is today called use-case modelling was first used in telecommunications software development. As its power for describing large systems has become known, it has become a popular technique for specifying object-oriented systems in general, especially user interfaces [4]. It is widely used for describing systems and subsystems where user-initiated events drive the application. However, use cases possess no specifically object-oriented characteristics. Indeed, they can be used most effectively as a precursor to either an object-oriented analysis/design or, via direct decomposition, to a functionally-oriented design [5].

A use-case-driven approach facilitates communication between the requirements engineer and the system sponsors during requirements elicitation. The concept of a use case can be described very simply to system users and hence can reduce the well-known communication gap that exists between the problem solving and problem owning communities. To the extent that they explore the user interfaces directly, early feedback can be obtained from the users on this crucial and volatile aspect of system specification [6]. In addition to capturing the requirements, they are meant to be of value during the analysis and design activities and can play a significant role in the testing process. However, use cases cannot capture non-functional requirements and, although it has been argued that use cases in their present form cannot replace systems requirements specifications entirely [7], as Cockburn [8] puts it: "they really are requirements but they are not all of the requirements".

The task of defining measures for the size of use cases requires consideration of many issues. We commence this paper with a discussion of the UML standard for use cases followed, in Section 3, by a survey of popular practices in the construction of use cases to ensure that any chosen definition is both theoretically sound and also fits with common practice. This background then gives us the foundation for our proposals for appropriate metrics for use cases (Section 4) before concluding in Section 5.

2 Defining Use Cases

A use-case model describes an external view of the system. It consists of actors and their interactions with a software system, described in terms of use cases, which aim to capture the functional requirements. Jacobson [9] argues that system-level responsibilities and use cases are related, although such a formal linkage is *not* included in the current version of the UML [10].

Use-case modelling is a technique for eliciting, understanding and defining functional system requirements in a way that both developers and users can understand [11]. The "story" of how the system behaves from the user's perspective can be told with the use case and its associated scenarios. It can be used to reach an agreement between the people who order the system and people who develop the system. Jacobson [12] argues that the use-case model is used to ensure that the right system is built.

It should also be noted that use cases only capture functional requirements, specifically those that interact with an actor. They cannot capture non-functional requirements or the actual internal processing of a function. Hence their size can only be used as an estimate for the effort needed to develop the functional requirements that involve an interaction with an actor.

In the OO world, use cases have been incorporated as one of the notations which comprise the notational suite known as the Unified Modeling Language or UML [10]. According to this OMG standard, the definition of a use case is:

"The use case construct is used to define the behavior of a system or other semantic entity without revealing the entity's internal structure. Each use case specifies a sequence of actions, including variants, that the entity can perform, interacting with actors of the entity." [10, p2-137]

"Use case diagrams show actors and use cases together with their relationships. The use cases represent functionality of a system or a classifier, like a subsystem or a class, as manifested to external interactors with the system or the classifier." [10, p3-94]

Notwithstanding these definitions, there remain serious ambiguities or at least ambiguous yet valid interpretations of the concept of "use case" as seen in the series of versions of the UML. This has led to the industry joke that if you gather together *n* experts in use cases in the one room, there will be at least *n* different definitions (Both Graham and Cockburn have validated this empirically [13, p244]).

Cockburn [8] also identifies "failures" with the current usage of use cases. He notes that the original ideas of Jacobson have been changed as a consequence of the drawing-tools influence of the OMG's committees, thus losing the original predominantly textual nature of the use case. Since a use case *is* text, he argues that nothing in the UML standard (which discuss only *use case diagrams*) describes the essence of the use case itself. Indeed, many developers think that a use case is the picture you can draw as a use case diagram whereas, as Cockburn [8, pxxi] points out, a use case fits *inside* one of the ellipses on a use case diagram. Consequently, any metrics suite for use cases needs to discriminate between these two elements in the use (and misuse) of use cases versus use case diagrams.

While use cases were intended originally to help in eliciting user requirements in an investigative rather than a documentary manner, prior to design, recent modifications are seen [14] as adding unnecessary complications. This leads to experienced developers having multiple conflicts of interpretation. In particular, users confuse the "for instance" and the "prototypical" interpretations – the former (usually in analysis) eliciting sample user interactions while the latter (usually in design) specifying typical courses of all interactions of this type. Refinements made as use cases became part of UML led to the formalization of two relationships between use cases which have been generally misunderstood and, throughout the various versions of UML, significantly altered in their definitions. The current (Version 1.4) stereotyped relationships of interest are named „include“ and „extend“, probably the latter causing the greater confusion of the two, generally understood to be offering support for exceptional cases. On the other hand, if the comment [15] that "The semantics of „extend“ cannot handle exceptions" is correct, then this represents further disorder in what the „extend“ stereotype is meant to represent. Their hard-hitting comments on use cases, together with the warnings in [16,17], underline the potential difficulty of creating a standard use-case metric for a far-from-unambiguous concept.

Use cases are defined in the context of a software system, whereas requirements engineering makes no such assumption. Consideration of contextual factors that may influence the time needed to implement the system segment specified by a use case is needed. Given a standard unit of measurement for use cases, rules for the consistent construction of use cases and the gathering of historical effort data, it becomes possible to investigate linking use cases with effort using use-case metrics.

3 Use-Case Models

Although use cases are included in the OMG's UML standard, as noted above, they appear to be ambiguously defined in the sense that different authors interpret and use them very differently. In order to identify appropriate metrics, it is therefore necessary to evaluate some of the major use-case variants. Here we evaluate use-case models as proposed in [8,18,19].

Cockburn template

1. Use-case Name
<the name should be the goal as a short active verb phrase>
2. Context of use: <a longer statement of the goal, if needed, its normal occurrence con-ditions>
3. Scope: <design scope, what system can be considered black-box under design>
4. Level: <one of: Summary, User-goal, Subfunction>
5. Primary Actor: <a role name for the primary actor, or description>
6. Stakeholders & Interests: <list of stakeholders/key interests in the use case>
7. Precondition: <what we expect is already the state of the world>
8. Minimal Guarantees: <how the interests are protected under all exits>
9. Success Guarantees: <the state of the world if goal succeeds>
10. Trigger: <what starts the use case, may be time event>
11. Main Success Scenario:
<step #> <action description>
12. Extensions
<step altered> <condition>: <action or sub-use case>
<step altered> <condition>: <action or sub-use case>
13. Technology and Data Variations List
<step or variation # > <list of variations>
<step or variation # > <list of variations>
14. Related Information
<whatever your project needs for additional information>

Fig.1. Use-case template proposed in [8]

3.1 Cockburn's Approach

Cockburn [20] focusses on the *goals* involved in use cases and identifies 18 use-case types along the four dimensions of purpose, context, multiplicity and structure, noting that the most common involves semi-formal structure. Use cases also can have different scope (e.g. system, organization); all of which tends to leave users lost in multi-dimensional space [21]. From these earlier ideas, Cockburn [8] has constructed a standard template for use cases with 14 major constituent elements. Figure 1 shows one of several alternatives he offers, another favourite being named as a "fully dressed" form, which is much the same in content but slightly differently laid out.

3.2 Rational Unified Process (RUP)

Figure 2 depicts six main fields in the RUP use case [18] which, although similar to those in Figure 1, are more skeletal and do not include context, scope etc., focussing instead on the technical descriptors (cf. items 7, 9, 11-13 in Figure 1). RUP's use case template focusses on the flow of events, which describe a sequence of actions within the use case, written in natural language. All possible alternative flows are mandated to be grouped within the single related use case, thus defining a "use case *class*" – or, more commonly, simply a "use case". Instances of the use case are scenarios, which emphasize one particular sequence of actions.

RUP Template

1. **Use-case Name**
   - 1.1 Brief Description
   - 1.2 Actions
   - 1.3 Triggers
2. **Flow of Events**
   - 2.1 Basic Flow
   - 2.2 Alternative Flows
     - 2.2.1 < First Alternative Flow >
     - 2.2.2 < Second Alternative Flow >
3. **Special Requirements**
   - 3.1 < First special requirement >
4. **Pre-Conditions**
   - 4.1 < Pre-condition One >
5. **Post-Conditions**
   - 5.1 < Post-condition One >
6. **Extension Points**
   - 6.1 < Extension Point 1 >

Fig. 2. Use-case template as used in RUP [18]

3.3 Regnell's Model

Regnell's use-case model [19] hides the complexity of the use case in three levels:

- Environment level
- Structure level
- Event level

Each level can have corresponding metrics for the size of the use case. For example, in the environment level, only the actors, stakeholders and their goals are considered together with the services offered to the actors/stakeholders to meet their goals. The structure level is mainly concerned with the normal flow and alternative flows indicating the breadth and the depth of the use case. In the event level, the individual actions are captured and, thus, in this level, the concept of atomic actions and the number of actions a measure of size seems appropriate. Regnell [19] also proposes a use-case algebra to express the actions at the event level. This proposed algebra attempts to add formality to what is, in essence, an informal approach [20].

3.4 A Brief Comparison

The RUP model concentrates on the structure and event levels and does not include environment level details such as stakeholders and goals. The structure and event levels are described in detail but the event level is expressed in unstructured natural language leading to ambiguities and problems in the interpretation of the use-case details. Thus, the RUP model for use cases appears to have serious limitations when the overall goals and the stakeholders' interests are not taken into account explicitly in the use case. In that sense, Cockburn's method seems more relevant since he adds the environment level details that the RUP model lacks. Cockburn's model expresses all three levels of Regnell's use-case model but, again, uses natural language to express event level details. This becomes a limitation for this method, since this introduces ambiguities in expressing the event level actions.

3.5 Writing Textual Use Cases

Whichever model of use cases is used, we need to finally write the use cases in natural language or some semi-formal or formal language that expresses the customer's requirements. This is the core part of the use case, since many of the errors in requirements that are not identified until the later phases are due to the informal way in which this part of the use-case construction is handled.

Use-case descriptions are often written in a natural language such as English. This introduces ambiguities in the expressions and frequently does not translate the real-world problem into precise requirements. Thus, a standard or template is required that constrains the user to write in a specific way. Some progress has been made in the CREWS-SAVRE project [22] in which they suggest an incrementally guided process of use-case specification. They discuss the linguistic patterns and structures that helps in the writing of use-case specifications and relate the use-case model to natural language. Cockburn [8] offers advice on style guidelines to assist in writing narrative prose together with contents guidelines to advise the author on the expected contents of the prose. Other guidelines are given in [23].

4 Metrics for Requirements

In engineering in general, it is important to be able to estimate the resources needed to construct a product. The size attribute is an important input to the process of resource estimation [24]. In software engineering, the estimation of the scale and scope of a project is difficult to do accurately at an early stage of development. At the same time, early estimates can be very important to the success of a project, since resource allocations are often made on their basis (e.g. [25]).

Metrics that can be gathered from requirements include

- requirements size (pages of specification, number of requirements, function points etc.)
- requirements completeness (everything the software is to do is included; all responses of software to realizable classes of input data in all realizable situations are included; all pages, figures, tables etc. are numbered and referenced & all terms and units provided; no sections marked TBD (to be determined) [26]
- requirements defect density (from inspection)
- traceability between requirements (ensures the origin of each requirement is clear; facilitates the referencing of each requirement in future enhancements)

Requirements quality can be measured in terms of volatility, traceability, consistency and completeness. Volatility is the degree that requirements change over a finite time period (e.g. [27]). Traceability can be from requirement to requirement, from requirement to design and from requirement to test [28]. Normally a requirements traceability matrix is used. Requirements completeness metrics are used to assess when a requirement is too complex, at the wrong level, or too superficial [25].

Cockburn [8] offers as measures the categories of small, medium, large and huge. With only four categories of size, the range of the size of a project within a category is significant. The ability to produce precise metrics depends on the available historical data and how past activities resemble present ones.

A similarly roughly quantitative approach [29] quotes work of Karner based on a function point approach. It is suggested that useful metrics can be derived from counts of

- number of actors, weighted by their complexity (weights of 1, 2 or 3)
- number of use cases, weighted by the number of transactions that they contain (weights of 5, 10 or 15) *or*
- number of analysis classes used to implement each use case, weighted by their complexity (weights of 5, 10 or 15)

Note that as well as the complexity factors being arbitrary and coarse-grained, use cases (for RE) are at a high abstraction level. They do not, therefore, contain information on either transactions or classes, these being too fine-grained. In addition, there is a many-to-many, not one-to-one as implied above, relationship between classes and use cases.

From these numbers, the authors simply create a cumulative sum called UUCP (unadjusted use-case points) which is then subject to further subjective (and complicated) weightings to get a final count for use-case points (UCP); these latter calculations bearing a strong resemblance to the weighting calculations of FPs. Effort is then calculated as x UCP where x is a figure representing effort in person hours per UCP, a value varying widely.

A very different approach is preferred by Constantine and Lockwood [30]. They suggest five metrics, linked to GUI and essential use cases. Those relating to essential use cases (three in number) are at a higher abstraction level than our focus here so are not discussed further in this paper.

Marchesi [31] suggests three primary metrics:

UC1 = total number of use cases
UC2 = overall number of communications between actors and use cases
UC3 = total number of communications between actors and use cases neglecting include and extend structures

Marchesi then argues that an estimate of global complexity of the system is given by

$$UC4 = K_1\, UC1^2 + UC3 + K_2\, [\, smm([C]) - smm([E])]$$

where coefficients K_1 and K_2 are computed empirically and smm[(M)] is the sum of all elements of matrix M and C and E are matrices for the communications between use cases and actors' and E is derived from C (for details see original paper). The squaring of UC1 is said to be "for homogeneity reasons"! UC4 is said to be proportional to system complexity although no coefficient of proportionality is discussed and no justification for the statement is given. There is stated to be significant subjectivity in the calculation of the metric.

Having chosen a use-case model and then using some guidelines for constructing the use cases, the use cases can be specified in a form ready to be measured. Here, we use primarily the hierarchical use-case model by Regnell together with the CREWS-SAVRE approach for writing the descriptions of the use case. Actions can be either atomic actions or a compound of atomic actions called a flow of actions. An atomic unit that is common to all representations of use cases would give any measures based on it the widest potential application. Since actions are common to all use-case representations, we propose that atomic actions should be used as a unit of measurement for use cases, where an atomic action is one that cannot be further decomposed without leaving the domain [13, p219].

Once we have something we can count, we can define metrics based on that. For example, we propose the following size measures:

1. Number of atomic actions in the main flow
2. The number of atomic actions in each alternative flow
3. The longest path between the first atomic action of the use case to the final atomic action of the use case
4. Number of alternative flows (represents the breadth of the use case [32])

Alternative flows are measured from the start of the use case to its termination.

Apart from the above metrics, we need to consider the environment level factors [19] that will contribute to the complexity of the use case independently of size measures. We suggest the following measures to account for environment factors:

5. Number of stakeholders
6. Number of actors
7. Total number of goals

We consider these as complexity factors in that a use case with the same number of atomic actions can have different values for each of the environment factors. When those latter values change, it will, intuitively, alter the effort associated with the use case. For instance, when more goals must be met, the use case must be reviewed for each one and conflicts must be resolved.

The following composite metrics can be derived from the above measures.

8. Total number of atomic actions in the alternative flows
9. Total number of atomic actions in all flows
10. Number of atomic actions per actor
11. Number of atomic actions per goal
12. Number of goals per stakeholder

As an example, we analyze the use case for "Identify Assets" from the small business loans system [33, pp191-193]. This is given in Table 1. Some use case actions are expressed as compound statements to avoid repeating similar statements; hence, a dimension factor is included to indicate how many times the action is required. The values of the calculated use case metrics are given in Table 2. It can be seen that there are no extreme values, suggesting reasonable balance across main and alternative flows. What is now required is for these metrics to be collected from industry projects and related to external characteristics [34] such as maintainability, effort of implementation etc.

Table 1. Use case example – modified from use case: Identify Asset [33]

Use Case Thumbnail UC100-IdentifyAsset (version 0.9)
Use Case Description This use case describes the process of identifying a single asset of a borrower, so that it can be used by the securities and assets officer of the bank in order to assess whether it can be used as collateral for the purpose of granting a loan to the borrower.
Pre-Conditions Asset details (as a single piece of free-form text) must be provided by the customers (potential borrower at this stage) before any classification and verification process can start. The A07-Securities&AssetsOfficer should already have such data in hard form (the actual loan application form) and/or soft copy at hand.

Post-Conditions
None

Actors
A03-SmallBusinessBorrower
A07-Securities&AssetsOfficer
A09-Database

Stakeholders
S01=A03-SmallBusinessBorrower
S02=A07-Securities&AssetsOfficer
S03 Business Manager
S04 Board of Directors

Goals
A03-SmallBusinessBorrower – to provide information related to their Asset; to assist in calculation of the net asset value available as collateral
A07-Securities&AssetsOfficer – to calculate the net asset of the borrowers; to calculate the collateral by balancing the net assets with the loan amount requested; to store all details in the database
A09-Database – to store the asset details
Assumptions:
1. Number of Asset Details =4 (used in main and alternative flow)

Use Case Text
1. A03-SmallBusinessBorrower provides name of asset to be offered as collateral
2. A03-SmallBusinessBorrower provides details of asset to be offered as collateral (dimension =4)
3. A07-Securities&AssetsOfficer records name of the asset
4. A07-Securities&AssetsOfficer records details of the asset (dimension =4)
5. A07-Securities&AssetsOfficer queries the system if the asset already exist in the system (Alternative 1)
6. System prompts for asset name
7. A07-Securities&AssetsOfficer records name of the asset
8. System prompts for asset details (dimension =4)
9. A07-Securities&AssetsOfficer records details of the asset (dimension =4)
10. Asset name is sent to the A09-Database
11. Asset details are sent to the A09-Database (dimension =4)

Alternative Courses
Alternative 1: Asset already exists in the system (as made available by the borrower as existing customers of the bank)
1. System provides asset details (dimension =4)
2. A07-Securities&AssetsOfficer verifies the details of the asset with A03-SmallBusinessBorrower (dimension =4)

Constraints
None

Table 2. Results of metrics for the use case example of Table 1

Metric	Value of metric
Number of atomic actions in main flow	26
Number of atomic actions in alternative flows	Alternative 1: 8
Longest path	26
Number of alternative flows	1
Number of stakeholders	4
Number of actors	3
Total number of goals	3
Derivative metrics	
Total number of atomic actions in alternative flows	8
Total number of atomic actions in all flows	34
Number of atomic actions per actor	11.33
Number of atomic actions per goal	11.33
Number of goals per stakeholder	0.75

5 Conclusion

Use case modelling, whilst commonly used for documenting requirements, needs to be standardized before reliable and repeatable metrics can be obtained. We have set out the requirements for such a standardization and also proposed the basic metrics likely to be useful. These are based primarily on use-case models of [8,19] and offer a first attempt to create a size measure for use cases. The next step is to evaluate the important research questions of whether use-case attributes such as size (and complexity) can be controlled and whether such use-case metrics can be sufficiently rigorous for estimating effort. Finally, we should note that this added rigour applied to use cases should improve the consistency and quality of communication between client and developer, helping to ensure that the right system is built.

Acknowledgements

This is Contribution number 02/13 of the Centre for Object Technology Applications and Research of the University of Technology, Sydney. We wish to thank the Australian Research Council for financial support through the ATN Grant scheme.

References

1. Nuseibeh, B and Easterbrook, S., 2000, Requirements engineering: a roadmap", in Future of Software Engineering (22nd IEEE Int. Conf. on Software Engineering), 35-46
2. Davis, A. M., Jordan, K, and Nakajima, T., 1997, Elements underlying specifications of requirements, Annals of Software Engineering, 3, 63-100

3. Jacobson, I., Christerson, M., Jonsson, P. and Övergaard, G., 1992, Object-Oriented Software Engineering: A Use Case Driven Approach, Addison-Wesley
4. Constantine, L.L., 1997, The case for essential use cases, Object Magazine, 7(3), 72-70
5. Korson, T., 1998, The misuse of use cases (managing requirements), Object Magazine, 8(3), 18-20
6. Leffingwell, D., Widrig, D., 2000, Managing Software Requirements, A Unified Approach, Addison-Wesley
7. Kosters, G. et al., 2001, Coupling use cases and class models as a means for validation and verification of requirements specification, Req. Eng. Journal, 6(1), 3-17
8. Cockburn, A., 2000, Writing Effective Use Cases, Addison Wesley
9. Jacobson, I., 1994a, Basic use-case modeling. ROAD, 1(2), 15-19
10. OMG, 2001, OMG Unified Modeling Language Specification, Version 1.4, September 2001, OMG document formal/01-09-67 [Online]. Available http://www.omg.org
11. Jacobson, I., 1994c, Use cases and object, ROAD, 1(4), 8-10
12. Jacobson, I., 1994b, Basic use-case modeling (Continued), ROAD, 1(3), 7-9
13. Graham, I., 1998, Requirements Engineering and Rapid Development. An Object-Oriented Approach, Addison-Wesley
14. Simons, A.J.H. and Graham, I., 1998, 37 things that don't work in object-oriented modelling with UML, BCS Obj.-Oriented Prog. Sys. Newsletter, 35 (eds. S Kent & R Mitchell)
15. Simons, A.J.H. and Graham, I., 1999, 30 Things that go wrong in object modelling with UML 1.3, chapter 16 in: Behavioral Specifications of Businesses and Systems, (Eds. H Kilov, B Rumpe and I Simmonds), Kluwer Academic Publishers, 237-257
16. Simons, A.J.H., 1999, Use cases considered harmful, Procs. TOOLS 29, (Eds. R. Mitchell, AC Wills, J Bosch and B Meyer), IEEE Computer Society, 94-203
17. Lilly, S., 1999, Use case pitfalls: top 10 problems from real projects using use cases, Procs. TOOLS 30 (eds. D. Firesmith, R. Riehle, G. Pour and B. Meyer), IEEE Computer Society Press, 174-183
18. Kruchten, Ph., 2000, The Rational Unified Process: An Introduction, Second edition, Addison Wesley
19. Regnell, B., 1996, Hierarchical use case modelling for requirements engineering, Report Number 120, Doctoral Thesis, Dept Communication Systems, Lund University, Sweden
20. Cockburn, A., 1997a, Goals and use cases, J. Obj.Oriented Progr., 10(5), 35-40
21. Cockburn, A., 1997b, Using goal-based use cases, J. Obj.Oriented Progr., 10(7), 56-62
22. Achour, C.B., Rolland, C., Maiden, N.A.M. and Souveyet, C., 1999, Guiding use case authoring: results of an empirical study, Procs. Fourth IEEE International Symposium on Requirements Engineering (RE99), University of Limerick, Ireland

23. Firesmith, D.G., 1999, Use case modeling guidelines, Procs. TOOLS 30 (eds. D. Firesmith, R. Riehle, G. Pour and B. Meyer), IEEE Computer Society Press, 184-193
24. Verner, J.M. and Tate, G., 1992, A software size model, IEEE Trans. Soft. Eng., 18(4), 265-278
25. Costello, R.J. and Liu, D.-B., 1995, Metrics for requirements engineering, Journal of Systems Software, 29, 39-63
26. Davis, A., 1993, Software Requirements Analysis and Specification (2nd ed.), Prentice Hall
27. Zowghi, D., Offen, R. and Nurmuliani, 2000, The impact of requirements volatility on the software development lifecycle, Procs Int Conf on Software, Theory and Practice (ICS2000), IFIP World Computer Conference, Beijing, China, August 2000
28. Gotel, O.C.Z and Finkelstein, A.C.W., 1994, An analysis of the requirements traceability problem, Procs. First Int. Conf. Requirements Engineering (ICRE94), 94-101
29. Schneider, G. and Winters, J.P., 1998, Applying Use Cases: A Practical Guide, Addison-Wesley
30. Constantine, L.L. and Lockwood, L.A.D., 1999, Software for Use, Addison-Wesley
31. Marchesi, M., 1998, OOA metrics for the Unified Modeling Language, Euromicro Conference on Software Maintenance and Reengineering
32. Whitmire, S.A., 1997, Object Oriented Design Measurement, John Wiley & Sons
33. Henderson-Sellers, B. and Unhelkar, B., 2000, OPEN Modeling with UML, Addison-Wesley
34. Fenton, N.E., 1994, Software measurement: a necessary scientific basis, IEEE Trans. *Soft. Eng.,* **20**, 199-206

Progressive Access: A Step towards Adaptability in Web-Based Information Systems

Marlène Villanova-Oliver, Jérôme Gensel, and Hervé Martin

Laboratoire LSR – IMAG, BP 72, 38402 Saint Martin d'Hères cedex, France
Tel.: (33) 4 76 82 72 80, Fax: (33) 4 76 82 72 87
{villanova,gensel,martin}@imag.fr

Abstract. Web-based Information Systems (WIS) are used for diffusing and processing information over the Internet. Because of the large amounts of information they manage, it is crucial to adapt the delivered information. This can be done by giving users a progressive access to information. For this purpose, we propose to stratify the Information Space of a WIS by decomposing it into personalized sub-Information Spaces. This stratification is described through a Progressive Access Model (PAM) written in UML. The PAM gives WIS users, first, access to some information considered as minimal and essential, and then, allows them to navigate through larger and/or smaller personalized Information Spaces. Together with the PAM, we present a specific query language which allows to query a stratified Information Space. This way, the stratification is taken into account in query expressions, while replies are formatted according to the different levels of detail available in the stratified user's Information Space.

1 Introduction

The Web is now considered a reliable medium for widely diffusing information and, unsurprisingly, more and more Information Systems, so-called Web-based Information Systems (WIS), are accessible on Internet. These WIS address various application domains such as e-business, education, geography, etc. As any other Information Systems, WIS are designed to manage very large sets of data and to offer specialized services. Moreover, in the context of the Web, they are supposed to offer navigation facilities (through hyperlinks and/or dynamic web pages) generally embedded into a multimedia presentation of information. Although this characteristic makes these systems attractive, the measurement of the quality of a WIS does *not* only rely on the graphical appearance or on the quantity of available information, but also on its usefulness. The appropriateness of information a WIS delivers to its users turns out to be an acute problem when, designing such systems, one ignores that 1) all users do *not* need the same information, and 2) users do *not* need all the available information all the time.

Z. Bellahsène, D. Patel, and C. Rolland (Eds.): OOIS 2002, LNCS 2425, pp. 422-433, 2002.

The first point can be addressed by distinguishing users profiles and is often referred to as *adaptability*. Recent systems, developed by commercial companies such as [1], announce a new generation of web applications able to track down the behaviour of their users and to dynamically react, by adapting the presentation of information. More generally, a WIS is said to be adaptable when the user gets the impression that the system has been specially designed for her/him. Then, adaptability (and its dynamic version called *adaptivity* [2]) can be defined as the ability a WIS has to provide its users with some relevant information with regard to their rights, needs, individual characteristics and material configurations (WAP, browser, etc.), in terms of both content and presentation.

The second point concerns the delivery of information by WIS and the fact that users may need occasionally only some parts of information. Indeed, even when information is appropriate, users can be confronted to a cognitive overload, due to a too massive and/or difficult to understand quantity of information. In order to spare users the trouble of getting "lost in the hyperspace", as described in [3], we propose to provide them with a gradual organization of information which allows them to progressively access it.

For this purpose, in [4], we have defined the notion of *mask* (we initially called *zoom*) for organizing, at a conceptual level, the data of a WIS so that it offers its users a progressive and personalized access to their own *Information Space*. An Information Space refers to a set of information related to the application domain generally described by a (Entity-Relation, Class-Association, XML, etc.) data model. The idea is to favor the adaptability of a WIS by stratifying the Information Space into different levels of detail which are exploited by progressive access mechanisms. This way, a user can navigate gradually from a level of detail to another. Such a stratification can be defined for a group of users but also for a single user.

The stratification is performed through a Progressive Access Model (we call PAM), which has been implemented in KIWIS, a platform for the design and the automatic deployment of WIS [5]. In KIWIS, the PAM is written using AROM [6], an Object-based Knowledge Representation System. We show in [4] how to provide users with a progressive access by stratifying a data model, which is described using the object-based formalism of AROM. Here, we propose a UML description of the PAM at a higher abstraction level, which constitutes a generalization of our previous works. The UML class diagram we present can be extended in order to describe how a stratification applies on a particular data schema (Entity-Relation, Class-Association, XML, etc.). We illustrate this extension in the case of an object-oriented data schema.

The second contribution of this paper consists in a query language, called PAM QL. PAM-QL is an OQL-like [7] query language which allows to query a stratified Information Space. On the one hand, query expressions can be formulated on the stratification, while levels of detail can be used in query expressions as well. On the other hand, replies are formatted by the WIS according to the stratification of the user's Information Space. More precisely, a query, whether it explicitly refers to the stratification or not, is processed by the WIS and its reply takes into account the levels of detail defined by the stratification associated with the user.

The paper is organized as follows. In section 2, we present the Progressive Access Model (PAM) in charge of describing the stratification of each personalized information space. In section 3, we introduce the PAM Query Language (PAM-QL) which allows to formulate queries taking into account the underlying stratification of an Information Space described using the PAM. The section 4 gives the architecture of KIWIS, a platform we currently develop for the design and deployment of WIS, and in which both the PAM and the PAM-QL have been integrated. Some related works are compared in section 5. Some conclusions and perspectives end the paper.

2 The Progressive Access Model

In our approach, adaptability of a WIS is addressed by allowing WIS designer to perform a stratification of the Information Space. This stratification consists in defining several levels of detail. A stratification can be associated with each group of users or single user, providing them with a progressive access to information, according to their interest.

The stratification of an Information Space is mainly based on the notion of *mask* [4], we briefly recall here for readability reasons. The notion of *mask* allows to represent more or less completely the structure a set of (structured) information, by masking a part of it. A *Maskable Entity* is a set of information which can be masked. Applying a mask, a *Representations of Maskable Entity* (RoME) is defined as a subset of information extracted from the Maskable Entity. Each RoME is associated with a level of detail: the higher the level, the more completely the Maskable Entity is represented. Moreover, we define an ordered relation between these RoMEs based on the set inclusion.

Let $ME=\{e_1, e_2, ..., e_n\}$ be a Maskable Entity, where e_i is an element of information and such as n = Card (ME) ≥ 2. In order to set-up a progressive access to the whole set of information corresponding to a ME, we define four rules, to which each RoME of ME has to comply:

- RoME $\in$ Set of parts of ME.
- $RoME_i$ corresponds to the level of detail i available on the ME, where $1 \leq i \leq m$, m being the maximum detail level authorized.
- $RoME_1 \neq \emptyset$, even at the first level of detail, at least one element of information is visible (*i.e.* can be accessed).
- for each i<j, $RoME_i \subset RoME_j$, so the elements of information visible at the level of detail i are also visible at each greater level of detail j. Moreover, at the level of detail $i+1$, at least one more element of ME is visible (strict inclusion).

In order to perform a personalized stratification of the Information Space, one initially needs information about both the application domain and the users of the WIS. The former is embedded in a model which represents the objects of the real world managed by the WIS. In our approach this model is called *Data Model* and is described using UML [8] notations. The latter necessitates an explicit modelling of users, we achieve through a model called the *Generic User Model* (GUM) shown in Fig. 1. The presented GUM is a minimal model which can be extended according to the characteristics of users and to the requirements of the application domain. The main classes of the GUM are described below.

User is an abstract class of the GUM dedicated to the description of users and groups of users. Its sub-classes *Group* and *IndividualUser* maintain information concerning respectively a group of users and an individual user. The membership of an individual user to one or more groups is modelled by the relation *is_member_of*. The Boolean attribute *isMainGroup* in the class association *Main_Group* links a user to one and only one group by default.

In the remainder of this section, we refer to the GUM *via* the class *User* and we call *user(s)* object(s) of this class.

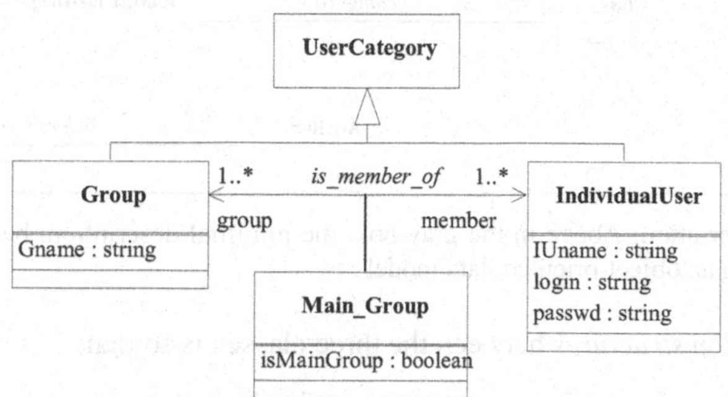

Fig. 1. Description of the Generic User Model in UML

2.1 Minimal and Extended Descriptions of the PAM

The Progressive Access Model (PAM) is dedicated to the stratification of the data model of the application domain addressed by the WIS in order to introduce different levels of detail in information. The PAM is coupled with both the Data Model and the GUM. The connections between the three models (Data Model, GUM and PAM) allow a WIS designer to define as many personalized stratifications on the data model as required. Such a modelling makes it possible to support adaptability for groups of users as well as for single users.

We give here a description of the PAM using UML. At the higher abstraction level, a minimal description is proposed (*cf.* gray box in Fig 2). This description has to be extended in order to specify the stratification according to the formalism (e.g. Entity/Relation, class/association, XML, etc) chosen for the data model of the application domain (as shown in Fig. 2 and described later in the section). The minimal description of the PAM contains three classes. The class *User* connects the PAM to the GUM. The class *MaskableEntity* corresponds to the set of information to be stratified. The stratification can be performed at different granularities. For instance, in an object data model, a Maskable Entity (ME) to be stratified can be either a schema, or a class, or an attribute. The class *Representation* denotes the different representations available for a Maskable Entity and which constitute the stratification of this ME. A *Representation of Maskable Entity* (RoME) corresponds to a level of detail at which the information (or Maskable Entity) is presented more or less completely.

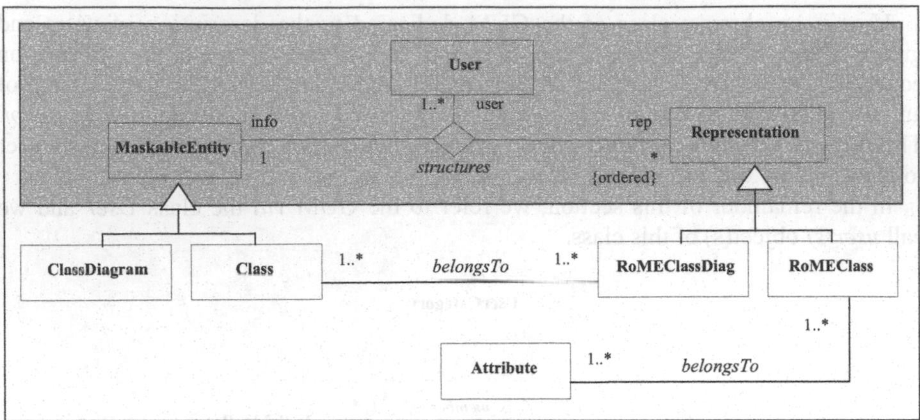

Fig. 2. PAM description. Above in the gray box, the minimal description, below the extended description fitting an object-oriented data model

The association *structures* between the three classes is so that:

- 0 to *n* instance(s) of *Representation* can be linked to one couple of instances (*User*, *MaskableEntity*). No (0) instance means no stratification: the user is given no progressive access to information which, in this case, is delivered as a whole. On the contrary, *n* instances of *Representation* offer to the user *n* levels of representation for this *MaskableEntity*. These levels correspond to subsets of information, ordered by the WIS designer, according to the users' needs, so that she/he can progressively access information.
- 1 to *n* instance(s) of *User* can be linked to one couple of instances (*MaskableEntity*, *Representation*), allowing several users to share the same stratification.
- one and only one instance of *MaskableEntity* is linked to one couple of instances (*User*, *Representation*).

Let us now suppose that the Data Model is described using an object-oriented paradigm (*i.e.* in terms of classes and attributes). In order to extend the PAM, one has to determine the set of information which can be seen as ME and to identify their associated RoME. Due to lack of space, we only consider here two levels of granularity. Fig. 2 shows the extended version of the PAM adapted to the object-oriented context considered here:

- the class diagram is a ME whose RoME are sets of classes;
- a class seen as a set of attributes is a ME whose RoME correspond to subsets of its attributes.

The class *MaskableEntity* is either a data model (class *ClassDiagram*) or a *Class*. The class *Representation* specializes into the class *RoMEClassDiag* and *RoMEClass* which are used to define respectively how a *RoME* is built for a *ClassDiagram* considered as a *MaskableEntity* and for a *Class* seen as a *MaskableEntity*. The class *RoMEClassDiag* is linked to the class *Class* through the association *belongsTo*.

Linking a set of instances of *Class* to one instance of *RoMEClassDiag* reflects that these classes are accessible at the level of detail to which corresponds this instance of *RoMEClassDiag*. The class *RoMEClass* is linked to the class *Attribute* through the association *belongsTo*. Linking a set of instances of *Attribute* to one instance of *RoMEClass* signifies that these attributes are accessible at the level of detail to which corresponds this instance of *RoMEClass*.

2.2 Example of Stratification Using the PAM

In this section, we introduce examples which illustrate the way a class diagram and a class can be stratified.

Fig. 3a) shows the whole Data Model of an application dedicated to the management of Academic trainings. One specific Information Space is delimited by the border of the darker gray area. This information space is supposed to meet the needs of one user in charge of the administration of students. Since it is assumed that the administration tasks performed by this user do *not* distinguish between temporary or permanent teachers, the two corresponding classes are out of the Information Space. This stratification would clearly not be the same for the Information Space of an accountant in charge of teachers' salaries. At the first level, the RoME 1 allows the user to access information related to the students and the training. The second level is supported by RoME 2 which extends the visibility on information by adding the class Course. RoME 3 corresponds to the third level of information and gives additionally access to information about teachers. It can be assumed that this stratification has been established considering which classes are the more usually accessed during the tasks performed by user.

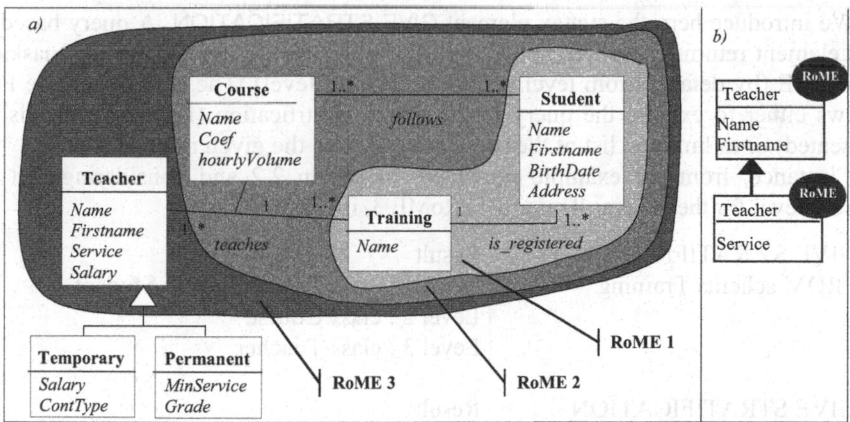

Fig. 3. a) Example of a class diagram stratified in 3 levels: the schema 'TRAINING'. b) Example of the stratification of a class in 2 levels

Fig. 3b) shows how the class *Teacher* can be considered as a ME stratified into two levels of detail. The black arrow and the labels 'RoME' express that this stratification can be seen as an internal specialization for the class. Each labelled box corresponds to a RoME of the class *Teacher*. At level 1, the content of an instance of *Teacher* will be displayed using only 2 attributes. At level 2, one more attribute is visible.

It can be noticed that by totally hiding the attribute *Salary* in the stratification of class *Teacher*, a certain level of confidentiality can be expressed and handled by the PAM at the class level. Similarly, Fig. 3a) illustrates confidentiality at the schema level by excluding the classes *Temporary* and *Permanent* from the Information Space. Instances of the class *Temporary* and *Permanent* are shown as instances of class *Teacher* (i.e. only the attributes defined in this classes are used to represent both *Temporary* and *Permanent*).

3 PAM QL: A Query Language for the PAM

The objective of the PAM Query Language presented in this section is twofold. On the one hand, the PAM-QL allows to query the stratification performed on the Information Space. On the other hand, according to the stratification (i.e. according to levels of detail), it aims at formatting the data in response to a query. These two aspects are presented below using an OQL-like formalism [7]. Once the stratification has been created or modified through the instantiation of the PAM, the PAM-QL can be used for the consultation of the stratified Information Space.

3.1 Queries on Stratification

We give below the general expression of a query on stratification:

```
GIVE STRATIFICATION
FROM maskable_entity ME
[ FOR all_levels | level_interval = [min, max] ]
```

We introduce here the syntax element GIVE STRATIFICATION. A query based on this element returns the different levels of the stratification defined for the maskable entity ME (by default, from level one to the current level). The optional clause FOR allows either to expand the query to the whole stratification (i.e. all the levels are presented) or to limit the list of the presented levels to the given interval.
For instance, from the example presented in section 2.2 and considering that the current level for the schema Training is RoME 3, it yields:

	Result
GIVE ST RATIFICATION FROM schema Training	Level 1 : class Training, class Student Level 2 : class Course Level 3 : class Teacher

	Result:
GIVE STRATIFICATION FROM schema Training FOR level_interval = [1, 2]	Level 1 : class Training, class Student Level 2 : class Course

Considering that the current level is the one of RoME 1 defined for the class Teacher, it yields:

	Result:
GIVE STRATIFICATION FROM class Teacher FOR all_levels	Level 1 : attribute Name, attribute Firstname Level 2 : attribute Service

3.2 Queries on a Stratified Information Space

In this section, we show how the PAM-QL exploits the stratification in the processing of a query. The displayed instances are formatted according to the levels of the stratification defined for the user.

```
SELECT ME.information
FROM maskable_entity ME
[WHERE expression]
[ FOR all_levels | level_interval = [min, max] ]
```

This query searches for the instances of ME, whose presentation is limited to the field(s) of the information associated with ME, and which respect the expression given in the optional clause WHERE. When ME is a schema, information concerns its classes, while when ME is a class, information concerns its attributes. If * is used in the SELECT, information corresponds to the RoME of the current level.
For instance, from the example presented in section 2.2 and considering that the current level for the schema Training is RoME 2.

SELECT * FROM Training	Result: All instances of classes Training, Student and Course are listed, which corresponds to RoME 2. Each of these classes are represented at their lower level of detail.

If the requested information does *not* belong to the current level, the result is automatically expanded to the first level at which information appears. Considering now that the current level for the class Teacher is RoME 1, it yields:

SELECT service FROM Teacher WHERE Service>200	Result All instances of Teacher whose service of teaching consists of more than 200 hours are shown, attributes Name, Firstname and Service being visible (RoME 2).

The optional clause FOR allows to:

- expand the query to the whole stratification (*all_levels*). In this case, instances are presented using the maximum level of detail available for the user;
- limit the visibility of information to the levels in the given interval.

4 Integration of the PAM in KIWIS

We briefly present here how the PAM is integrated and exploited in KIWIS [5], a platform we currently develop for designing and deploying adaptable WIS. KIWIS integrates the progressive access to information approach based on the PAM.

4.1 KIWIS: General Overview

In KIWIS, the PAM is implemented using AROM, an Object-based Knowledge Representation System whose representation language is based on UML-like notations. For a designer, modeling a WIS using KIWIS consists in instantiating five different models:

- the Generic User Model. This model describes the users (single or groups) needs and profiles;
- the Data Model. This model describes the application domain supported by the WIS;
- the PAM. This model describes the progressive access modalities;
- the Operation Model. This model describes the functionalities of the WIS (consultation, modification, etc.) and the related security aspects;
- the Hypermedia Model. This model describes the presentation features in terms of Web pages composition and graphical aspects specified by a charter.

Once instantiated, each of these models is translated into XML or associated languages (such as XML Schema, or XSL) files. The deployment of the so-specified WIS is controlled by different managers which constitute the kernel of KIWIS. The architecture is shown in Fig. 4. For more details concerning these models and managers, please see [5].

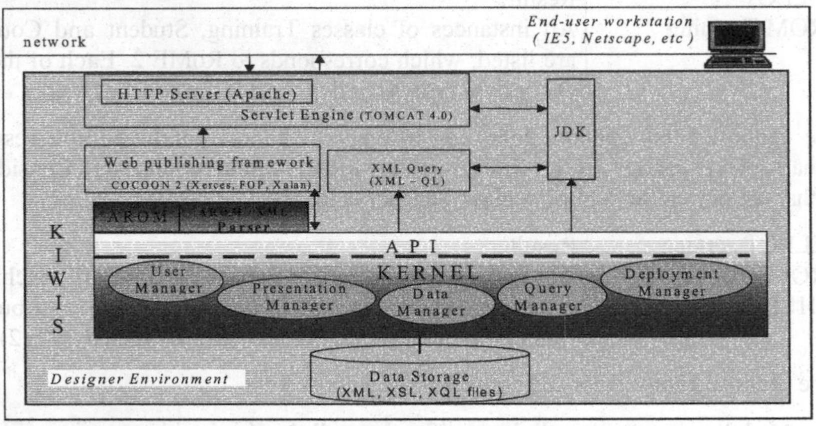

Fig. 4. Architecture of KIWIS

4.2 Query Processing Using the PAM

Fig. 5 illustrates the way the different Managers mentioned in the previous section work together for processing a PAM-QL query sent by a user to a WIS built with KIWIS.

A PAM-QL query sent to the generated WIS by a user is first processed by the User Manager ①, which consults[1] information from the GUM and the PAM in order to reinterpret the query. The GUM ② informs about who is the user and which are her/his rights on data. The PAM ③ provides information about the data stratification features specified for this user. Then, the User Manager transmits the reinterpreted

[1] The Query Manager is called each time the other Managers extract information from their corresponding models, although this does *not* appear in the figure for a matter of visibility.

query to the Data Manager ④, which executes the query on the Data Model ⑤. This Manager then creates an XML files ⑥ which contains the result of the query.

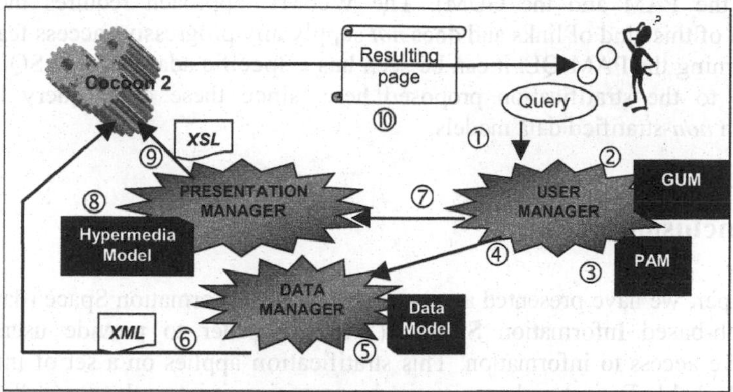

Fig. 5. Query processing in a WIS deployed with KIWIS

At this stage, the content to be returned is adapted to the user's presentation preferences which are also extracted from GUM ② and are transmitted from the User Manager to the Presentation Manager ⑦.

The Presentation Manager queries the Hypermedia Model ⑧ for delivering the adequate presentation in an XSL files ⑨. XML and XSL files are sent to Cocoon in order to publish the page corresponding to the reply to the query. This page, adapted from both content and presentation viewpoints, is finally returned to the user ⑩.

5 Related Work

We compare here our work with proposals integrating notions close to the stratification one. *Views* [9] which were first defined in relational Data Bases (but since broadly applied to OODBMS [10], to XML [11], etc.) are also used to provide the user with a convenient representation of information, according to her/his needs. Defined from a conceptual schema, they constitute several specific *external schemas* of it. Then RoMEs can be considered as ordered series of views. But, to our knowledge, there is no work dealing with a stratification relying on several views as the one presented in this paper and favouring a progressive access to information.

The notion of *context* (a higher order conceptual entity that describes a group of conceptual entities from a particular standpoint) [12] can also be considered as a basis for stratifying an information space into RoME, at a schema level. Masks can be seen as a specification of contexts having a variable size: the information space is stratified in order to be either enlarged or reduced. Our approach is close to the proposal of [13] where the notion of context is enriched in order to partially mask information. However, this approach does *not* put the emphasis on adaptability to user needs.

In WebML [14], a *data unit* enables the definition of short or long, multimedia or textual, versions of an entity, what could be assimilated to our approach. Entities in WebML only correspond to the notion of class whereas our work handles different granularities. Moreover we define, at the conceptual level, navigation mechanisms based on the stratification and automatically adapted to users (thanks to the link between the PAM and the GUM). The WebML approach requires the explicit definition of this kind of links and does *not* supply any progressive access features.

Concerning the PAM-QL, it can be seen has a specific adaptation of SQL or OQL standards to the stratification proposed here, since these other query languages operate on *non*-stratified data models.

6 Conclusion

In this paper, we have presented a way to stratify the Information Space (data model) of a Web-based Information System (WIS) in order to provide users with a progressive access to information. This stratification applies on a set of information (called Maskable Entity) and consists in decomposing it into sub-sets (called RoME) ordered by a set inclusion relation. The description of this stratification is achieved through a Progressive Access Model (PAM) written in UML. In order to personalize the progressive access, the PAM is linked to both the data model of the application domain and a model, called Generic User Model (GUM) which maintains knowledge about users. Based on stratifications processed at different levels of granularity, users of a WIS can access, first, essential information, and then, more or less information, depending on their interest, time or material configuration, etc. To our opinion, the stratification features proposed here through the PAM could be applied more generally on any kind of Information Systems, not only on Web-based ones, and not only on those adopting an object-oriented model as the one presented here.

In this paper, we have also proposed a query language in order to exploit the PAM. The PAM Query Language (PAM-QL) is an OQL-like query language which allows to query an Information Space whose stratification is described through the PAM. The PAM-QL allows to query the WIS about the stratification performed on the Information Space. But it also aims at formatting the data contained in a reply to a query, according to the stratification (i.e. according to levels of detail).

The results of this study have been implemented into KIWIS, a platform for designing and deploying adaptable WIS. KIWIS integrates five models a WIS designer has to instantiate for describing the adaptable WIS to be deployed. Once instantiated, these models are translated in XML before KIWIS automatically generates the so-specified WIS. From the stratification described in the PAM, the associated navigation mechanisms and graphical charters for presentation, users of the generated WIS are given a progressive and personalized access to information.

Using KIWIS, the stratification and PAM-QL proposed here have been first experimented in the SPHERE project [15] consisting of an Information System dedicated to geographic and historical data on river flooding. Masks have shown to be of a rather intuitive use for different categories of users (experts, city hall employees, etc.) who consult data about the same topic (flooding) but at different levels of detail.

Our research concerning KIWIS are now directed towards dynamic adaptability techniques in order to react more efficiently to end-users actions. The idea is to dynamically elaborate and modify both the stratification and the navigation schema of a WIS, learning from the user's behavior. The use of cookies technology to track information about users' sessions in order to automatically adapt information, coupled with some meta-rules of navigation, is one way we have started to explore.

References

1. Interligo. Available from http://www.interligo.com (2001)
2. C. Stephanidis, A. Paramythis, D. Akoumianakis and M. Sfyrakis, *Self-Adapting Web-based Systems: Towards Universal Accessibility*, 4th Workshop on User Interface For All, Stockholm, Sweden, October, 1998
3. Theng, Y.L., Thimbleby, H.: Addressing Design and Usability Issues in Hypertext and on the World Wide Web by Re-Examining the "Lost in Hyperspace" Problem. J. of Univ. Computer Science. Vol. 4. Issue 11. Springer (1998), 839-855
4. M. Villanova, J. Gensel and H. Martin, *Progressive Access to Knowledge in Web Information Systems through Zooms*, 7th Int. Conf. on Object Oriented Information Systems, Calgary, Canada, August, 2001,467-476
5. M. Villanova-Oliver, J. Gensel, H. Martin and C. Erb, Design and Generation of Adaptable Web Information Systems with KIWIS, ITCC 2002
6. Page, M., Gensel, J., Capponi, C., Bruley, C., Genoud, P., Ziébelin, D., Bardou, D., Dupierris V.: A New Approach in Object-Based Knowledge Representation: the AROM System. 14th Int. Conf. on Industrial and Engineering Applications of Artificial Intelligence and Expert Systems, IEA/AIE 2001, Hungary, (2001) 113-118
7. S. Cluet, Designing OQL: Allowing Objects to be Queried, Information Systems, 23(5), 1998
8. J. Rumbaugh, I. Jacobson and G. Booch. The Unified Modeling Language Reference Manual. Addison-Wesley, (1999)
9. Tsichritzis D., Klug, A.: The ANSI/X3/SPARC DBMS Framework Report of the Study Group on Data Base Management Systems, AFIPS Press (1977)
10. Abiteboul S., Bonner A.: Objects and Views. SIGMOD (1991) 238-347
11. Abiteboul S.: On Views and XML. ACM Symposium on Principles of Database Systems. (1999) 1-9
12. Motschnig-Pitrik, R.: Contexts and Views in Object-Oriented Languages. In P. Bouquet, L. Serafini, P. Brézillon, M. Benerecetti, F. Castellan (Eds.): Modeling and Using Context. 2nd Int. and Interdisciplinary Conference, CONTEXT'99, Trento, Italy (1999)
13. Theodorakis, M., Analyti, A., Constantopoulos P., Spyratos, N.: Contextualization as an Abstraction Mechanism for Conceptual Modelling. 18th International Conference on Conceptual Modeling, Paris, France (1999)
14. Ceri, S., Fraternali P., Bongio, A.: Web Modeling Language (WebML) : a modeling language for designing Web sites. WWW9 Conference. Amsterdam (2000)
15. Davoine, P.A., Martin, H., Trouillon, A., Cœur, D., Lang, M., Bariendos M., Llasat C.: Historical Flood Database for the European SPHERE Project: modelling of historical information, 21th General Assembly of the European Geophysical Society, Nice (2001)

A Contribution to Multimedia Document Modeling and Organizing

Ikram Amous, Anis Jedidi, and Florence Sèdes

Univ. Paul Sabatier, Team SIG-IRIT
118 route de Narbonne, 31062 Toulouse Cedex 4
{amous,jedidi,sedes}@irit.fr

Abstract. This paper presents a solution to resolve the problem of multimedia documents collection reorganizing. This solution is based on a documentary warehouse enriched by metadata (for each media type) elicited, modeled and structured in XML meta-documents. To homogenize these meta-document representation, we based our annotation on a document indexing and segmentation process.
The warehouse thus created is seen as the hyperbase to which the user will apply personalization and querying mechanisms. The personalization enables dynamic re-structuring and re-construction of documents answering to the user queries. This approach is based on the OOHDM methodology extension with the use of the metadata.

1 Introduction

Building personalized web application is a challenging task. For that, we use a documentary warehouse to propose a local structure to documents in order to be able to reorganize them dynamically.

The approach we propose relies a modeling extension based on a set of textual and media-based metadata (specific each media type). The metadata extraction is carried out by specific functions for each media. In our laboratory (IRIT), libraries are developed and are dedicated to each media [9][10]. Once the metadata extracted, they are structured in XML documents called "meta-document", employed to enrich the documentary warehouse thus created [4].

To create dynamic documents, we propose to use the hypermedia design application methodology OOHDM (Oriented Object Hypermedia Methodology Design) [15]. So, we propose to extend this methodology by the introduction of metadata into documents. To dynamically re-organise the documents, we use the abstract view (built from the diagrams of context navigation) defined using ADVs (Abstract Data View).

In this paper, we will present the metadata modeling already detailed in [3] and the use of OOHDM methodology in order to create dynamic views of documents answering to the user's needs expressed through queries. In section 2, we present our motivation. In section 3, we present metadata likely to be extracted and modeled. In section 4, we present our proposition which consists in extending OOHDM by introducing metadata and we conclude in section 5.

Z. Bellahsène, D. Patel, and C. Rolland (Eds.): OOIS 2002, LNCS 2425, pp. 434-444, 2002.

2 Motivations

The lack of knowledge on multimedia document structure prevents from easily locating and re-covering them [1]. These problems led to several works proposing metadata to improve document consultation. Among these works [7] presents a metadata classification and an identification for the multimedia documents. [2] proposes an oriented object model for spatio-temporal representation of multimedia documents. Other approaches such as MPEG7 [14] aim at offering a complete set of tools for audio-visual description, creating descriptions on the documents and giving access to the contents. All these works propose useful sets of metadata for document annotation but do not take into account the legacy databases nor elicited and modeled non-textual metadata (instantiated by an audio or image value). To cope with these insufficiencies, we propose on the one hand, the introduction and modeling of non-textual metadata [3] on addition to the existing textual metadata.

On the other hand, we propose to create dynamic view of documents. Several works propose methods to dynamically restructure documents. [5] proposes the Araneus System which extracts information and integrates them into views of databases. [8] proposes the WebML language implemented to design complex web sites. Its proposals include HDM, RMM, OOHDM [15] and Araneus.

All these works propose useful concepts to the document collection design but does not consider the elicited metadata. So, we propose to integrate into the generated dynamic view of documents, metadata elicited in the first part of this paper.

3 Metadata

The need of powerful solution for quickly and efficiently identifying various types of audiovisual content of interest to the user, using also non text-based technologies, directly follows from the urge to efficiently use the available multimedia content and the difficulty of doing so. To this end, MPEG initiated a new work item, formally called "Multimedia Content Description Interface", known as MPEG-7 [14]. MPEG-7 specifies a standard to describe various media types information, including still pictures, video, speech, etc. These descriptions enable the retrieval and the filtering of the next audio-visual data with a predefined structure, but do not provide any representation of "legacy databases".

In order to integrate these applications, we propose a set of elicited metadata in meta-document. Extracting metadata is based on a document indexing and segmentation process elaborated medium by medium. In this section, we present briefly the metadata modeling for each media type. The detail of each one is present in [3].

3.1 Text Media

We propose the annotation of this media by a set of metadata extracted by different tools like Exrep (Extended Regular Expression Processor) [9] (IRIT). These metadata are structured in a meta-document having the root tag "text_file", enriched by the generic attributes "name", "language", "size" and "type".

Each text file is composed of documentary granules (indexed by key word) identified by a structure recognition process. The documentary granule can be chapter, section, paragraph, … We propose to identify by "Text_Unit" (TU) any documentary granule chosen by the user. All these metadata are structured in a meta-document modeled as follows:

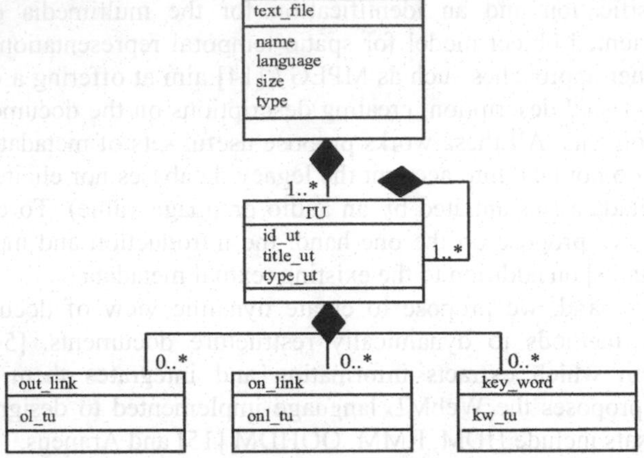

Fig. 1. Text model

3.2 Audio Media

The representation and the description of the audio documents require procedures and techniques developed within the framework of several researches in segmentation, indexing and extraction :

Indexing processes using for example speech recognition enable to elaborate indexing motives (recognized key words, orthography...).

Segmentation processes based on a time-localized abrupt changes in significative parameters of sound have to be detected and classified as diagnostic cues for understanding change in the content of the sonic flow (word, music, noise) [12].

Extraction signal tools allow the annotation of various sound by amplitude, width, speed... like the Transcriber tool [6].

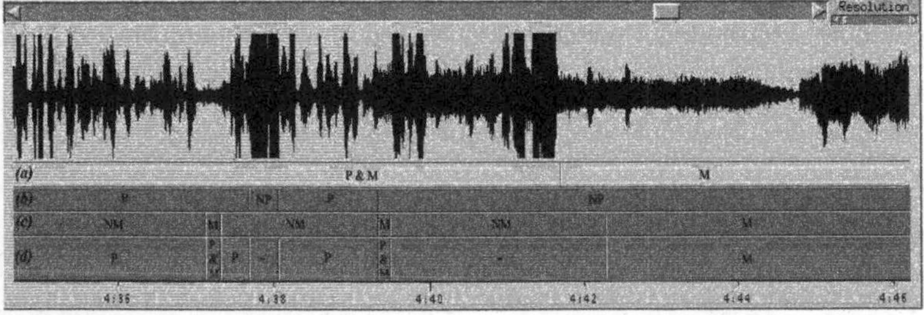

Fig. 2. The Transcriber segmentation

These process results are integrated to annotate the audio documents by metadata. They are structured in a meta-document having the root tag "audio_file" modeled as follows:

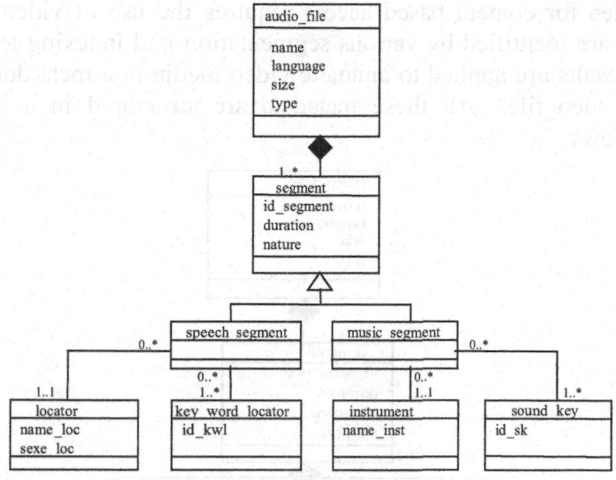

Fig. 3. Audio model

3.3 Image Media

For the image media, we propose textual and graphical metadata, extracted by means of image analysis and recognition techniques [10] (IRIT). The segmentation/generation process is similar to that of digital documents in which one segment characterizes a chunk of text, an image, a page, ... and for which the Optical Character Recognition (OCR) enables to develop motives for indexing segments. The image segmentation process attempts to identify regions to which are associated features such as color, texture [11]. The process results consist in segmenting an image into several regions to annotate the image media by metadata. All these metadata are structured in a meta-document modeled as follows:

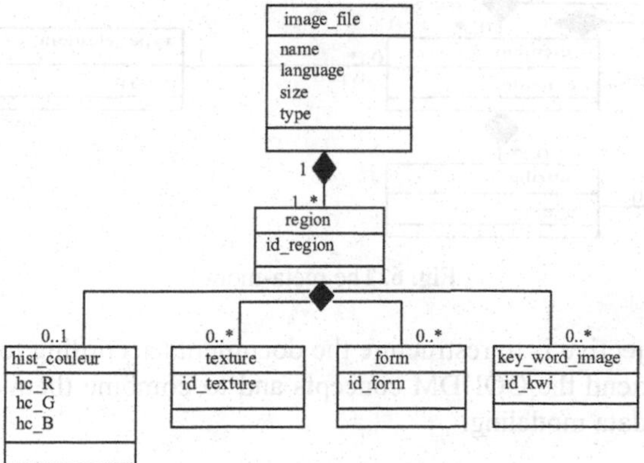

Fig. 4. Image model

3.4 Video Media

Video is composed of audio-visual information. Providing content based access to video data is essential for the successful integration of video into computers. Organizing video for content based access requires the use of video metadata. All these metadata are identified by various segmentation and indexing techniques [13]. The indexing results are applied to annotate video media in a meta-document having the root tag "video_file". All these metadata are structured in a meta-document modeled as follows:

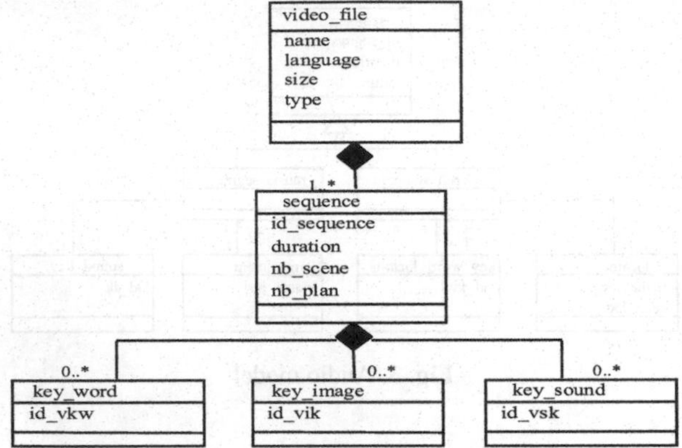

Fig. 5. Video model

3.5 The Basic Meta-model

Our first objective is the annotation of different media documents, by an homogenate structure. For that, we propose a meta-model designed to fit to the different meta-documents of all media types. The meta-model is as follows:

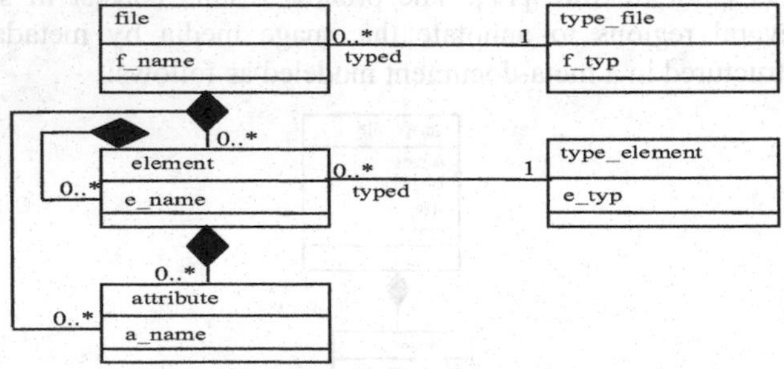

Fig. 6. The meta-model

Our second objective is to restructure the documents according to the user's needs. We propose to extend the OOHDM concepts and to combine them with the previous approach of metadata modeling.

4 Dynamic Views of Documents with OOHDM

OOHDM [15] proposes concepts and mechanisms to structure the access to a web sites. It is a model-based approach for building hypermedia applications. It consists of four different steps namely conceptual design, navigational design, abstract interface design and implementation.

We present then our proposition which consists in extending OOHDM by introducing metadata in all its steps and also in the document contents. We illustrate this methodology on an application example about the laboratory activities.

4.1 Conceptual Design

During the conceptual design, a model of the application domain is built, using object-oriented modeling principles. For each domain class, we add a class meta [4] containing the extracted metadata and including all the "meta-document" of each data type. Each class meta is composed of zero or more files (files containing metadata of an image media, files containing metadata of a video media, etc.). The conceptual model of our application is as follows:

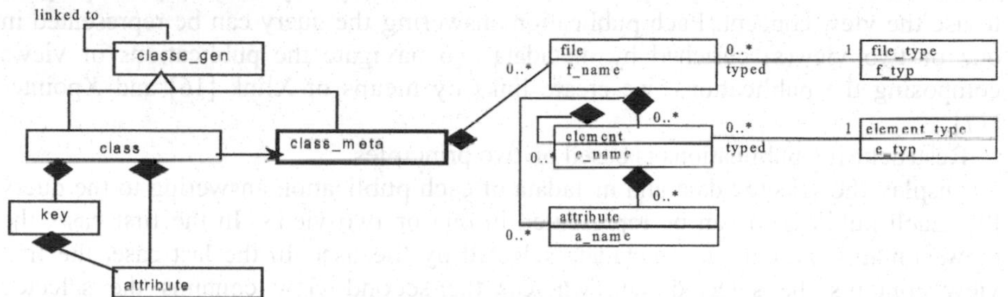

Fig. 7. The conceptual meta-model

4.2 Navigational Design

The navigational design is expressed in two diagrams: the navigational classes diagram and the navigational contexts diagram.

4.2.1 Navigational Classes Diagram

The navigable objects of an hypermedia application are defined by a navigational diagram classes which reflect a selected view around the application domain. The predefined types of navigational classes are organized into navigational contexts.

We represent in this diagram only the important elements and also the 'Anchor' attributes representing links between classes.

4.2.2 Navigational Contexts Diagram

In OOHDM the main structuring primitive of a navigational schema is the notion of navigational context. This latter is a set of nodes, links, context classes and other (nested) navigational contexts induced from navigational classes. An index or a guided tour can define a navigational context. The principal point to build these contexts is the node which introduces the 'Anchor' attribute, whose behavior definition defines the navigation semantics [15]. We propose to extend the OOHDM methodology by introducing metadata in the conceptual schema and also in the navigational context. Thus, navigation (context) can be activated by metadata.

4.3 Abstract Interface Design

Once the navigational structure has been defined, it must be made perceptible to the user through the application's interface, done by defining an abstract interface model. In OOHDM we use the ADV design approach for describing the user interface of an hypermedia application. In our approach, the generated metadata will be taken into account in the ADVs and can be even visualized in the new dynamically created documents [4].

4.4 Experiments

To explain our generic approach, we use an example of a documentary warehouse representing publication of our team. To answer the query "display the publications interested to 'OOHDM' by key word" with XML and by a dynamic way, we propose to use the view concept. Each publication answering the query can be represented in one or two view(s) enriched by metadata. To navigate the publications or views composing the publications, we create links by means of Xlink [16] and Xpointer [17].

Restructuring publications is based on two principles:

Display the selected data and metadata of each publication answering to the query [4]. Each publication can be represented in one or two views. In the first case, the view contains the data and metadata selected by the user. In the last case, the first view contains the selected data whereas the second view contains the selected metadata.

Display for each publication, only the documentary units answering to the query ('OOHDM' in the example) and their metadata. Each publication can be presented in one or two views. In the first case, the view contains the documentary units answering to the user query and their metadata. In the last case, the first view contains the documentary units whereas the second view contains the metadata of the documentary units displayed in the first view.

We illustrate these query types by examples elaborated by OWS (Oracle Web Server).

4.4.1 First Principle

To have an answer to the query presented above, we propose to display the data (title, subject, type, etc.) and metadata (key word, inlinks, onlinks, image forms, etc.) of each publication answering to the user queries ('OOHDM' in the example).

Fig. 8 shows a Web site view presented with the WebML language [8]. The hypertext is composed of four pages. Each page presents a set of information to be displayed.

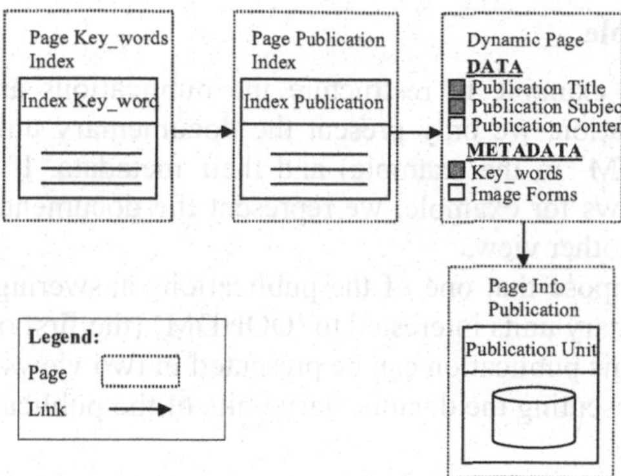

Fig. 8. A Web site view with the graphical WebML notation

The page "Page Key_words Index" presents an index on the key_words used in all publications. The page "Page Publication" presents a set of Publications using the key word selected in the page "Page Key_words Index". To reconstitute each publication, we use a "Dynamic Page". This last allows to the user to select all information what he want to display.

Example: if the user select to display in a view the publication data like title and subject and the publication metadata like key_words, the view is then presented as follows:

```
<?xml version="1.0"?>
<VIEW id="view1">
    <DATA>
            <title> title 1 </title>
            <subject> subject 1 </subject>
    </DATA>
    <METADATA>
            <key_word kw_tu_1= "word1"  kw_tu_2= "word2" />
    </METADATA>
    <A xml:link="simple"
    href="http://www.irit.fr/proto.affich_pub?numpub=2"> next publication </A>
</VIEW>
```

Gathering data and metadata, the content of each views of documents is different from one to another, according to the user needs expressed into his queries and his selection.

We can use in this case the Xlink links to browse the documents created dynamically.

Let us see an example of a publication seen in one view:

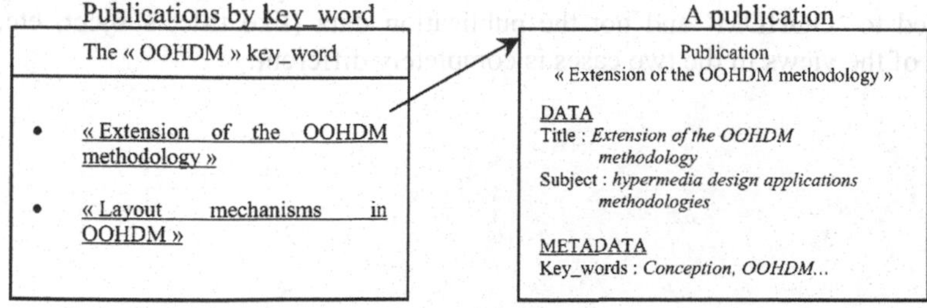

Fig. 9. A publication viewed in one view

4.4.2 Second Principle

We propose an other example to restructure the publications answering the same query. In each publication, we only present the documentary units relevant for the user's query ('OOHDM' in the example) and their metadata. If we represent each publication in two views for example, we represent the documentary units in a view and the metadata in another view.

Example: if we suppose that one of the publications answering to the user needs contains two documentary units interested to 'OOHDM' (the first one is text while the second is an image), this publication can be presented in two views as follows:

The first view representing the documentary units of the publication is presented as follows:

```
<?xml version="1.0"?>
<VIEW id="View1_1">
    <DATA>
        <DU id="1"> ud1
        <xlink:simple
          href='http://www.irit.fr/proto.affich_d_pub?numpub=1#xpointer
        (VIEW/DATA/DU[position()&lt;=2])'/>
        </DU>                    //the first DU which type is text
        <DU id="2"> ud3
        <xlink:simple
        href='http://www.irit.fr/proto.affich_d?numpub=1
          #xpointer(VIEW/DATA/DU[position()&lt;=1])'/>
        </DU>          //the second documentary unit which type is image
    </DATA>
    <A xml:link="simple"
    href="http://www.irit.fr/proto.affich_md?numpub=1"> next page </A>
</VIEW>
```

In this first view, we add Xpointer links to navigate the documentary units.

The second view representing the metadata of the documentary units (DU) is presented as follows:

```
<?xml version="1.0"?>
<VIEW id="View1_2">
    <METADATA>
        <MD-DU id_du="1">     //metadata of the first DU which is text
          <key_word  kw_tu_1= "word1"  kw_tu_2= "word2"/>…
        </MD-DU>
        <MD-DU id_du="2"> //metadata of the second DU unit which is image
          <form  id_form_1= "form1"  id_form_2= "form2"/> …
        </MD-DU>
    </METADATA>
    <A xml:link="simple"
    href="http://www.irit.fr/proto.affich_d?numpub=1"> previous page </A>
</VIEW>
```

Let us see an example of a publication which can be seen in two views (cf. Fig.10)

The difference between this second case and the first one consists in the user choice. The user can select in this second case to display the documentary units interested to 'OOHDM' and not the publication data (like title, subject, etc.). The content of the views in the two cases is completely different.

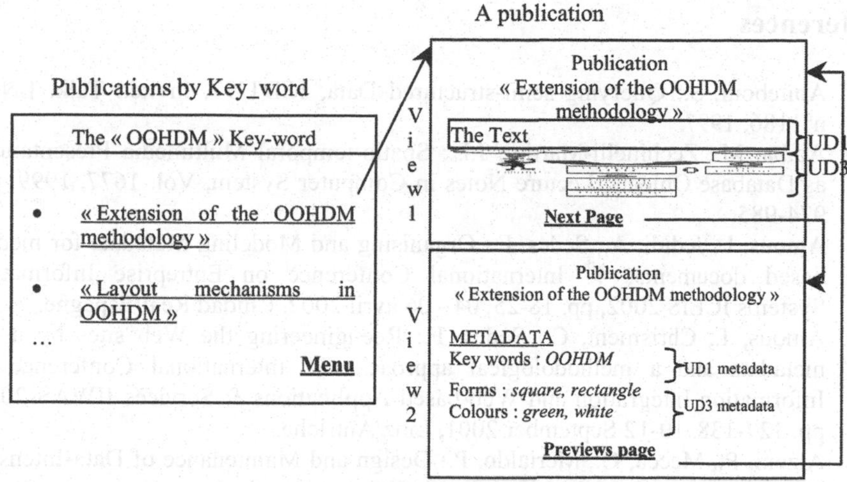

Fig. 10. A publication viewed in two views

5 Conclusion

The semi-structured data context led to introduce the metadata concept, concept that we propose to model and to add in our model to improve search process. The various metadata families process is based on the indexing process and is carried out by extraction (elicitation, synthesis) from the multimedia contents. It can be supplemented by a more or less assisted manual process. The metadata modeling presented in the section 2, is more detailed in [3]. We use this modelisation to enrich the OOHDM methodology in order to build dynamic documents. They are created by the use of views containing the data and metadata answering to the user's requests. Our approach is generic and can be applied on all application type, but to clarify our method, we have chosen a given example.

We propose in this paper with comparison to the paper [4] to use metadata modeling and not only the elicited metadata to build dynamic documents. We propose also to create one or tow views according to the user's needs. The created view contains not only the selected data and metadata but also the documentary units answering the query and respective metadata.

The future prospects of our work concern on the one hand the improvement of metadata modeling by a lower granularity level for all media type. We focus here to the scalable metadata. They can be represented at various levels according to the evolution of the document, the user's needs, the indexing tools. So it is necessary to define and create the scalable operators for a better metadata modeling. For video medium, for example, we can considerate the spatial and temporal features as "inter-media metadata" integrating image and audio media.

On the other hand, we can propose to extend query languages by operator applied for multimedia document querying.

References

1. Abiteboul, S.: Querying semi-structured Data, ICDT'97, Invited Talk, LNCS n°1186, 1997.
2. Adiba, M., Zechinelli-Martini, J.L.: Spatio-temporal Multimedia Presentations as Database Objects, Lecture Notes in Computer System, Vol. 1677, 1999, pp. 974-985.
3. Amous, I., Jedidi, A., Sèdes. F.: Organising and Modeling Metadata for media-based documents, 4th International Conference on Entreprise Information Systems ICEIS 2002, pp. 18-25, 04 - 06 avril 2002, Cuidad Real/Espagne.
4. Amous, I., Chrisment, C., Sèdes. F.: Reengineering the Web sites by using metadata and a methodological approach, 3rd International Conference on Information Integration and Web-based Applications & Services IIWAS 2001, pp. 127-138, 10-12 September 2001, Linz/Autriche.
5. Atzeni, P., Mecca, G., Merialdo, P.: Design and Maintenance of Data-Intensive Web Sites, Proc. EDBT 1998, pp. 436-450.
6. Barras, C., Geoffrois, E., Wu, Z., Liberman, M.: Transcriber: a Free Tool for Segmenting, Labeling and Transcribing Speech, 1st International Conference on Language Resources and Evaluation (LREC), pp. 1373-1376, May 1998.
7. Böhm, K., Rakow, T.C.: Metadata for multimedia documents, SIGMOD-RECORD, Vol. 23, n°4, pp. 21-26, décembre, 1994.
8. Ceri, S., Fraternali, P., Bongio, A.: Web Modeling Language (WebML): a modeling language for designing Web sites, 9th International World Wide Web Conference The Web, Amsterdam, May 15-19, 2000.
9. Lambolez, P.Y., Queille, J.P., Voidrot, J.F., Chrisment, C.: EXREP: a generic rewriting tool for textual information extraction, Ingéniérie des Systèmes d'Information, Vol. 3, n°4, pp. 471-485, 1995.
10. Desachy, J.: Image processing, signal processing, and synthetic aperture radar for remote sensing, SPIE proceedings series, Vol. 3217, September, 1997, London, UK.
11. Gong, Y.: Advancing content-based image retrieval by exploiting image color and regions features, Multimedia Systems, Vol. 7, n°6, pp. 449-457, November 1999.
12. Gauvain, J.L., Lamel, L., Adda, G.: Transcribing Broadcast News for Audio and Video Indexing, Communication of the ACM, Vol. 43, n°2, pp. 64–67, February 2000.
13. Lienhart, R., Effelsberg, W.: Automatic text segmentation and text recognition for video indexing, Multimedia Systems, Vol. 8, n°1, pp. 69-81, January 2000.
14. Mpeg-7.com: a gateway into the world of content management and the interface between industry and the MPEG community. http://www.mpeg-7.com.
15. Schwabe, D., Rossi, G., Barbosa, S. DJ.: Abstraction, composition and layout definition mechanism in OOHDM, 1995. http://www.cs.tufts.edu/~isabel/schwabe/MainPage.html
16. W3C: XML Linking Language (XLink) Version 1.0, 2000. http://www.w3.org/TR/xlink/
17. W3C: XML Pointer Language (XPointer) Version 1.0, 2001. http://www.w3.org/TR/xptr

An Object Oriented Collaboration Flow Management System for Virtual Team Support

Jacques Lonchamp

LORIA
BP 239, 54506 Vandœuvre lès Nancy Cedex, France
jloncham@loria.fr

Abstract. Collaboration flow management is a new paradigm for virtual team support which aims at assisting the opportunistic flow of collaboration within a distributed project, considered as a living and self-organizing system. Such a flow includes informal and formal, synchronous and asynchronous, task-oriented and project management-oriented collaborative sessions. Some of them are elements of model-driven session-based process fragments. The paper defines the collaboration flow management paradigm and describes our Java prototype of collaboration flow management system through a realistic scenario. The paper also discusses how a high level of flexibility is obtained through a set of design choices and object oriented implementation techniques.

1 Introduction

A virtual team (VT) is a *team,* i.e. a group of people who work interdependently with a shared goal, *distributed across space, time, and organization boundaries*, and *linked by webs of interactive technology*. VTs can improve work performance by reducing costs (cutting travel costs and time), shortening cycle time (moving from serial to parallel processes), increasing innovation (permitting more diverse participation, and stimulating creativity), and leveraging learning (gaining wider access to expertise, and sharing best practices). The success of a VT approach depends on a set of psychological, organizational, and cognitive factors [10]. A computerized support for VTs should take into account these factors and include them in its basic requirements. First, a sense of identity and membership is necessary for VTs. Periodically performing informal virtual meetings is not sufficient for developing a collaborative attitude. Participants must feel that the supporting environment help them to *do important and constructive things together, in synergy*. Secondly, traditional authority is minimized in VTs, which develop an inner authority based on competencies. In VTs, power comes from information, expertise, and knowledge, not from position. The important things done together through the supporting environment should include *expression of competencies, externalization of knowledge and mental models* related to the task in hand. Third, trust is the key to VTs. People work together because they trust one an-

Z. Bellahsène, D. Patel, and C. Rolland (Eds.): OOIS 2002, LNCS 2425, pp. 445-457, 2002.

other. People make deals, set goals, and lend one another resources. Trust can build with *the recognition of the contribution that everyone makes, the clarity of positions and commitments*. Finally, project and process management is a critical ingredient for successful distributed work. Co-located teams can quickly clarify goals, correct misunderstandings, and work through problems. VTs need to be *more explicit in their planning and their processes*. When considering these requirements, we claim that no existing paradigm for cooperative systems, neither the workflow management paradigm nor the workgroup computing paradigm, is satisfying. A *new paradigm* is required for VT support. The next section elaborates this idea and defines such a paradigm, called the 'collaboration flow management paradigm'. Section three describes our current Java prototype of collaboration flow management system through a realistic scenario. Section four discusses how a high level of flexibility is obtained through a set of design choices and object oriented implementation techniques. Finally, the last section compares our proposal with related work and draws some perspectives.

2 The Collaboration Flow Management Paradigm

2.1 Motivations

The first section stresses the importance of supporting the VT life cycle process. VT projects usually follow a life cycle with an alternation of divergence phases, during which people work individually, and collaborative convergence phases, during which people *build some shared understanding*, discuss for *discovering and solving the divergences accumulated during individual work*, and *drive the project*. A classical Workflow Management System (WfMS) provides support for coordinating individual activities, as those occurring during divergence phases. Generally, a WfMS provides no support for collaborative activities. Conversely, a VT environment should mainly support convergence phases. The 'workgroup computing paradigm' is not a satisfying solution because it considers collaborative tasks in isolation and does not support the life cycle process as a whole. A computerized environment for VTs should support-processes *whose steps are collaborative sessions* either synchronous or asynchronous, informal or formal. Following the requirements of the first section, we analyze these sessions as working sessions, during which participants express their views, competencies, positions, and commitments about the task in hand. At a very abstract level, we feel that *issue resolution* is the basic building block which can be used for describing all these activities. Participants discuss and solve many issues about the artifacts, the shared context, and the collaboration process itself. The environment should support *the definition and management of processes whose steps are issue-based synchronous or asynchronous, informal or formal, collaborative sessions*.

Otherwise, a VT is a *living and self-organizing system*. As Peter and Trudy Johnson-Lenz explain [6], 'post-mechanistic groupware', like all living systems, are 'rhythmic' and made of 'containers' with flexible and permeable 'boundaries'. The VT computerized environment should support in particular a range of session types (containers types) providing different 'collaboration rhythms', in accordance with the task urgency and the required depth of issue analysis, and different 'group boundaries', through the evolving definition of a 'core team' and an 'extended team'. Procedures (process models), context, and timing are the three other primitives of post-mechanistic groupware [6]. The choice between these forms (containers, rhythms, boundaries, procedures) should be made *dynamically and collectively during the course of the project.*

2.2 Basic Functionalities of a Collaboration Flow Management System

From above, the following four basic functionalities are identified:

(1) Support different types of *short/rapid, more or less formal, synchronous sessions for the core team*, such as artifact-centered informal sessions (around a shared document or a free hand drawing) or formal argumentation sessions (with different rhythms and styles of interaction: 'free', 'turn talking', 'circle', 'moderated', ...). Composite synchronous sessions can mix formal and informal times.

(2) Support *longer/slower/deeper, formal, asynchronous sessions for the core team, controlled through the enactment of issue-based and session-based collaborative process model fragments*. Such model fragments specify for instance various brainstorming processes, document review or inspection processes, knowledge elicitation processes, solution evaluation processes. When needed, an asynchronous issue-based session within a process fragment can be *transformed* into a synchronous session for continuing with a faster rhythm the resolution of conflicting issues (see Fig.1). *Process model fragments can be built, refined, or changed dynamically, at run time.*

(3) Support the overall *collaboration flow:* some initial asynchronous *Project Management (PM) process* enables project initiators to launch the synchronous sessions and the asynchronous process fragments (see Fig.1). This initial PM process is the spring of the *opportunistic flow of collaboration that the VT generates*, which can include in particular other PM processes better suited to the circumstances and which *replace* the initial one (see section 3.3).

(4) Play the role of a *project memory*, storing all project related information: artifacts, debates, free hand drawings, messages, process trace, etc. These elements can be *externalized*, for instance as HTML/XML documents, for easier access and feedback from the extended team during *asynchronous informal sessions* on the Web.

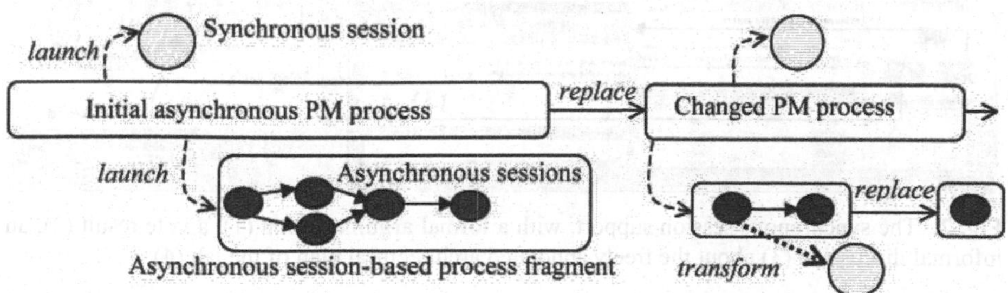

Fig. 1. Main elements of a collaboration flow

3 A Prototype of Collaboration Flow Management System

In this section, we describe a scenario supported by our prototype of object oriented *Collaboration flow Management System* (CfMS). Our lab plans an extension of its building. A VT has been created for discussing different aspects of the project. The team includes representatives of lab members and participants coming from the university, the town, and the firm of architects. A kick-off informal orientation meeting has first planned a set of virtual meetings about specific questions. These synchronous sessions are organized through the asynchronous PM process (see section 3.3).

3.1 Synchronous Session Support

The session described here is about car parking near the lab. Such a synchronous session does not follow any predefined execution path: the session moderator can describe the problem and organize the work by using the audio channel.

In our scenario, the problem is first informally discussed through textual or graphical annotations on the overall building plan (see Fig.2). Social protocols, such as author identification with colors, can be negotiated. Clarifications may be obtained through the chat tool. In a second time, each emerging controversial issue can be formally discussed with explicit arguments and a 'turn talking' policy ('free' and 'moderated' policies are also available). On the basis of the resulting argumentation trees (similar to those produced during asynchronous sessions which are described in more details in section 3.2.2), the moderator can select some solutions and measure the consensus within the core team with the voting tool. All documents (annotated plans, argumentation trees, vote results) can be saved as HTML documents for feedback from other lab members.

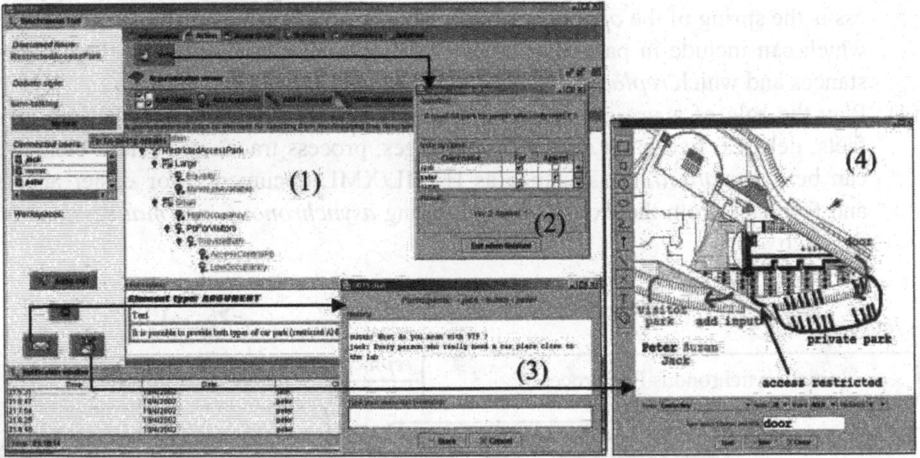

Fig. 2. The synchronous session support, with a formal argumentation (1), a vote result (2), an informal discussion (3) about the freely annotated architectural plan of the lab (4)

3.2 Model-Driven Collaborative Process Fragment Support

Later in the course of the project, the VT has planned an asynchronous model-driven process fragment for a systematic study of the existing cafeteria dysfunctions and for proposing a consensual list of possible causes and solutions for the new cafeteria.

3.2.1 The Meta Model

The process modeling language is defined by a *meta model*, which extends the classical *process view* and *organizational view* of WfMSs with a *decision view* and a *knowledge view* (see Fig.3).

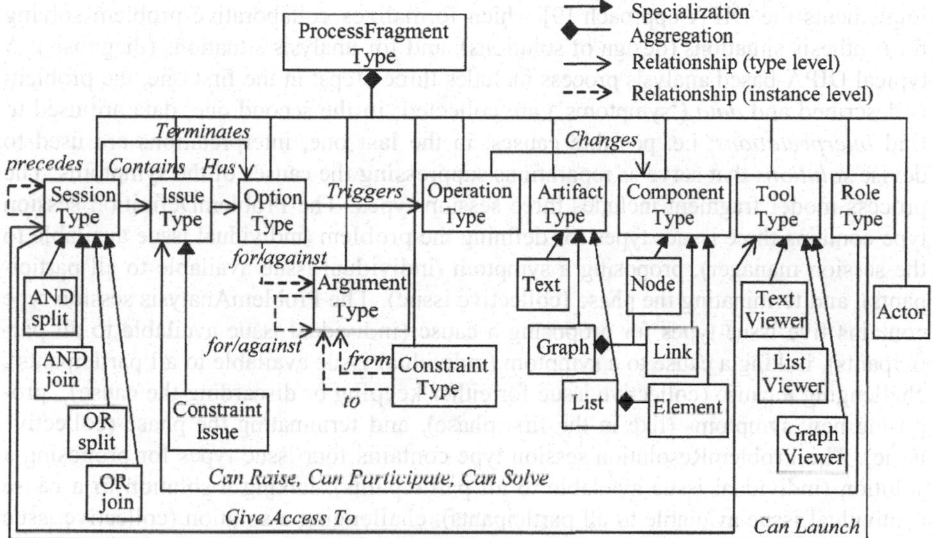

Fig. 3. The basic elements of the meta model

The *process view* mainly includes ProcessFragment and Session types. Each process fragment instance is structured into a network of session instances (also called 'phases'), with precedence relationships, and special phase instances corresponding to the classical workflow operators (AND split, OR split, AND join, OR join phase types). The *knowledge view* mainly includes Artifact, Component, and ApplicationTool types. Artifact types specialize generic types such as Text, List, Table, Graph (concept map), or Image. Component types specialize generic types such as ListElement, GraphNode, or GraphEdge. ApplicationTool types mirror the specialization of artifact types, with specializations of generic types such as TextViewer, ListViewer, TableViewer, or GraphViewer. Each Session type grants access to some ApplicationTool types. The *organizational view* mainly includes Role and Actor types. The *decision view* describes collaborative work at a fine grain level. Each Session type is defined internally by a set of Issue types, which must be solved either individually or collectively. Each Issue type is characterized by a set of Option types, which describe the possible solutions. At run time, one option is chosen trough an argumentation process. Each Option type can trigger, when it is chosen, some Operation type, which can change some Component, or change the process state (e.g. termination of a Session), or change the process definition itself. This meta model is implemented as an object oriented class model. Core classes implement the basic environment mechanisms (enactment, awareness, ...). Application specific classes specialize core classes and are generated by compiling a process fragment model description. Instantiation of specialized classes takes place statically for instances which are necessary for starting the process or dynamically at run time. All instances are persistent.

3.2.2 The Scenario

A process model fragment is selected and instantiated (see section 3.3). The fragment implements the DIPA approach [9] which formalizes collaborative problem solving for synthesis situations (design of solutions), and for analysis situations (diagnosis). A typical DIPA-based analysis process includes three steps: in the first one, the problem is described and *data* ('symptoms') are collected; in the second one, data are used to find *interpretations*, i.e. possible causes; in the last one, interpretations are used to devise *solutions* that serve as reparations suppressing the causes of the symptoms. The process model fragment includes three session types. The ProblemDefinition session type contains three issues types for defining the problem (individual issue available to the session manager), proposing a symptom (individual issue available to all participants), and terminating the phase (collective issue). The ProblemAnalysis session type contains five issue types for proposing a cause (individual issue available to all participants), linking a cause to a symptom (individual issue available to all participants), challenging a cause (collective issue for either keeping or discarding the cause), proposing new symptoms (like in the first phase), and terminating the phase (collective issue). The ProblemResolution session type contains four issue types for proposing a solution (individual issue available to all participants), linking a solution to a cause (individual issue available to all participants), challenging a solution (collective issue for either keeping or discarding the solution), and terminating the phase (collective issue). The instantiated process is a sequence with one phase of each type.

When a user, say Jack, logs in a process fragment where he plays a role, he can use the What can I do? guidance query and the Whats'new? awareness query (for knowing elements that have changed since his last logout). He can also browse various textual and graphical representations of the model types and the process instances. All participants only act by solving typed issue instances. If Jack wants to propose a new cause, he raises an individual ProposeCauseIssue. Then he has to explain his intention as an argument. This individual issue is automatically solved and triggers an operation which creates a new Cause component. If Jack wants to challenge a cause given by Peter, he raises a collective ChallengeCauseIssue. Then, he gives an argument in favor of the Discard option. Other participants can react (e.g. support the Keep option or challenge Jack's argument). The debate takes the form of an argumentation tree, possibly with qualitative importance constraints between arguments. Such a constraint (more/less/equally important than) opens a sub issue, called a 'constraint issue', for debating about the value of the constraint. Participants can access various representations of argumentations, as a threaded discussion form (Fig.3) or a graphical form with a 'playback' facility (Fig.5). At each argumentation move, the system computes a preferred option by using an *argumentative reasoning technique* close to the approach proposed in Zeno [4]. The system provides also statistical charts about the participation, the favorite option of each participant, and the level of conflict, based on the number of changes of the global preferred option. Suzan, who plays a role giving the capability to solve this type of issue, terminates the debate by choosing one option. The issue resolution triggers an operation that either keep or discard the challenged cause. Different tools, like table or graph viewers, are available to the session participants for accessing the process artifacts, such as the symptom/cause/solution concept graph of Fig 5.

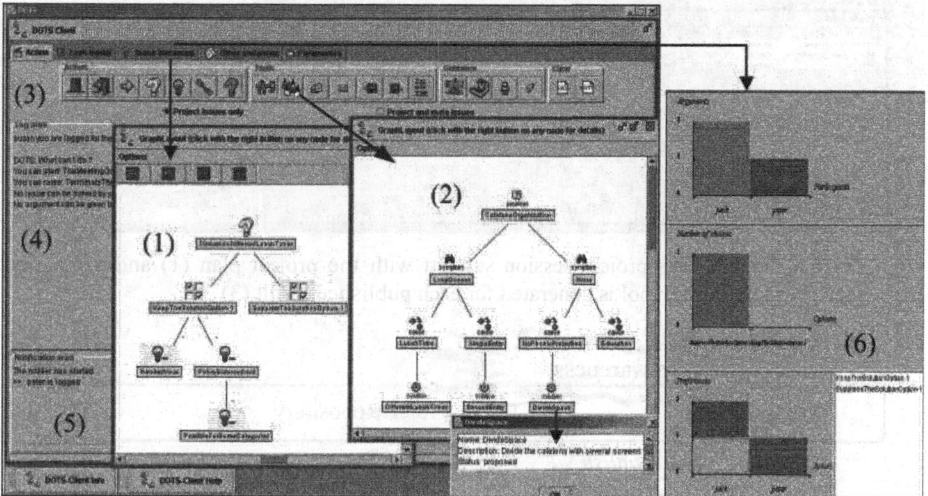

Fig. 4. The asynchronous process centered support, with a graphical view of an issue (1), the DISA concept graph built during the session (2), the action panel (3) with a 'What Can I do?' guidance query (4), the notification panel (5), the statistical analysis of the debate (6)

3.3 The Project Management Process

In our scenario, the initial PM process follows a very simple model: participants playing the role of ProjectManager can plan synchronous sessions and asynchronous process fragments by solving CreateSessionOrProcess individual issue instances. Each resolution adds a new description (name, date, objective, participants, status, results, ...) to a ProjectPlan artifact and calls people for participation through email generation. This planning activity can also result from synchronous orientation meetings with the core team. The ProjectManager can also publish in a ProjectRepository artifact, HTML documents produced by the terminated processes/sessions (PublishResult issue type). A dedicated tool for accessing them is generated and appears in the tool list of the PM session (see Fig.6). The 'What's new?' awareness query at the level of the PM process can help to coordinate concurrent process fragments: for instance, when a first one (pf1) publishes a new result, a second one (pf2) can start a phase taking the new document into account (see Fig.6). This mechanisms also work for individual activities which are out of the control of the CfMS.

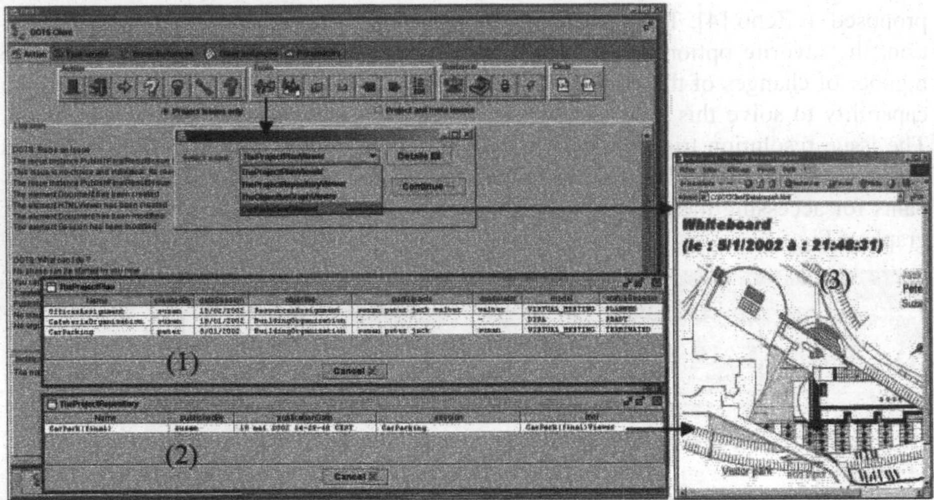

Fig. 5. The asynchronous project session support with the project plan (1) and the project repository (2). A dedicated tool is generated for each published result (3)

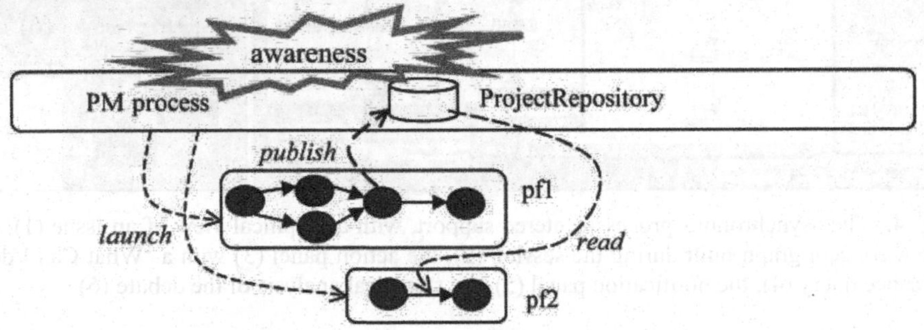

Fig. 6. Synchronization of process fragments

4 Flexibility of the CfMS Prototype

Flexibility is a central requirement for CfMSs. We briefly emphasizes nine points which contribute to the flexibility of our prototype.

(1) The overall design enables switching between *informal and formal support*. For instance, during a synchronous session, an informal debate around a document can switch to formal argumentations. A collaborative problem solving session can either be organized as an informal meeting or as a formal model-driven asynchronous session. At the end of such a formal process among the core team, the produced artifacts can be proposed to an extended team for informal discussion on the Web.

(2) The overall design also enables switching *between asynchronous and synchronous work*. An issue resolution can start asynchronously and terminate synchronously or the opposite.

(3) The concept of *process model fragment* is important for ensuring the fluidity of the global process. There is no rigid overall process model and each fragment allows to redefine many organizational parameters contributing to the global fluidity: fluidity of the core team and extended team boundaries, fluidity of the roles and the assignment of the actors, fluidity in the definition and organization of the sessions, fluidity in the rhythms between different styles of interaction, etc.

(4) A process fragment is a *data object* not a program or a script. The information about the process state and the process evolution is distributed over the process elements. This object orientation allows a process fragment to be modified during its enactment for exception handling or opportunistic adaptation to new situations. However, we favor as far as possible disciplined predefined changes (see point 5).

(5) A model fragment can include *open points* for refining the model at run time. In our model an open point takes the form of an instance of a model refinement phase type which includes a *model refinement issue type*, with one option type for each possible refinement. At run time, one of these options is chosen, either individually by the project manager, or collectively by the core team. The corresponding refinement is deployed, by instantiating new phase instances and new phase precedence relationships. By this way, artifact production and process refinement are performed similarly. For instance, such a refinement phase at the end of PM model fragments can enable the project manager (or the core team) to change the PM policy. In our scenario, a richer PM model could include an issue type for publicizing individual tasks by publishing them in the ProjectPlan. Participants could commit themselves to do a given task, and their commitments could be published in the ProjectPlan.

(6) The *implementation makes easy run time evolutions of the process fragments*. In a model each specific type is the specialization of one of the generic types of Fig.3. Relationships *at the type level* (e.g. the ProblemAnalysis session type contains the ProposeCause issue type) are expressed and stored persistently as relationships between instances of "meta classes" which are associated to all model classes (see Fig.7).

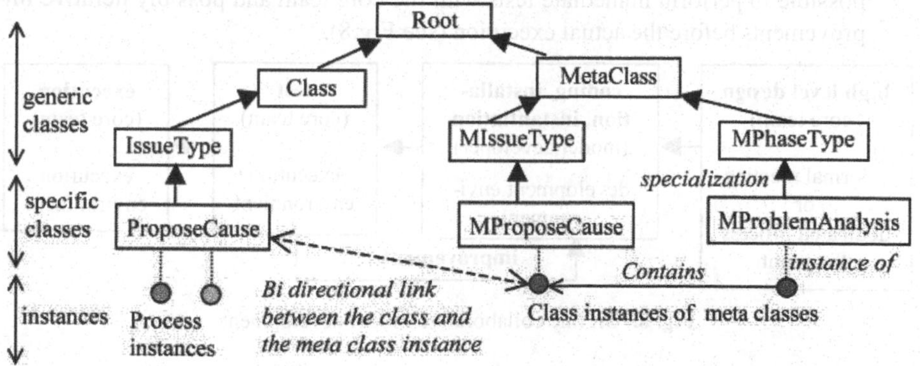

Fig. 7. The implementation organization

Thus, many *process model structural changes between existing components* are performed dynamically through predefined 'meta issue' types (e.g. AddIssueTypeToPhaseType) in the same way as changing process instances. It is worth noting that, unlike many other systems the 'meta interface' of our system (i.e. the set of the 'meta issues') is a *collaborative interface*.

(7) For *creating new model classes* (and the corresponding meta classes) we use the *'linguistic reflection' technique* [8]. Predefined meta issues generate new classes in the form of Java code, compile, and instantiate them dynamically. This technique is effective when the code can be generated on the basis of a few number of parameters provided by end users at run time. It is quite frequent, because specific classes are specializations of the predefined core classes and most elements are inherited from the super classes. For instance, creating new role types is easy, because no specific code is necessary: all the semantics of the role type is expressed in terms of relationships at the class level (see the Can Raise, Can Participate, Can Solve, Can Launch relationships of Fig.3). In some other cases, such as creating new operation types, potentially complex code has to be created. The solution is to allow dynamic coding in the process model language followed by the whole transformation process (starting with our specific compiler producing Java code followed by the persistency pre processor, the regular Java compiler, and the instantiation process [13]). This approach is possible under the control of a single participant by calling the integrated development environment (editor, compiler, instantiation tool, verifier) from the PM process. We describe in the next point another approach which allows the core team to participate to the model definition even if its members have no detailed knowledge of the process modeling language.

(8) In this approach, the general design of the model fragment is collaboratively defined either during an informal virtual meeting or by using *a dedicated model fragment which guides the model elicitation process* (definition of main phase, issue, and role types, and generation of the model skeleton). Then, on the basis of this rough design, a model developer can complete immediately the code and install/instantiate the new fragment with the development environment. Finally, it is possible to perform immediate tests with the core team and possibly iterative improvements before the actual execution (see Fig.8).

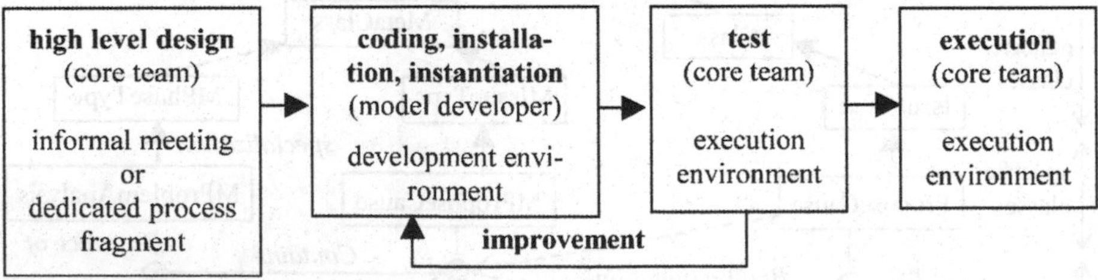

Fig. 8. On line collaborative model development

(9) The last aspect of flexibility is related to the idea of *core services and substitutable external services*. In our vision, a CfMS should only provide the core serv-

ices necessary to support collaboration. Even if the prototype provides low level services for exchanging files and managing a basic file/directory-based repository, in most cases, a document sharing system for distributed teams such as BSCW [1] or our Java Motu prototype [16] should complement the CfMS for managing (sharing, versioning) the shared application artifacts created during individual steps, such as the architectural plans in our scenario. By this way, *collaboration is not tied to some particular document management policy*. Similarly, no integrated support is provided for coordinating the execution of individual tasks. *A cooperative WfMS or ad-hoc WfMS* could also complement our CfMS from this point of view.

In summary, all the *evolution work* (model refinement at open points, punctual changes with the meta interface, and on line model development) is performed through specific issue types (refinement issues, meta issues, model elicitation issues) and is similar to the *application-oriented work* and the *project management work*.

5 Related Work and Perspectives

Our approach is rooted in a wealth of research projects. Among the most important precursors, we can cite Conversation Builder [7] (for genericity, process model fragments, asynchronous collaboration), Cognoter/Argnoter [17] and gIBIS [3] (for argumentation and concept mapping). We can also emphasize, in many application domains, a trend from hard-coded tools to model-based generic environments. It is the case for instance for review/inspection systems, moving from specialized tools such as ICICLE, Scrutiny, etc. [15] to generic review/inspection environments such as CSRSv3 [18] or ASSIST [14].

More specifically, two recent systems have strong similarities with our proposal. We share with Compendium [2] the idea of modeling collaborative work through a set of issue types, called 'question-based templates' in Compendium. We share with SCOPE ('Session-based Collaborative Process-centered Environment')[5] the idea of 'session based process modeling'. SCOPE roughly coincides with our definition of a CfMS. But SCOPE, on the one hand does not provide high level interaction services, such as our argumentation and decision-making services, and on the other hand imposes some low level mechanisms, such as a specific concurrency control mechanism, that we exclude from our core services. At the commercial level, VT support systems are mainly collaborative portals such as Livelink virutalteams for instance [11] which provides six 'walls' (rooms) for six themes: people, purpose, links (between people and work), time, meetings, and content (documents). Such a portal does not provide a real process support and is not 'proactive' as our proposal.

For extending the core services of our CfMS prototype, future work will be directed towards a better support *for the VT project memory* by using XML technologies. Such a memory should store and restore *both in human-readable and machine-readable forms* all kinds of information, such as the collaboration artifacts, the process history, the argumentation trees, and even the process model fragments themselves. Another important objective is to provide a larger *library of reusable process model fragments*, either task-oriented or PM-oriented, and to evaluate them through scenarios and experiments, such as those already performed with our previous prototype [13].

Acknowledgments

This work is part of the INRIA ECOO project. Bruno Denis and Fabrice Muller have contributed to the CfMS prototype development.

References

1. Bentley, R., Appelt, W., Busbash, U., Hinrichs, E., Kerr, D., Sikkel, K., Trevor, J., and Woetzel, G.: Basic support for cooperative work on the World Wide Web. International Journal of Human-Computer Studies, 46 (1997)827-846
2. Conklin, J., Selvin, A., Buckingham Shum, S., Sierhuis M.: Facilitated Hypertext for Collective Sense making: 15 Years on from gIBIS. Tech. Report KMI-TR-112, Knowledge Media Institute (2001)
3. Conklin, J., Begeman, M.: gIBIS: A hypertext tool for exploratory policy discussion. ACM Transaction on Office Information System, 6, 4 (1988) 303-331
4. Gordon, T.F., Karacapidilis, N.: The Zeno argumentation framework. Proc. 6th Int. Conf. on AI and Law (ICAIL'97), Melbourne, Australia, ACM Press (1997) 10-18
5. Haake, J.M., Wang: W. Flexible support for business processes: extending cooperative hypermedia with process support. Information and Software Technology, 41, 6 (1999)
6. Johnson-Lenz, P., Johnson-Lenz, T.: Post mechanistic groupware primitives: rhythms, boundaries and containers. Int. Journal Man-Machine Studies, 34 (1991) 395-417
7. Kaplan, S., Caroll, A.: Supporting collaborative processes with Conversation Builder. Computer communications, 15, 8 (1992)
8. Kirby, G.N.C., Morrison, R., Stemple, D.W.: Linguistic reflection in Java. Software Practice & Experience, 28, 10 (1998) 1045-1077
9. Lewkowicz, M., Zacklad, M.: MEMO-net, un collecticiel utilisant la méthode de résolution de problème DIPA pour la capitalisation et la gestion des connaissances dans les projets de conception. Proc. IC'99, Palaiseau, France (1999) 119-128
10. Lipnack, J., Stamps, J.: Virtual teams. John Wiley & Sons, New York (2000)
11. Livelink virtualteams system (http://www.opentext.com/)
12. Lonchamp, J., Muller: Computer-Supported Deliberations for Distributed Teams. Proc. I2CS 2001, Ilmenau, Germany, LNCS, Springer-Verlag (2001) 167-174
13. Lonchamp, J., Denis, B.: Fine-grained process modeling for collaborative work support: experiences with CPCE. Journal of Decision Systems, 7 (1998) 263-282

14. Macdonald, F., Miller, J.: Automatic generic support for software inspection. Proc. 10th International Quality Week, San Francisco (1997)
15. Macdonald, F., Miller, J., Brooks, A., Roper, M., Wood, M.: A review of tool support for software inspection. Proc. 7th Int. Workshop on CASE (1995)
16. Motu system (available at http://motu.sourceforge.net/)
17. Stefik, M., Foster, G., Bobrow, D., Kahn, K., Lanning, S., Suchman, L.: Beyond the chalkboard: computer support for collaboration and problem solving in meetings. CACM, 1,(1987) 32-47
18. Tjahjono, D.: Building software review systems using CSRS. Tech. Report ICS-TR-95-06, University of Hawaii, Honolulu (1995)

Connectors for CORBA Components

Bruno Traverson[1] and Nesrine Yahiaoui[2]

[1] EDF R&D
1 avenue du Général de Gaulle F-92140 Clamart France
Bruno.Traverson@der.edfgdf.fr
[2] UVSQ PRiSM
45 avenue des Etats-Unis F-78035 Versailles France
syahiaou@ens.uvsq.fr

Abstract. To enable integration of heterogeneous components, the description of offered interfaces (services offered by the component to its environment) of the components is not always sufficient. To support complex assemblies, two additional concepts have to be handled: required interfaces (services offered by the environment to the component) and connectors (mechanisms needed to interconnect components). CCM (CORBA Component Model) has recently been proposed as a component model on top of CORBA middleware: it integrates the concept of required interfaces but not yet the concept of connectors. Our proposal is to add this concept to CCM. We illustrate it with different varieties of connectors, like interface adaptors and mediators integrating mechanisms such as load balancing and fault tolerance.

1 Introduction

Nowadays, a discussion is been held about the fact that software components may achieve goals that have been targeted - and missed - by object-oriented approaches. The purpose of this paper is not to participate to this debate but rather to understand what is new in component-oriented technologies regarding to what has been generally done in object-oriented technologies. From our analysis, we found some fundamental differences especially regarding the description of dependencies among software elements. In object-oriented approaches, the focus was essentially on offered interfaces - describing services offered by the object to its environment. In component-oriented approaches, also exist the notions of required interfaces (describing services offered by the environment to the component) and connectors (mechanisms needed to interconnect components). We will expend on this in the first part of this paper.

Anyway, we must objectively note that the industry marketplace has shown a real interest in component-oriented approaches and its main actors have recently introduced different component platforms. Hence, OMG (Object Management Group) is currently specifying CCM (CORBA Component Model) which is a component plat-

Z. Bellahsène, D. Patel, and C. Rolland (Eds.): OOIS 2002, LNCS 2425, pp. 458-463, 2002.

form built on top of CORBA (Common Object Request Broker Architecture) object-oriented middleware.

Our contribution is based on the draft specification of CCM and proposes to add to it the concept of connector. We illustrate our work on a banking application realizing a fund transfer. Also, we exhibit some examples of useful connectors, like interface adaptors and mediators integrating mechanisms such as load balancing and fault tolerance.

This paper is structured in two parts. The first part is two folds: some further details on component and connector concepts and, then, a brief description of the CCM specification. The second part describes our proposal by giving the main design principles and some illustrating examples. The conclusion gives some information on related work and further perspectives.

2 CORBA Components

Benefits in using software components are clear: to minimize software production costs but also to reduce maintenance costs and to encourage reuse. However, this is not always simple in practice. Thus, paramount is the integration process of heterogeneous components to get the desired result in an efficient way. This is the reason why connectors (ways of interconnecting components) should be considered at the same degree of importance as components.

2.1 Components and Connectors

A priori, a component is designed and developed independently to the applications that use it. This is the reason why it is necessary that this component be, on the one hand, adaptable according to the application that uses it and be, on the other hand, usable in various environment systems. These two levels of adaptation correspond to what is called parameter setting (or configuration). It consists, in both cases, of positioning values of parameters influencing the behavior of the component. In the case of our banking application, the setting of application parameters consists, for example, in defining the amount that can be overdrawn up on an account. The setting of system parameters will allow, for instance, to decide what interaction mode will be used within the application: interactive with on-line responses or message-driven with differed responses.

Beyond the aspect of configuration just described, reuse allows cost reduction. However, this property tends to imply that a component offers a " standard " service sufficiently common for a great number of applications that leaves less room to innovative features. In addition, reuse is only possible, if a disciplined design and development approach such as that defined by Bertrand Meyer (design by contract) [6] and adequate organization (definition of a component repository) are set up. The banking application may be reusable in any banking establishment or for inter-bank transfers and even in another application domain. In each one of these three assumptions, the difficulties of reuse a component can come as well from potentially different technical choices (in different branches of the same bank), possibly incompatible marketing

policies (in different bank establishments) or of a lack of genericity of the component itself (in another application model).
The component-based approach is viable only if it is simple to connect the components between them to build, by assembly, a particular application. The assembly of several components that can be of various origins is facilitated if there is a flexible and powerful way to carry out the necessary adaptations - as well at the application level as at the system level - to make a successful integration. Thus, the banking application may be built directly by assembly of components that can carry out deposit and withdraw operations. On the other hand, difficulties may emerge when the basic components – realizing local deposit and local withdraw operations - are not always co-localized and thus implies a distributed implementation of the transfer operation.

A characteristic, often indicated to differentiate a component-based approach from an object-based approach, is the possibility, for a component, to support several interfaces. This permits to express in the form of interfaces the pre-requirements that the component has towards its environment. Thus, two kinds of interfaces can be distinguished: the offered interface or server interface corresponds to services offered by the component to its environment, interfaces used by the component are called required interfaces or client interfaces. We can realize our banking application by assembling four components: a first one asking for the transfer operation, a second one realizing the transfer operation, and the two others respectively realizing the deposit and the withdraw operations. The second component, in addition to the transfer interface it offers, has to use the interfaces of the last two components.

The integration of software modules from various origins poses a certain number of problems as well from a business point of view as from a technical point of view. From a business point of view, the description of a module by using an interface description language (IDL) or via an application programming interface (API) in programming language can lead to errors related to the homonyms (two interfaces that have the same syntactical description but that are semantically incompatibles) and to synonyms (two interfaces that give the same service but have different syntax), that are badly controlled. Moreover, no instructions for use of the service parameters offered by the module are described, the risk of using them out of their validity domain is important and can lead to disastrous consequences. From a technical point of view, the environment where a software component is deployed may be inadequate for its normal behavior (insufficient system resources). Moreover, the co–existence of components from various origins where each one need a quota of system resources may provoke access conflicts to these resources and thus may lead to a global collapse of the system. To solve these problems, we need a notation for describing more precisely the component and the way they are assembled [9].

2.2 CCM

The future version of CORBA (Common Object Request Broker Architecture) specification proposed and maintained by the OMG (Object Management Group) includes a component model called CCM (CORBA Component Model) [7]. The CCM specification particularly describes the following aspects: design of components (abstract model), implementation of components (programming model), assembly and deployment mechanisms on component infrastructure.

In this paper, we will only present the abstract model that corresponds to the specification level we are considering.
Interfaces of a CORBA component (called ports in the CCM specification) are described by using the OMG interface description language (IDL). They can have different kinds. The offered interfaces (called facets in the CCM specification), respectively the required interfaces (called receptacles in the CCM specification) allows to declare the service offered by the component, respectively the service needed for its operation. The event-driven interfaces (event source and event sink) allow asynchronous exchanges in *push* mode (this means that the transmission of an event to one or more event receptors is triggered by the event emitter). Finally, the attribute interface allows the component configuration.

Our banking application may be described using three kinds of components: the client component which issues the transfer requests, the bank component which receives them and dispatches it into deposit and withdraw requests to account components that implement locally the respective operations.

Synchronous communications are used to communicate between components. So, we are using facet and receptacle interfaces. Attribute interface of the account component may be used to define the amount of overdrawn up for the withdraw operation.

3 Adding Connectors to CCM

As we have seen in the previous section, CCM model introduces the concepts of offered interfaces and required interfaces but not yet the concept of connectors. Thus, interconnection between CORBA components operates directly between interfaces of the same type. Another problem is that the interconnection between components is not explicitly described in the IDL description. Our proposal intends to fill this gap in defining "CORBA connectors" at the same level as CORBA components i.e. in the IDL description.

3.1 Main Design Principles

Connectors are classified according to the classification given in [4]. Four categories are used in this classification:

Communication services: where the connector provides the data transmission service among components. This data may be messages, data to process, results of computation (e.g. request/response, event queue).

Co-ordination services: where the connector provides the control transfer service among components (e.g. synchronous, asynchronous invocation).

Conversion services: where the connector converts the interaction required by one component to that provided by another. Conversion services allow components that have not been especially tailored for each other to interacting (e.g. interface adaptation).

Facilitation services: where the connector provides the service of negotiation and improvement of component interactions (e.g. load-balancing and fault-tolerance).

In order to minimize impact on the current specification, connectors are described like components. To distinguish them from components, connector descriptions use a distinct terminology. We decide to reuse a common terminology used in ADL (Architecture Description Languages) [5]. For instance, instead of speaking of ports, roles define the interconnection points.

3.2 Assessment

In this section, we exhibit some examples to illustrate the use of different kinds of connectors.

Firstly, let us consider the case of interface adaptation. This connector consists in adapting two syntactically different but semantically compatible interfaces. Thus, it allows the components that have this kind of interface to interacting. The benefit of this connector is that it permits to remove the re-writing phase of the component code and its compilation. Another benefit of this kind of connector is that it supports evolution. Indeed, if two components are directly linked and that one has changed its interface, the second one must be written and compiled again. If the interface adaptation connector is used, the adaptation is taken into account in the connector without change in components.

Secondly, let us consider the case of load balancing. This connector, as its name indicates it, consists in load balancing requests among multiple components offering the same interface. When a component transmits a request to an interface, the connector intercepts it and dispatches it to the component that has fewer loads, according to a selection criterion.

Lastly, let us consider the case of fault-tolerance. This connector consists in maintaining interaction between components even if the component that offers the interface breaks down. For instance, when the caller component transmits a request to an interface, the fault-tolerance connector intercepts it and dispatches it to one instance of the called component. If this component does not respond or throws an exception, the connector can catch it and start a new instance of a component offering the same interface, then connects to it and finally dispatches a second time the request. All these operations are transparent to the caller component.

4 Conclusion

We have proposed, in this paper, an extension to the CCM specification in order to integrate, in IDL descriptions, the connector concept. Indeed, we think this concept is paramount for successful integration of heterogeneous components.

Presently, we are defining a meta-model of our CCM implementation using UML (Unified Modeling Language). This will enable us to have specifications of components and connectors that are platform-independent. This will open the possibility to integrate components from different platforms (CCM, EJB, .Net).

We are also considering the integration of the configuration concept in CCM. The configuration concept permits to describe particular assemblies of components and connectors. This will enable us to support composite components also known as a greybox approach [2].

Lastly, we are looking at the recent evolutions of UML [8]. It is expected that UML 2.0 will integrate number of concepts discussed in this paper. We are also very interested by contract-based design, as for instance described in [1] and [3], to support dynamic reconfiguration and contract negotiation.

References

1. A. Beugnard, J.M. Jézéquel, N. Plouzeau, D. Watkins, Making Components Contract Aware. Computer, July 1999, pp 38-45.
2. M. Büchi, W. Weck, The Greybox Approach: When Blackbox Specifications Hide Too Much. TUCS Technical Report No. 297, August 1999. ISBN 952-12-0508-3. ISSN 1239-1891.
3. L. Andrade, J. Fiadero, Interconnecting Objects With Contracts. ECOOP'2001. Hungary, June2001.
4. N. K. Mehta, N. Medvidovic, S. Phadke, Towards a Taxonomy of Software Connectors. Proceedings of the 22th International Conference on Software Engineering (ICSE 2000), pages 178-187. Limerick, Ireland, June 4-11, 2000.
5. N. Medvidovic, R.N. Taylor, A Classification and Comparison Framework for Software Architecture Description Languages. IEEE transactions on Software Engineering, vol. 26, N°1, pp. 70-93, 2000.
6. B. Meyer, Object-oriented Software Construction, Second Edition. Prentice-Hall, 1997.
7. OMG, CORBA Components. OMG Document, August 1999.
8. OMG, Unified Modeling Language. OMG Draft Document, 2002.
9. M. Shaw, D. Garlan, Software Architecture: Perspective on an Emerging Discipline. Prentice-Hall, 1996.

Non-functional Replication Management in the Corba Component Model*

Vania Marangozova and Daniel Hagimont

INRIA Rhône-Alpes
655 avenue de l'Europe, Montbonnot 38334 St Ismier cedex, France
{Vania.Marangozova,Daniel.Hagimont}@inrialpes.fr

1 Introduction

Component-based programming is a promising approach to distributed application development [1]. It encourages software reuse and promotes the separation (as in aspect-oriented programming[5]) between the components' business implementations and the code managing the used system services. One system service of particular importance to the distributed computing domain is replication.

Managing replication as a separate (non-functional) aspect in a component-based environment is a way to provide a generic replication solution which can be applied to a wide range of applications. It allows the association of different replication/consistency protocols with components according to their contexts of (re)use.

If many projects have addressed the issue of managing replication in contemporary middleware (and more specifically in Corba [3][6][9]), providing configurable replication management in a component-based environment is still an open issue.

This paper presents our approach to component replication, based on the CORBA Component Model (CCM [8]). We show that replication can be managed as a configurable non-functional aspect in a component-based system.

The article is organized as follows. Section 2 presents our motivations and Section 3 provides a rapid overview of CCM. Our infrastructure for replication and consistency configuration, as well as its application to a specific scenario, are presented in Section 4. Sections 5 concludes this article.

2 Motivations

We investigate the integration of a replication service in a component-based infrastructure. We aim at providing a solution which allows the implementation of various replication scenarios for a given component-based application. We are particularly interested in scenarios in which replication is used for cache management, fault tolerance and mobile disconnection.

Replication management includes two major points: replication and consistency management. Replication involves the choice and the mechanisms for creating and

* This work is supported by the Réseau National des Technologies Logicielles (RNTL Arcad).

Z. Bellahsène, D. Patel, and C. Rolland (Eds.): OOIS 2002, LNCS 2425, pp. 464-469, 2002.

placing copies on different network nodes. Consistency is concerned with the relations established between these copies. In consequence, in order to support various replication scenarios, the target infrastructure should provide adequate solutions to the following issues:

- Replication configuration (What, when & where?). The replication service should allow deciding *what* entities should be replicable. Moreover, such a solution should allow to decide of the most appropriate moment for replication (*when*) and to control optimal copy placement (*where*).
- Consistency configuration (How?). There is a need for mechanisms enabling consistency management policy configuration depending on the context of replication use (caching, availability during disconnection, etc.).

Therefore, replication and consistency management should be configurable.

3 The CCM Platform

CCM [8] is a component model specification from OMG. The experiments reported in this article are based on the OpenCCM implementation [7] of this specification. We overview the CCM features that we used.

The abstract model is concerned with component descriptions. The defined descriptions are richer than standard IDL declarations as they consider both the interfaces used and provided by a component. This is made possible thanks to an IDL extension which introduces the notion of *port*. Ports define connection points (used and provided) for a component. Ports have a type which is an interface. They are used at runtime by clients for business method invocations and during deployment for component connections configuration. Given that the model imposes the static definition of all components' ports, the deployment phase makes all interconnections explicit.

The deployment model defines the deployment process which involves component implementations' installation (archives defined by the packaging model), component instances' creation, component configuration and port (component) interconnection, and application launching. In OpenCCM, application deployment is done by a deployment program. Therefore, the architecture of the application, defined as a set of components with interconnected ports, is described in the deployment program.

4 Replication Management in OpenCCM

The design choices allowing to respond to the needs of an adaptable replication management infrastructure are first discussed. Then, we present an experiment in which we apply the principles of the proposed infrastructure to two replication/consistency scenarios for an simple agenda application.

4.1 Principle

As we have seen in section 2, replication management includes copy creation and placement control, as well as copy consistency management.

Given that copy creation and placement modify the global architecture of an application and that the application architecture is defined in the deployment model, replication configuration can be naturally specified in the deployment model. Replication configuration in the deployment model is described in section 4.1.1.

In our approach, we suppose that consistency between copies can be managed using specialized treatments executed before and/or after normal (business) method invocations. Consistency management implementation relies therefore on invocation interception. This interception is done at the interface level, separately from the component implementation, and is closely related to the component definitions given in the abstract model. Consistency management configuration is described in section 4.1.2.

4.1.1 Replication Configuration

By defining what and where components are to be deployed as well as how these components are to be interconnected, the CCM deployment model describes the initial architecture of an application. Even if to date, CCM does not consider reconfiguration (the when aspect), the deployment model is the right place where reconfiguration actions should be defined.

Since replication configuration consists in creating and interconnecting additional entities in the application's architecture, replication configuration can be naturally specified in the deployment model. In fact, a deployment model including replication will have to specify the set of replicable components (what), define the most appropriate moment for replication (when) and the best copy placement (where). The definition of a dynamic copy creation is to be part of the future reconfiguration specification features of the deployment model.

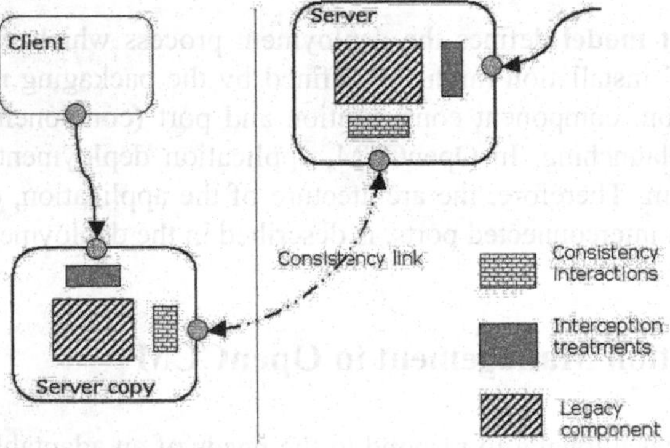

Fig. 1. A simple replication scheme

Replication configuration in OpenCCM is added in the deployment programs. As these programs control component instance creation and interconnection, they are also given the responsibility of creating component replicas and connecting them to other components. In a cache management system for instance (Fig. 1), the deployment program has to connect a client component to a local copy of a server component in replacement of the remote one. As the copies have to be kept consistent, there is a need for connections between the copies. In fact, following a specific consistency protocol, a deployment program has to establish consistency links between component replicas (examples of consistency links are described later).

4.1.2 Configuration of Consistency Management

Consistency management in a replicated object system generally relies on interception objects triggering consistency actions upon copy invocations. The use of interception mechanisms in a component-based system allows the integration of the consistency management aspect without modification of components' functional code. The consistency actions take the form of pre and post treatments for the business method invocations which continue to be delegated to the initial component implementations.

Consistency protocols define consistency relations between copies and provide treatments to maintain these relations valid. Logically, these treatments require the existence of copy interconnections to propagate consistency actions. These connections are the consistency links mentioned in the previous section and settled during deployment. In the example of a cache management system, consistency actions may consist in the invalidation of a given copy and the acquisition of a fresh one which are implemented using consistency links.

Most consistency protocols require access to components' internal data. In the example of a cache management system, component's data need to be copied upon component's caching or update. The access to components' internal state may be based on global component capture/restoration or on application-specific selector/mutator functions. In our prototype, we preserve the component encapsulation principle by leaving the responsibility of implementing component state access primitives to the component developer. Consistency protocol implementations can thus rely on these primitives and ignore component implementation details.

The previously described interception objects and consistency links are the basis of consistency management. Their implementations depend of course on the specific consistency protocol chosen for a given application.

4.1.3 Implementation

We have implemented such a support for replication and consistency management on top of the OpenCCM middleware.

For consistency management, we implemented our own interception mechanism, but a similar feature should be soon integrated into OpenCCM, in the form of adaptable component containers. Replication configuration only relies on adaptations of deployment programs. Overall, replication and configuration can be managed as an adaptation of the application, relying on CCM features without requiring any extension to OpenCCM.

4.2 Experience

In our experiment, we have used a simple agenda application. In this application, users can connect to an agenda server and register, edit or remove rendezvous from their planning. The application is composed of two components: a client which includes a graphical interface and a server which includes the agenda's persistent data.

We have applied the above infrastructure principle to two replication scenarios. The first one implements a simple disconnection scenario while the second one implements a caching system.

4.2.1 Disconnection Protocol

In the case of the disconnection protocol, we proceeded as follows. The agenda's components' implementations remain the same apart minor modifications in the Server in order to make it `Serializable` and to implement a default state management procedure.

The consistency implementation in this scenario distinguishes between master and slave server copies. A slave server is a disconnected copy of a master server. When a disconnection process is launched, the slave server is created on the machine getting disconnected and initialized with the state of the master. The client is connected to this slave server. At reconnection, the possibly diverged slave and master states are reconciled, and the client is reconnected to the master server. Reconciliation is based on a simple redo protocol using a log of disconnected operations (managed in the slave server).

4.2.2 Caching Protocol

We have also experimented with a caching system for the agenda application. This caching system allows to deploy copies of the server component on several client machines and to keep consistent portions of the agenda database. We have implemented a version of the entry consistency protocol [2], which follows a multiple-readers/single-writer protocol.

The implementation of the consistency protocol is very close to the one implemented in the Javanaise system [4]. Each method of the agenda server component is associated with a component locking policy, depending on the method's nature (read/write) The interception treatment ensures that a consistent copy is cached before forwarding the invocation to it.

The deployment program specifies the sites where caching should be applied. A master site stores the persistent version of the server component and a client may address either the remote master copy or a local replica.

The consistency links between replicas implement an interface which defines operations for fetching (in read or write mode) an up-to-date component copy and for copy invalidation. There are actually two consistency links between a client and the server: one is used by the client in order to fetch copies (in read or write mode), the other is used by the server in order to invalidate copies and locks held by the clients.

5 Conclusion and Future Work

We have investigated the integration of replication and consistency management in a component-based platform. We have shown that it is possible to manage replication as an adaptable non functional property in a component-based system.

We have identified two places where the non functional integration of replication management takes place. The first place is at the level of the components' interfaces. We use interception objects in order to capture invocation events and to trigger consistency actions. These interception objects could be replaced by adaptation mechanisms at the container level when they are available (many research groups are working on adaptable containers, both in the EJB and CCM environments). The second integration place is the deployment model. Given that the deployment model is the place where an application's architecture is described and since replication impacts this architecture, it is logical to describe the replication aspect configuration in the deployment model.

As mot of the configuration is done by hand, an immediate perspective of this work is to provide the tools which would assist the definition of replication policies.

References

1. R. Balter, L. Bellissard, F. Boyer, M. Riveill and J.Y. Vion-Dury, ``Architecturing and Configuring Distributed Applications with Olan", *Proc. IFIP Int. Conf. on Distributed Systems Platforms and Open Distributed Processing (Middleware'98)*, The Lake District, 15-18 September 1998.
2. N. Bershad, Matthew J. Zekauskas, and Wayne A. Sawdon. The Midway Distributed Shared Memory System. In Proceedings of the 38th IEEE Computer Society International Conference, pages 528--537. IEEE, February 1993.
3. G. Chockler, D. Dolev, R. Friedman, and R. Vitenberg. Implementing a Caching Service for Distributed CORBA Objects. In Proceedings of Middleware '00,1-23, April 2000.
4. D. Hagimont, F. Boyer. "A Configurable RMI Mechanism for Sharing Distributed Java Objects". IEEE Internet Computing, Vol. 5, 1, pp. 36-44, Jan.-Feb. 2001.
5. G. Kiczales, E. Hilsdale, J. Hugonin, M. Kersten, J. Palm, and W. G. Griswold. An Overview of AspectJ. In J. L. Knudsen, editor, ECOOP 2001, Object-Oriented Programming, volume 2072 of LNCS. Springer-Verlag, June 2001.
6. R. Kordale and M. Ahamad. Object caching in a CORBA compliant system. USENIX Computing Systems, 9(4):377404, Fall 1996-
7. The OpenCCM Platform, http://corbaweb.lifl.fr/OpenCCM/
8. Corba Components – Volume I, OMG TC Document orbos/99-07-01.
9. Chris Smith, Fault Tolerant CORBA (Fault tolerance joint initial submission by Ericsson, IONA, and Nortel supported by Alcatel), ftp://ftp.omg.org/pub/docs/orbos/98-10-10, October 20, 1998.

A Responsive Client Architecture with Local Object Behavior Deployment

Ana Paula V. Pais, Bárbara O. B. Corrêa, Carlo E. T. Oliveira, and Gilson Tavares

Universidade Federal do Rio de Janeiro, NCE-CCMN Bloco C
PO. Box 2324, Rio de Janeiro Brazil
{anapais,barbara,carlo,gilson}@nce.ufrj.br
http://tedmos.nce.ufrj.br

Abstract. Information Systems with a large user base require thin client technology due to deployment issues. Configuration and version management, added to maintenance cost are major players on this decision. However, heavy traffic loads and network latency impose severe penalties on users. Candidate solutions to this problem must optimize users ergonomics whilst keeping maintenance costs low. In a straightforward approach, client architectures should provide web deployable local processing facilities. This paper describes an architecture based on the MVC paradigm capable of porting portions of the system to client executable scripts. Required entities are encapsulated in XML carriers and exchanged on demand between client and server side systems. Numerous user interactions are executed on the client side, relieving the network and improving responsivity. This solution not only enhances ergonomics but is also highly scalable, delegating tasks to the greater number of client machines, whereas focusing server activity on more relevant operations.

1 Introduction

Web information systems can be hard on users that expect responsivity. Solving this problem should not impact on development or maintenance costs. A responsive client system must be capable of handling local legs of use case logic without interfering with architectural robustness of entire application. Most of the time, users are dealing with data that can be resolved locally or involve read only access to entity lists. Discretionary additions of client side scripting may solve the user problem at cost of system integrity flaws, interweaving of GUI and business logic, high increase of maintenance complexity. An engineering approach should commit to architectural soundness, preserving at client level the quality standards employed at the server side. A client scaled reproduction of the server design can live up to the paradigm advantages, running the local logic in conformance with business constraints and keeping layout design apart from control code. Keeping the MVC (Model, View, Controller) paradigm [1], the client architecture can operate safely on objects, transporting them back and forth from the server. Local interaction constrained by the

Z. Bellahsène, D. Patel, and C. Rolland (Eds.): OOIS 2002, LNCS 2425, pp. 470-481, 2002.

same behavior stated at server level maintain system integrity and reuse use case design.

2 The Stunt Architecture (SA)

The stunt architecture [2,3] is designed to support automatic code generation from model diagrams. It embodies the MVC paradigm allowing the possibility of detaching each layer as a stand-alone system.

2.1 Stunt Architecture Concepts

The elaboration of the robustness diagram [4] from the use case script is the starting point to the stunt architecture. The conception of the robustness diagram is ideal for modeling systems that implement the MVC architecture. This architecture splits the system in three parts: model, view and control. The model is responsible for storing all the information about the current state of the application. The view determinates the visual representation of the information contained in the model. The control is responsible for the behavior, stating how and when the application must react to user input. The robustness diagram constitutes a graphical representation of a use case. This diagram possesses a set of stereotypes and rules of formation, constraining the class relations in the use case.

The stunt architecture defines a new set of stereotypes and rules, refining the robustness diagram formality and expressivity. This allows the automatic generation of the remaining UML diagrams from the interpretation of the robustness diagram. The designer makes the necessary adjustments in the resultant diagrams to fill the gaps left over by the automatic generation. From the diagrams, it is possible to generate Java source code, an abstract description of the user interface and a description of the entities. The abstract description of the visual interface allows its implementation in different types of user interface.

The application of the stunt architecture targets the construction of a system from the definition of the use cases. This approach has limitations in projects using a preexisting database. Reusing a data model would be advantageous in the migration of legacy systems.

In web systems, the user interface resides in the client layer, while model and control modules reside in the server. The client layer does not execute any type of validation.

The access control is fundamental for the majority of currently developed systems. Users of a system possess different privileges. As an example, all users can know which are the available products of a store, but not all of them can modify the information of a product. The stunt architecture currently does not cover this aspect.

2.2 Reverse Stunt Architecture (RSA)

The high benefit of the stunt architecture comes from tracking use cases scripts right down to its implementation. However, in the case of legacy systems, use case logic is tangled all over the code, requiring refined computational intelligence to extract it. A simpler approach to this case is to rely on the data model underlying the legacy system. In most cases, the data model can be extracted from database metadata information. This relevant information is not taken into account by the stunt architecture, since the data model is generated from use cases. The Reverse Stunt Architecture is a modification on SA to make use of existing data models.

The Reverse Stunt Architecture was designed to tackle specifically this problem. It uses the relational schema to automatically generate various modules of the new system on the top of a robust and reliable architecture. The generated classes map entities extracted from the database tables. The RSA also generates a set of support classes, building a minimal functionality to the system. These classes prepare the system to carry through basic operations as modify, insert or exclude an entity. RSA integrate in its architecture mechanisms to improve system management and configuration, commonly found in many corporations. On the other hand, the business rules are engaged. In this aspect, the architecture stunt is well fuller. Table 1 presents a comparison of SA and RSA.

Table 1. Comparison of SA and RSA

Feature	RSA	SA
MVC	Poor	Complete
Traceability	ER	UML
Customization	Easy	Hard
Maintenance	Hard	Moderate

The RSA embeds many other aspects for business applications. It supports access control based on user profiles; users profiles scope management; calendar based access control and declarative specification of entity visualization. As this architecture is sufficiently flexible, new aspects can easily be added. This information is stored in the database, and can be configured by administrative users in the proper interface of the system. When a user enters the system, the pertinent information is extracted from the database to configure its environment. The system matches all the information against the user profile, showing only the options available to this user. Data representing model, view and control objects are obtained from the application server and passed to the client layer to allow possible local processing.

2.3 The Memento – Proxy – Prototype Pattern

The classes that represent entities store valuable information, which together form the system domain model. For this reason, there is a great concentration of operations and responsibilities that these classes accumulate. As the model information to be presented in diverse parts of the system, the same classes that are used in the model layer may appear in control and view layers. The resulting tightly coupled dependence increases the development and maintenance costs.

Complex use cases requiring the execution of extensive operations can lock entities for long periods. This overhead on the model classes impairs the performance and maintenance of the system. Prototypes had been considered as a solution for this problem. They are classes that impersonate the entity in diverse parts of the system. As a common point uniting SA and RSA architectures, the board stunt or simply prototype, is responsible for system functionality mobility. Since it can be rendered into XML [5], the prototype can cross system boundaries using many available protocols.

In order to cross system borders, domain entities must change its representation into a prototype form. The entity that will be represented constructs its own prototype. The prototype attributions in the architecture contemplate three roles: memento [6], proxy [6] and prototype [6]. The memento role externalizes entity state and allows it to travel across the system. The proxy role allows it to operates on the behalf of the entity. The prototype role itself allows it to incorporate new data for the creation of new entities.

A great variety of prototypes can be generated from an entity, in accordance with the needs imposed by use case modeling. Prototypes accommodate to the uses cases in which they will participate, keeping a subgroup of the original entity attributes. The prototype takes the responsibility for the entity that it represents, and accesses it in operations as inclusion, update and exclusion. To achieve platform independence, the information is interchanged in XML format, as shown in Figure 1.

This mechanism offers advantages as decoupling between the system layers and adaptation of the model to the necessities of the use case. Operations can be carried through without compromising the integrity of the entities or performance of the system. The representation in XML guarantees an efficient carriage of information.

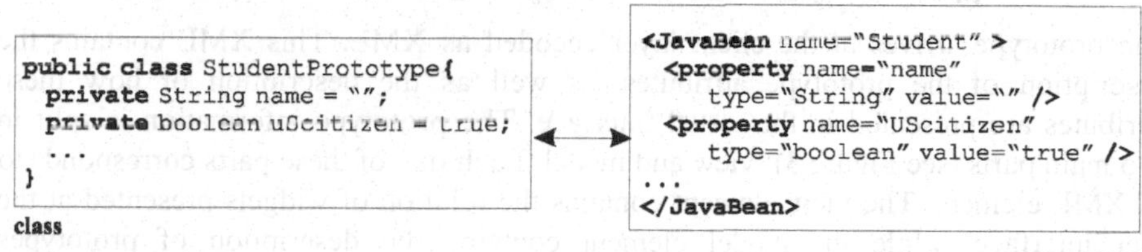

public class StudentPrototype{
private String name = "";
private boolean UScitizen = true;
...
}
class
<JavaBean name="Student" >
<property name="name"
type="String" value="" />
<property name="UScitizen"
type="boolean" value="true" />
...
</JavaBean>
XML

Fig. 1. Prototype-carrier translation

2.4 Visualization Widgets

The entities cross the system borders in the form of prototypes. When arriving at the client layer, the entity assumes a form with which the user can interact. Widgets constitute the bridge between the user and the entity.

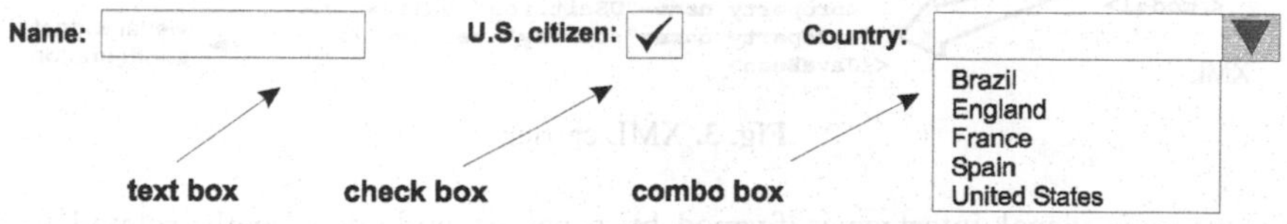

Fig. 2. Common widgets

The state of an entity is represented by the value of its attributes. These values can be classified in some categories, which can be associated with one or more widgets. Figure 2 shows the most common widgets: textboxes, checkboxes and combo-boxes.

The form that the attribute will take in the user interface is stored in the database. Each attribute is associated with a set of features:

- Visual – identification of the widget that represents the entity attribute in the editing screen;
- Title – text attached to the widget, labeling the information showed in it;
- isListItem –indicates if the attribute is a entity qualifier for query results. When a query result screen is presented, it only shows attributes with this flag set;
- isQueryItem – indicates if the attribute is used as a key in a query screen.

This set of information is used to dynamically construct screens that display the entities for simple operations. For instance, the edition screen of an entity lists its attributes, in addition to the insertion, modification and exclusion buttons. This screen is constructed from an inspection in the database, which results in the description of how the entity will be presented. This inspection determines how the attributes of the entity will be shown, and verify which operations the user can execute. If the user does not have permission to modify the entity data, only the insertion option will be available.

2.5 Prototype and Widget Information Binding

The prototype arrives at the client layer encoded as XML. This XML contains the description of the prototype attributes, as well as the description of how these attributes are presented in the visual interface. The prototype information is split in two main parts (see Figure 3): view and model. Each one of these parts corresponds to an XML element. The view element contains the relation of widgets presented at the user interface, while the model element contains the description of prototypes necessary to the execution of the use case.

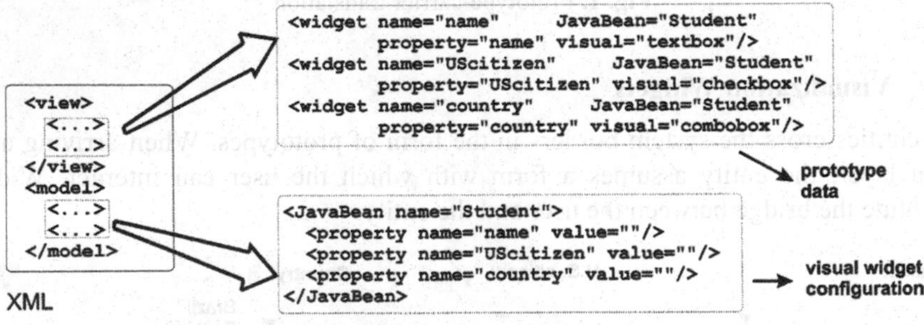

Fig. 3. XML carrier

The use case visual interface is formed by a set of widgets directly related to the attributes of prototypes. Each widget is associated with an XML element that describes its type and the identification of the corresponding entity and attribute. All prototypes required to the execution of the use case are included in the XML carrier, where each element identifies an attribute of the prototype. An attribute is described by a name and the value that it stores.

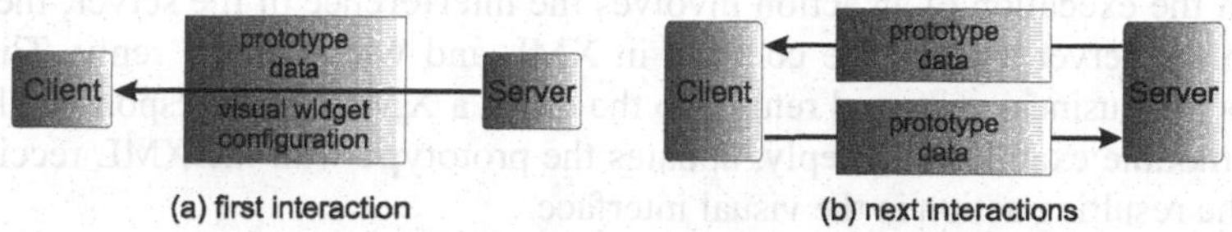

Fig. 4. XML carrier operation

When the use case initiates, the client receives the XML carrier containing both view and model elements, as shown in Figure 4.a. The XML carrier is translated into objects responding to local user interaction in the client layer. The objects that implement prototypes are initiated with information proceeding from the server. These objects are locally modified due to user interaction with visual widgets. Widgets wrappers are associated to the attributes of a prototype. When the user modifies the value shown for one widget, the wrapper is notified and modifies the corresponding prototype. On the other hand, when the prototype suffers some modification, all wrapper listeners are notified, updating the visual interface.

When user action implies in data transfer to the server, the prototype is translated into XML. The server receives the XML carrier, and executes the required operations. Client/Server interchange carries on by passing the XML back and forth, synchronizing model and view representations, as the depicted in Figure 4.b.

3 The Enhanced Client Architecture

The RSA was developed to cover some deficiencies of the SA. The current development of the RSA centers on the construction of web systems. Moreover, one of the objectives of the RSA is the construction of a client layer capable of local use case operation.

The client layer of the RSA encloses HTML pages and scripts responsible for local operations. The HTML Page possesses a standard format that can be constructed from the information contained in the database. The developer can also create new forms to suit use case requirements, observing the established standards.

3.1 General Client Architecture

The RSA client layer has the responsibility of renderize the use case interface in HTML as well as most of the feasible local functionalities. This enhanced client encompasses a self-contained full-fleshed MVC representation of the entire system.

The view encloses widgets wrappers responsible for user interaction. The local model contains prototypes corresponding to the entities involved in the use case. The local view and model synchronize in an observer pattern [6] fashion. The control commands the execution of the use case. It locally answers for some actions of the user that do not need server interference. The control only transfers to the server the validations that are not of the ability of the client layer.

When the execution of an action involves the interference of the server, the control sends to the server a prototype codified in XML and waits for the reply. The server executes the business rules and returns to the client a XML coded response. The client control module examines the reply, updates the prototype with the XML received and shows the resulting action in the visual interface.

The isolation between the data and the visual interface allows the same information to be presented by different components of the interface at the same time, and guarantees that these components will reflect eventual modifications of the information. The implementation of the client control determines the local response autonomy to user interaction.

3.2 View: DHTML Forms

The use case is formed by a set of screens, and web systems can implement the use case script using a set of HTML or JSP pages [7]. Web systems users generally demand prompt response to its solicitations. As can be seen in Figure 5, web request processing involves several steps from browser to server and back. An HTTP invocation for a JSP page involves the execution of business rules, the alteration of JSP beans, and finally, the presentation of the HTML page to the client.

Fig. 5. Dynamic HTML page load

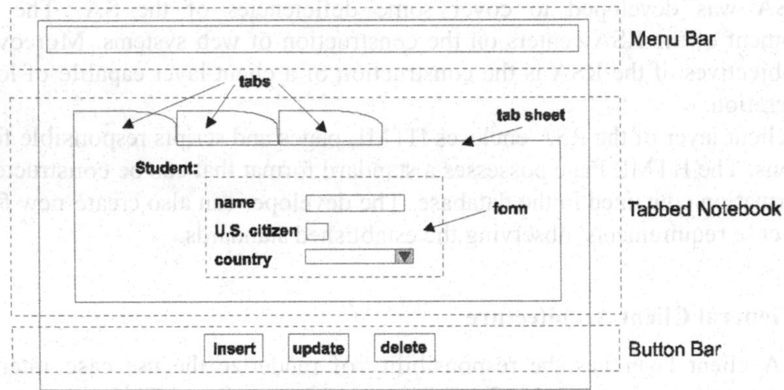

Fig. 6. Standardized layout

Despite the cost to load a dynamic page, web applications frequently present the same page to the user, just varying the value of some fields. As a solution, HTML pages can be assembled just once and the field values modified through scripts executed in the client.

Moreover, a single HTML page can contain all the required code covering the full set of screens needed in a use case. That is made through a set of layers, where a single layer is visible at a time. Each layer consists of a block of HTML code that becomes visible when renderized in a specific place of the screen. The client executes a set of scripts written in Javascript [8], capable of managing layers as well as modifying the content of fields in the corresponding HTML forms.

Use case view is committed to a standardized layout, as shown in Figure 6. Overlaid panes are built in advance to achieve fast user interaction. Three containers form the HTML page: a menu bar, one tabbed notebook and a button bar.

Menu bar is the entry point for the execution of the main system use cases. It corresponds to the set of accessible options to an user. Meanwhile buttons in the button bar represent user actions that modify the use case state.

Tabbed notebook contains the set of screens (tab sheets) for a use case. The tab sheet consists of a HTML form specified in one DHTML [9] layer. A single tab sheet is visible at a time. When the user selects a tab, the corresponding tab sheet becomes visible.

Input fields in the HTML form constitute the graphical representation of attributes pertaining to one or more prototypes. Figure 7 represents the interrelation between these elements. The form allows the user to visualize and modify prototypes content.

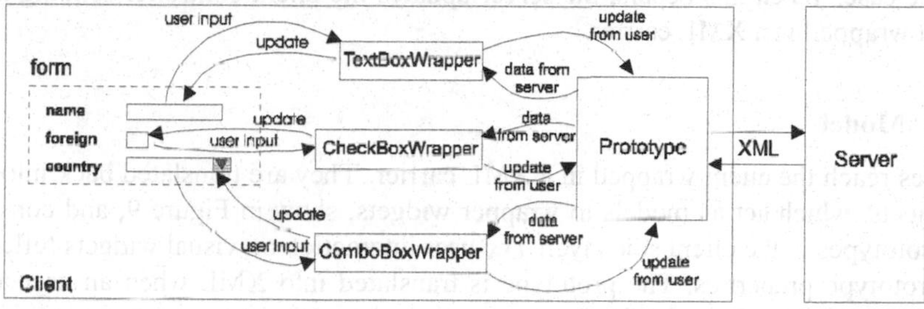

Fig. 7. Model-view-control interaction

3.3 Control

A client control module that implements the use case state machine allows local processing, enhancing system scalability. Some transitions in the state machine require little or none processing. States can be reached by the simple user interaction with the interface.

The control module encompasses a collection of controller, state and action objects. Controller objects are implementations of finite state machines representing use cases. A state object represents a step in a use case sequence. Action objects encapsulate events responsible for state transition.

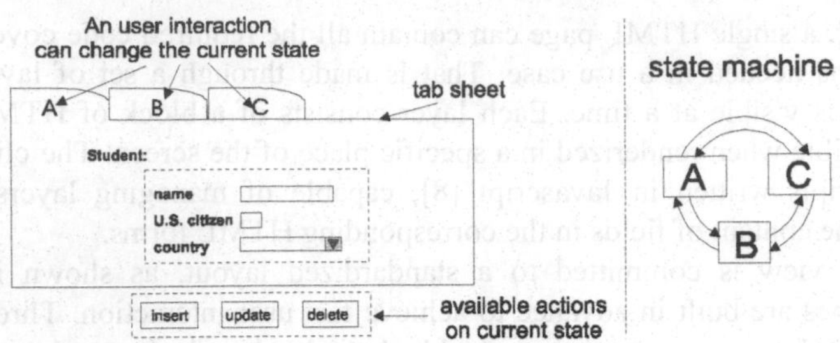

Fig. 8. Use case renderization sequence

The controller keeps a collection of states. Each state aggregates a set of actions that can be executed within. Each state corresponds to a tab sheet on the screen. The visible tab sheet represents the current state of the controller. Figure 8 shows the correspondence between tab sheets and controller states. Buttons, links and images dispatch actions to the controller, which represent events to the controller state machine. The controller change state or execute an action without accessing the server. Controller construction defines the initial state and the collection of valid states and actions. However, the client controller configuration can change in the course of the use case. When this occurs, the server updates the client controller sending a new object wrapped in a XML carrier.

3.4 Model

Entities reach the client wrapped in a XML carrier. They are translated back into a set of objects, which act as models to wrapper widgets, show in Figure 9, and constitute the prototypes in the client side layer. The user interaction on visual widgets reflects in the prototype properties. The prototype is translated into XML when an user action needs to be executed on server side.

Prototypes, in the client context, are formed by three types of objects: JavaBean, Composite and Element. The JavaBean object corresponds to an entity and aggregates a set of Elements. The Element object corresponds to an attribute of the entity. Elements, generally, are used as models for textboxes and checkboxes. A Composite is a collection of JavaBeans. It represents aggregations between entities.

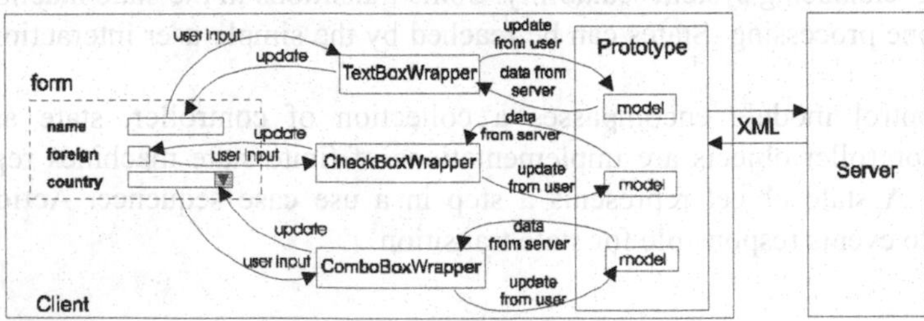

Fig. 9. Widget-attribute binding

4 Local Client Operation

Use case renderization involves the generation of a XML carrier and a client side controller. While the carrier is just the encoding of view and model data, the controller logic must be entirely developed in Javascript. Factoring similar functionalities on usual use case scenarios leads to a set of primitive reusable operations. These operations can be aggregated to handle a default use case.

A basic client controller implements the default use case. This controller encompasses the query, list, edition, message and help states. In the query state, attributes of an entity can be specified and submitted as query parameters. The list state shows a table with query results, where each item links to the edition state presenting the target entity. Edition state provides inclusion, modification and exclusion operations. Message and help states provide information to the user. Besides controlling the state of the use case, the local controller prevents unnecessary server calls.

The XML necessary for the default use case execution is generated dynamically from meta-information stored in the database. The controller objects support inheritance, allowing functionalities of the basic controller to be reused. Sophisticated use cases demand the creation of specific controllers.

5 Implementation

The RSA System is implemented using the J2EE [10] application server technology. The process initiates with an HTTP invocation coming from the client starting a server side script. This script invokes a controlling object that analyzes the invocation options and assembles a DHTML page to handle the chosen use case. This page contains all the required forms to the course of the use case packed in DHTML layers. The client side scripts are added to the page and sent as reply to the HTTP invocation. Before finishing the reply, the controlling object loads the XML carrier in a Javascript variable.

The client layer implemented in this work was developed in Javascript. The objects that play the role of model, view and control are instantiated in the beginning of the use case, when the HTML page is loaded. The loading script examines the received HTML page and binds the wrappers with widgets contained in the page.

Figure 10 represents the schematic flow action of script loading and execution. Wrappers capture the events fired by HTML objects. The wrapper examines the HTML object, gets the value that was modified and notifies the prototype. The wrapper updates the HTML object whenever it is notified of changes in prototype. The modifications made in HTML objects can be as simple as modify the value of a textbox, or more complex as to modify the value list of a combobox.

Since that Javascript is not a standardized language, distinct browsers exhibit different behaviors. To simplify the design, a single browser was used as development tool. The chosen browser was MS Internet Explorer 6.0. Although some peculiarities of explorer have been used to speed up the development, these will have to be neglected by forms that are more adaptable to other browsers.

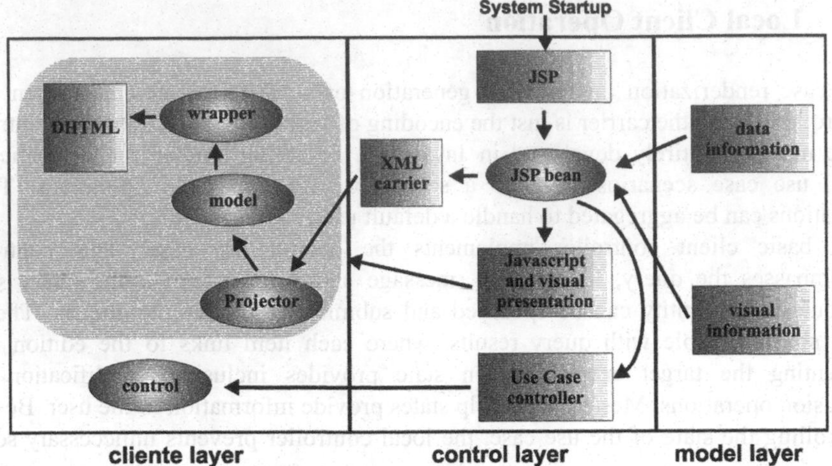

Fig. 10. Client initialization flow

The main objective of this implementation is to reuse the data proceeding from server requests, managing its access locally in the client layer. These data remain in the client, preventing the submission of successive identical requests to the server. Previously loaded screens with requested data that are common to several use case extensions are kept for posterior use. This technique reduces the number of client/server interactions.

6 Assessments

The RSA is being used in a university academic management system called SIGA. This system involves all academy features with personalized user interaction. Teachers, students and academic managers work together in the same environment with different access privileges configured by declarative clauses.

The SIGA system is appropriate to evidence the features proposed by RSA since its first implementation was developed in Cobol language, hosted on a mainframe. In a first attempt of system migration, the development schedule was overdue. The critical points on this process pointed out the requirements to conceive the RSA. At the current version, RSA is ready to present better results for this process.

The addition of specific functionalities beyond the basic RSA controller is still a hard task. Due to generation by the diagram models the SA can build complete use case implementation much easier. The absence of use case modeling in RSA incurs in high development costs.

Once migrated, the new SIGA system covers well the basic operations required to manipulate data on the domain entities. Built on top of a robust and modern architecture, the RSA approach achieves excellent results among users. An attractive web presentation combined with a fine performance, achieve high acceptance among the academic users. Some clients still sluggish due to underpowered hardware, whereas machines fitting specifications succeed. On other hand, client application restrictions concern some users. This version requires browser compatibility with MS-Internet Explorer 6. As a work in progress, the implementation is being refactored to support other browsers.

7 Conclusion

Enterprise applications are growing exponentially and evolving into high volume web systems. This work presents an architectural solution to cope with stricter requirements of development turnaround and performance specifications.

The Reverse Stunt Architecture provides automatic generation compatibility together with responsive implementation enhancements. A high-level metadata specification drives the generation of a robust and scalable implementation.

Applied design pattern solutions together with MVC paradigm contributes to a consistent architectural soundness.

The performance solution preserves system and design integrity through a client side scaled reproduction. The main contribution of this work is to depict how state of art web service can derive from theoretical system design guidelines.

The production status working application serves a community of over 60.000 users and can handle a peak loads over 300 simultaneous connections. This indicates how real world system development can be improved through careful architectural conception.

References

1. Developer's Guide - Borland - JBuilder 2, Borland, 1998
2. Pais, A.P.V., Oliveira, C.E.T., Leite, P.H.P.M.: Robustness Diagram: A Bridge between Business Modeling and System Design. Proceedings of the 7th International Conference on Object-Oriented Information Systems, OOIS'01 – Calgary, Canada – August 27-29, 2001, Vol. 1, Springer-Verlag, 530-539
3. Pais, A.P.V., Oliveira, C.E.T.: Enhancing UML Expressivity towards Automatic Code Generation. Proceedings of the 7th International Conference on Object-Oriented Information Systems, OOIS'01 – Calgary, Canada – August 27-29, 2001, Vol. 1, Springer-Verlag, 335-344
4. Rosemberg, D.; Scott, K.; Use Case Driven Object Modeling With UML: A Practical Approach; Addison-Wesley; 1999
5. Harold, E. R., XML Bible. IDG Books Worldwide, Inc.
6. Gamma, E., Helm, R.; Johnson, R., Vlissides, J., Design Patterns – Elements of Reusable Object-Orient Software. Addison-Wesley, 1998
7. Hall, M., Core Servlets and JavaServer Pages. Sun Microsystems
8. Wagner, R., et al., JavaScript Second Edition. Sams Net
9. DHTML References. Available at: http://msdn.microsoft.com/library/default.asp?url=/workshop/author/dhtml/reference/dhtmlrefs.asp. Access on march/2002
10. Shannon, B., Hapner M., Matena V., Davidson J., Pelegri-Llopart E., Cable L., Java 2 Platform, Enterprise Edition: Platform and Component Specifications. Sun Microsystems

Structuring Product-Lines: A Layered Architectural Style

Tommi Myllymäki, Kai Koskimies, and Tommi Mikkonen

Institute of Software Systems, Tampere University of Technology
Box 553, FIN-33101 Tampere, Finland
{tommikm,kk,tjm}@cs.tut.fi

Abstract. A product-line is a set of software systems sharing the same architecture and implementation platform. Based on an analysis of several industrial product-lines, a general layered model is proposed as the main structuring principle of a product-line. It is demonstrated that the model can be used to explain and clarify several existing product-line architectures.

1 Introduction

The current focus in industrial software development is to find techniques that optimize the software development process within the domain of an enterprise. This has led to the proliferation of *software product-lines* ([1], [2]). A (software) product-line is a set of systems that share a common architecture and a set of reusable components, which jointly constitute a software platform supporting application development for a particular domain.

Although the idea of software product-lines has been widely adopted, the design of product-line architectures has proved to be hard. Typically, product-lines make use of a variety of existing techniques like architectural styles [3], components [4], frameworks [5], design patterns [6], and generative programming approaches [7]. The overwhelming options of existing technologies make it difficult for a software architect to come up with a well-structured high-level solution for a product-line architecture. In many cases, the platform is seen as an unstructured set of assets, some of which are then selected to be part of a product build. Then, it is not clearly understood how the platform should be structured, what kind of variability is supported by the different parts of the platform, what kind of specialization or usage interfaces are offered by each part, and how the different parts are versioned. Another indication of the lack of understanding of product-lines is that the terminology is often confusing, not clearly separating the constituent concepts of product-lines.

In this paper, our aim is to study the structuring principles of the software platforms enabling product-lines, propose a general model based on a layered architectural style for such platforms, and clarify the product-line terminology on the basis of that model. The work builds on case studies carried out in a research project investigating industrial product-line practices. The model is not new in the sense that

Z. Bellahsène, D. Patel, and C. Rolland (Eds.): OOIS 2002, LNCS 2425, pp. 482-487, 2002.

it has been actually used in a number of product-lines, but we argue that it has not been previously clearly recognized and analyzed. We hope that this model and the terminology it implies will help software architects to understand product-line organization and to communicate about product-lines.

We proceed as follows. In Section 2 we give an account of the proposed layered model, followed by real-life examples sketched in Section 3. Finally, some discussion and concluding remarks are presented in Section 4.

2 Layered Platform: A Product-Line Architectural Style

A software asset (say, a component) may depend on architectural aspects at different levels of abstraction and generality. Firstly, a software asset may depend only on the form and semantics of some general resources common to a wide spectrum of products. Secondly, a software asset may depend on a particular, general architectural style. Thirdly, a software asset may depend on the design decisions related to a particular application domain. Finally, a software asset may depend on the design decisions required for a particular product. On the basis of these dependencies, we divide the assets of a software system into four categories, each constituting a layer. The layers are called the *resource platform*, the *architecture platform*, the *product platform*, and the *product* layer, respectively. The resulting layered architecture is depicted in Fig. 1.

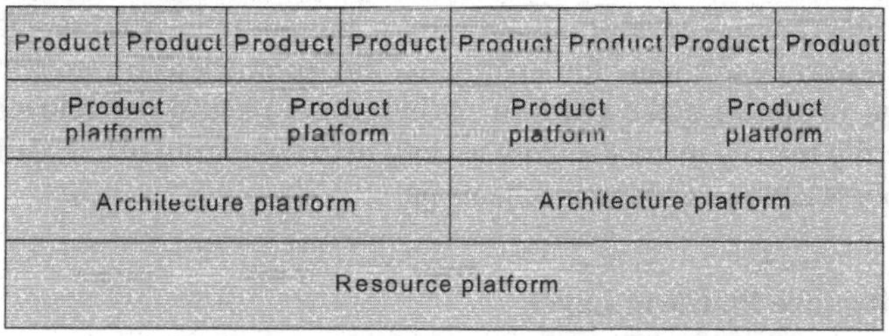

Fig. 1. Layered platform architecture

The layers are naturally ordered on the basis of generality: the categories were listed above in the order of decreasing level of generality. If a software asset depends only on the way general resources are provided but not on any particular architectural style, it belongs to the resource platform layer (i.e., the lowest layer in the figure). If a software asset depends on a chosen architectural style, but not on a particular domain, it belongs to the architecture platform layer. If a software asset depends on an application domain but not on a particular product, it belongs to the product platform layer. Finally, if a software asset depends on a particular product, it belongs to the product layer (uppermost layer). All the software artifacts belonging to any of these layers are collectively called a product-line.

The products built on a product-line can be divided into a system hierarchy based on the level of shared layers. Products that share the same product platform are called a *product family*. These products have a significant amount of common functionality, and they share the same architecture. Products that share the same architecture platform are called a *product tribe*. These products have a common high-level architecture but not necessarily common functionalities. Products that share the same resource platform are called a *product culture*. Such products have neither common architecture nor common functionality, but they have a common set of resource abstractions.

2.1 Resource Platform Layer

The lowest layer, the resource platform, provides an API for accessing the basic services and resources of the environment. Depending on the system, these services might be related, for example, to communication (distributed systems), process scheduling (embedded systems), or persistence (business systems). The provided services do not depend on a predefined architectural style or domain of the products. The services are called through a simple API: the caller becomes dependent on the form and semantics of the service, but not on the internal structure of the resource platform. Sometimes the resource platform may possess a state, in which case the order of the service calls may be restricted. In that case the resource platform should inform the caller about incorrect usage (e.g. with exceptions), allowing the caller to respond accordingly.

The task of the resource platform is to attach the software system to its external resource environment (hardware, graphics, networking etc.), and to facilitate the changing of that environment. For the latter purpose, the layer should map the underlying resources and services of the environment to an abstract, environment-independent interface. The abstract API may be an industrial standard, and the platform itself may be available for a particular environment as a commercial product.

The design of the resource platform is based on identifying relevant horizontal domains like file management, database access, network protocols, threading facilities and inter-process communication mechanisms.

2.2 Architecture Platform Layer

The architecture platform defines the architectural style of the product-line. It provides specific component roles as implied by the style, to be played by various components of the product platforms, and points where these components can be attached. It also provides a set of conventions or design patterns that must be followed by those components. Within the object-oriented paradigm, a role can be represented by a base class (interface) in the architecture platform, to be subclassed (implemented) in the product platform. Hence an object-oriented architecture platform can be implemented as a framework. Such a framework can be called *architecture framework*, to distinguish it from the more conventional *application framework*. Note that the extension points of the architecture framework are domain-independent, pertaining only to the architectural style.

The interface provided by the architecture platform may also include API-like service interfaces. However, an essential difference with the resource platform is that each caller is in some role with respect to the architecture, and that role may imply certain interaction patterns that must be followed, whereas the callers of the resource platform are in a uniform position with respect to the platform.

The design of the architecture platform is based on the quality requirements of the products and on the functional requirements related to the chosen architecture. For example, in a platform based on the implicit invocation architecture [3] the functional requirements specify the communication mechanisms of the components. The architecture platform may be developed by the same company that builds the products, or it may be a third-party component, possibly based on a standard interface.

2.3 Product Platform Layer

The product platform builds on the general architectural style provided by the architecture platform, and provides a skeleton for products in a particular product category (or domain). The skeleton may embody refined architectural solutions for this domain, within the boundaries of the underlying architectural style. The product platform provides a specialization interface that allows for variance in the functional requirements of the products. The design of the product platform is affected both by the common, domain-specific functional requirements and by the quality requirements of the products.

A possible form for the product platform is a framework together with supplementary components, each component being used in at least two different products. Such a framework is called an *application framework*.

A product platform is usually developed by the same company that develops the products: from the business viewpoint, a product platform allows the company to store its knowhow on building software for a particular domain, so that this knowhow can be easily reused for new products.

2.4 Product Layer

The product layer implements product-specific functional requirements. The product layer is written against the specialization interface provided by the product platform. This interface may hide the underlying architectural style. It is often possible to generate the product-specific parts, or a large portion of them, automatically on the basis of a description of the desired functional properties of the product. The product layer is typically company-specific.

3 Examples

In this section, we will show how the discussed principles fit various systems we have studied as part of this research. The selection of systems introduced here covers different domains, which demonstrates the genericity of the approach.

3.1 Symbian OS

Symbian OS is a software platform targeted for mobile systems [8], in which the layers discussed above have the following contents. The resource platform of the

Symbian architecture is constituted by the kernel. In the simplest form, it can be understood as a context-switching machine. In addition, as the platform is targeted to mobile systems, special measures are required against memory garbaging. The architecture platform layer in the Symbian environment provides an infrastructure that can be easily adapted to different kinds of mobile devices. The most important decision in the architectural sense is that hardware (and also many software) resources are predominantly protected with servers, and therefore, client-server sessions are built in the system. Moreover, the architecture platform defines the basic application structure. The programmer must comply with the defined practices, which is often enforced in a framework-like fashion. The product platform is populated by the core application logic of the applications built in the environment. Device specific user interface adaptations also reside in this layer. Applications in the Symbian environment are coded by attaching application specific code into a predefined MVC-like framework defined by the lower layers.

3.2 Insurance Product-Line

EJB (Enterprise JavaBeans) is a component architecture for distributed business applications provided by Sun Microsystems [9]. Currently several commercial and non-commercial products implement the EJB specification.

An EJB-based insurance system product-line supports the development of (distributed) insurance applications for various sub-domains of insurance business. In this case the resource platform consists of the services of the underlying technological infrastructure, most notably relational database and communication protocols (ORB, Object Request Broker). The architecture platform is represented by an EJB implementation, providing general services for the EJB component model. An application platform constitutes an application framework for life insurance systems, based on the EJB component model. Finally, a product is a particular life insurance application. Note that other insurance application frameworks can be built on top of the same architecture platform.

3.3 3G Network Elements

IP multimedia services [10] in 3G telecommunications network is supported by several inter-connected database like network elements. Each element performs different functions and handles different data, but essential quality goals like high availability and high performance remain the same. Development of these elements in Nokia Networks is organized roughly according to the presented layered model. In their case, the resource platform layer offers network element independent services like inter-process communication facilities and database access. These services are not limited to supporting IP multimedia only, but can be used in the development of other kinds of network elements too. The architecture platform layer provides a very flexible architecture framework implementing design solutions ensuring high availability and high performance. The framework also implements key concepts that can be specialized significantly in order to enable differences in functionality. The product platform layer consists of complete implementation of each network element. The elements are then fine tuned for customer specific needs according to the configuration information contained in the product layer.

4 Discussion

We have witnessed the same structure in several industrial systems; therefore, we consider it an emerging pattern. The proposed layered model based on this structure is expected to facilitate organizing product-lines in several ways. Foremost, it can be used as a base to organize development of software assets shared between individual products and product families in an enterprise. It also alleviates estimating the amount of work required to introduce a new product into an existing product family or to build an entirely new product family. The model localizes the effects of changes in the requirements, allowing the reuse of large portions of the system even when the domain changes significantly. The introduction of the model also helps in communicating about product-lines, because a terminology is available for addressing assets at different levels of generality and different sets of products.

Ongoing application of the model in the industry will provide further confirmation of these expectations. Hopefully it also provides other interesting insights and reveals potential downsides of the model.^

References

1. Bosch J., Design & Use of Software Architectures: Adopting and evolving a product-line approach. Addison.Wesley, 2000.
2. Clements P., Northrop L., Software Product Lines: Practices and Patterns. Addison.Wesley, 2002.
3. Shaw M., Garlan D., Software Architecture: Perspectives on an Emerging Discipline. Prentice Hall, 1996.
4. Szyperski C., Component Software: Beyond Object-Oriented Programming. Addison-Wesley, 1998.
5. Fayad M., Schmidt D., Johnson R., (eds.), Building Application Frameworks — Object-Oriented Foundations of Framework Design. Wiley, 1999.
6. Gamma E., Helm R., Johnson R., Vlissides J., Design Patterns: Elements of Reusable Object-Oriented Software. Addison-Wesley, 1995.
7. Czarnecki K., Eisenecker U., Generative Programming, Methods, Tools, and Applications. Addison.Wesley, 2000.
8. Tasker M., Allen J., Dixon J., Shackman M., Richardson T., Forrest J., Professional Symbian Programming: Mobile Solutions on the EPOC Platform. Wrox Press Inc, 2000.
9. Sun Microsystems: http://developer.java.sun.com/developer/products/j2ee/, 2002.
10. IP Multimedia (IM) Subsystem - Stage 2, 3GPP TS 23.228, http://www.3gpp.org, 2002

Integrating Heterogeneous Communication and Messaging Systems in an Object-Oriented Middleware Framework

George Kogiomtzis* and Drakoulis Martakos**

Department of Informatics and Telecommunications
National and Kapodistrian University of Athens
Panepistimioupolis, Ilisia, 15784, Athens, Greece
g.kogiomtzis@interworks.gr
martakos@di.uoa.gr

Abstract. Integrated communications have been largely associated with message-oriented middleware in collaborative distributed computing environments, both on small and large scales. Past experience has shown that monolithic architectures based on large executables are extremely difficult to maintain and very unresponsive to change. This paper aims at proposing an intelligent, object-oriented communications and messaging architecture based on interrelated business objects and components, designed to support business-to-business communication. The philosophy behind our approach has been to construct a scalable and flexible system architecture that enables the incorporation of new services at minimum effort. The framework allows for the implementation of reusable components, independently from the core architecture, that can be automatically discovered, configured and plugged-in to the system and used as "cartridges" on demand, according to the communication requirements of the application that will make use of the bearers linked to the system.

1 Introduction

In the last decade companies focus on building enterprise-wide messaging and communication infrastructures in order to meet the ever-increasing requirements for inter- and intra-enterprise communications. In this perspective, enterprise services are crafted to facilitate and improve the communications within the enterprise, with the goal of reducing the overall cost of communication for the enterprise as a single entity. Communications and messaging in information systems development, an ever growing and rapidly changing milieu itself, have nowadays become the fastest growing kind of middleware and are constantly being extended to support new

* Corresponding Author, PhD. Candidate
** Associate Professor

Z. Bellahsène, D. Patel, and C. Rolland (Eds.): OOIS 2002, LNCS 2425, pp. 488-493, 2002.

technologies and infrastructures as they emerge [2]. The exchange of application data that support day-to-day transactions and activities lies beyond a simple file transfer or transmission of an email message. As a result, the existence of a sophisticated communications infrastructure is often highly desirable by both small companies and large enterprises with numerous business units dispersed all over the world.

In this paper, we propose a well-defined communication management system architecture that supports application integration across diverse business environments and applications. It represents a generic, open middleware architecture that can be applied to a variety of organizational models regardless of the purpose, content and structure of the information to be transmitted. As such, the aim of the proposed framework has been to integrate heterogeneous communication services in an object-oriented and component-based architecture by incorporating transport service-related operations into pluggable transport modules that can be automatically configured and plugged-in to the system in a plug-and-play fashion.

The rest of the paper is structured as follows. Section 2 provides a detailed overview of the proposed architecture and presents the conceptual framework of the system. The paper concludes in Section 3, where we summarize the presented work and identify areas of further research.

2 Conceptual Overview of the Proposed Architecture

The proposed system introduces a framework that allows the implementation of reusable components that can be automatically plugged-in to the system and used as cartridges on demand, according to the communication requirements of the application that uses them. One such class of components is designed to wrap the functionality of standard communication, networking and messaging protocols into a middleware component with a defined set of properties and methods conforming to a standard interface–components that manage FAX, SMTP, FTP and TCP sessions for example [3], [4]. This implementation only needs to package program functionality in a way such that the capabilities of the component are discoverable by the container during assembly or at run time [6].

Over the last few years, it has become apparent that creating an *n-tier* environment, where developers can be shielded from platform and data storage specifics, in order to concentrate on implementing the necessary business logic, is an effective solution [6]. As such, the system (hereafter abbreviated as CMS) is modeled as a *four-layer* architecture, depicted in Figure 1, separating the low-level messaging service components and communication protocols from the business logic, and data layers. These layers and their subsystems are analyzed in subsequent sections.

2.1 The User Interface (Application) Layer

This is the application user interface offering direct user interaction with the system and is responsible for manipulating the core application-programming interface (API) exposed by CMS. It provides a well-defined console for configuring the communication service parameters as well as managing the communication objects.

The Workbench Console resides on the client and issues calls through CORBA or DCOM to the common program interfaces exposed by the lower-level components of CMS. As far as CMS is concerned, this console constitutes the user's single point of administration where queues can be added and removed and communication services can be plugged-in and assigned to queues.

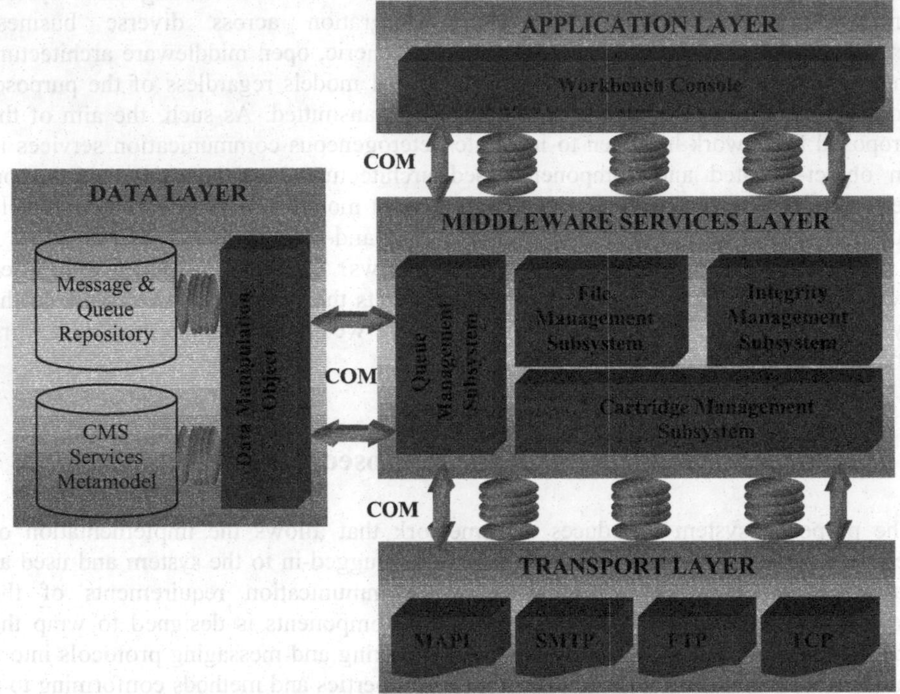

Fig. 1. Conceptual Framework of the CMS Architecture

2.2 The Middleware Services Layer

This layer implements the main engine of the communication system and the Cartridge Support Services and is responsible for co-ordinating all processes and modules under CMS. This middleware services layer is responsible for providing access to a queue and message management engine that controls the message and queue repository (message store) as well as binding the User Interface Console to specific cartridge components for administration purposes and maintains a common communication service metamodel for that reason. This layer's subsystems are analysed below.

File Management. The file management subsystem is primarily responsible for converting the transmission data to a CMS-specific standard format while protecting the data's integrity by ensuring that the original is not changed in transit. To maintain the CMS architectural consistency at the highest level, a common standard format has been derived to which all transmission data must conform. The standard specifies that all message data be wrapped into a message package that contains the original message data and a message header (in XML file format) with all relevant communication information. In this way, CMS dictates the way in which the communication data is structured, so that it can be understood by all enterprise-wide CMS installations.

Data Integrity Management. This subsystem provides assured message delivery by ensuring that messages arrive at the destination intact and in the correct order. In doing so, the system incorporates a message tracking mechanism with which all CMS installations across the enterprise know at any time what message to expect from any given queue. For this purpose, the system implements an algorithm, which checks the message counters and issues warnings for lost messages.

Cartridge Management. The Cartridge Manager provides a single point for the administration, authentication and management of cartridges and a place for components to register and provide their services. In the proposed plug-and-play approach to communication components, a challenging design issue is to enable the set-up of components that implement diverse requirements and use different settings without ever modifying the source code that manages the cartridges and configures their settings. This subsystem is therefore responsible for collecting all data from the relevant data repositories in RDBMS and passing them in batch mode to the appropriate cartridge. In doing so, it consults the service metamodel to obtain a reference to the required service and then generates an XML tree at run-time containing all the settings referring to that service. This process is repeated for both service and message settings after initialization of the CMS cartridge component. Once the XML tree generation is complete, the cartridge manager will forward the XML metadata to the cartridge, which will evaluate the data and configure itself accordingly for operation.

Queue and Message Management (QMS). Realizing the growing importance of message queuing middleware, the CMS philosophy relies on a ubiquitous message queue-based approach [1], [7]. In this approach each application sends it message to an intermediary queue. The message is then forwarded to its ultimate target. If the target cannot respond, the message is maintained in the queue and resent until it is accepted. However, some of the main mechanisms of QMS have been incorporated in CMS in an effort to decentralize some core functionality in CMS service modules, such as the data integrity mechanism. The QMS still maintains the message and queue management mechanisms but it is not responsible for message routing or protocol convergence. As such, it exposes an API that allows application modules to control the flow of messages between queues and constitutes a common access system in which the user or higher-level systems (such as workflow) can deposit message objects and from which CMS can collect messages for transmission to the destination queue objects. The QMS conceptual framework is depicted in Figure 2.

Core Engine Controller. Most of the CMS functionality is encapsulated in a middleware server component called the Core Engine Controller. This component is vital to the architectural consistency of CMS in that it ensures interoperability between the different subsystems and acts as a component manager, similar to a *CORBA Request Broker* to provide a single point of authentication and engine session management [1], [5], [8].

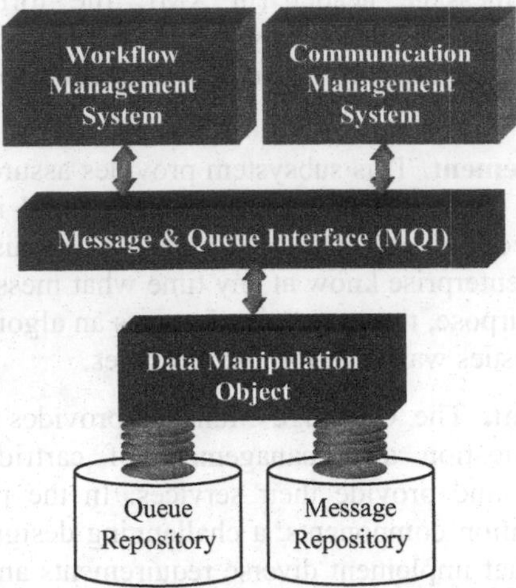

Fig. 2. Conceptual Framework of the QMS subsystem

2.3 The Communication Services (Transport) Layer

This layer maintains a collection of software components that encapsulate the low-level messaging services and communication protocols. Each component is responsible for providing a specific service and must conform to a common set of properties, methods and interfaces. A separate module implements each communication service object. We define these independent communication modules as *Cartridges*. Common examples of communication services and protocols currently supported include MAPI, cc:Mail, X.400, MHS, FAX, TCP, FTP and HTTP.

2.4 The Relational Database Management System (Data) Layer

This is where CMS persists all information required for its normal day-to-day operation. At this layer, CMS maintains a common Message and Queue Repository, which can be accessed by the Queuing Management System module containing an abstract database implementation template that is used for database connection, navigation and other operations in the RDBMS. Finally, the CMS maintains repositories for each of the core engine services such as the Data Integrity Management, the History Management and the Scheduler Management Services as well as a metamodel of all supported communication services.

3 Conclusion

For years companies have been interested in integrating enterprise applications to offer solutions that range from improved operating systems to relational databases, bridges and APIs that made it possible to exchange data between applications. In this paper, we have presented an enterprise framework for inter-enterprise co-operation and communication. The idea behind the proposed system architecture emerged in an attempt to provide a different approach to application integration by providing a Message-Oriented Middleware Platform for collaborative computing environments. The architecture is based on an n-tier component-based, object-oriented model, which provides heterogeneous transport services and infrastructure support for automatic service discovery and configuration, security policies and integrated message and queue management.

The CMS philosophy has been to construct a highly scalable and flexible system architecture that enables incorporation of new services at minimum effort, offering advantages such as complete control of service customization, increased system flexibility, easy adaptation to custom requirements, scalability through the use of pluggable transport modules and coexistence of heterogeneous messaging and communication systems.

In the real application environment, a commercial implementation of the proposed system architecture is currently being implemented and evaluated for the purposes of the Market Maker project.

Acknowledgments

This paper is based on research conducted and funded by MarketMaker, "Wiring Smart Enterprises in the Digital World through Process Orchestration", Information Society Technology (IST), 5th Framework Programme of the European Commission, Project Number IST-2001-33376.

References

1. Expersoft Corporation, "*Integrating CORBA with Message-oriented Middleware (MOM)*", Expersoft Corporation, White Paper, 1997.
2. Johnsson D., "The Changing Requirements of Inter-Company Messaging: Electronic Commerce Trends", GE Information Services Inc, White Paper, 1998.
3. Lhotka R., "*Visual Basic 6 Business Objects*", Wrox Press Ltd, 1998.
4. Moniz J., "*Enterprise Application Architecture*", Wrox Press Ltd, 1999.
5. Orfali, R., Harkey D., "*Client/Server Programming with JAVA and CORBA*", Wiley Publishing, 1997.
6. Spitzer T., "Component Architectures", *DBMS*, September 1997.
7. Thomson M., "*Technology Audit*", MQSeries Product Family, Butler Direct Limited, September 1999.
8. Vinoski S., "*Distributed Object Computing With CORBA*", Hewlett-Packard Company, 1993.

Object Schizophrenia Problem in Object Role System Design

K. Chandra Sekharaiah and D. Janaki Ram

Distributed Object Systems Lab, Dept. of Computer Science & Engg.
Indian Institute of Technology, Madras, India
{chand,djram}@cs.iitm.ernet.in

Abstract. This paper argues for strong notions of Object Schizophrenia (OS) and Object Schizophrenia Problem (OSP) and makes subtle distinction between them. It presents how OSP can occur in modeling is-part-of and is-role-of relationships. Basically, we assert that OS-condition of an object does not necessarily entail OSP. The occurrence of OSP is investigated in the realm of role modeling. Broken consultation, wrong message interpretation and security schizophrenia problem that arise due to reusing mechanisms in role modeling such as delegation are incorporated as new symptoms into the semantic scope of the notion of OSP. We introduce plurality of OS and OSP by categorizing OSs and OSPs based on various models for object relationships and OSP symptoms. A comparison picture of the existing role models is presented with regard to OSP. We assert that there can be different approaches for handling the OSP and that a solution to OSP works out only in a model-specific way. In the realm of role modeling, this work emphasizes that modeling the role paradigm should ensure that the role model is OSP-free. We argue for strong notion of object identity for role-playing objects in terms of the Oid integrity principle.

Keywords: Object Schizophrenia (OS), Object Schizophrenia Problem (OSP), Role Modeling Problem (RMP), Subject Oriented Programming (SOP), Whole-Part Association (WPA), Role Paradigm Conformance Model (RPCM).

1 Introduction

Object schizophrenia problem [1,2] is a major obstacle in role-based object oriented software development. OS [1,2] is an inherent, common phenomenon in role modeling, subject oriented programming [3], and some design patterns. There is no clear difference between OS and OSP in the literature. This paper provides deeper insights to understanding OS and OSP in modeling dynamically evolving objects with roles. We relate broken semantics of abstraction, encapsulation, identity and message passing with the notions of OS and OSP.

Our findings on OS and OSP in modeling objects with roles yielded certain semantics of importance for object community [1]. Further accepted findings on OS and OSP are in an earlier version of this paper in [2].

Z. Bellahsène, D. Patel, and C. Rolland (Eds.): OOIS 2002, LNCS 2425, pp. 494–506, 2002.

The rest of the paper is organized as follows: The next section presents details of the notion of object identity as related to object role systems. In section 3, we explain the object schizophrenia problem given in [1,2]. Section 4 explains a classification of OSPs. Section 5 compares and contrasts OSP with OS. Section 6 relates OS and OSP with the existing literature on role modeling. Section 7 explains how object schizophrenia problem is more probable in modeling composite objects with roles. Section 8 concludes the paper and gives future directions for research.

2 Object Identity at the Core of the OSP

Object community have emphatically addressed the identity semantics of object [3,4,5] and obstacles in development [6]. Object identity is a modeling concept. Oids are defined for real-world objects as well as for objects residing in a computer [7]. Two parts of the identity principle for the Oids are in [7].

Even as each object is associated with a unique identifier regardless of its current state, a stronger notion of identity has to be incorporated [5]. *Identity* is more relevant than other properties of an object since it is not simply a value describing an object; it cannot be changed in the same way other values describing the object can be changed. In [3], *identity* was emphasized to be the guiding principle for inter-operating, integrated applications that are based on the decentralized development of objects. In [4], object identity was given the highest priority among the properties of objects. In [8], a revised notion of object identity is suggested in the realm of roles since real-world entities are represented by multiple objects. Entity identity is contrasted with role identity-entity identity is the unique system-defined identifier and is provided by the object identity of the root instance of an object-role hierarchy; every particular role of a real-world entity is identified by the object identity of the instance representing the entity in that role.

In an object role system [9,10], two role objects are entity-equivalent if they correspond to one and the same real world entity i.e., they have a common root object, the player object [8]. The root object's identity is independent, global identity. It is not dependent on the role instances. However, the identities of the role, subrole instances are existence dependent on a particular root object identity. This means that role objects export behavior only in conjunction with identification of a particular root object. A role is a handle/agent that the root object holds to export the role-specific behavior. Role hierarchies [8,11,12] are designed such that the role objects and the subrole objects are entity-equivalent. Thus, the identity of the root object is called *integral identity*. An object with roles should have *integral identity*- its own identity, role, subrole identities and *entity-equivalence* [8] of roles and subroles. The *Oid integrity principle* is based on the notion of entity equivalence [8]. In modeling objects with roles, it provides a third dimension to Oid principle.

The **Oid integrity principle**: The objects representing roles/subroles/multiple views of any relevant object (called the root object/intrinsic object) should be entity-equivalent. That is, an operation such as *find_root()* on them should be able to generate one and the same Oid i.e., the Oid of the root object.

The principle provides a stronger notion of Oid in the realm of role modeling. The prevalence of multiple identities for object with roles is called *broken identity.* In role modeling, Oid integrity principle paves the way to satisfy the Oid principle in the presence of broken identity. Broken identity is a concept in modeling the role paradigm [1,2,9]. Also, a composite object is said to have broken identity by supporting state and properties in terms of the Oids of its component objects. Different from broken identity, *split identity* is the concept in modeling the "nominally part-of" relationship. In this relationship, a part object could be meaningful as part of a composite object as well as an independent object. For instance, a Department object may get messages directly or as a result of delegation from higher level composite objects such as a College object or a University object. Thus, different identity semantics are found meaningful in different object relationships. The categorization of identity semantics helps for deeper insights into understanding various OSPs. In the later sections, we discuss how the concepts of broken identity and split identity together with OSP symptoms facilitate the classification of OSs and OSPs.

2.1 Broken Identity vs. Violation of the Identity Principle

Many applications require the ability to define and manipulate a set of objects as a single logical entity for purposes of semantic integrity, and efficient storage and retrieval. For example, in role modeling, it should be possible to handle and manipulate object with roles as having one and the same identity. Similarly, a composite object hierarchy requiring the component objects to be necessarily dependent objects is handled and manipulated as one and the same object. Such composite objects are often used in locking, recovery management etc.

Broken identity is an inevitable feature in modeling the role paradigm. However, the condition of broken identity does not necessarily mean violation of the identity principle. Violation of the identity principle means violation of at least one of the three parts of the identity principle. Traditional objects fulfill the Oid principle by just following the first two parts. Objects with roles fulfill the Oid principle by satisfying the Oid integrity principle too. Mere prevalence of broken identity is indicative of OS only. When Oid integrity principle is not satisfied in the presence of broken identity, the result is OSP. For example, in role modeling, the usage of delegation together with violation of the Oid integrity principle results in multiple ways for message processing resulting in bugs of the sort that are very hard to find.

The prevalence of broken identity or split identity is indicative of OS. We classify OS as inter-object schizophrenia and intra-object schizophrenia. In inter-OS, the state and/or interface and identity of the object are in broken condition. There are multiple objects that together represent one and the same object identically. The implementations of the objects are captured in multiple classes. All role models that conform to role paradigm have inter-OS. In intra-OS, an object has single Oid and yet supports multifarious interfaces/states. The IP model [13,14] and the Aspects model [15] are beset with this kind of OS.

3 Object Schizophrenia Problem: What It Means

OS is a necessary but not sufficient condition for OSP. OSP is an offshoot of OS, but not the vice versa. The difference between intended method semantics and the processed method semantics in the presence of OS is OSP. OSP is the error in the semantics of a message forwarding mechanism in a role model. OSP is the broken semantics of concerns such as method execution, security, contracts, assumptions etc. in a method lookup scheme in the presence of OS.

Basically, an object has a set of "operations" and a "state" that remembers the effect of operations [16]. Objects are contrasted with functions which have no memory. OSP is mainly due to the memory loss in message forwarding semantics. When a role model can not provide memory identification semantics of interest, there is OSP in the role model. A message forwarding mechanism has to necessarily have tight coupling with memory identification semantics. A coupling can be delegation coupling, consultation coupling, nearest neighbor slave coupling etc. The problems of various couplings are illustrated in the next section while explaining BD-OSP and BC-OSP. The coupling is with regard to the applicability of the "self" semantics. In [17], object is defined as an entity whose behavior is characterized by the actions that it suffers and that it requires of other objects. In line with this, an OS object suffers for its actions which are inherent to it and lets other objects suffer for the actions it requires of them. The difference between the suffering of the actions of an OS object with respect to a viewpoint and the suffering of its actions with respect to another viewpoint is OSP. The viewpoints are held by the different stakeholders involved in the system development.

In [18], three symptoms of OS are provided as broken delegation, broken assumptions and dopplegangers. In this paper, they are appropriately categorized as symptoms of OSP to avoid the confusion between OS and OSP. OSP symptoms are explained in the context of role modeling. Message forwarding mechanisms such as *delegation* and *consultation* [19] are the causes of OSP in role modeling. A role model has to provide non-intrusive evolution (problems can be addressed at without modifying the existing code) of objects playing roles. If OSP symptoms prevail, this requirement can not be met. Hence, a role model has to be free from the OSP. In terms of the identity semantics, split identity is sure to result in OSP. Broken identity may or may not result in OSP.

4 OSP Classification

In this section, we explain various kinds of OSPs. In [18], the symptoms of OSP are explained in cases where "nominally part-of" relationship exists between objects. The relationship "B is nominally part-of A" could mean that B can exist as either part of A or as a stand-alone object.

We say that each symptom defines one kind of OSP. This means that as many symptoms are there, so many kinds of OSPs are there. As the number of symptoms are more, we say that the *degree of OSP* is more. As the number of symptoms are less, we say that *the degree of OSP* is less. We make a preliminary classification of OSPs based on the problems encountered with message forwarding semantics. The OSPs are: WMI-OSP, BD-OSP, SP-OSP, BA-OSP, DG-OSP. We explain these varieties of OSP in the next section.

4.1 WMI-OSP: OSP Due to Wrong Message Interpretation Semantics

WMI-OSP is a kind of OSP. For example, method lookup semantics in the implementation of roles in [11] may lead to WMI-OSP. Here, resolution mechanism for methods first goes down the role hierarchy and the most specialized behaviors prevail. Each time a new role is acquired, the dispatch table of an object is updated. The get_payment() method of a super role may be obtained and interpreted as relevant to a subrole in a false manner [1,2]. Because this problem is due to OS, it is considered as WMI-OSP.

4.2 BD-OSP: OSP Due to Broken Delegation

Secure delegation is said to occur when an object (called the delegator/initiator object) authorizes another object (called the delegate/destination object) to perform some task using (some of) the rights of the delegator. The authorization lasts until some target object (end-point) provides the service. Essentially, secure delegation is the ability to verify that an object that claims to be acting on another's behalf, is indeed authorized to act on its behalf.

BD-OSP may be due to interpreting the "self" semantics in favor of the locality of the method holder object i.e. due to consultation, or in favor of the locality of the nearest neighbor slave object etc.

4.3 SP-OSP: OSP Due to Unprovided Security Semantics in Message Forwarding Mechanism

Where multiple delegation paths are there to the root object, different security concerns may have to be figured out. Where it may be secure for an object to respond to a message forwarded in one delegation path, it may be insecure to respond to a message forwarded in a different delegation path. In other words, security concerns of a role player object are not the same in all directions. By modeling security as message filter [9,20], message filter hierarchy can be used to avoid the security problems at any one node in the role hierarchy. However, such extra security concerns that arise due to delegation are unaddressed and unprovided in literature. We see this as an OSP symptom because this problem occurs not merely due to delegation but in the added context of modeling OS objects/RPCM objects [1].

4.4 BA-OSP: OSP Due to Broken Assumptions

The symptom of broken assumptions in [1] is categorized appropriately as a kind of OSP under this heading.

4.5 DG-OSP: OSP Due to Dopplegangers

Dopplegangers [18] is an OSP symptom which is found in such systems that involve composite objects, for instance shutdown-management, indexing, locking, recovery management wherein a registry is maintained for maintaining a set of objects that register and de-register as part of the mechanism involved. For instance, consider a shutdown-management system which allows objects to register for notification when the system shuts down. For accomplishing this, each participating object is registered with the manager and the manager keeps a set of object identifiers that need to be notified. In cases where "nominally part-of" relationship is applicable, it is possible to send the notification in two ways- one through the whole object, and another to the stand-alone instance which could be the part object too. The result of notification results in bugs that are hard to find.

Similarly, a locking protocol may recognize a composite object as a single lockable granule. Such a locking protocol is applicable to composite objects that consist of composite references (i.e., physical part hierarchies). Different lock modes may be applicable to prevent a transaction from updating/reading a part object) while another transaction is reading/updating the composite object, as a whole. The "nominally part-of" relationship leads to violation of locking semantics involved in this kind of locking protocol since a part object can exist notwithstanding the existence of the composite object.

In role modeling, the problems of using part-of relationship for modeling the role paradigm have already been explained in [21]. Existing role models have not used part-of relationship of any kind and are free from the symptom of dopplegangers. Amongst the OSPs, split identity semantics are peculiar to DG-OSP.

4.6 BC-OSP: OSP Due to Broken Consultation

BC-OSP is an OSP that is associated with the usage of *consultation* as the message forwarding mechanism. It is the inability of an object with roles to implement consultation correctly. Where there is loss of semantics between expected method execution semantics and obtained method execution semantics when consultation is used, we categorize it as BC-OSP. BC-OSP may be due to interpreting the "self" semantics in favor of the locality of the message receiver object i.e. due to delegation, or in favor of the locality of the nearest neighbor slave object etc..

In the existing role models, delegation and not consultation is used. However, which one is a better method lookup scheme in role modeling is a moot question.

Type of OSP	Identity Semantics	Modeling Composite Objects based on is–part–of Relationships		Modeling the Role Paradigm
		Modeling nominally–part–of Relationship i.e. Modeling the Confusion in is–part–of Relationships	Modeling necessarily–part–of Relationship (Aggregation)	
BD–OSP is possible in	Broken Identity	✓	✓	✓
BA–OSP is possible in	Broken Identity	✓	✓	✓
DG–OSP is possible in	Split Identity	✓	✗	✗
WMI–OSP is possible in	Broken Identity	? (not known)	? (not known)	✓
SP–OSP is possible in	Broken Identity	✓	✓	✓
BC–OSP is possible in	Broken Identity	✓	✓	✓

BD= Broken Delegation
BA= Broken Assumptions
DG= Dopplegangers

SP= Security Problem
WMI= Wrong Method Interpretation
BC= Broken Consultation

Fig. 1. An OSP classification picture

OSPs such as WMI-OSP, BA-OSP, SP-OSP tend to arise not only with delegation but also with the usage of consultation. OSP is mainly due to the difference in the localities of reference of interests of the stakeholders in the usage of the message forwarding semantics in the role model.

A classification picture of OSPs is given in Figure 1 based on various kinds of OSP symptoms. Needless to say, eliminating OSP due to delegation does not necessarily mean introducing consultation. A solution to OSP can work only in a model-specific way. In other words, as long as the method lookup semantics are fixed, a solution to OSP is definitely possible within the scope of that model.

5 OS or OSP?

OS and OSP are different. In software development that captures separation of concerns, OSP arises iff OS exists and results in at least one OSP symptom. Thus, OSP is a specialized condition of OS. OSP is a bottleneck for supporting non-invasive evolution of objects in role modeling. OSP is, mainly, the result of undisciplined usage of message forwarding mechanism such as delegation. Violation of the encapsulation principle results in OSP. The condition of broken encapsulation is not necessarily violation of the identity principle. For example, in a role hierarchy, the implementation of the objects in the higher level is exposed to the objects in the lower level. However, the identity principle is preserved because the Oid integrity principle is followed. Non-violation of the identity principle does not necessarily avoid OSP. Gottlob's role model [8] preserves the identity principle but has OSP on account of the usage of delegation. Subject oriented programming community [18] claim that OSP is avoided just because the identity principle is preserved. Most of the existing role models have OSP besides OS on account of the usage of delegation for method lookup. Subject oriented model involves broken encapsulation by supporting decentralized development of objects because ownership and encapsulation of a software object are treated as synonyms by some researchers [22,23,24]. However, subject oriented composition involves the usage of single object identity. Preserving the Oid principle is a necessary but not sufficient condition for avoiding OSP. As such, there are scenarios where object schizophrenia prevails and yet OSP does not prevail. [18] shows "nominally part-of relationship" as causing OSP. However, "role-of" relationship and not "nominally part-of" relationship is used in the role models in [8,10]. Further, we have seen how OSP can occur in modeling the "role-of" relationship.

In role modeling, whereas OSP is avoidable, OS is inevitable. By itself, OS is not a problem. Together with one or more symptoms, OS manifests as OSP. Figure 2 shows that OS and OSP can occur differently in role models. The IP model [13,14], the Aspects model [15], the Typehole model [9,25,26] and the DMMA model [27] are OSP-free role models. Based on the distinction made between OS and OSP, while providing various features in the role models, researchers should consider as the primary objective that the model conforms to the role paradigm and is yet OSP-free.

6 The Role Modeling Problem

Roles provide restricted, complementary perspectives of a complex object, and dynamic object composition and decomposition. In [14], role modeling was proposed for mobile collaborative applications. In [13], office objects were modeled with different roles for different contexts in the lifetime of the object playing roles.

Objects with roles have to satisfy such properties as visibility, dependency, identity, multiplicity, dynamicity, and abstractivity [21]. This set of properties constitute role paradigm [1,9]. A role paradigm conformance model (RPCM) satisfies the role paradigm. The works in [8,21] explain that traditional object oriented techniques such as specialization, aggregation and association are not adequate for RPCM design. The role models in [8,25] are RPCMs. Objects with roles that conform to the role paradigm are called RPCM objects. RPCM objects belong to the category of OS objects [1].

In [16], an object may learn from experience. Its reaction to an operation is determined by its invocation history. OSP objects can not learn from experience in that the same kind of OSP can occur even for multiple invocations. As a solution, a separate design object may be incorporated into the role model. The design object may capture the various couplings of "self" semantics. It may capture the variability requirements in regard of the "self" semantics. It may capture a switching mechanism amongst the three kinds of couplings explained earlier. A particular coupling mechanism can be dynamically selected.

		Conforms to Roleparadigm	Broken Interface	Broken Identity	Split Identity	Identity Principle Violated	OS is there?	OSP is possible?
Role Models	Aspects	No	Yes	No	No	No	Yes	No
	ORM	No	Yes	No	No	No	Yes	No
	Albano's Model	No	Yes	No	No	No	Yes	Yes
	Gottlob's Model	Yes	Yes	Yes	No	No	Yes	Yes
	Raymond's Model	No	Yes	Yes	No	No	Yes	Yes
	Typehole Model	Yes	Yes	Yes	No	No	Yes	No
	Split Object Model	No	Yes	No	No	No	Yes	Yes
	IP Model	No	Yes	No	No	No	Yes	No
	DMMA Model	No	Yes	Yes	No	No	Yes	No
Composition Techniques	Subject Composition	not applicable	Yes	No	No	No	Yes	No
	Object Composition: nominally part–of relationship e.g. Adapter pattern	not applicable	not applicable	Yes	Yes	Yes	Yes	Yes
	Object Composition: necessarily part–of relationship	not applicable	not applicable	not applicable	No	No	Yes	Yes

Fig. 2. OSP in various role models: A comparative picture

RMP is defined as the requirement of designing an OSP-free RPCM. The existing role models [8,11,10] do not solve the RMP. Gottlob's role model captures the role paradigm. However, it is based on delegation for method lookup and, hence, has the object schizophrenia problem. None of the existing role models have strong claims as being OSP-free RPCM.

Figure 2 gives a comparison of various existing role models as regards the OSP and the Oid semantics. In the Aspects model [15], *aspects* extend the role-playing object's state and behavior. It does not support multiple role instantiation. So, it is not an RPCM. Maintaining a single Oid, it does not specify method dispatch for aspects. Consequently, it is OSP-free. Pernici's role model, ORM [28] maintains multiple objects in the form of role-playing object and the role objects but does not discuss anything about the method lookup. In [11], an object with its roles has a single Oid. The model does not support multiplicity property [21]. Hence, it is not an RPCM. Method dispatch is based on a role type hierarchy down and up the hierarchy based on delegation. Consequently, it is not OSP-free. The DOOR model [10] provides seven delegation schemes. Consequently, it is not OSP-free. Typehole model [9,25,26] conforms to role paradigm. Messages are sent directly to the destination role objects. No message forwarding mechanism is used. The model has OS. However, dispensing with delegation mechanism which is the usual message forwarding mechanism in most of the role models, the model is an OSP-free role model. Gottlob's model [8] involves broken Oid, but satisfies the identity principle by following the Oid integrity principle. Objects and its roles have different Oids. It is an RPCM. Method dispatch is based on delegation only up the hierarchy and late binding is followed. Thus, it is not OSP-free. In the IP model [13,14], multiple interfaces are captured in a single class. The various interfaces refer to the different behaviors of a role-playing object. Single object identity is followed. The model does not provide multiple role instantiation. The objects allow one role behavior at a time in addition to the time-invariant behavior captured by the public interface. Similar to the Aspects model and the ORM, the model supports only rudimentary aspects of role modeling and no message forwarding mechanism is used. Hence, OSP does not arise in the model. It is not an RPCM.

Split Object Model [29] investigates the semantics of delegation and emphasizes disciplined use of delegation. *Pieces* in this model are like roles. They do not have an object status. Single object identity is maintained. The pieces in this model are much akin to the multiple interfaces supported by the IP model and the DMMA model. Together they are like *role type hierarchy* of Albano's model. Message forwarding from lower pieces in the hierarchy to the ascendent pieces is followed. This is a case where there is broken interface and yet single Oid is possible. This concept is similar to the IP model. The split object model does not support multiple role instantiation. Consequently, it is not an RPCM. The usage of message forwarding mechanism makes it OSP-prone. The DMMA model [27] avoids OSP by dispensing with delegation. Messages are sent directly to destination roles. No message forwarding mechanism is used. Multiple role instantiation is followed.

In [30], roles were proposed for composing different perspectives on a problem domain. However, Kristensen's work in [30] on subject composition by roles does not address the OSP. In [18], subject composition has no OSP in contrast with object composition.

7 Object Schizophrenia Problem in Modeling Composite Objects with Roles

Composite object classes are defined using references to other object classes. They are basically aggregates of subparts that involve the definition of other objects. A dependency relationship between the component objects and the composite object must be provided if the semantics of the composite objects has to be applicable on the component objects. A composite object is based on the Is-Part-of relationship. Further, the relationship may be qualified as either "nominally-part of" relationship or "necessarily part-of" relationship.

The complexity in modeling composite objects with roles is not addressed by researchers. The term "composite object with roles" is used for a composite object wherein either the composite object or the component object or both play roles. In modeling composite objects with roles, providing a message forwarding mechanism raises interesting issues. Message forwarding semantics are applied for objects that capture *is-role-of* relationship or *has-a* relationship, but have not addressed as to how the method lookup mechanism can be provided when both the diverse relationships are in design. The University Database Example in [2,9] is illustrative of the OSP complexity in modeling composite objects with roles. OSP complexity is more in modeling WPAs that capture "nominally part-of" relationship.

8 Conclusions and Future Work

In this paper, OS and OSP are interrelated and differentiated. OSP is a specialized condition of OS. The mere prevalence of OS is not a problem. OSs and OSPs have been classified. The significance of addressing the OSP while designing an RPCM has been brought out. Message forwarding mechanisms such as delegation and consultation require disciplined usage to avoid OSP. The classification of OSs and OSPs and the contrast between the two concepts will give new insights to the researchers to come up with OSP-free RPCMs. Solving one kind of OSP in a model may often amount to not solving another kind of OSP. Hence, we say that a solution to OSP is only model-specific. It is limited to the scope of concerns addressed in the model. To whatever extent the concerns are addressed in the model, OSP can be solved definitely to that extent. Beyond that, OSP of some kind or the other appears as a live problem. A comparison picture of OS and OSP in various existing role models shows that no role model has strong claims as being an OSP-free RPCM. Stronger notion of object identity has been built with new semantics in terms of broken identity, split identity and Oid integrity principle as relevant to is-part-of and is-role-of relationships. Role model designs where OS may prevail but the *Oid integrity principle* is preserved pave the way to eliminate OSP.

The issues that arise with the complexity of OSP in the design of object role systems involving composite objects with roles require deeper investigation. OSP is a more complex issue in modeling objects with distributed roles. Migrating objects with roles in distributed applications together with ensuring the identity characteristic requires further investigation. An object may export different role hierarchies at different sites or it may have different roles at different sites. Decentralizing the object-role hierarchies for role model designs in distributed, mobile systems has potential for research. We are working on making a definitional formalism for OSP in terms of behavior calculus. Based on the contrast made between OS and OSP, the role modeling community can focus on addressing the OSP in the next generation role models.

References

1. Chandra Sekharaiah K., Janaki Ram D.: Object Schizophrenia Problem in Modeling Is-Role-of Inheritance. In: Inheritance Workshop in 16th European Conference on Object-Oriented Programming, University of Málaga, Spain (2002) 494, 495, 496, 498, 499, 501
2. K.Chandra Sekharaiah, D.Janaki Ram: Object Schizophrenia Problem in Object Role Database System Design. In: Tech. Report no IITM-CSE-DOS-02-04, Distributed and Object Systems Group, Dept. of C. S. E. IIT Madras, Chennai, India (2002) 494, 495, 496, 498, 503
3. William Harrison, Harold Ossher: Subject-Oriented Programming (A Critique of Pure Objects). In: Proceedings of OOPSLA. (1993) 411–428 494, 495
4. M.Sakkinen: Disciplined Inheritance. In: Proceedings of ECOOP'89. (1989) 39–56 495

5. Koshafian, G.Copeland: Object Identity. In: Proceedings of OOPSLA. (1986) 406–416 495
6. Mehmet Aksit, Lodewijk Bergmans: Obstacles in Object-Oriented Software Development. In: Proceedings of OOPSLA, Vancouver, Canada (1992) 341–358 495
7. Roel Wieringa, Wiebren DeJonge: The Identification of Objects and Roles - Object Identifiers Revisited. In: Technical Report IR-267, (Vrije Universiteit, Amsterdam) 495
8. George Gottlob, Michael Schrefl, Brigitte Röck: Extending Object-Oriented Systems with Roles. ACM Transactions on Information Systems **14** (1996) 268–296 495, 500, 501, 502
9. K.Chandra Sekharaiah, Arun Kumar, D.Janaki Ram: A Security Model for Object Role Database Systems. In: International Conference on Information and Knowledge Engineering (Accepted, to appear), Las Vegas, Nevada, USA (2002) 495, 496, 498, 501, 502, 503
10. Raymond K. Wong, H.Lewis Chau, Frederik H.Lochovsky: A Data Model and Semantics of Objects with Dynamic Roles. In: Proceedings of the 13th International Conference on Data Engineering, IEEE CS Press, University of Bermingham, Birmingham, U. K. (1997) 402–411 495, 501, 502
11. A.Albano, R.Bergamini, G.Ghelli, R.Orsini: An Object Data Model with Roles. In: Proceedings of the 18th VLDB Conference, Dublin, Ireland (1993) 39–51 495, 498, 502
12. E.Sciore: Object Specialization. ACM Transactions On Information Systems **7** (1989) 103–122 495
13. Janaki Ram D., Ramakrishnan R, Srinivas Rao Ch., Vivekananda N: CO-IP: An Object Model for Office Information Systems. In: Proceedings of the Third International Conference on Object Oriented Information Systems (OOIS'96), London (1996) 31–43 497, 501, 502
14. Anjaneyulu P, D.Janaki Ram: PolyConstraints: A Design Pattern for Flexible Collaboration in Heterogeneous Mobile Environments. In: Proceedings of 24th International Conference on Technology of Object Oriented Languages and Systems (TOOLS ASIA), Beijing (1997) 205–214 497, 501, 502
15. Joel Richardson, Peter Schwarz: Aspects: Extending Objects to Support Multiple, Independent Roles. In: Proceedings of the ACM SIGMOD Int. Con. on Management of Data. Volume 20. (1991) 298–307 497, 501, 502
16. Peter Wegner: Dimensions of Object-Based Language Design. OOPSLA Proceedings in ACM Sigplan Notices (1987) 168–182 497, 501
17. Grady Booch: Object-Oriented Development. IEEE Transactions on Software Engineering **12** (1986) 211–221 497
18. IBM Research: Subject-oriented Programming Group: Subject-Oriented Programming and Design Patterns, (http://www.research.ibm.com/sop/) 497, 499, 500, 501, 503
19. Günter Kniesel: Type-Safe Delegation for Run-Time Component Adaptation. In: ECOOP, Lisbon, Portugal (1999) 497
20. Rushikesh K. Joshi, N.Vivekananda, D.Janaki Ram: Message Filters for Object-Oriented Systems. Software-Practice and Experience **27** (1997) 677–699 498
21. Bent Bruun Kristensen: Object Oriented Modeling with Roles. In: Proceedings of the Second International Conf. on Object Oriented Information Systems(OOIS), Dublin, Ireland, Springer Verlag (1995) 57–71 499, 501, 502
22. Coad P., Yourdon E.: Object Oriented Analysis 2nd Edition. Yourdon Press, Prentice Hall (1990) 501

23. Atkinson C.: Object Oriented Reuse, Concurrency, and Distribution: An Ada-based approach. ACM Press, Addison Wesley (1991) 501
24. Franco Civello: Roles for Composite Objects in Object-Oriented Analysis and Design. In: Proceedings of OOPSLA. (1993) 376–393 501
25. K.Chandra Sekharaiah, D.Janaki Ram, A. V. S. K.Kumar: Typehole Model for Objects with Roles in Object Oriented Systems. In: Fourteenth Europeon Conference on Object Oriented Programming, Workshop Reader, LNCS 1964, Sophia Antipolis, France, Springer Verlag (2000) 301–302 501, 502
26. D.Janaki Ram, Chitra Babu: A Framework for Dynamic Client-Driven Customization. In: Proceedings of Object Oriented Information Systems (OOIS). (2001) 245–258 501, 502
27. D.Janaki Ram, K.Chandra Sekharaiah: Dynamically Mutable Multiple Abstractions. In: Proceedings of the Second National Conference on Object Oriented Technology (NCOOT'98), Pondicherry, India (1998) 26–32 501, 503
28. Barbara Pernici: Objects with Roles. In: IEEE/ACM Conference on Office Information Systems ACM SIGOIS. Volume 1., Cambridge, Massachutes (1990) 205–215 502
29. Daniel Bardou, Christophe Dony: Split Objects: A Disciplined Use of Delegation within Objects. In: Proceedings of OOPSLA. (1996) 122–137 503
30. Bent Bruun Kristensen: Subject Composition by Roles. In: Proceedings of the Fourth International Conf. on Object Oriented Information Systems(OOIS), Brisbane, Australia (1997) 503

Roles and Aspects: Similarities, Differences, and Synergetic Potential

Stefan Hanenberg and Rainer Unland

Institute for Computer Science, University of Essen, 45117 Essen, Germany
{shanenbe,unlandR}@cs.uni-essen.de

Abstract. Both, the role concept and aspect-oriented programming are techniques which permit a flexible adaptation of object-oriented constructs and therefore can be used to adjust existing software to new challenges. While the former one is already well known in the object-oriented world, the latter was only recently introduced. Currently, both techniques co-exist without affecting each other and therefore concrete software projects either use the one or the other approach. There are some situations where the result of utilizing the one or the other is approximately the same. Therefore, it is reasonable to analyze each approach in respect to its underlying philosophy and its impact on the implementation level and to compare them on the basis of those observations. This paper discusses the equivalences and differences between the role concept and aspect-oriented programming and reveals potential synergies between both approaches.

1 Introduction

In the traditional object-oriented literature real-world entities are represented by objects which interact with their environment. Entities in this environment interact with an object by using its intrinsic properties. Nevertheless, as pointed out by Harrison and Ossher in [11] users have different perspectives on an object. In that way the observable properties are not only objective, intrinsic properties, but also subjective, extrinsic properties which depend on a user's perspective.

The core assumption of the role concept is that there are (extrinsic) properties and behavior of an object which may change during its lifetime. In other words, it is assumed that the original classification of an object may change during life-time. A similar argumentation was done against class-based programming languages, for example Lieberman argues in [17] that people do not think in classes but in prototype object whose "essential properties" represent people's view on a class.

The concept of roles and its relation to object-oriented programming has been already widely discussed (cf. [20,16,15,7]). Nevertheless, popular programming languages like C++ or Java do not support roles as first class entities on the language

Z. Bellahsène, D. Patel, and C. Rolland (Eds.): OOIS 2002, LNCS 2425, pp. 507-520, 2002.

level. So developers who need to apply the role concept usually make use of a framework.

In the recent past, aspect-oriented programming (AOP) became more and more popular. One of the major observation in [14] is that there are concerns which cannot be cleanly encapsulated using traditional composition techniques and therefore are somehow tangled with other modules. Aspect-oriented programming is about modularizing such concerns, which are called *aspects*. [3] introduces AOP as "the idea that computer systems are better programmed by specifying the various concerns (...) of a system and some description of their relationships". The underlying aspect-oriented environment is responsible for assembling those concerns together. The result of such a composition is that there are numerous (object-oriented) building blocks stemming from different concerns spread all over the object hierarchy. Hence, an object's member and the classification of objects are not only determined by the corresponding class definition, but also by all aspects which influence the class definition after the (aspect-oriented) composition.

The equivalences between the role concept and aspect-oriented programming are obvious. Both approaches soften the strict restrictions of static typed, class-based programming languages, since the association of class, members and behavior is not completely determined at class-definition time. If such a characteristic is needed in a class-based programming language, developers have to determine which approach serves better the needs at hand and what implementation techniques are the most adequate for the given problem. Currently, there is no known combination of both approaches so they can just be used mutually exclusive. For deciding what technique to use it is necessary to analyze the intention of both approaches, their equivalences, trade-offs and their impact on the resulting code.

In this paper we discuss the similarities and differences between the role concept and aspect-oriented programming. We introduce both concepts in section 2 and 3. Afterwards we discuss both approaches with respect to their similarities, differences and potential synergies. In section 5 we propose a software framework to support the role concept. In section 6 we discuss the result of applying this framework and aspect-oriented programming simultaneously. Finally, we summarize the paper.

2 The Role Concept

Roles are temporary views on an object. A role's properties can be regarded as subjective, extrinsic properties of the object the role is assigned to. During its lifetime an object is able to adopt and abandon roles. Thus, an object's environment can access not only the object's intrinsic, but also its extrinsic properties. In [15] and [16] Kristensen formulates some characteristics of roles:

- *Identity*: An object and its actual role can be manipulated and viewed as one entity
- *Dynamicity*: Roles can be replaced during an object's lifetime
- *Dependency*: Roles only exists together with its corresponding object

- *Extension only*: A role can only add further properties to the original object, but not remove any
- *Multiplicity*: An object can have more than one instance of the same role at the same time
- *Abstractivity*: Roles are classified and organized in hierarchies
- In [7] Gottlob et al. emphasize another characteristic of roles:
- *Behavior:* A role may change an object's behavior.

The feature *abstractivity* emphasizes that roles are well-planed and organized in hierarchies similar to object-oriented hierarchies. On the other hand, this characteristic insinuates that the role concept is highly connected to class-based programming languages and hence roles are classified by classes. Nevertheless, it should be emphasized that role concepts can also be used in class-less object-oriented programming languages.

An important characteristic of roles is that roles are dynamically added to objects whereas a role itself has properties (fields and methods). Hence, the accessible properties of a single object differ from perspective to perspective and from time to time. The *root object* describes the intrinsic object, i.e. the original object without any roles. A *role object* is the instance of a role which is added to a certain root object. A *role* is a generalization of its roles similar to classes. For reason of simplification we use the term role instead of role object except in situations where it is necessary to stress the difference. A *subject* is a special perspective on a root object including (some of) its roles. A root object has several subjects whereby every subject contains a different set of included roles. The interface of a subject is an aggregate consisting of the root object's interface plus every role object's interface.

One interesting property of roles (in comparison to aspect-oriented programming) is the behavior characteristic. A role when added to an object may change the object's behavior. While [7] describes this as an intrinsic role feature, [15] and [16] regard it as a special kind of role which they call a *method role*. A method role is a role's method which is bound to an intrinsic method of the root object. It is important to emphasize for later examinations that the cardinality between intrinsic method and method role is `1:n`, i.e. every intrinsic method may have several method roles, but every method role has exactly one intrinsic method.

If and how a method role changes an object's behavior depends on what kind of method role it is. There are method roles, which alter a root object's behavior because the object's user is aware of the role, i.e. the role containing the method role is part of a subject used by the user. In that case we call the role method to be *subjective*. In the other case there are method roles which replace the root object's behavior independently of the user's perspective. Although such a behavior is not part of the root object's intrinsic behavior it is independent of a user's perspective. We call such method roles *non-subjective*.

It is obvious that there are several conflicting situations, since more then one role can be assigned to an object. Whenever an object's intrinsic methods are invoked the underlying environment has to determine if and how the corresponding roles influence the resulting behavior. The following conflict situations occur:

- *multiple subjective method roles*: there is more than one subjective method role assigned to the invoked method.
- *multiple non-subjective method roles*: there is more than one non-subjective method role assigned to the invoked method.
- *mixed method roles*: there are at least one subjective and one non-subjective method role assigned to the invoked method.

Furthermore, there is a conflict if there are at least two members from different roles with the same selector within the same subject. If an object uses such a selector to access a member it has to be determined what member to choose.

Figure 1 illustrates a person that has two jobs in parallel as a bartender. A job is a temporal role, because persons usually do not keep their job for the whole lifetime. The person has some properties like name and day of birth which are not influenced by any role. On the other hand there are the properties phone number and income. The phone number is on the one hand an intrinsic property, because it describes a person's private phone number. On the other hand it is an extrinsic property, because it describes a phone number specific to the bartender role (and contains a pub's phone number). If the phone number property is realized as a method, then the bartender's phone number methods are subjective, since if someone asks a person in private for his number he expects to get the private number, but if he asks a bartender for his number he expects to get the bar's number. On the other hand, a person's income directly depends on the income at his jobs. So the income methods of both bartender roles are non-subjective roles methods.

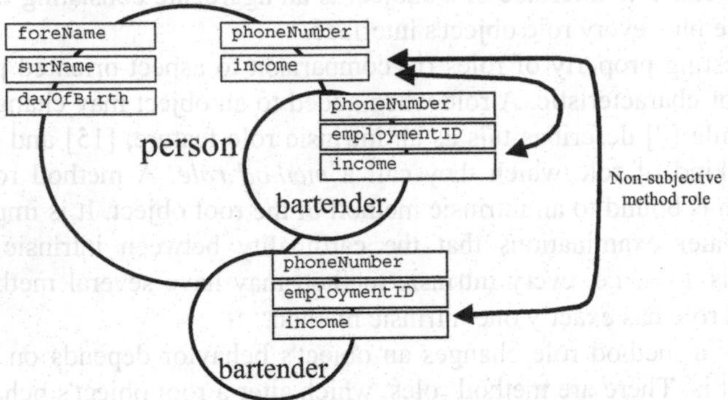

Fig. 1. Object person with two roles bartender

Although the benefit of role concepts has been accepted widely, popular object-oriented programming languages like C++ or Java do not support roles as first class entities on language level. The reason for it is quite simple: the underlying assumption for static typed, class-based programming languages is that an object's properties are entirely known at compile-time and can therefore be classified. Hence, class-based programming languages do not distinguish between intrinsic and extrinsic properties ([17] discusses this topic in detail). Therefore additional techniques are needed to support roles in class-based languages.

3 Aspect-Oriented Programming

In [3] aspect-oriented programming (AOP, [14]) is introduced as "the idea that computer systems are better programmed by specifying the various concerns (...) of a system and some description of their relationships". The underlying aspect-oriented environment is responsible for composing those concerns. The aspect-oriented term for such a composition is *weaving*. The composition consists of a transformation of all influenced building blocks at certain points specified by the developer which are called *join points*. They represent input parameters for the weaver.

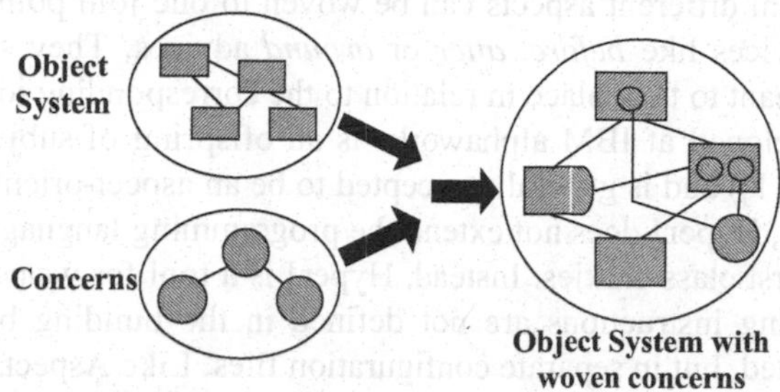

Fig. 2. Weaving Concerns into a software system

The major observation in [14] is that there are concerns which cannot be cleanly encapsulated using traditional composition techniques and therefore the resulting code is tangled with other modules. So aspect-oriented programming is about modularizing such concerns, called *aspects* which cannot be cleanly separated by traditional composition techniques. A typical example of an aspect is *synchronization* that has no satisfactory pure object-oriented solution (cf. [18]).

Figure 2 illustrates the weaving process. There are different concerns and an object system defined in separated modules. The weaver is responsible for combining those concerns with the object system. How each concern is represented in the final woven system depends on the weaver.

Although there are already numerous works on AOP, there is until now no common agreement about what the core ingredients of aspect-oriented programming are, i.e. there is no agreement on what kind of composition mechanisms are necessary for a technique to be called aspect-oriented. In [4] Filman proposes *quantification* to be a major idea of AOP and describes quantification as "the idea that one can write unitary and separate statements that have effect in many, non-local places in a programming system". However, Filman does not propose how such a characteristic impacts the underlying programming languages. So the current situation is that different aspect-oriented techniques provide different mechanisms to achieve such a quantification and/or different kinds of quantification (cf. [10]). Nevertheless, there are already different techniques available which are generally accepted to be aspect-oriented.

The most popular ones are *AspectJ* [1] and *HyperJ* [8]. In the following we briefly discuss the communalities between both to work out the core ingredients of aspect-oriented programming. Afterwards we discuss the impact of different kinds of weaving.

3.1 AspectJ and HyperJ

AspectJ [1] is currently the most popular general purpose aspect language built on top of the programming language Java and offers additional composition mechanisms to modularize cross-cutting concerns. It supports *aspects* as first class entities that permit to define cross-cutting code. Aspects contain definitions of join points which are used by the weaver to change the behavior of objects or to change class definitions. Changing the behavior of objects is achieved by a method-like language construct called *advice* which specifies the new behavior. One advice can be connected to several different join points which may be spread all over the object structure. Moreover, several advices from different aspects can be woven to one join point. There are different kinds of advices like *before*, *after* or *around* advices. They specify when the new behavior is meant to take place in relation to the corresponding join points.

HyperJ [8] developed at IBM alphaworks is an offspring of subject-oriented programming (SOP, [11]) and is generally accepted to be an aspect-oriented technique. In contrast to AspectJ, HyperJ does not extend the programming language. So aspects are not supported as first class entities. Instead, HyperJ is a tool for weaving Java classes, whereas the weaving instructions are not defined in the building blocks which are about to be combined, but in separate configuration files. Like AspectJ it is possible to add fields or methods to classes and to change the behavior of objects.

Another equivalence between HyperJ and AspectJ is that both permit to change an object's behavior depending on its context: the behavior of an object may depend on the client who sends a message to the object (AspectJ even permits to define behavior for certain control flows). Furthermore, both approaches have in common they allow to group join points based on lexical similarities. A typical example is the grouping of all method calls where the method selector begins with the tokens "`set`".

3.2 Static and Dynamic Weaving

Above we introduced weaving as a mechanism for composing separate defined concerns into a software system. The underlying system is responsible for weaving the concerns. Nevertheless, the question is when concerns are to be woven to the system. Weaving may either occur *before* or *at* runtime. The first case is usually called *static weaving*, the latter one *dynamic weaving*. The point in time when static weaving occurs may correspond to the compile time of the concerns (as implemented in AspectJ), or it is after compile time and before runtime (HyperJ). If weaving occurs during runtime, concerns can be woven and unwoven depending on the systems state. Moreover, there are *load-time approaches*, like *Binary Component Adaption* (BCA, [12]) which utilize the Java-specific class-loading for transforming the concerns to be woven and the classes they affect. Load-time approaches are a special kind of dynamic weaving since the transformations are done during runtime.

The underlying weaving mechanism has a direct impact on what kind of quantification can be supported. Static weaving permits to use all kinds of static information (type information, syntax tree, etc.), while dynamic approaches only use state information. An aspect which appears only at runtime cannot influence the whole system since parts of the system are already executed without the aspect's influence. On the other hand dynamic weaving reduces the preplanning restrictions: instead of determining already at compile time what aspects appear in the system, this can also be achieved at runtime.

3.3 Characteristics of AOP

Based upon the observations above we can extract the following characteristics of aspect-oriented programming:

- *Aspect Proclamation*: Aspects arise by declaring them, i.e. the underlying environment is responsible at weaving time for identifying the objects influenced by the aspects and generating the new woven objects.
- *Context dependence*: Aspects allow to change objects' behavior depending on a certain context. E.g. HyperJ and AspectJ permit to define an object's behavior depending on the caller.
- *Split aspects*: A single aspect may influence several objects. An aspect may touch every part of an object structure at weaving time.
- *Cardinality between method and advice*: AspectJ and HyperJ permit a cardinality of `n:m` between the original methods and the added behavior. I.e. for every method there may be several advices and every advice may be added to several methods.

It is emphasized by numerous authors that aspect-oriented programming is not just restricted to object-oriented programming, but may also be applied to other paradigms. Nevertheless, almost all known approaches are built on object-oriented languages. Assuming an underlying object-oriented language, the characteristics above show that aspect-oriented programming represents an extension to object-oriented programming. In the traditional object-oriented literature it is accepted that "an object may learn from experience. Its reaction to an operation is determined by its invocation history" [22]. In aspect-oriented programming an object's behavior is additionally determined by its invocation context and the existence of other concerns.

4 Comparing Aspects and Roles

In the previous sections we have seen that both concepts permit to adapt the behavior and structure of objects. Here, we compare both approaches based on the above mentioned characteristics.

First of all we analyze in what way aspects match the characteristics of roles.

- *Identity:* Aspects do not have to be instantiated for each object they are woven to. This is done by the underlying environment. Furthermore, a single aspect may influence numerous objects (split aspect) which means that an aspect and the objects it is woven to do not form one single entity/unit.
- *Dynamicity:* The question whether aspects can be added dynamically depends on the underlying aspect-oriented system. Dynamic weavers permit it while

static weavers do not. Therefore dynamicity is not a mandatory characteristic of aspects.

- *Dependency*: Aspects do not exist on their own. Instead they depend on the object-oriented structure they are woven to. Hence, aspects have this characteristic.
- *Extension only:* Based on the above introduction of AOP the answer needs to be: yes, like roles aspects are extension only. On the other hand, systems like AspectJ permit to declare restrictions on the object-oriented structure. It is possible to e.g. declare that "a class `A` must not have a method `B`. Otherwise class `A` will not be compiled". This means that aspects are not extension only. However, up to now there is no common agreement on whether this is an essential aspect-oriented feature or not. Hence, it cannot be finally decided whether aspects meet this characteristic.
- *Multiplicity*: From the technical point of view there is no reason why an aspect may not be applied to the same object twice. Nevertheless, the major focus of AOP is to weave different concerns at the same time into a system. Usually a single concern is not applied to an object or class for more than one time. This implies that multiplicity is not a characteristic of AOP.
- *Abstractivity*: Like roles, aspects can be organized in hierarchies. In AspectJ aspects are treated like classes. In HyperJ it is possible to define dependencies between the configuration files. So, aspects meet this characteristic.
- *Behavior*: Aspects and roles can change the behavior of the structure they are woven to. While a role may change the behavior of single objects using method roles, aspects may change the behavior of larger units (collection of objects). Usually aspects are woven to classes and not to single objects.
- On the other hand we have to check if roles share some properties of aspects:
- *Aspect Proclamation*: Roles are always assigned to objects. Therefore, aspect proclamation is not supported by roles.
- *Context dependence*: Roles do not permit to change an object's behavior depending on the context. Either a method role is added to a root object or not. E.g. a method role does not vary its behavior in dependence of the clients sending a message to the root object.
- *Cardinality between method and advice*: As already mentioned, the cardinality between method and its roles is (usually) 1:n. AspectJ and HyperJ permit a cardinality of `n:m` between the original methods and the added behavior. However, it is possible to implement the role concept in a way that is supports this `n:m` relationship.
- *Split aspect*: A role instance can only influence the behavior of the object it is assigned to. A role cannot be split so that each subpart influences a different object.

The overall conclusion is that aspects (especially based upon dynamic weaving) match almost every characteristic of roles while roles do not match the characteristics of aspects. Nevertheless, it should be emphasized that current aspect-oriented approaches (like AspectJ or HyperJ) provide only static weaving and, therefore, do not support dynamicity. But dynamicity is one of the most important characteristics of roles.

The above discussion clearly indicates that developers currently have to decide whether they need dynamicity. In case they do they cannot use current aspect-oriented techniques. If developers need to exploit context dependent object behavior they cannot use roles. Moreover, if developers want to declare concerns in their system, i.e. want to adapt numerous classes and objects without the additional effort of identifying and modifying the sources to be changed, they need the characteristic of aspect proclamation which is not supported by the role concept.

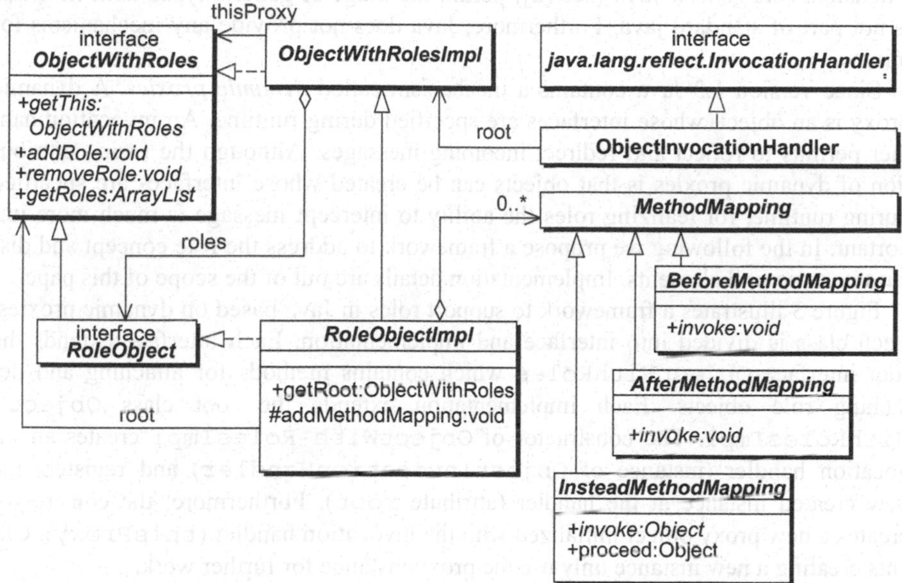

Fig. 3. Framework to Support Roles in Java

5 Implementing Roles in Java

There are mainly two different directions for realizing roles. On the one hand there are approaches on the implementation level which directly depend on language specific features. E.g. Gottlob et al propose in [7] a Smalltalk implementation, which is based on the Smalltalk specific feature of handling incoming messages on the meta level. [15] discusses implementations in BETA by extending the compiler. In [21] VanHilst and Notkin use C++ class templates to implement roles and Neumann and Zdun propose in [19] *per-object-mixins* which use message interception techniques. [13] proposes an aspect-oriented implementation of the role concept but neglects the impact of static weaving for the characteristic of dynamicity.

On the other hand, there are approaches for supporting roles at design time. E.g. Fowler discusses in [5] different ways for designing roles based on some design patterns [6]. The usual argument against the latter approach is the *preplanning problem*, i.e. "the use of the patterns for extension must be done in advance of an actual need to exploit its flexibility for a particular piece of software" [9]. For realizing roles this means that the designer has to decide what type of object may realize what kind of roles. On the other hand this is a limitation to the dynamicity characteristic, since at design time is must be determined which objects may have what roles (if any) at runtime.

The approaches above cannot be applied to Java, since Java does not provide the necessary features: It does neither permit to alter the implementation of meta classes nor to cxtend the compiler. Likewise, Java does not support class templates. Although extensions like *generic java* (see [2]) permit the usage of generic types until now this is not part of standard java. Furthermore, Java does not providc any mechanisms for mixins.

Since version 1.3 Java contains a mechanism called *dynamic proxies*. A dynamic proxy is an object, whose interfaces are specified during runtime. An invocation handler permits to reflect and redirect incoming messages. Although the main contribution of dynamic proxies is that objects can be created whose interfaces are specified during runtime, for realizing roles the ability to intercept message is much more important. In the following we propose a framework to address the role concept and discuss its structural elements. Implementation details are out of the scope of this paper.

Figure 3 illustrates a framework to support roles in Java based on dynamic proxies. Each class is divided into interface and implementation. Each interface extends the root interface `ObjectWithRoles` which contains methods for attaching and detaching role objects. Each implementation extends the root class `ObjectWithRolesImpl`. The constructor of `ObjectWith-RolesImpl` creates an invocation handler (instance of `ObjectInvocationHandler`) and registers the new created instance at the handler (attribute `root`). Furthermore, the constructor creates a new proxy object initialized with the invocation handler (`thisProxy`). Clients creating a new instance only use the proxy instance for further work.

Each class, which represents a role must also be split into interface and implementation and extends the interface `RoleObject` respectively `RoleObjectImpl`. The constructor of `RoleObjectImpl` has an `ObjectWithRoles` parameter which represents the root object. Furthermore, the framework contains *method mappings*. A method mapping is an object which determines which methods of the root object are influenced by which method roles. The framework supports three kinds of role methods: *before*, *after* and *instead* mappings. A before method mapping allows method roles to be executed before the original invocation takes place, after and instead mapping behave correspondingly. Instead method mappings differ slightly from the other ones: they have a method `proceed()` which allows the root method to be invoked.

The invocation handler receives messages sent to the root object and analyzes if there are attached roles that contain method mappings matching the called method. Afterwards the invocation handler invokes the method role with the highest priority (in our implementation the role added at last has the highest priority). Details about how the handler works are out of scope of this paper.

Figure 4 shows how an income method role of the type mentioned in section 2 is implemented: the income of a person is calculated by adding the income of all roles. The method `proceed()` returns the value of the next method role (either the next method role registered to the same method or the target method itself). The parameter `ic` contains some context information necessary for method roles. The constructor of the method mapping contains parameters to determine to what entity the method role is registered. The parameters in figure 4 determine that the method role is registered to a method `getIncome()` without any parameters.

```
public class BartenderImpl extends
        RoleObjectImpl implements Bartender {
    {
      addMethodMapping(
      new InsteadMethodMapping ("getIncome", new Class[0]) {
        public Object invoke(InvocationContext ic)
                throws Throwable {
            return getIncome()+ proceed(ic);
        }
      });
    }

    float income;
    public float getIncome() { return income; }
    ...
  }
```

Fig. 4. Implementation of an income method role

6 Collaboration with AspectJ

In the previous section we introduced a framework to support the role concept. Here we discuss how the proposed framework collaborates with aspect-oriented programming by using AspectJ[1] as the most popular general purpose aspect language. The proposed framework fulfills the characteristics of the role concept. Especially the characteristic of dynamicity which is not provided by AspectJ is supported.

Since AspectJ is an extension of Java it seems to be reasonable to use it in addition to the framework. Nevertheless, for the following reasons there are some difficulties: AspectJ uses the compilation unit's syntax trees for weaving. The framework (or more precisely: the invocation handlers) on the other hand uses reflection to redirect incoming messages which are not transformed in AspectJ. The consequences of this are not that obvious:

- *Double advice invocation*: Each context independent advice, i.e. each advice that adapts an object's behavior independently of the calling object, is invoked twice. The reason for this is that AspectJ tests the type of the target object for each redirected call in the woven code. If the class does not match the place where the advice is woven to the advice (more precisely: the advice's Java representation) is invoked directly. However, in the proposed framework the target object is always a dynamic proxy. So AspectJ invokes the advice twice.

[1] The observations in this paper are based on AspectJ, v 1.0.3

- *Inelegant weaving in method roles*: For mainly two reasons there is no elegant solution for weaving advices to method roles: in the framework the method mapping classes are abstract and it turned out to be a good idiom to use anonymous classes for registering method roles (see figure 4). Since AspectJ uses lexical similarities to identify join points, these classes can hardly be identified.
- *No context dependent behavior in method roles*: The static weaver in AspectJ cannot accomplish call dependent weavings in method roles, since the root object's invocation handler is responsible for invoking method roles and reflective calls are not transformed by the weaver.
- *Non-natural parameter passing*: parameters which arc related to the calling object or the target object are always instances of implementations. Nevertheless, the framework assumes clients to work on the proxy instances. Hence, advices always need to execute the `thisProxy` instance for each passed parameter. Therefore, parameter passing is in a way not natural.

It should be mentioned that technical solutions exist for all above mentioned problems. Nevertheless, the developer has to be aware of these problems, because they influence the usage of both, the underlying framework for roles and AspectJ.

7 Conclusion

In this paper we discussed the similarities and differences between the role concept, introduced in section 2, and aspect-oriented programming. In section 3 we elaborated some aspect-oriented characteristics based on AspectJ and HyperJ. Moreover, we discussed the impact of different weaving techniques. Afterwards we compared both approaches. In section 5 we proposed a software framework for the support of the role concept. Section 6 discussed the consequences of applying the proposed framework and AspectJ simultaneously.

The paper provides two important contributions. First, we showed that there is a difference between aspects and roles. This conclusion is quite interesting, since both approaches are about object adaptation and there are numerous identical coding examples which claim to be typical applications for only one approach (e.g. an implementation of the observer pattern). Moreover our comparison showed that there is a difference between dynamic weaving and the role concept. Second, we discussed the consequences of using roles and aspects at the same time by introducing a framework based on AspectJ that supports roles. We showed that this leads to undesired results and restricts the usage of both approaches.

Both, roles and aspects offer valuable mechanisms for adapting software systems which have some characteristics in common. Nevertheless, it has to be considered that an integration of both techniques requires more effort than a first glimpse may pretend.

References

1. AspectJ Team, The AspectJ Programming Guide, http://aspectj.org/doc/dist/progguide/
2. Gilad Bracha, Martin Odersky, David Stoutamire, and Philip Wadler, Making the future safe for the past: Adding Genericity to the Java Programming Language, OOPSLA 98, Vancouver, October 1998.
3. Tzilla Elrad, Robert E. Filman, Atef Bader, Aspect-oriented programming: Introduction, Communications of the ACM, Volume 44 , Issue 10, October 2001, pp. 29-32.
4. Robert E. Filman, What is Aspect-Oriented Programming, Revised, Workshop on Advanced Separation of Concerns, ECOOP 2001.
5. Fowler, M., Dealing with Roles, Proceedings of the 4th Annual Conference on the Pattern Languages of Programs, Monticello, Illinois, USA, September 2-5, Washington University Technical Report 97-34, 1997.
6. Erich Gamma, Richard Helm, Ralph Johnson, John Vlissides. Design Patterns: Elements of Reusable Object-Oriented Software, Addison-Wesley, 1995.
7. Georg Gottlob, Michael Schrefl, Brigitte Röck, Extending Object-Oriented Systems with Roles, ACM Transactions on Information Systems, Vol. 14, No. 3, July 1996.
8. IBM alphaworks, HyperJ Homepage, http://www.alphaworks.ibm.com/ tech/hyperj, last access: February 2001.
9. IBM Research, Subject-Oriented Programming and Design Patterns, http://www.research.ibm.com/sop/sopcpats.htm, last access: January 2001.
10. Hanenberg, S., Unland, R.: A Proposal For Classifying Tangled Code, Workshop Aspekt-Orientierung der GI-Fachgruppe 2.1.9, Bonn, February, 2002.
11. William Harrison, Harold Ossher, Subject-Oriented Programming (A Critique of Pure Objects), Andreas Paepcke (Ed.): Conference on Object-Oriented Programming Systems, Languages, and Applications (OOPSLA), SIGPLAN Notices 28(10), October 1993.
12. Keller, R., Hölzle, U., Binary Component Adaption, ECOOP 1998, LNCS, 1445, 1998, pp. 307-329.
13. Elizabeth A. Kendall, Role Model Designs and Implementations with Aspect-Oriented Programming, Proceedings of Conference on Object-Oriented Programming Systems, Languages and Applications (OOPSLA '99), SIGPLAN Notices 34 (10), 353-369.
14. Kiczales, G., Lamping, J., Mendhekar, A., Maeda, C., Lopes, C., Loingtier, J.-M., Irwing, J., Aspect-Oriented Programming. Proceedings of ECOOP '97, LNCS 1241, Springer-Verlag, pp. 220-242.
15. Bent Bruun Kristensen, Object-Oriented Modeling with Roles, Proceedings of the 2nd International Conference on Object-Oriented Information Systems (OOIS'95), Dublin, Ireland, 1995.
16. Bent Bruun Kristensen, Kasper Østerbye, Roles: Conceptual Abstraction Theory & Practical Language Issues". Theory and Practice of Object Systems, Vol. 2, No. 3, pp. 143-160, 1996.

17. Lieberman, Henry, Using Prototypical Objects to Implement Shared Behavior in Object Oriented Systems, Proceedings of OOPSLA 1986, SIGPLAN Notices 21(11) pp. 214-223.
18. Matsuoka, S., Yonezawa A., Analysis of Inheritance Anomalies In Object-Oriented Concurrent Programming Languages, In: Agha, G., Wegner, P., Yonezawa, A. (eds.), Research Directions in Concurrent Object-Oriented Programming Languages, MIT-Press, 1993, pp. 107-150
19. Gustav Neumann and Uwe Zdun. Enhancing object-based system composition through per-object mixins. In Proceedings of Asia-Pacific Software Engineering Conference (APSEC), Takamatsu, Japan, December 1999.
20. Pernici, Objects with Roles, Proceedings of OOIS, 1990
21. VanHilst, M., D. Notkin, "Using Role Components to Implement Collaboration-Based Designs," Proceedings of the Conference on Object-oriented Programming Systems, Languages, and Applications (OOPSLA'96), ACM Press, 1996, pp. 359-369.
22. Peter Wegner. The Object-Oriented Classification Paradigm. In: Bruce Shriver and Peter Wegner (eds.), Research Directions in Object-Oriented Programming, MIT Press, 1987, pp 479-560.

Flexible Object-Oriented Views Using Method Propagation

Daniel Pfeifer

Institute for Program Structures and Data Organisation (IPD)
Universität Karlsruhe, Germany
{pfeifer}@ira.uka.de

Abstract. Object-oriented views play a key role when giving accessing applications a new or restricted perspective on persistent object-oriented data. However, traditional object-oriented view systems only allow for limited changes when it comes to restructuring a database schema and the related persistent objects in a view. We present a new approach for defining object-oriented views that enables view schemas and view objects whose structure is highly flexible with respect to the underlying database structure. Nevertheless we can guarantee complete type-safety of view schemas and a well-defined and consistent behavior when running updates on view objects as well as on underlying database objects.
We reach this goal through the concept of method propagation: given that a method of a persistent base class fulfills certain conditions, it can be attached to view classes after its signature is appropriately adjusted. At runtime a method call on a view object is delegated to a corresponding base object and executed there.
In the course of this paper we introduce a formal model for object-oriented databases which serves as a basis for defining method propagation conditions. We then present a view language that is derived from our formal approach and highlight the architecture of a prototypical view system.

1 Introduction

In the 1980s and 1990s, research as well as business discovered object-oriented databases as a means of extending the metaphor of object-oriented programming to the world of databases. Nowadays, they gather new momentum in the context of object relational mappings for application server architectures such as EJB (Enterprise Java Beans). As a result, the ability to conveniently adapt and to version object-oriented schemas in real-life programming environments gains new importance.

In this paper, we solve a part of this problem by applying the concept of method propagation for creating flexible object-oriented views: given that a method of a persistent base class fulfills certain conditions, it can be attached to view classes after its signature is appropriately adjusted. At runtime a method call on a view object is delegated to a corresponding base object and executed there.

Z. Bellahsène, D. Patel, and C. Rolland (Eds.): OOIS 2002, LNCS 2425, pp. 521–535, 2002.

The remainder of this paper is structured as follows: the next section outlines our research contributions and compares them to related work. Section 3 gives a brief formal introduction of a simple object-oriented data model, which serves as a basis for the following sections. In Section 4, we introduce a generic but simple formalism for defining views, concluding with an initial characterization of resulting view schemas. Then follows a formal introduction of the concept of method propagation and a discussion of its conditions in Section 5.1. The initial view schemas from Section 4 are enriched by propagated methods and inheritance relationships (Section 5.2). Furthermore, Section 5.3 states how propagated methods can be executed at runtime.

In order to realize our theoretical considerations, we discuss various aspects of REPLOP, a declarative view definition language (Section 6), and give an example of its application in Section 7. Section 8 presents a prototypical implementation of a view system for REPLOP. The paper closes with a conclusion (Section 9) and comments on future work.

2 Our Contribution in Respect to Related Work

Since its first discussion in [2], there have been various publications in the field of object-oriented views. It is beyond the scope of this paper to summarize all the proposed directions—we refer to [10] and [16] for this purpose. However, the following paragraphs give an impression of how our contribution can be positioned in respect to competing research.

Object-oriented views can be split in two important categories: object generating and object preserving. While object preserving approaches exclusively reuse base object identifiers for defining view objects ([2, 7], [14]), object generating views apply special functions for creating view object identifiers. As [13, 10] and [11], our work follows the latter, more powerful concept, which allows for splitting and merging objects in a view.

It has been argued that object generating approaches hinder clean view update strategies [19]. Our paper will demonstrate that this is not the case: we support view updates by propagating set-methods and any other kinds of state changing methods from base objects to view objects. So far, updates for object generating views have only been briefly considered in [10], whereas we present a corresponding view update strategy that covers formal as well as implementation aspects.

In [11], Heiler and Zdonik introduce the term of equivalence preservation, which postulates that changes on a base object o are immediately reflected by all view objects to which o is mapped. We regard this as an essential part of view consistency, hence it is fully supported by our approach.

Also, we enable more or less arbitrary reorganizations of a view's class graph in respect to its underlying base schema as long as view schema consistency and static type-safety of view methods can be asserted. Most other publications impose restrictions on the placement of view classes in the class graph ([7, 19]) or favor a completely automated placement by the view system ([14]). Unfortunately this reduces the control of a view designer and obstructs him from creating an accurate object-oriented design for a related view.

Despite the amount of research that has been spent on object-oriented views, we could not find many contributions that address the problem of mapping relationships and typed references from base objects to view objects and vice versa. [4, 10, 8] treat this problem for situations of one-to-one mappings between base and view objects. In contrast, we can also deal with n-to-m mappings by resolving reference arguments and results of propagated methods at runtime. At view generation time, a view's schema is automatically completed by additional types so that type safe view method signatures are guaranteed.

Our approach is based on the work of [15, 17] and [20]. Although the goal of these publications was the design of an objectbase evolution system, some of the suggested concepts could be reused for the design of our sample view definition language.

The idea of using base methods for the definition of view methods has been first treated in [11]. In their solution the authors suggest to refer to base methods and base object attributes when implementing view method bodies. Our paper fosters an automatic generation of view methods through method propagation, which frees a view designer from manually reimplementing view methods. Still, customized view method implementations can also be easily supported by our approach. The authors of [18] and [4] consider method propagations, but only for the case of 1-to-1 mappings between base and view objects and special 1-to-n mappings respectively. Also, they do not address a necessary adjustment of method signatures on the view level.

3 A Data Model for OODBs

In this section we give a brief formal definition of a data model for creating object-oriented schemas as well as related databases. The included concepts—namely class types, multiple inheritance, method signatures and objects—are standard to most object-oriented systems. They form the basis for a formal approach to our view system as presented in the following sections.

For simplicity, class attributes as well as primitive types are omitted as they are not required for our considerations. Besides, the former concept can be captured through get/set-methods, while primitive types can be represented by equivalent classes with suitable methods.

An OODB schema S is a tuple $(T, \prec)$ of a class type set $T = \{t_1, \ldots, t_n\}$ and an inheritance relation $\prec$. Every class type $t \in T$ consists of a unique name and a set of methods whose names are unique within t. So every t a is tuple of the form $(tname,\ F)$ with $F = \{f_1, \ldots, f_m\}$. Uniqueness of class type names can be expressed as $\forall t_a, t_b \in T : t_a \neq t_b \Rightarrow t_a.tname \neq t_b.tname$.[1] It allows for the mapping of a class type name to its class type $t \in T$ by a function *type* with $type(t.tname) = t$.

[1] We use the dot notation to refer to tuple elements.

The inheritance relation $\prec \subseteq T \times T$ is a transitive and acyclic relation. We say that $t_a \in T$ is supertype of $t_b \in T$, if $t_a \prec t_b$ holds and write $t_a \preceq t_b$, if $t_a \prec t_b \vee t_a = t_b$.

Every method $f \in t.F$ is a triple $(fname, rtname, (ptname_1, \ldots, ptname_p))$, where $fname$ represents the method's name, $rtname$ its result type and $ptname_i$ its i-th parameter type.[2] Note that the number of parameters p depends on the method f. In order to refer to a method's number of parameters, we write $p(f)$. The result type and the parameter types are name references of types in T, more formally: $rtname$, $ptname_i \in \{t.tname \mid t \in T\}$. Uniqueness of method names per class can now be expressed as follows: $\forall t \in T : \forall f, g \in t.F : f \neq g \Rightarrow f.fname \neq g.fname$.[3]

For the final part of our definition we introduce the concept of contravariance for methods. Let t_a, t_b be two class types in T. A method $f \in t_a.F$ is said to be contravariant to a method $g \in t_b.F$, if and only if $g.fname = f.fname \wedge type(g.rtname) \preceq type(f.rtname) \wedge p(f) = p(g) \wedge \forall\, k = 1 \ldots p(f) : type(f.ptname_k) \preceq type(g.ptname_k)$. We express this formally by writing $g \trianglelefteq f$.[4]

Using the contravariance relationship we claim that the inheritance relation $\prec$ constrains the methods of every class type $t_b \in T$ in the following way: if a method g is contained in a supertype of t_b, then a method f which is contravariant to g must be contained in t_b, thus: $\forall t_a, t_b \in T : g \in t_a.F \wedge t_a \prec t_b \Rightarrow \exists f \in t_b.F : g \trianglelefteq f$.

Based on the definition of schemas, the formal structure of OODBs becomes very simple, because of a lack of attribute values in objects: an OODB $B(S)$ for a schema S is a set of objects $\{o_1, \ldots, o_m\}$. Every o_i is a tuple $(oid, tname)$ where oid is the object's unique identifier and $tname$ is a name reference to a class type $t \in S.T$.

In order to obtain all objects of a class type and its subtypes, we define a function obj on the set of types $S.T$:

$$obj : S.T \rightarrow \wp(B(S)),\ t \mapsto \{\, o \in B(S) \mid t \preceq type(o.tname) \,\}$$

Here, $\wp(s)$ specifies the powerset of a set s.

For further considerations we define $\mathcal{B}(S)$ as the set of all valid databases B that can be created for a schema S.

4 A Generic Formalism for View Definitions

This section introduces a simple and generic formalism for specifying views, which is based on the data model from above. Two functions, the identity function and the type assignment function, form the heart of the view formalism.

[2] We do not discuss method implementations in this context but only their declarations.

[3] Unique method names are here enforced for simplifying other definitions below. They are not crucial to the presented concepts.

[4] In general, contravariance is important to guarantee statically type safe method overriding in object-oriented programming. For a more thorough discussion on this topic, refer to [6].

The former function maps base objects to view objects, while the latter one assigns a type to each view object.

The identity function ϕ associates base objects with names that eventually represent object identifiers of view objects for every database of a $B \in \mathcal{B}(S)$. Assuming that these names are taken from a set $VOids$, we obtain:

$$\phi_B \subseteq B \times VOids,\ \phi : \mathcal{B}(S) \to \bigcup_{B \in \mathcal{B}(S)} \{\phi_B\},\ B \mapsto \phi_B$$

Given a database $B \in \mathcal{B}(S)$, tuples $(o, oid_v) \in \phi_B$ indicate that an object $o \in B$ is mapped to a view object, whose object identifier will be oid_v. As ϕ_B is a relation, we support n-to-m mappings between base objects and view objects, and if an object o is in no tuple of ϕ_B, o will not be represented by any objects in a corresponding view database. The resulting function ϕ associates a relation ϕ_B with its database $B \in \mathcal{B}(S)$.

The type assignment τ is a function that maps identifiers of view objects to identifiers of a set $TNames$ for every database $B \in \mathcal{B}(S)$. We obtain it from a set of functions τ_B in a similar fashion as ϕ:

$$\tau_B : \phi_B(B) \to TNames,\ oid_v \mapsto tname, \tau : \mathcal{B}(S) \to \bigcup_{B \in \mathcal{B}(S)} \tau_B,\ B \mapsto \tau_B{}^5$$

Later, the identifiers $tname \in TNames$ will become type names of class types in a resulting view schema S'.

We are now able to define a view $V(S)$ for a schema as a pair (ϕ, τ) with ϕ and τ as above. Note that our definition of a view depends on S but not on a particular database $B(S)$ since ϕ and τ are defined for all databases that can be created for S.

Based on $V(S)$, we can already derive a simple view schema $S' = (T', \prec')$ and a corresponding set of view databases that form a subset of $\mathcal{B}(S')$:

1. We set $\prec' = \{\}$, so there are no inheritance relationships yet.
2. $T' = \{(tname, \{\}) \mid \exists \tau_B \in \tau(\mathcal{B}(S)) :\ tname \in \tau_B(B)\}$, so we create types for just those type names that are referenced in τ. Methods are not yet included.
3. Given a database $B \in \mathcal{B}(S)$ we construct a corresponding view database $B' = \{(oid_v, \tau_B(oid_v)) \mid oid_v \in \phi_B(B)\}$.

Depending on $V(S)$, the view databases B' that are constructed this way can form a real subset of $\mathcal{B}(S')$ that we declare as $\mathcal{VB}(S')$.

[5] Through the course of this paper, we denote the image of a function $f : A \to B$ as $f(A)$. The inverse of f is denoted by f^{-1}. f^{-1} turns out to be a relation, if f is not injective.

5 Method Propagation

We now discuss how a view schema S', as created in the previous section, can be enriched by method declarations and inheritance relationships. We introduce the concept of method propagation as a means to redeclare methods from base classes in view classes.

As the type structure in a view schema might be entirely different from the corresponding base schema, the signatures of propagated methods must be adjusted accordingly. A set of conditions, which go with a method propagation, ensure that view method invocations can be resolved at runtime and can be delegated to method calls on base objects.

Before we can specify propagation conditions, we need to introduce type relations: depending on a base schema $S = (T, \prec)$, a view $V(S) = (\phi, \tau)$ and a resulting view schema S', a type relation $TRel$ states what base types are mapped to what view types by examining the corresponding objects in databases over S. A type relation can be formally specified as follows:

$$TRel \subseteq S.T \times S'.T, TRel = \{(t, t') \mid \exists B \in \mathcal{B}(S) : t'.tname \in \tau_B(\phi_B(obj(t)))\}$$

5.1 Conditions for Method Propagations

Let $S = (T, \prec)$ be a an OODB schema as defined in Section 3 and $f \in t.F$ be a method of a type $t \in T$. Further, let $V(S) = (\phi, \tau)$ be a view on S, S' the schema derived from $V(S)$ according to Section 4 and $\mathcal{VB}(S')$ be the corresponding view databases.

Then f can be *propagated* to type $t' \in TRel(t)$, if the following conditions hold for every database $B \in \mathcal{B}(S)$:

1. Every view object, which might occur as the i-th method argument, can be uniquely related to a base object, which holds the type or subtype of the i-th base method parameter:
$$\forall i = 1 \dots p(f) : \forall oid_v \in \phi_B(B) : type(\tau_B(oid_v)) \in TRel(type(f.ptname_i)) \Rightarrow$$
$$\exists_1 o \in \phi_B^{-1}(oid_v) : type(f.ptname_i) \preceq type(o.tname)$$
2. For every view object of type t', there exists only one related base object that contains a base method g being contravariant to f:
$$\forall oid_v \in \tau_B^{-1}(t'.tname) : \exists_1 o : \phi_B^{-1}(oid_v) : \exists g \in type(o).F : f \trianglelefteq g$$ [6]
3. The mapping of base objects to a method's result type is unique or not existing:
$$\forall o \in obj(type(f.rtname)) : |\phi_B(o)| \leq 1$$ [7]

[6] The $\exists_1$-quantifier may be replaced by $\exists$ if there is a selection function that determines which contravariant method to choose if o and thus g is not unique. This idea is applied for the implementation in Section 6.

[7] This condition was added for the sake of a more convenient presentation. Its omission leads to set valued return types of view methods, which is taken into account in our prototypical implementation.

Method propagations offer a way of binding methods of base types to view types. Applying the propagation, those methods may be called on view objects much in the same way as on underlying base objects. Essentially, the definition ensures that for a view method invocation, all related view objects can be uniquely resolved and mapped to base objects through the identity function ϕ. Eventually a method call is delegated to and performed on the corresponding base objects. Its result is then propagated to the view level by mapping the resulting base object to its view object as defined by ϕ as well. Section 5.3 describes this mechanism in more detail.

5.2 Deriving Methods and Inheritance Relationships for Views

The conditions for method propagations ensure that methods calls, which should be performed on view objects, can be delegated to method calls on base objects. What is still missing are signatures for propagated methods in a view schema. We now describe how to derive those signatures and related inheritance relationships.

Let $f \in t.F$ be a method of a type $t \in S.T$ as defined in Section 3. f shall fulfill the propagation conditions of Section 5.1 and shall be propagated to a view type $t' \in S'.T$. Then $f' = (f.fname,\ rtname', (ptname'_1,\ \ldots,\ ptname'_{p(f)}))$ will be the signature of the corresponding propagated method f' that is to be added to $t'.F$.

As a requirement for statically type-safe method invocations, the result type of $rtname'$ and the parameter types of $ptname'_i$ ought to have the following qualities:

1. The view result type should be of the same type or a supertype of all the view types to which the base result type and its subtypes are mapped:

$$\forall t \in T : type(f.rtname) \preceq t \Rightarrow \forall t' \in TRel(t) : type(f'.rtname') \preceq' t'$$

2. A view parameter type should be of the same type or a supertype of all the view types to which the corresponding base parameter type is mapped and the view parameter type should have no further subtypes.

$$\forall i = 1 \ldots p(f) : \forall t' \in T' : type(f'.ptname'_i) \preceq' t' \Leftrightarrow$$

$$\exists t \in T : type(f.ptname_i) \preceq t \ \wedge t' \in TRel(t)$$

One can prove that, together with the method propagation conditions from Section 5.1, these two qualities guarantee type-safe method invocations when delegating method calls from base to view objects.

By applying them to all propagated base methods, a new schema S'' can be computed. It is derived from S' by adding propagated methods to view types $t' \in S'.T$ and inheritance relationships to $\preceq'$ such as claimed above. In order to satisfy the two qualities, S'' might also contain additional types which represent some view method's return type or some parameter type.

In this paper, we assume that a corresponding view management system automatically adds view return types, view parameter types and related inheritance relationships, if necessary. Additional inheritance relationships must be explicitly declared by the view designer. Their consistency is checked by the view management system and in case of an inconsistency the related view definition will be rejected.[8]

It is noteworthy that according to Section 3, the way of adding methods to a type t' causes conflicts, if propagated methods with equal names were to be added to t'. In this case we assume that exactly one of those methods will be added. Thus, we can conclude that for every t', there is a functional mapping from a propagated method f' to its corresponding base method, which shall be expressed by $BaseF(t', f') = f$.

5.3 Resolving View Method Calls at Runtime

Let $o'.f'(a'_1, \ldots, a'_{p(f)})$ be the corresponding method call on a view method $f' \in t'.F$. Based on Section 5.1, we now describe in detail, how to resolve and execute this call on the view object o' at runtime:

1. $BaseF(type(o'.tname), f') = f$ returns the base method from which f' was derived.
2. Condition 2 in Section 5.1 guarantees that there is exactly one $o \in B$ so that o's type $type(o)$ contains a method that is contravariant to f.
3. Condition 1 in definition 5.1 ensures that for every argument a'_i, we obtain exactly one base object a_i which holds $type(f.ptname_i)$ or a corresponding subtype as its type.
4. Hence, the method call $r = o.f(a_1, \ldots, a_{p(f)})$ can be executed on the underlying database B.
5. Condition 3 in 5.1 provides a unique mapping of the result object r to view object r'. So r' will be returned as a value on the view level.

6 REPLOP - A Language for Defining Flexible Views

In order to realize our formal approach in practice, we developed a view definition language called REPLOP, which stands for *repl*ace *op*erator. Originally REPLOP stems from an objectbase evolution language that was first introduced in [15, 20] and [17]. For our purposes, we modified the language in order to facilitate the expression of method propagations.

6.1 Structure of REPLOP Statements

A REPLOP program consists of a set of statements that describe how to map base objects to view objects. A statement is preceded by a query that selects base

[8] For a lack of space, we do not present the formal conditions for manually added inheritance relationships.

objects, which should be affected by the statement's mapping. The structure of queries is similar to those of SQL or OQL and so we only present them as part of an example in Section 7.

The basic form of a REPLOP statement s (without a corresponding query) is as follows:

var_1 , ... , var_n -> $idExpr_1$, ..., $idExpr_q$ AS $statementName_s$ $classTypeName$
[var_{i_1}.$methodName_1$->$viewMethodName_1$,...,
  var_{i_k}.$methodName_s$->$viewMethodName_k$]

The variables $var_1, \ldots, var_n$ are typed and bound to base objects through the query that precedes a statement. They refer to base objects that are mapped to view objects by the statement.

Next, there follows a sequence of identity expressions that, when evaluated, form the identifier of a new view object. In this context the use of expressions allows for very general mappings of base object to view objects, since it depends on the equality of the expressions whether base objects from different query result tuples are mapped to the same view object or a different one. E.g. the case $q = 1$ and $idExpr_1 = 0$ states that all queried view objects that are bound to $var_1, \ldots, var_n$ in s will be mapped to exactly one view object (being identified by 0).

At evaluation time, base objects bound to $var_1, \ldots, var_n$ are then mapped to the new view object. This way, every statement forms a partial definition of the function ϕ from Section 4. Note that a view object identifier also depends on the statement by which it was created. So, even if two different statements created the same value tuple for identifying view objects, the view objects would obtain different identities (and thus would differ).

classTypeName identifies the name of the view class which will become the type of a generated view object. Hence, it serves for implementing function τ from Section 4.

The optional statement name $statementName_s$ is a unique name for the program statement s. It aids in refering to view objects generated by s in other program statements. In Section 7, we demonstrate its use for defining get-methods in views.

The last section of a statement defines which base methods should be propagated to what view methods. By separating base method names from view method names, we enable method renaming for a propagation. Also, not all possible method propagations are automatically applied, but only those that are explicitly declared by the arrow notation (->). Obviously, view method signatures do not need to be specified, since they can be automatically derived according to Section 5.2. However their uniqueness must be explicitly checked by a corresponding view system.

6.2 Verifying Method Propagation Conditions for Statements

The structure of statements raises the question of how to verify the method propagation conditions from Section 5.1 for a declarative view definition language

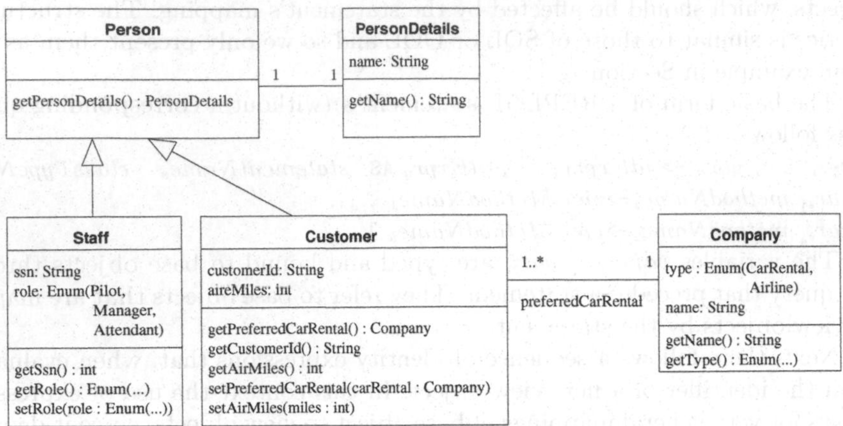

Fig. 1. Base schema for a simple person database

such as REPLOP. Below, we give a criterion that shows how Condition 1 of Section 5.1 can be verified for a method that is to be propagated.[9]

An important means for verifying Condition 1 is the analysis of functional variable dependencies in REPLOP statements and their preceding queries. We assume that the concept of functional dependencies is known and refer to [3] for a related introduction. $var_j \rightarrow var_i$ states that a variable var_i of a REPLOP statement is functionally dependent on another variable var_j. A brief example shall illustrate how functional dependencies can be inferred from REPLOP expressions: if the select condition of a query is `a == b.x` for two variables `a` and `b`, the dependency `b` $\rightarrow$ `a` follows.

Lemma. Let S be our base schema, $t \in S.T$. The function $f \in t.F$ should be propagated in a REPLOP program prg, $f = (fname,\ rtname,\ (ptname_1,\ \ldots,\ ptname_p))$. The function $idExprs(s)$ is to provide a tuple of the identification expressions $idExpr_1, \ldots, idExpr_q$ of s.

Then, the following criterion implies Condition 1 from Section 5.1:

$$\forall i = 1 \ldots p : \forall s \in Stats(prg) : \exists v \in Vars(s) : type(v) \preceq type(ptname_i) \Rightarrow$$
$$(\exists_1 v \in Vars(s) : type(v) \preceq type(ptname_i) \wedge idExpr(s) \rightarrow v)$$

7 A Sample View

In this section we give an example how to use REPLOP for defining a view. The sample view is based on a very simple person database whose schema is presented in Figure 1, using UML notation ([5]).

[9] For a lack of space we do not present the related proof and the corresponding criteria for Conditions 2 and 3.

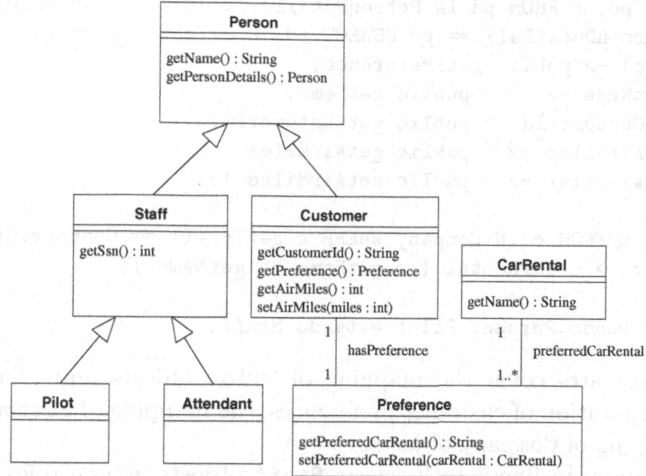

Fig. 2. Resulting view schema

The schema models an airline's staff and customer information. `Person` is the super class of `Staff` and `Customer`. Information about person details is represented by a separate class `PersonDetails`. For simplicity it only holds a person's name. The `Staff` class keeps the social security number and an employee's role. The roles are represented by an enumeration type. For customers we added a car rental preference which references a car rental company, a customer's ID and his or her air miles.

In order to point out the effects of method propagations, we have also added the get/set-methods for every class.

Figure 2 presents the targeted view schema, which implies drastic changes. The methods `getPreferredCarRental()` and `setPreferredCarRental()` from class `Customer` highlight the view definition's impact on method signatures. Because of a mapping of `Company` to `CarRental`, the view methods' signatures have been adjusted to `getPreferredCarRental() : CarRental` and `setPreferredCarRental(CarRental)`, respectively.

In the following we give an extract of a REPLOP program that defines a corresponding view:

```
REPLACE pd, s FROM pd IN PersonDetails, s IN Staff WHERE
s.getPersonDetails() == pd && s.getRole() == Staff.PILOT
OBJECT pd, s -> s Pilot [
  pd.getName -> public getName,
  s.getSsn -> public getSsn ];

REPLACE c FROM c IN Customer OBJECT c -> c AS pref Preference [
  c.getPreferredCarRental -> public getPreferredCarRental,
  c.setPreferredCarRental -> public setPreferredCarRental ];

```

```
11  REPLACE pd, c FROM pd IN PersonDetails, c IN Customer WHERE
12  c.getPersonDetails() == pd OBJECT pd, c -> c Customer [
13    pref(c) -> public getPreference,
14    pd.getName ->       public getName,
15    c.getCustomerId -> public getCustomerId,
16    c.getAirMiles ->    public getAirMiles,
17    c.setAirMiles ->    public setAirMiles ];
18
19  REPLACE c FROM c IN Company WHERE c.getType() == Company.CARRENTAL
20  OBJECT c -> c CarRental [ c.getName -> getName ];
21
22  Staff extends Person; Pilot extends Staff;
```

The first four parts cover the mapping of `Pilot` objects and related person details, the separation of customer preferences, the mapping of `customer` objects and the mapping of `Company` objects.

E.g. the query in line 1 to 2 selects `Staff` objects, whose roles are `PILOT`, and person details that are related to each pilot. Line 3 maps the selected `Staff` objects and related `PersonDetails` objects to view objects with the view type `Pilot`. The `-> s` part denotes that variable `s` is used as an identity expression. Thus, the object identifier of a `Staff` object will be used to identify `Pilot` view objects, which are generated by this statement.

Line 4 shows of how the method `getName()` is propagated for every object bound to `pd`. The propagated method carries the same name, and the visibility modifier `public` is associated with it.

Most other parts of the program extract can be interpreted in similar ways. An exception is line 13, where the view identity function `pref` is used for declaring the view method `getPreference()`. As mentioned in Section 6.1, `getPreference()` will return a `Preference` view object at runtime, whose identifier is equal to `c`, the argument of `pref()`. Line 22 specifies some inheritance relationships that should hold for the view schema.

8 Implementation

In order to study the feasibility and usefulness of our ideas, we developed a prototypical view system in Java, which is presented next. Our implementation is based on a simple but easy to use OODBMS called db4o ([1]).

Concerning the system's architecture, we distinguish two phases: view generation time and runtime. At view generation time, the system reads and analyzes a REPLOP program, and depending on the program's statements, view classes are generated. At runtime, the corresponding view class binaries are used to establish a view and to access data from an underlying object-oriented database.

The dataflow of the system's view generation part is as follows: first a REPLOP program that defines a view is read, parsed and semantically analyzed. This process involves loading base schema classes for resolving references to base types. After that the system discovers functional dependencies between variables of the REPLOP program's abstract syntax tree (AST). Based on this information, all method propagations of the program can be verified. If the check happens to be successful, in memory representations of the view classes including view method signatures are generated. Finally source code for all view classes is generated, written to the file system, and compiled.

Figure 3 mainly presents dependencies of the system's runtime components (as indicated by dashed arrows). At the top of the picture, an accessing application invokes methods on view objects. However, for initialization purposes and for accessing a view's root objects, the application first consults a view manager. The latter establishes a connection to the database and creates a view mapping component. Apart from initializing the view through the view manager, it remains transparent to the application that it navigates on view objects instead of real database objects.

The view mapping component serves as a bridge when accessing base objects through view method calls. In order to support the mapping between view and base objects, it obtains an AST of the same REPLOP program that was processed at view generation time.

When looking up the base objects of a view object, the view mapping component performs an interpretation on the AST, which results in a query for the base objects at the database manager. In turn, the database manager instantiates the base objects or just returns them if they are already loaded. This process takes place for every view method call and for all view objects being involved in a call.

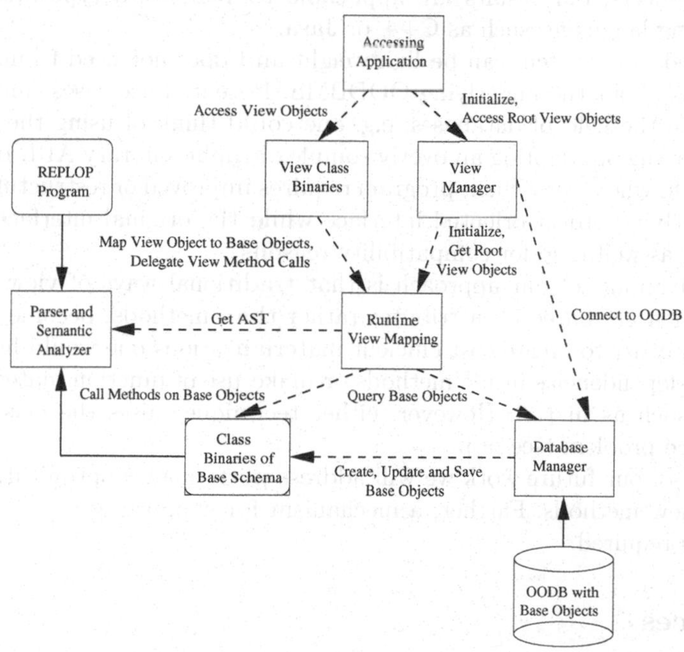

Fig. 3. Component and data dependencies at runtime

Eventually a method's result is mapped to a view object. If the resulting view object has never been accessed before, the view mapping performs a second interpretation on the AST to evaluate the REPLOP statement which is in charge of generating the view object. As an effect, the view object is instantiated but holds a reference to the view mapping component as its only internal state. The view mapping component itself keeps a backpointer to the view object and maintains the values that represent the view object's identifier such as described in Section 6. As a consequence, view object implementations are very lightweight, while the view mapping component keeps track of the mapping information.

Note that the system never runs into view update problems since the view objects only act as proxies and always represent the current state of the underlying database. Therefore, state changing operations can easily be handled on both ends, the view and the database itself. If a view method call cannot be passed on, because some of the related base objects have been deleted, the system throws a "view object deleted" exception which must be caught by the accessing application.

9 Conclusion

This paper has been discussing the formal basis as well as practical aspects of method propagation in the context of object oriented views. A sample declarative view definition and a prototypical view system demonstrated that the approach can be utilized in practice. Although we support n-to-m mappings between base and view objects, our results are applicable to real world type systems and programming languages such as C++ or Java.

A related view system can be lightweight and does not need to make many assumptions about the underlying OODBMS. Potential use cases can be found even outside the field of databases; e.g. one could think of using the approach when versioning or adapting an overly complex graphics library API. In general, it can pay off, whenever a client program requires improved or restructured access to an underlying object oriented interface while the original interface must be maintained as well (e.g. for compatibility reasons).

A disadvantage of our approach is that traditional ways of view materialization, which are based on attributes rather than methods, become harder to support. In order to create cost efficient materializations one would have to analyze data dependencies inside methods or make use of function materialization strategies such as in [12]. However, either technique raises the classical view maintenance problem (see [9]).

As part of our future work we will address performance optimizations when invoking view methods. Further, a mechanism for supporting view object constructors is required.

References

[1] http://www.db4o.com. WWW reference only. 532

[2] Serge Abiteboul and Anthony J. Bonner. Objects and views. In *Proc. of the ACM SIGMOD '91*, pages 238–247. ACM Press, 1991. 522

[3] W. W. Armstrong. Dependency structure of database relations. *Information Processing*, pages 580–583, 1974. 530

[4] Elisa Bertino. A view mechanism for object-oriented databases. In Alain Pirotte, Claude Delobel, and Georg Gottlob, editors, *Advances in Database Technology (EDBT '92)*, volume 580 of *LNCS*, pages 136–151. Springer, 1992. 523

[5] Grady Booch, James Rumbaugh, and Ivar Jacobson. *The Unified Modeling Language User Guide.* Addison-Wesley, 1999. 530

[6] Giuseppe Castagna. Covariance and contravariance: Conflict without a cause. *ACM Transactions on Programming Languages and Systems*, 17(3):431–447, 1995. 524

[7] M. Dobrovnik and J. Eder. Adding view support to ODMG-93. In *Proc. of the Intl. Workshop on Advances in Databases and Information Systems (ADBIS '94)*, pages 62–73, 1994. 522

[8] Michael Dobrovnik and Johann Eder. Logical data independence and modularity through views in oodbms. In *Proc. of ESDA '96*, pages 13–20, 1996. 523

[9] D. Gluche, T. Grust, C. Mainberger, and M. H. Scholl. Incremental updates for materialized OQL views. *LNCS*, 1341:52–69, 1997. 534

[10] Giovanna Guerrini, Elisa Bertino, Barbara Catania, and Jesus Garcia-Molina. A formal model of views for object-oriented database systems. *Theory and Practice of Object Systems (TAPOS '97)*, 3(3):157–183, 1997. 522, 523

[11] Sandra Heiler and Stanley B. Zdonik. Object views: Extending the vision. In *Proc. of the Sixth International Conference on Data Engineering*, pages 86–93. IEEE Computer Science Press, 1990. 522, 523

[12] Alfons Kemper, Christoph Kilger, and Guido Moerkotte. Function materialization in object bases. In James Clifford and Roger King, editors, *Proc. of the ACM SIGMOD '91*, pages 258–267. ACM Press, 1991. 534

[13] Michael Kifer, Won Kim, and Yehoshua Sagiv. Querying object-oriented databases. In Michael Stonebraker, editor, *Proc. of the ACM SIGMOD '92*, pages 393–402. ACM Press, 1992. 522

[14] Harumi A. Kuno and Elke A. Rundensteiner. The multiview oodb view system: Design and implementation. *Journal of Theory and Practice of Object Systems (TAPOS '96), Special Issue on Subjectivity in Object-Oriented Systems*, 2(3):202–225, 1996. 522

[15] Guido Moerkotte and Andreas Zachmann. Towards More Flexible Schema Management in Object Bases. In *Proc. of the Intl. Conf. on Data Engineering*, pages 174–181. IEEE, 1993. 523, 528

[16] Renate Motschnig-Pitrik. Requirements and comparison of view mechanisms for object-oriented databases. *Information Systems*, 21(3):229–252, 1996. 522

[17] D. Pfeifer. *Ein System zur typsicheren Objektbankevolution.* Master's thesis, Universität Karlsruhe, IPD, Germany, 1999. Only available in German. 523, 528

[18] B. Schiefer. *Eine Umgebung zur Unterstützung von Schemaänderungen und Sichten in objektorientierten Datenbanksystemen.* PhD thesis, Universität Karlsruhe, FZI, Germany, 1993. Only available in German. 523

[19] Marc H. Scholl, Christian Laasch, and Markus Tresch. Updatable views in object-oriented databases. In *Proceedings of 2nd International Conference on Deductive and Object-Oriented Databases*, LNCS, pages 189–207. Springer, 1991. 522

[20] A. Zachmann. *Typsichere Objektmigration.* PhD thesis, Universität Karlsruhe, IPD, Germany, 1997. Only available in German. 523, 528

Towards an Assisted Reorganization of Is_A Hierarchies

Samira Si-Said Cherfi and Nadira Lammari

Laboratoire CEDRIC, Conservatoire National des Arts et Métiers
292, Rue Saint Martin, 75141, Paris cedex 03, France
{sisaid,lammari}@cnam.fr

Abstract. This paper presents the specification of an Is_A hierarchies reorganization method, called REORG, with a process modeling language called MAP. REORG proposes two complementary mechanisms: the splitting and the restructuring mechanisms. The first one derives Is_A hierarchies concealed in existing entities. The second one performs grouping of existing entities without losing the inheritance semantics by introducing several types of constraints. MAP is a process modeling language that provides a formalism combining visual facilities and formal descriptions of information systems processes. The specification of REORG with MAP supplies a process model, which makes explicit modeling practices and then allows the integration of these practices into any CASE tool.

1 Introduction

According to [1] a software development environment in general and a CASE tool in particular consists of three components namely, structure, mechanisms and policies. Structures refer to objects manipulated by the mechanisms. The latter are the visible and underlying tools. Policies are rules and guidelines imposed by the tools. The existing CASE tools assist developers essentially through their structure component by providing editors and browsers allowing artifacts production and manipulation. They however lack mechanisms and policies implementing methods rules and guidelines destined to support difficult and tedious tasks. Our contribution is twofold. First we propose a method for inheritance hierarchies reorganization named REORG. Second we provide a specification of REORG as a detailed and formalized process model using MAP process language.

REORG is a method supporting Is_A inheritance hierarchies reorganization for both EER and object-oriented schemas. It proposes two complementary mechanisms: the splitting and the restructuring mechanisms. The first one derives Is_A hierarchies concealed in existing classes or entities. The second one performs grouping of existing classes or entities without losing the inheritance semantics by introducing several types of constraints. MAP is a process language that increases both understanding and implementation of methods. It provides a formalism combining visual facilities and formal descriptions of information systems processes. The

Z. Bellahsène, D. Patel, and C. Rolland (Eds.): OOIS 2002, LNCS 2425, pp. 536-548, 2002.

specification of REORG with MAP supplies a process model which makes explicit modeling practices and then allows their integration into any CASE tool.

The remainder of the paper is organized as follows. Section 2 presents the REORG method. Section 3 formalizes REORG with MAP. Finally, Section 4 concludes and presents some perspectives.

2 Reorganizing Is_A Hierarchies Using REOG

REORG is a method supporting Is_A inheritance hierarchies reorganization for both EER and object-oriented schemas. In this paper, the method is illustrated on EER schemas. It proposes two mechanisms, namely the splitting and the restructuring mechanism. The first one allows inheritance derivation. Other inheritance derivation mechanisms exist in the literature ([2,3,4]). They are based on class factorizations, that is they compare class characteristics from a syntactic (same name) and/or semantic (same type or signature) point of view. Therefore they ignore possible inclusion relations between instance sets. Thus the derived inheritances are indifferently IS-A or implementation inheritances. Furthermore, none of them take into account optional attributes: they can derive equivalencies of classes that are semantically different.

The first mechanism of REORG performs transformations of an EER sub-schema into a schema where new IS_A links have been brought out. It takes into account relationships cardinality constraints and existence constraints defined between entity's attributes. The second mechanism is used to restructure a sub-schema by merging entities belonging to the same hierarchy. The execution of a merge preserves the semantics of the initial sub-schema. In other words, the suppressed IS_A links are replaced by existence constraints and/or cardinality constrains.

Existence constraints are of four kinds: non-null, mutual, exclusive and conditional existence constraints. *A non-null constraint* defined for an entity-type attribute expresses the fact that this attribute is mandatory. *A mutual existence constraint*[1] defined between two attributes x and y of an entity-type, denoted $x \leftrightarrow y$, describes the simultaneous presence or absence of a value for x and y in the instances of the entity-type. *An exclusive existence constraint*[1] defined between two attributes x and y of an entity-type, denoted $x \not\leftrightarrow y$, translates the non coexistence of x and y in the entity-type instances. Finally, a *conditional existence constraint*[1] defined between two attributes x and y of an entity-type, denoted $x \mapsto y$, captures the fact that any tuple where x is applicable, y is also applicable. We read this constraint " x requires y ".

2.1 The Splitting Mechanism

The idea carried by the splitting mechanism is to find, among entity-types, entities (subset of instances) that share the same structure and then to construct Is_A hierarchies according to the inclusion links between the structures of the deduced

[1] The formal definitions of these constraints and their generalization to a set of attributes can be found in [5].

entities. In the context of conceptual modeling, the splitting mechanism can be applied either for an entity-type or for an entity-types set. For lack of space, we focus on splitting an entity-type.

The identification of the different entities represented by an entity-type is performed by analyzing the existence constraints supplied by the designer. For example, let TouristPlace be an entity-type representing all the tourist places of a country such as museums, historical monuments, etc. Its structure is defined by the mandatory attributes Name, IdPlace, Address and EntranceFee and by the optional attributes Century and ClosingDay. We suppose for this example that only museums have a closing date and that there is no museum that is also a historical monument. This hypothesis is translated into the entity-type TouristPlace by adding this exclusive existence constraint: Century $\not\leftrightarrow$ ClosingDay.

As described, TouristPlace gathers only three interesting subsets of instances. These subsets are not disjoint. The first one represents all the tourist places (it is the set of all instances of the entity-type). The second one represents all the museums and the third one all the historical monuments. Each of these subsets gathers instances sharing the same subset of not null attributes. For example, all the museums have a name, a IdPlace, an address and a closing date. Therefore the entity-type TouristPlace can be split into three entity-types E1, E2, E3 associated to the three subsets of instances. This decomposition is based on the existence constraints deduced from the type of the attributes (mandatory or optional) and on the above exclusive existence constraint. The resulting entity-types are organized into an inclusion graph (see Figure 1-a), and by inversing the direction of the graph inclusion arrows, we obtain an Is_A hierarchy (see Figure 1-b) where the specializations are disjoint. The designer can thereafter give a name for each of these entity-types. For instance, he can call the entity-type E1 'TouristPlace', the entity-type E2 'Museum' and the entity-type E3 'HistoricalMonument'.

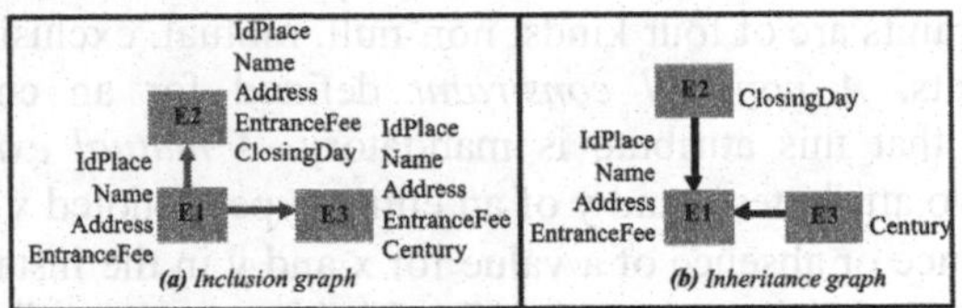

(a) Inclusion graph (b) Inheritance graph

Fig. 1. The result of splitting TouristPlace

This technique that allows us to deduce the different structures of entities concealed into an entity-type is described in [5]. It consists in deducing, from the entity-type structure (its attributes set), all the valid sub-structures (substructures that are compatible with the existence constraints). Let S be a subset of the attributes set of an entity-type T. S is said to be a valid sub-structure of T if and only if S satisfies the following three rules:

- *Homogeneity*: any attribute of T linked to an attribute of S by a mutual existence constraint is in S,
- *Non-partition*: There are no exclusive existence constraints between attributes of S,
- *Convexity*: any attribute of T required by a group of attributes of S is in S

For example, the sub-structure composed by the attributes Name, ClosingDay and Century don't verify the three described rules and then it is a non valid sub-structure. The algorithm used to derive valid sub-structures from an entity-type is based on this definition.

Remark 2. If the designer is not capable to specify the existence constraints of the entity-type to split, the splitting mechanism is preceded by a reverse engineering process that derives them by analyzing a representative sample of instances given by the designer. It proceeds in three steps. First it determines a Boolean equation describing all the different types of instances encountered in the given set of instances. Then, it transforms the left part of this Boolean equation from a disjunctive form to a conjunctive form. Finally, by analyzing the different minterms of the transformed expression it derives the existence constraints. The derived existence constraints are proposed to the designer for validation. The latter can either confirm the deduced set of constraints or modify it. The designer has also the possibility to revise its sample. This process of collecting constraints is repeated until the resulting set is approved by the designer and qualified by the process as consistent. To illustrate this technique let us suppose that instead of the set of existence constraints (those used to derive the hierarchy of Figure 1-b), we have the following representative sample of instances for the entity-type TouristPlace:

IdPlace	Name	Address	EntranceFee	ClosingDay	Century
10	Grottes de Lombrives	Arieges	100	null	null
11	Ascenseur des bateaux	Thieu	200	null	null
12	Observatoire de Paris	Paris	55	Sunday	null
46	Selestat	Alsace	0	null	19
30	Musée de l'elecropolis	Mulhouse	100	Sunday	null
50	Tour Eiffel	Paris	95	null	19

Fig. 2. A representative sample of ToutistPlace

This set of instances identifies three types of instances for the entity-type TourisPlace regarding the presence or the absence of attributes: instances having only the four first attributes valued, instances having the five first attributes valued and, finally, instances having IdPLace, Name, Address, EntranceFee and Century valued,

To express the types of instances which exist in TouristPlace, we exploit the notion of Boolean expression. If we associate to each of the attributes IdPLace, Name, Address, EntranceFee, ClosingDay and Century respectively the Boolean variable X1, X2, X3, X4, X5, X6 that take the value 1 for a type of instances if the associated attribute is valued for this type and 0 otherwise, we can translate the presented types of instances by the Boolean equation:

$$X1.X2.X3.X4.\overline{X5}.\overline{X6}+X1.X2.X3.X4.X5.\overline{X6}+X1.X2.X3.X4.\overline{X5}.X6=1$$

To solve this Boolean equation we can transform its left part from this disjunctive form to a conjunctive one and solve a set of equations. For our example, we have to solve the equivalent Boolean equation:

$$X1.X2.X3.X4.(\overline{X5}+\overline{X6})=1$$

that can be solved by the resolution of the following equations:

$$(X1 = 1), (X2 = 1), (X3 = 1), (X4 = 1) \text{ and } (\overline{X5} + \overline{X6} = 1)$$

Each equation gives a solution that can be materialized by an existence constraint. In this example, the four first equations means respectively that the four first attribute must be mandatory. The last equation means that every instances of TouristicPlace having EntranceFee valued don't have ClosingDay valued and vice versa. These attributes are therefore related by an exclusive existence constraint. A formal description of this technique can be found in [6].

Remark 3. Entity-types are linked to relationships. Their participation to the relationships are described by cardinality constraints. A null participation of an entity-type to a relationship may has two semantics: some instances of the entity-type never participate or some instances can temporarily not participate. For deriving IS_A links only the first semantic must be taken into account. For example, if the entity-type TouristPlace was linked to an entity-type Photo via the relationship "Has" and to an entity-type Topic via the relationship "Presents" (see Figure 3-a) and if some tourist places do not have photos and if only tourist places that have closing dates present topics, then the splitting mechanism leads to the hierarchy of Figure 3-b.

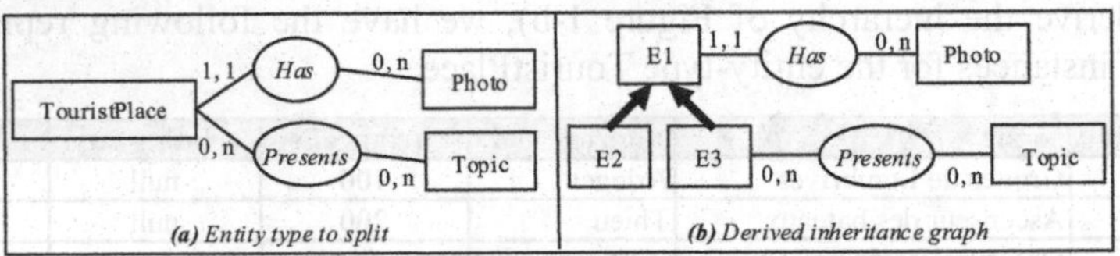

Fig. 3. Another example of entity-type to split

This supposes that the designer has supplied the mechanism by the constraint: "Participation-to-Present" ↔ ClosingDay.
The specification of such constraints concerns also reflexive relationships.

Remark 4. The existence constraints constitute the entries of the splitting mechanism. Before using them, the mechanism proceeds to their validation, according to validation rules. The inconsistent constraints are indicated to the designer, sometimes with possible solutions. For instance, if, in addition to the constraints of TouristPlace, the designer supplies the mechanism by the constraint Century ↮ Name then the mechanism will detect an inconsistency of the constraints set and will propose the elimination of either this constraint or the constraint Century↦Name.

2.2 The Restructuring Mechanism

The restructuring mechanism aims at replacing a sub-schema by a unique entity-type. As for the splitting mechanism, the sub-schema can either be proposed by a CASE tool or by the designer. For example, let us consider the initial schema presented in Figure 4-a. The gray colored part corresponds to the schema to restructure. This selection is made by the designer or suggested by the CASE tool. After schema restructuring, the selected sub-schema is replaced by the entity-type named E in Figure 4-b.

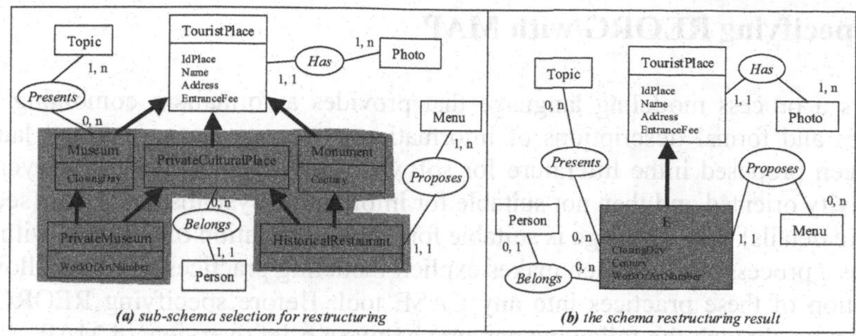

Fig. 4. Applying the restructuring mechanism

Moreover, the restructuring mechanism adds a set of existence constraints corresponding to the IS_A links initially contained in the restructured schema. These constraints are deduced by applying the following rules:

- *Coexistence rule*: If two attributes coexist in an entity-type then they are linked by a mutual existence constraint in the generated entity-type.
- Generalization/specialization rule: If an entity-type B inherits from an entity-type A, then every specific attribute-type of B requires every specific attribute-type of A in the generated entity-type.
- *Specialization exclusion rule*: if two entity-types A and B do not share any sub-types in the sub-schema, then the existence of every specific attribute of A excludes the existence of every specific attribute of B in the generated entity-type.
- *Multiple inheritance rule*: if D is the only direct sub-type of entity-types A and B then every couple composed of an attribute of A and an attribute of B requires every attribute of D in the generated entity-type.

For the example of Figure 4, the restructuring mechanism will deduce the existence constraints described in Figure 5.

"Participation-to-Presents"↔ClosingDay
WorkOfArtNumber→ClosingDay
WorkOfArtNumber→"Participation-to-Presents"
WorkOfArtNumber→"Participation-to-Belongs"
"Participation-to-Proposes"↦"Participation-to-Belongs"
"Participation-to-Proposes"↦Century
Century ↮ ClosingDay
Century ↮ "Participation-to-Presents"
"Participation-to-Belongs", ClosingDay ↦WorkOfArtNumber
"Participation-to-Belongs", "Participation-to-Presents" ↦WorkOfArtNumber
"Participation-to-Belongs", Century ↦"Participation-to-Proposes"

Fig. 5. Existence constraints derived by the restructuring mechanism

Remark. The restructuring mechanism, as presented in this paper, can only be applied when all the entity-types composing the sub-schema to restructure share the same ascendants. This is due to the fact that, at the conceptual level, a sub-type inherit all the properties of the super-type whereas in object-oriented languages some inherited properties could be hidden.

3 Specifying REORG with MAP

MAP is a process modeling language that provides a formalism combining visual facilities and formal descriptions of information systems processes. Other langages have been proposed inthe litterature for software processes [7, 8, 9]. However, they are activity oriented and then not suitable for information systems processes (see [10]) for more details).This language is suitable for The specification of REORG with MAP supplies a process model which makes explicit modeling practices and then allows the integration of these practices into any CASE tool. Before specifying REORG with MAP, let us, through the following paragraph, give a brief overview of MAP.

3.1 Overview of MAP Process Language

From a process view, we can say that to construct an EER schema the designer proceeds on two steps. He first constructs a draft of the entity relationship schema, and then incrementally refines the schema.
In the MAPs vocabulary, the process is described as a set of intentions to achieve and the ways to progress from an intention to another. An intention corresponds to a goal which achievement leads to an artifact production or transformation. Let us consider the situation sketched in Figure 6a. This schema is an initial draft that is further refined to construct a more complete schema. In this example we identify two intentions: construct a schema draft and refine it.

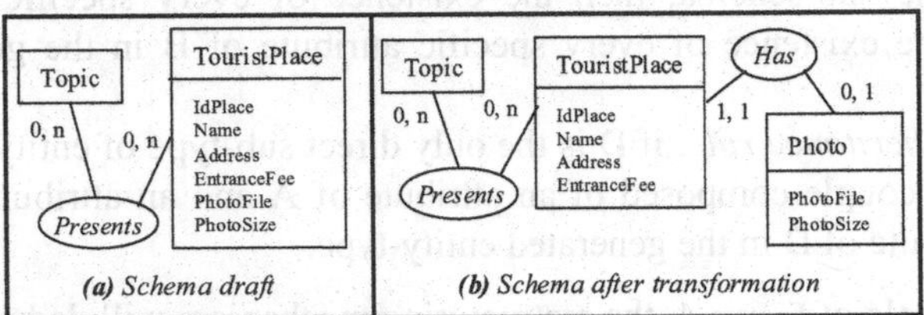

Fig. 6. A schema draft and its transformation

There are several ways to refine an EER schema: by refining an existing entity-type, relationship-type or an attribute-type or by adding new elements (entity-types, relationship-types or attribute-types). Each refinement corresponds to a progression from the process view. For example, to progress from the entity-type TouristPlace of Figure 6a, we can use the so-called *normalization heuristics*[2] stipulating that if attribute-types do not contribute to a description of an entity-type, remove them to a separate entity-type. In our exemple, the attribute-type PhotoSize does not describe the entity-type TouristPlace but the other attribute-type PhotoFile. The application of this heuristics moves the two attribute-types PhotoFile and PhotoSize into a new entity-type Photo (see Figure 6b).
The applied heuristics illustrates one way to progress from an entity-type. Other possible progressions from an entity-type are summarized in Figure 7.

[2] This heuristic is inspired from the third normal form in relational databases.

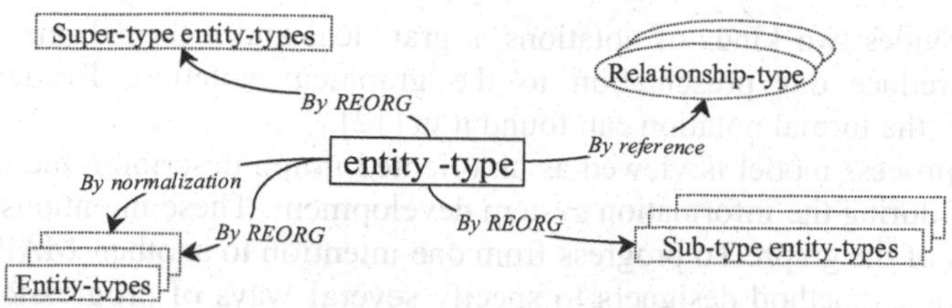

Fig. 7. Progressing from an entity-type

Each progression corresponds to a strategy in the MAP vocabulary. Figure 7 enumerates three strategies: the normalization strategy, applying the normalization heuristics, the reference strategy that recognizes that an attribute-type refers to an existing entity-type and the REORG strategy that allows the extraction of IS_A hierarchies concealed in existing entity-types.

The MAP Notation. In MAP, a process model corresponding to a method specification is composed of a set of guidelines (see Figure 8). A guideline corresponds to a set of detailed actions to execute. It can be strategic or tactical. Strategic guidelines are related to the achievement of high-level intentions in the information system development whereas tactical guidelines enable a fine-grained specification of more automatic process aspects [10, 11]. A strategic guideline could be described informally using textual descriptions or more formally as a structured process. A structured process describes a decomposition of the intention related to the strategic guideline into more precise intentions.

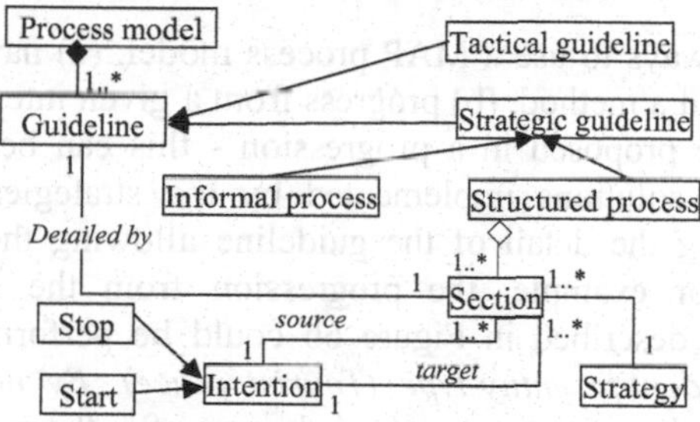

Fig. 8. The MAP process language

More formally, a *structured process* is composed of a collection of *sections* (at least one). A section is a triplet: <*source* intention, *target* intention, *Strategy*> expressing the possible progression from the source intention to the target intention applying the proposed strategy. We distinguish two generic intentions that are S*tart* (as a source intention) and *Stop* (as a target intention) which are mandatory in any structured process. MAP details each section by a guideline to specify how to apply the strategy to progress from the source intention to the target intention. This guideline could be tactical or strategic providing a mean to incremental and progressive process models specification.

MAP provides two kinds of notations, a graphical and a formal one. For lack of space, we reduce our presentation to the graphical notation. Readers who are interested by the formal notation can found it in [12].

A MAP process model is viewed as an oriented graph describing the intentions to be achieved during the information system development. These intentions correspond to the nodes of the graph. To progress from one intention to another, MAP allows and even encourages method designers to specify several ways of progression described as *strategies*. The process model presented in Figure 9 is a partial representation of our vision of how to construct an entity-relationship schema. A designer can start by identifying one or several entity-types performing, from a progression from *Start* intention to *Identify entity-type* intention by a non-assisted strategy. For further progressions, the process model of Figure 9 suggests among others progression to new entity-types identifications using three different strategies namely, *By reference, By normalization* or *By REORG*. Each strategy expresses a different way to progress towards intention achievement. This introduces more flexibility in the development process and consequently increases the satisfaction of the method user.

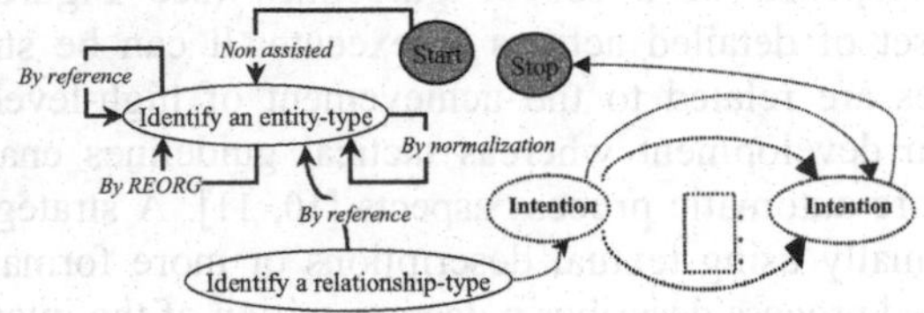

Fig. 9. MAP graphical notation

There are several ways to use a MAP process model: (a) navigate in the graph to browse and understand a method, (b) progress from a given intention by selecting one strategy among those proposed in a progression - this can be done to compare or simulate the several solutions implemented by the strategies- or (c) achieve an intention by exploring the detail of the guideline allowing the achievement of the desired intention. For example, the progression from the schema described in Figure 6a to the one described in Figure 6b could be performed by executing the following section <*Identify entity-type (Tourist_place), By normalization, Identify entity-type(x)*>. The value of entity-type(x) is known after the guideline execution.

3.2 Formalizing REORG with MAP

The starting point for the formalization process presented in this section was an informal synthetic vision established for the REORG method. A part of the specification validation was done by executing manually the resulting process model on the 'Tourist Place' example used in the second section of the paper. The result of the experience is detailed below.

REORG Intentions. In addition to ' *Start* ' and *'Stop'* intentions, the establishment of the synthetic vision of the REORG method led to the identification of three intentions which are: (1)'Choose sub-schema', (2)'Construct new-hierarchy' and (3) 'Integrate into the initial schema' (see Figure 10). Indeed, reorganizing an existing schema starts practically by a selection of the part of the schema to reorganize. This reorganization leads to a new hierarchy that must be integrated into the initial schema.

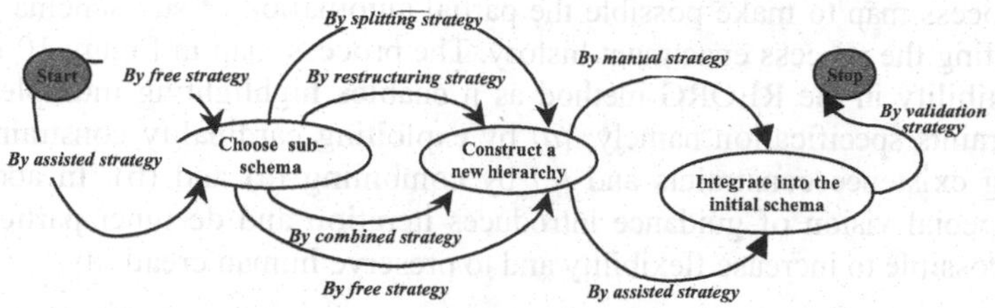

Fig. 10. The REORG process model

To choose a sub schema to reorganize two strategies are possible, a free strategy applying a selection by the designer and an assisted strategy where a proposition of the sub-schema to reorganize is done by the CASE tool.

To progress from a sub-schema selection 4 strategies are suggested: by the splitting strategy applying the splitting mechanism of REORG, by the restructuring strategy applying the restructuring mechanism of REORG,by a combined strategy applying both the splitting and the restructuring mechanisms and, finally, by a free strategy which allows designers working freely on the sub-schema without assistance. The result of the progression is the new hierarchy construction. The user can further progress in the schema construction by integrating the obtained hierarchy into the initial schema. The process model proposes again two strategies: the assisted strategy that integrates automatically the hierarchy or a free strategy that allows manual integration by the user. The verification of the resulting schema correctness is implemented by the validation strategy.

To reduce the complexity of the REORG process model and to increase its understanding, we have organized it into several levels of abstraction. Remember that each section is detailed by a guideline that can be either strategic or tactical. For lack of place, we have not given the detail of all the sections constituting the process model. We restrict this list to two examples illustrating both kinds of guidelines.

Refining a Process Model: An Example of Strategic Guidelines. In the process model described in Figure 10, the major part of the sections have a strategic nature. We have chosen to describe the section allowing the construction of a new hierarchy using the splitting strategy: <Choose sub-schema, By splitting strategy, Construct new hierarchy >. The process model detailing the chosen section is described in Figure 11.

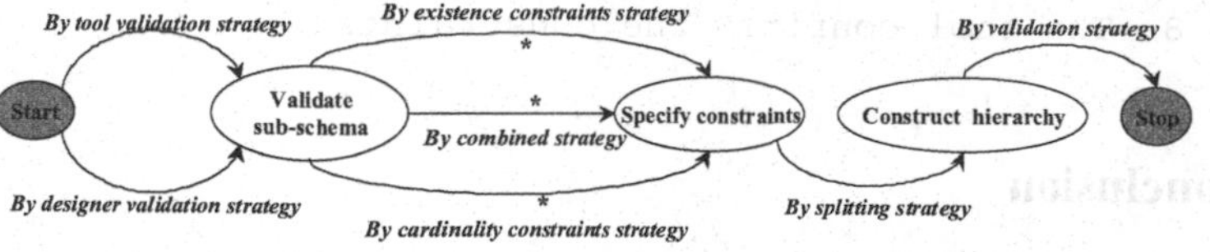

Fig. 11. Detailing new hierarchies construction using the splitting strategy

The specification of the details shown in Figure 11 allowed us to understand that the sub-schema on which reorganization should be applied depends on the reorganization strategy selected by using the process map in Figure 10. This led us to put the validation at the second level of abstraction and not in the first one of the whole process map to make possible the partial automation of sub-schema validation by exploiting the process enactment history. The process map in Figure 10 introduces more flexibility in the REORG method as it enables highlighting multiple solutions for constraints specification namely: *(a)* by exploiting cardinality constraints, *(b)* by exploiting existence constraints and *(c)* by combining (a) and (b). In addition, the MAP's special vision of guidance introduces iteration and designer participation as often as possible to increase flexibility and to preserve human creativity.

Refining a Process Model: An Example of Tactical Guidelines. Tactical guidelines correspond to fine grained processes that could be implemented by automatic actions. One of these guidelines implements the section <Sub-schema validation, By existence constraints strategy, Specify constraints> (see Figure 11).

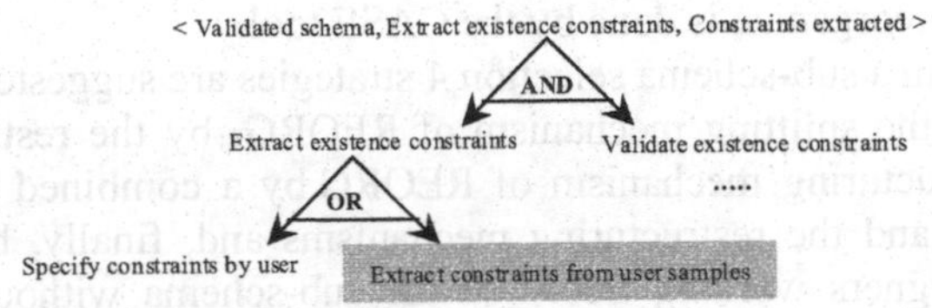

Fig. 12. Example of tactical guideline

The example expressed in Figure 12 describes a very fine grained process more concerned with actions to execute automatically than with intentions to achieve. The grey coloured action is associated to the following steps:

```
Step 1- The designer supplies the sample instances.
Step 2- The tool extracts the existence constraints.
Step 3- The designer validates the extracted constraints. If
        accepted go to Step 8.
Step 4- The tool proposes either the modification of the
        sample or the constraints set if the constraints set
        is rejected.
Step 5- The designer modifies either the sample or the
        constraints set.
Step 6- The tool validates the constraints set if it has been
        modified. The result of the validation allows going
        either to Step 3 or Step 4.
Step 7  Go to Step 2 if the sample has been modified.
Step 8- The tool confirms the constraints.
```

4 Conclusion

The work presented in this paper offers an assisted reorganization of Is_A hierarchies through the specification of the REORG method with the MAP formalism.
Describing the process model of REORG with MAP has allowed us:

- the investigation of supplementary aspects in the method which where highlighted during the process enactment simulation
- the introduction of a modular specification which will facilitate future method evolution and its integration into a CASE tool.

This work is on the one hand an extension to the work presented in [11] and is on the other hand a part of the E-MeRCI project [13] which objective is to construct an environment for round-trip information systems development. This work is more precisely related to the assistance module aiming at providing guidance during the development process using several methods such as REORG, MeRCI [14]. Other similar experiences where developed in [12,15]. This experience was a mean to validate the MAP process language by applying it to a new method. It provided a good example to check the ability of MAP to specify methods at several levels of detail. It brought concrete examples on tactical guidelines. The next step in the project will be to specify the other methods needed in E-MeRCI using the MAP process language and implement the assistance module.

References

1. Perry M., Kaiser G., Models of Software Development Environments, IEEE transactions on Software Engineering, vol 17: 3, March 1998.
2. Godin R., Mili H., Mineau G. W., Missaoui R., Arfi, A. & Chau T.-T., Design of Class Hierarchies based on Concept (Galois) Lattices. Theory and Practice of Object Systems, 4(2), 117-134, 1998.
3. Lieberherr L., Bergstein P. and Silva-Lepe I., From Objects to Classes: Algorithms for Optimal Object-oriented Design. Software Engineering, vol.6, n°4, july 1991.
4. Thieme C. and Siebes A., Schema Integration in Object-Oriented Databases. CAISE'93. Lecture Notes in Computer Science n°685, Springer-Verlag, Paris, France, June 1993.
5. Lammari N., Laleau R., Jouve M., Multiple viewpoints of Is_A Inheritance Hierarchies through Normalization and Denormalization Mechanisms. Proc. of OOIS'98, Springer-Verlag, Paris, September 9-11, 1998.
6. Lammari N., An Algorithm to Extract IS-A Inheritance Hierarchies from a Relational Database, Proc. of ER'99, LNCS 1728, Paris, 1999.
7. Armenise P., Bandinelli S., Ghezzi C., Morzenti A., A survey and assessment of software process representation formalisms, Int. Journal of Software Engineering and Knowledge Engineering, Vol. 3, No. 3, 1993.
8. Dowson M., Fernstrom C., Towards requirements for Enactement Mechanisms, Proc. of the th European Workshop on Software Process Technology, 1994.
9. Finkelstein A., Kramer J., Nuseibeh B., 'Software process modelling and technology', Research Studies Press LTD, 1994.
10. Si-said S., Rolland C.: "Guidance for Requirements Engineering Processes", Proc. of the 8th Int. Conf. and workshop on Database and Expert Systems Applications, DEXA'97, September1-5, 1997, Toulouse, France.

11. Si-Saïd S., Proposition pour la modélisation et le guidage des processus d'analyse des systèmes d'information, PhD thesis, Université Paris-1 La Sorbonne, Feb. 1998.
12. Assar S., Ben Achour C., Si-Said S., Un Modèle pour la Spécification de Processus d'Analyse des Systèmes d'Information. 18ème Congrès of INFORSID, Lyon, France, 16-19 Mai 2000.
13. Akoka J., Assar S., Comyn-Wattiau I., Lammari N., Laleau R., Noiseau Y., Si-Said S., E-MeRCI: Un Environnement et Une Méthode pour la Rétro-Conception Intelligente d'applications de bases de données, Technical report ISID-1-01, CEDRIC-CNAM, Paris, February 2001.
14. Comyn-Wattiau I., Akoka J., Relational Database Reverse Engineering: Logical Schema Conceptualization. Revue Networking and Information Systems, Hermès, 1999.
15. Benjamen A., Une approche Multi-démarches pour modélisation des démarches méthodologiques, PhD Thesis, Université Paris 1-La Sorbonne, October 1999.

Author Index

Lecture Notes in Computer Science

For information about Vols. 1–2358
please contact your bookseller or Springer-Verlag

Vol. 2359: M. Tistarelli, J. Bigun, A.K. Jain (Eds.), Biometric Authentication. Proceedings, 2002. X, 197 pages. 2002.

Vol. 2360: J. Esparza, C. Lakos (Eds.), Application and Theory of Petri Nets 2002. Proceedings, 2002. X, 445 pages. 2002.

Vol. 2361: J. Blieberger, A. Strohmeier (Eds.), Reliable Software Technologies – Ada-Europe 2002. Proceedings, 2002 XIII, 367 pages. 2002.

Vol. 2362: M. Tanabe, P. van den Besselaar, T. Ishida (Eds.), Digital Cities II. Proceedings, 2001. XI, 399 pages. 2002.

Vol. 2363: S.A. Cerri, G. Gouardères, F. Paraguaçu (Eds.), Intelligent Tutoring Systems. Proceedings, 2002. XXVIII, 1016 pages. 2002.

Vol. 2364: F. Roli, J. Kittler (Eds.), Multiple Classifier Systems. Proceedings, 2002. XI, 337 pages. 2002.

Vol. 2365: J. Daemen, V. Rijmen (Eds.), Fast Software Encryption. Proceedings, 2002. XI, 277 pages. 2002.

Vol. 2366: M.-S. Hacid, Z.W. Raś, D.A. Zighed, Y. Kodratoff (Eds.), Foundations of Intelligent Systems. Proceedings, 2002. XII, 614 pages. 2002. (Subseries LNAI).

Vol. 2367: J. Fagerholm, J. Haataja, J. Järvinen, M. Lyly. P. Råback, V. Savolainen (Eds.), Applied Parallel Computing. Proceedings, 2002. XIV, 612 pages. 2002.

Vol. 2368: M. Penttonen, E. Meineche Schmidt (Eds.), Algorithm Theory – SWAT 2002. Proceedings, 2002. XIV, 450 pages. 2002.

Vol. 2369: C. Fieker, D.R. Kohel (Eds.), Algorithmic Number Theory. Proceedings, 2002. IX, 517 pages. 2002.

Vol. 2370: J. Bishop (Ed.), Component Deployment. Proceedings, 2002. XII, 269 pages. 2002.

Vol. 2371: S. Koenig, R.C. Holte (Eds.), Abstraction, Reformulation, and Approximation. Proceedings, 2002. XI, 349 pages. 2002. (Subseries LNAI).

Vol. 2372: A. Pettorossi (Ed.), Logic Based Program Synthesis and Transformation. Proceedings, 2001. VIII, 267 pages. 2002.

Vol. 2373: A. Apostolico, M. Takeda (Eds.), Combinatorial Pattern Matching. Proceedings, 2002. VIII, 289 pages. 2002.

Vol. 2374: B. Magnusson (Ed.), ECOOP 2002 – Object-Oriented Programming. XI, 637 pages. 2002.

Vol. 2375: J. Kivinen, R.H. Sloan (Eds.), Computational Learning Theory. Proceedings, 2002. XI, 397 pages. 2002. (Subseries LNAI).

Vol. 2377: A. Birk, S. Coradeschi, T. Satoshi (Eds.), RoboCup 2001: Robot Soccer World Cup V. XIX, 763 pages. 2002. (Subseries LNAI).

Vol. 2378: S. Tison (Ed.), Rewriting Techniques and Applications. Proceedings, 2002. XI, 387 pages. 2002.

Vol. 2379: G.J. Chastek (Ed.), Software Product Lines. Proceedings, 2002. X, 399 pages. 2002.

Vol. 2380: P. Widmayer, F. Triguero, R. Morales, M. Hennessy, S. Eidenbenz, R. Conejo (Eds.), Automata, Languages and Programming. Proceedings, 2002. XXI, 1069 pages. 2002.

Vol. 2381: U. Egly, C.G. Fermüller (Eds.), Automated Reasoning with Analytic Tableaux and Related Methods. Proceedings, 2002. X, 341 pages. 2002 .(Subseries LNAI).

Vol. 2382: A. Halevy, A. Gal (Eds.), Next Generation Information Technologies and Systems. Proceedings, 2002. VIII, 169 pages. 2002.

Vol. 2383: M.S. Lew, N. Sebe, J.P. Eakins (Eds.), Image and Video Retrieval. Proceedings, 2002. XII, 388 pages. 2002.

Vol. 2384: L. Batten, J. Seberry (Eds.), Information Security and Privacy. Proceedings, 2002. XII, 514 pages. 2002.

Vol. 2385: J. Calmet, B. Benhamou, O. Caprotti, L. Henocque, V. Sorge (Eds.), Artificial Intelligence, Automated Reasoning, and Symbolic Computation. Proceedings, 2002. XI, 343 pages. 2002. (Subseries LNAI).

Vol. 2386: E.A. Boiten, B. Möller (Eds.), Mathematics of Program Construction. Proceedings, 2002. X, 263 pages. 2002.

Vol. 2387: O.H. Ibarra, L. Zhang (Eds.), Computing and Combinatorics. Proceedings, 2002. XIII, 606 pages. 2002.

Vol. 2388: S.-W. Lee, A. Verri (Eds.), Pattern Recognition with Support Vector Machines. Proceedings, 2002. XI, 420 pages. 2002.

Vol. 2389: E. Ranchhod, N.J. Mamede (Eds.), Advances in Natural Language Processing. Proceedings, 2002. XII, 275 pages. 2002. (Subseries LNAI).

Vol. 2390: D. Blostein, Y.-B. Kwon (Eds.), Graphics Recognition. Proceedings, 2001. XI, 367 pages. 2002.

Vol. 2391: L.-H. Eriksson, P.A. Lindsay (Eds.), FME 2002: Formal Methods – Getting IT Right. Proceedings, 2002. XI, 625 pages. 2002.

Vol. 2392: A. Voronkov (Ed.), Automated Deduction – CADE-18. Proceedings, 2002. XII, 534 pages. 2002. (Subseries LNAI).

Vol. 2393: U. Priss, D. Corbett, G. [illegible]ova (Eds.), Conceptual Structures: Integration and [illegible]faces. Proceedings, 2002. XI, 397 pages. 2002. (S[illegible]ies LNAI).

Vol. 2394: P. Perner (Ed.), Advan[illegible]n Data Mining. VII, 109 pages. 2002. (Subseries L[illegible]

Vol. 2395: G. Barthe, P. Dybjer, L. P[illegible]. Saraiva (Eds.), Applied Semantics. IX, 537 pages. 2002.

Vol. 2396: T. Caelli, A. Amin, R.P.W. Duin, M. Kamel, D. de Ridder (Eds.), Structural, Syntactic, and Statistical Pattern Recognition. Proceedings, 2002. XVI, 863 pages. 2002.

Vol. 2398: K. Miesenberger, J. Klaus, W. Zagler (Eds.), Computers Helping People with Special Needs. Proceedings, 2002. XXII, 794 pages. 2002.

Vol. 2399: H. Hermanns, R. Segala (Eds.), Process Algebra and Probabilistic Methods. Proceedings, 2002. X, 215 pages. 2002.

Vol. 2400: B. Monien, R. Feldmann (Eds.), Euro-Par 2002 – Parallel Processing. Proceedings, 2002. XXIX, 993 pages. 2002.

Vol. 2401: P.J. Stuckey (Ed.), Logic Programming. Proceedings, 2002. XI, 486 pages. 2002.

Vol. 2402: W. Chang (Ed.), Advanced Internet Services and Applications. Proceedings, 2002. XI, 307 pages. 2002.

Vol. 2403: Mark d'Inverno, M. Luck, M. Fisher, C. Preist (Eds.), Foundations and Applications of Multi-Agent Systems. Proceedings, 1996-2000. X, 261 pages. 2002. (Subseries LNAI).

Vol. 2404: E. Brinksma, K.G. Larsen (Eds.), Computer Aided Verification. Proceedings, 2002. XIII, 626 pages. 2002.

Vol. 2405: B. Eaglestone, S. North, A. Poulovassilis (Eds.), Advances in Databases. Proceedings, 2002. XII, 199 pages. 2002.

Vol. 2406: C. Peters, M. Braschler, J. Gonzalo, M. Kluck (Eds.), Evaluation of Cross-Language Information Retrieval Systems. Proceedings, 2001. X, 601 pages. 2002.

Vol. 2407: A.C. Kakas, F. Sadri (Eds.), Computational Logic: Logic Programming and Beyond. Part I. XII, 678 pages. 2002. (Subseries LNAI).

Vol. 2408: A.C. Kakas, F. Sadri (Eds.), Computational Logic: Logic Programming and Beyond. Part II. XII, 628 pages. 2002. (Subseries LNAI).

Vol. 2409: D.M. Mount, C. Stein (Eds.), Algorithm Engineering and Experiments. Proceedings, 2002. VIII, 207 pages. 2002.

Vol. 2410: V.A. Carreño, C.A. Muñoz, S. Tahar (Eds.), Theorem Proving in Higher Order Logics. Proceedings, 2002. X, 349 pages. 2002.

Vol. 2412: H. Yin, N. Allinson, R. Freeman, J. Keane, S. Hubbard (Eds.), Intelligent Data Engineering and Automated Learning – IDEAL 2002. Proceedings, 2002. XV, 597 pages. 2002.

Vol. 2413: K. Kuwabara, J. Lee (Eds.), Intelligent Agents and Multi-Agent Systems. Proceedings, 2002. X, 221 pages. 2002. (Subseries LNAI).

Vol. 2414: F. Mattern, M. Naghshineh (Eds.), Pervasive Computing. Proceedings, 2002. XI, 298 pages. 2002.

Vol. 2415: J.R. Dorronsoro (Ed.), Artificial Neural Networks – ICANN 2002. Proceedings, 2002. XXVIII, 1382 pages. 2002.

Vol. 2417: M. Ishizuka, A. Sattar (Eds.), PRICAI 2002: Trends in Artificial Intelligence. Proceedings, 2002. XX, 623 pages. 2002. (Subseries LNAI).

Vol. 2418: D. Wells, L. Williams (Eds.), Extreme Programming and Agile Methods – XP/Agile Universe 2002. Proceedings, 2002. XII, 292 pages. 2002.

Vol. 2419: X. Meng, J. Su, Y. Wang (Eds.), Advances in Web-Age Information Management. Proceedings, 2002. XV, 446 pages. 2002.

Vol. 2420: K. Diks, W. Rytter (Eds.), Mathematical Foundations of Computer Science 2002. Proceedings, 2002. XII, 652 pages. 2002.

Vol. 2421: L. Brim, P. Jančar, M. Křetínský, A. Kučera (Eds.), CONCUR 2002 – Concurrency Theory. Proceedings, 2002. XII, 611 pages. 2002.

Vol. 2423: D. Lopresti, J. Hu, R. Kashi (Eds.), Document Analysis Systems V. Proceedings, 2002. XIII, 570 pages. 2002.

Vol. 2425: Z. Bellahsène, D. Patel, C. Rolland (Eds.), Object-Oriented Information Systems. Proceedings, 2002. XIII, 550 pages. 2002.

Vol. 2426: J.-M. Bruel, Z. Bellahsene (Eds.), Advances in Object-Oriented Information Systems. Procedings, 2002. IX, 314 pages. 2002.

Vol. 2430: T. Elomaa, H. Mannila, H. Toivonen (Eds.), Machine Learning: ECML 2002. Proceedings, 2002. XIII, 532 pages. 2002. (Subseries LNAI).

Vol. 2431: T. Elomaa, H. Mannila, H. Toivonen (Eds.), Principles of Data Mining and Knowledge Discovery. Proceedings, 2002. XIV, 514 pages. 2002. (Subseries LNAI).

Vol. 2435: Y. Manolopoulos, P. Návrat (Eds.), Advances in Databases and Information Systems. Proceedings, 2002. XIII, 415 pages. 2002.

Vol. 2436: J. Fong, C.T. Cheung, H.V. Leong, Q. Li (Eds.), Advances in Web-Based Learning. Proceedings, 2002. XIII, 434 pages. 2002.

Vol. 2438: M. Glesner, P. Zipf, M. Renovell (Eds.), Field-Programmable Logic and Applications. Proceedings, 2002. XXII, 1187 pages. 2002.

Vol. 2440: J.M. Haake, J.A. Pino (Eds.), Groupware: Design, Implementation and Use. Proceedings, 2002. XII, 285 pages. 2002.

Vol. 2442: M. Yung (Ed.), Advances in Cryptology – CRYPTO 2002. Proceedings, 2002. XIV, 627 pages. 2002.

Vol. 2443: D. Scott (Ed.), Artificial Intelligence: Methodology, Systems, and Applications. Proceedings, 2002. X, 279 pages. 2002. (Subseries LNAI).

Vol. 2444: A. Buchmann, F. Casati, L. Fiege, M.-C. Hsu, M.-C. Shan (Eds.), Technologies for E-Services. Proceedings, 2002. X, 171 pages. 2002.

Vol. 2445: C. Anagnostopoulou, M. Ferrand, A. Smaill (Eds.), Music and Artificial Intelligence. Proceedings, 2002. VIII, 207 pages. 2002. (Subseries LNAI).

Vol. 2447: D.J. Hand, N.M. Adams, R.J. Bolton (Eds.), Pattern Detection and Discovery. Proceedings, 2002. XII, 227 pages. 2002. (Subseries LNAI).

Vol. 2451: B. Hochet, A.J. Acosta, M.J. Bellido (Eds.), Integrated Circuit Design. Proceedings, 2002. XVI, 496 pages. 2002.

Vol. 2453: A. Hameurlain, R. Cicchetti, R. Traunmüller (Eds.), Database and Expert Systems Applications. Proceedings, 2002. XVIII, 951 pages. 2002.

Vol. 2454: Y. Kambayashi, W. Winiwarter, M. Arikawa (Eds.), Data Warehousing and Knowledge Discovery. Proceedings, 2002. XIII, 339 pages. 2002.

Vol. 2455: K. Bauknecht, A M. Tjoa, G. Quirchmayr (Eds.), E-Commerce and Web Technologies. Proceedings, 2002. XIV, 414 pages. 2002.